9427

P9-EDF-043

(Continued on back endsheets)

Dictionary of Literary Biography® • Volume One Hundred Forty-Four

Nineteenth-Century British Literary Biographers

Nineteenth-Century British Literary Biographers

Edited by
Steven Serafin
Hunter College of the City University of New York

A Bruccoli Clark Layman Book
Gale Research Inc.
Detroit, Washington, D.C., London

Printed in the United States of America

Published simultaneously in the United Kingdom
by Gale Research International Limited
(An affiliated company of Gale Research Inc.)

The paper used in this publication meets the minimum requirements
of American National Standard for Information Sciences–Permanence
Paper for Printed Library Materials, ANSI Z39.48-1984. ∞ ™

Library of Congress Catalog Card Number 94–076961
ISBN 0–8103–5558–2

The trademark **ITP** is used under license.

10 9 8 7 6 5 4 3 2 1

Contents

Plan of the Series

. . . Almost the most prodigious asset of a country, and perhaps its most precious possession, is its native literary product – when that product is fine and noble and enduring.

Mark Twain*

The advisory board, the editors, and the publisher of the *Dictionary of Literary Biography* are joined in endorsing Mark Twain's declaration. The literature of a nation provides an inexhaustible resource of permanent worth. We intend to make literature and its creators better understood and more accessible to students and the reading public, while satisfying the standards of teachers and scholars.

To meet these requirements, *literary biography* has been construed in terms of the author's achievement. The most important thing about a writer is his writing. Accordingly, the entries in *DLB* are career biographies, tracing the development of the author's canon and the evolution of his reputation.

The purpose of *DLB* is not only to provide reliable information in a convenient format but also to place the figures in the larger perspective of literary history and to offer appraisals of their accomplishments by qualified scholars.

The publication plan for *DLB* resulted from two years of preparation. The project was proposed to Bruccoli Clark by Frederick C. Ruffner, president of the Gale Research Company, in November 1975. After specimen entries were prepared and typeset, an advisory board was formed to refine the entry format and develop the series rationale. In meetings held during 1976, the publisher, series editors, and advisory board approved the scheme for a comprehensive biographical dictionary of persons who contributed to North American literature. Editorial work on the first volume began in January 1977, and it was published in 1978. In order to make *DLB* more than a reference tool and to compile volumes that individually have claim to status as literary history, it was decided to organize volumes by topic, period, or genre. Each of these free-

standing volumes provides a biographical-bibliographical guide and overview for a particular area of literature. We are convinced that this organization – as opposed to a single alphabet method – constitutes a valuable innovation in the presentation of reference material. The volume plan necessarily requires many decisions for the placement and treatment of authors who might properly be included in two or three volumes. In some instances a major figure will be included in separate volumes, but with different entries emphasizing the aspect of his career appropriate to each volume. Ernest Hemingway, for example, is represented in *American Writers in Paris, 1920–1939* by an entry focusing on his expatriate apprenticeship; he is also in *American Novelists, 1910–1945* with an entry surveying his entire career. Each volume includes a cumulative index of the subject authors and articles. Comprehensive indexes to the entire series are planned.

With volume ten in 1982 it was decided to enlarge the scope of *DLB*. By the end of 1986 twenty-one volumes treating British literature had been published, and volumes for Commonwealth and Modern European literature were in progress. The series has been further augmented by the *DLB Yearbooks* (since 1981) which update published entries and add new entries to keep the *DLB* current with contemporary activity. There have also been *DLB Documentary Series* volumes which provide biographical and critical source materials for figures whose work is judged to have particular interest for students. One of these companion volumes is entirely devoted to Tennessee Williams.

We define literature as the *intellectual commerce of a nation:* not merely as belles lettres but as that ample and complex process by which ideas are generated, shaped, and transmitted. *DLB* entries are not limited to "creative writers" but extend to other figures who in their time and in their way influenced the mind of a people. Thus the series encompasses historians, journalists, publishers, and screenwriters. By this means readers of *DLB* may be aided to perceive literature not as cult scripture in the keeping of intellectual high priests but firmly positioned at the center of a nation's life.

From an unpublished section of Mark Twain's autobiography, copyright by the Mark Twain Company

DLB includes the major writers appropriate to each volume and those standing in the ranks immediately behind them. Scholarly and critical counsel has been sought in deciding which minor figures to include and how full their entries should be. Wherever possible, useful references are made to figures who do not warrant separate entries.

Each *DLB* volume has a volume editor responsible for planning the volume, selecting the figures for inclusion, and assigning the entries. Volume editors are also responsible for preparing, where appropriate, appendices surveying the major periodicals and literary and intellectual movements for their volumes, as well as lists of further readings. Work on the series as a whole is coordinated at the Bruccoli Clark Layman editorial center in Columbia, South Carolina, where the editorial staff is responsible for accuracy of the published volumes.

One feature that distinguishes *DLB* is the illustration policy – its concern with the iconography of literature. Just as an author is influenced by his surroundings, so is the reader's understanding of the author enhanced by a knowledge of his environment. Therefore *DLB* volumes include not only drawings, paintings, and photographs of authors, often depicting them at various stages in their careers, but also illustrations of their families and places where they lived. Title pages are regularly reproduced in facsimile along with dust jackets for modern authors. The dust jackets are a special feature of *DLB* because they often document better than anything else the way in which an author's work was perceived in its own time. Specimens of the writers' manuscripts are included when feasible.

Samuel Johnson rightly decreed that "The chief glory of every people arises from its authors." The purpose of the *Dictionary of Literary Biography* is to compile literary history in the surest way available to us – by accurate and comprehensive treatment of the lives and work of those who contributed to it.

The *DLB* Advisory Board

Introduction

"In the formula invented and perfected by James Boswell," Harold Nicolson writes in *The Development of English Biography* (1928), "our national talent for biography found its full expression." Boswell is regarded as the first consummate artist of biography and its most important innovator; yet in actuality he neither invented a new formula of biographical writing nor produced a perfect specimen of the genre. He is, nonetheless, a pivotal figure in biographical writing, and his contribution to the development of biography as a form of artistic expression is immeasurable. Boswell's *The Life of Samuel Johnson, LL.D.* (1791) remains one of the most significant works in the history of English literature, and the biographical methodology described by Nicolson as "essentially suited to the British temperament" has exerted a major influence on the course of English biography throughout the nineteenth century and into the present. As noted by Reed Whittemore in *Pure Lives: The Early Biographers* (1988), Boswell represents a "dividing point" in the history of biography, shifting the subject of biography "decisively over to a character as himself." Despite the magnitude of his influence, there was little attempt by nineteenth-century biographers to imitate the Boswellian formula; instead, the genre would be redefined in the spirit of the age.

According to Richard D. Altick in his *Lives and Letters: A History of Literary Biography in England and America* (1965), "English biography in the nineteenth century was a rich but unstable compound of history, journalism, eulogy, inspiration, and materials suitable to the study of the mind." Aided by the technical improvements in printing as well as increased literacy among the public, biography enjoyed unprecedented popularity; and, with the rise of the contemporary man of letters to public prominence, literary biography emerged as the biographical genre of primary importance. There was, however, considerable debate concerning biographical theory. As the genre developed in the nineteenth century it came to display what Ira Bruce Nadel calls "an allegiance to documents and facts" and most often reflected an impersonal portrait of the subject. On the other hand, from early in the century Thomas Carlyle would advocate the development of biography as an art rather than a process of compilation, and

this element would have the most significant impact on the development of the genre.

In the preface to *English Biography in the Early Nineteenth Century, 1801–1838* (1966) Joseph W. Reed writes: "The early nineteenth century was not (as it was for autobiography) a golden age of biography. It is more notable for the quantity of production than quality of workmanship, more significant for suppression than revelation, more noted for rules and checks on development than for biographical innovation." Beginning with the publication of Sir Walter Scott's life of John Dryden (1808), however, there appeared a succession of biographical works of distinctive value, including Robert Southey's *Life of Nelson* (1813), Thomas Campbell's biographical sketches in his *Specimens of the British Poets* (1819), Carlyle's *The Life of Friedrich Schiller* (1825), Thomas Moore's life of George Gordon, Lord Byron (1830), and Allan Cunningham's life of Robert Burns (1836). The most significant biography produced in the first half of the century was John Gibson Lockhart's *Memoirs of the Life of Sir Walter Scott, Bart.* (1837–1838). Drawing extensively on Scott's correspondence, diary and journal entries, and autobiographical fragments, *Memoirs of the Life of Sir Walter Scott, Bart.* holds a unique position in the development of nineteenth-century biography; according to Leslie Stephen, it "may safely be described as, next to Boswell's *Johnson,* the best in the language."

"It all began splendidly," Nicolson observes, "We had Moore and Southey and Lockhart; but then came earnestness, and with earnestness hagiography descended on us with its sullen cloud, and the Victorian biographer scribbled laboriously by the light of shaded lamps." The artistic problem confronting the nineteenth-century biographer was the value and function of personal detail. It was Boswell who had "established the lavish use of concrete detail as a principle of biographical art"; the Victorian biographer, however, had to function within the accepted boundaries of decorum and discretion. Conforming to the social, political, and religious orthodoxy of the age, biographers would often consider it part of their purpose to suppress, alter, or distort detail as a means to develop and preserve an idealized version of their subjects. Altick observes: "The conditions under which nineteenth-century biography normally was produced made it unlikely that men and women of boldly original, innovating talent would be attracted to the form." The problem was not so much what the truth really was but how much truth it was permissible for a biographer to tell.

The most notable feature within the development of the genre is what Waldo H. Dunn refers to in his *English Biography* (1916) as "reconstructing a biography; that is, the gathering together of all available historical documents, facts, and traditions relative to some person and from these distilling something like the true story of this person's pilgrimage through life." This methodology is illustrated in Scott's lives of Dryden and Jonathan Swift (1814), Lucy Aikin's *The Life of Joseph Addison* (1843), Carlyle's *The Life of John Sterling* (1851), Elizabeth Cleghorn Gaskell's *The Life of Charlotte Brontë* (1857), David Masson's *The Life of John Milton* (1859–1880), James Spedding's *The Letters and the Life of Francis Bacon* (1861–1874), Alexander Gilchrist's *Life of William Blake, "Pictor Ignotus"* (1863), Sir George Otto Trevelyan's life of Thomas Babington Macaulay (1876), and James Anthony Froude's life of Carlyle (1882–1884).

Of additional importance within nineteenth-century biography, as noted by Nadel in his *Biography: Fiction, Fact and Form* (1984), is the emergence of the professional biographer as "a respected if not admired figure in the literary landscape." Although biography throughout the century was written primarily by individuals drawn to the genre for the purpose of writing a commemorative life, the popularity and commercial prominence of the genre proved, for some, an inviting and often profitable undertaking. For the professional biographer the commemorative instinct in writing a life was replaced by the ability to produce a responsive and dependable product to satisfy public demand or expectation. There gradually emerged, however, a professional who would combine scholarly objectivity, analytical study, and detached interpretation of the subjects to create biographies of artistic merit, accuracy, and completeness.

Among the first to be recognized in this capacity was John Forster. In addition to writing political biographies, notably *Lives of Eminent British Statesmen* (1836–1839), Forster produced literary biographies of Oliver Goldsmith (1848), Walter Savage Landor (1869), Charles Dickens (1872–1874), and Swift (1875). According to Nadel, "The professional status Forster creates for the biographer is more than social or financial recognition; it is the realization that the identity and even existence of the subject is solely with and through what the biography has created, the organic union of the subject and his work, or of history and the individual. Hence, the obligation to correct inaccuracies, or discover new material in order to prove the responsibility of the genre and the sincerity of the biographer. No longer can the biographer be thought of as a casual journeyman, indifferent to his task and irresponsible in his art." The biographical progression initiated by Forster is realized later in the century by such writers as Stephen, John Morley, and Edmund Gosse and extends into twentieth-century biography.

The institutionalization of lexicography in the nineteenth century emphasizes the Victorian predilection for collective lives, and among the most important compilations were *The Dictionary of National Biography (DNB)* and Macmillan's English Men of Letters series. Published in sixty-three volumes from 1885 to 1901, the *DNB* was edited by Stephen and later by Sir Sidney Lee. According to Nadel the *DNB* represents "the apex of the Victorian belief in, and commitment to, fact, reflecting the importance of science and history in the age." The first series of the English Men of Letters, edited by Morley, consisted of thirty-nine volumes published from 1878 to 1892, including Morley's *Burke* (1879), Froude's *Bunyan* (1880), Stephen's *Alexander Pope* (1880), Masson's *De Quincey* (1881), Gosse's *Gray* (1882), Austin Dobson's *Fielding* (1883), and John Addington Symonds's *Sir Philip Sidney* (1886). The English Men of Letters series was of particular importance for enhancing the reputation of literary biography within the nineteenth century; the contribution of such distinguished biographers was instrumental in the success of the series in reaching the attention of a wide public.

Of the early-nineteenth-century biographers, Carlyle was the most influential in developing a substantial body of biographical theory. He also provided the impetus for English biographers to write lives of foreign subjects. Following the example of Carlyle's *The Life of Friedrich Schiller,* nineteenth-century biographers produced such diverse works as Thomas Campbell's *Life of Petrarch* (1841), George Henry Lewes's *The Life and Works of Goethe* (1855), Morley's *Voltaire* (1872) and *Rousseau* (1873), and Symonds's *The Life of Michelangelo Buonarroti* (1893). In the latter half of the century the most important biographical theorist was Gosse, who railed against the Victorian biography of manners and advocated the concise and introspective interpretation of a subject. As one of the most versatile of late-Victorian biographers, Gosse, in addition to his life of Thomas Gray for the English Men of Letters series, produced lives of Sir Walter Ralegh (1886), William Congreve (1888), and John Donne (1899), and remained productive into the early twentieth century with lives of Coventry Patmore (1905), Henrik Ibsen (1907), and A. C. Swinburne (1912).

By virtue of the quantity and quality of literary production, the nineteenth century was, as noted by Dunn, a "century of triumph for men of letters." *Nineteenth-Century British Literary Biographers* is designed to introduce the lives and works of those individuals who influenced the development of the genre and helped solidify biography as an artistic as well as a professional endeavor. Extending from the Romantic tradition to the Victorian age to the emergence of modernism, the nineteenth century witnessed a transformation of unprecedented proportions. In his evaluation of its intrinsic worth, Dunn writes: "A century which produced so many men worthy of record, so many biographies worthy of their subjects, and readers in such abundance, is a century worthy of the most careful study, and one destined to leave a lasting impression upon the life of mankind."

— Steven Serafin

Acknowledgments

This book was produced by Bruccoli Clark Layman, Inc. Karen L. Rood is senior editor for the *Dictionary of Literary Biography* series. Philip B. Dematteis was the in-house editor.

Production coordinator is George F. Dodge. Photography editors are Josephine A. Bruccoli and Joseph Matthew Bruccoli. Layout and graphics supervisor is Penney L. Haughton. Copyediting supervisor is Bill Adams. Typesetting supervisor is Kathleen M. Flanagan. Julie E. Frick is editorial associate. The production staff includes Phyllis A. Avant, Ann M. Cheschi, Melody W. Clegg, Patricia Coate, Wilma Weant Dague, Brigitte B. de Guzman, Denise W. Edwards, Sarah A. Estes, Joyce Fowler, Laurel M. Gladden, Stephanie C. Hatchell, Leslie Haynesworth, John Lorio, Rebecca Mayo, Kathy Lawler Merlette, Pamela D. Norton, Delores I. Plastow, Patricia F. Salisbury, Paul Smith, and William L. Thomas, Jr.

Walter W. Ross and Deborah M. Chasteen did library research. They were assisted by the following librarians at the Thomas Cooper Library of the University of South Carolina: Linda Holderfield and the interlibrary-loan staff; reference librarians Gwen Baxter, Daniel Boice, Faye Chadwell, Cathy Eckman, Gary Geer, Qun "Gerry" Jiao, Jean Rhyne, Carol Tobin, Carolyn Tyler, Virginia Weathers, Elizabeth Whiznant, and Connie Widney; circulation-department head Thomas Marcil; and acquisitions-searching supervisor David Haggard. Special thanks are due to Roger Mortimer and the staff of Special Collections at the Thomas Cooper Library. The following librarians generously provided material: William Cagle and Joel Silver of the Lilly Library, Indiana University, and Ann Freudenberg, Kendon Stubbs, and Edmund Berkeley, Jr., of the University of Virginia Library.

Nineteenth-Century British Literary Biographers

Dictionary of Literary Biography

Lucy Aikin

(6 November 1781 – 29 January 1864)

Elise F. Knapp
Western Connecticut State University

BOOKS: *Epistles on Women, Exemplifying Their Charac-*
ter and Condition in Various Ages and Nations: With
Miscellaneous Poems (London: Printed for J.
Johnson, 1810; Boston: Wells & Wait, 1810);

Juvenile Correspondence, or Letters, Designed as Examples
of the Epistolary Style, for Children of Both Sexes
(London: J. Johnson, 1811; Boston: Cummings & Hilliard, 1822);

Lorimer: A Tale (London: Printed for Henry Colburn, Sold by G. Goldie, Edinburgh; and J.
Cumming, Dublin, 1814; Philadelphia: Carey / Boston: Wells & Lilly, 1816);

Memoirs of the Court of Queen Elizabeth, 2 volumes
(London: Printed for Longman, Hurst, Rees,
Orme & Brown, 1818; Boston: Wells & Lilly,
1821);

Memoirs of the Court of King James the First, 2 volumes
(London: Longman, Hurst, Rees, Orme &
Brown, 1822; Boston: Wells & Lilly, 1822);

Memoir of John Aikin, M.D.: With a Selection of His Mis-
cellaneous Pieces, Biographical, Moral, and Critical,
2 volumes (London: Baldwin, Cradock & Joy,
1823; Philadelphia: A. Small, 1824);

An English Lesson Book, for the Junior Classes (London:
Printed for Longman, Rees, Orme, Brown &
Green, 1828); republished as *Holiday Stories for*
Young Readers (London: Groombridge, 1858);

Memoirs of the Court of King Charles the First, 2 volumes
(London: Longman, Rees, Orme, Brown,
Green & Longman, 1828; Philadelphia: Carey,
Lea & Blanchard, 1833);

The Life of Joseph Addison (London: Longman,
Brown, Green & Longmans, 1843; Philadelphia: Carey & Hart, 1846);

Lucy Aikin; silhouette by J. Kendrick (Cushing/Whitney
Medical Library, Yale University)

Memoirs Miscellanies, and Letters of the Late Lucy Aikin,
Including Those Addressed to the Rev. Dr. Channing
from 1826 to 1842, edited by Philip Hemery Le

Breton (London: Longman, Green, Longman, Roberts & Green, 1864).

OTHER: *Poetry for Children: Consisting of Short Pieces to Be Committed to Memory,* edited by Aikin (London: Printed for Richard Phillips, 1801);

Louis François Jauffret, *The Travels of Rolando: Containing, in a Supposed Tour round the World, Authentic Descriptions of the Geography, Natural History, Manners and Antiquities of Various Countries,* translated by Aikin, 4 volumes (London: Printed for Richard Phillips, 1804);

Jean Gaspar Hess, *The Life of Ulrich Zwingli,* translated by Aikin (London: J. Johnson, 1813);

Anna Laetitia Barbauld, *The Works of Anna Laetitia Barbauld,* edited, with a memoir, by Aikin (2 volumes, London: Longman, Hurst, Rees, Orme, Brown & Green, 1825; 3 volumes, Boston: Reed, 1826);

Barbauld, *A Legacy for Young Ladies: Consisting of Miscellaneous Pieces, in Prose and Verse,* edited by Aikin (London: Printed for Longman, Hurst, Rees, Orme & Green, 1826; Boston: Reed, 1826);

Elizabeth Ogilvy Benger, *Memoirs of the Life of Anne Boleyn, Queen of Henry VIII,* includes "Memoir of Miss Benger" by Aikin (London: Printed for Longman, Hurst, Orme & Brown, 1827);

The Juvenile Tale Book: A Collection of Interesting Tales and Novels for Youth, contributions by Aikin (London, 1837);

John Aikin, ed., *Selected Works of the British Poets with Biographical and Critical Prefaces,* edited by Aikin (London: Longman, Brown, Green & Longmans, 1845);

John Aikin, *The Arts of Life,* edited by Aikin (London: Longman, Brown, Green, Longmans & Roberts, 1858);

Daniel Defoe, *Robinson Crusoe in Words of One Syllable,* edited by Aikin as Godolphin (London & New York: Routledge, 1868 [i.e., 1867]);

Thomas Day, *Sandford and Merton: In Words of One Syllable,* edited by Aikin as Mary Godolphin (London & New York: Cassell, Petter & Galpin, 1868?);

Aesop's Fables: In Words of One Syllable, edited by Aikin as Godolphin (New York: Miller, 1869; London: Cassell, Petter & Gilpin, 1873);

John Bunyan, *The Pilgrim's Progress, in Words of One Syllable,* edited by Aikin as Godolphin (London: Routledge, 1869; New York: McLoughlin, 1884);

Johann David Wyss, *The Swiss Family Robinson, in Words of One Syllable,* edited by Aikin as

Godolphin (London, 1869; Philadelphia: Altemus, 1899).

Lucy Aikin was the first woman biographer in England to base her writing on extensive research in original documents. In long and scholarly volumes on Queen Elizabeth I, King James I, and King Charles I she illuminated not only royal figures and their courts but also the relationships between their reigns and the evolving culture of the English nation; in her biographies of English writers she linked her subjects' creative work to their education, their experiences as children, and the circumstances of their adult lives. She declined to follow a set theory of biography: "Every life should be written on the plan suited to itself," she asserted in *The Life of Joseph Addison* (1843). At a time when serious education for women was a controversial issue, even in her own family, she argued for equality of education for the sexes. Her work is overtly didactic; its objective is to produce informed and independent citizens. A member of a family of educators, Aikin wrote, translated, and revised literature for children. Her popularity was strong and enduring; editions of her works appeared on a regular basis until well into the twentieth century. While her contemporaries Jane Austen and the Brontë sisters wrote under pseudonyms, Aikin used her own name for most of her works.

Aikin was born in Warrington, Lancashire, on 6 November 1781 to John Aikin, M.D., and Martha Jennings Aikin, his first cousin. Lucy Aikin's grandfather John Aikin, D.D., had been a tutor in the classics and theology at the Warrington Academy, a Dissenting institution devoted to training young men for the Christian ministry. At the time of his daughter's birth, the younger John Aikin was also a tutor in the classics at Warrington Academy. Joseph Priestley, the scientist and radical theologian, was a friend of the Aikin family, as were other distinguished philosophers, Dissenting theologians, and literary figures.

As the fifth child and only daughter, Lucy was indulged and admired by her father and his colleagues. She was saved from being spoiled, she later acknowledged, by the "good sense, the firmness, the parental affection well understood by my excellent mother," who "taught me what flattery was, and strongly warned me against being led away by it." The contrasting but powerful influences of her father and mother shaped their daughter's theory of education. Two early experiences contributed to her beliefs about teaching. When she was three years old, her grandmother Aikin, whose own daughter, Anna Laetitia Barbauld, had been an infant prodigy who read at the age of twenty months, became exasperated at Aikin's apparent obtuseness and dismissed her, calling her a "little dunce." The emotional scar left by this incident remained with Aikin permanently; she later described her feeling of "incurable deficiency," adding: "How soon may the tender spirit of a child be broken, and its faculties dulled by such treatment!"

Quite a different experience, this one positive, set Aikin on her life's work of writing. When her mother reprimanded her for not sharing with her brother George, Aikin justified her action heatedly and at length. Although her mother continued to disapprove, her father exclaimed, "Why, Lucy, you are quite eloquent!" Aikin's reaction reveals both the impression her father's praise had on her and her assumptions about sexual roles: "Had I been a boy, it might have made me an orator; as it was, it incited me to exert to the utmost, by tongue and pen, all the power of words I possessed or could ever acquire – I had learned where my strength lay." Her father's encouragement and guidance led Aikin to undertake increasingly independent and challenging intellectual tasks. He also inspired her with an enduring love of nature, especially of the Lancashire hills and the sea. Her education was entirely private except for a brief and unhappy period at a day school, where she found herself intellectually advanced far beyond her classmates.

After the dissolution of the Warrington Academy in 1783 the Aikins settled in Yarmouth, where Dr. Aikin hoped to set up a medical practice. When these expectations dimmed, they moved to London in 1792 and lived there until 1797, when Dr. Aikin's health began to fail. Convinced that rural surroundings would invigorate him, they moved to Stoke Newington.

By the time she was seventeen Aikin was fluent in Latin, French, and Italian, and she began to have short articles and reviews published in the *Annual Register*. Caught up by her family's commitment to education, she began to translate and adapt informational works, simplifying and shortening them for young readers. Her books for children laid the groundwork for the kinds of knowledge and research that were to distinguish her memoirs of English royal courts. In 1804 she translated and adapted Louis François Jauffret's *The Travels of Rolando,* a travel adventure that provided accurate descriptions of the geography, natural and social history, manners, and ancient sites of countries around the world. Her *Poetry for Children: Consisting of Short Pieces to Be Committed to Memory* (1801) came

out in at least eleven further editions before 1836; its title reflects the author's belief that a strong memory can be built through practice and training.

A clear didactic purpose marks all of Aikin's work for the young, but in every case moral lessons are veiled by dramatic or sentimental surface appeal, notably in *Juvenile Correspondence, or Letters, Designed as Examples of Epistolary Style, for Children of Both Sexes* (1811), *The Life of Ulrich Zwingli* (1812), and *An English Lesson Book, for the Junior Classes* (1828).

Aikin's *Epistles on Women, Exemplifying Their Character and Condition in Various Ages and Nations,* a history of women in verse, appeared in 1810. This curious piece is Augustan in form, consisting of heroic couplets, but it is forward-looking in its argument that women ought to be recognized and treated as men's equal partners. Aikin asserts that women "have been the worthy associates of the best efforts of the best men" and that "no talent, no virtue, is masculine alone; no fault or folly exclusively feminine" and predicts that "the Juvenals and Popes of future ages will abstain from making [women] the butt of scorn or malice . . . nor will even the reputation of our great Milton himself secure him from the charge of blasphemous presumption in making his Eve address to Adam the acknowledgement, 'God is thy head, thou mine.'" In the four epistles, tracing women's position from primitive societies to her own, Aikin argues that "man always suffers by degrading women"; finally, she exhorts Englishmen to "look with favor on the mental improvement of females." Aikin's liberal position is more remarkable in that her celebrated aunt, the poet Barbauld, consistently opposed higher education for women. When the bluestocking Elizabeth Montagu invited her to help set up a college for young ladies, Barbauld emphatically declined: women, she said, need only "such a general tincture of knowledge as to make them agreeable companions to a man of sense." Women should be "subject to a regulation like that of the ancient Spartans; the thefts of knowledge in our sex are only connived at while carefully concealed, and if displayed, punished with disgrace." Aikin's willingness to take a position so radically different from one supported by the family's foremost author, who was also her father's collaborator on literary projects, reflects considerable strength and independence; that she was also her aunt's devoted friend and admirer reveals her open-mindedness, a quality that distinguishes her biographies.

In 1814 Aikin experimented with the gothic novel, producing *Lorimer: A Tale*. After his father's death the melancholy Eustace Lorimer travels to

*Lucy Aikin's father, John Aikin, M.D., whose biography she
published in 1823 (Cushing/Whitney Medical Library,
Yale University)*

France, where he meets and falls in love with the beautiful Bertha Fermor. They endure daunting trials and dangerous threats before being finally united. The plot is ingenious, but the characters are flat. *Lorimer* was Aikin's last attempt at adult fiction.

By this time in her early thirties, Aikin chafed at the necessity of asking her father for money. She had written her works for children in part because there was a good market for didactic children's books, but she felt ready for something more challenging. "Of the two," she wrote her brother Edmund in 1818, "I believe I had rather amuse men and women than instruct children." In an earlier letter to Edmund dated December 1814, she outlined her plan for writing a history of the court of Queen Elizabeth. "I am glad you like the notion of my Queen Elizabeth project. I know not how I shall succeed in the execution, but the preparation is delightful to me. I mean to call it 'a view of the court of Queen Elizabeth,' or some such thing, and intend to collect all the notices I can of the manners of the age, the state of literature, arts &c., which I shall interweave, as well as I am able, with the biographies

of the Queen and the other eminent characters of her time, binding all together with as slender a thread of political history as will serve to keep other matters in their places. Of books I shall certainly want a great number, but the Red Cross Street Library will furnish a good many – Mr. Roscoe has kindly promised me several of his – from other friends I can borrow some, and when all these are exhausted, perhaps I may contract with a bookseller to supply me."

The letter describes the method she followed to produce her first highly successful biography: she brought into a harmonious combination evidence from many primary and printed sources, including the John Strype collection of manuscripts, which had been published as *Annals of the Reformation and Establishment of Religion* (1708–1731); the papers of William Cecil, Lord Burghley; and those of Sir Philip Sidney, published as *Collins's Letters and Memorials of State, &c.,* commonly called the *Sydney Papers* (1746); and Birch's *Memoirs of the Reign of Queen Elizabeth* (1754). *Memoirs of the Court of Queen Elizabeth* (1818) includes full characterizations of all the major figures who surrounded the queen, as well as many minor characters. Henry VIII is depicted as a dangerous, unpredictable, volatile, and cruel man who could also be sentimental: he was "moved to tears on reading the tender and pious letter from the dying hand of Catherine [of Aragon]." Elizabeth is brilliant, scholarly, vain, and deeply divided on the executions of Mary, Queen of Scots, and Robert Devereux, second Earl of Essex. One of the most interesting characters is Robert Dudley, Earl of Leicester, for whom the queen had an abiding passion. One of the book's many anecdotes has to do with the power he had over the queen because they were both born on the same day. "It was believed by the superstition of the age, that this coincidence of their nativities produced a secret and invincible sympathy which secured to Dudley, during life, the affections of his sovereign lady." Throughout the work Aikin argues the need for a strong monarch independent from European entanglements. After detailing the uncertainty and constant shifting of alliances marking Elizabeth's rise to power, the book concludes with the happiness and stability of the English people under a strong queen who might be vain or unjust but who puts her people first. A parallel theme is the sustained religious struggle between Catholics and Protestants. Other topics have to do with cultural history: the flowering of English poetry during Elizabeth's reign, the erudition and education of women in the court, and the widespread ignorance about disease.

Aikin's youngest brother, Edmund, a Liverpool architect, contributed "On the Domestic Architecture of the Reign of Elizabeth," which was appended to the second volume of the biography and describes the construction and furnishings of castles the queen occupied and visited. Aikin wrote to Edmund in March 1818, "At length I can say here is my book — *our* book, rather, since the appendix is yours . . . it is a nervous thing to face the critics of these days! I am not quite mercenary enough altogether to prefer solid pudding to empty praise, but solid pudding may reasonably enough surely be preferred to dry beating; therefore, I may be excused for saying that, at present, the money is my most agreeable matter of anticipation."

Memoirs of the Court of Queen Elizabeth was an immediate success, going into eight editions by 1869. Her publishers approached Aikin with suggestions that she write again immediately, but it took Aikin four years to research and write her next important biography, *Memoirs of the Court of King James the First* (1822). This two-volume examination of the life and times of James I begins with his birth in 1566 and traces his loss of power and popularity until his

death in 1625. The volumes are laced with contemporary accounts from journals, letters, diaries, and court papers. The reader becomes an imaginary member of the court; only occasionally does the author intrude with historical or literary judgments. Subjects of particular importance include James's right to the throne, which was questionable because of legal restrictions enacted by Elizabeth to bar Mary, Queen of Scots, or her issue from the succession. James's legendary frigidity of temperament and feebleness of judgment are countered by his deep love of learning, his long periods of genial goodwill, and his loyalty to friends. The reader realizes what a strange figure he cut in the English court with his coarse manners, vulgarity, and unintelligible Scottish dialect. Biographies and histories of prominent families in the court are treated at length, as are literature, manners, medicine, superstition, and abuses of the system of justice, especially torture by the rack.

A principal theme in *Memoirs of the Court of King James the First* is the bitter struggle between Catholics and Protestants. The implications of this religious contest extend through the fabric of society. The connections between literature and its social context are pointed out in fine detail. Aikin discusses all the great seventeenth-century dramatists, noting that Ben Jonson wrote many masks to accommodate the notions of King James and Queen Anne and to give parts to members of the court. She sketches John Donne's life and career, including his resistance to taking holy orders; when he finally agreed, James promptly rewarded him by making him dean of Saint Paul's Cathedral. In a sharp judgment of Donne's poetry, Aikin condemns his experiments with their "strange conceits" and "gross language." She reserves her highest praise for Donne's meditations, letters, and satires. Aikin stresses throughout her work the need for a monarch who puts the happiness and welfare of his people before all else, and James I fails this test. Her final evaluation is that his "intentions were better than his performance."

Like its predecessor, *Memoirs of the Court of King James the First* gained immediate popular recognition; it went through three editions in less than two years. Critical acknowledgment was harder for a woman to achieve; but it came, although in unusual form. The *Edinburgh Review* for June 1822 included a review of Sir Walter Scott's *The Fortunes of Nigel* (1822); a reference to King James I in the review prompted a footnote that testifies to the popular response to Aikin's work: "We cannot refer, in any way, to the reign or character of this Sovereign, without thinking of the

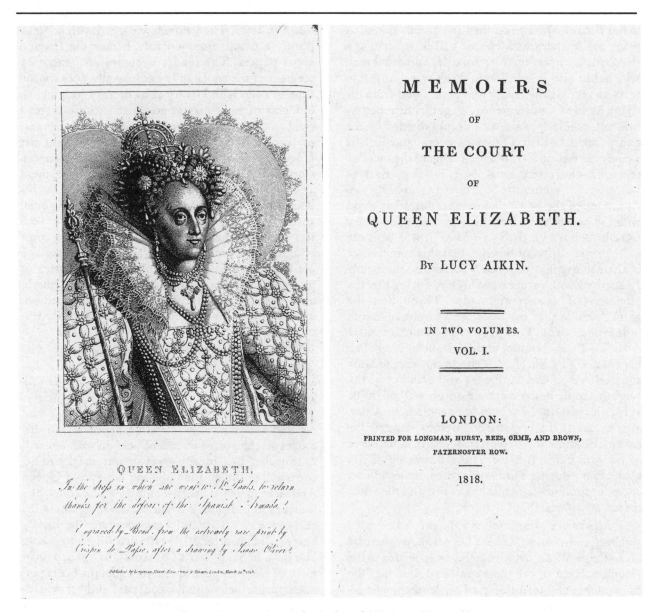

QUEEN ELIZABETH,

In the dress in which she went to St. Pauls, to return thanks for the defeat of the Spanish Armada.

Engraved by Bead from the extremely rare print by Crispin de Passe, after a drawing by Isaac Oliver.

Published by Longman Hurst, Rees, Orme & Brown, London, March 14th 1818.

MEMOIRS

OF

THE COURT

OF

QUEEN ELIZABETH.

By LUCY AIKIN.

IN TWO VOLUMES.
VOL. I.

LONDON:

PRINTED FOR LONGMAN, HURST, REES, ORME, AND BROWN,
PATERNOSTER ROW.

1818.

Frontispiece and title page for the first of Aikin's royal biographies

admirable account of him and his court which Miss Aikin has lately given to the world, in a work very nearly as entertaining as a novel, and more instructive than most histories. This is not only full of interest and curiosity, but is written throughout with the temperance, impartiality, and dispassionate judgment of a true historian, and in a style always lucid and succinct, and frequently both animated and elegant. We regret that it did not fall into our hands till the public opinion had been so decidedly pronounced on it as to make it unnecessary, if not presumptuous in us to interpose our own. We can only say that we are now fully inclined to trust her with the continuation of the work she has begun; and earnestly exhort her to proceed to the reigns of the two Charleses, and the Protector who steps between them – in all respects the most difficult and important part of our national story."

Before Aikin could respond to the challenges raised by the anonymous reviewer, the deaths of her father and aunt diverted her energy to family biography. Her father died in 1822, and her two-volume *Memoir of John Aikin, M.D.: With a Selection of His Miscellaneous Pieces, Biographical, Moral, and Critical* appeared the following year. The exceptional range of John Aikin's talents and interests is revealed: a doctor of medicine by profession, he studied and wrote extensively about English literature, the history of medicine in Britain, children's education, English trees and plants, and the geography of England.

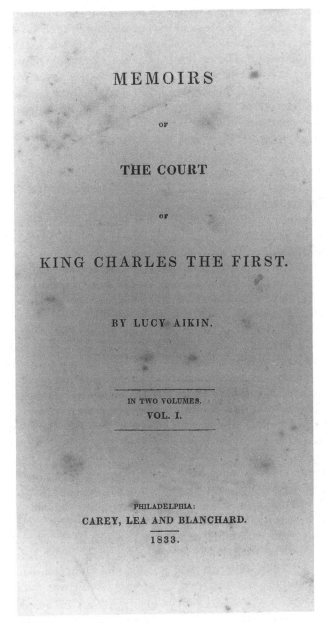

Title page for the third and last of Aikin's royal biographies

A defender of liberty and civil rights, he argued against the workhouse and in favor of rights to security and freedom for the poor. Dr. Aikin's support for the French Revolution cost him most of his medical practice in Yarmouth. His interest in practicing medicine was consistently weaker than his passion for literary studies, theology, and political theory. He spoke out for women's rights and women's education. Women should be "the *companions,* contradistinguished from the *playthings* of men," he asserted in an argument in favor of equal education for both sexes. His friends were many and influential; in addition to Priestley, they included the geographer Thomas Pennant.

His daughter's account of his life gives scant information about Dr. Aikin's family, with the striking exception of his relationship with his sister, Anna Laetitia Aikin Barbauld. The two worked closely together on literary projects, notably *Evenings at Home* (1792–1796), and were in daily correspondence for long periods. Perhaps the most startling indication of their close bond was Dr. Aikin's agreement to let his sister and her husband, who were unable to have children, raise his son Charles as their own.

The review of *Memoir of John Aikin, M.D.* in the *Gentleman's Magazine* for November 1823 acknowledged the scholarly excellence of Dr. Aikin's writing but noted that "It is not prudent for a Medical Man to take a conspicuous part in any study not evidently connected with his profession." The review goes on: "We cannot dismiss this work, without congratulating Miss Aikin upon [her] judicious manner . . . and elegant style. [Her] taste . . . confers high honour upon her literary character."

Barbauld died on 9 March 1825. That year her niece published a selection of Barbauld's poetry, correspondence, and essays, for which she wrote a highly complimentary biographical essay. Aikin emphasizes Barbauld's childhood experiences, especially at the intellectually stimulating Warrington Academy, and her strong family ties, especially to John Aikin, whose encouragement of her writing led to its initial publication. Each of Barbauld's published works is discussed in the context of her life. Women's education is treated at length. Barbauld disagreed with her friend Elizabeth Montague that women's education should be the same as men's, observing in a letter that "to have too great fondness for books is little favorable to the happiness of a woman." Barbauld's opposition to slavery is emphasized in a discussion of her "Epistle to Mr. Wilberforce," which praises his efforts to abolish the slave trade. Barbauld's commitment to children's education and – despite her opposition to equal education for women – her support for women writers are sustained themes. Philip Hemery Le Breton, the husband of Aikin's niece, evaluated the biographies of Dr. Aikin and Barbauld in his introduction to Lucy Aikin's memoirs and letters (1864): "Both may be regarded as works of filial piety; for her aunt shared with her father in the reverence and affection with which she regarded the union of virtue and talent. The cast of her own mind fitted her better for sympathizing with the strong practical sense, the liberal views, and the literary diligence of her father, than with the sensibility and poetical elegance of her aunt."

Her family biographies completed, Aikin turned once again to British history. *Memoirs of the Court of King Charles the First* (1828) traces the record of the king and his court from his birth in 1600 to his beheading in 1649. Social and cultural developments are woven into the text as it unfolds the great matters of the state. Literary history, art and architecture, manners, women's education, and medical history are reported in the context of the widening chasm between king and commoner.

During the course of the two volumes Aikin builds a sense of the inevitability of Charles's tragic fate. His undisguised sympathy for the Catholic cause, his French Catholic wife, Henrietta, his recurring hopes of establishing absolute monarchy, and his haughty manner combine to prevent him from making peace with a punitive and unyielding Protestant force bent on severely restricting, if not eliminating, the monarchy. As a strong liberal and a Dissenter, Aikin finds little to admire in Charles. After quoting at length from court papers describing his repeated requests for a hearing before his beheading, she declares herself "unequal . . . in many ways" to measuring the justice of his trial and execution.

Aikin had nothing further published for fifteen years; then, in 1843, *The Life of Joseph Addison* appeared. Several considerations prompted her choice of subject. Edward Tickell, a descendant of Addison's executor, had presented her with important private papers and previously unpublished letters. In addition, Addison had always been a favorite author of the Aikin family; Lucy Aikin's library included a thirty-three-volume collection of Addison's works that had belonged to her father. Finally, she wished to correct what she saw as "a real deficiency in our literature," noting that biographies and critical essays had been written on Alexander Pope, Jonathan Swift, and John Dryden but that nothing had been done on Addison except Thomas Tickell's introduction to Addison's collected works (1721) and Samuel Johnson's essay in his *Prefaces, Biographical and Critical, to the Works of the English Poets* (1779–1781). She believed that Johnson's judgment was swayed by an "unfavorable bias" against Addison because Addison was a strong Whig, noting that Johnson's "judicial scales were never held with an unswerving hand when the character, whether personal or literary, of a decided Whig was placed in the balance."

Aikin's biography begins with an extensive discussion of the life and writings of Addison's father, Dr. Lancelot Addison, who strongly influenced his son's literary production. Another powerful early influence was the younger Addison's education at the Charterhouse, where he met Richard Steele and became a serious classical scholar. Aikin uses Addison's correspondence to trace his political and literary careers, including his friendships with Pope, Swift, and Lady Mary Wortley Montagu. She builds an impressive account of his long and influential political career, from his election to Parliament as a member for Malmsbury and his development as spokesman for the Whig party in the periodical *Whig Examiner*. His political activities brought about a coolness in his relationship with Swift, a relationship Aikin follows closely throughout her work. Aikin examines Addison's writing in the context of its creation, always emphasizing his wit, humor, imagination, and subtle moral and aesthetic purposes. Finally, she evaluates his merit as critic, describing it as "that of the restorer, or first promulgator among ourselves, of a pure and correct taste; that taste of which good sense is the law." Her warm defense of Addison prompted a response from Thomas Babington Macaulay, who charged her in the *Edinburgh Review* (July 1843) with having "often fallen into errors of a very serious kind." His claim is exaggerated, as American editors were quick to point out, but Aikin wrote no more literary biographies.

After her father's death Aikin and her mother had moved to Hampstead, where Martha Aikin died in 1830. During the last twenty years of her own life, Aikin lived with Anna Letitia Le Breton, the daughter of her brother Charles, and Anna's husband Philip. In 1874 Anna Le Breton published her aunt's letters to William Ellery Channing, an American clergyman whom Aikin met in Stoke Newington. Their lively correspondence from 1826 to 1842 covers a great variety of moral, political, literary, and theological topics. The letters in which American and English attitudes are compared and contrasted illuminate the cultural differences between the two nations in informal but striking observations.

After the uncertain success of *The Life of Joseph Addison* Aikin began to use a pseudonym, Mary Godolphin, for some successful children's books: adaptions of Thomas Day's *Sandford and Merton* (1868?), *Aesop's Fables* (1869), Daniel Defoe's *Robinson Crusoe* (1882), John Bunyan's *The Pilgrim's Progress* (1884), and Johann Davis Wyss's *The Swiss Family Robinson* (1914). These works, which went through many editions, were all published after her death from influenza on 29 January 1864. She was buried in Hampstead next to her old friend, the author Joanna Baillie.

Aikin's achievement was remarkable, almost unique. As a literary biographer she was a leader in placing emphasis on hereditary propensities, childhood experiences, and education as factors that shape the development of an author. She used anecdotes and letters to enliven her books, to support her interpretations, and to provide contemporary literary history. She wrote lively but objective period biographies based on extensive research in primary materials; she was an outspoken champion of equal education and rights for women; she knew and corresponded with many distinguished public figures and writers; and she supported herself by writing under her own name.

Letters:

Correspondence of William Ellery Channing, D.D., and Lucy Aikin, from 1826 to 1842, edited by Anna Letitia Le Breton (Boston: Roberts, 1874).

James Dykes Campbell

(2 November 1838 – 1 June 1895)

Alun R. Jones
University of Wales

BOOK: *Samuel Taylor Coleridge: A Narrative of the Events of His Life* (London & New York: Macmillan, 1894; republished with memoir of Campbell by Leslie Stephen, London & New York: Macmillan, 1896).

OTHER: Alfred Tennyson, *Poems MDCCCXXX. MDCCCXXXIII,* edited by Campbell (N.p., 1862);

Some Portions of Essays Contributed to The Spectator by Mr. Joseph Addison: Now First Printed from His Ms. Notebook, edited by Campbell (Glasgow: Printed for J. D. Campbell by Bell & Bain, 1864);

The Poetical Works of Samuel Taylor Coleridge, with a biographical introduction, edited by Campbell (London: Macmillan, 1893);

Coleridge's Poems: A Facsimile Reproduction of Proofs and Mss. of Some of the Poems with Preface and Notes by W. Hale White, edited by Campbell (London: Constable, 1899);

Charles Lamb: Specimens of English Dramatic Poets Who Lived about the Time of Shakespeare, with Extracts from the Garrick Plays, edited by Campbell (London: Routledge, 1907; New York: Dutton, 1907).

James Dykes Campbell's biography of Samuel Taylor Coleridge (1894) is a landmark in the history of the genre in that it defines the standards of scholarship, accuracy, documentation, and impartiality by which every biographer of Coleridge has since been measured. Moreover, despite his lack of formal education, Campbell's dedication to his research, his passion for truth, and his love of literature, combined with a warm understanding of humanity, enabled him to write a work that did much to establish biography at the center of literary studies.

Campbell was born at Port Glasgow, Scotland, on 2 November 1838; he was the second son and third child of Peter Campbell and Jean Dykes Campbell. At six he was sent to the burgh school in Port Glasgow, where he received an education that included French and Latin. He left school at fourteen and joined the office of a local merchant. On the death of his father in 1854 the family moved to Glasgow; there Campbell found employment with R. Cochrane & Co., which manufactured Verreville pottery. It was at that time that he seems to have begun his study of English literature.

In April 1860 he went to Toronto, Canada, as a representative of his employers. He quickly became a member of a distinguished group with literary and scientific interests that included Edwin Hatch, later Bampton Lecturer and Reader in Ecclesiastical History at the University of Oxford but at that time Professor of Classics at Trinity College, Toronto. He collected early editions of the poetry of Alfred Tennyson and made a close textual study of the poems. In 1862 he privately printed a small volume in which he reprinted poems from *Poems, Chiefly Lyrical* (1830) and *Poems* (1833) that Tennyson had suppressed in subsequent editions of his work. He also gave a full list of all revisions that the poet had made in poems that he had allowed to be republished. The privately printed *Poems MDCCCXXX. MDCCCXXXIII* is a foolscap octavo of 120 pages in plain paper wrappers, blue in some copies and green in others. Tennyson's name does not appear anywhere in the book. John Camden Hotten, a London publisher, attempted to sell copies of the book, and Sotheby's auction catalogue for 17, 18, and 19 June 1862 describes the book as having been produced by a gentleman in "the wilds of Canada." Tennyson took legal action against Hotten to protect his copyright, obtaining first an injunction prohibiting the sale of the book and then an apology from Hotten, who was also fined one hundred pounds and ordered to deliver up all copies in his possession. As a consequence, this work is now a scarce collector's item.

Campbell returned to Glasgow in 1862 and started in business for himself as a commission mer-

James Dykes Campbell (engraving from the Illustrated London
News, *8 June 1895)*

chant and agent for the Jarrow Iron Company and later for Palmer's Shipbuilding and Iron Co. He applied unsuccessfully for the post of librarian at the Universities of St. Andrews and Glasgow, wrote reviews for the *Glasgow Herald,* and contributed to *Notes and Queries.* Among his earliest contributions to the latter was "Coleridge's Early Poems. Published 1796" (1863). Between February 1863 and February 1866 he had almost seventy items on a wide variety of topics published in the magazine, testifying to the breadth and detail of his reading and his curiosity about words, meanings, and literature. His contributions are marked by their attention to precision, definition, and fact. Some are on Scottish literary history and some are concerned with etymology and distinctions of meaning of words.

In 1864 he privately printed 250 copies of a blue-covered pamphlet entitled *Some Portions of Essays Contributed to The Spectator by Mr. Joseph Addison.* In "An Advertisement" he says that he knows nothing of the provenance of these papers, but that the manuscript, from which he printed excerpts from the essays "Of Imagination," "Of Jealousie," and "Of Fame," was contained in an "old calf-bound octavo volume" that he had acquired from a London dealer in 1858. In an article, "Addison's 'Spectator' *MSS,*" in the *Athenæum* (1 November 1890), Campbell says: "I was young in 1864, and in the introduction to the tract I assumed too confidently that my

own firm belief in the genuineness of the MS. would be accepted by the critics as evidence enough. The *Athenæum* in a long article [27 August 1864] very soon and very properly undeceived me by calling for the history of the MS., and the controversy was taken up somewhat warmly by several London and provincial papers. . . . I purchased it in 1858 from Mr C. J. Skeet then a well-known second-hand bookseller in King William Street, Strand." He points out that it had since been accepted as authentic by Leslie Stephen, who referred to the manuscript in his entry on Addison in the *Dictionary of National Biography* and by W. J. Courthope in his book on Addison in the English Men of Letters series (1884).

In 1866 Campbell joined a mercantile firm in Port Louis, Mauritius, and soon after set up a firm in his own name. According to the memoir of Campbell by Stephen in the 1906 edition of the Coleridge biography, Campbell made a trip to Bombay shortly after reaching Mauritius and in 1869 visited Australia on business. The writer Walter Besant had arrived in Mauritius in 1861 to take up a teaching post; in his autobiography (1902) he recalls Campbell as one of a group of young merchants "who have literary proclivities without any particular gifts of imagination or expression. Most of this kind try the impossible and produce bad verse and bad fiction. Campbell did nothing of the kind; he kept up his reading, he went on with his work, and at the age of forty or so he found he could retire with a competence."

Among Campbell's correspondents was William Michael Rossetti, who was at that time preparing his edition of the works of Percy Bysshe Shelley (1870). In his diary Rossetti describes Campbell as "my Shelleyan correspondent in the Mauritius"; later he found Campbell to be "a man of remarkable genial and friendly address." In June 1872 Besant took Rossetti the manuscript belonging to Campbell that had been the subject of their correspondence, which contained the originals of writings published in the *Keepsake* for 1828. One of these was a poem, "Sadok the Wanderer," which the index to the manuscript attributed to Shelley; Rossetti, however, was of the opinion that neither the poem nor the handwriting was Shelley's, which has proved to be the case.

In 1873 Campbell became a partner in Ireland, Fraser & Co., the leading firm of merchants on the island. On 13 November 1875 he married Mary Sophia Chesney, the elder daughter of General F. R. Chesney; the marriage was childless. He seems to have devoted much of his time in Mauritius to reading, studying, and preparing himself for the life of the scholar that he afterwards became. As Stephen remarked in his memoir of Campbell, "He must have had from nature the scholar's instincts of accuracy and minute observation. They were no doubt heightened by his experience of a merchant's office, which taught him how to work systematically; to keep accounts, whether of money or of facts, clearly; and to appreciate the bearing of minute indications with unfailing commonsense." Besant remembered in Campbell's obituary in the *Athenæum* (8 June 1895) that "he was attracted towards Coleridge as the centre of a group of writers about whom he was always reading and extending his knowledge." On a visit to England with his wife in 1878 Campbell explored every corner of the Lake District, carefully going over the ground made memorable by Coleridge and William Wordsworth.

Campbell was so successful in business that he was able to retire in June 1881 and return to England. After a tour of Italy, during which he became friendly with the American writer Charles Dudley Warner, he settled in a flat at 29 Albert Hall Mansions, Kensington Gore. He quickly became part of London's literary life and was soon on terms of close friendship with some of London's leading literary figures. Among them was Anne Procter, the widow of Bryan Waller Procter (Barry Cornwall) then in her eighties, who also lived in Albert Hall Mansions. Through her he gained entry into the lit-

erary world that stretched back to the time of Coleridge and the Romantics of which she and her husband had been a part. He also developed a friendship with Robert Browning, who valued Campbell not only as a friend but also as a bibliographer and book collector. Campbell established the authenticity of Browning's copy of Thomas Coryate's *Crudities* (1611) by collating it with the uniquely perfect copy in Chetham's Library, Manchester. Campbell was elected to the committee of the Browning Society in July 1883; by June 1884 he had been elected Secretary and Treasurer, serving until July 1886. He initiated a notes-and-queries section in the society's "Monthly Abstract," which he edited. He was also jointly responsible with his successor as Secretary and Treasurer, Walter B. Slater, for launching a fund to meet the damages and legal fees incurred by the society's president, F. J. Furnival, for libeling the director of Browning's *Strafford* (1837), which was put on for the society in December 1886.

Owing to his friendship with Browning, Campbell was able to make a significant contribution to the reputation of the poet Thomas Lovell Beddoes. On his death in 1849 Beddoes had left his papers to a friend, the solicitor Thomas Forbes Kelsall; Kelsall, in turn, bequeathed Beddoes's manuscripts, together with the biographical information he had collected on Beddoes, to Browning, who, Kelsall thought, would edit Beddoes's poetry. Beddoes's relatives did not wish his suicide to be disclosed; but in 1881 this problem was resolved with the death of his cousin, Zoe King, and Browning invited Edmund Gosse to examine the papers with a view to the production of a new edition of Beddoes's works. Gosse went through the black tin box in which Browning kept the papers, but he produced his edition of Beddoes's poetry in 1890 without using in any significant way the materials from the box. After the death of Browning's son in 1912 neither the box nor its contents were found among his effects. Browning, however, had also allowed Campbell to examine the box's contents. According to H. W. Donner, who edited Beddoes's works in 1935, "Dykes Campbell did not miss his chance. With unsparing labour he transcribed everything of importance that had been left unpublished ... poems, fragments, letters, down to single lines that had been omitted, and all the important biographical and other material in the Browning box. Everything that remained of what Beddoes had ever written or deleted was copied and deleted all over again by Dykes Campbell going through the whole process of creation and revision as it had once happened in the poet's mind. . . . [Campbell's transcrip-

Page from Campbell's transcription of the manuscript for Thomas Lovell Beddoes's play Death's Jest-Book *(Bodleian Library, Oxford)*

tion] is thus the most authoritative text in existence." This transcription is now in the Bodleian Library. "It is a matter for profound regret," in Donner's opinion, "that Dykes Campbell, who did all the spadework preparatory to a complete edition, should not have been permitted to edit the poet he so devoutly admired. But it was Browning's wish that Edmund Gosse should edit the Works of Beddoes, and Dykes Campbell's scribal activities remained obscure for wellnigh fifty years."

Although Anne Procter claimed a close friendship with Tennyson, Campbell never seems to have established any kind of relationship with him — which, in view of his piratical edition of Tennyson's early poems, is hardly surprising. He did write to Tennyson, however, concerning another of the suppressed poems, and received a reply from Hallam Tennyson giving his father's reluctant permission to publish the original version. Campbell published the poem, "Lines on Cambridge of 1830," together with Hallam Tennyson's letter, in both the *Times* (15 March 1884) and *Notes and Queries* (15 March 1884) under the heading "An Early Sonnet by the Poet Laureate."

Other literary figures with whom Campbell sustained close relationships included Alfred Ainger, with whom he first corresponded when Ainger was preparing his edition of Charles Lamb's letters, and Stephen, with whom he corresponded when Stephen was preparing the entry on Addison for *The Dictionary of National Biography*. Campbell and Ainger visited the area where Lamb had grown up; they also visited the Quantocks to renew acquaintance with the places where Coleridge and Wordsworth had lived in their younger days. Stephen recalled that Campbell "brought to my notice the curious discovery which he had made of some of Addison's early drafts of *Spectators*. Our acquaintance speedily ripened into friendship, and when I was writing upon Coleridge for the same work he supplied me most liberally — perhaps I should say he almost overwhelmed me — with information upon the subject." When Arthur Symons was preparing his study of Browning (1886) he was put in touch with Campbell by Furnival and was given every assistance, including an introduction to Browning. Symons described his debt in the introduction to the second edition of his book (1906), published after Campbell's death: "I am conscious how much I owed, at that time, to the most helpful and judicious friend whom I could possibly have had at my elbow, Dykes Campbell. There are few pages of my manuscript which he did not read and criticise, and not a page of my proofs which he did not labour

over as if it had been his own. He forced me to learn accuracy, he cut out my worst extravagances, kept me sternly to my task. It was in writing this book under his encouragement and correction that I began to learn the first elements of literary criticism."

Campbell reluctantly moved from London to St. Leonards, Sussex, in May 1889 because the doctors had said that the sea air would be beneficial for his wife's health. He continued to visit London and his club, the Savile, and he entertained his friends at St. Leonards. He also made new friends, in particular the poet Coventry Patmore, who lived in the Hastings area.

Between 1883 and 1893 Campbell worked single-mindedly on Coleridge and the Coleridge circle. He published many articles, mainly in the *Athenæum,* and mainly on textual matters. He became a recognized authority on the period even before his biography was published, and he was one of a select group invited to be present on 9 June 1893 when a tablet in honor of Coleridge was affixed to the cottage Coleridge had occupied in Nether Stowey nearly a hundred years before.

He was much in demand as a reviewer, though several of his reviews demonstrate his intolerance of anything that fell short of his own exceptionally high standards. Ainger chided him for the severity of his attack on Benjamin E. Martin's *In the Footsteps of Charles Lamb* (1890) in the *Athenæum* (28 February 1891), which concluded, "In short this book is worthless." In the same review Campbell also savaged W. C. Hazlitt's "Some Unpublished Letters of Charles and Mary Lamb," published in the *Atlantic Monthly* (February 1891). Patmore wrote to Campbell, "We shall go to the heaven of the Vikings, slaying our enemies all morning for ever, and sipping claret over their corpses all night." This irascibility is exemplified also by Campbell's last contribution to *Notes and Queries* (6 April 1895), "Tomb of Sir James Mackintosh," which betrays contempt as well as impatience with a contributor who had failed to find Coleridge's satiric poem on Mackintosh. Ainger, however, makes a scholarly virtue out of these attacks: "Thoroughness and accuracy were his cardinal virtues," he says in his obituary notice of Campbell, "slovenliness and scamped work his detestation; and if he had a critical intolerance, it was of any fresh would-be editor and critic who palmed off his carelessness and inefficiency upon the world of unsuspecting readers."

Campbell's edition of *The Poetical Works of Samuel Taylor Coleridge* was published in 1893. For his text Campbell used the 1829 edition of Coleridge's

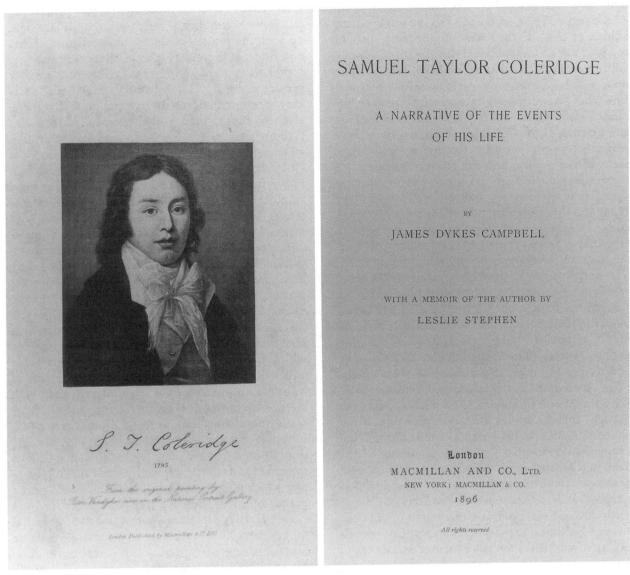

Frontispiece and title page for Campbell's biography of the Romantic poet

poems rather than the 1834 edition, which was the last to be published in Coleridge's lifetime. In an article in the *Athenæum,* "The 1828 Edition of Coleridge's Poems" (10 March 1888), Campbell says: "The conclusion to which I am led is that the edition of 1829 alone contains the author's final selection and text, and that it should be adopted as the basis of any further reproduction of Coleridge's poems. I have shown that the edition of 1828 was very deliberately discarded by the poet, and that those who had the best means of knowing the facts have put on record that the edition of 1834 was the work not of Coleridge, but of his son-in-law. There can be no doubt that that of 1829 really occupies the position mistakenly assigned by Coleridge's son

and daughter to that of 1828, of being 'the last upon which Coleridge was able to bestow personal care and attention,' and that it 'may be held to represent the author's matured judgment upon the larger and more important part of his poetical productions.' "

Taking the 1829 edition as authoritative has not recommended itself to modern Coleridge scholars, who follow Ernest Hartley Coleridge in using the 1834 edition. In the preface to his edition of *The Poetical Works of Samuel Taylor Coleridge* (1912) Ernest Hartley Coleridge writes: "I have adopted the text of 1834 in preference to that of 1829, which was selected by James Dykes Campbell for his monumental edition of 1893. I should have deferred to his authority but for the existence of conclusive proof that, here and there, Coleridge altered and emended the text of 1829, with a view to the forthcoming edition of 1834. In the Preface to the 'new edition' of 1852, the editors maintain that the three-volume edition of 1828 (a mistake for 1829) was the last upon which Coleridge was 'able to bestow personal care and attention,' while that of 1834 was 'arranged mainly if not entirely at the discretion of his latest editor, H. N. Coleridge.' This, no doubt, was perfectly true with regard to the choice and arrangement of the poems, and the labour of seeing the three volumes through the press; but the fact remains that the text of 1829 differs from that of 1834, and that Coleridge himself, and not his 'latest editor,' was responsible for that difference." On the other hand, Ernest Hartley Coleridge does not hesitate to describe Campbell's edition as "monumental," and Norman Fruman has spoken of "the most excellent edition of Dykes Campbell, who was more scrupulous than most later editors in excluding from the Coleridge canon works known not to be his." Campbell edited by strict principles not only as to inclusion and exclusion but also in establishing and dating the texts. He refused to accept Coleridge's own dates and demonstrated how unreliable the poet was on this count as on others. Campbell thought that Coleridge affixed improbable, if not impossible, dates to his poems to amuse himself, but Fruman suggests that Coleridge manipulated the dates and settings of his poems so as "to be thought of as a poet with astounding creative powers who as a schoolboy had been a *Wunderkind*." Fruman's suggestion would seem to be an expression of the cynicism of his times, just as, presumably, Campbell's explanation reflects the good-natured innocence of his.

The introduction to the volume, revised and enlarged, became *Samuel Taylor Coleridge: A Narrative of the Events of His Life,* published in 1894. In his letter to Patmore of 21 October 1892, Campbell referred to the biography as "my big print 'Life of S. T. C.' which of course is only the Old Obadiah expanded by say 20% to 25%. I am hoping to be able to read the thing myself in this big print — and see if I can detect any of the merits my partial friends like yourself see in it." Besant observed that "Few books have ever caused their writers labour more conscientious or more assiduous. He hunted up everything that could concern his subject: he visited every spot once trodden by the feet of Coleridge; he spared no pains, no expense. Sitting at his great table in the study of his house at St. Leonards, he was surrounded by books, papers, letters, memoranda, all bearing on the subject; he also had always

ready to his hand his great pipe; it was pleasant to talk it over with him, if only to watch his face light up with the joy that belongs to one who searches and finds. If there was labour, there was also joy. Never was a book written that afforded the writer greater pleasure." The work set standards of accuracy, documentation, and thoroughness that thereafter, all biographies had at least to try to attain. Campbell describes his intentions in his preface when he says that as "no authoritative biography of Coleridge existed, I was obliged to construct a narrative for my own purpose. With this in view, I carefully sifted all the old printed biographical materials, and so far as possible collated them with original documents. I searched all books of memoirs, etc., likely to contain incidental information regarding Coleridge; and, further, I was privileged by being permitted to make use of much important matter, either absolutely new, or previously unavailable. My aim has been, not to add to the ever-lengthening array of estimates of Coleridge as a poet and philosopher, but to provide something which appeared to be wanting — a plain, and as far as possible, an accurate narrative of the events of his life. Explanations have been offered when such seemed necessary or desirable, but comment, especially moralising, has been studiously avoided." Campbell did not attempt a full biography, he says, since he regarded his narrative as "something which might serve until the appearance of the full biography which is expected from the hands of the poet's grandson, Mr. Ernest Hartley Coleridge." In 1884 Ernest Hartley Coleridge had warned off potential biographers by announcing in the *Academy* that he was preparing a biography, but it was never completed. Reviewers generally agreed with Frederick Greenwood, who described Campbell's biography in the *Illustrated London News* (3 March 1894) as "a model of what a biography should be." Some criticized Campbell for not doing what he specifically said he would not do, a point made by Edward Dowden in the *Saturday Review* (8 August 1895): "Campbell did not aspire to estimate the character of Coleridge, nor to expound his spiritual life, nor to pronounce judgment on his poetical work, nor to interpret his body of thought or the rich suggestions which he contributed to the speculations of his time. He sought to determine the external facts of the poet's biography, and to apply these to the illustration of the poems; and what he attempted he achieved." Henry James wrote in his notebook on 17 April 1894: "In reading Dykes Campbell's book on Coleridge — it is so good that one almost forgets how much better a little more of the power of evocation might have made it — I was infinitely struck with the suggestiveness of S. T. C's figure — wonderful, admirable figure — for pictorial treatment" (James's story "The Coxon Fund" [1895] was inspired by his reading of Campbell's biography). Campbell deliberately eschewed "evocation," as he also, as far as possible, avoided the speculation that bedeviled Coleridge studies before him and since. But the achievements, confusions, and disappointments of his subject's life have never been better or more sympathetically stated than they are in his final summary: "I would fain leave the foregoing narrative to work its own impression on the mind of the reader. If its somewhat fuller and more orderly presentment of what I believe to be the truth, be not found to tend, on the whole, to raise Coleridge in the eyes of men, I shall, I confess, feel both surprised and disappointed. It is neither by glossing over his failings, nor by fixing an exclusive eye on them, that a true estimate of any man is to be arrived at. A better way is to collect as many facts as we can, set them in the light of the circumstances in which they were born, sort them fairly into the opposing scales, and weigh them in an atmosphere as free as possible from cant and prejudice. To my own mind it seems that Coleridge's failings are too obvious to require either all the insistence or all the moralising which have been lavished on them: and that his fall is less wonderful than his recovery. His will was congenitally weak, and his habits weakened it still farther; but his conscience, which was never allowed to sleep, tortured him; and, after many days, its workings stimulated the paralysed will, and he was saved. A brief dawn of unsurpassed promise and achievement; 'a trouble' as of 'clouds and weeping rain'; then, a long summer evening's work done by 'the setting sun's pathetic light' — such was Coleridge's day, the after-glow of which is still in the sky. . . . men and women who neither shared nor ignored his shortcomings, not only loved him but honoured and followed him. . . . We may read and re-read his life, but we cannot know him as the Lambs, or the Wordsworths, or Poole, or Hookham Frere, or the Gillmans, or Green knew him. Hatred as well as love may be blind, but friendship has eyes, and their testimony may wisely be used in correcting our own impressions." Ainger's comment on this passage is just: "The plea for a kindly judgment of the character of Coleridge, as summed up in the final words of the biography, is not only one of the most eloquent and pathetic pieces of criticism given to the world in our generation, but will live in the hearts of all who knew the writer as a sure index of the gentle and truth-loving

nature that has been so early removed from among them."

The authority of Campbell's biography is best judged by the attitudes of those Coleridge scholars who drew freely on his work. John Livingstone Lowes described him (albeit while pointing out one of his errors) as "the most rigorously accurate of Coleridgean scholars . . . whose scrupulous exactness is proverbial." All agree with E. K. Chambers, who in the preface to his own biography (1938) says without qualification that "Every writer about Coleridge must be conscious of his debt to the *Narrative* of James Dykes Campbell."

During their residence in St. Leonards, Campbell's wife's health had improved, and since they had come to find the Sussex air too mild they moved in early 1895 to Tunbridge Wells, about equidistant from the coast and London. Campbell himself had been in failing health for several months; on a visit to London he was persuaded to consult a doctor, who, immediately recognizing the seriousness of his condition, sent him home. A week later, on 1 June 1895, Campbell died of heart disease. He was buried in the churchyard of St. Alban's Church, Frant, under a cross about ten feet high bearing some Celtic tracery and the inscription:

> "Friendship is a sheltering tree.
> He prayeth best who loveth best.
> All things both great and small."

He would, of course, have been shocked by the impropriety of running together quotations from two separate poems.

Stephen paid tribute to his friend in his *Athenæum* obituary: "His nature was mellow to the core: kindly, genial, and equally fitted for social meeting and the quieter display of intimate friendship in a solitary companion. This combination of moral and intellectual qualities showed itself in the charming humour which was always bubbling up in his chat and gleaming over his graver conversation. . . . Campbell like a true humorist, could enjoy the incongruities of Coleridge's practice as heartily as he could appreciate the essential lovableness of Coleridge's character. It was, I think, this union of qualities not always combined, of absolute impartiality in his treatment of evidence with a cordial recognition of all that was really estimable and attractive, which is the peculiar merit of his book. His judgment is thoroughly sane, without being hurried into sentimentalism or tinged by cynicism. We love Coleridge all the better when we perceive that his biographer's admiration has never induced him to throw the reins upon the neck of judgment."

Campbell's friend William Hale White (better known under his pseudonym, Mark Rutherford) provided two prefaces and notes for an edition of proofs and manuscripts of some of Coleridge's poems that Campbell had had printed shortly before his death. This work was published in 1899. The edition of Lamb's *Specimens of English Dramatic Poets Who Lived about the Time of Shakespeare* that Campbell had prepared for the press was not published until 1907. Campbell's wife died in 1919.

References:

Thomas Lovell Beddoes, *The Works of Thomas Lovell Beddoes,* edited by H. W. Donner (London: Oxford University Press, 1935), pp. li–lii;

Walter Besant, *Autobiography of Sir Walter Besant* (London: Hutchinson, 1902), pp. 115–116, 139;

E. K. Chambers, *Samuel Taylor Coleridge: A Biographical Study* (Oxford: Clarendon Press, 1938), p. vii;

Norman Fruman, *Coleridge: The Damaged Archangel* (New York: Braziller, 1971), pp. 11–12, 506;

Henry James, *The Complete Notebooks,* edited by Leon Edel and Lyall H. Powers (New York: Oxford University Press, 1987), p. 89;

"Obituary Notice," *Athenæum,* no. 3528 (8 June 1895): 738–739;

Coventry Patmore, *Memoirs and Correspondence,* 2 volumes, edited by Basil Champneys (London: Bell, 1900), I: 265–266; II: 395;

William Michael Rossetti, *The Diary of W. M. Rossetti, 1870–1873,* edited by O. Bornand (Oxford: Oxford University Press, 1977), pp. 55, 243;

Edith Sichel, *The Life and Letters of Alfred Ainger* (London: Constable, 1906);

Arthur Symons, *An Introduction to the Study of Browning,* revised edition (London: Dent, 1906), p. x.

Papers:

Some of James Dykes Campbell's papers are in the British Library.

Thomas Campbell

(27 July 1777 – 15 June 1844)

Fiona Robertson
University of Durham

See also the Campbell entry in *DLB 93: British Romantic Poets, 1789–1832, First Series.*

BOOKS: *The Wounded Hussar* (Glasgow, 1799);

The Pleasures of Hope; with other Poems (Edinburgh: Printed for Mundell & Son and for Longman & Rees and J. Wright, London, 1799; New York: Printed by John Furman for Jones Bull, 1800);

Poems (Edinburgh: Printed by James Ballantyne, 1803);

Annals of Great Britain from the Ascension of George III to the Peace of Amiens, 3 volumes (Edinburgh: Printed for Mundell, Doig & Stevenson, Constable, and J. Fairbairn, Edinburgh; J. & A. Duncan, Glasgow; and T. Ostell, London, 1807);

Gertrude of Wyoming, a Pennsylvanian Tale; and other Poems (London: Printed by T. Bensley & published for the author by Longman, Hurst, Rees & Orme, 1809; New York: Printed & published by D. Longworth, 1809);

Specimens of the British Poets; with Biographical and Critical Notices, and an Essay on English Poetry, 7 volumes (London: John Murray, 1819);

Miscellaneous Poems (London: W. Dugdale, 1824);

Theodric, a Domestic Tale; and other Poems (London: Longman, Hurst, Rees, Orme, Brown & Green, 1824; Philadelphia: H. C. Carey & I. Lea, 1825);

Inaugural Discourse of Thomas Campbell, Esq. on Being Installed Lord Rector of the University of Glasgow, Thursday April 12th, 1827 (Glasgow: John Smith & Son; Bell & Bradfute, Edinburgh; and Henry Colburn, London, 1827);

Letters on the History of Literature, Addressed to the Students of the University of Glasgow (Glasgow: Distributed by J. Smith, 1829);

Address of the Literary Polish Association to the People of Great Britain to which is added a Letter from Samuel T. Howe, Esq. of the United States, to Thomas Campbell, Esq. (London: George Eccles, 1832);

Life of Mrs. Siddons (2 volumes, London: Wilson, 1834; 1 volume, New York: Harper, 1834);

Letters from the South, 2 volumes (London: Colburn, 1837); republished as *The Journal of a Residence in Algiers,* 2 volumes (London: Colburn, 1842);

Life of Petrarch (2 volumes, London: Colburn, 1841; 1 volume, Philadelphia: Carey & Hart, 1841);

The Pilgrim of Glencoe, and other Poems (London: Moxon, 1842).

Collections: *The Poetical Works of Thomas Campbell. Including several pieces from the original manuscript, never before published in this country. To which is prefixed a biographical sketch of the author, by a gentleman of New-York* [Washington Irving] (Baltimore: Printed by Fry & Kammerer for Philip H. Nicklin & Co., also for D. W. Farrand & Green, Albany; D. Mallory & Co., Boston; Lyman & Hall, Portland, Maine; and E. Earle, Philadelphia, 1810);

The Poetical Works of Thomas Campbell, edited by W. Alfred Hill (London: Edward Moxon, 1851; Boston: Little, Brown, 1854); republished, with a biographical sketch, by William Allingham, Aldine Edition (London: G. Bell & Sons, 1875);

The Complete Poetical Works of Thomas Campbell, Oxford Edition, edited by J. Logie Robertson (London & New York: Printed by Henry Frowde for Oxford University Press, 1907).

OTHER: *New Monthly Magazine and Literary Journal,* edited by Campbell, 1821–1830;

Metropolitan: A Monthly Journal of Literature, Science, and the Fine Arts, edited by Campbell, 1831–1832;

The Scenic Annual, for 1838, edited by Campbell (London: Virtue, 1838);

The Dramatic Works of William Shakspeare, with remarks on his life and writings, edited by Campbell (London: Routledge, 1838);

Engraving by E. Finden, after a portrait by Sir Thomas Lawrence

Frederick Shoberl, *Frederick the Great, His Court and Times,* 2 volumes, edited, with an introduction, by Campbell (London: Colburn, 1842, 1843);
History of Our Own Times, 2 volumes, edited by Campbell (London: Colburn, 1843, 1845).

SELECTED PERIODICAL PUBLICATIONS – UNCOLLECTED: "Lectures on Poetry, the Substance of Which Was Delivered at the Royal Institution," *New Monthly Magazine,* new series 1–17 (January 1821–November 1826);
"Proposal on a Metropolitan University in a Letter to Henry Brougham, Esq.," *Times* (London), 9 February 1825;
"Suggestions Respecting the Plan of an University in London," *New Monthly Magazine,* new series 13, no. 52 (1825): 404–419; part 2, "Suggestions Respecting Plan of a College in London," 14, no. 55 (1825): 1–11.

Thomas Campbell's neglected biographical works spring not from a curiosity about individuals but from opinions about literature and from a desire to make a wider range of earlier poetry accessible to a popular readership. His most important biographical project, *Specimens of the British Poets; with Biographical and Critical Notices, and an Essay on English Poetry* (1819) is an ambitious extension of the plan of Samuel Johnson's *Prefaces, Biographical and Critical, to the Works of the English Poets* (1779–1781), dealing with 238 named (and many anonymous) authors from Geoffrey Chaucer to Christopher Anstey. The biographical sketches in this work are, Campbell says, "necessarily and designedly only miniatures of biography," but they reveal important assumptions about the relationship between life and writing, and they bring to biography the fastidiousness and refinement of taste for which Campbell was renowned. His other biographical works are his *Life of Mrs. Siddons* (1834), his introduction to *The Dramatic Works of William Shakspeare, with remarks on his life and writings* (1838), and his *Life of Petrarch* (1841).

In *The Spirit of the Age; or, Contemporary Portraits* (1825) William Hazlitt characterizes Campbell as "a *high finisher* in poetry, whose every work must bear inspection, whose slightest touch is precious." This reputation as a poet and perfectionist gave authority to Campbell's other works and helped to popularize a carefully and self-consciously crafted, sometimes overly rhetorical style of biography. He is the least prying of biographers, filtering out improprieties in the lives of individuals, but he is alert to the importance of literary communities and to the ways in which writers interact as influences, critics, detractors, and rivals. Campbell's model for literary lives was clearly social rather than solitary, and that orientation, though never made explicit or explored theoretically, was a significant development in literary biography.

Campbell was born in Glasgow on 27 July 1777 and was the youngest of the eleven children of Alexander Campbell and Margaret Campbell, née Campbell. His father was a tobacco merchant who had set up business in Falmouth, Virginia, before returning to Glasgow and marrying the sister of his business partner in 1756. Previous generations of his father's family had lived in Kirnan in Argyllshire – roots that Campbell celebrates in his poem "Lines on Visiting a Scene in Argyllshire," written in 1800 and published in his *Poems* (1803). Although Alexander Campbell's business was badly damaged by the disruptions in trade during the American Revolution, the family maintained important links with America, and America would be a favorite subject for the writer throughout his life. The Campbells took great pride in the intellectual precosity of their youngest child, who was educated at Glasgow University from 1791 to 1796; he won several prizes for Greek and Latin translation and for his own poems. By that time his liberal sympathies had been aroused by the French Revolution, and he would remain a prominent campaigner for political and social freedom.

In 1797 Campbell moved to Edinburgh, working as a clerk in the Register House and in a law office, but with the publication of *The Pleasures of Hope; with other Poems* in April 1799 he entered on a literary career. He visited Germany in 1800–1801, con-

tracting there the venereal disease that would undermine his health and the health of his wife and children. He married his second cousin Matilda Sinclair on 10 October 1803 and settled in London. They had two sons, Thomas Telford, born in 1804, and Alison, who was born a year later and died in 1810. Campbell's financial problems were eased by the grant of a royal pension of two hundred pounds per annum in 1805 and by a family legacy of nearly five thousand pounds in 1815.

The publication of *The Pleasures of Hope; with other Poems* brought Campbell immediate and lasting fame. He went on to produce a series of lyric poems, the best known being "Ye Mariners of England," first published in the London *Morning Chronicle* in 1801, and "The Battle of the Baltic," included in *Gertrude of Wyoming, a Pennsylvanian Tale; and other Poems* (1809). His later collections of poetry were *Theodric, a Domestic Tale; and other Poems* (1824) and *The Pilgrim of Glencoe, and other Poems* (1842). His prose works include *Annals of Great Britain from the Ascension of George III to the Peace of Amiens* (1807) and *Letters from the South,* first published in the *New Monthly Magazine* in 1835–1836 and in book form in 1837. He edited two literary periodicals, the *New Monthly Magazine and Literary Journal* (1821–1830) and the *Metropolitan* (1831–1832). His preface to his first volume as editor of the *New Monthly Magazine* reveals much about the ideals that govern his literary discussions: the magazine is to be a "calm spot in the world of periodical literature where all minds of common charity and candour may meet without the asperities of party feeling."

There were few "calm spots" in his own writing life. Cyrus Redding, assistant editor of the *New Monthly Magazine,* wrote scathingly in his *Literary Reminiscences and Memoirs of Thomas Campbell* (1860) of the chaotic work practices from which Redding was undoubtedly a sufferer:

> It was unfortunate that his habits of study were not long fixed upon any subject, but were discursive, and were not directed to carry out a single object to the end. . . . Often wholly engrossed by any chance literary subject that occupied his attention at the instant, he could scarcely be prevailed upon to divert it to another for ever so short a time. Hence, whatever article came to him he would put it by, as he intended, for future inspection, and not think of it again. He had no method, no arrangement, his papers lay about in confusion, and if he wanted for a moment to put them aside, he would jumble them into a heap, or cram them into a drawer.

Campbell's letters continually express anxiety about money and irritation at the literary projects

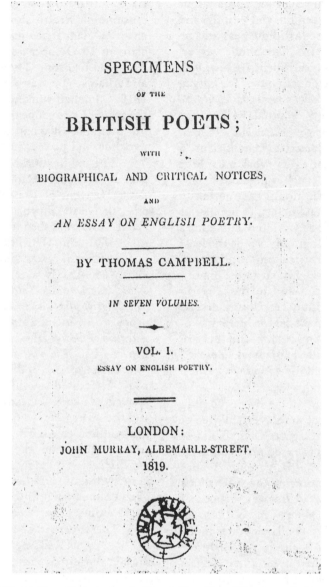

SPECIMENS

OF THE

BRITISH POETS;

WITH

BIOGRAPHICAL AND CRITICAL NOTICES,

AND

AN ESSAY ON ENGLISH POETRY.

BY THOMAS CAMPBELL.

IN SEVEN VOLUMES.

VOL. I.

ESSAY ON ENGLISH POETRY.

LONDON:
JOHN MURRAY, ALBEMARLE-STREET.
1819.

Title page for the first volume of Campbell's most important work of literary biography, which was conceived as a continuation of Samuel Johnson's
Prefaces, Biographical and Critical, to the Works of the English Poets

this anxiety obliged him to undertake. It would be a mistake, however, to see his prose works merely as forced mercenary productions.

Specimens of the British Poets originated in an earlier project that Campbell first mooted in a letter to Sir Walter Scott in March 1805. Campbell hoped to gather the opinions of "first-rate judges" such as Scott and to base a selection of poetry on their suggestions. Having discovered that Scott had plans for a similar collection, however, by June he was proposing that they work jointly on the project. The collection was to be based on the poets in Johnson's *Prefaces, Biographical and Critical, to the Works of the English Poets,* with Scott adding material on the older

and Campbell on the more recent poets. Under pressure from his publishers to reduce the scope of the selection, Campbell implored Scott's support "in rejection of their proposal to put the great plan of our national poetry and poetical biography on a dirty little scale." In 1806 Campbell was revising the biographies of the poets in Johnson's work and selecting examples of their writings. His publishers expressed the hope that although his scheme for the proposed "British Poets" was too unwieldy, the lives might appear separately. Campbell's views on his project varied over these years of gestation, but he came to believe that its true value lay in the combination of poetry and biographical information.

Material for *Specimens of the British Poets* accumulated over the next ten years, although publication was delayed from April 1816 until 1819 while Campbell painstakingly revised and added materials in proof. "The fastidious delicacy of Campbell's taste is proverbial," writes his physician, executor, and biographer Dr. William Beattie; "the fear of a misprint would have caused him a sleepless night, and sent him to the printer's early in the morning – were it only to alter a letter, or substitute these for those."

In a letter to his friend John Richardson in 1809, Campbell explains that his primary concern lay with the accurate representation of the "main currents" of his subjects' lives, leaving the "tributaries" to antiquarian scholars. He describes the project in metaphors drawn from natural history and anthropology: "A man, or rather a god, like Milton, is to be described in all his attributes, as a great unity. Those minor beings are to be classed, male and female, according to their tribes. I shall endeavour, with as much industry as I can employ, to analyze them individually, like a natural historian; and then attempt as much philosophical generality as possible. I mean to class them in groups. . . ." The emphasis on classification gives added significance to his choice of title (already made in his first letter to Scott), which links his work to George Ellis's *Specimens of Early English Romances in Metre* (1805) and Robert Southey's *Specimens of the Later English Poets* (1807). The idea of the specimen had begun to acquire associations with scientific investigation and analysis in the second half of the eighteenth century. Campbell's specimens present for investigation a version of a national literary tradition. Therefore, its inclusions (notably, antimonarchic as well as royalist poets from the seventeenth century) and exclusions are significant. Only 3 of the 238 authors are women: Katherine Philips, Aphra Behn, and Frances Greville. Campbell emphasizes vernacular, native poetry; none of John Milton's Latin poems is included. He also aims to find an audience for poets left out of many contemporary anthologies. Extracts from the works of William Shakespeare and other frequently cited poets are kept to a minimum, making way for treatment of Richard Edwards, William Hunnis, Thomas Storer, Joshua Sylvester, Richard Niccols, William Habington, Richard Braithwaite, Edward Ward, Leonard Welsted, James Grainger, Cuthbert Shaw, Thomas Penrose, William Whitehead, and John Bampfylde. Campbell includes one American writer: Timothy Dwight. In volumes six and seven, which deal with late-eighteenth-century writers, biographies and extracts are fuller, and there is more sustained atten-

tion to Scottish writers: Michael Bruce, William Falconer, Tobias Smollett, Robert Fergusson, John Armstrong, John Logan, William Julius Mickle, Thomas Blacklock, and James Beattie.

Campbell's prefatory "Essay on English Poetry," which takes up the first volume of *Specimens of the British Poets,* is lucid and uncontentious. It seeks to locate the start of specifically English rather than Saxon poetry, pausing to explain its exclusion of the "rude voice" of William Langland. Its major contributions are the discussion of Elizabethan poetry and the defense of Alexander Pope against the criticisms of his most recent editor, William Lisle Bowles – a defense that led to counterattack from Bowles. The essay says nothing about biographical methodology, but it includes asides on the personal characters of John Skelton, Thomas Sackville, Ben Jonson, and Philip Massinger and demonstrates a concern with historical context as a determinant of the temper of poets. At several points Campbell attempts to sketch the personal character of a historical period, but he avoids detailed comment on the social and political conditions in which his poets wrote. Therefore, his Milton stands "alone, and aloof above his time, the bard of immortal subjects."

After the second volume, which covers the long period from Chaucer to Sir John Beaumont, the extracts are organized into volumes covering between twenty and fifty-five years each, the breakdown into more-equal periods, representing an attempt to improve on the erratic coverage of Johnson's *Prefaces, Biographical and Critical, to the Works of the English Poets*. Of Campbell's many sources, the most consistent are previous editions of the poets' works and a few standard reference works, including Alexander Chalmers's *General Biographical Dictionary* (1812–1817), Anthony Wood's *Athenae Oxonienses* (1691–1692), and John Nichols's *Literary Anecdotes of the Eighteenth Century* (1812–1815). The importance of Johnson's *Prefaces, Biographical and Critical, to the Works of the English Poets* is explicit from the earliest stages of work on *Specimens of the British Poets.* When Campbell comes to write on those poets he shares with Johnson, however, he is less forthcoming than usual and tends not to mention Johnson as a major source. His life of Wentworth Dillon, Earl of Roscommon, quotes Thomas Warton rather than Johnson as its authority. He takes issue with Johnson in defending Milton, of whom he provides a distinctly romanticized and depoliticized portrait. He also disagrees with "the grave doctor of the last century" on the character of John Philips, and with his "malignant and exaggerated" criticisms of Thomas Gray. His single sentence on Richard Savage per-

Portrait by Sir Joshua Reynolds of Mrs. Sarah Siddons as the Muse of tragedy (Henry E. Huntington Memorial Library and Art Gallery, San Marino, California). Campbell's biography of the actress was published in 1834.

haps reveals most clearly the inhibiting effect of Johnson as precursor, but his final protest is to give no biographical sketch whatsoever of Johnson himself.

Campbell's biographical notices are uneven in length and scholarship, ranging from twenty-eight pages to one sentence. Although they can be evocative and imaginative, as in the account of the meeting between Edmund Spenser and Sir Walter Ralegh, they do not always strive for precision. Of Thomas Nabbes, Campbell writes: "He seems to have been secretary or domestic to some nobleman or prelate, at or near Worcester." Curiously, in the light of his own family interest in Virginia, he makes no mention in his account of George Sandys of the ten years during which Sandys acted as treasurer to the Virginia colony, drawing predominantly on Sandys's own accounts of his travels and

claiming that "Few incidents of his life are recorded." Some of the entries decline even to provide the information on which Campbell has based his judgment, as in the note on Barton Booth, which reads in its entirety: "An excellent man, and an eminent actor." Eighteen poets receive no biographical notice at all, and several of those omissions – notably John Dryden, Joseph Addison, William Congreve, and Jonathan Swift – are surprising. Campbell's biographical skills are demonstrated most clearly in the twelve entries that exceed ten pages (on Chaucer, Spenser, Jonson, Whitehead, Allan Ramsay, Thomas Chatterton, Oliver Goldsmith, Sir William Jones, Robert Burns, William Mason, Joseph Warton, and William Cowper). By far the longest entry is on Cowper, and it is concluded only in deference to "the reader's patience" and "the boundaries which I have been obliged to prescribe to myself, in the length of these notices." Another long entry, the earnest biography of Ramsay, implicitly gives the Scottish writer an important place among the much briefer depictions of his English contemporaries. It describes Ramsay's importance in Scottish culture, discusses in some detail the context of continuing Scottish resistance to union with England, and gives an unusually intimate sketch of Ramsay's appearance, manners, and conversation. Campbell provides a sensitive discussion of Chatterton and comes closest to a detailed estimate of personality in his account of Goldsmith. He also takes great care with Burns, whose education, early reading, fame, and social circumstances he describes in depth. Campbell is primarily concerned to absolve Burns of any charge of vulgarity, setting him up as a "deep and universal" genius and showing a marked lack of interest in the sexual adventures that preoccupied many of Burns's early critics.

His tendency to elevate and romanticize the subjects of his biographies is in keeping with the purifying impetus of his critical selection. He is quick to condemn any supposed failures in morality or good taste in the works he describes, and he tailors his biographical accounts accordingly. In his life of Richard Corbet, Campbell passes over the anecdotes that enliven John Aubrey's account of the bishop in his *Brief Lives* (1813) and emphasizes instead Corbet's humane treatment of Puritans. His accounts are occasionally prudish; of Francis Beaumont and John Fletcher – "names, united by friendship and confederate genius" – Campbell relates: "we are told by Aubrey, that Fletcher and he lived together in London, near the Bankside, not far from the theatre, had one bench in the same house between them, the same clothes, cloak, &c." Campbell's attention rarely descends to items of furniture, so the "bench" here is an oddity. The explanation lies in Aubrey's account: "They lived together on the Banke side, not far from the Play-house, both batchelors; lay together; had one Wench in the house between them, which they did so admire; the same cloathes and cloake, &c. betweene them." Campbell's revision of this sentence is a perfect example of his attention to propriety.

Campbell states his critical opinions decisively, and several entries contain far more criticism than biography. The entry on Edward Young is dominated by a critique of *Night Thoughts* (1742–1746), while the life of William Mason contains a long digression on Greek drama. Mark Akenside, it would appear, had no life at all independent of his poem *The Pleasures of Imagination* (1744). In keeping with this primarily critical impulse, Campbell tends to deduce personal character from literary tone and choice of subject matter, although he sporadically (as in the life of Samuel Rowlands) recognizes the limits of this method. Only occasionally does he allude to original research into the life of a subject. More frequently he takes issue with previous commentators, although his tone is seldom disputatious and only once (when dismissing Southey's opinion of John Pomfret's poem "Choice") openly sarcastic. His critical comments can be both perceptive and pithy, as when he describes John Armstrong's revision of his blank-verse sex manual, *The Oeconomy of Love* (1736): "He corrected the nefarious production, at a later period of his life, betraying at once a consciousness of its impurity, and a hankering after its reputation." Nonliterary interests are occasionally woven into his account. Unable to bestow much praise on the "strong misguided energy" of Christopher Marlowe, he spends much of the brief entry musing on the coincidence between a scene in a play attributed to Marlowe and recent events in Napoleonic Spain. When noting Spenser's reputed preeminence in pastoral, he cannot resist making a patriotic case for Ramsay, the Scot. His inclination to dwell on sentimental incidents in his subjects' romantic lives is notable in the case of John Donne, whose life Campbell declares more interesting than his poetry. In contrast, George Herbert receives only two distinctly disengaged sentences.

Specimens of the British Poets was widely reviewed. *Blackwood's Edinburgh Magazine* (March 1819) praised Campbell's gentleness and generosity as a critic, finding his appreciation of Spenser particularly admirable and "delicately characteristic," though, like several others, the reviewer objects to the claim that Spenser was "the Rubens of English poetry." Like others, similarly, he criticizes Campbell for underestimating Marlowe. With the exception of Francis Jeffrey in the *Edinburgh Review* (March 1819), the reviewers made no comment on Campbell's skills as a biographer except to find his sketches too short – especially in the case of the older poets. Instead they concentrate on the selection of writers and works and on the "Essay on English Poetry," which the *British Critic* (April 1819) criticized as "too poetical." The *Monthly Review* (December 1819) described the biographical notices as "rather capricious, and always too short." Although he describes *Specimens of the British Poets* as a "very excellent and delightful" collection, Jeffrey finds the commentary underweight and the mixture of biography and criticism inconsistent. He appreciates Campbell's generosity as a critic, although he suspects him of "indulgent, and, perhaps, latitudinar-

LIFE

OF

MRS. SIDDONS.

BY THOMAS CAMPBELL.

" Pity it is that the momentary beauties flowing from a harmonious elocution
cannot, like those of poetry, be their own record;—that the animated graces of the
Player can live no longer than the instant breath and motion that represent them;
or at least can but faintly glimmer through the memory and imperfect attestation of
a few surviving spectators."

CIBBER.

VOL. I.

LONDON:
EFFINGHAM WILSON, ROYAL EXCHANGE.

1834.

Title page for Campbell's biography of Siddons

ian opinions." He also recognizes the special quality of the entry on Chatterton, which most clearly reveals "the amiable but equitable and reasonable indulgence of Mr. Campbell's mind." Scott told his publisher in 1821 that he had been discouraged by Campbell's work from preparing a collection titled "Lives of the Poets" as a continuation of his series Ballantyne's Novelist's Library (1821–1824): "I fear it would be difficult to give novelty. Consider there is Dr. Johnson & Tom Campbell. Certainly a good selection would throw out one half of what is commonly cramd into these formidable collections." Clearly Scott had not changed his mind about the principles of selection that originally prevented his working jointly with Campbell on the project.

While working intermittently on *Specimens of the British Poets,* Campbell lectured on poetry at the Royal Institution. He delivered the first series of lectures in 1812, the second in 1813, repeated them in Liverpool and Birmingham, and gave some additional lectures in London in 1820. Under the title "Lectures on Poetry, the Substance of Which Was Delivered at the Royal Institution," they were published in revised form in the *New Monthly Magazine* between January 1821 and November 1826. Hazlitt describes their style as "at once chaste, temperate, guarded, and just," but a letter to *Blackwood's Edinburgh Magazine* (September 1827) argued that Campbell had plagiarized some of his material from Friedrich von Schlegel.

Campbell planned a revised and enlarged edition of *Specimens of the British Poets,* but he was reluctant to begin work on it. Redding noted with some asperity Campbell's refusal to correct the errors that were pointed out to him by Byron and others: "As to fame, while he had Pope's 'voracity' for it, he had an inveterate dislike to pay the purchase-money." The new edition eventually appeared, revised not by Campbell but by Peter Cunningham, in 1841. Meanwhile, the 1820s were times of change and considerable unhappiness for Campbell. His surviving son, Thomas, suffered increasingly from mental illness and was eventually placed in an asylum, where he remained until after Campbell's death. His wife died on 9 May 1828, after which Campbell became known for his sentimental attachments: "A sad fellow, you will say, is this incorrigible old flirt, your friend," he wrote to Beattie in 1836. On the other hand, in 1825 Campbell became involved in the founding of London University; the university opened in 1828, by which time Campbell had resigned from its council. In November 1826 the students of the University of Glasgow elected him rector, and he was twice reelected. This post prompted his *Letters on the History of Literature, Addressed to the Students of the University of Glasgow,* which was published in the *New Monthly Magazine* between July 1827 and August 1828 and in book form in 1829.

In 1830 he started work on a biography of the painter Sir Thomas Lawrence but soon abandoned it to his collaborator, D. E. Williams. He campaigned for British intervention on behalf of the Poles after the fall of Warsaw in 1831 and formed a Polish Committee that led to the establishment of the Literary Polish Association in 1832.

Campbell's next biographical project was undertaken at the request of its subject just before her death. Campbell had long been an admirer and friend of the great tragic actress Sarah Siddons, who, he said in a letter of 1802, "confers her friendship with a dignity that elevates the object of her attention to a temporary share of her own importance." His *Life of Mrs. Siddons* was begun just after her death in June 1831 and published in 1834. Early in the project, doubtful of his capabilities, he considered bringing in John Payne Collier as co-author, and the work brought him more anxiety than pleasure. In some ways he was inhibited by reverence: Redding would describe the book as "a biography on stilts." Campbell's letters, however, testify to the care he took in gathering information about Siddons and to the range of materials and memoirs to which he was given access by her family. He dili-

gently consulted Siddons's friends and theatrical associates as well as published sources and at the last minute became obsessively concerned to settle doubts about the version of Shakespeare's *King Lear* (1608) in which Siddons had played Cordelia early in her career. On completing his work in one volume in December 1832, he discovered to his surprise that his publishers had envisaged two, but he was confident that his material would "bear diffusion."

The *Life of Mrs. Siddons* is primarily an account of the actress's career, and it is hampered by Campbell's lack of theatrical knowledge. Campbell also had a competitor: James Boaden's *Memoirs of Mrs. Siddons* had appeared in 1827. Campbell benefited, however, from access to personal memoranda and family materials unavailable to Boaden, and he is able to tell key parts of Siddons's life in her own words. After the first chapters domestic details are sporadic and minimal, and it is not until reporting her husband's death that Campbell mentions — only because they are raised by Boaden, and only to deny them — rumors that her marriage had been unhappy. In chapter 3 he digresses to give the histories of eleven great actresses before Siddons, and he later gives briefer accounts of the leading male actors of Siddons's day as preparation for an analysis of her acting partnership with her brother John Philip Kemble. Much of the biography is taken up with critiques of the parts Siddons performed, in the course of which Campbell delivers his opinions about plays and dramatic convention. Two chapters are devoted to Siddons's most celebrated role, Lady Macbeth, and include her own notes on the character; Campbell also gives particular weight to her performances as Desdemona in Shakespeare's *Othello* (1622). After quoting Siddons's written account of her first introduction to the Edinburgh stage, Campbell retells the incident in the more lively and colloquial language that he remembers her using at social gatherings: "How much more pleasantly people tell their history in social converse than in formal writing." The work as a whole lacks the immediacy and warmth that Campbell adds to this episode, with the result that some of the enlivening details, such as Siddons's interest in clay modeling, are unintentionally bathetic. Campbell keeps his subject at a distance by blurring the distinction between her and her roles; discussing her performance as Katherine in Shakespeare's *Henry VIII* (1632), he finds "a strong moral resemblance between the historical heroine and her illustrious representative." In the "Eulogium" at the end of the biography, Campbell reveals the feelings that have inhibited him: "my predominant sensation, whilst writing her Life, has been a consciousness of my incompetence to do her justice." He also includes, at last, some small incidents from his own acquaintance with her, with an apologetic reminder to readers "to recollect how frequently our truest estimates of human nature are drawn from trifling incidents."

Reviewers were, on the whole, disappointed in the book. The *Gentleman's Magazine* (October 1834) puzzled over Campbell's failure to take full advantage of the resources at his command, while *Tait's Edinburgh Magazine* (August 1834) regretted that Campbell had "fancied himself bound, in biographical decorum, or social propriety, to suppress . . . the many characteristic traits and anecdotes with which he has the power of interweaving a *Boswellian* life of the great actress." The most ruthless of the reviews, which opens by declaring the work "a real *superfetation*," was written by John Wilson Croker for the *Quarterly Review* (August 1834). After Boaden's biography, Croker declared, nothing more on Siddons was required, yet Campbell's work is "equally voluminous and more expensive," poorly written in a style of "obscure bombast," derivative, inflatedly hypothetical, and negligent: in short, an "*abuse of biography*." He considered the extracts from Siddons's memoranda too short and inconsistently selected and Campbell's theatrical knowledge inadequate for his subject. Croker concluded by calling Campbell "the worst theatrical historian we have ever read." Reviews in the *Athenaeum,* the *Monthly Review,* and the *Literary Gazette* were more moderate, while the *New Monthly Magazine,* loyal to its former editor, published a warm appreciation.

After publication of the *Life of Mrs. Siddons* Campbell traveled to France and to North Africa, the subject of his *Letters from the South,* and made an extended visit to Edinburgh, where he was made a freeman of the city. In 1838 appeared *The Dramatic Works of William Shakspeare, with remarks on his life and writings* (Campbell was strongly committed to the spelling *Shakspeare*). Of the seven chapters of the "Remarks," the two longest are devoted to critical discussion of the plays. Campbell reveals a preference for the comedies and romances as well as an extensive knowledge of both the sources of the plays and the work of earlier critics. With a display of his now-familiar national pride, he pauses over Schlegel's commentary on the Scotsman Captain Jamy from *Henry V* (1600). Several of the discussions are repeated from the *Life of Mrs. Siddons,* particularly the defense of the marvelous in drama, the attack on the character Beatrice in *Much Ado About Nothing* (1600), and the evaluations of *Cymbeline*

(1623) and *Henry VIII.* The biography itself opens with a lament that the "Genius of Biography" has preserved so few records of Shakespeare's life and takes some care over establishing the likely social status of Shakespeare's family – an account in which one detects certain similarities to Campbell's own background – and the extent of his education. The tradition by which Shakespeare's birthday is celebrated on Saint George's day prompts Campbell not to sentimental patriotism but to a denunciation of the unworthiness of the "swindler and cutthroat" George of Cappadocia. Continuing to expand on personal opinions, he considers the inhibiting effect of "laboriously acquired erudition" on poetic imagination. Campbell's prudery is again in evidence in the way in which he discusses Anne Hathaway's pregnancy, the possible biographical referents of the *Sonnets* (1609), and the question of Shakespeare's infidelities. Employing a time-honored technique for passing on gossip, he declares: "The story of young Davenant saying, that he was going to see his godfather, and being told that he ought not to take the name of God in vain, is old enough for Joe Miller, and need not be repeated." The "Remarks" are noteworthy for what they reveal of the general opinion about Shakespeare's life in Campbell's time and for Campbell's personal, sometimes unusual, perspective on the plays. Although they touch on stage history, they make little attempt to set the plays in historically, politically, or biographically specific contexts. Redding declares Campbell's edition of Shakespeare "utterly worthless" and detects in it "the natural effect of early senility." Reviewers had little to say about it, but the fact that it went through several editions over the next thirty years indicates some success in reaching its targeted popular readership.

Immediately after completing "the stuff which I have to write about old Shakey" Campbell began to edit a biography of Petrarch that had been left in manuscript by William Coxe, archdeacon of Wiltshire, although he confessed himself at a loss to explain his motives for accepting the project. As the work progressed, however, he became intrigued by Petrarch's history and particularly, as his letters show, by Petrarch's relationship with Laura. By September 1839 he had developed a genuine and informed interest in the historical and political materials to which his researches had led him, and in March 1841 the *Life of Petrarch* was published in two volumes. In his prefatory "Advertisement" Campbell explains the origin of the project and is scathing about Coxe's manuscript, "an incomplete biography, that stops short of the poet's death by twelve

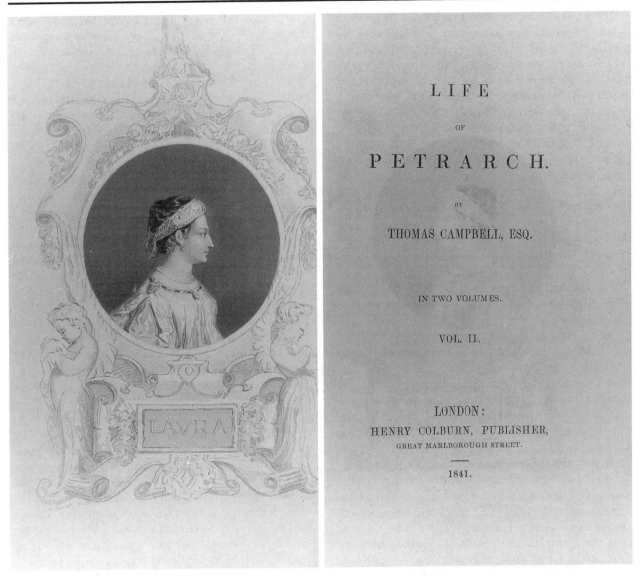

Frontispiece and title page for the second volume of Campbell's biography of the fourteenth-century Italian poet

years, written in a style so sprawlingly diffuse that, where three words would serve, the Archdeacon is sure to employ nine . . . [I] found that the reverend man's verbosity defied all power of packing." Although Campbell rapidly abandoned Coxe, he remained closely indebted to previous scholarly work on Petrarch. Most of his material is derived from the Abbé Jacques François Aldonçe de Sade's *Mémoires pour la vie de F. Pétrarch* (1764–1767), corrected where necessary by Giovanni Battista Baldelli Boni's *Del Petrarca e delle sue opere libri quattro* (1797).

In his preface Campbell surveys the history of biographies of Petrarch, but even in this comparative context he gives no explicit indication of the principles governing his own biography. He again views character through literary expression: the first chapter approaches Petrarch via the fame and influence of his works. Campbell's heavily fanciful style does not augur well: "After the deluge of barbarism in modern Europe had subsided, he stood, like a post-diluvian patriarch, connecting our knowledge of the old world with that of the new: and he had over his head a rainbow of genius, promising that the flood of ignorance should never return." Yet there are more instances than before of an attempt to see events through his subject's eyes. Campbell takes considerable trouble over Petrarch's political activities and has an informed grasp of cultural and historical contexts. On the subject of Laura, Campbell deals decisively with what he sees as the errors of previous commentators and expresses strong sympathy for her. He is inclined to read Petrarch's sonnets as straightforward autobiographical accounts of the relationship. His most outspoken commentary is reserved for Petrarch's relationship with the mother of his children; the omission of this private passion from Petrarch's literary works defies the close correspondence Campbell posits between life and the expression of it in art. Although most of Campbell's account is scholarly in tone, there are some energetic intrusions of personal opinion. A footnote on Coxe, for example – "I copy this twaddle from Archdeacon Coxe, though even with him it was not original" – prompts a discussion of that fashionable literary attitude, solitude: "I abominate all this slang about solitude . . . I have generally found the devotees of loneliness among the most stupid of their species."

Campbell begins volume two with an account of the life of Petrarch's friend Giovanni Boccaccio, again interweaving personality and creative work. Petrarch's "moral, political, and poetical" character is considered in detail in the final two chapters, where, for the first time, Campbell explicitly discusses some of the conventions of biography. His presentation of character proceeds from the belief that biographers "must take a broad and collective view of its physiognomy, and not decide by minute differences from its general expression. The truly great portrait-painter studies, first of all, the predominant physiognomical expression of the face he paints, and does not depend for collective effect on that microscopic elaboration of minute traits, which always leads to exaggeration." The description recalls the emphasis on "scientific" classification in Campbell's letter about the methodology of *Specimens of the British Poets*. Arguing against the common practice of biographers, Campbell resists drawing up "a balance-sheet of [Petrarch's] good qualities and defects, placing them like so many pounds sterling in a debtor and creditor account"; he insists on a more complex analysis, couching his comments in scientific terms: "There is a moral chemistry in the combining materials of our spiritual nature which is not to be judged of mechanically, according to the disunited qualities of those materials. The *tertium quid* produced by mixture varies according to its adverse ingredients." The passage expresses a greater awareness of the problems implicit in biographical analysis than Campbell had shown before. Appended to the biography are a selection of Petrarch's sonnets, translated by T. H. Sealy and Susan Wollaston; a chronology of his life, abridged from Baldelli; and a "Description of the Coins Relating to the Age of Petrarch," by J. G. Pfister.

Most reviewers agreed with the *Gentleman's Magazine* (August 1841) that the life was a judicious sketch of Petrarch's character, "the history of a poet, written by one of kindred feeling and inspiration." The *Athenaeum* (May 1841) described it as "a reflection of his own image of the man, unsophisticated by pedantic alembication, unstained by preconceived theories, but refined perhaps and exalted by the tint of his own views of human nature, and his own poetic temperament." The *Spectator* (May 1841), however, declared that it lacks a "lifelike air" as a result of Campbell's detachment and thin scholarship.

Campbell's health had been failing for some time, and the decline became even more marked after publication of the *Life of Petrarch*. He continued to work, editing Frederick Shoberl's *Frederick the Great, His Court and Times* (1842, 1843) and carrying out research for new projects. In 1841 his niece Mary Campbell joined him as his housekeeper; in 1843, to reduce expenses, they moved to Boulogne, France. By June 1844 his health had deteriorated so much that Beattie traveled to be with him. Campbell died on 15 June and was buried on 3 July in the Poets' Corner of Westminster Abbey.

During Campbell's lifetime his work as a literary critic and biographer was overshadowed by his fame as a poet, and the decline of his poetic reputation has reduced recognition of his criticism and biography still further. Yet his work is both significant in itself and characteristic of its times. Although they espouse no theory of biography, Campbell's studies rest on certain assumptions about decorum, consensus, balance, and objectivity. They look for a subject's defining characteristics in his or her work rather than in the life. The reviewer's lament that he had missed the opportunity to provide "a *Boswellian* life" of Siddons seems to indicate a bland and inhibited biographer, but Campbell emphasized the primacy of literature and aimed to free biography from gossip and speculation. As poet, editor, educationist, and political campaigner he assumed a moral importance for literature that gives purpose to his biographies of literary figures. In his summary of "The Pleasures of Hope," book 1, Campbell expresses his faith in "the wide field that is yet open for the progress of humanising arts among uncivilised nations." His biographies, like his poetry, aim to assist that progress.

Letters:

Life and Letters of Thomas Campbell, edited by William Beattie, 3 volumes (London: Moxon, 1849; New York: Harper, 1850).

Biographies:

Cyrus Redding, *Fifty Years' Recollections, Literary and Personal, with Observations on Men and Things,* 3 volumes (London: Skeet, 1858);

Redding, *Literary Reminiscences and Memoirs of Thomas Campbell,* 2 volumes (London: Skeet, 1860);

J. Cuthbert Hadden, *Thomas Campbell,* Famous Scots Series (Edinburgh: Oliphant Anderson, 1899).

References:

H. Hale Bellot, *University College London, 1826–1926* (London: University of London Press, 1929);

George M. C. Brandes, "The British Spirit of Freedom," in his *Main Currents in Nineteenth Century Literature,* 6 volumes (London: Heinemann / New York: Macmillan, 1906), IV: 189–194;

James Coutts, *A History of the University of Glasgow* (Glasgow: Maclehose, 1909);

W. Macneile Dixon, *An Apology for the Arts* (New York: Longmans, 1944), pp. 165–178;

Charles Duffy, "Thomas Campbell: A Critical Biography," Ph.D. dissertation, Cornell University, 1939;

Duffy, "Thomas Campbell and America," *American Literature,* 13 (January 1942): 346–355;

Frank G. Garvin, Jr., "Thomas Campbell and the Reviewers: A Study of Evolving Literary Criteria in the Periodical Reviews, 1798–1824," Ph.D. dissertation, University of Illinois, Urbana-Champaign, 1973;

William Hazlitt, *The Spirit of the Age; or, Contemporary Portraits* (London: Printed for Henry Colburn, 1825);

Lafcadio Hearn, "Note on Thomas Campbell," in his *On Poets,* edited by R. Tanabe, T. Ochiai, and I. Nishizaki (Tokyo: Hokeuseido, 1938), pp. 640–653;

Ian Jack, *English Literature 1815–1832* (Oxford: Clarendon Press, 1963);

Peter S. Macaulay, "Thomas Campbell: A Revaluation," *English Studies,* 50 (February 1969): 39–46;

Mary Ruth Miller, "Five Recently-Found Letters by Thomas Campbell," *Modern Language Review,* 83 (April 1988): 287–296;

Miller, *Thomas Campbell* (Boston: Twayne, 1978);

Frederick E. Pierce, *Currents and Eddies in the English Romantic Generation* (New Haven: Yale University Press, 1918);

George Richards, "Thomas Campbell and Shelley's *Queen Mab,*" *American Notes & Queries,* 10 (September 1971): 5–6;

Sir Walter Scott, *The Letters of Sir Walter Scott,* 12 volumes, edited by H. J. C. Grierson (London: Constable, 1932–1937), VII: 15;

Daniel B. Shumway, "Thomas Campbell and Germany," in *F. E. Schelling Anniversary Papers by His Former Students* (New York: Russell, 1923), pp. 233–261.

Papers:
Important collections of Thomas Campbell's manuscript poems, prose, and letters are held by the National Library of Scotland, Edinburgh; the British Library, London; the Bodleian Library, Oxford; University College, London; the University of Glasgow; and the Huntington Library, San Marino, California. Notes, drafts, and other papers associated with Campbell's biographical work are held by the Houghton Library, Harvard University; the Pierpont Morgan Library, New York; and the Folger Library, Washington, D.C.

Thomas Carlyle

(4 December 1795 – 5 February 1881)

Ann W. Engar
University of Utah

See also the Carlyle entry in *DLB 55: Victorian Prose Writers Before 1867.*

SELECTED BOOKS: *The Life of Friedrich Schiller* (London: Printed for Taylor & Hessey, 1825; Boston: Carter, Hendee, 1833);

German Romance (4 volumes, Edinburgh: William Tait / London: Charles Tait, 1827; 2 volumes, Boston: Munroe, 1841);

Sartor Resartus (Boston: Munroe, 1836; London: Saunders & Otley, 1838);

The French Revolution: A History (3 volumes, London: Fraser, 1837; 2 volumes, Boston: Little, Brown, 1838);

Critical and Miscellaneous Essays, 4 volumes (Boston: Munroe, 1838; London: Fraser, 1839);

Chartism (London: Fraser, 1839; Boston: Little, Brown, 1840);

On Heroes, Hero-Worship & the Heroic in History (London: Fraser, 1841; New York: Appleton, 1841);

Past and Present (London: Chapman & Hall, 1843; Boston: Little, Brown, 1843);

Latter-Day Pamphlets (London: Chapman & Hall, 1850; Boston: Phillips, Sampson, 1850);

The Life of John Sterling (London: Chapman & Hall, 1851; Boston: Phillips, Sampson, 1851);

Occasional Discourse on the Nigger Question (London: Bosworth, 1853);

History of Friedrich II. of Prussia, called Frederick the Great, 6 volumes (London: Chapman & Hall, 1858–1865; New York: Harper, 1858–1866);

Inaugural Address at Edinburgh, April 2nd, 1866 (Edinburgh: Edmonston & Douglas / London: Chapman & Hall, 1866); enlarged as *On the Choice of Books* (London: Hotten, 1869; Boston: Osgood, 1877);

Shooting Niagara: and After? (London: Chapman & Hall, 1867);

The Early Kings of Norway: Also An Essay on the Portraits of John Knox (London: Chapman & Hall, 1875; New York: Harper, 1875);

Reminiscences by Thomas Carlyle, edited by James Anthony Froude (2 volumes, London: Longmans, Green, 1881; 1 volume, New York: Scribners, 1881);

Reminiscences of my Irish Journey in 1849 (London: Low, Marston, Searle & Rivington, 1882; New York: Harper, 1882);

Last Words of Thomas Carlyle, on Trades-Unions, Promoterism and The Signs of the Times (Edinburgh: William Paterson, 1882);

Reminiscences, 2 volumes, edited by Charles Eliot Norton (London & New York: Macmillan, 1887);

Last Words of Thomas Carlyle (London: Longmans, Green, 1892; New York: Appleton, 1892);

Carlyle's Unpublished Lectures: Lectures on the History of Literature or the Successive Periods of European Culture, Delivered in 1838, edited by R. P. Karkaria (London & Bombay: Kurwen, Kane, 1892); also published as *Lectures on the History of Literature, Delivered by Thomas Carlyle, April to July 1838,* edited by J. Reay Greene (London: Ellis & Elvey, 1892);

Wotton Reinfred, A Posthumous Novel (New York: Waverly, 1892);

Montaigne and Other Essays, Chiefly Biographical (London: Gowans, 1897; Philadelphia: Lippincott, 1897);

Historical Sketches of Notable Persons and Events in the Reigns of James I. and Charles I., edited by Alexander Carlyle (London: Chapman & Hall, 1898; London: Chapman & Hall / New York: Scribners, 1898);

Two Note Books of Thomas Carlyle from 23rd March 1822 to 16th May 1832, edited by Norton (New York: Grolier Club, 1898);

Collectanea. Thomas Carlyle, 1821–1855, edited by Samuel Arthur Jones (Canton, Pa.: Kirgate Press, 1903).

Collection: *The Works of Thomas Carlyle,* Centenary Edition, 30 volumes, edited by H. D. Traill

Thomas Carlyle

(London: Chapman & Hall, 1896–1899; New York: Scribners, 1896–1901).

OTHER: *Oliver Cromwell's Letters and Speeches,* edited by Carlyle (3 volumes, London: Chapman & Hall, 1845–1846; 2 volumes, New York: Wiley & Putnam, 1846; revised and enlarged, 3 volumes, London: Chapman & Hall, 1846; revised and enlarged, 4 volumes, London: Chapman & Hall, 1850);

Letters and Memorials of Jane Welsh Carlyle, prepared for publication by Carlyle, edited by James Anthony Froude (3 volumes, London: Longmans, Green, 1883; 2 volumes, New York: Scribners, 1883);

New Letters and Memorials of Jane Welsh Carlyle, 2 volumes, annotated by Carlyle, edited by Alexander Carlyle (London & New York: John Lane/Bodley Head, 1903).

TRANSLATIONS: A. M. Legendre, *Elements of Geometry and Trigonometry; with Notes,* translated, with an introductory chapter, by Carlyle, ed-

ited by David Brewster (Edinburgh: Oliver & Boyd, 1824); revised edition, edited by Charles Davis (New York: Ryan, 1828);

Johann Wolfgang von Goethe, *Wilhelm Meister's Apprenticeship: A Novel,* 3 volumes (Edinburgh: Oliver & Boyd / London: Whittaker, 1824; revised edition, London: Fraser, 1839; Philadelphia: Lea & Blanchard, 1840).

Thomas Carlyle's writings so influenced nineteenth-century British social, political, and aesthetic thought that he has been called a Victorian prophet or sage. He rejected both traditional Christianity and the skepticism of the eighteenth century in favor of a secular faith based on wonder, vitality, and imagination – what Carlyle called "natural supernaturalism." He emphasized the necessity of the destruction of old institutions and modes of thought by permanent revolution, but he also condemned democracy. Most people, he argued, are followers and need the gifted leadership of a hero. Carlyle's interest in great men and in the decay and regeneration of ideas and social structures impelled him toward history and biography; for Carlyle, "History is the essence of innumerable biographies."

Carlyle produced important works of literary biography and criticism, particularly of German Romantic writers. Between 1822 and 1832 he wrote some twenty major essays (collected in his *Critical and Miscellaneous Essays,* 1838) that helped shape the attitude of the educated British audience toward German literature. In essays such as "Biography" (1832) and "Sir Walter Scott" (1838), which begin as reviews of recently published biographies, he formulates principles for writing good biography. Finally, his most widely read work, the novel *Sartor Resartus* (1836), is a purported literary biography. Thus Carlyle contributed importantly to the theory and practice of literary biography, and this genre forms an essential part of his work.

Carlyle was born on 4 December 1795 in the Scottish village of Ecclefechan to James and Margaret Aitken Carlyle. His father, who was a stonemason and later a farmer, instilled Scottish Calvinist principles of self-denial and hard work into his large family. Carlyle attended Annan Academy from 1806 to 1809 and Edinburgh University from 1809 to 1814 but left the university without taking a degree. His parents hoped that he would become a clergyman, but his reading of the works of skeptical writers such as David Hume and Edward Gibbon shook his faith in religion. He was already dreaming of literary fame, but in the meantime he supported himself as a tutor. Despising what he called the "wretchedness" of teaching, he began to study German and started his literary career by translating and by writing reviews and encyclopedia articles.

In 1823 the *London Magazine* asked Carlyle to write a short biographical sketch of Friedrich Schiller; the essay expanded during the writing to book length and became Carlyle's first literary biography. It is written in his early, more eighteenth-century style rather than the more dramatic, complex "Carlylese" of later works. *The Life of Friedrich Schiller* (1825) was the first extended English study of the poet.

Carlyle begins *The Life of Friedrich Schiller* by explaining why one would read biography. "We are anxious to know," he writes, "how so great a man passed through the world, how he lived, and moved, and had his being." The aim of a biographer, Carlyle claims, is to help the reader to see as the subject saw and feel as the subject felt. To do so, the biographer must almost become the subject, but he thus runs the risk of subsuming the subject's self in his own. Carlyle often ran into such difficulties

and is frequently criticized for self-projection. For example, Albert J. LaValley says that Carlyle's early writings on German literary figures are "autobiographical acts of self-discovery, closely analogous to Carlyle's mode of letter writing or notebook jotting." Of *The Life of Friedrich Schiller,* LaValley comments, "the first part of the book could almost as easily [have] been Carlyle's biography as it is Schiller's."

In *The Life of Friedrich Schiller* Carlyle says that the value of literary biography is that it allows readers to see whether the subject's life bears out the thoughts and feelings that seem to come through in the literature. This notion influenced later literary critics such as Walter Pater and Matthew Arnold in emphasizing the use of biography in literary criticism.

Carlyle begins by acknowledging the difficulties he faced in writing the biography of Schiller, including the few and incomplete records as well as differences in language and culture. He recognizes two problems in learning about a man from his writings but hopes that his biography will satisfy readers' curiosity about Schiller's "fortunes" and chief "peculiarities" and will help them enjoy the "magnificent and fragrant beauty" of Schiller's creations.

After his introductory remarks on biography, Carlyle notes for his British readers that Schiller was born in the same year as Robert Burns. He gives information about the authors whose works Schiller read, including ones he preferred. He discusses the strengths and weaknesses of Schiller's works; he praises the force of *The Robbers* (1782), for example, but claims that Schiller's early skill in composition surpassed his knowledge of the world.

Carlyle's sources include Schiller's letters and Madame Anne-Louise-Germaine de Staël's three-volume *Germany* (1813). His standard practice in writing was to read voluminously and take notes but then to throw the notes aside when actually writing. Despising the mechanical transcription of documents, he wrote under what he considered a form of mystical inspiration. Without his sources before him, however, he was prone to use only facts that led to his predetermined conclusions.

Despite Carlyle's excesses and some flagrant errors, *The Life of Friedrich Schiller* was praised by reviewers of its time and continues to be cited today. The *Eclectic Review* and *Gentleman's Magazine* lauded its spirit, its soundness, and Carlyle's thorough knowledge of his subject matter. Carlyle made German literature alive and important for several generations of English audiences. Recent studies such as T. J.

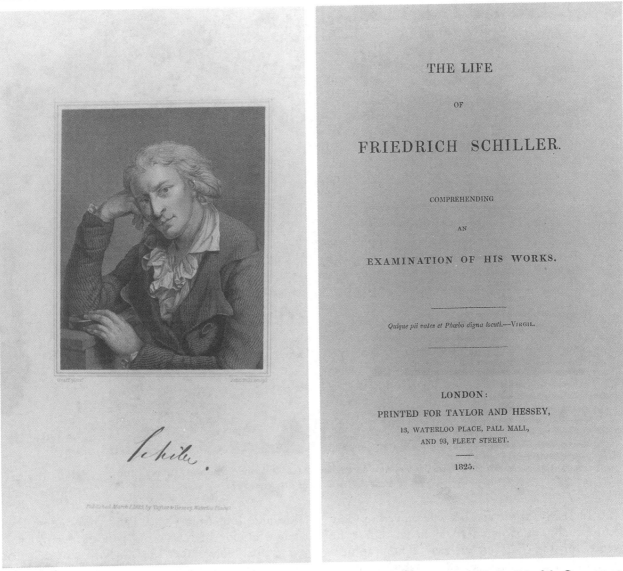

THE LIFE

OF

FRIEDRICH SCHILLER.

COMPREHENDING

AN

EXAMINATION OF HIS WORKS.

Quique pii vates et Phœbo digna locuti.—VIRGIL.

LONDON:

PRINTED FOR TAYLOR AND HESSEY,

13, WATERLOO PLACE, PALL MALL,
AND 93, FLEET STREET.

1825.

Frontispiece and title page for Carlyle's first literary biography, which was also the first full-length study in English of the German poet

Reed's *Schiller* (1991) recommend Carlyle's work, and other twentieth-century biographies of Schiller continue to quote Carlyle and use his translations.

In 1824 Carlyle visited London for the first time. He stayed with his friend Edward Irving, who introduced him to London literary society; among those Carlyle met was Samuel Taylor Coleridge, whom he thought tedious and weak-willed. After resigning his tutoring position Carlyle returned to Scotland and settled at Hoddam Hill farm. In 1821 he had met Jane Baillie Welsh, an ambitious and witty daughter of a doctor. They married on 17 October 1826, much to her family's dismay. Their forty-year marriage was childless.

From 1826 to 1828 Carlyle worked on a novel, *Wotton Reinfred,* which was published posthu-

mously in 1892. During this period he met Francis Jeffrey, editor of the *Edinburgh Review.* His first piece for Jeffrey, "Richter" (June 1827), was a brief essay on Jean Paul Friedrich Richter (Johann Paul). Ostensibly a review of Heinrich Doring's biography of Richter, the essay, like *The Life of Friedrich Schiller,* bears marks of Carlyle's self-projection. Carlyle judges Richter to be an original and independent genius, possibly because Richter's style coincided with Carlyle's developing one: both use concrete imagery, extended metaphor, and a syntax that demands that the reader stay alert until the ends of sentences. In "Richter" Carlyle derides the current state of biographical writing and hopes that his own work will help reform biography.

Jane Welsh Carlyle in the year of her marriage to Carlyle; portrait by Kenneth Macleary (from John Stewart Collis, The Carlyles, *1971)*

In 1828 Carlyle and his wife moved to Craigenputtoch, an isolated rural farm. There he wrote for the *Edinburgh Review* a biographical essay, "Burns" (December 1828), which starts as a review of John Gibson Lockhart's *Life of Robert Burns* (1828). Carlyle is more interested in estimating Burns's moral and spiritual worth, especially for Carlyle's own struggles, than in examining Burns's achievement as a poet. Burns "interests and affects us," he writes, "not chiefly as a poet, but as a man." Burns's excellence is his sincerity, "his indisputable air of Truth. Here are no fabulous woes or joys; no hollow fantastic sentimentalities; no wiredrawn refining." Burns, however, does not conquer in his religious struggle as Carlyle claims Johann Wolfgang von Goethe or Richter did; this failure to conquer is his tragic defect. "His heart, indeed, is alive with trembling adoration, but there is no temple in his understanding."

During a nine-month stay in London in 1831–1832, Carlyle met and became friends with the philosopher John Stuart Mill. While in London, Carlyle wrote for the *Edinburgh Review* the essay "Characteristics" (December 1831), in which he says that the strongest force within the human being is unconscious and mysterious: God is in man, literature is a branch of religion, and the artist's goal is to represent the mysterious and God-like deliverances of his deepest unconscious.

In his essays "Biography" and "Boswell's *Life of Johnson,*" which appeared in *Fraser's Magazine* in April and May 1832, respectively, Carlyle evaluates John Wilson Croaker's new edition of James Boswell's *Life of Samuel Johnson, LL.D.,* first published in 1791. Carlyle argues that biography is useful for gaining "some acquaintance with our fellow-creatures," for learning "how they got along in those old days, suffered and doing; to what extent, and under what circumstances, they resisted the Devil and triumphed over him, or struck their colours to him." Biography, thus, has moral import. To Carlyle, Boswell illustrates the ennobling virtues of hero worship, the inspiration that comes from a great man's example: Boswell had enough greatness in himself, Carlyle says, to recognize Johnson's moral and religious leadership.

In "Biography" and "Boswell's *Life of Johnson*" Carlyle follows some of his typical biographical practices: avoidance of aesthetic theory, creation of a hero, and self-projection. The man rather than his works interests Carlyle. Neither piece contains much discussion of Johnson's voluminous writings, but Johnson's life fits Carlyle's heroic pattern in many respects: his antecedents are undistinguished; his childhood is the story of an awakening, proud genius; he suffers from extreme poverty and lack of recognition; fame comes to him, but he remains an independent man, more concerned with teaching people than with pleasing them. Carlyle identified strongly with Johnson's guilty feelings about his treatment of his father and at the same time looked to Johnson as a father figure.

One topic Carlyle emphasizes in discussing Johnson's life but barely touches on in his other biographical writings is politics. Carlyle's discussion of this topic is partly motivated by a desire to rebuke an astringent piece Thomas Babington Macaulay had written on Johnson, but it also results from Carlyle's need to find answers to his own problems in the biographies of others. The review was written at the time of the passage of the Reform Bill, which widened the electoral franchise. Carlyle was beginning to fear democracy and was turning toward a study of the French Revolution to try to discover why a revolution occurred in France but not in England. For Carlyle, Johnson, as a central figure in English society, held the social fabric together by supporting the English heritage of ideas. Carlyle followed Boswell in viewing Johnson as a hero in an unheroic world, one who maintained a vision of coherence in an age of spiritual crisis. Carlyle's own need for faith and order in the disarray of the nineteenth century echoes Boswell's similar need in the disarray of the late eighteenth century.

At the time the two Johnson articles were appearing, Carlyle was having difficulty finding a publisher for what is today his best-known work; finally, *Fraser's Magazine* ran *Sartor Resartus* in installments from November 1833 to August 1834. The response was almost entirely negative; some readers canceled their subscriptions.

Sartor Resartus, though fiction, tells much about Carlyle's ideas about and practice of the art of writing biography. The work sounds his message about the importance and pleasure of biography and the use of biography to find heroes: "Biography by nature is the most universally profitable, univer-

sally pleasant of all things: especially the Biography of distinguished individuals." The main character of *Sartor Resartus,* the philosopher Diogenes Teufelsdröckh, is known to the reader through the Editor, who valiantly tries to serve as Teufelsdröckh's biographer and critic. The Editor at first has no biographical documents but seeks to understand Teufelsdröckh by reading his book again and again. The early part of *Sartor Resartus* is, thus, similar to the book review/biographies that Carlyle had been writing. Just as the Editor begins to think he understands Teufelsdröckh's meaning, he receives six bags of disorganized material about Teufelsdröckh. The documents, which the Editor inserts into his text, show that he has been mistaken about many of Teufelsdröckh's ideas. The Editor despairs of ever completely understanding Teufelsdröckh, and his health is affected. The Editor's difficulties and uncertainties seem to represent Carlyle's own feelings about biography or any other kind of understanding at this time: all perceptions and knowledge will remain partial and tentative no matter how hard one tries to achieve certitude. A major theme of *Sartor Resartus* is that one must renounce happiness and certainty, assume that there is divine justice, and continue with one's work.

In August 1833 Ralph Waldo Emerson visited Carlyle at Craigenputtoch. Their friendship, conducted mostly by mail over the years, was beneficial for Carlyle: Emerson convinced a Boston publisher to publish *Sartor Resartus* in book form in 1836 (it did not appear in that form in England until 1838), funded the American edition (1838) of Carlyle's *The French Revolution* (published in England in 1837), and introduced Henry David Thoreau to Carlyle's works and Carlyle to Walt Whitman's.

In June 1834 the Carlyles moved to 5 Cheyne Row, London. For the next three years Carlyle worked on *The French Revolution*. During this time he met William Wordsworth, Robert Southey, and the man who was to become his most cherished friend for the next nine years and the subject of one of his best biographies: the poet, novelist, and dramatist John Sterling.

The French Revolution was well received by the critics and popular with the public, but Carlyle still needed to work to support himself and his wife. Though he did not want to write for periodicals, he wrote a review of Lockhart's *Memoirs of the Life of Sir Walter Scott, Bart.* (1837–1838) for Mill's *London and Westminster Review* (January 1838). This review contains more seeds of the hero-worship ideas that Carlyle was to develop in *On Heroes, Hero-Worship & the Heroic in History* (1841). Carlyle observes that humans are instinctively curious about the "distinguished" and that this curiosity is the impulse to reading and writing biographies. "This perpetual fact of hero-worship," he claims, is also the foundation of politics, religion, loyalty, and "all the highest human interests." Carlyle also argues that biographers must tell the truth. He disparages current English biographies that are so carefully written not to offend that they end up not being biographies at all. Carlyle says that all men go through life giving and receiving offense and that these offenses should be recorded. This insistence on truth would lead Carlyle to choose James Anthony Froude to write his biography and edit his wife's papers.

Turning to Scott himself, Carlyle asserts that the primary question is whether Scott was a great man. Carlyle answers with hesitancy: Scott certainly was popular, and many lesser men than he have been called great. Carlyle's final verdict is that Scott was not heroic and does not help other men in their struggles with faith and life. Instead, Scott was worldly and ambitious. "There is nothing spiritual in him; all is economical, material, of the earth earthy." His writings suffer because of his character: he "had, as it were, no message to deliver to the world; wished not the world to elevate itself, to amend itself, to do this or that, except simply pay him for the books he kept writing." Scott's Waverley novels are "not profitable for building up or elevating in any shape! The sick heart will find no healing here, the darkly-struggling heart no guidance: the Heroic that is in all men no divine awakening voice." Biography, for Carlyle, is, thus, self-discovery and self-teaching: one finds one's own life in the biography and gains moral strength from it. If Carlyle finds what is useful and helpful for himself in a man's life, then that man's life was successful.

From 1837 to 1841 Carlyle gave annual lectures on German literature, literature in general, revolution, and heroes. *On Heroes, Hero-Worship & the Heroic in History,* the published version of the May 1840 lectures, delineates the unconscious and mysterious forces that underlie the personalities of great men. In his discussions of poets and writers – Johnson, Burns, Dante, William Shakespeare, and Jean-Jacques Rousseau – Carlyle repeats the claim he made in "Characteristics" that the artist is the priest of the divine force in the universe. He also theorizes that great literature occurs when ages of belief are beginning to unravel: in the Elizabethan Age, for example, literature flourished because the power of Catholicism and feudalism was dissipating. Dante and Homer, however, do not exactly fit Carlyle's theory, so, instead of being considered as

The Carlyles' house at 5 Cheyne Row, Chelsea, London, where they moved in 1834

literary figures, Dante becomes a religious and Homer a historical one.

Carlyle also has problems deciding whether his heroes are representative men who embody the characteristics of their ages or great men who rise above their age. Burns and Johnson, he contends, are great men who were out of place in the eighteenth century, a century whose representative figures are Hume and Voltaire. Carlyle says that any man's achievement is limited by the character of the age in which he lives, since not all actions are possible at any given moment.

Carlyle's method of presentation in the lectures is to identify enthusiastically with the hero, trying to *become* him for the audience. At times the method becomes theatrical, which may have worked well in a lecture but seems overwrought and almost fraudulent in written form. The hero-worshiping identification finally results in Carlyle's painting a portrait of himself rather than of the people whose lives and ideas he tries to represent. As A. O. J. Cockshut writes, "We are left half-convinced that the man was really the man the biographer saw."

The soundproof upstairs study, added to the Carlyles' house in 1853, where Carlyle wrote his biography of Frederick the Great

During the late 1830s and early 1840s Carlyle formed friendships with members of a new generation of writers, including Robert Browning, Alfred Tennyson, Charles Dickens, Richard Monckton Milnes, John Forster, William Makepeace Thackeray, and Edward FitzGerald. He planned a biography of Oliver Cromwell, but the work stagnated and he decided instead to edit Cromwell's letters and speeches and let Cromwell speak for himself. The edition was published in 1845–1846.

In the 1840s tensions developed in the Carlyles' marriage. Carlyle frequently left to visit friends; Jane Carlyle had headaches and was frequently depressed and exhausted. His moodiness tried her already-strained nerves, and they bickered. Carlyle became more and more interested in Harriet Baring, Lady Ashburton, while Geraldine Jewsbury became Jane's closest friend and fell in love with her. As Browning, Dickens, Tennyson, and Thackeray became famous in their own right, Carlyle gained new disciples in Froude, William Allingham, and John Ruskin. Froude, whom he met in 1849, was a frequent visitor to the Carlyle home for the next ten years and developed a strong affection for both Carlyles.

Carlyle's *Latter-Day Pamphlets* (1850) attacks modern democratic culture and received a storm of criticism. Even in this work Carlyle waxes strong in praise of biography, which, he says, above all other forms of literature, can teach us how to live. Also, since every life displays the struggle between the divine spirit and worldly chaos, biography becomes a message out of heaven from which we can discover the will of God. On 17 June 1850 Carlyle wrote to Leigh Hunt after reading Hunt's autobiography (1850), "In fact, this book has been like an exercise of *devotion* to me; I have not assisted at any sermon, liturgy or litany, this long while, that has had so *religious* an effect on me." Carlyle thus fuses biography and religion.

Carlyle's next work, *The Life of John Sterling* (1851), is quite different from *Latter-Day Pamphlets:* instead of writing on social issues as an Isaiah-like prophet, he writes gently and persuasively about the life of his friend, who had died of tuberculosis in 1844. Carlyle's deep affection for Sterling and sympathy for the conditions of human existence, expressed in his rich language, produced a work that George Eliot – then Mary Ann Evans, writing anonymously in the *Westminster Review* (January 1852) – judged to be "a touching monument of the capability human nature possesses of the highest love, the love of the good and beautiful in character, which is, after all, the essence of piety. The style of the work, too, is for the most part at once pure and rich; there are passages of deep pathos which come upon the reader like a strain of solemn music, and others which show that aptness of epithet, that masterly power of close delineation, in which, perhaps, no writer has excelled Carlyle."

As with the other biographies, *The Life of John Sterling* is as much about Carlyle as it is about Sterling. It includes a hostile portrait of Coleridge based partly on Carlyle's visit with Coleridge in 1824. In showing Sterling's rejection of Coleridge's liberal orthodoxy Carlyle revealed his own rejection of Christianity, a view that had been present but not overtly expressed in earlier works and that offended some readers of the Sterling biography. Carlyle also used Sterling to embody the confusion and corruption of modern culture: Sterling was a brilliant, noble young man who loved life but who was not strong enough (as Carlyle felt himself to be) to fight the destructive tendencies of society, including the propensity toward self-deception and evasion that modern society encourages.

Carlyle faced several problems in writing Sterling's biography. One was to downplay but not eliminate the religious aspects of Sterling's life. The impetus for writing the biography was to rescue Sterling from the biography Archdeacon Julius Charles Hare had written for Sterling's *Essays and Tales* (1848). Hare had known Sterling longer than had Carlyle and, thus, had direct acquaintance with more incidents of Sterling's life. But, for Carlyle, Hare's biography emphasized Sterling's relationship with the church far too much, to the exclusion of other important parts of his life. Another problem was Sterling's limited artistic achievement: Carlyle respected Sterling's attempts to be a poet but not his actual poems. He gives few examples of Sterling's work. More important to Carlyle is Sterling the man, as an emblem of his times. A minor writer whose highest claims to public attention were his friendships with great men becomes, under Carlyle's pen, representative of the struggle to find the "right" in the confusion of religion and politics, to live "manfully." Sterling is a hero not in the sense of being perfect and unconquerable but in the sense of standing as a model in an unheroic era. In *The Life of John Sterling* Carlyle transcends the problems and, through evocative language and sincere sentiment, creates a masterpiece of biography.

In 1851 Carlyle began studying the life of Frederick the Great; in 1852 he traveled to Ger-

many to continue his research. The first two volumes of the *History of Friedrich II. of Prussia, called Frederick the Great* were not published until 1858; Carlyle in the meantime had struggled with problems with sources, his own lack of enthusiasm about the project, and sorrow over his mother's death. In 1858 Carlyle traveled to Germany again, visiting battlefields to gather material for the remaining four volumes. It took seven more years, however, for Carlyle to finish the work.

In 1865 Carlyle was elected rector by the students of the University of Edinburgh. On 2 April 1866 he delivered an inaugural address in which he discussed his ideas about duty, work, art, heroes, history, reverence, religion, and lifelong learning from both books and life. While he was polishing the speech for publication, he received word that his wife had died.

Shortly after Jane's death Jewsbury gave Carlyle a short biographical sketch of her. Carlyle, critical of the sketch's inaccuracies and feeling remorse for making Jane submerge her own talents to become his chief source of support, wrote his own personal memoir of her life and their relationship. He also began annotating a long biographical article about himself written by Friedrich Althaus for the periodical *Unsere Zeit* and started a memoir of Edward Irving, the friend of his and Jane's youth. On a vacation to the Riviera he finished the memoir of Irving and wrote sketches of Jeffrey, Southey, and Wordsworth.

In 1868 Carlyle, with the help of his niece, Mary Aitken, organized Jane's letters, which he considered evidence of her brilliance; he also wrote annotations for a biography of her. He turned this material over to Froude in 1871.

By 1871 Carlyle wrote only by dictation to Aitken. In the winter of 1871–1872 he dictated a history of the early kings of Norway in which he finds new heroes in Olaf Tryggveson, King Olaf the Saint, and Magnus the Good. "The Early Kings of Norway" was published in *Fraser's Magazine* in 1875 and in book form later that year along with "An Essay on the Portraits of John Knox," written in late 1874 and early 1875 and published in *Fraser's Magazine* in April 1875. In the latter essay Carlyle finds the "Torpichen Portrait" of Knox inadequate to his own vision of Knox as a "heaven-inspired" seer and leader and proposes that a bronze statue of Knox modeled on the "Somerville Portrait" be put in College Square, Edinburgh. His depiction of Knox is, again, an unintentional portrait of himself. Knox, he says, had "utmost sharpness of discernment and discrimination . . . a beautiful and simple but com-

Thomas and Jane Welsh Carlyle in 1854

plete incompatibility with whatever is false in word or conduct; inexorable contempt and detestation of . . . *humbug*. . . a pure, and mainly silent, tenderness of affection. . . . Touches of genial humour are not wanting under his severe austerity; an occasional growl of sarcastic indignation against malfeasance, falsity, and stupidity . . . a most clear-cut, hardy, distinct, and effective man."

Carlyle died in his sleep on 5 February 1881. He was buried in Ecclefechan.

Carlyle was one of the most influential figures of the Victorian age; his attitudes affected a wide audience, particularly the writers of his day. His convictions that modern life was too "mechanical" and analytical, that greed and selfishness had replaced feelings of blessedness and brotherhood, and that spiritual rebirth was needed to bring coherence to modern life drew many to regard him with awe and reverence. In his later writings, such as *Latter-Day Pamphlets*, however, his prophetic stridency and antidemocratic ideas turned many away. Late-twentieth-century readers do not revere Carlyle uncritically but find him a remarkable stylist whose vivid and energetic prose helps them experience

past events, whose clear-sighted delineation of character helps them empathize with and understand the person about whom they are reading, and whose ideas on justice, purpose, and heroism still provoke thought.

Carlyle's contributions to literary biography are both theoretical and practical. "Man is," he says in "Biography," "properly the *only* object that interests man." The boundaries separating history, biography, literature, and social criticism are not rigid for Carlyle: in a sense all his works are a nineteenth-century epic poem. To him, history is a procession of great men rather than the interplay of economic, political, and social forces, and a good biography portrays both the character of the subject and the times in which he lived.

Carlyle advised biographers to give a full sense of their subjects, not just dry-as-dust facts about them; to reveal the importance of their lives; to re-create their experiences; and to tell the truth no matter how unpopular it might be. Though Carlyle tended to identify too strongly with his subjects, so that their biographies became his autobiography, he produced two masterpieces of literary bi-

Carlyle's grave, Ecclefechan, Scotland

ography, *The Life of Friedrich Schiller* and *The Life of John Sterling,* which, respectively, helped introduce German literature and thought to British readers and postulated how much of human life is culturally determined.

Letters:

The Correspondence of Thomas Carlyle and Ralph Waldo Emerson, 1834–1872, 2 volumes (Boston: Osgood, 1883; London: Chatto & Windus, 1883); supplementary volume (Boston: Ticknor, 1886);

Early Letters of Thomas Carlyle, 2 volumes, edited by Charles Eliot Norton (London & New York: Macmillan, 1886);

Correspondence between Goethe and Carlyle, edited by Norton (London: Macmillan, 1887);

Letters of Thomas Carlyle, 1826–1836, 2 volumes, edited by Norton (London & New York: Macmillan, 1888);

Letters of Thomas Carlyle to His Youngest Sister, edited by Charles Townsend Copeland (Boston & New York: Houghton, Mifflin, 1899; London: Chapman & Hall, 1899);

New Letters of Thomas Carlyle, 2 volumes, edited by Alexander Carlyle (London & New York: John Lane/Bodley Head, 1904) ;

The Love Letters of Thomas Carlyle and Jane Welsh, 2 volumes, edited by Alexander Carlyle (London & New York: John Lane/Bodley Head, 1909);

Letters of Thomas Carlyle to John Stuart Mill, John Sterling and Robert Browning, edited by Alexander Carlyle (London: Unwin, 1923; New York: Stokes, 1923);

Letters of Thomas Carlyle to William Graham, edited by John Graham (Princeton: Princeton University Press, 1950);

Thomas Carlyle: Letters to His Wife, edited by Trudy Bliss (Cambridge, Mass.: Harvard University Press, 1953);

The Correspondence of Emerson and Carlyle, edited by Joseph Slater (New York: Columbia University Press, 1964);

The Letters of Thomas Carlyle to His Brother Alexander, edited by Edwin W. Marrs, Jr. (Cambridge: Harvard University Press, 1968);

The Collected Letters of Thomas and Jane Welsh Carlyle, volumes 1– , edited by Charles Richard Sanders, K. J. Fielding, Clyde de L. Ryals, and others (Durham, N.C.: Duke University Press, 1970–);

Thomas and Jane: Selected Letters from the Edinburgh University Library Collection, edited by Ian Campbell (Edinburgh: Friends of Edinburgh University Library, 1980);

The Correspondence of Thomas Carlyle and John Ruskin, edited by George Alan Cate (Stanford, Cal.: Stanford University Press, 1982).

Bibliographies:

Isaac Watson Dyer, *A Bibliography of Thomas Carlyle's Writings and Ana* (Portland, Maine: Southworth, 1928);

Rodger L. Tarr, *Thomas Carlyle: A Descriptive Bibliography* (Pittsburgh: University of Pittsburgh Press, 1989).

Biographies:

R. S. Shepherd, with the assistance of C. N. Williamson, *Memoirs of the Life and Writings of Thomas Carlyle* (London: Allen, 1881);

James Anthony Froude, *Thomas Carlyle, A History of the First Forty Years of His Life, 1795–1835,* 2 volumes (London: Longmans, Green, 1882);

Froude, *Thomas Carlyle, A History of his Life in London, 1834–1881,* 2 volumes (London: Longmans, Green, 1884);

David Alec Wilson, *Life of Thomas Carlyle,* 6 volumes (London: Kegan Paul, 1929–1934);

John Stewart Collis, *The Carlyles: A Biography of Thomas and Jane Carlyle* (London: Sidgwick & Jackson, 1971);

Ian Campbell, *Thomas Carlyle* (London: Hamilton, 1974);

A. L. LeQuesne, *Carlyle* (Oxford: Oxford University Press, 1982);

Fred Kaplan, *Thomas Carlyle* (Ithaca, N.Y.: Cornell University Press, 1983).

References:

Harold Bloom, ed., *Thomas Carlyle* (New York: Chelsea House, 1986);

John Clubbe, ed., *Carlyle and his Contemporaries: Essays in Honor of Charles Richard Sanders* (Durham, N.C.: Duke University Press, 1976);

A. O. J. Cockshut, *Truth to Life: The Art of Biography in the Nineteenth Century* (London: Collins, 1974; New York & London: Harcourt Brace Jovanovich, 1974);

Frederic Ewen, *The Prestige of Schiller in England, 1788–1859* (New York: Columbia University Press, 1932);

K. J. Fielding and R. L. Tarr, eds., *Carlyle Past and Present: A Collection of New Essays* (London: Vision, 1976);

Elliot L. Gilbert, "Rescuing Reality: Carlyle, Froude, and Biographical Truth-Telling," *Victorian Studies,* 34 (Spring 1991): 295–314;

Kenneth Marc Harris, "Transcendental Biography: Carlyle and Emerson," in *Studies in Biography,* edited by Daniel Aaron, Harvard English Studies, 8 (Cambridge, Mass.: Harvard University Press, 1978), pp. 95–112;

Charles Frederick Harrold, *Carlyle and German Thought: 1819–1834* (New Haven, Conn.: Yale University Press, 1934);

Albert J. LaValley, *Carlyle and the Idea of the Modern* (New Haven, Conn.: Yale University Press, 1968);

Charles Richard Sanders, *Carlyle's Friendships and Other Studies* (Durham, N.C.: Duke University Press, 1977);

J. P. Seigel, ed., *Thomas Carlyle: The Critical Heritage* (London: Routledge & Kegan Paul, 1971);

Hill Shine, *Carlyle's Early Reading to 1834* (Lexington: University of Kentucky Libraries, 1953);

G. B. Tennyson, *Sartor Called Resartus: The Genesis, Structure, and Style of Thomas Carlyle's First Major Work* (Princeton: Princeton University Press, 1966).

Papers:

The National Library of Scotland in Edinburgh has the most complete collection of Thomas Carlyle's letters and manuscripts; the Edinburgh University Library also has a distinguished collection of the Carlyles' correspondence, particularly Jane's. Other manuscripts are in the British Museum Library, the Victoria and Albert Library, the Carlyle House in Chelsea, the Berg Collection of the New York Public Library, the Houghton Library at Harvard, and the university libraries of Yale and Duke.

Allan Cunningham

(7 December 1784 – 30 October 1842)

Richard Greene
Memorial University of Newfoundland

See also the Cunningham entry in *DLB 116: British Romantic Novelists, 1789–1832.*

BOOKS: *Remains of Nithsdale and Galloway Song: With Historical and Traditional Notices Relative to the Manner and Customs of the Peasantry,* edited by Robert Hartley Cromek (London: T. Cadell & W. Davies, 1810);

Songs: Chiefly in the Rural Language of Scotland (London: Printed for the author by Smith & Davy and sold by J. Hearne, 1813);

Sir Marmaduke Maxwell, a Dramatic Poem; The Mermaid of Galloway; The Legend of Richard Faulder; and Twenty Scottish Songs (London: Taylor & Hessy, 1822);

Traditional Tales of the English and Scottish Peasantry, 2 volumes (London: Taylor & Hessy, 1822; London & New York: Routledge, 1887);

Paul Jones: A Romance, 3 volumes (Edinburgh: Oliver & Boyd, 1826; Philadelphia: Carey & Lea, 1827);

Sir Michael Scott, a Romance, 3 volumes (London: Colburn, 1828);

The Lives of the Most Eminent British Painters, Sculptors and Architects, 6 volumes (London: Murray, 1829–1833); excerpts republished as *The Lives of the Most Eminent British Painters and Sculptors,* 5 volumes (New York: Harper, 1831–1834);

Some Account of the Life and Works of Sir Walter Scott (Boston: Stimpson & Clapp, 1832);

The Maid of Elvar: A Poem, in Twelve Parts (London: Moxon, 1832);

The Cabinet Gallery of Pictures, Selected from the Splendid Collections of Art, Public and Private, Which Adorn Great Britain: With Biographical and Critical Descriptions, 2 volumes (London: Major, 1833, 1834);

Biographical and Critical History of the British Literature of the Last Fifty Years (Paris: Baudry, 1834);

Lord Roldan: A Romance (3 volumes, London: Macrone, 1836; 1 volume, New York: Harper, 1836);

The Life and Correspondence of Robert Burns (London: Cochrane, 1836);

The Life and Land of Burns (New York: Langley, 1841);

The Life of Sir David Wilkie: With His Journals, Tours, and Critical Remarks on Works of Art; and a Selection from His Correspondence, 3 volumes, edited by Peter Cunningham (London: Murray, 1843);

Poems and Songs, edited by Peter Cunningham (London: Murray, 1847).

OTHER: *The Songs of Scotland, Ancient and Modern: With an Introduction and Notes, Historical and Critical, and Characters of the Lyric Poets,* 4 volumes, edited by Cunningham (London: Taylor, 1825);

The Anniversary, 2 volumes, edited by Cunningham (London: Sharpe, 1829, 1830);

The Works of Robert Burns, 8 volumes, edited, with a biography, by Cunningham (London: Cochrane & M'Crone, 1834);

The Poems, Letters, and Land of Burns, 2 volumes, edited, with a memoir, by Cunningham (London: Virtue, 1838, 1840);

James Thomson, *The Seasons, and The Castle of Indolence,* edited, with a biography of Thomson, by Cunningham (London: Tilt & Bogue, 1841).

Allan Cunningham was a prolific author in a variety of genres. His poetry, much of it in dialect, is generally accomplished and memorable, although his drama and fiction are only of historical interest. During the latter part of his career he became a literary biographer, producing a reference work on British literature and biographies of Sir Walter Scott, Robert Burns, and James Thomson.

Cunningham was born in a cottage in the parish of Keir in Dumfriesshire, Scotland, on 7 December 1784. His father, John Cunningham, was employed at that time as a factor at Blackwood House, the estate of a Mr. Copeland. Two years later the

*Allan Cunningham (engraving by J. Jenkins after a portrait by
J. Moore)*

family moved to Dalswinton, where John Cunningham took a similar position on the estate of Patrick Miller, an eminent businessman who was associated with the development of steam navigation. Allan Cunningham's mother, Elizabeth Harley Cunningham, was the daughter of a Dumfries merchant; Cunningham's biographer, David Hogg, describes her as "a lady of great personal attractions and accomplishments, shrewd in judgment, poetic in fancy, and altogether possessing a very superior intellect, which she transmitted to her family, both sons and daughters...."

The family faced financial difficulties, and the children's formal education was limited; the dame schools they attended did little more than teach their students how to read the Bible. Cunningham learned nothing of grammar or composition but eventually made up these deficiencies by private study. He read extensively, as did his four brothers and four sisters. His eldest brother, James, born in 1775, later wrote for newspapers and magazines and maintained a correspondence with the Romantic poet and novelist James Hogg, the "Ettrick Shep-

herd." Another brother, Thomas Mounsey, born in 1776, would contribute poems to Scottish magazines and would also become a friend of Hogg. The youngest brother, Peter Miller, born in 1789, would be the best-educated member of the family, studying medicine at Edinburgh University and becoming a naval surgeon; his two-volume account of his experiences in New South Wales would be published in 1827.

During Cunningham's childhood Burns was for three years a neighbor across the river Nith at Ellisland; he was a good friend of John Cunningham and a regular visitor to the Cunningham home. He is said to have recited "Tam O' Shanter" (1791) for the first time at the Cunningham's table while Allan stood listening in the inglenook. When Cunningham was eleven years old he attended Burns's wake and funeral; he would write an essay for the *London Magazine* (August 1824) comparing that occasion with the spectacle surrounding the interment of George Gordon, Lord Byron.

By his eleventh year Cunningham was apprenticed to his brother James, who had become a stonemason. The two brothers shared a strong interest in poetry; on one occasion they went to meet James Hogg, who was working near Dalswinton. On another occasion Allan walked to Edinburgh to catch a glimpse of Scott.

In 1807 Cunningham began to have some of his poetry published in *Literary Recreations,* a London periodical edited by Eugenius Roche. In the summer of 1809 Cunningham met Robert Hartley Cromek, an engraver and antiquarian, for whom he undertook to collect old songs of Nithsdale and Galloway. The "collection," which was published in December 1810 as *Remains of Nithsdale and Galloway Song,* consisted almost entirely of Cunningham's original compositions. Although the book was generally admired, many readers detected the imposture. It is difficult to believe that Cromek did not know that Cunningham was the true author of the songs.

At Cromek's request Cunningham moved to London in April 1810. He soon found work with a sculptor, James George Bubb, and by September had established himself as, in David Hogg's words, "the soul and nerve of the shop." By December, however, he had taken a job with Roche, who was then editing the *Day,* reporting parliamentary debates and contributing poems. On 1 July 1811 he married Jean Walker, a domestic servant from Preston Mill, near Dalswinton; they had five sons and a daughter. Through the early years of their marriage Cunningham earned his living as a professional writer for various publications, including the *Literary Gazette.* In 1813 his second book of poems, *Songs: Chiefly in the Rural Language of Scotland,* was published.

In 1814 he took a job as assistant to Francis Chantrey, a well-known sculptor. He was responsible for correspondence, and he sometimes supervised the execution of stone figures from the sculptor's clay models. He would remain in this job until Chantrey's death, which preceded his own by about a year. Chantrey's clientele included many of the prominent poets and writers of the time, and these contacts helped Cunningham establish himself as a literary figure. He met Scott in 1820, when Chantrey sent him to arrange a sitting. Scott had already expressed admiration for Cunningham's songs, and the two became close friends. Scott seemed to regard Cunningham as a gifted poet but was more reserved about his other writings. He read the manuscript for Cunningham's *Sir Marmaduke Maxwell, a Dramatic Poem* (1822) and offered precise, though diplomatic, criticism of the play: "Many parts of the poetry are eminently beautiful,

though I fear the great length of the piece, and some obscurity of the plot, would render it unfit for dramatic representation. There is also a fine tone of supernatural impulse spread over the whole action, which I think a common audience would not be likely to adopt or comprehend – though I own that to me it has a very powerful effect." Cunningham was easily annoyed by adverse criticism; he continued to rely on Scott's advice, however, such as the suggestion that he attempt romance fiction.

Cunningham usually worked twelve hours a day in Chantrey's studio, yet he wrote extensively for various periodicals. While writing for the *London Magazine* between 1821 and 1823 he became a friend of Thomas De Quincey, who was also a contributor. In 1822 his *Sir Marmaduke Maxwell, a Dramatic Poem; The Mermaid of Galloway; The Legend of Richard Faulder;* and *Twenty Scottish Poems* and a two-volume collection, *Traditional Tales of the English and Scottish Peasantry,* were published. Three years later he edited a four-volume anthology, *The Songs of Scotland, Ancient and Modern* (1825). His first romance, *Paul Jones,* appeared in 1826; he wrote two other novels, *Sir Michael Scott* (1828) and *Lord Roldan* (1836).

Cunningham's first important biography arose directly out of his work with Chantrey. *The Lives of the Most Eminent British Painters, Sculptors and Architects* (1829–1833) opens with a synoptic essay on British art before William Hogarth, then provides individual accounts of the most prominent figures of the eighteenth and early nineteenth centuries. The series was highly popular, with initial volumes selling out print runs in excess of ten thousand copies. Cunningham also included some biographical notices in his *The Cabinet Gallery of Pictures* (1833, 1834), and his substantial biography of the painter Sir David Wilkie was published posthumously in 1843.

Cunningham's first biography of a literary figure appeared in 1832. *Some Account of the Life and Works of Sir Walter Scott* is a brief memoir, based largely on Cunningham's personal knowledge. Although the book was eclipsed by John Gibson Lockhart's monumental biography (1837–1838), it remains an attractive work. Cunningham's admiration for Scott was profound; his memoir opens with Henry Fuseli's observation that biography is "the unequivocal homage of inferiority offered to the majesty of genius." As with Burns and Thomson, the subjects of his other literary biographies, Cunningham saw in Scott a man from his own country whose genius was incontestable. Yet the work is not slavish in its regard for Scott: "I write of [him], however, less from a sense of inferiority, than from an earnest love and an enthusiastic admiration of the subject; or rather from a desire to afford some relief to my own feelings." Cunningham doubtless felt some inferiority when he compared himself to Scott, not least because his own background as a laborer set the two men apart in terms of class. Cunningham was not, however, servile or falsely modest; his respect for Scott had chiefly to do with the latter's talent as a writer. He does not hesitate to record Scott's criticism of *Sir Marmaduke Maxwell*, nor other episodes that cast his own abilities in a poor light: "We talked of Romance writing: 'When you wish to write a story,' he said, 'I advise you to prepare an outline – a skeleton of the subject; and when you have pleased yourself with it, proceed to endow it with flesh and blood.' I remember (I said) that you gave me much the same sort of advice before. 'And did you follow it?' he said, quickly. 'I tried (I answered) but I had not gone far on my way till some will-o-wisp or another dazzled my sight; so I deviated from the path, and never got on it again.' ' 'Tis the same way with myself,' he said, smiling: 'I form my plan, and then in executing it I deviate.' 'Ay, ay! (said I) I understand; but You deviate into excellence, and I into absurdity.' " Cunningham's debt to Scott was both literary and personal: the memoir records that Scott found places for two of Cunningham's sons in the service of the East India Company when Cunningham lacked the money to launch them in careers.

Cunningham places Scott in the context of the literary scene of the 1820s; he also discusses the Scottish background of Scott's life and works. An amusing aspect of the biography is Cunningham's interest in Scott's attempt to conceal his authorship of the Waverley novels; having begun his own career with a minor fraud, Cunningham seems to have been fascinated by even the most innocent forms of literary subterfuge.

As one who had enjoyed his generosity, Cunningham describes the financial difficulties of Scott's last years with a barely concealed anger that Scott should have been allowed to struggle under his debts by a nation that would eventually raise statues to his memory. The book, published in the year of Scott's death, is a personal tribute written "to afford some relief to my own feelings." Cunningham's most readable biography, the work can be described as a good writer's tribute to a better one.

In his *Biographical and Critical History of the British Literature of the Last Fifty Years* (1834) Cunningham discusses the works and careers of various authors in the years between the death of Samuel Johnson in 1784 and that of Scott. He expresses a general contempt for the prosaic qualities of poetry after John Milton but sees that the American and French revolutions created a "free and investigating tone" that encouraged men of genius to recover poetry for the imagination. The work reflects Cunningham's own tastes; he writes in the opening section: "I shall draw my information from the best sources to which I have access, and sketch the characters of the dead and the living with all possible impartiality. To secure this, I have come under no obligations for information; and I write chiefly from a memory seldom faithless in matters concerning genius." It is no surprise, then, that the work contains much more critical opinion than biographical information.

The book is divided into sections dealing with poetry, romance, history, biography, drama, and criticism. While such favorites of Cunningham's as Scott, James Hogg, Burns, Robert Southey, and William Cowper are much praised, the book is most memorable for its strictures. Of Maria Edgeworth, whom he generally admires, he writes: "She walks by the side of her characters as Mentor by the side of Telemachus, keeping them out of all manner of pleasant mischief, and wagging the monitory head, and waving the remonstrating finger, should their eyes brighten or their breath come thick at approaching adventures." With other authors he is less gentle. George Crabbe, for example, is judged to be out of sympathy with humanity: "the Englishman is a cold and remorseless dissector, who pauses, with the streaming knife in his hands, to explain how strongly the blood is tainted, what a gangrene is in the liver, how completely the sources of health are corrupted, and that the subject is a thorough bad one." He struggles particularly with his assessment of Byron; he is in no doubt about the poet's literary merits but despises almost everything about him: "The cynical, sneering, and sarcastic spirit of our times – the doubting of everything, and believing in nothing – found a poet in George Gordon, Lord Byron." Cunningham expresses some sympathy for Byron's financial difficulties but in the end can only praise his poetry. Even then, he sees the brilliance of *Don Juan* (1819–1824) as chiefly diabolical: "The poet seems to have been sitting between angels of light and darkness when he wrote it, and to have been influenced by the former at the rate of ten stanzas to the canto."

As a reference work Cunningham's book has long ceased to have any use. As an assessment of the literature of his time, however, it is of great interest. Many of his judgments reflect contemporary

THE

WORKS

OF

ROBERT BURNS;

WITH

HIS LIFE,

BY

ALLAN CUNNINGHAM.

"HIGH CHIEF of Scottish song!
That could'st alternately impart
Wisdom and rapture in thy page;
And brand each vice with satire strong,
Whose lines are mottoes of the heart,
Whose truths electrify the sage."
CAMPBELL.

IN SIX VOLUMES.

VOL I.

LONDON:
COCHRANE AND M'CRONE,
11, WATERLOO PLACE.

1834.

Title page for the first volume of Cunningham's edition of Burns's works, which includes Cunningham's biography of the poet

fashion – an obvious example is his enthusiasm for Southey. Yet he discusses with something like impartiality the works of several women authors, and he treats with fairness the works of many males who have vanished from the literary canon.

The history ends with a remarkable essay discussing the influence of Oriental texts on British literature. Cunningham surveys the work of dozens of scholars through the eighteenth and nineteenth centuries and mocks the popular notion "that Oriental literature is a uniform something, compounded of the Bible and the Arabian Nights' Entertainments, of which the Hebrew language was the most valuable portion." In particular, he objects to the lumping together of literatures of different languages and different nations. He claims that Hindu philosophy makes Plato's speculations appear tame, and he de-

scribes Sanskrit as "a language of unrivalled richness, variety, and extent." He draws attention to the distinctiveness of Arabian, Persian, Turkish, and Chinese writings and speculates that Armenian, Tartar, and Sinhalese works would likewise appear distinctive if they were studied in greater depth. He laments that there is no satisfactory account of Buddhism in English, and he ends by appealing for additional funds for translators. Eighteenth- and nineteenth-century orientalism is now widely judged guilty of racism and imperialism; while Cunningham's ideas are obviously conditioned by the age in which he lived, it is hard to condemn his view of translated literatures as a "flood of light from the East."

Cunningham's most substantial literary project was his edition of the works of Burns, which appeared in 1834. The first volume includes a biography that displays Cunningham's reverence for Burns, who, even more than the urbane Scott, inspired in Cunningham a sense of kinship both as a Scottish poet and a member of the laboring class. In its first printing the work sold more than six thousand copies.

"The Life of Burns" opens with firm emphasis on the poet's poverty: "Robert Burns, the chief of the peasant poets of Scotland, was born in a little mud-walled cottage on the banks of Doon. . . ." Of course, Cunningham numbered himself among the peasant poets. He knew well that in a literary culture that expected its writers to have been educated in the classics, laboring poets had to claim a higher competence. Since the days of Stephen Duck a succession of English, Scottish, and Irish poets had been described as "natural geniuses." The primitivist argument allowed for native ability to triumph over circumstance and for plowmen and stonemasons to be taken seriously as writers. Yet the claim was always open to challenge; Cunningham observes that some of the Scottish literati "spoke of [Burns] as a chance, or an accident: and though they admitted that he was a poet, yet he was not one of settled grandeur of soul, brightened by study." Cunningham, who had actually made his way in polite society and was noted for his civility, describes how Burns's assertive manner and occasional lapses of courtesy alienated many admirers in Edinburgh. Cunningham is, nonetheless, aware of the typical experience of laborer poets as they find that they are no longer lionized: "the marvel of the inspired ploughman had begun to subside; the bright gloss of novelty was worn off, and his fault lay in his unwillingness to see that he had made all the sport which the Philistines expected, and was required to make room for some 'salvage' of the season, to paw, and roar, and shake the mane." It is hard to imagine that Cunningham's sensitivity on this point does not arise from having been himself treated as a curiosity or a "salvage" (savage) prodigy.

While Cunningham's allegiances are always clear, he is in some respects unable to draw close to the object of his admiration. Despite his childhood acquaintance with Burns and his knowledge of Burns's letters, which he collected, the biography lacks immediacy when compared to the memoir of Scott. That work draws considerable force from Cunningham's anecdotes and his recollection of table talk; with Burns he is obliged to rely on secondhand accounts, and the work is lacking in descriptions of significant or revealing incidents. This difficulty is overcome to some extent toward the end of the book when Cunningham describes the poet's burial, a subject he had written about before: "On reaching the northern nook of the kirk-yard, where the grave was made, the mourners halted; the coffin was divested of the mort-cloth, and silently lowered to its resting-place, and as the first shovelfull of earth fell on the lid, the volunteers, too agitated to be steady . . . [fired] three ragged volleys. He who now writes this very brief and imperfect account was present: he thought then, as he thinks now, that all the military array of foot and horse did not harmonize with either the genius or the fortunes of the poet, and that the tears which he saw on many cheeks around, as the earth was replaced, were worth all the splendor of a show which mocked with unintended mockery the burial of the poor and neglected Burns." Despite such colorful passages, the work is diminished by the quality of Cunningham's research. The stories he recounts are sometimes unreliable, and Burns's subsequent biographers have been cautious about accepting them where they are not confirmed by other sources.

Although "The Life of Burns" has obvious limitations, it is valuable as an attempt to raise Burns's reputation. The claim Cunningham ultimately makes for Burns is solidly Romantic: "he perceived the tie of social sympathy which united animated with unanimated nature, and in many of his finest poems most beautifully he has enforced it."

Cunningham's sense that Burns was undervalued because of class prejudice is evident throughout "The Life of Burns" and is the starting point for a second biographical essay, "The Land of Burns," which appeared in the first volume of Cunningham's *The Poems, Letters, and Land of Burns* (1838, 1840). In the first chapter he makes almost no attempt to hide the anger he feels toward Byron, who claimed that Burns had "as much dirt as deity about him." Cunningham insists that, apart from Byron's disregard for virtue and morality, "the peer and the peasant seem of imagination all compact. . . ." The snobbery of Byron and others is seen as a denial of the power of the imagination, Romanticism's great leveler.

The quality of Burns's imagination and his response to his surroundings are the central issues of "The Land of Burns." The work is essentially a reading of some of Burns's most important compositions in relation to the landscapes that inspired them. Although the account is often charming, its nostalgic lyricism is sometimes cloying, and the writing is generally unfocused. For example, Cunningham discusses "The Wounded Hare" (1793): "The field on which the hare was wounded is still pointed out, as well as the spot where the poet and the farmer had the angry parley. The latter is where the highland of the farm sinks into the holm, the poet's favorite musing place; for there he composed 'Tam O' Shanter,' and several of his finest lyrics; and there also some visitors from the south found him, with a rough fur cap on his head, a broadsword at his side, and a rod in his hand, angling for salmon. The place of itself is beautiful. . . ." Such a passage is representative of the essay's leisurely ramble through its subject's life and career. "The Land of Burns" is Cunningham's act of devotion both to Burns and to the country of their birth. As biography, however, it is slight, and as criticism it is unenlightening. Cunningham was not the first to write about Burns from this perspective, and there is little of significance in the work. Only the brief attack on class prejudice in the early part of the essay renders it memorable.

Cunningham's last literary biography, of Thomson, was included in his edition of Thomson's *The Seasons, and The Castle of Indolence* (1841). It reiterates many of the concerns of his writings on Burns: "the chief rural poets of Scotland were natives of scenes which biographers imagine had some influence on the character of their compositions. . . ." Cunningham's description of the effect of environment on Thomson's poetry could easily have been transplanted from either of his accounts of Burns: "The place of his birth, and the scenes where he was educated, are celebrated in Scottish song: to such influences he was not insensible: he could not walk out without seeing a hill or a stream famous in story; nor could he stroll in either wood or field without treading in the yet uneffaced footsteps of patriots and poets; nor wander by a rivulet side, nor drink out of a fountain – and of this he was fond – without feeling they were celebrated in imperishable verse: add to this the presence of a magnificent landscape, which united the wild beauties of nature with those of civilization – the pastoral with the agricultural – scenes sure to awaken verse of an undying kind; for in them resided the Muse which first inspired him." Passages of this sort proliferate in Cunningham's biographies. They reflect, perhaps, his sense of distance from his homeland: he returned there for visits only twice in thirty-two years. In this sense the real subject of Cunningham's biographies of individual writers is the poetical character of Scotland as the author, as much as his subjects, had experienced it.

His sense of literary value is, as ever, Romantic; he speaks of Thomson as "the great author of 'The Seasons' – a poem which gives a tongue to inanimate nature, while it elevates and chastens the human heart." His account of Thomson's life is characteristically short of reliable details. At one point he recounts at length the story of Thomson, who had been arrested for debt, being given one hundred pounds by the actor James Quin. This gift was meant to be an advance on the money Quin would leave the poet in his will as payment for the pleasure he had received from *The Seasons* (1730). Cunningham describes the dinner, the wine, and the conversation that is supposed to have occurred in the jail; at this point he confesses that there is no proof of the truth of the story except that Johnson gives it as a "report" and that it seems in character for Quin. Cunningham's sense of evidence was defective, and his works show signs of haste. His huge output – thirty volumes in thirty-three years, not counting the books he edited – entailed that he had little time to check his information. As with the biographies of Burns, few claims can be made for Cunningham's treatment of Thomson.

In the last year of his life Cunningham suffered from two strokes, of which the second was fatal. He died on 30 October 1842.

As a literary biographer Cunningham suffers by comparison with some of his contemporaries, notably Lockhart, though his memoir of Scott and his literary history have a lasting value. Southey believed that Cunningham was the finest stylist, next to David Hume, born north of the Tweed. This judgment is too generous. Yet his prose style is, at its best, engaging and robust, and that quality is one of his chief claims on the attention of readers in the twentieth century.

Biography:

David Hogg, *The Life of Allan Cunningham, With Selections from His Works and Correspondence* (London: Hodder & Stoughton / Dumfries: Anderson / Edinburgh: Grant, 1875).

References:

"Allan Cunningham," *Times Literary Supplement,* 31 October 1942, p. 535;

David Groves, "De Quincey, Allan Cunningham, and the *Edinburgh Saturday Post,*" *Review of English Studies,* 41, no. 162 (1990): 230–232.

Papers:

Collections of Allan Cunningham's papers are in the Bodleian Library, Oxford; in the British Library; and at the University of Iowa.

Thomas De Quincey

(15 August 1785 – 8 December 1859)

Ayse Agis
Yale University

See also the De Quincey entry in *DLB 110: British Romantic Prose Writers, 1789–1832, Second Series.*

BOOKS: *Close Comments upon a Straggling Speech* (Kendal: Printed by Airey & Bellingham, 1818);

Confessions of an English Opium Eater (London: Printed for Taylor & Hessey, 1822; Philadelphia: E. Littell / New York: R. Norris Henry, 1823);

The Stranger's Grave, possibly by De Quincey (London: Longman, Hurst, Rees, Orme, Brown & Green, 1823);

Klosterheim; or the Masque (Edinburgh: Blackwood / London: Cadell, 1832);

The Logic of Political Economy (Edinburgh & London: William Blackwood & Sons, 1844);

De Quincey's Writings, 22 volumes, edited by James T. Fields (Boston: Ticknor, Reed & Fields, 1851–1859);

Selections Grave and Gay from Writings, Published and Unpublished, of Thomas De Quincey, Revised and Arranged by Himself, 14 volumes (Edinburgh: Hogg, 1853–1860);

China: A Revised Reprint of Articles from Titan, with Prefaces and Additions (Edinburgh: Hogg / London: Groombridge & Sons, 1857);

The Collected Writings of Thomas De Quincey, 14 volumes, edited by David Masson (Edinburgh: Adam & Charles Black, 1889–1890);

The Uncollected Writings of Thomas De Quincey, 2 volumes, edited by James Hogg (London: Printed by S. Sonneschein for James Hogg, 1890; New York: Scribner & Welford, 1890);

The Posthumous Works of Thomas De Quincey, 2 volumes, edited by Alexander H. Japp (London: Heinemann, 1891, 1893);

A Diary of Thomas De Quincey, 1803, edited by Horace A. Eaton (London: Noel Douglas, 1927; New York: Payson & Clarke, 1927);

New Essays by De Quincey: His Contributions to the Edinburgh Saturday Post and the Edinburgh Evening Post, 1827–8, edited by Stuart M. Tave (Princeton: Princeton University Press, 1966).

Editions: *Recollections of the Lake Poets,* edited by Edward Sackville-West (London: Lehmann, 1948);

Confessions of an English Opium-Eater in Both the Revised and the Original Texts with its Sequels, Suspiria De Profundis and the English Mail Coach, edited by Malcolm Elwin (London: Macdonald, 1956);

Reminiscences of the English Lake Poets 1834–1840, edited by John E. Jordan (London: Dent, 1961; New York: Dutton, 1961).

OTHER: *Walladmor: "Freely Translated into the German from the English of Sir Walter Scott" and Now Freely Translated from the German of G. W. Haering into English,* 2 volumes (London: Taylor & Hessey, 1825);

Niels Klim: Being an Incomplete Translation by Thomas De Quincey from the Danish of Ludvig Holberg, edited by Sydney Musgrove (Auckland, New Zealand: Auckland University College, 1953).

Best known as the author of the *Confessions of an English Opium Eater* (1822), Thomas De Quincey was an innovative master of English prose style whose importance has been eclipsed by the modern tendency to consider poetry the major Romantic genre, as well as by the lack of a reliable collected edition of his works. Considered by his contemporaries as one of the best writers of his time, De Quincey wrote digressive and fragmented articles, stories, biographies, and autobiographies that are often reminiscent of prose poetry in their style and imaginative reach. His autobiography and the biographies he wrote of the Lake Poets share the psychological and narrative concerns of Romantic poetry and criticism and are successful examples of the transmutation of Romantic poetics into prose.

De Quincey was born Thomas Penson Quincey on 15 August 1785 in Manchester but lived "the whole of [his] childhood . . . in a rural seclusion"

just outside the city. He was the fourth child and second son of Thomas Quincey, a textile merchant, and Elizabeth Penson Quincey, whose London family held a somewhat higher social position than her husband's. His father, a man of some culture, owned what seemed to Thomas a "vast" library and had contributed "Account of a Tour in the Midland Counties" to the *Gentleman's Magazine* in 1774.

Young Thomas early formed close ties with his sisters rather than with his "horrid, pugilistic brothers"; his rather distant, authoritarian mother; or his frequently absent father. His most important childhood experiences centered around the deaths of three family members within three years. The death of his younger sister Jane when he was four and a half was "less sorrowful than perplexing" because "death was then scarcely intelligible to me." Two years later, however, the death of his nine-year-old sister Elizabeth devastated him. "Blank anarchy and confusion of mind fell upon me. . . . I wish not to recall the circumstances of that time." Yet this remained one of the seminal experiences of his life and was later re-created in one of the most powerful passages of *Autobiographic Sketches,* the first volume of *Selections Grave and Gay from Writings, Published and Unpublished, of Thomas De Quincey, Revised and Arranged by Himself* (1853–1860).

In 1793 the elder Thomas Quincey died; he left an estate of sixteen hundred pounds a year, sufficient for the family to continue living in comfort. After the death of their father, Thomas's elder brother William came home from boarding school, and the brothers were sent to a guardian, the Reverend Samuel Hall, for tutoring. On the way to their lessons William would compel Thomas to get involved in his fights with the factory boys of their district, but he was also instrumental in the invention of the imaginary kingdoms of Gombroon and Tigrosylvania, each represented by one of the brothers and at continual war with each other. After William died of typhus at sixteen, Thomas and his younger brother Richard, known as "Pink," were sent to the Bath Grammar School. There Thomas became so well known for his facility with classical languages, especially Greek, that his teacher told a visitor: "That boy could harangue an Athenian mob, better than you or I could address an English one."

After two years he was removed from the school by his mother and, after a period at home, sent to a school at Winkfield, Wiltshire, where he wrote for the boys' weekly paper, the *Observer,* and won prizes for translation. Around 1799 the Quinceys changed their names to De Quincey on the basis of a tradition that they were descendants of de Quincis, who had come over with William the Conqueror. In the summer of 1800 De Quincey went to Ireland to visit Howe Peter Browne, Lord Westport, a young friend from Bath who was the son of John Denis Browne, Lord Altamont, an Irish peer. At their country house he met King George III, who talked to him about the De Quincey family. He was also present at the last sitting of the Irish House of Lords before the passage of the Act of Union. He visited London for the first time that summer and felt "a delightful fear" at the acoustic magic of the Whispering Gallery at St. Paul's Cathedral, where he imagined that a whisper at one end reached him at the other "as a deafening menace in tempestuous uproars," even though the gallery actually conducts sound without amplification.

In 1801 De Quincey's mother and guardians sent him to Manchester Grammar School, where he would have a chance to win one of several scholarships of forty guineas to Brasenose College at Oxford University. The master, Charles Lawson, was old and left the students mostly to their own devices. There De Quincey read the *Lyrical Ballads* (1798) of William Wordsworth and Samuel Taylor Coleridge and the poetry of Thomas Chatterton and made the acquaintance of the Reverend John Clowes, an elderly Swedenborgian who introduced him to the tradition of Christian mysticism. Soon realizing, however, that he could not bear the monotonous routine of this dingy school for three years, De Quincey asked his guardians and his mother for permission to leave. When it was refused, he ran away.

De Quincey spent some time rambling in Wales, often sleeping in the open and eating little in order to economize. Determined to be independent of his guardians, he went to London to borrow money against his expectations; his London adventures would provide material for some of the most interesting chapters of *Confessions of an English Opium Eater*. The moneylenders proving intractable, De Quincey suffered great poverty; unable to afford food and lodging, he was reduced to sleeping on a bare floor in the house of an attorney he had consulted. He shared his sleeping space with "a poor friendless child" who served as a maid to the lawyer and on whom, it is said, Charles Dickens later based the character of the Marchioness in *The Old Curiosity Shop* (1841).

Perhaps the most important element in De Quincey's London adventures was his meeting Ann, a young prostitute who became one of the focal points of his autobiographical writings. He writes that his "poor orphan companion, who had herself met with little but injuries in this world," saved his life by spending her last money on him when he collapsed in the street of hunger and exhaustion. Soon after, he went to Eton to procure a guarantee of credit from a young peer, on which he hoped to borrow enough money to support himself and Ann. When he returned to London, however,

he was unable to find her, and he never heard of her again. In De Quincey's personal mythology the image of the noble, protective, maternal child-woman seems to have played a central role. Later his wife and daughters were to play such a role for this diminutive man, who himself looked childlike to the end of his life.

After reconciling with his guardians De Quincey went to Worcester College, Oxford, in December of 1803, with an allowance of one hundred pounds a year. At Oxford he concentrated on extending his knowledge of German and English literature. It was during his time at Oxford that he started taking opium, which he purchased in the form of laudanum for a toothache on a visit to London in 1804.

De Quincey's connection with the Romantic authors also started at this time. In 1805, on another visit to London, he made the acquaintance of Charles and Mary Lamb. He had been corresponding with Wordsworth since 1803, and in 1807 he sought out Coleridge at Bridgewater; De Quincey escorted Coleridge's wife, Sara, and their children to Grasmere, where he met Wordsworth and his sister, Dorothy. Later that year he anonymously gave five hundred pounds, about a quarter of the patrimony at his disposal, to Coleridge, whose poverty, as well as his opium addiction, were hindering his ability to complete his work. This spontaneous generosity was typical of De Quincey's impulsive kindness and unbusinesslike nature.

De Quincey never took his degree; in his final examinations in 1808 he performed brilliantly in Latin but left before taking the Greek exam the next day, even though his excellence in the subject was acknowledged at the university. After leaving Oxford, De Quincey superintended the printing of Wordsworth's pamphlet *The Convention of Cintra* (1809) in London before moving to Dove Cottage, Grasmere, with so many books that Coleridge, who was living with the Wordsworths, would sometimes borrow five hundred volumes at once. In the next few years De Quincey read Wordsworth's *The Prelude* (1850) in manuscript and formed close ties with the Wordsworth children, especially Catherine, whose death in 1812 deeply affected him in its reminder of the losses of his sister Elizabeth and his London friend Ann. He also visited Edinburgh with his friend John Wilson and through him met John Gibson Lockhart, the son-in-law and future biographer of Sir Walter Scott; William Hamilton; the editor and publisher James Hogg; and other members of the Scottish literary scene. He made an immediate impact even though he had not yet had a single line published.

De Quincey's parents, Thomas and Elizabeth Penson Quincey (left: The Bodley Head; right: Collection of Rosemary Blok van Cronesteyn)

On 15 February 1817 De Quincey married Margaret Simpson, of a farming family near Grasmere, with whom he had had a son, William, the previous November. Margaret proved a loyal, loving, capable, and long-suffering wife, putting up with poverty and neglect without complaint. Gradually his relationship with the Wordsworths cooled, mainly due to their disapproval of his marriage and his opium addiction.

The consumption of opium had become habitual with De Quincey in 1813, when he started taking 340 grains daily to cure stomach problems that probably resulted from his earlier starvation in Wales and London. After his marriage he would often try to cure himself of the habit by reducing his dose to 40 grains a day. He was unable to keep his resolve, however, and as a consequence suffered profound depression. When obliged to contribute regularly to journals, he would be able to reduce his opium intake temporarily but was never able to give it up completely. De Quincey's opium use led to overwhelming dreams during which he would sometimes feel as if he had lived through a century in a single night.

De Quincey had already been contributing to *Blackwood's Edinburgh Magazine* and to the *Quarterly Review* when, in the summer of 1819, he became editor of the *Westmorland Gazette*. In October and November 1821 *Confessions of an English Opium Eater* appeared in the *London Magazine*. It was successful enough to be reprinted as a book in 1822, with a second edition the following year. By the end of 1824 he had contributed other articles to the *London Magazine,* among them "Letters to a Young Man Whose Education has been Neglected" (January–May 1823) and "The Dialogue of the Three Templars on Political Economy" (April–May 1824). In 1825 his translation of *Walladmor* — a bad German romance that had been passed off in Germany as the translation of a new Scott novel — was published. De Quincey was becoming quite well known as a writer both in England and on the Continent. He was introduced into the "Noctes Ambrosianae" series in *Blackwood's Edinburgh Magazine* by his friend Wilson, and he contributed a translation of Gotthold Ephraim Lessing's *Laokoon* (1766) to *Blackwood's* in November 1826 as well as the first part of "On Murder Considered as One of the Fine Arts"

Page from the manuscript for De Quincey's "William Wordsworth and Robert Southey," part of his "Lake Reminiscences" series for Tait's Edinburgh Magazine *(MA 903; Pierpont Morgan Library). This installment appeared in the July 1839 issue.*

in February 1827. He moved to Edinburgh in 1828. Between 1828 and 1830 he contributed to the *Edinburgh Literary Gazette*. In 1832 his novel *Klosterheim* came out; although never popular, it is distinguished by powerful descriptive passages prescient of Edgar Allan Poe's stories. It was successfully dramatized in London.

De Quincey's career as a biographer began with a collective biography of the more lurid of the Roman emperors. These witty and urbane essays, "The Caesars," were serialized in *Blackwood's Edinburgh Magazine* from 1832 to 1834. Then, deciding that his recollections and impressions of the literary figures he had known might be interesting to readers, he wrote a series of twenty-three biographical essays that were published irregularly in *Tait's Edinburgh Magazine* from 1834 through 1841. In addition to essays on Coleridge, William and Dorothy Wordsworth, Charles and Mary Lamb, and Robert Southey, De Quincey wrote the essays "The Society of the Lakes" and "Rambles from the Lakes" about less well known figures, including Hannah More; Sarah Siddons; Charles Lloyd, a minor poet; Elizabeth Smith, a friend of More's as well as a translator and compounder of a Hebrew-Arabic-Persian dictionary; the Sympsons, a family of literary clergymen; and Wilson, a figure of small talent who enjoyed positions of power beyond his literary capabilities. After being appointed professor of moral philosophy at the University of Edinburgh, Wilson wrote urgent letters asking De Quincey to define moral philosophy and to write discreetly the lectures Wilson was to deliver; De Quincey complied.

Coleridge died on 25 July 1834; De Quincey's four-part essay "Samuel Taylor Coleridge" appeared in *Tait's* between September 1834 and January 1835. This essay revealed that Coleridge's marriage had not been happy and that he had been "forced [to marry] upon his sense of honour" by the more morally scrupulous Southey. De Quincey also mentioned Sara Coleridge's jealousy of Dorothy Wordsworth, whom she considered her intellectual superior, as well as Coleridge's opium addiction. Most important, he revealed Coleridge's plagiarisms from such writers as Friedrich Schelling and Frederica Braun, while at the same time praising Coleridge's inventiveness in spinning "daily . . . theories more gorgeous [than] Schelling – no, nor any German that ever breathed . . . could have emulated in his dreams." Although angered like the rest of Coleridge's family and friends at the breach of trust, Coleridge's daughter, Sara, wrote that De Quincey "has characterized my father's genius and peculiar mode of discourse with great eloquence

and discrimination. . . . I cannot believe that he has any enmity to my father, indeed he often speaks of his kindness of heart." Similarly, Thomas Carlyle thought that the articles had been written "with no wish to be untrue . . . or hurt anybody, though not without his own bits of splenetic conviction."

De Quincey's relationship with the Wordsworths, on the other hand, ended up tinged with feelings of "hostility – nay, something, I fear, too nearly akin to vindictive hatred" at their denial of moral support at the time of the birth of his first child and of his marriage shortly thereafter to a wife the Wordsworths deemed socially unacceptable. (De Quincey had been told nothing of Caroline, the illegitimate daughter of Wordsworth and Annette Vallon who had been born in 1792 and was living in France.) The Wordsworths' rejection seemed especially bitter to De Quincey, who felt that he had offered Wordsworth the strength and comfort of a warm friendship and, more important, of a rare literary understanding at a time of artistic isolation when Wordsworth was writing *The Prelude* between 1798 and 1805. De Quincey's essays "Lake Reminiscences: William Wordsworth" appeared in *Tait's* between September 1834 and January 1835. "William Wordsworth and Robert Southey" appeared in July 1839 and "Southey, Wordsworth and Coleridge" in August 1839. The Wordsworths found offensive the references to William Wordsworth's appearance: "not a well-made man . . . a crooked walk . . . manners . . . not always perfect . . . slovenly"; to his scholarship: "did not read much"; and to Dorothy Wordsworth's nervous stammer. De Quincey also compared William Wordsworth's supposed incapacity for passionate love to his own devotion to his wife. The most accurate text of the "Literary Reminiscences," in the Ticknor, Reed and Fields edition of *De Quincey's Writings* (1851–1859), was superseded by the 1854 abridgment De Quincey made in *Selections Grave and Gay* to mollify his subjects' families and by David Masson's 1889–1890 edition of *The Collected Writings of Thomas De Quincey*, which randomly recombines the essays.

In addition to the "Literary Reminiscences" that appeared in *Tait's*, De Quincey provided contributions on Johann Wolfgang von Goethe, John Milton, Schiller, and William Shakespeare to the *Encyclopædia Britannica*. "The Shakespeare article cost me more intense labour than any I ever wrote in my life," De Quincey said in a 16 July 1838 letter to the editor of the *Britannica*, Macvey Napier.

In 1833 De Quincey's youngest son, Julius, died at the age of four; in 1835, his promising eldest son, William, died of a brain disease at eighteen; in

Last page of the manuscript for an essay on Charles Lamb, written by De Quincey for the November 1848 issue of the North Britain Review
(Historical Manuscript Collection, Boston University)

1837 his wife died of typhus. "His mind was unhinged by these sorrows," wrote his daughter Florence later. Nevertheless, with his eldest daughter, Margaret, taking over the responsibility of looking after her brothers and sisters, De Quincey continued writing. In January 1838 one of his most effective pieces of fiction, "The Household Wreck," appeared in *Blackwood's*. A Kafkaesque story about a narrator who loses his wife to a nightmarish, impersonal bureaucracy, it seems to be connected with De Quincey's guilty feelings about having left his wife alone so much while pursuing his literary activities in London and Edinburgh. In August another story, "The Avenger," appeared in *Blackwood's*. A book, *The Logic of Political Economy,* was published in 1844. In spite of his activity, this period was one of great poverty and debt; feeling persecuted and dejected, De Quincey lapsed into an excessive use of opium. Only in 1844 was he able to reduce his daily intake to six grains, an amount he did not exceed for the rest of his life.

Between 1851 and 1859 De Quincey's collected works were published in twenty-two volumes by Ticknor, Reed and Fields in Boston; although there was no copyright agreement between Britain and the United States, the editor and publisher, James T. Fields, gave the author a share of the profits. In his old age De Quincey was finally beginning to enjoy some financial security. Meanwhile, he was helping Hogg produce a fourteen-volume edition of his works, which came out between 1853 and 1860 as *Selections Grave and Gay.* Of the two, the Boston edition is considered the more complete and reliable.

In his literary efforts De Quincey was plagued not only by his opium use but also by procrastination and lack of organization. He would accumulate books and papers until he was forced to move out of his rooms and take other lodgings; at the time of his death six such "storehouses" existed. Conscientious landladies would care for his papers, while others would hold them hostage until his debts were settled. The "charm of his conversation" and his "gentle courtesy," however, attracted many friends throughout his life. He was always "pathetically and conscientiously anxious" to make up for the trouble caused by his shortcomings. He died on 8 December 1859 in Edinburgh.

De Quincey shared Wordsworth's and Coleridge's revolt against the philosophical and literary principles of the eighteenth century. Stylistically, he considered himself the literary descendant of the great prose writers of the seventeenth century, such as Jeremy Taylor and Sir Thomas Browne, and

tried to restore their traditions. He became a master of what he called in the preface to *Selections Grave and Gay* "the department of impassioned prose." As a biographer his model was Samuel Johnson's *Prefaces, Biographical and Critical, to the Works of the English Poets* (1779–1781), with its fragmentary, impressionistic prose, rather than the all-encompassing approach of James Boswell's *The Life of Samuel Johnson, LL.D.* (1791). His "Literary Reminiscences" have been called "autobiographic biography," a form that eludes generic classification in its "fragmented, digressive, ahistorical" style. This difficulty of categorizing his work, which is a mixture of scholarship, journalism, translation, meditation, and reminiscence, contributed to its obscurity; De Quincey himself complained that "The advantage lies in doing anything which has a name, an assignable name."

Letters:

H. A. Page (Alexander H. Japp), *Thomas De Quincey: His Life and Writings. With Unpublished Correspondence* (2 volumes, London: Hogg, 1877; New York: Scribner, Armstrong, 1877; revised and enlarged edition, 1 volume, London: Hogg, 1890);

De Quincey Memorials: Being Letters and Other Records, 2 volumes, edited by Japp (London: Heinemann, 1891; New York: United States Book Company, 1891);

De Quincey at Work: As Seen in One Hundred and Thirty New and Newly Edited Letters, edited by W. H. Bonner (Buffalo, N.Y.: Airport Publications, 1936);

Unpublished Letters of Thomas De Quincey and Elizabeth Barrett Browning, edited by Sydney Musgrove (Auckland, New Zealand: Auckland University College, 1954);

John E. Jordan, *De Quincey to Wordsworth: A Biography of a Relationship, With the Letters of Thomas De Quincey to the Wordsworth Family* (Berkeley & Los Angeles: University of California Press, 1962).

Bibliographies:

David Masson, "Appendix Chronological and Bibliographical," in volume 14 of *The Collected Writings of Thomas De Quincey* (Edinburgh: Black, 1890);

J. A. Green, *Thomas De Quincey: A Bibliography Based upon the De Quincey Collection in the Moss Side Library* (Manchester: Free Reference Library/Moss Side Library, 1908);

W. E. A. Axon, "The Canon of De Quincey's Writings, with References to Some of His Unidentified Articles," in *Transactions of the Royal Society of Literature,* second series 32 (1914): 1–46;

John E. Jordan, "Thomas De Quincey," in *The English Romantic Poets & Essayists: A Review of Criticism and Research,* revised edition, edited by Carolyn Washburn Houtchens and Lawrence Huston Houtchens (New York: Published for the Modern Language Association of America by New York University Press, 1966), pp. 289–331;

Harold O. Dendurant, *Thomas De Quincey: A Reference Guide* (Boston: G. K. Hall, 1978).

Biographies:

H. A. Page (Alexander H. Japp), *Thomas De Quincey: His Life and Writings. With Unpublished Correspondence* (2 volumes, London, Hogg, 1877; New York: Scribner, Armstrong, 1877; revised and enlarged edition, 1 volume, London: Hogg, 1890);

David Masson, *De Quincey* (London: Macmillan, 1880; New York: Harper, 1901);

J. R. Findlay, *Personal Recollections of Thomas De Quincey* (Edinburgh: Black, 1886);

James Hogg, ed., *De Quincey and His Friends: Personal Recollections, Souvenirs and Anecdotes* (London: Sampson Low, Marston, 1895);

Malcolm Elwin, *De Quincey* (London: Duckworth, 1935);

Horace A. Eaton, *Thomas De Quincey: A Biography* (London & New York: Oxford University Press, 1936);

Edward Sackville-West, *A Flame in Sunlight: The Life and Work of Thomas De Quincey* (London & Toronto: Cassell, 1936); also published as *Thomas De Quincey: His Life and Work* (New Haven: Yale University Press, 1936);

John Calvin Metcalf, *De Quincey: A Portrait* (Cambridge, Mass.: Harvard University Press, 1940);

John E. Jordan, *De Quincey to Wordsworth: A Biography of a Relationship, with the Letters of Thomas De Quincey to the Wordsworth Family* (Berkeley & Los Angeles: University of California Press, 1962);

Grevel Lindop, *The Opium-Eater: A Life of Thomas De Quincey* (London: Dent, 1981; New York: Taplinger, 1981).

References:

M. H. Abrams, *The Milk of Paradise: The Effect of Opium Visions on the Works of De Quincey, Crabbe,* *Francis Thompson and Coleridge* (Cambridge, Mass.: Harvard University Press, 1934);

John Barrell, *The Infection of Thomas De Quincey: A Psychopathology of Imperialism* (New Haven: Yale University Press, 1991);

Edmund Baxter, *De Quincey's Art of Autobiography* (Edinburgh: Edinburgh University Press, 1990);

Elizabeth Bruss, *Autobiographical Acts: The Changing Situation of a Literary Genre* (Baltimore: Johns Hopkins University Press, 1977);

A. W. Cafarelli, *Prose in the Age of Poets: Romanticism and Biographical Narrative from Johnson to De Quincey* (Philadelphia: University of Pennsylvania Press, 1990);

Hugh Sykes Davies, *Thomas De Quincey* (London: Longmans, Green, 1964);

Vincent A. De Luca, *Thomas De Quincey: The Prose of Vision* (Toronto: University of Toronto Press, 1980);

David D. Devlin, *De Quincey, Wordsworth, and the Art of Prose* (New York: St. Martin's Press, 1983; London: Macmillan, 1983);

Albert Goldman, *The Mine and the Mint: Sources for the Writings of Thomas De Quincey* (Carbondale & Edwardsville: Southern Illinois University Press, 1965);

Michael Haltresht, "The Meaning of De Quincey's 'Dream Fugue on . . . Sudden Death,' " *Literature and Psychology,* 26, no. 1 (1976): 31–36;

Ian Jack, "De Quincey Revises His *Confessions,*" *PMLA,* 72 (March 1957): 122–146;

Mary Jacobus, "The Art of Managing Books: Romantic Prose and the Writing of the Past," in *Romanticism and Language,* edited by Arden Reed (Ithaca, N.Y.: Cornell University Press, 1984), pp. 215–246;

F. Samuel Janzow, "De Quincey Enters Journalism: His Contributions to the *Westmorland Gazette,* 1818–1819," Ph.D. dissertation, University of Chicago, 1968;

John E. Jordan, *Thomas De Quincey, Literary Critic: His Method and Achievement* (Berkeley: University of California Press, 1952);

Karen M. Lever, "De Quincey as Gothic Hero: A Perspective on *Confessions of an English Opium Eater* and *Suspiria de Profundis,*" *Texas Studies in Literature and Language,* 21 (Fall 1979): 332–346;

Judson S. Lyon, *Thomas De Quincey* (New York: Twayne, 1969);

Robert M. Maniquis, " 'Lonely Empires': Personal and Public Visions of Thomas De Quincey," in *Mid-Nineteenth Century Writers: Eliot, De*

Quincey, Emerson, volume 8 of *Literary Monographs,* edited by Eric Rothstein and Joseph Anthony Wittreich, Jr. (Madison: University of Wisconsin Press, 1976), pp. 49–127;

Thomas McFarland, *Romantic Cruxes: The English Essayists and the Spirit of the Age* (Oxford: Clarendon Press, 1987);

J. Hillis Miller, *The Disappearance of God: Five Nineteenth Century Writers* (Cambridge, Mass.: Harvard University Press, 1975);

Sigmund K. Proctor, *Thomas De Quincey's Theory of Literature* (Ann Arbor: University of Michigan Press, 1943);

Robert L. Snyder, ed., *Thomas De Quincey: Bicentenary Studies* (Norman: University of Oklahoma Press, 1985);

René Wellek, "De Quincey's Status in the History of Ideas," *Philological Quarterly,* 23 (July 1944): 248–272;

John C. Whale, *Thomas De Quincey's Reluctant Autobiography* (London: Croom Helm, 1984; Totowa, N.J.: Barnes & Noble, 1984);

Virginia Woolf, "De Quincey's Autobiography," in her *The Common Reader, Second Series* (London: Hogarth Press, 1932).

Papers:

Thomas De Quincey's papers are at Dove Cottage, Grasmere, and in the Berg Collection of the New York Public Library; the Gluck Collection of the Buffalo and Erie County Library; the Henry E. Huntington Memorial Library and Art Gallery, San Marino, California; the National Library of Scotland; the British Library; the Liverpool County Libraries Record Office; the Boston Public Library; Brown University Library; the University of Chicago; the University of Edinburgh; the Folger Shakespeare Library, Washington, D.C.; the Grey Collection, Auckland Public Library, New Zealand; the Houghton Library, Harvard University; the Historian's Papers, 1779–1942, Duke University Library; King's School, Canterbury; Magill University; the Montague Collection, New York Public Library Manuscript Division; the Pierpont Morgan Library; the Robert J. Taylor Collection, Princeton University; Worcester College, Oxford; the Wordsworth Collection, Cornell University; Yale University; the Bodleian Library, Oxford University; Boston University; Georgetown University; the Samuel Carter Hall and Anna Maria (Fielding) Hall Collection, Knox College Archives; the Tracy William McGregor Collection, University of Virginia; the University of California at Berkeley; the Manchester Central Library; the Carl H. Pforzheimer Library; and the Thomas Cooper Library, University of South Carolina. A description of the works in many of these collections is included in the article on De Quincey in *Index of English Literary Manuscripts, Volume IV, 1800–1900, Part I: Arnold to Gissing,* compiled by Barbara Rosenbaum and Pamela White (London & New York: Mansell, 1982), pp. 681–693.

Austin Dobson

(18 January 1840 – 2 September 1921)

Brian McCrea
University of Florida

See also the Dobson entry in *DLB 35: Victorian Poets After 1850.*

BOOKS: *"The Drama of the Doctor's Window": A Brief Statement Concerning That Poem since Its Appearance in "Saint Paul's Magazine," for February, 1870; with Appendices Respecting Its Earlier "History"* (London: Privately printed, 1872);

Vignettes in Rhyme and Vers de Société (London: King, 1873); revised as *Vignettes in Rhyme, and Other Verses* (New York: Holt, 1880); revised as *Old-World Idylls, and Other Verses* (London: Kegan Paul, Trench, 1883); republished as *Poems on Several Occasions,* volume 1 (London: Kegan Paul, Trench, 1889; revised and enlarged edition, London: Kegan Paul, Trench, Trübner, 1895; New York: Dodd, Mead, 1895);

The Civil Service Handbook of English Literature (London: Lockwood, 1874); revised and enlarged as *A Handbook of English Literature for the Use of Candidates for Examinations, Public Schools, and Students Generally* (London: Lockwood, 1880 [i.e., 1879]);

Proverbs in Porcelain, and Other Verses (London: King, 1877);

Hogarth (London: Low, Marston, Searle & Rivington, 1879; New York: Scribner & Welford, 1879); enlarged as *William Hogarth* (London: Low, Marston, 1891; New York: Dodd, Mead, 1891; enlarged again, London: Kegan Paul, Trench, Trübner, 1898; Philadelphia: Lippincott, 1900; revised edition, London: Heinemann / New York: McClure, Phillips, 1902; enlarged edition, London: Heinemann, 1907);

Fielding (London: Macmillan, 1883; New York: Harper, 1883);

Thomas Bewick and His Pupils (London: Chatto & Windus, 1884; Boston: Osgood, 1884);

At the Sign of the Lyre (London: Kegan Paul, Trench, 1885; New York: Holt, 1885; revised and enlarged, 1889); republished as *Poems on Several Occasions,* volume 2 (London: Kegan Paul, Trench, 1889; revised and enlarged edition, London:

Kegan Paul, Trench, Trübner, 1895; New York: Dodd, Mead, 1895);

Richard Steele (London: Longmans, Green, 1886; New York: Appleton, 1886);

Life of Oliver Goldsmith (London: Scott, 1888; Port Washington, N.Y.: Kennikat Press, 1972);

The Sun Dial: A Poem (New York: Dodd, Mead, 1890);

Four Frenchwomen (London: Chatto & Windus, 1890; New York: Dodd, Mead, 1890);

Horace Walpole: A Memoir with an Appendix of Books Printed at the Strawberry Hill Press (London: Osgood, McIlvaine, 1890; New York: Dodd, Mead, 1890);

Eighteenth Century Vignettes, 3 volumes (London: Chatto & Windus, 1892–1896; New York: Dodd, Mead, 1892–1896; volume 1 revised and enlarged, London: Chatto & Windus, 1897);

The Ballade of Beau Brocade and Other Poems of the XVIIITH Century (London: Kegan Paul, Trench, Trübner, 1892);

The Story of Rosina, and Other Verses (London: Kegan Paul, Trench, Trübner, 1895; New York: Dodd, Mead, 1895);

A Postscript to Dr. Goldsmith's Retaliation, Being an Epitaph on Samuel Johnson, LL.D. (Oxford: Privately printed, 1896);

Verses Read at the Dinner of the Omar Khayyám Club, on Thursday, 25th March, 1897 (London: Printed at the Chiswick Press, 1897);

Collected Poems (London: Kegan Paul, Trench, Trübner, 1897; enlarged, 1902; enlarged again, 1909; enlarged again, 1913);

Miscellanies, 2 volumes (New York: Dodd, Mead, 1898, 1901);

A Departmental Ditty, to T. W. H. P. (London: Chiswick Press, 1899);

Oliver Goldsmith: A Memoir (New York: Dodd, Mead, 1899);

A Paladin of Philanthropy, and Other Papers (London: Chatto & Windus, 1899; London & New York: Humphrey Milford, Oxford University Press, 1925);

Henry Fielding: A Memoir (New York: Dodd, Mead, 1900);

Carmina Votiva and Other Occasional Verses (London: Privately printed, 1901);

Samuel Richardson (London & New York: Macmillan, 1902);

Side-Walk Studies (London: Chatto & Windus, 1902; London & New York: Humphrey Milford, Oxford University Press, 1924);

Fanny Burney (Madame d'Arblay) (London & New York: Macmillan, 1903);

To William John Courthope on His Dining with the Johnson Club: A Welcome by Austin Dobson (London: Privately printed, 1903);

De Libris: Prose and Verse (London: Macmillan, 1908; New York: Macmillan, 1908; enlarged edition, London: Macmillan, 1911);

Old Kensington Palace, and Other Papers (London: Chatto & Windus, 1910; New York: Stokes, 1910);

At Prior Park and Other Papers (London: Chatto & Windus, 1912; New York: Stokes, 1912);

Eighteenth Century Studies (London: Dent, 1914);

Rosalba's Journal, and Other Papers (London: Chatto & Windus, 1915);

Poems on the War, edited by Clement Shorter (London: Privately printed, 1915);

A Bookman's Budget (London & New York: Oxford University Press, 1917);

Later Essays, 1917–1920 (London & New York: Humphrey Milford, Oxford University Press, 1921);

Three Unpublished Poems (Winchester: Mr. Blakeney's Private Press, 1930).

Collections: *An Anthology of Prose and Verse,* edited by Alban Dobson (London & Toronto: Dent / New York: Dutton, 1922);
The Complete Poetical Works of Austin Dobson (London & New York: Oxford University Press, 1923).

OTHER: Manuel (Ernest Louis Victor Jules L'Epine), *The Authentic History of Captain Castagnette, Nephew of the "Man with the Wooden Head,"* translated by Dobson (London: Beeton, 1866);

Frederick A. White, *The Civil Service History of England: Being a Fact-Book of English History,* revised by Dobson (London, 1870; revised, 1871; revised, 1882; revised, 1884; revised, 1887; revised, 1890; revised, 1896);

Andrew Lang, *The Library,* chapter on modern English illustrated books by Dobson (London: Macmillan, 1881);

Fables of Mr. John Gay, memoir by Dobson (London: Kegan Paul, 1882; New York: Appleton, 1883);

Selections from the Poetry of Robert Herrick, edited by Dobson (New York: Harper, 1882; London: Low, 1883);

Daniel Defoe, *The Life and Strange Surprising Adventures of Robinson Crusoe: Being a Facsimile Reprint of the First Edition Published in 1719,* introduction by Dobson (London: Stock, 1883 [i.e., 1882]);

Eighteenth Century Essays, edited by Dobson (London: Kegan Paul, 1882; New York: Appleton, 1882);

Oliver Goldsmith, *The Vicar of Wakefield,* edited by Dobson (London: Kegan Paul, 1883);

Pierre Augustin Caron de Beaumarchais, *Beaumarchais' Le Barbier de Séville,* edited by Dobson (Oxford: Clarendon Press, 1884);

Lang, *Ballades and Verses Vain,* selected by Dobson (New York: Scribners, 1884);

Goldsmith, *The Vicar of Wakefield: Being a Facsimile Reproduction of the First Edition Published in 1766,* introduction by Dobson (London: Stock, 1885);

Richard Steele, *Selections from the Tatler, Spectator, and Guardian,* edited by Dobson (Oxford: Clarendon Press, 1885);

A Memoir of Thomas Bewick, Written by Himself, edited by Dobson (London: Quaritch, 1887);

Goldsmith, *She Stoops to Conquer, a Comedy,* introduction by Dobson (New York: Harper, 1887);

Goldsmith, *Selected Poems,* edited by Dobson (Oxford: Clarendon Press, 1887);

The Poems and Plays of Oliver Goldsmith, 2 volumes, edited by Dobson (London: Dent, 1889);

Selected Poems of Matthew Prior, introduction by Dobson (London: Kegan Paul, 1889);

"The Quiet Life": Certain Verses by Various Hands, prologue and epilogue by Dobson (New York: Harper, 1890);

The Citizen of the World, 2 volumes, edited by Dobson (London: Low, 1890);

Henry Fielding, *The Journal of a Voyage to Lisbon,* edited by Dobson (London: Chiswick Press, 1892);

Hans Holbein, *The Dance of Death,* introductory note by Dobson (London & New York: Bell, 1892);

The Poems of Oliver Goldsmith, edited by Dobson (London: Dent, 1893);

Coridon's Song and Other Verses from Various Sources, introduction by Dobson (London: Macmillan, 1894);

The Little Passion of Albert Dürer, introduction by Dobson (London: Bell, 1894);

Old English Songs from Various Sources, edited by Dobson (London & New York: Macmillan, 1894);

The Poetical Works of Oliver Goldsmith, revised and edited by Dobson (London: Bell, 1895);

Jean Marteilhe, *The Memoirs of a Protestant Condemned to the Galleys of France for His Religion: Written by Himself,* 2 volumes, translated by Goldsmith, introduction by Dobson (London: Dent, 1895);

Thomas Hood, *The Haunted House,* introduction by Dobson (London: Lawrence & Bullen, 1896);

Jane Austen, *Emma,* introduction by Dobson (London & New York: Macmillan, 1896);

Austen, *Mansfield Park,* introduction by Dobson (London: Macmillan, 1897);

Austen, *Northanger Abbey and Persuasion,* introduction by Dobson (London: Macmillan, 1897);

Austen, *Pride and Prejudice,* introduction by Dobson (London & New York: Macmillan, 1897);

Austen, *Sense and Sensibility,* introduction by Dobson (London & New York: Macmillan, 1897);

The Spectator, 8 volumes, edited by G. Gregory Smith, introductory essay by Dobson (London: Dent, 1897–1898);

Izaak Walton, *Lives of John Donne, Henry Wotton, Richard Hooker, George Herbert, and Robert Sanderson,* 2 volumes, edited by Dobson (London: Dent, 1898);

Bibliographical Notes on a Collection of Editions of the Book Known as "Puckle's Club," introduction by Dobson (Cleveland, Ohio: Rowfant Club, 1899);

Charles Reade, *Peg Woffington,* introduction by Dobson (London: George Allen, 1899);

Walton, *The Compleat Angler,* edited by Dobson (London: Dent, 1899);

William Hazlitt, *Lectures on the Comic Writers,* edited by Dobson (London: Dent, 1900);

The Works of William Hogarth, Including the Analysis of Beauty and Five Days' Peregrination, edited by Dobson (Philadelphia: Barrie, 1900);

James Puckle, *The Club; or, A Grey Cap for a Green Head: Containing Maxims, Advice & Cautions, Being a Dialogue between a Father & Son,* introduction by Dobson (London: Printed at the Chiswick Press & are to be sold in London by Freemantle & Co., and in New York by Trueslove, Hanson & Combs, 1900);

James Boswell, *The Life of Samuel Johnson, LL.D.,* 3 volumes, edited by Arnold Glover, introduction by Dobson (London: Dent, 1901; New York: Dutton, 1925);

William Cosmo Monkhouse, *Pasiteles the Elder, and Other Poems,* prefatory note by Dobson (London: R. Brimley Johnson, 1901);

Goldsmith, *The Deserted Village,* edited by Dobson (London & New York: Harper, 1902);

Leigh Hunt, Herbert Railton, Claude Shepperson, and Edmund J. Sullivan, *The Old Court Suburb; or, Memorials of Kensington, Regal, Critical, and Anecdotal,* edited by Dobson (London: Freemantle, 1902);

Frances Burney d'Arblay, *Evelina; or, A Young Lady's Entrance into the World,* introduction by Dobson (London: Macmillan, 1903);

Goldsmith, *The Bee, and Other Essays,* edited by Dobson (London: Dent, 1903);

Goldsmith, *The Good Natur'd Man and She Stoops to Conquer,* edited by Dobson and George P. Baker (Boston & London: Heath, 1903);

Tales from Maria Edgeworth, introduction by Dobson (London: Wells Gardner, 1903; New York: Stokes, 1908);

Alfred Barbeau, *Life & Letters at Bath in the xviijth Century,* preface by Dobson (London: Heinemann / New York: Dodd, Mead, 1904);

The Diary of John Evelyn, introduction by Dobson (London: Cassell, 1904);

Frederick Locker-Lampson, *London Lyrics,* edited by Dobson (London: Macmillan, 1904);

D'Arblay, *Diary and Letters of Madame d'Arblay (1778–1840) as Edited by Her Niece Charlotte Barrett,* 6 volumes, preface and notes by Dobson (London & New York: Macmillan, 1904–1905);

William Makepeace Thackeray, *The History of Henry Esmond,* introduction by Dobson (London: Macmillan, 1905);

Selected Essays of Joseph Addison, introduction by Dobson (London: Heinemann, 1906);

The Diary of John Evelyn, 3 volumes, edited by Dobson (London & New York: Macmillan, 1906);

The Complete Poetical Works of Oliver Goldsmith, Oxford Edition, edited by Dobson (London: Frowde, 1906; New York: Frowde, 1911);

Sir Walter Scott, *Lives of the Novelists,* introduction by Dobson (London, New York & Toronto: H. Frowde, Oxford University Press, 1906);

John Brown, *Horae Subsecivae,* introduction by Dobson (London & New York: H. Frowde, Oxford University Press, 1907);

Lewis Carroll, *Alice's Adventures in Wonderland,* proem by Dobson (London: Heinemann / New York: Doubleday, Page, 1907);

Hunt, *The Town: Its Memorable Characters and Events,* edited by Dobson (London: Grant Richards, Oxford University Press, 1907);

The Discourses of Sir Joshua Reynolds, to Which Are Added His Letters to "The Idler," introduction by Dobson (London: Grant Richards, Oxford University Press, 1907; London & New York: H. Frowde, Oxford University Press, 1933);

William Shakespeare, *The Merry Wives of Windsor,* edited by Sidney Lee, introduction by Dobson, volume 8 of *The Complete Works of William Shakespeare,* Renaissance Edition (London: Murray, 1907);

Rose of My Life, prefatory poem by Dobson (London: Jenkins, 1916);

Goldsmith, *The Citizen of the World and The Bee,* edited by Dobson (London & Toronto: Dent / New York: Dutton, 1934).

Recognized in the nineteenth century as, in Francis Edwin Murray's words, "the lineal descendant of [Joseph] Addison, [Oliver] Goldsmith, and [Thomas] Gray," Austin Dobson adumbrates the present-day university professor who specializes in a literary period – in Dobson's case, the eighteenth century. Dobson, however, was not a professor but a clerk at the Board of Trade, and he first achieved notice as a writer – although he later chafed against the designation – of vers de société. Edmund Gosse claimed that Dobson achieved the widest "circulation" and the greatest "popularity" of any "English verse-writer of his immediate generation." But Dobson probably had his greatest impact on British society with *The Civil Service Handbook of English Literature* (1874) and in his contributions to *The Civil Ser-*

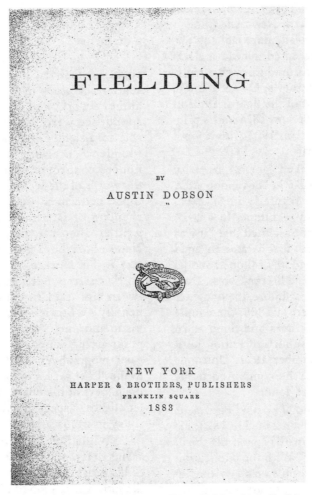

FIELDING

BY

AUSTIN DOBSON

NEW YORK
HARPER & BROTHERS, PUBLISHERS
FRANKLIN SQUARE
1883

*Title page for Dobson's biography of Henry Fielding for the English
Men of Letters series*

vice *History of England* (1870). These books, designed
to prepare young men for examinations for civil-
service positions, reflect nineteenth-century assumptions about the broad relevance of literary
study; they also reflect the tendency in Dobson's
day to link the study of literature with the study of
history. Murray praises the literature handbook as
"compendious, complete, accurate, and convenient" – adjectives that can be applied also to
Dobson's studies of Goldsmith, John Gay, Richard
Steele, Henry Fielding, Samuel Richardson, Alexander Pope, Horace Walpole, Fanny Burney, William
Hogarth, and Jane Austen. Dobson's work, then,
provides a fine example of literary biography as
written by a Victorian man of letters, although
in his personal life, particularly his widely noted
"abstemiousness," Dobson departed from the man
of letters type. As Stewart M. Ellis noted in his eulogy on Dobson: "He was not gregarious or fond of
club life. . . . He rarely dined out, even before his

health failed." Dobson's attendance at a 1904 dinner celebrating the restoration of Hogarth's house
at Chiswick was notable precisely because it was so
rare. While anthologists such as Jerome Hamilton
Buckley typically note of Dobson that "Until 1884
his work was largely in verse, thereafter in prose,"
the connections between Dobson's verse and his
prose – particularly his tendency to seek in both an
alternative to the "conditions of modern life" –
have not been widely noted.

Henry Austin Dobson was born in Plymouth on
18 January 1840, the eldest son of George Clarisse
Dobson and Augusta Harris Dobson. When Austin
was still quite young, the family moved to Holyhead,
where his father, a civil engineer, worked on the great
breakwater. Dobson's first schooling was at
Beaumaris Grammar School; later he attended a
school in Coventry kept by J. W. Knight. He finished
his formal education at the Gymnase Strasburg, where
he was the only English student. At age sixteen he re-

turned to England, declined an offer of employment by the Armstrong Ship Works at Newcastle (though he was a good mechanical draftsman, Dobson disliked mathematics), and accepted instead a clerkship at the Board of Trade secured through a Holyhead acquaintance of his father's, Owen Stanley, the brother of the president of the board. Dobson would become a first-class clerk in 1874 and a principal clerk in 1884 and retire in 1901 with a Civil List pension of £250 per year.

Dobson's first published poem, "A City Flower," appeared in *Temple Bar* in 1864. Soon after, his poems began to appear regularly in *St. Paul's Magazine*, edited by Anthony Trollope. In a 1914 *Morning Post* interview Dobson claimed that "It was largely through Trollope that I first became engaged in literary pursuits"; he found in Trollope a model for combining government and literary work. Dobson married Francis Mary Beardmore, the daughter of a successful civil engineer, in 1868; the couple had five sons and five daughters and lived at 75 Eaton Rise in the London suburb of Ealing until Dobson's death on 2 September 1921. Dobson's poems were composed after he commuted home from his work at the Board of Trade.

Dobson's first collection of poetry, *Vignettes in Rhyme and Vers de Société*, was published in 1873; his second, *Proverbs in Porcelain*, in 1877; and his third, *At the Sign of the Lyre*, in 1885. With the publication of *At the Sign of the Lyre* Dobson's verse writing tapered off, and his work as a literary biographer quickened. *The Civil Service Handbook of English Literature* had appeared in 1874, but in Ellis's view Dobson's *Hogarth* (1879) "was the touchstone or pre-eminent factor of his literary life," leading him "to the study of the life and art of the eighteenth century." In 1883 John Morley persuaded Dobson to write the volume on Fielding for the English Men of Letters series. In 1884 Dobson published a book on the engraver Thomas Bewick, followed by biographies of Steele (1886); Goldsmith (1888); Walpole (1890); an enlargement of his biography of Hogarth (1891); a three-volume series, *Eighteenth Century Vignettes* (1892–1896); and volumes for the English Men of Letters series on Richardson (1902) and Burney (1903). *The Dictionary of National Biography* notes that "From this time [1903] onwards any publisher intending to reissue an eighteenth-century work went to Austin Dobson for an introduction. Altogether fifty such volumes with Dobson's editorial superintendence are catalogued." Whether as an "introducer" or as a memoirist, Dobson's works made him appear to his contemporaries as, in the words of George Edward Woodberry, "a seasoned

habitué of the haunts of Queen Anne's city. He knows London like an antiquary and rebuilds it like a dramatist."

As the rapid appearance of his biographies suggests, Dobson defined quite narrowly the research necessary to write a memoir. For him the author's works and, if available, the author's correspondence were the heart of any biography. His role consisted of summarizing the works and correspondence, drawing significant and previously unnoticed connections between them, and evaluating the worth of the work – that is, the moral and emotional betterment that it encourages. The opening chapters of Dobson's biography of Walpole are written almost entirely from Walpole's "Short Notes of My Life" (first published in Walpole's Letters to Sir Horace Mann [1844]) and from Walpole's correspondence, particularly the letters between him and Gray; his biography of Steele relies heavily on Steele's correspondence – particularly his memoranda to his wife, "Dear Prue" – at one point giving ten pages to direct quotation; the Hogarth biography, in all its versions, refers repeatedly to the "brief sketch of his life" that Hogarth left with his papers at his death. Dobson is always ready to let authors "speak for themselves," quoting extensively from his sources or paraphrasing them.

While Dobson's attitude toward his subjects seems deferential insofar as he turns large portions of his biographies over to them, he claims that it is the biographer's job to distinguish between superior and inferior achievement. Dobson, in a way few contemporary academic critics would risk, arbitrates between the claims for attention of competing authors and painters, informing his audience, with missionary unabashedness, why they should read or view works by his subjects. He views art as a contest for popular favor; in a typical passage, he opens his anthology *Eighteenth Century Essays* (1882) by noting that "people continue to pit Fielding against [Tobias] Smollett, and [William Makepeace] Thackeray against [Charles] Dickens" and assuming that "there will always be a party for [Joseph] Addison and a party for Steele." In this contest Dobson sets himself the task of assuring that virtue is recognized and rewarded. He defends Steele against Thomas Babington Macaulay's charges of carelessness, even fecklessness; he defends Fielding against unsubstantiated allegations about his "dissolute" personal life by Arthur Murphy and others.

Dobson's sense of his role as a biographer perhaps appears most clearly in his preface to the 1907 edition of his *William Hogarth*. This edition, he says, concludes the project he had begun in 1879 with a "smaller book" on Hogarth "in the 'Great Artists' series." Dobson admits that in 1879 he had "neither hope nor thought" that the book would be so successful. But by 1907 the book had gone through many reprintings, as well as new editions in 1891, 1898, and 1902, so Dobson can speak confidently of the "popular character" of the work and of changes he has made to enhance it. From 1879 to 1907 he has received compelling and gratifying evidence that a large audience waits upon his judgments.

The 1907 preface also reveals Dobson's concern with assessing the value of art through the ranking of artists and their works. In the early editions Dobson had taken it upon himself to correct contemporary misapprehension of Hogarth's achievement: "so far from being an indifferent colourist, William Hogarth, at his best, was really a splendid painter." In 1907, however, Dobson worries that the emphasis on Hogarth as painter has gone too far, and he resets the balance: "while it is manifest that the efforts of Hogarth as a painter pure and simple have been strangely underrated, it would be undesirable now to pass to the other extreme, and ignore his specific mission as a pictorial moralist." Dobson had earlier drawn attention to such paintings as *The Shrimp Girl* and *The March to Finchley,* but in the 1907 edition he focuses on the famous sets of engravings: *The Rake's Progress, The Harlot's Progress,* and *Marriage a la Mode.* Dobson admires these series for their moral clarity, claiming of *The Harlot's Progress* that Hogarth "had a plain and straightforward message to deliver. If you do that — this will follow — and this — and this." Revealingly, Dobson rates Hogarth's *Four Stages of Cruelty* lower than the other "progress" pieces because while the engravings in that series "have all the downright power of Hogarth's best manner . . . they are unrelieved by humour of any kind, and are consequently painful and even repulsive." The *Four Stages of Cruelty* engravings are too intense to allow for the moral clarity that Dobson values (Dobson uses *painful* and *repulsive* synonymously, setting a standard that would judge against tragedies by William Shakespeare and Sophocles), and thus they must suffer in his ranking.

Important to note in Dobson's dismissal of the *Four Stages of Cruelty* is his confidence that he can distinguish between "manner" and worth, between what today might be called form and content. For Dobson the value of a work of art is never defined by its form; nor does he share with the New Critics of the mid twentieth century the assumption that form and content are inseparable. Rather, for Dobson, art must ennoble the human spirit, and that

end may be achieved apart from technical or formal merit. Thus, in his introduction to the Oxford Edition of Goldsmith's *Complete Poetical Works* (1906), Dobson judges that "in grace and tenderness of description *The Deserted Village* in no way falls short of *The Traveller;* and . . . its central idea, and its sympathy with humanity give it a higher value as a work of art." Dobson's emphasis on ranking works of art is manifest here, but perhaps most remarkable is his assumption that he can locate both the "central idea" and the "higher value" of a poem without appealing to formal standards ("grace . . . of description"). Similarly, in his volume on Richardson, Dobson claims that "there can be no doubt" that *Clarissa* (1747–1748) is Richardson's "masterpiece" but complains about the novel's "extraordinary diffuseness and inordinate prolixity." For Dobson a great book can be sloppily or awkwardly written.

While Dobson will tolerate "prolixity," he will not countenance works lacking in that "sympathy with humanity" that he finds in Goldsmith's *The Deserted Village* (1770). He turns away from the *Four Stages of Cruelty* because its graphic portrayal of human viciousness has become, for him, "repulsive." Similarly, while the verbiage of Richardson's *Clarissa* can be pardoned, the novel cannot be excused for its central event — the vile Lovelace's rape of the heroine. While conceding that the novel is a masterpiece, Dobson describes it as "this, in some respects repulsive, but in all respects remarkable" work. He greatly concerns himself to discover upon whom Lovelace was modeled, so as, perhaps, to account for his villainy. When Dobson finally determines that he cannot find a historical precedent, he describes the character growing "with the progress of the story in the heated mind of his inventor." Masterpiece or not, for Dobson such villainy must be owing to distortion — to "heat," not to "humanity."

In his confident dismissal of works or parts of works that he finds "repulsive," Dobson himself points to his limits as a critic and a memoirist. As Ellis says, for all Dobson's fame as an expert on the eighteenth century, "his interest and delight in his subject must have been, in the main, sentimental. . . . He could never have been in sympathy with the laxity and corruption of the eighteenth century or with its modes of speech and social habits." Gosse, a friend of Dobson's from their early days together at the Board of Trade, seconds Ellis's description of Dobson as "almost puritanical in his code of morals," claiming that Dobson "shut his eyes to the violence of instinct and all the squalors of passion. In his otherwise almost faultless per-

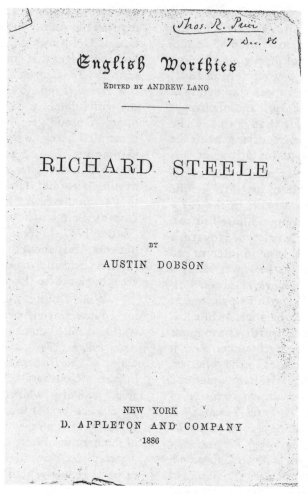

Title page for Dobson's biography of the eighteenth-century essayist and dramatist

sonal character, timidity was a feature which could not but be regretted." Gosse says that this "prudery . . . increased with advancing years" and that because of it Dobson eventually "deprived himself of some of his beloved eighteenth-century authors." Looked at too closely, without the "relief" of humor, much of eighteenth-century life and art was "repulsive." As Thomas Earle Welby observes, Dobson's eighteenth century was a "fanciful rearrangement of the materials his learning gave him"; it was "a world in which forgetfulness of the actual world was possible."

Gosse's notion that Dobson finally "deprived himself" of his eighteenth-century authors finds validation in Dobson's biographies, early as well as late. Dobson's prefaces frequently concern themselves with what he will *not* discuss. Thus he opens his Fielding volume by praising Leslie Stephen's recent work on Fielding (which is "now in everyone's hands," according to Dobson) and then claiming

that Stephen's achievement allows Dobson to "confine my attention more strictly to the purely biographical side of the subject." Rather than advancing new interpretations of *Joseph Andrews* (1742) and *Tom Jones* (1749), "I have made it my duty, primarily, to verify such scattered anecdotes respecting Fielding as have come down to us; to correct . . . a few misstatements . . . to add such supplementary details as I have been able to discover for myself." Perhaps most striking here is Dobson's happiness with the confines within which he works. He makes no large claims for the book, and the few claims he does make are comfortably mundane: "I am able to give, for the first time, the date and place of Fielding's second marriage, and the baptismal dates of all the children by that marriage, except the eldest. I am also able to fix approximately the true period of his love affair with Miss Sarah Andrew. From the original assignment at South Kensington I have ascertained the exact sum paid . . . for *Joseph An-*

drews." In all these details of "getting and spending," the power of Fielding's satire, and his sometimes unsettling anger, are lost.

Dobson's volume on Burney, his last contribution to the English Men of Letters series, is similarly timid. Brief chapters on Burney's novels are surrounded by highly detailed chapters on her father's family history and career. The volume concludes with an evaluation of Burney's *Diary* (1842–1854) in which, freed from the burden of dealing with her major works, Dobson writes with great force: "The *Diary* of Mme. D'Arblay deserves to rank with the great diaries of literature." But Dobson uses the diary to shield himself from the difficult question of the literary status of Burney's novels. Throughout the Burney volume, as in the Walpole, Steele, Hogarth, and Richardson books, the author speaks for himself or herself. And Dobson, cheerfully confined by the need to give the authors their space, can look away from "repulsive" features of both eighteenth-century and contemporary life: discrimination based on class and gender, deceit in the service of bad passion, and political and moral turpitude.

Dobson achieved fame as a poet by working within the tradition of older French lyrics and the tradition of Horace's *Odes;* he only briefly flirted with Pre-Raphaelitism before developing a polished and urbane style. He eschews the contemporary in his verse forms, and in poems such as "A Dead Letter" and "To Lydia Languish" he complains that "the time is out of joint." In his biographies Dobson continues the project he began in his verse. Fancifully reconstructing the eighteenth century, the biographies manifest and elaborate Dobson's tendency in his verse to take, as Arthur Symons describes it, an "indirect, smiling, deliberate way of dealing with life." The biographies manifest a shaping motive similar to that of the poems: a past world, an older model allows Dobson both to express and to mediate his distaste for the "modern," to assuage his anxiety that his "time" is one for which he, with his "timidity" and "prudery," is not fit. When Dobson concludes his Richardson volume by suggesting that Richardson will not achieve "popularity" again because "the conditions of modern life appear to be hopelessly averse from the perusal of novels in seven or eight volumes," the "smile" to which Symons refers is hardly broad or ebullient. Rather, his lips are tightly pursed, his distaste barely concealed. The smile is even weaker when he opens *Eighteenth Century Essays* with an explanation of why he has included sketches of social life rather than philosophical or moral essays: "With the march of time philosophy has taken new

directions . . . if we are didactic now, we are didactic with a difference." The "if" suggests that eighteenth-century morality and philosophy – the beauties of the improved version of eighteenth-century life that Dobson constructed – are lost on the modern world.

When Dobson cannot maintain his distance from the "squalors of passion" or the ugliness of the "stages of cruelty," when his material – Clarissa's rape, for example – no longer permits him to be "indirect," then the smile breaks; he turns away from his subject with the dismissal "repulsive." When Dobson prefaces *Hogarth* by wistfully claiming that "it would be a pleasant task to loiter for a space in that vanished London of Hogarth, of Fielding, of [David] Garrick," the words *pleasant, loiter,* and *vanished* say much about his motives as a biographer. The London Dobson set about "rearranging" from "the materials his learning gave him," as Welby put it, offered a respite from the disjointed modern world; it was a nonexistent, "vanished" place to "loiter," to relax. When the materials for "rearranging" ceased to be "pleasant," then Dobson reached his limits as a biographer, and his efforts at comprehensive sympathy ceased.

Perhaps nowhere are Dobson's virtues and limitations as a literary biographer more evident than in his work on Steele for the English Worthies series. Published in 1886, *Richard Steele* reveals the range of Dobson's sympathy with his subjects as well as his persistent need to rank authors according to their "humanity." As Woodberry points out, the conflicting versions of Steele offered by his attacker Macaulay and his defender Thackeray meant that Dobson faced "tremendous rhetorical odds" as he tried "to give us only a natural picture." In Woodberry's view Dobson successfully navigates between "the hen-pecking manner of Macaulay" and "the patronizing charity of . . . Thackeray." Dobson claims that Thackeray's portrait, while "doing justice to Steele's generosity, kindliness, amiability . . . leaves the impression that he was weaker, frailer, more fallible than the evidence warrants." Dobson's biography focuses almost entirely on matters of personal conduct; impatient with formal questions, Dobson assumes silently that Steele's characters – Isaac Bickerstaff and Mr. Spectator, most notably – directly express his views. Unlike recent academic critics, Dobson pays scant attention to the possibilities for irony and ambiguity created by these personae.

When not discussing Steele's behavior, Dobson directs his commentary on Steele's works away from the texts themselves to their emotional or moral impact. Dobson reserves his highest praise for those papers in which he discovers emotional openness and power. This standard leads him to value Steele's sincerity over Addison's stylishness; he claims that Steele's "virtues redeemed his frailties" and that Steele's humor "is so cheerful and good-natured, so frank and manly that one is often tempted to echo the declaration of Leigh Hunt – 'I prefer open-hearted Steele with all his faults to Addison with all his essays.'" Seeking sincerity, Dobson asserts that Steele reaches his "highest mark" in *Tatler* number 181 (in which Steele describes his family's response to the death of his father), number 95 (an account of an old friend of Isaac Bickerstaff who lives a life of perfect domestic tranquillity and happiness), and number 114 (an account of the response of the friend's family to the death of the wife). Dobson's need to rank works is, again, clear: the *Tatler* is better than the *Spectator,* and these three issues are the best of the best. The Steele volume also is typical of Dobson's work in its tendency to let Steele speak for himself: he quotes at length from both *Tatler* number 95 and number 114.

Dobson devotes large portions of his book to direct quotation because he appreciates Steele's works for their ability to stir emotion, and he wants to evoke those emotions in his own readers. In his account of *Tatler* numbers 181, 95, and 114 Dobson uses the word *pathetic* positively; they are, in today's terms, "tearjerkers," but Dobson values them as such. His commentary attends closely and carefully to the text – becoming something like the explication of the New Critics – only as he studies how Steele achieves these effects: "A month after [*Tatler* number 95], in *Tatler* number 114 comes a pathetic account of her death, and the grief of her heartbroken husband and children – an account so vivid in its realism that it is hardly possible to not believe it based upon an actual occurrence. Steele – the story goes – overpowered by his emotion, was unable to complete the paper, and a frigid academic close was supplied by Addison. . . . There are other examples of Steele's descriptive power in *The Tatler,* but in these he attains the measure of his strength." As the Victorians are said to have practiced "Muscular Christianity," this passage might be called muscular criticism; the emphasis is on "descriptive power" and "the measure of . . . strength." Such emotional effects, however, are not susceptible to extended or close analysis: the emotion tends to fade as the intellect charts its origin and techniques. Dobson comments on the account in *Tatler* number 114 not by analyzing specific passages but by guessing that the event must really have happened. He does not bother to check out the story of Steele's collapse, which first appeared in an essay by John Forster.

Perhaps most revealing about Dobson's commentary is his failure to push harder when he describes the disparity between the bulk of the paper and its "frigid academic close." Dobson, as is typical of him as a literary biographer, turns the question into one of personality and value: for him this is one of many instances that show the contrast between the coldly rational Addison and the passionate and frank Steele. Dobson's basic insight is astute enough; the tone of the paper does change. But Dobson has little to say about the means by which this change is effected or the ambiguity that it creates. He skirts around the opportunities the paper offers for explication and analysis.

Throughout *Tatler* number 114 characters (particularly Bickerstaff) alternate between bereavement and tenuous control of their emotions. Called to his friend's home at this moment of crisis, Bickerstaff tries to gauge the "greatness" of his friend's grief and wonders how he will bear his loss. In the dying woman's room the opposition becomes particularly intense. While her family weeps, she speaks and acts with gracefulness and resignation. Bickerstaff describes his "Heart . . . torn in Pieces to see the Husband on one Side suppressing and keeping down the Swellings of his Grief, for Fear of disturbing her in her last Moments; and the Wife even at that Time concealing the Pains she endured, for Fear of increasing his Affliction." At odds here are strong passion and the "suppressing" of it, and Bickerstaff, too, is split between the conflicting impulses. The wife's last words are to Bickerstaff: "Take care of your Friend – don't go from him," and they intensify his conflict because they remind him of his duty when he might prefer to give in to his feelings.

With the wife's death, Dobson claims, Steele's contribution to the paper ends: "In the Moment of her Departure, my Friend (who thus far had commanded himself) gave a deep Groan, and fell into a Swoon by her Bed-side." Grief overwhelms the children as well: "The Distraction of the Children, who thought they saw both their Parents expiring together, and now lying dead before them, would have melted the hardest Heart." Whether or not Addison took over from the faltering Steele here, this sentence does make a slight but important shift in focus. Moving away from excessive and, thus, dangerous passion, Bickerstaff begins to exert some control over himself and the situation by turning the discussion toward general cases. Hearts are still melting, but they are hearts in general, not Bick-

HORACE WALPOLE

A MEMOIR

WITH AN APPENDIX OF BOOKS PRINTED AT THE
STRAWBERRY HILL PRESS

BY

AUSTIN DOBSON

WITH ILLUSTRATIONS BY
PERCY AND LEON MORAN

NEW-YORK
DODD, MEAD & COMPANY
1890

Frontispiece and title page for Dobson's biography of the creator of the Gothic novel

erstaff's own heart, earlier "torn in Pieces." The father recovers from his swoon, and Bickerstaff helps "to remove [him] to another Room, with a Resolution to accompany him till the first Pangs of his Affliction were abated." Bickerstaff now stands as a figure of "resolution," and passion is understood to be a force that abates. Bickerstaff reinforces his resolution by recalling classics of literature: Pliny's *Epistles*; John Milton's *Paradise Lost* (1667), book 4, lines 639 to 656 (Eve's speech claiming that she can enjoy Paradise only in Adam's company), and book 2, lines 557 to 561 (the fallen angels "in wand'ring mazes lost"); and John Dryden's criticism of Milton in the preface to his translation of Juvenal. Thus Dobson complains about "a frigid and academic close" and attributes it to Addison's bad hand: even if the story of Steele being overcome by emotion and dropping his pen is a bit implausible, the reference to Pliny and the admiring citations of *Paradise Lost* might seem to point to Addison. But Steele, too, knew his Pliny and his Milton; indeed, Eve's speech

corresponds well with his own notions of happy domesticity. Dobson is a careful enough reader to sense the change in tone, but he does not take that change to be interesting in itself. By focusing on the question of authorship Dobson avoids the dark truth the paper suggests: grief so intense cannot be shared and perhaps defies solace.

In his *Morning Post* interview Dobson claimed that his long career as a civil servant actually helped him as a poet and biographer by teaching him "habits of punctuality and regularity.... A man who has been a government clerk is not likely to say, as some poets have done, 'I must wait for inspiration.'" Whether in his catalogue of Hogarth's paintings and prints, his appendix summarizing the publications from Walpole's Strawberry Hill Press, or his researches into the family backgrounds of Fielding and Burney, Dobson is diligent and, within his limitations, thorough: he has taken the time, for example, to discover to whom Hogarth sold his works, how much he received for them, and where they were then located. Dobson the clerk is good at keeping track of the pounds and shillings that his subjects had available to them, and Dobson the father of ten is good at sorting out the sometimes tangled webs of eighteenth-century family relations.

Dobson told Ellis, "I have tried very hard to write prose, and I am always more pleased when I write a successful piece of prose than verse, though poetry comes easier to me." In this comment, taken in conjunction with his praise for the discipline encouraged by a government clerkship, can perhaps be found the measure of his work as a biographer. For Dobson, biography involved the making of a world, the creation of an alternative to modern disjointedness. The needs that biography fulfilled for him encouraged his sympathy with writers such as Fielding and Steele and prompted him to seek out the "facts" that would scotch the bad rumors about them. But the anxiety that motivated his biographies sharply limited the range of his sympathy. The "squalors of passion," the "stages of cruelty," were finally to be dismissed as "repulsive." Ambiguous texts, such as *Tatler* number 114, he treated as problems in attribution, not as problems in interpretation.

Dobson moved smoothly from poetry to biography because his outlook in both genres remained the same: an indirect, wryly humorous view of life. Within his limited range, he pursued biography with remarkable diligence and energy. While his work has been superseded in all cases by more recent biographies, it remains an instructive, even compelling example of biography as written by a man of letters, an intelligent and learned nonspecialist who is not afraid to reveal his prejudices and tastes. The biographies testify that the "ease" Dobson seeks is hard won, the humanity he encourages a rare virtue, the "indirect . . . way of dealing with life" he pursues a product of both great effort and considerable learning.

Interview:

"Interview with Austin Dobson," *Morning Post* (London), 17 January 1914, pp. 8–13.

Bibliographies:

Francis Edwin Murray, *A Bibliography of Austin Dobson* (Derby: Murray, 1900);

Alban Dobson, *A Bibliography of the First Editions of Published and Privately Printed Books and Pamphlets by Austin Dobson* (London: First Edition Club, 1925);

Dobson, *Catalogues of the Collection of the Works of Austin Dobson, 1840–1921* (London: University of London Library, 1960).

References:

Jerome Hamilton Buckley, "Henry Austin Dobson . . . Biographical Sketch," in his *Poetry of the Victorian Period* (Glenview, Ill.: Scott, Foresman, 1965), pp. 1022–1023;

Alban Dobson, *Austin Dobson: Some Notes* (London: Oxford University Press, 1928);

Stewart M. Ellis, "Austin Dobson," in his *Mainly Victorian* (London: Hutchinson, 1925), pp. 211–221;

John Forster, "Sir Richard Steele," *London Quarterly Review,* 96 (April 1855): 263–293;

Edmund Gosse, "Austin Dobson," in his *Silhouettes* (New York: Scribners, 1925), pp. 183–190;

William Ernest Henley, "Austin Dobson," in his *Views and Reviews: Essays in Appreciation* (New York: Scribners, 1902), pp. 120–123;

Herbert C. Lipscomb, "Horace and the Poetry of Austin Dobson," *American Journal of Philology,* 50 (1929): 1–20;

James Keith Robinson, "A Neglected Phase of the Aesthetic Movement: English Parnassianism," *PMLA,* 68 (September 1953): 733–754;

Robinson, "Austin Dobson and the Rondeliers," *Modern Language Quarterly,* 14 (March 1953): 31–42;

Arthur Symons, "Austin Dobson," in his *Studies in Prose and Verse* (London: Dent, 1904), pp. 224–226;

A. W., "Austin Dobson: A Poet of Two Worlds," *Times Literary Supplement,* 13 January 1940, p. 22;

Thomas Earle Welby, "Austin Dobson," in his *Back Numbers by "Stet" of The Saturday Review* (London: Constable, 1929), pp. 6–10;

Cornelius Weygandt, "Austin Dobson, Augustan," in his *Tuesdays at Ten* (Philadelphia: University of Pennsylvania Press, 1928), pp. 232–239;

George Edward Woodberry, "Addison and Steele Revisited," in his *Studies of a Littérateur* (New York: Harcourt, Brace, 1921), pp. 116–124.

Papers:

The Austin Dobson Collection at the University of London includes books, manuscripts, notebooks, reviews, and correspondence.

John Forster

(2 April 1812 – 1 February 1876)

John J. Fenstermaker
Florida State University

BOOKS: *Lives of Eminent British Statesmen,* volumes 44, 45, 46, 48, and 49 of *Lardner's Cabinet Cyclopædia* (London: Longman, Orme, Brown, Green & Longmans, 1836–1839); enlarged as *The Statesmen of the Commonwealth of England: With a Treatise on the Popular Progress in English History,* 5 volumes (London: Longman, Orme, Brown, Green and Longmans, 1840);

The Life and Adventures of Oliver Goldsmith: A Biography; in Four Books (London: Bradbury & Evans, 1848); revised and enlarged as *The Life and Times of Oliver Goldsmith,* 2 volumes (London: Bradbury & Evans, 1854; London & New York: Ward, Lock, 1871);

Daniel De Foe and Charles Churchill, 2 volumes (London: Longman, Green, Brown & Longmans, 1855);

Historical and Biographical Essays, 2 volumes (London: Murray, 1858; revised and enlarged, 1860);

The Arrest of the Five Members by Charles I: A Chapter of English History Rewritten (London: Murray, 1860);

The Debates on the Grand Remonstrance, November and December, 1641 With an Introductory Essay on English Freedom under the Plantagenet & Tudor Sovereigns (London: Murray, 1860);

Sir John Eliot: A Biography, 2 volumes (London: Longman, Green, Longman, Roberts & Green, 1864);

Walter Savage Landor: A Biography, 2 volumes (London: Chapman & Hall, 1869; Boston: Fields, Osgood, 1869);

The Life of Charles Dickens, 3 volumes (London: Chapman & Hall, 1872–1874; Boston: Estes & Lauriat, 1872–1874);

The Life of Jonathan Swift: Volume the First, 1667–1711 (London: Murray, 1875; New York: Harper, 1876);

Dramatic Essays: Reprinted from the "Examiner" and the "Leader," by Forster and George Henry Lewes, edited by William Archer and Robert W. Lowe (London: Scott, 1896).

OTHER: John Fletcher, *The Elder Brother,* adapted by Forster (London: Bradbury & Evans, 1846);

Diary and Correspondence of John Evelyn: To Which Is Subjoined the Private Correspondence between King Charles I. and Sir Edward Nicholas, and between Sir Edward Hyde, Afterwards Earl of Clarendon, and Sir Richard Browne, 4 volumes, edited by William Bray, revised and enlarged by Forster (London: Colburn, 1854);

George Nugent Grenville, Baron Nugent, *Memorials of John Hampden, His Party and His Times,* fourth edition, edited, with a memoir of Nugent, by Forster (London: Bohn, 1860);

Selections from the Poetical Works of Robert Browning, edited by Forster and Bryan Waller Proctor (London: Chapman & Hall, 1863 [i.e., 1862]);

The Works and Life of Walter Savage Landor, 8 volumes, edited by Forster (London: Chapman & Hall, 1876).

SELECTED PERIODICAL PUBLICATIONS – UNCOLLECTED: "Our Early Patriots," *Englishman's Magazine,* 1 (April–August 1831): 351–356;

"Our Early Patriots – John Pym," *Englishman's Magazine,* 1 (April–August 1831): 499–512;

"Our Early Patriots – Sir John Eliot," *Englishman's Magazine,* 1 (April–August 1831): 623–637;

"Sir Henry Vane's Scheme of Parliamentary Reform," *Englishman's Magazine,* 2 (September 1831): 1–13;

"John Hampden," *New Monthly Magazine,* 34 (1832): 288–289;

"Encouragement of Literature by the State," *Examiner,* 5 January 1850, p. 2;

"The Dignity of Literature," *Examiner,* 19 January 1850, p. 35;

"Ill-Requited Services," *Examiner,* 12 July 1851, pp. 433–434.

As critic, historian, and biographer, John Forster was a ubiquitous and powerful presence in the literary world of early- and mid-Victorian England.

Painting by C. E. Perugini (Victoria and Albert Museum)

He befriended and exerted significant influence over many contemporary English writers, including William Harrison Ainsworth, Robert Browning, Edward Bulwer, Thomas Carlyle, Charles Dickens, Leigh Hunt, Walter Savage Landor, and William Makepeace Thackeray. Chief literary and drama critic of the *Examiner* for more than twenty years and editor from 1847 to 1856, Forster was called by the *Eclectic Magazine* (October 1852) "perhaps the one most influential critic of the metropolitan press." His essays appeared in the major British periodicals, and he was editor or business manager of the *New Monthly Magazine,* the *Foreign Quarterly Review,* and the *Daily News.* Moreover, in his time he was considered one of the foremost authorities on the history of the Commonwealth of the seven-

teenth century. Between 1836 and 1864 he had many of his studies of that era published, the best known of which were his five volumes of *Lives of Eminent British Statesmen* (1836–1839) in Dionysius Lardner's *Cabinet Cyclopædia* and the two-volume biography *Sir John Eliot* (1864). His greatest achievements, however, were the literary biographies of Oliver Goldsmith and of Dickens; the latter is one of the finest English biographies written in the nineteenth century.

In person, too, Forster was impressive. He was a huge man who lived a life overflowing with expletives and superlatives – "Prodigious!" "Monstrous!" "Incredible!" "In*tol*-er-able!" Yet, according to his friend Percy Fitzgerald, "you could not but be struck by the finished shapes in which his sentences ran. There was a weight, a power of illustration, and a dramatic colouring, that could only have come of long practice. He was gay, sarcastic, humourous, and it was impossible not to recognize that here was a clever man and a man of power."

Forster was born on 2 April 1812 in Newcastle and was the eldest of four children. His father, Robert Forster, and uncle, "Gentleman John" Forster, were butchers; his mother, Mary, from Gallowgate, was the daughter of a farmer. Noting Forster's reputation as a star pupil, his voracious reading, and his obvious precociousness, "Gentleman John" determined that his nephew should go to the university. Forster entered Cambridge in 1828 but remained only a month before enrolling at the new University College in London.

While studying law, he promptly began his career as a critic in *Newcastle Magazine* for January 1829 with "Remarks on Two of the Annuals." Within the year he met Hunt and, shortly thereafter, Bulwer and Charles Lamb; each impressed on him that literature was a dignified and prestigious calling. With the help of these mentors, Forster began in the early 1830s to contribute criticism and historical sketches of Commonwealth figures to the *Athenaeum, New Monthly Magazine,* and *Englishman's Magazine* and criticism to the newspapers *True Sun, Courier,* and *Examiner.* In 1832 he became drama critic for the *True Sun;* by 1834 he was subeditor and chief literary and drama critic for the *Examiner.* Although called to the bar in 1843, Forster never practiced law; by the mid 1830s literature had become his vocation and his profession.

For the *Examiner* he wrote careful and scholarly criticism that owed its foundation to the influence of Lamb and can be best understood as part of Forster's unrelenting advocacy of the rights and dignities owed professional authors. He developed a consistent set of criteria for assessing books he reviewed: the work must be true – that is, faithful to reality; must provide a humane perspective on fundamental human passions and experiences; and must have a form so exactly embodying a unified concept and purpose as to produce a single effect or emotion. Additionally, Forster would speak of the "spirit of the book," a concept he explained in the *Examiner* for 9 July 1853: "A book that *is* a book, no simulacrum, but a living mass of thoughts and feelings grouped in their particular way, made visible under their own peculiar form, cannot be characterised in a sentence. The spirit of such a book, in its lights and shades and wonderful varieties, not only resembles, but it really is – the spirit of a man." Only a man whose essential nature was just could

write a positive and moral book. Armed with this aesthetic and a commitment to the dignity of authorship, Forster set out, as the *Eclectic* put it, "to estimate and to control the progress of the national literature"; pursuing that end, he soon became the "most influential critic of the metropolitan press." Positive reviews in his *Examiner* columns significantly advanced the early reputations of such authors as Dickens, Browning, and Alfred Tennyson.

Throughout his career Forster also made time for historical research and publication. The greatest concentration of such work came during the years 1836 to 1840, even as his duties at the *Examiner* were making substantial daily demands. During these years he contributed to Lardner's *Cabinet Cyclopædia* historical portraits of leading figures in the struggle against Charles I: Eliot, Thomas Wentworth, John Hampden, John Pym, Sir Henry Vane, Henry Marten, and Oliver Cromwell; in 1840 these studies were republished as *The Statesmen of the Commonwealth of England,* to which Forster added an introductory "Treatise on the Popular Progress in English History." In 1854 he edited anonymously, in four volumes, the diary and letters of John Evelyn. "The Civil Wars and Cromwell," a lengthy review essay in the *Edinburgh Review,* followed in 1856; it would be republished in the second volume of Forster's *Historical and Biographical Essays* (1858).

Forster's histories and historical biographies offer an eloquent and forcefully expressed Whig view of the Commonwealth period based on a Carlylean conception of the hero in history. His purpose in his historical writing was to explain the gradual winning by the people of individual freedoms and civil liberties, beginning at the time of the first Norman kings and culminating when an all-powerful House of Commons defied a tyrannical sovereign in the 1640s. His powerful advocacy in these texts grows out of two passionate beliefs: liberty can best be preserved by understanding the past; and the central historical event the people of England must properly understand and value is the revolution against the tyranny of Charles I that resulted in the establishment of the Commonwealth. The strengths and weaknesses of his commitment to these beliefs are most dramatically evident in his earliest historical sketches. Pym, who brought about Wentworth's execution for treason and who later led the debates on the Grand Remonstrance, was to Forster an "eloquent" orator, a "great statesman" and "patriot," the "most popular" man of his time. The "manly," "enthusiastic," "eloquent," and "immortal" Vane devised a system for parliamentary reform only to have it appropriated by the "hypocritical tyrant and military usurper" Cromwell, about whom Forster's opinion would later soften under Carlyle's influence. His histories are, thus, filled with heroes and villains. Yet, as the historian Samuel Gardiner pointed out in 1876, Forster's fervor never creates history that is false or wrong: "He never attached himself to unworthy objects. . . . His portraits have in them the life which springs from sympathy. From them the world learned, not quite all that Eliot, and Pym, and Hampden really were, but what they wished to be."

In 1856 Forster gave up the editorship of the *Examiner,* became secretary of the Lunacy Commission, and married Eliza Ann Colburn, the widow of his longtime friend the publisher Henry Colburn. Eliza Forster shared her husband's busy social and work schedule and helped him as he struggled with chronic poor health and a series of ravaging illnesses. In 1860 appeared *The Arrest of the Five Members by Charles I* and a companion volume, *The Debates on the Grand Remonstrance, November and December, 1641.* Perhaps his greatest triumph of historical research, the two-volume *Sir John Eliot: A Biography* was published in 1864.

By the middle of the 1840s, then, Forster had established a reputation as one of the principal literary critics of the day and as a historian of the Commonwealth period. His great interest in literary biography, however, lay outside both these periods, centering instead on eighteenth-century writers: Goldsmith, Charles Churchill, Daniel Defoe, Samuel Foote, Richard Steele, and Jonathan Swift.

His first literary biographies – those of Churchill and Defoe – appeared as review essays in the *Edinburgh Review* in 1845; review essays on Foote and Steele appeared in the *Quarterly Review* in 1854 and 1855 respectively. All were republished in *Historical and Biographical Essays,* and the Defoe and Churchill essays were also published separately in 1855. They grew out of Forster's concern that the lives of these men had been improperly understood in the books under review. The biographies of Goldsmith and Swift, on the other hand, were fully documented book-length or multivolume works, the labor of years of research and study: ten years on Goldsmith, twenty on Swift. On its appearance in 1848 *The Life and Adventures of Oliver Goldsmith* prompted such acclaim that Forster began almost immediately to work on an enlarged version; the two-volume *The Life and Times of Oliver Goldsmith* was published in 1854. *The Life of Jonathan Swift* (1875), projected for three volumes, was cut off at a single volume by Forster's death. Yet Forster is known today not for his studies of eighteenth-century au-

thors but for his biographies of two eminent literary contemporaries: *Walter Savage Landor* (1869) and, particularly, *The Life of Charles Dickens* (1872–1874).

The sketches of Churchill, Defoe, Foote, and Steele and the full-length study of Goldsmith illustrate Forster's theory of biography. He offers idealized portraits of men whose literary subjects and perspectives seemed right to him. A sensitive reading of their major works convinced Forster that the authors were essentially moral and optimistic. He believed, as did Carlyle, Browning, and John Ruskin, that great literature expressed a moral vision because the author was a moral person. An author's character flaws were important only in that they showed what the person had had to overcome. Hence, in his biographies Forster does not try to balance the good and the evil in his subjects' characters; rather, he introduces only those details that suggest the individual's true nature as revealed in his finest works. A biographer could, of course, be accused of suppression and distortion in such selectivity; as James A. Davies points out in the *Dickens Studies Annual* (1978), "Goldsmith's envy, coarseness in company, extravagant gambling, and failure to honour contracts; Churchill's hatred and harrying of [Tobias] Smollett and vindictive satirical attacks on the man who thwarted him of his father's living, his participation in the rites of Medmenham Abbey, the hedonism of his epitaph; Defoe's uncontrollable anger; Foote, fat and flabby, leaving his estate to his illegitimate sons; Steele's heavy drinking, homicidal dueling, mercenary marriage, illegitimate children, and flagrant dishonesty; Swift as absentee parish priest and congenital misanthrope – all are silently omitted from Forster's pages."

Shaping his portraits with his eye on a Victorian middle-class readership, Forster creates a unified vision of each that is dependent on that author's major literary work; focusing mainly on these writers as men of letters, he presents little biographical detail unrelated to their struggles as professional authors. As with the subjects of his historical biographies, each of these literary men stands before the reader as courageous, independent, and uncompromised – as a hero.

Forster viewed literary history, beginning with John Dryden, as moving from dependence on patronage and on capricious and greedy publishers and booksellers to control by a discerning middle-class readership whose purchases determined which authors would be rewarded. In each biography he stresses the dignity of literature as a profession, the importance of middle-class values, and the author's struggle for respectability and financial reward.

The house at Lincoln's Inn Fields, London, where Forster lived from 1834 until his marriage. Forster's quarters were on the ground floor of Number 58, the entrance to which is partially hidden by the columns (photograph by T. W. Tyrell).

Of the four shorter sketches, those of Churchill and Foote are less notable than those of Defoe and Steele. Although Churchill is a minor literary figure and his life would seem singularly inappropriate as a heroic model for the Victorian middle-class reader, Forster's biography of him typifies the pattern of each of these studies.

As a student, Churchill was quick and able. But an impetuous marriage to a woman who saddled him with heavy debts, and his abandonment of literature in deference to his father's wish that he become a clergyman, soon led to unhappiness, followed by his abandonment of his wife, creditors, and religious vocation. His return to literature produced two quick failures; but his third effort, *The Rosciad* (1761) – a satire on actors and the theater of his day – was an instant success. Following subsequent good fortune with satire and other poetry, Churchill settled amicably with his wife (although he did not return to her) and paid the creditors.

Most important, he found in literature a profession that offered dignity and financial security. Forster's final judgment sets the pattern for these eighteenth-century biographies: Churchill overcame much in his personal life, and his best work was consistently moral, positive, and timeless; he attacked corruption and hypocrisy, and "that their vile abettors . . . have not carried him into utter oblivion with themselves, sufficiently argues for the sound morality and permanent truth expressed in his manly verse."

In "Daniel De Foe" and "Sir Richard Steele" Forster's concern centers on reputation: "It is with De Foe dead, as it was with De Foe living. He stands apart from the circle of the reigning wits of his time, and his name is not called over with theirs"; "A magnificent eulogy of [Joseph] Addison is here built upon a most contemptuous depreciation of Steele; and if we are content to accept without appeal the judgment of Mr. [Thomas Babington] Macaulay's Essay, there is one pleasant face the less in our Walhalla of British Worthies."

Trying to survive as a professional author with his integrity intact, Defoe disseminated his political and social ideas in virtually every type of writing practiced in his time (including producing his journal, the *Review,* while in prison), and he suffered virtually every conceivable impediment: censorship, quarrels with publishers and booksellers, literary piracy, incarceration. Forster sympathizes with his political efforts in the interests of Whigs and Dissenters, seeing Defoe as "our only famous politician and man of letters, who represented, in its inflexible constancy, sturdy dogged resolution, unwearied perseverance, and obstinate contempt of danger and of tyranny, the great Middle-class English character." Forster calls Defoe "immortal" and a master of realism: "The art of natural story-telling, which can discard every resort to mere writing or reflection, and rest solely on what people . . . say and do . . . has had no such astonishing illustrations." After a detailed examination of *Robinson Crusoe* (1719) and *Moll Flanders* (1721), he awards Defoe the accolade "father of the illustrious family of the English novel."

Forster's defense of Steele in response to Macaulay's high praise for Addison confronts directly the issue of character. Forster proceeds, he admits, not "without partiality" but also "not without frank and full allowance for the portion of evil which is inseparable from all that is good, and for the something of littleness mixed up with all that is great." To offset anything of evil or littleness, Forster quotes affectionate passages from Steele's letters to his wife, favorable comments from such eminent contemporaries as Swift and Alexander Pope and, of course, Addison; as in all of his literary biographies, however, Forster's "brief" depends finally on the literary works — in Steele's case, his finest essays — that capture the author's essential and best self. Using work written before the partnership with Addison as well as later pieces, Forster demonstrates Steele's originality and considerable achievements in the periodical essay and points to the unwavering judgment of the reading public over time: Steele's works have always been considered witty, moral, positive correctives for the manners and morals of his age.

Clearly the lives of Defoe and Steele, as viewed by Forster, embodied critical values: Defoe's *Review* defined periodical journalism in new ways and offered a model followed in Steele's *Tatler* and, later, in the *Spectator* of Steele and Addison. These journals ranged broadly over contemporary mores and preached middle-class morality — for the "citizen classes" in the former case and for the "beauties and wits" in the latter two. More particularly, these sketches of Defoe and Steele, highlighting their efforts as men of letters, touch directly on the moral and ethical dimensions of authorship (Defoe was censored and jailed; Steele was victimized by inadequate copyright protection) — the dignity, rights, and privileges of such professionals that constitute the primary focus in Forster's work throughout the 1840s and 1850s. And nowhere was he to make the argument more fully and cogently than with the life of Goldsmith.

The Life and Adventures of Oliver Goldsmith, a seven-hundred-page volume, received such critical and popular acclaim that Forster devoted much of the next six years to revision and expansion. Dickens, who shared Forster's concerns regarding the dignity of professional authorship, offered high praise in a letter of 22 April 1848 to Forster: the "gratitude of every man who is content to rest his station and claims quietly on Literature, and to make no feint of living by anything else, is your due for evermore." The second edition, three hundred pages longer than the first, appeared in two volumes in 1854 as *The Life and Times of Oliver Goldsmith;* it went through six reprintings in Forster's lifetime.

In his biography of Goldsmith, Forster achieved two related goals: to record compellingly the life of the hero-as-man-of-letters who wrote such renowned works as *The Vicar of Wakefield* (1766), *The Deserted Village* (1770), and *She Stoops to Conquer* (1773); and to show the general plight of the man of letters attempting to find dignity and reward in the absence of the grand patron, at a time when the professional writer often labored at the mercy of unscrupulous bookmen in the Grub Street world of the mid eighteenth century.

The life of Goldsmith presents a detailed portrait of Goldsmith as a man who was conspicuously inept: an early failure in his efforts at professions in religion, education, law, and medicine, he then wrote, largely friendless, in penury and anonymity while struggling for respect and social position. On the other hand, as in Forster's earlier sketches, character flaws and other troubling personal details are eventually mitigated by the artist's literary genius, which achieves fruition despite the incredible odds he has had to overcome: "Nor let us omit from . . . consideration the nature to which he was born, the land in which he was raised, his tender temperament neglected in early youth, the brogue and the blunders he described as his only inheritance. . . .

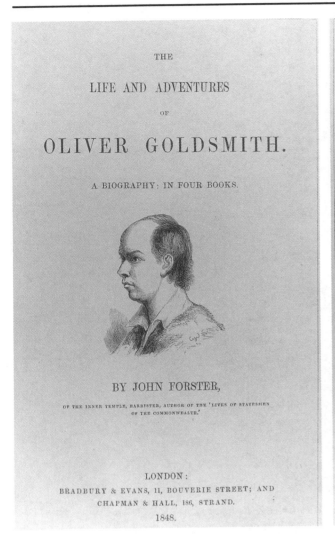

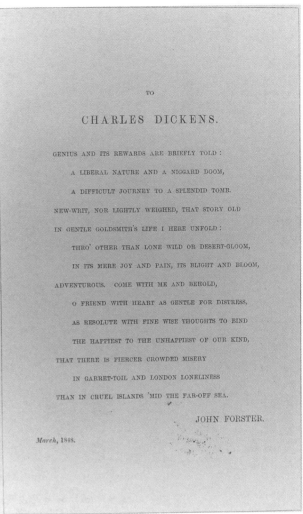

Title page and dedication from Forster's first literary biography

Manful, in spite of all, was Goldsmith's endeavor and noble its results."

When Landor died in 1864, Forster had been his friend for almost thirty years, had supervised publication of his writing since the late 1830s, and held copyright to all of his works. As a biographical subject for Forster, however, Landor presented distinct problems: born to wealth, Landor lost or gave away most of his money in his youth; undisciplined and impetuous, he was forced to leave Oxford for firing a fowling piece into the occupied room of a fellow student he detested for Tory sympathies; as a young man he recorded in verse a series of sexual exploits and may have fathered an illegitimate child; when he was nearly sixty, he abandoned his wife and three children in Italy (although he continued to support them financially); at eighty-three he left England to avoid the costs arising from a libel case involving a sixteen-year-old girl; throughout his life he fought, often publicly, with friends, neighbors, critics, and publishers. Further, Landor's art did not entertain or morally enlighten the middle class, nor was he a hero-as-man-of-letters struggling for dignity and respect: he wrote primarily to please himself, gave away what he earned, and cared little for popularity. Landor's life would seem to render impossible development of the central points in Forster's previous biographies: the dignity of the profession of authorship and the importance to posterity of recovering and appreciating the works and essential character of writers worthy of the highest public esteem. Forster struggled for five years; the result was the eleven-hundred-page, two-volume *Walter Savage Landor: A Biography*.

The volumes are not easy reading; they suffer from inadequate organization and are padded with long extracts of criticism of each of Landor's works drawn from reviews. They do include some new

Crayon sketch by Sir William Boxall of Forster's wife, the former Eliza Ann Colburn (Victoria and Albert Museum)

materials – letters and minor works not previously published – and Forster did believe that Landor's writings were worthy and demonstrated a genius that had been unfairly neglected. On the issues of how to give Landor his due, to be truthful regarding the facts of his life, and not to violate the biographer's own aesthetic principles, however, Forster is surprisingly successful. He distances himself from his old friend, dealing with Landor as a historical figure. He abandons the idea of "hero," instead describing Landor as a "genius," an "original," "unique," "special." He does not suggest that Landor's character was essentially moral or that his personal excesses were rendered unimportant by the value of his works. Forster believed that Landor's egocentric and undisciplined life substantially reduced the stature of the man and the writing: "Though I place him in the first rank as a writer of English prose; though he was also a genuine poet. . . . Even the ordinary influences and restraints of a pro-

fessional writer were not known to him. Literature was to him neither a spiritual calling, as [William] Wordsworth regarded it; nor the lucrative employment for which [Sir Walter] Scott valued it. Landor wrote without any other aim than to please himself, or satisfy the impulse as it arose. Writing was in that sense an indulgence to which no limits were put, and wherein no laws of government were admitted."

These judgments show Forster's adherence to his most important critical principle: that the artist's essential nature, the "spirit of the man," will necessarily be reflected in his art. Landor's writing does lack discipline; the art is limited by the nature of the man. In recording this truth Forster qualifies his otherwise generous final assessment of Landor's works: "There is hardly a conceivable subject, in life or literature, which they do not illustrate by striking aphorisms, by concise and profound observations, by wisdom ever applicable to the needs of

Palace Gate House, 46 Montague Square, London, where Forster moved after his marriage in 1856

men, and by wit as available for their enjoyment." Hence, Landor is not a hero-as-man-of-letters, a worthy middle-class companion of the literary figures from Defoe to Dickens whose "lives" constitute Forster's best biographical writing.

When Dickens died on 9 June 1870, Forster was not only the best qualified person to write his biography but was the novelist's own choice. His 1848 letter praising *The Life and Adventures of Oliver Goldsmith* had concluded: "I desire no better for my fame when my personal dustyness shall be past the controul of my love of order, than such a biographer and such a Critic."

Dickens's life and especially his works presented excellent subjects for Forster as the advocate of the dignity of authorship as a profession. The novelist's private life was full of public acts of charity, including efforts with Forster, Bulwer, and others to assist struggling authors; his writings were universally acknowledged for their positive moral and social content. The breakup of his marriage, which had been handled ineptly in its public phase,

and other character weaknesses appeared simply as human failings, in no way compromising the hero nor contradicting the positive moral character that is revealed in his greatest works. Despite serious ill health, which forced him to resign from the Lunacy Commission in 1872, Forster toiled at his task of duty and affection. The resulting three-volume study, *The Life of Charles Dickens,* was his last completed work and, clearly, his crowning achievement.

These volumes are organized similarly to *Walter Savage Landor:* Dickens's letters form much of the text, and a history of the writing and publishing of each work is followed by analyses of it most often from reviews. But these materials are better assimilated, and the overall organization is more coherent than in the Landor biography. High praise flowed from many sources, published and private. Carlyle, who deeply admired Forster's biography of Goldsmith, was typical in writing to Forster on 16 February 1874: "you have given to every intelligent eye the power of looking down to the very bottom of Dickens's mode of existing in this world; and I say I have performed a feat which, except in [James] Boswell, the unique, I know not where to parallel. So long as Dickens is interesting to his fellow-men, here will be seen face to face, what Dickens's manner of existing was. . . . "

The only serious negative criticisms touched on the idealizing strain obvious in all of Forster's biographies and the problem of Forster's ubiquitous presence as Dickens's sole correspondent. The *Saturday Review* for 23 November 1872 claimed: "The book should not be called the Life of Dickens but the History of Dickens's Relations to Mr. Forster. . . . It is the [Samuel] Johnson giving us the life of his Boswell." This criticism prompted a response from Forster in the third volume. Wishing to make "Dickens the sole central figure" and to give the biography the feeling of autobiography, Forster selected the letters to himself as serving these ends perfectly: "It is the peculiarity of few men to be to their most intimate friend neither more nor less than they are to themselves, but this was true of Dickens." The essential Dickens was the Dickens of his books and of the letters to his principal friend and confidant of more than three decades.

The issue of idealization is, of course, pertinent to each of the biographies. Recent scholarship tracing Forster's manipulation of materials reveals how an "improved" Dickens was effected. The editors of the Pilgrim Edition of *The Letters of Charles Dickens* (1965–) note that Forster altered letters by rephrasing or rearranging to emphasize his own importance, by changing dates, by improving the style, and by implying that letters to others were written to him. In the end, however, the editors find in *The Life of Charles Dickens* what is also evident in the other studies: Forster "had his subject remarkably in perspective. He was, moreover, concerned not simply with public image . . . but with truth, as he conceived it. The *Life* contains numerous small distortions of fact, but paradoxically, these distortions were in the interest of a larger, or ideal, truth."

Dickens emerges in Forster's view a complicated man of letters whose life became tragic as he grew older. In the period 1830 to 1850 he is unequaled in energy and popularity, creating positive books peopled by hundreds of memorable characters; his private life unfolds as a blur of travel, social gatherings, and charitable undertakings. Experimentation leads to the Christmas books and, after some missteps, to the editing of the weekly *Household Words* in 1850. His efforts to raise money to assist struggling professional authors first develops through amateur theatricals and then, more formally, through the Guild of Literature and Art. But

Forster records darker intimations, too, even in the early years, the fruit of which will include the collapse of Dickens's marriage in 1858.

Early in volume one Forster identifies the major character flaw in his subject: a "too great confidence in himself, a sense that everything was possible to the will that would make it so." To this fault or tendency Forster ascribes the hurtful decisions — both large, such as separation from his wife and his public readings from his works, and small, such as his squabbles with publishers and using real persons as models for characters — Dickens made throughout his life, particularly in the final two decades. Forster strongly disapproved of the public readings for personal gain that Dickens began in earnest after 1858, feeling that they touched on the dignity-of-literature issue: "It was a substitution of lower for higher aims; a change to commonplace from more elevated pursuits; and it had so much of the character of a public exhibition for money as to raise, in the question of respect for his calling as a writer, a question also of respect for himself as a gentleman." Forster is unrelenting in showing Dickens's obsession with the money he made from the readings and suggests that this fascination finally became a self-destructive urge. Throughout the volumes Forster seems unfailingly to offer the advice that most befits the dignified man of letters; whenever Dickens disregards his adviser, he is uniformly found wanting.

Nevertheless, the achievement of the biography resides in its charting of the complexity of Dickens's character. However aggrieved he may have felt personally on occasion, Forster held an unfailingly positive vision of Dickens's achievement; he never lost sight of what was noble in Dickens's character. The greatness that was bodied forth in the novelist's best works, forming "the whole of that inner life which essentially constituted the man," went far in Forster's mind to mitigate the sad confusions of the later years.

After *The Life of Charles Dickens* Forster turned his attention to Swift, but Forster died suddenly on 1 February 1876. His wife was his only living relative. He is buried at Kensal Green cemetery in the same tomb as his sister Elizabeth.

According Forster a just appraisal is difficult: his criticism is buried in the files of the *Examiner,* other newspapers, and some quarterlies; his historical writings and eighteenth-century literary biographies have been largely superseded; his only widely known work, *The Life of Charles Dickens,* serves primarily as a reference tool for persons studying Dickens. Further, he was sometimes a

WALTER SAVAGE LANDOR.

A BIOGRAPHY.

By JOHN FORSTER.

IN EIGHT BOOKS.

BOSTON:
FIELDS, OSGOOD, & CO.,
SUCCESSORS TO TICKNOR AND FIELDS.
1869.

Title page for Forster's biography of his old friend

too-perfect and too-voluble embodiment of Victorian middle-class respectability in his personal life. Nevertheless, Forster gave invaluable assistance to writers such as Browning, Bulwer, Tennyson, Landor, Dickens, and Carlyle, all of whom – except Tennyson – dedicated to him individual works or collected editions or named him literary executor. Moreover, his criticism and his historical and literary biographies provide a comprehensive gloss on the moral aesthetics of the cultivated, middle-class reader of the early- and high-Victorian age.

In virtually all of his writing, and particularly in the literary biographies, Forster argued vigorously and unequivocally for the dignity of the profession of authorship, consistently urging a more just evaluation of the profession of letters. He saw himself as a critic in company with Lamb, Hunt, and William Hazlitt, and he truly was their heir. In his honest striving to recognize, encourage, and publicize both the best and the most promising writers and to record as exemplars the lives of literary geniuses, he assisted many to the reputations and rewards they deserved. Judged by his own best writings, Forster emerges as one with the writers he most cherished: a hero-as-man-of-letters.

Biographies:
Henry Morley, "Biographical Sketch of Mr. Forster," in *Handbook of the Dyce and Forster Collections in the South Kensington Museum* (London: Chapman & Hall, 1880);

Whitwell Elwin, "John Forster," in *Catalogue of Printed Books, Forster Collection* (London: H. M. Stationary Office, 1888);

Percy Fitzgerald, *John Forster by One of His Friends* (London: Chapman & Hall, 1903);

Richard Renton, *John Forster and His Friendships* (London: Chapman & Hall, 1912);

James A. Davies, *John Forster: A Literary Life* (Leicester: Leicester University Press, 1983).

References:

Alec Brice, "The Compilation of the Critical Commentary in Forster's *Life of Charles Dickens,*" *Dickensian,* 70 (September 1974): 185–190;

James A. Davies, "Striving for Honesty: An Approach to Forster's *Life,*" *Dickens Studies Annual,* 7 (1978): 34–48;

John Fenstermaker, *John Forster* (Boston: Twayne, 1984);

Samuel Gardiner, "Mr. John Forster," *Academy,* 9 (5 February 1876): 122;

Madeline House, Graham Storey, and Kathleen Tillotson, eds., *The Letters of Charles Dickens,* Pilgrim Edition, 5 volumes (Oxford: Clarendon Press, 1965–   );

Charles Richard Sanders, "Carlyle's Letters," *Bulletin of the John Rylands University Library of Manchester,* 38 (September 1955): 223;

Rosalind Vallance, "Forster's *Goldsmith,*" *Dickensian,* 71 (January 1975): 21–29;

David Woolley, "Forster's *Swift,*" *Dickensian,* 70 (September 1974): 191–204.

Papers:

John Forster materials are widely scattered in library collections in the United Kingdom and the United States. The Forster Collection of the Victoria and Albert Museum in London contains Forster's massive personal library, a holding of more than eighteen thousand bound volumes as well as paintings, sketches, prints, and autographs and manuscripts of literary and political figures of the seventeenth, eighteenth, and nineteenth centuries — including the world's largest collection of Samuel Richardson manuscripts and a major collection of Swiftiana.

James Anthony Froude

(23 April 1818 - 20 October 1894)

Elizabeth McCrank
Boston University

See also the Froude entries in *DLB 18: Victorian Novelists After 1885* and *DLB 57: Victorian Prose Writers After 1867.*

BOOKS: *Shadows of the Clouds,* as Zeta (London: Ollivier, 1847);

A Sermon Preached at St. Mary's Church, on the Death of the Rev. George May Coleridge (Torquay: Croyden, 1847);

The Nemesis of Faith; or, The History of Markham Sutherland (London: Chapman, 1849; Chicago: Belfords, Clarke, 1879);

The Book of Job (London: Chapman, 1854);

History of England, 12 volumes: volumes 1–10 published as *History of England from the Fall of Wolsey to the Death of Elizabeth* (volumes 1–6, London: Parker, 1856–1860; volumes 7–8, London: Longmans, Green, Longmans, Roberts & Green, 1864; volumes 9–10, London: Longmans, Green, 1866); volumes 11–12 published as *History of England from the Fall of Wolsey to the Defeat of the Spanish Armada* (London: Longmans, Green, 1870); 12 volumes, with titles as above (New York: Scribners, 1865–1870);

Short Studies on Great Subjects, 4 volumes (London: Longmans, Green, 1867–1883; New York: Scribners, 1871–1883);

Inaugural Address Delivered to the University of St. Andrews, March 19, 1869 (London: Longmans, Green, 1869);

The Cat's Pilgrimage (Edinburgh: Edmonston & Douglas, 1870; New Haven, Conn.: East Rock Press, 1949);

Calvinism: An Address Delivered at St. Andrews, March 17, 1871 (London: Longmans, Green, 1871; New York: Scribners, 1871);

The English in Ireland in the Eighteenth Century, 3 volumes (London: Longmans, Green, 1872–1874; New York: Scribner, Armstrong, 1873–1874);

The Life and Times of Thomas Becket (New York: Scribner, Armstrong, 1878);

Caesar: A Sketch (London: Longmans, Green, 1879; New York: Scribners, 1879);

Bunyan (London: Macmillan, 1880; New York: Harper, 1880);

Two Lectures on South Africa Delivered Before the Philosophical Institute, Edinburgh, Jan. 6 & 9, 1880 (London: Longmans, Green, 1880);

Thomas Carlyle, A History of the First Forty Years of His Life, 1785–1835, 2 volumes (London: Longmans, 1882; New York: Harper, 1882);

Luther: A Short Biography (London: Longmans, Green, 1883; New York: Scribners, 1884);

Thomas Carlyle, A History of His Life in London, 1834–1881, 2 volumes (London: Longmans, Green, 1884; New York: Harper, 1884);

Oceana; or, England and Her Colonies (London: Longmans, Green, 1886; New York: Scribners, 1886);

The Knights Templars (New York: Alden, 1886);

The English in the West Indies; or, The Bow of Ulysses (London: Longmans, Green, 1888; New York: Scribners, 1888);

Liberty and Property: An Address (London: Liberty and Property Defence League, 1888);

The Two Chiefs of Dunboy; or, An Irish Romance of the Last Century (London: Longmans, Green 1889; New York: Munro, 1889);

Lord Beaconsfield (London: Low, Marston, Searle & Rivington, 1890; New York: Harper, 1890);

The Divorce of Catherine of Aragon: Being a Supplement to The History of England (London: Longmans, Green, 1891; New York: Scribners, 1891);

The Spanish Story of the Armada and Other Essays (London: Longmans, Green, 1892; New York: Scribners, 1892);

Life and Letters of Erasmus (London: Longmans, Green, 1894; New York: Scribners, 1894);

English Seamen in the Sixteenth Century (London: Longmans, Green, 1895; New York: Scribners, 1895);

James Anthony Froude

Lectures on the Council of Trent (London: Longmans, Green, 1896; New York: Scribners, 1896);
My Relations with Carlyle (London: Longmans, Green, 1903; New York: Scribners, 1903).

OTHER: "A Legend of St. Neot," in *Hermit Saints,* volume 4 of *Lives of the English Saints,* edited by John Henry Newman and others (London: Toovey, 1844);
"Suggestions on the Best Means of Teaching English History," in *Oxford Essays* (London: Parker, 1855);
Reminiscences by Thomas Carlyle, edited by Froude (2 volumes, London: Longmans, Green, 1881; 1 volume, New York: Scribners, 1881);
Letters and Memorials of Jane Welsh Carlyle, prepared for publication by Thomas Carlyle, edited by Froude (3 volumes, London: Longmans, Green, 1883; 2 volumes, New York: Scribners, 1883).

SELECTED PERIODICAL PUBLICATIONS – UNCOLLECTED: "Arnold's Poems," *Westminster Review,* 61 (January 1854): 146–159;
"Lord Campbell as a Writer of History," *Westminster Review,* 61 (April 1854): 446–479;

"Lord Macaulay," *Fraser's Magazine,* 93 (June 1876): 675–694;
"A Few Words on Mr. Freeman," *Nineteenth Century,* 5 (April 1879): 618–637;
"A Sibylline Leaf," *Blackwood's Magazine,* 133 (April 1883): 573–592;
"A Leaf from the Real Life of Byron," *Nineteenth Century,* 14 (August 1883): 228–242.

James Anthony Froude, historian of the English Reformation, is also well known as the friend and biographer of Thomas and Jane Welsh Carlyle. In addition to the Carlyle volumes, in the last sixteen years of his life Froude wrote well-received biographies of Benjamin Disraeli, Desiderius Erasmus, Martin Luther, Julius Caesar, John Bunyan, and Thomas Becket; he also produced biographical sketches of Robert Burns, Francis Bacon, Henry VIII, and many other figures from English history. His early historical works received mixed reactions in his own time: he was praised for his fluid writing style but criticized for careless errors and oversights. Later critics often appraised Froude on moral and theological grounds, rather than on the basis of historical accuracy and argument. His friends, including Thomas Carlyle, strongly supported his works, all of which stemmed from extensive original research. Although Froude's histories are read today primarily as clear representations of the Whig historical tradition and its biases, his biographies are read because of the fullness of the portraits that Froude drew.

The last of eight children, Froude was born on 23 April 1818 to Robert Hurrell Froude, a modestly well-off clergyman in Dartington, Devonshire, and Margaret Spedding Froude. His mother died when Froude was two years old, and the boy was left to the supervision of his aunt and his brothers Robert and Hurrell. Although Robert was kind to the boy, the aunt and Hurrell subjected him to tests of physical endurance that were almost beyond the capacity of the sickly youth to endure.

Froude was sent to Buckfastleigh School, in the neighborhood of Dartington, in 1827. Froude remembered this small school with fondness, although his academic progress was limited by its meager capabilities. This pleasant time ended when Froude's father pushed him into the Westminster School in 1830 in the hope of getting him into Oxford as soon as possible. In his later writings Froude referred to Westminster as a "den of horrors" and the time spent there as "purgatorial discipline." Eventually Froude took an interest in history, and he applied himself enough to be admitted to Oriel College, Oxford. Hurrell Froude had played a prominent role in the Oxford movement of John Henry Newman but had died shortly before Froude arrived, and because of his brother's reputation Froude was introduced to Newman. Temporarily mesmerized by Newman's presence, Froude engaged in his first biographical effort, "A Legend of St. Neot" (1844). It was characteristic of Froude that he approached the subject not as a hagiographer but, already under the influence of Carlyle's writings, as a storyteller relating a fable with a moral at the end.

After initiating steps to take holy orders, the usual prerequisite for a university position, Froude made a sensation with the publication of a semiautobiographical novel titled *The Nemesis of Faith* (1849), in which a young minister struggles over remaining in the Anglican church against his conscience or entering the Catholic church. The protagonist applies his reason to faith, and the resulting skepticism drives him to distraction. In the end his skepticism — "the nemesis of faith" — loses out to his need for comfort, and he enters a Catholic monastery. Anglicans were angered by Froude's suggestion that Catholicism was a more comforting faith, while virtually all religious groups abhorred the

skepticism he depicted. The book was publicly burned, and Froude was forced to resign the fellowship he had gained at Exeter College and to leave Oxford.

His family, disappointed by the scandal that Froude had provoked, provided no support for him, and he was forced to fend for himself. In June 1849 he was introduced to Carlyle by James Spedding, a relative of his mother's; in October he married Charlotte Maria Grenfell in London. Froude had obtained a position as a tutor to a wealthy family in Manchester; but in 1850 he resigned, and the couple moved to a cottage in Plas Gwynant, Wales. There Froude set about doing what interested him most: writing history. He did so with the same skeptical eye that he had applied to faith, in an attempt to remove what he conceived of as the superstitions and myths that obscured truth from readers. In October 1853 the Froudes moved to Babbicombe, Devon; later they settled in Bideford, in the same county.

His first work written there was a critical reappraisal of the English Reformation, written in direct response to the teachings of Newman. Immediately on publication of the first of the twelve volumes of his *History of England* (1856–1870) Froude was attacked by Goldwin Smith, Regius Professor of Modern History at Oxford. Smith, in two carefully worded reviews in the *Edinburgh Review* (July and October 1858), admitted that much of Froude's work was based on newly examined materials, unseen by other historians, making final judgment of the work impossible; but he concluded that significant errors and misrepresentations had occurred often enough to call into doubt Froude's competence as a historian. Smith's attack, measured and contained as it was, proved to be by far the most significant criticism of Froude's work during his lifetime. Later critics — particularly Edward Augustus Freeman, in a series of reviews in the *Saturday Review* from 1864 to 1892 — weakened their criticisms by their unfeigned hostility toward their subject. On the other hand, Froude received praise from the general public and from reviewers such as William Bodham Donne. Six volumes of the *History of England* had appeared by 1860.

Charlotte Froude died in the spring of 1860, leaving Froude with three children: Georgina Margaret, age ten; Rose Mary, eight; and Pascal Grenfell, six. In November Froude moved to London to take up the editorship of *Fraser's Magazine;* most of the biographical sketches he produced would appear first in the pages of *Fraser's*. In September 1861 he married Henrietta Warre, a close friend of his

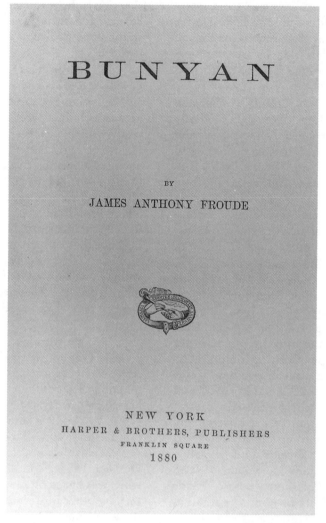

BY

JAMES ANTHONY FROUDE

NEW YORK
HARPER & BROTHERS, PUBLISHERS
FRANKLIN SQUARE
1880

Title page for Froude's biography of the author of The Pilgrim's
Progress *for the English Men of Letters series*

deceased wife, with whom he subsequently had a son, Ashley Anthony, and a daughter, Mary Caroline. Soon after his marriage he set off for Valladolid, Spain, to read the newly available papers of Philip II's archives.

The 1860s were a successful decade for Froude. The Longmans publishing house purchased the rights to the *History of England* from John William Parker and Son; Froude added volumes nine and ten in 1866 and eleven and twelve in 1870. At the conclusion of the work Longmans republished the series in the Cabinet Edition. A succession of honors followed, including election to the Massachusetts Historical Society, the rectorship of the University of St. Andrews, and membership in the Metaphysical Society. He vacationed in Ireland in 1870, traveling to places that he had visited in the early 1840s and gathering material for the magazine and for books.

Froude ended his tenure at *Fraser's* in 1874; the same year brought the publication of the third and final volume of his *The English in Ireland in the Eighteenth Century* (1872–1874). He left almost immediately for a speaking tour in the United States, in which he attempted to present the English position on Ireland. The tour was cut short by the furor stirred up by Irish sympathizers. Froude, rather than endanger his American sponsors and hosts, declined to speak more than four times, believing that the newspaper reports and pamphlet editions of his speeches would carry his message as far as any further appearances would have. Shortly after Froude's return from the United States, his second wife died.

Later in 1874 Froude began a career as an unofficial diplomat and correspondent to Disraeli's colonial secretary, Henry Howard Molyneux Herbert, fourth Earl of Carnarvon. He traveled to South Africa, becoming embroiled in the disputes over federation of the Cape Town Colony, the Orange Free State, the Transvaal, and Natal. He returned to England in January 1875, then went back to Cape Town in June and stayed until the year ended. In the midst of the Cape Town debates Froude's *The Life and Times of Thomas Becket* was serialized in the magazine *Nineteenth Century;* it was published in book form in 1878.

Froude portrays Becket as a treasonous, power-hungry scoundrel who manipulated the hapless Pope Alexander III while trying the patience, goodwill, generosity, and social conscience of King Henry II. Becket, according to Froude, engaged Henry not in a moral struggle but in a power struggle. Time and again Froude's Becket deliberately defies laws, issues ultimatums, and countermands the king's attempts to resolve the conflicts over jurisdiction. Froude dismisses Becket's self-imposed penitentials, legendary hair shirts, and much-vaunted charity as pretentious posing, charades designed to dupe the credible. He ascribes to Becket the desire for nothing less than total domination of the country and even sees Becket's death as stage-managed martyrdom. His death was Becket's final triumph over Henry, who had valiantly attempted to hold the church at bay. Ultimately, Froude argues, the struggle between church and king was decided in favor of the church by the Magna Carta – the document from which, according to Froude, nearly all of the corruptions of the pre-Reformation English church stemmed.

In 1879 Froude's *Caesar: A Sketch* was published. In the study, which was inspired by Froude's concern about colonial issues in South Africa and Ireland, he ponders the effects of colonial expansion on a constitutional government. Froude argues that the side of the "people" is actually the side of despotism. He presents the century of the Roman commonwealth as a time of civil war between the aristocrats, championed by Sulla, Cicero, and Pompey, and the populace, led by the Gracchi, Gaius Marius, and Julius Caesar. The Gallic wars and African campaigns of Caesar are, in Froude's hands, intimately connected with the efforts of the senate to dominate and pollute the constitution. The book is rife with minute biographical sketches: Froude draws Cicero as a conceited prig, although possessing a conscience, whose great downfall is his vanity; Pompey is a dupe who has risen above his level of competence; Cato the Younger is a fanatic and a schemer; Caesar is a loner who refuses to be a mere mob leader but recognizes the necessity of reforming Rome if the constitution is to survive at all. In the ensuing struggle the constitution was defended by those who had corrupted it – the aristocracy – for the purpose of continuing to abuse it, and, thus, it perished. Froude presents the story as an ironic one, maintaining a Burkean resignation about the dangers of reforming a bad government.

Caesar was followed by *Bunyan* (1880). Froude detaches himself from some of John Bunyan's convictions, particularly the latter's idea that children should be taught how miserable they are – a notion that must have reminded Froude of his own harsh childhood. Bunyan's trial over the Act of Uniformity is covered in detail. Bunyan saw attempts by officials to reach a compromise with him as temptations designed to test his faith; for twelve years he remained in prison, refusing to compromise, and ultimately outlasted the government that had placed him there. Froude dismisses exaggerated stories of Bunyan's suffering; he points out that Bunyan was released from prison each day and only required to return at nightfall. In the latter portion of the book Froude outlines the plot of Bunyan's *The Life and Death of Mr. Badman* (1680), includes a critique of John Milton's *Paradise Lost* (1667), and comments on Bunyan's *The Holy War* (1682). Froude suggests that Bunyan's topics were beyond mortal understanding and suffered in his attempt to portray them. While Froude pronounces these works failures, he praises the first half of *The Pilgrim's Progress* (1678) for overcoming sectarianism and addressing the spiritual journey of all human beings; still, he says, by the end the story has become a dull imitation of itself. Froude paints Bunyan as a champion of religious liberty, but one who failed to see the point behind the Indulgences of 1672.

Meanwhile, Froude had been charged with the biographical enterprise for which he is best known: the commission as literary executor and biographer for Thomas and Jane Welsh Carlyle. After thirty-two years of friendship – the last fifteen notable for Froude's care of Carlyle after Jane Carlyle's death in 1866 – Carlyle presented the younger man with the entirety of his wife's correspondence, bidding Froude to edit the material; additionally, although Carlyle had requested that no biography be written of him, he asked Froude to undertake the project when he found out that others were writing his life. Froude had set his heart on writing about Charles V and Philip II, but he agreed that it was better for a biography to be written by one who had known the person and had possession of the subject's papers.

The publication of Jane Carlyle's papers in 1883 revealed some less pleasant aspects of her mar-

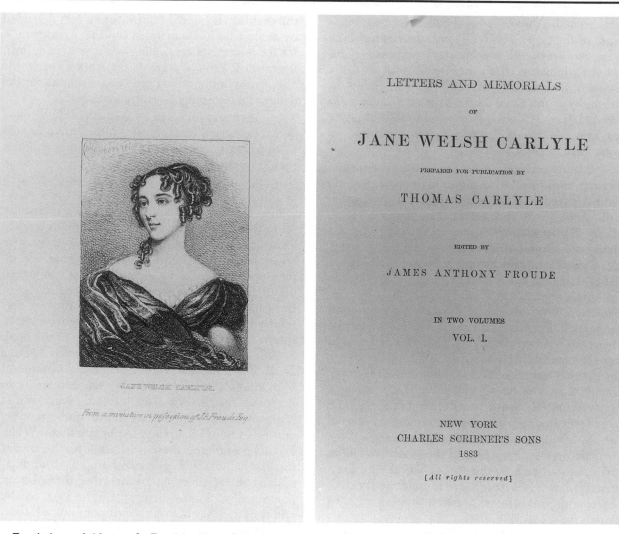

LETTERS AND MEMORIALS

OF

JANE WELSH CARLYLE

PREPARED FOR PUBLICATION BY

THOMAS CARLYLE

EDITED BY

JAMES ANTHONY FROUDE

IN TWO VOLUMES
VOL. I.

NEW YORK
CHARLES SCRIBNER'S SONS
1883

[All rights reserved]

Frontispiece and title page for Froude's edition of the papers that revealed the unhappiness of Thomas Carlyle's wife in her marriage

riage. Jane Welsh had sacrificed her own prospects as a literary personage in favor of her husband's career. Carlyle, focused on himself, had both neglected her and demanded unceasing care from her. When he had read the papers after her death, he had been grieved by what he found there and had implored Froude to publish the papers and Carlyle's own memoir of her as a kind of literary atonement for his neglectfulness.

Carlyle died on 5 February 1881; one month later Froude's edition of Carlyle's memoir, *Reminiscences,* was published. Immediately, controversy broke out. Carlyle's niece, Mary, challenged Froude's possession of and right to publish any of Carlyle's papers, despite Carlyle's will, and demanded a share in the profits from *Reminiscences.* The first two volumes of Froude's biography of Carlyle appeared in 1882, the third and fourth in 1884. The controversy with Mary Carlyle continued as she chal-

lenged what she believed to be Froude's incorrect representation of the Carlyles' marriage as unhappy. The contest was eventually settled out of court; this result prevented Froude from publicly vindicating himself. In 1887 he wrote an explanation of his conduct in the Carlyle affair; it was a private document, written for friends and acquaintances, not for publication. In 1903, nine years after Froude's death, his children had the memoir published as *My Relations with Carlyle* in an attempt to clear their father's name.

The first two volumes of Froude's biography of Carlyle deal with the first forty years of Carlyle's life. Froude wished to present Carlyle as the product of Scottish peasant stock, a devoted son and brother. But on Carlyle's own principle that a biographer should let the subject speak for himself whenever possible, Froude quotes heavily from Carlyle's letters; from the first the letters reveal

Carlyle's demanding and selfish nature. His years of study in Edinburgh were lean ones for the young scholar, although the letters that Froude includes do not suggest any overly harsh or unusual circumstances. Nonetheless, the letters are filled with complaints and irritations of the most minor sort.

Carlyle's friendship with the Reverend Edward Irving fills a great portion of Froude's account of Carlyle's early life. It was through Irving that Carlyle met Jane Welsh; Froude portrays Carlyle's relationship with Welsh as the product of a failed romance between her and Irving that had developed when she was Irving's pupil. According to Froude, Welsh and Irving were prevented from marrying because of an earlier commitment by Irving; Carlyle, in this version, was Welsh's replacement for Irving.

The relationship between Carlyle and his wife proved to be the most controversial aspect of Froude's biography. While he greatly admired Thomas Carlyle, Froude also admired Jane Welsh Carlyle. It was part of his creed as a historian to show whatever evidence he felt was before him, and so Froude portrayed the discord in the Carlyles' marriage the way he had found it in her papers. Froude argued that Jane Welsh Carlyle was a literary genius herself and that she had sacrificed her own talents and ambitions for her husband's benefit. Carlyle was unaware of how his demands had crushed his wife: his own complaints so absorbed his attention that he never noticed her difficulties. Froude makes this situation clear in his description of the years that the Carlyles spent on their Scottish farm, Craigenputtoch. As usual, Carlyle complained about everything connected with the farm, but he had convinced Jane to move there against her wishes. It was, in Froude's opinion, a horribly lonely time for Jane; her health suffered from conditions there and never fully recovered. On the other hand, Carlyle, despite his complaints at the time, later remembered the Craigenputtoch years as one of the happiest periods of his life.

The years from 1834, when the Carlyles moved to London, until Carlyle's death are covered in the last two volumes of Froude's biography. In London Carlyle's relations with Lady Harriet Ashburton, a well-known hostess, were intimate enough to arouse jealousy in Jane Welsh Carlyle and to attract the attention of others. As with all of the sections of Froude's work that suggested anything less than perfect harmony between the Carlyles, the hint of any infamous connection between Carlyle and Lady Ashburton was denounced and denied by Mary Carlyle and her husband, Alexander Carlyle.

Throughout the work Froude attempted, despite his immense admiration for his longtime friend, not to engage in the sort of idealizing biography that Carlyle despised. His contemporaries generally agreed that Froude did not glamorize his subject: he drew a picture of a curmudgeon who was hard to get along with when young and grew more impatient, self-indulgent, and egoistic as he became more famous. Carlyle brooked no disagreement on public issues and held himself aloof from nearly all private engagements. As Carlyle's reputation grew, the man himself seemed to grow smaller and meaner.

The portrait that Froude painted was not a pleasant one, and attacks on the work were immediate and sustained. Alexander and Mary Carlyle found anti-Froude allies in Charles Eliot Norton, David Wilson, and Sir James Crichton-Browne, but Carlyle's acquaintances, siblings, and admirers such as John Ruskin were adamant in their defense of Froude. Modern critics lament the absence of certain details of Carlyle's life; nonetheless, as Froude's own biographer Waldo Hilary Dunn has observed, Froude's biography of Carlyle cannot be superseded. The combination of personal knowledge as well as access to the Carlyles' letters and papers gave Froude an unchallengeable authority on the subject.

In the midst of the Carlyle controversy Froude did a great deal of traveling and writing. In 1881 and 1884 he vacationed in Norway with his son Ashley. In 1885 the two went to Australia, New Zealand, and across the United States from San Francisco to New York; following this tour Froude wrote *Oceana; or, England and Her Colonies* (1886), a description of the British Empire. Afterward he went to the West Indies to develop his theories on federation as a replacement for empire; in 1888 this trip resulted in *The English in the West Indies; or, The Bow of Ulysses*. He produced a novel, *The Two Chiefs of Dunboy* (1889), in which his final views on Irish political matters were most clearly expressed.

In 1889 it was proposed to Froude that he write a series of biographical sketches of Disraeli. Froude had met Disraeli at least once, and the two had exchanged pleasantries over Disraeli's novel *Lothair* (1870). Froude's book on Disraeli, *Lord Beaconsfield,* appeared in 1890.

According to Froude, Disraeli had been a supremely confident youth who picked his fights with care. His political education had culminated with a great attack on the leader of his party, Sir Robert Peel. Froude presents this attack as the product of conviction: Disraeli remained true to his campaign

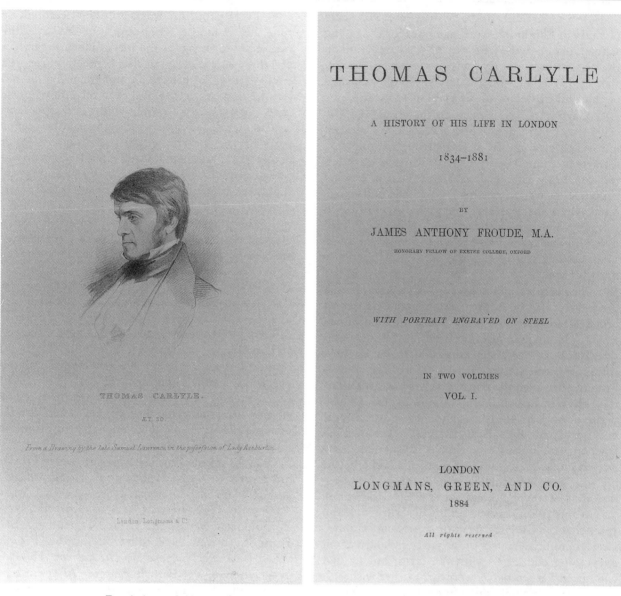

THOMAS CARLYLE

A HISTORY OF HIS LIFE IN LONDON

1834–1881

BY

JAMES ANTHONY FROUDE, M.A.
HONORARY FELLOW OF EXETER COLLEGE, OXFORD

WITH PORTRAIT ENGRAVED ON STEEL

IN TWO VOLUMES
VOL. I.

LONDON
LONGMANS, GREEN, AND CO.
1884

Frontispiece and title page for the second part of Froude's controversial biography of Carlyle

promises, while Peel abandoned his. Disraeli is drawn as ambitious for power, not money; his marriage to the wealthy widow of Wyndham Lewis is described as a perfect business arrangement. There is more of the conservative approach that appeared in *Caesar:* Froude uses Disraeli's life as an opportunity to reiterate his rejection of revolution as well as of any religious practices that could be characterized as superstitious. Disraeli is shown as, simultaneously, an absolute monarchist and a populist, again calling Caesar to mind. As an opposition leader he accomplished little, says Froude, but prevented much harm. Disraeli saw a regenerated aristocracy as the nation's greatest hope. Although he produced no lasting legislation and solved no major

problems, nonetheless, Froude argues, Disraeli was the dominant parliamentary member of his day.

In 1892 Froude's career climaxed in a manner that his friends considered fittingly ironic: he was appointed Regius Professor of Modern History at Oxford, the position that his implacable enemy, Freeman, had held previously. As tradition held that the Regius Professor must praise his predecessor in his inaugural lecture, Froude did so — although lukewarmly.

At Oxford Froude gave a series of twenty lectures on the life and letters of Erasmus. The lectures gave him room to develop the topic that had first brought him to the study of history: what he considered to be the oppressiveness of the pre-Reformation

MY RELATIONS WITH

CARLYLE

BY

JAMES ANTHONY FROUDE

TOGETHER WITH A LETTER FROM THE LATE
SIR JAMES STEPHEN, BART., K.C.S.I.
DATED DECEMBER 9, 1886

LONGMANS, GREEN, AND CO.
39 PATERNOSTER ROW, LONDON
NEW YORK AND BOMBAY
1903

Title page for the posthumous publication of Froude's response to
attacks on him by Carlyle's niece and her husband

Catholic church and the liberating nature of the Reformation. Froude paints the young Erasmus as a clear-minded boy forced into the church against his will by a pair of incompetent and unscrupulous guardians. Freeing himself from the clutches of the church courts, Erasmus traveled about Europe, always on the verge of poverty but unwilling to indenture himself either to the aristocracy or to the church. Erasmus's growth in fame and respect throughout Europe serves as the backdrop for Froude to ruminate on the various corruptions of the church. In Froude's hands Erasmus's life is a tragedy and a holy war: at the outbreak of the Reformation, Erasmus found himself pitted against all the monks of Europe while desperately maintaining against the Lutherans the need to reform the church, not destroy it. The scholar was gradually ground down between the forces of change that he himself had helped to bring into being and the church that, despite its flaws, he believed to be the only true one. At the end of his life Erasmus was partially reconciled at least to the people of the church, if not to the church as an institution.

In the spring of 1894 Froude retired to his home in Salcombe Harbour, Devonshire, where he edited the Erasmus lectures for publication. By the end of the summer he was quite ill and took to his bed; on 18 October he lost consciousness and never regained it, dying on 20 October.

Froude's biases were strong, but that they were not far from the mainstream is evidenced by the tremendous popularity of his books in his own time. Attempts by his critics to replace his biography of Carlyle fell far short. For modern historians and scholars, Froude's intimate knowledge of Carlyle, his reliance on original research, and his clear and straightforward writing style mark his works as valuable, if opinionated, portraits of his time and his contemporaries.

Letters:

John Skelton, *The Table-Talk of Shirley: Reminiscences of and Letters from Froude, Thackeray, Disraeli, Browning, Rossetti, Kingsley, Baynes, Huxley, Tyndall and Others* (Edinburgh & London: Blackwood, 1895);

Raymond M. Bennett, ed., "Letters of James Anthony Froude," *Journal of Rutgers University Library,* 11 (December 1947): 1–15; 12 (June 1949): 38–53; 25 (December 1961): 10–23; 26 (December 1962): 14–22;

The Froude-Ruskin Friendship as Represented Through Letters, edited by Helen Gill Viljoen (New York: Pageant, 1966).

Bibliography:

Robert Goetzman, *James Anthony Froude: A Bibliography of Studies* (New York: Garland, 1977).

Biographies:

Herbert Paul, *The Life of Froude* (London: Pitman, 1905);

Waldo Hilary Dunn, *James Anthony Froude: A Biography,* 2 volumes (Oxford: Clarendon Press, 1961–1963).

References:

Richard D. Altick, *Lives and Letters: A History of Literary Biography in England and America* (New York: Knopf, 1965);

L. M. Angus-Butterworth, *Ten Master Historians* (Aberdeen: Aberdeen University Press, 1961);

Kingsbury Badger, "The Ordeal of Anthony Froude, Protestant Historian," *Modern Language Quarterly,* 13 (March 1952): 41–55;

John Clubbe, "Grecian Destiny: Froude's Portraits of the Carlyles," in *Carlyle and His Contemporaries,* edited by Clubbe (Durham: Duke University Press, 1976), pp. 317–353;

Clubbe, Preface to *Froude's Life of Carlyle,* edited by Clubbe (Columbus: Ohio State University Press, 1979);

A. O. J. Cockshut, *Truth to Life: The Art of Biography in the Nineteenth Century* (London: Collins, 1974);

Waldo Hilary Dunn, *Froude and Carlyle: A Study of the Froude-Carlyle Controversy* (London: Longmans, Green, 1930);

K. J. Fielding, "Froude and Carlyle: Some New Considerations," in *Carlyle Past and Present: A Collection of New Essays,* edited by Fielding and Roger L. Tarr (London: Vision, 1976), pp. 239–269;

Andrew Fish, "The Reputation of James Anthony Froude," *Pacific Historical Review,* 1 (1932): 179–192;

G. P. Gooch, *History and Historians in the Nineteenth Century* (London: Longmans, Green, 1913), pp. 301–316;

Frederic Harrison, *Tennyson, Ruskin, Mill and Other Literary Estimates* (London & New York: Macmillan, 1899);

Gertrude Himmelfarb, "James Anthony Froude: A Forgotten Worthy," in her *Victorian Minds* (New York: Harper & Row, 1970);

Rosemary Jann, *The Art and Science of Victorian History* (Columbus: Ohio State University Press, 1985), pp. 105–140;

Howard Murphy, "The Ethical Revolt Against Christian Orthodoxy in Early Victorian England," *American Historical Review,* 60 (July 1955): 800–817;

Edward Sharples, Jr., "Carlyle and His Readers: The Froude Controversy Once Again," Ph.D. dissertation, University of Rochester, 1964;

Leslie Stephen, *Studies of a Biographer,* 4 volumes (New York: Putnam, 1902);

Lytton Strachey, "Froude," in his *Portraits in Miniature* (New York: Harcourt, Brace, 1931), pp. 191–202;

James Westfall Thompson, *A History of Historical Writing,* 2 volumes (New York: Macmillan, 1942);

Basil Willey, *More Nineteenth Century Studies: A Group of Honest Doubters* (New York: Columbia University Press, 1956).

Papers:

Collections of James Anthony Froude's unpublished correspondence, manuscripts and other materials are at the Beinecke Rare Book and Manuscript Library, Yale University; the Perkins Library, Duke University; the Huntington Library, San Marino, California; the University of Illinois Library at Urbana-Champaign; and the Harry Ransom Humanities Research Center, University of Texas at Austin. Collections of Froude's unpublished correspondence are also at the Bodleian Library, Oxford; the British Library, London; the Lambeth Palace Library, London; the University of Edinburgh Library; and the Tennyson Research Centre, City Library, Lincoln.

Elizabeth Cleghorn Gaskell

(29 September 1810 – 12 November 1865)

Barbara Mitchell
University of Leeds

See also the Gaskell entry in *DLB 21: Victorian Novelists Before 1885.*

BOOKS: *Mary Barton: A Tale of Manchester Life,* anonymous (2 volumes, London: Chapman & Hall, 1848; 1 volume, New York: Harper, 1848);

Libbie Marsh's Three Eras: A Lancashire Tale, as Cotton Mather Mills, Esquire (London: Hamilton, Adams, 1850);

Lizzie Leigh: A Domestic Tale, from "Household Words," attributed to Charles Dickens (New York: De Witt & Davenport, 1850);

The Moorland Cottage, anonymous (London: Chapman & Hall, 1850; Boston: Crosby & Nichols, 1851);

Ruth: A Novel, anonymous (3 volumes, London: Chapman & Hall, 1853; 1 volume, Boston: Ticknor, Reed & Fields, 1853);

Cranford, anonymous (London: Chapman & Hall, 1853; New York: Harper, 1853);

Lizzie Leigh and Other Tales, anonymous (London: Chapman & Hall, 1855; Philadelphia: Hardy, 1869);

Hands and Heart and Bessie's Troubles at Home, anonymous (London: Chapman & Hall, 1855);

North and South, anonymous (2 volumes, London: Chapman & Hall, 1855; 1 volume, New York: Harper, 1855);

The Life of Charlotte Brontë, Author of "Jane Eyre," "Shirley," "Villette," etc., 2 volumes (London: Smith, Elder, 1857; revised, 1857; New York: Appleton, 1857; edited by Alan Shelston, Harmondsworth, U.K.: Penguin, 1975);

My Lady Ludlow: A Novel (New York: Harper, 1858);

My Lady Ludlow and Other Tales (London: Smith, Elder, 1859);

Round the Sofa (London: Low, 1859; London & New York: Oxford University Press, 1913);

Right at Last, and Other Tales (London: Low, 1860; New York: Harper, 1860);

A Dark Night's Work (London: Smith, Elder, 1863; New York: Harper, 1863);

Sylvia's Lovers (3 volumes, London: Smith, Elder, 1863; 1 volume, New York: Dutton, 1863);

Cousin Phillis: A Tale (New York: Harper, 1864);

Cousin Phillis and Other Tales (London: Smith, Elder, 1865);

The Grey Woman and Other Tales (London: Smith, Elder, 1865; Philadelphia: Peterson, 1865);

Wives and Daughters: An Every Day Story (2 volumes, London: Smith, Elder, 1866; 1 volume, New York: Harper, 1866);

"My Diary": The Early Years of My Daughter Marianne (London: Privately printed by Clement Shorter, 1923).

Collections: *The Works of Mrs. Gaskell,* Knutsford Edition, 8 volumes, edited by A. W. Ward (London: Smith, Elder, 1906–1911);

The Novels and Tales of Mrs. Gaskell, 11 volumes, edited by Clement K. Shorter (Oxford: Oxford University Press, 1906–1919).

OTHER: "Clopton House," in *Visits to Remarkable Places, Old Halls, Battlefields, and Scenes Illustrative of Striking Passages in English History and Poetry,* by William Howitt (London: Longmans, 1840).

SELECTED PERIODICAL PUBLICATION – UNCOLLECTED: "Sketches among the Poor," *Blackwood's Edinburgh Magazine,* no. 1 (January 1837): 48–50.

Upon hearing of the death of her friend Charlotte Brontë on 31 March 1855, Elizabeth Cleghorn Gaskell wrote, "I loved her dearly, more than I think she knew. I shall never cease to be thankful that I knew her; or to mourn her loss." It was out of this love and respect for Brontë that Gaskell consented to the Reverend Patrick Brontë's proposal to write a biography of his daughter. In her two-volume *The Life of Charlotte Brontë* (1857) Gaskell

Elizabeth Cleghorn Gaskell, circa 1864 (reproduction of a painting by Samuel Lawrence used as a frontispiece for a volume of the Knutsford Edition of Gaskell's works; location of original unknown)

hoped, she said, to give "a right understanding of the life of [her] dear friend" to that "solemn public who know . . . how to admire . . . genius, and how to reverence . . . virtue." *The Life of Charlotte Brontë* remains unparalleled for its intimate, moving, and authentic telling of Brontë's life story. It was Gaskell's only biography, and it has the distinction of being the only biography written about Brontë by someone who had known her.

Elizabeth Cleghorn Stevenson was born on 29 September 1810 in Lindsey Row, Chelsea. Her father, William Stevenson, had been a Unitarian minister; but in 1797 he had resigned from the ministry and taken up farming under the direction of his friend, James Cleghorn, after whom his daughter was named. In the same year he had married Elizabeth Holland, from Sandlebridge in Cheshire. They had eight children, but only John, born in 1798, and Elizabeth survived.

The farm failed in 1801, and William Stevenson moved to Edinburgh, where he wrote newspa-

per and magazine reviews. He became editor of *Scots Magazine* in 1803. In 1804 he moved to London, where he held the post of Keeper of the Treasury Records until he died. He also contributed articles on agriculture, commerce, and navigation to various newspapers and magazines.

Mrs. Stevenson died when Elizabeth was thirteen months old, and Elizabeth was taken in by an aunt, Mrs. Lumb, in Knutsford. Knutsford was to appear in many of Gaskell's stories and novels. She would stay there for the next twelve or thirteen years and would frequently return later for respite from the turmoil of her life: "I am so much better for Knutsford — partly air, partly quiet and partly being by myself a good piece of every day."

William Stevenson remarried when Elizabeth was four. He visited Elizabeth only occasionally, and Elizabeth appeared to be unhappy when visiting him and his new wife. Although there are similarities between Gaskell's childhood and that of her subject, Brontë — they were both motherless, brought up in the north, and of a somewhat nervous temperament – Gaskell's life appears to have been more stable and happy than Brontë's.

Elizabeth attended school at Warwickshire from 1821 to 1826, first at Barford House near Warwick, then at Avonback in Stratford-upon-Avon. She also spent time in London with her father, who taught her languages, which she was later to put to good use in her travels on the Continent. After leaving school she spent most of her time at Knutsford "studying on her own," according to her recent biographer, Jenny Uglow. Her father died in 1829, and for two years she moved among relatives and friends in London, Newcastle, and Edinburgh. On a visit to Manchester in 1831 she met the Reverend William Gaskell; five years older than Elizabeth, he had been a minister at Cross Street Unitarian Chapel since 1828. They were married on 30 August 1832 in Knutsford. Outside of his pastoral duties William Gaskell was a lecturer in English literature at Manchester New College and then at the Workingmen's College, wrote articles and hymns, translated sacred verse, and served on civic committees. He took an interest in his wife's work, frequently correcting her manuscripts; she helped him with his lectures and did relief work among the poor.

Gaskell had a lively, generous, affectionate personality; her biographer Winifred Gérin describes her as having "a special quality of radiance" that made even the most shy, such as Brontë, feel comfortable with her. Gérin quotes Gaskell's friend Susanna Winkworth's initial impression of Gaskell: "she seemed always surrounded by an atmosphere of ease, leisure, and playful geniality, that drew out the best side of everyone who was in her company. When you were with her, you felt as if you had twice the life in you that you had at ordinary times."

The Gaskells had six children between 1833 and 1846. Their first child was stillborn, and their only son died of scarlet fever when he was ten, but four girls survived. Gaskell was a devoted mother – she wrote only occasionally during the early years of her marriage, but not for publication (for example, *"My Diary": The Early Years of My Daughter Marianne,* which was published posthumously in 1923). It was to overcome the death of her son in 1845 that she began writing seriously.

His death scarred her permanently; to this event has been linked what her biographer Annette Brown Hopkins calls "her preoccupation with death and other forms of disaster," and certainly arising from it is her great empathy for Brontë's grief over the deaths of her four sisters and brother.

Gaskell's first novel, *Mary Barton,* was published anonymously on 25 October 1848 and concerned the conflict between mill workers and owners. It was well received in literary circles, but the conservative press felt that Gaskell had presented a distorted picture by siding entirely with the laborers against the employers. Against these accusations she defended herself in a late-1848 letter in much the same way as she was to defend herself against accusations that *The Life of Charlotte Brontë* was not entirely true: "I can only say that I wanted to represent the subject in the light in which some of the workmen certainly consider to be *true,* not that I dare to say it is the abstract absolute truth." Gaskell worked from what she called "personal evidence." *Mary Barton* launched Gaskell's writing career, and she was soon invited by Charles Dickens to contribute to his new periodical, *Household Words.* She would write more than twenty-five stories and three serialized novels for the magazine.

Gaskell's first introduction to Brontë was through Brontë's novels *Jane Eyre* (1847) and *Shirley* (1849). Gaskell expressed uneasiness about both books, although she described them as "uncommon" and "wonderful." Mostly, like many other readers in England, she was curious about the identity of the writer, and when she received a copy of *Shirley* she wrote a letter of praise to Brontë's pseudonym, "Currer Bell." This letter is not extant, but Brontë's reaction to it is recorded in a letter to her editor. Gaskell's note "brought tears to my eyes. She is a good, she is a great woman. Proud I am that I can touch a chord of sympathy in souls so noble."

When the friendship between Brontë and Gaskell began, Brontë had just suffered the loss of her last sibling, Anne, and was alone in the parsonage at Haworth with her seventy-two-year-old father. Finding a replacement, both intellectual and emotional, for her writer sisters could not have occurred at a more fortunate time. Gaskell identified with Brontë's grief, having been motherless herself and having lost two children. Although she wrote to a friend on 14 May 1850 that she was "half amused to find you think I could do [Brontë] good," this objective seems to have been part of her impulse to form the friendship. Certainly it is the impetus behind *The Life of Charlotte Brontë,* which was written to make Brontë, as Gaskell says in a 23 December 1848 letter, "valued as one who had gone through such a terrible life." Curiosity and an instinct for a fascinating life story were also part of Gaskell's initial attraction. Although the two women discussed

Number 84, Plymouth Grove, Gaskell's home in Manchester

literary issues, Gaskell was primarily drawn to Brontë as a person rather than as an author. Indeed, Gaskell wrote in the 14 May 1850 letter that she was more interested in *Shirley* for "the glimpses one gets of" Brontë than for the story itself.

The five meetings between the two friends — in August 1850, June 1851, April 1853, September 1853, and May 1854 — are documented in *The Life of Charlotte Brontë*. Gaskell wrote long letters to friends describing the visits, and she incorporates portions of these letters in her biography, thus re-creating the freshness of initial impression. There were fundamental differences between the two women in writing styles, subject matter, temperament, and beliefs; after their first meeting Gaskell wrote to Charlotte Froude, circa 25 August 1850, "She and I quarrelled & differed about almost every thing, — she calls me a democrat & can not bear Tennyson — but we like each other heartily. . . . and I hope we shall ripen into friends." During these visits Gaskell heard many of the sad details of Brontë's life; after the first visit she wrote on 25 August 1850 to Catherine Winkeworth, "Such a life as Miss Brontë's I never heard of before. . . . " Gaskell was able to observe Brontë's interaction with female friends, male visitors, children, and her father. They also engaged in conversations about religion, superstition, writing, and marriage. At the end of 1852 Brontë was proposed to by Arthur Bell Nicholls, her fa-

ther's curate. She was unsure of her love for him, and her father was adamantly opposed to the marriage. This period was fraught with emotional crises for Brontë. Finally, in April 1854 she and Nicholls announced their engagement, and during Brontë's last visit with Gaskell matters of the heart were discussed fairly openly. Gaskell's portrait, which emphasizes Charlotte's nervous and somber temperament, reflects this period. But it is too simple to say that Gaskell saw only the tragic side of Brontë's life. During Gaskell's only visit to Haworth, in September 1853, the two women spent hours walking over the moors and talking before the fire. Gaskell balances the happy and the sad in her recollection of the visit: "Copying this letter has brought the days of that pleasant visit very clear to me, — very sad in their clearness. We were so happy together; we were so full of interest in each other's subjects. . . . I understood her life the better for seeing the place where it had been spent — where she had loved and suffered."

Brontë died on 31 March 1855. On 31 May Gaskell wrote to George Smith, Brontë's publisher, that she was thinking of writing some years hence a memoir of Brontë to "publish what I know of her, and make the world (if I am but strong enough in expression,) honour the woman as much as they have admired the writer." On 16 June Mr. Brontë wrote to Gaskell asking her to write "a brief account of [Charlotte's] life." This request had been precipitated by a letter from Charlotte's longtime friend Ellen Nussey to Mr. Brontë complaining that various writers were reporting inaccurately on Brontë's life and suggesting that Gaskell was the person best qualified to set the record right. After weighing the offer for two days, Gaskell accepted "this grave duty."

It was not unusual for a friend or relative to undertake a biography in this era; John Forster wrote a life of his friend Dickens (1872, 1874) and John Walter Cross wrote a biography of his wife, George Eliot (1885). Portraying the subject in a flattering light and writing an interesting narrative were goals of the Victorian biographer; while truth was not disregarded and faults could be pointed out, Victorian biographers subscribed to an unspoken code of ethics that involved decorum and propriety. Gaskell unabashedly admitted in an 18 June 1855 letter to Smith that with Nicholls and Mr. Brontë still living she would have to "omit a good deal of detail as to [Brontë's] home, and . . . circumstances. . . . "

The correspondence for the years from 1855 to August 1857, when the revised third edition of the biography came out, illustrates the tireless dedication with which Gaskell attacked the project. In a 26 December 1856 letter to Smith she says, "the amount of labour bestowed on the Biography, (to say nothing of anxiety in various ways,) has been more than double at least what the novel [*North and South*, 1855] cost me." Although sometimes called — by her and her contemporaries — a memoir, the work is much more than the rambling selection of personal reminiscences that Gaskell had first thought of writing. Gaskell wanted to honor, not flatter, and she set out to give a "right understanding," not a personal testimony. By Victorian standards *The Life of Charlotte Brontë* is well researched. Gaskell visited nearly every location where Brontë had been; she interviewed not just the accessible, obvious people, such as Mr. Brontë, Nicholls, and Nussey, but also traveled to London to interview Smith and to Brussels to interview Brontë's tutor, Constantin Heger. She was allowed access to Nussey's correspondence with Brontë — about 350 letters — and obtained letters from others, such as William Smith Williams, Brontë's editor at Smith, Elder and Company.

She attempted, as she said, to ascertain the truth, not simply record what Brontë had told her. For example, Gaskell was quite aware that Lowood — the school in *Jane Eyre* — and the Clergy Daughters' School at Cowan Bridge were not identical and that Brontë's memories of the school might not have been accurate, so she visited the school, obtained records, interviewed a member of the staff and some of the former pupils, and attempted to locate the real Miss Temple. Although Gaskell was criticized at the time (and even now) for confusing fact and fiction in this section, Margaret Lane, in her corrective biography, writes that "it does not seem that [Gaskell] has been seriously unjust" in her assessment of this episode.

A personal-relationship biography carries significant weight, both negative and positive. To offset her own presence in the work, Gaskell chose to let Brontë be her own biographer through profuse use of her letters. In this respect Gaskell was following others, such as William Mason in his biography of Thomas Gray (1775) and John Gibson Lockhart in his work on his father-in-law, Sir Walter Scott (1837–1838). In the first half of the biography Gaskell had fewer letters and had to fill in Brontë's early history; but in the second half, as she wrote to Smith on 19 August 1856, she let Brontë express everything as much as possible "in her own words" because "her language . . . is so powerful & living." An inherent problem in this technique is that the personality revealed in a letter tends to vary according to the recipient; in this case the recipient was Nussey, a serious, pious, martyrish woman with little interest in the arts. The "self" that Brontë chose to reveal to Nussey was only one of her many selves, but because those letters dominate the biography, so, too, does that "self" — the dutiful and often despondent Brontë. Readers have to be acute to notice the changes in temper portrayed in the few letters to Smith, Williams, Miss Wooler, and Gaskell herself. Although Gaskell was aware of this phenomenon — she wrote in a 15 December 1855 letter to Williams that "it is curious how much the spirit in which she wrote varies according to the correspondent whom she was addressing" — she does not remark on it in her biography. Modern critics tend to criticize Gaskell for what Katharine Frank calls "didactic" or "novelistic vision" in presenting Brontë as a tragic, suffering "heroine"; this view is, however, not simply imposed by Gaskell. Although largely a result of Gaskell's heavy dependence on the Brontë-Nussey correspondence which drew out the suffering and dutiful side of Brontë's character, this view reflects the social and cultural values of the Victorian period and is inherent in Brontë's own language.

The view of Brontë as a divided personality is a common one, although Gaskell, unlike more-recent biographers, mentions it only to avoid discussing it. Here she did have a predetermined thesis. Gaskell writes: "Charlotte Brontë's existence becomes divided into two parallel currents – her life as Currer Bell, the author; her life as Charlotte Brontë, the woman. There were separate duties belonging to each character – not opposing each other; not impossible, but difficult to be reconciled." Later biographers deal with this division as a crisis of creativity or a feminist struggle, but Gaskell decided to separate the woman from the author and concentrate on the former. In part, she did not think it her responsibility to engage in literary analysis, but she was also uncomfortable with Brontë's creative self. Unable to deal with the intense passion of Brontë's fiction (called "coarseness" by some Victorian reviewers of the day), Gaskell attempted to excuse it by saying that it arose "not from the imagination – not from internal conception – but from hard, cruel facts, pressed down, by external life. . . ." Although Gaskell writes that she "cannot measure or judge of such a character as hers . . . cannot map out vices, and virtues," it is mainly the vices that she finds difficult to discuss. Gaskell shows herself sensitive to many forces in Brontë's life, such as her physical environment, religion, and family, but can only speak in veiled terms of Brontë's creative energy, with its focus on passion.

The writer Charles Kingsley was so moved by Gaskell's biography, which, he said, presented a "valiant woman made perfect by suffering," that he began to read Brontë's works. But Gaskell did not make Brontë "perfect." She revered Brontë for her genius, her intelligence, her sense of duty, and her fortitude; but she points out, sometimes with a hint of frustration, Brontë's early "wild weird writing," which ran "to the very borders of apparent delirium"; her later "coarseness," which Gaskell calls "mistakes"; her inability to control her shyness, her hopelessness, and her fear of "loving too much" – which led her to restrain her own feelings.

Gaskell says in a July 1855 letter to Smith that her goal was to tell Brontë's story "distinct and delicate and thoroughly well," which suggests that she was concerned about technique as well as fact. She uses strategies she employed in her fiction, such as anecdote, vivid and poetically descriptive scenes, contrast, and emotional appeal. Gaskell's gift for describing landscape is notable in both her fiction and her biography. Such passages are more than backdrops, for she believed that environment influenced character. In the first chapter of the biography Gaskell suggests that the distant "sinuous wave-like hills" of Yorkshire and the view of the Haworth main street, which is like a "wall," affect the mind,

creating an "oppressive" and "monotonous" mental state, a feeling of an "illimitable barrier." Gaskell leads the reader through this landscape into the graveyard, "terribly full of upright tombstones," and finally into the church – at which point, with an absolutely right sense of the power of simplicity, she records without comment the inscriptions on the memorials to all the dead Brontës, ending with Charlotte's, which is set apart from the others. It is a memorable beginning, evoking disaster and death.

At the basis of Gaskell's landscape descriptions is the implicit contrast between the wildness of the moors and the order of the parsonage or of the cultivated world of London and Brussels – a contrast that supports her thesis of a woman divided between lawlessness and moral purpose. Describing Emily and Charlotte in Brussels for the first time, she exclaims, "What a contrast to ["the wild Yorkshire village"] must the Belgian capital have presented to those two young women . . . !" One such predilection for contrast got her into trouble: writing to Smith on 26 December 1856 about Branwell's involvement with Mrs. Lydia Robinson, she says, "I put that in [that Mrs. Robinson was enjoying London high society] . . . to point the contrast of her life, & Branwell's death." Obviously, in this instance, she was less concerned with the laws of libel than she was with the techniques of narration. She had just written *North and South,* a novel whose theme is contrast, and that preoccupation carried over into *The Life of Charlotte Brontë.* Contrast as a dramatic device did not, however, necessarily distort truth. The moors, although primarily seen as wild, dark, and lawless, are recognized, as well, as the Brontës' "true home," rich with heather and radiant in the sunlight.

With an eye and ear finely tuned to the emotional content of pictorial vignettes and anecdote, Gaskell creates many moving moments. The ending of the biography, like the beginning, evokes a strong emotional response with its return to the images of parsonage, church, and tombstone that were announced in the opening chapter: "Early on Saturday morning, March 31st, the solemn tolling of the Haworth church-bell spoke forth the fact of her death to the villagers who had known her from a child, and whose hearts shivered within them as they thought of the two [Mr. Brontë and Nicholls] sitting desolate and alone in the old grey house."

Gaskell collected anecdotes from villagers and servants who recalled the deaths of Branwell, Emily, and Anne. Charlotte herself told Gaskell of one poignant moment as Emily neared death; Gaskell immortalized it in her retelling, with Charlotte's

Page from the manuscript for Gaskell's The Life of Charlotte Brontë *(from Annette Brown Hopkins,* Elizabeth Gaskell: Her Life and Work, *1952)*

helplessness at her sister's death deftly underscored by the break in the rhythm of words: "I remember Miss Brontë's shiver at recalling the pang she felt when, after having searched in the little hollows and sheltered crevices of the moors for a lingering spray of heather – just one spray, however withered – to take in to Emily, she saw that the flower was not recognized by the dim and indifferent eyes."

The Life of Charlotte Brontë was finished on 7 February 1857, and Gaskell left for a holiday in Rome on 13 February. She was worn down by the concentrated writing, and as she usually did when one of her works was published, she wanted to escape the reviews. The biography came out on 25 March. The reviews were generally good, and both Mr. Brontë and Nussey seemed pleased with it. Mr. Brontë protested only "a few trifling mistakes," and a few months later he wrote Gaskell with high words of praise: "And my opinion and the reading World's opinion of the 'Memoir,' is that it is every way worthy of what one Great Woman should have written of Another, and that it ought to stand, and will stand, in the first rank of Biographies till the end of time. . . ." Henry Chorley in the *Athenaeum* (4 April 1857) called the book a "work of Art" and repeated, at the beginning and at the conclusion of his review, that Gaskell had "produced one of the best biographies of a woman by a woman." Other reviews were equally positive. George Henry Lewes called the book "exquisite," writing Gaskell on 15 April 1857 that "the early part is a triumph for you; the rest a monument for your friend." Eliot admitted to crying over it and wrote to a friend on 16 April 1857 that "Mrs. Gaskell has done her work admirably, both in the industry and care with which she has gathered and selected her material, and in the feeling with which she has presented it." She does, however, criticize Gaskell for weakening "the effect of philippics against the woman who hurried on [Branwell's] utter fall" by attributing "Branwell's conduct entirely to remorse" rather than to "germs of vice" long since present.

Mrs. Robinson, who by then had married Sir Edward Dolman Scott, soon had these "philippics" brought to her attention. She heard that she had been identified in the biography as the "wretched woman" who had seduced Branwell Brontë, and she threatened a libel suit. None of this news reached Gaskell until she picked up her mail in Paris when she was en route home at the end of May. On 30 May William Gaskell – in the name of his wife, who was still away – was forced to print a public retraction of material concerning "a certain widowed lady." On 6 June the *Athenaeum* printed an editorial retracting its praise of Elizabeth Gaskell as "an accurate collector of facts" and insisted that the book be withdrawn and modified. On 16 June – exactly two years after Mr. Brontë's proposal that she write the biography – Gaskell wrote Nussey "I am in the Hornet's nest with a vengeance."

The "Hornet's nest" involved three major issues, and even today the controversy surrounding them has not been resolved. The first was Gaskell's treatment of the former Mrs. Robinson. Branwell, when a tutor for the Robinsons' son, had fallen in love with Mrs. Robinson and had been dismissed by her husband, the Reverend Edmund Robinson. Branwell hoped that his love would be reciprocated when Mr. Robinson died less than two years later, but he was rejected by Mrs. Robinson. This rejection, in Gaskell's opinion, caused Branwell's rapid decline, his abuse of opium and alcohol, and, because of their distress over his condition, the "premature deaths" of Emily and Anne. While she did not name the woman in question, Gaskell called her "depraved" and "wretched." Gaskell had been aware that this situation was potentially libelous; after a warning from Smith she had attempted to conceal the woman's identity even further. Although most critics believe that Gaskell was fundamentally correct in her assessment of the affair, she was certainly not discreet, and the reason would seem to be that she allowed her novelist side to exploit the situation. Furthermore, she was able to use the incident to imply that Charlotte's "coarseness" was a result of *what she had to bear; and what she had to hear,* as she said in a 6 June 1857 letter to Kingsley.

Equally contentious were Gaskell's comments on the Reverend William Carus Wilson, who administered the Clergy Daughters' School. Gaskell acknowledges in the biography that Brontë may have taken "her conception of the truth for the absolute truth" and that it is difficult to sort out the evidence and "arrive at the truth." Nevertheless, Gaskell asserts that Wilson "certainly committed" errors, that he loved "authority," and that he ruthlessly lectured the children "on the sin of caring over-much for carnal things," thereby excusing the substandard food and sanitation at the school. Although she concludes that Brontë presented only one side in *Jane Eyre* and that Wilson did have a "noble and conscientious" side, Wilson and his son threatened a libel suit. A debate over the school took place in the newspapers, with letters from Wilson, from former students and from Nicholls who adamantly defended his wife's and Gaskell's position. When Gaskell rewrote this section for the

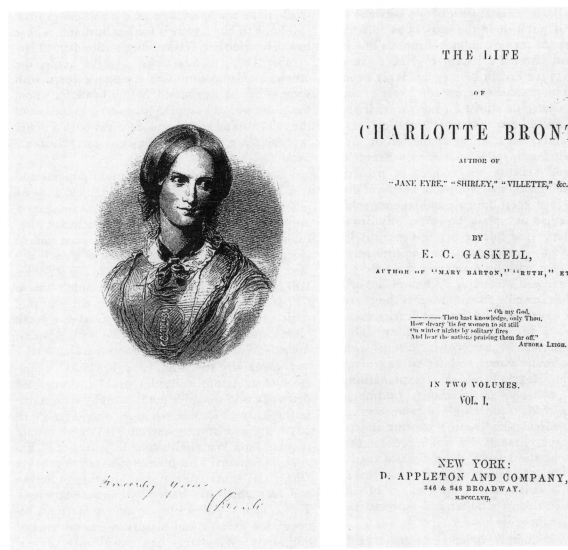

THE LIFE

OF

CHARLOTTE BRONTË,

AUTHOR OF

"JANE EYRE," "SHIRLEY," "VILLETTE," &c.

BY

E. C. GASKELL,

AUTHOR OF "MARY BARTON," "RUTH," ETC.

" Oh my God.
———— Thou hast knowledge, only Thou,
How dreary 'tis for women to sit still
On winter nights by solitary fires
And hear the nations praising them far off."
AURORA LEIGH.

IN TWO VOLUMES.
VOL. I.

NEW YORK:
D. APPLETON AND COMPANY,
346 & 348 BROADWAY.
M.DCCC.LVII.

Frontispiece and title page for Gaskell's only biography

third edition, she withdrew some of the more critical personal comments and also said that she had only heard Brontë refer to the school on one occasion. Gaskell had gleaned some of her information from *Jane Eyre,* although she had attempted to corroborate it by testimony from a laundress and some of Brontë's former fellow pupils. It seems quite clear that Gaskell, as she herself asserted in the 16 June 1857 letter to Nussey, "*did so try* to *tell the truth*"; and Alan Shelston notes in his edition of *The Life of Charlotte Brontë* (1975) that most of her accusations as to "the harshness of the regimen" and problems of sanitation have been "verified."

The third major issue was the question of Mr. Brontë's eccentricities. Although at first he called them only "trifling mistakes," he asked Gaskell to remove from the third edition the instances of his refusing meat to the children, sawing up chairs, burning the hearth rug, and cutting up his wife's silk gown. Some of these anecdotes Gaskell apparently got from a nurse who had been discharged, and they may have been exaggerated or misinterpreted; but the Haworth villagers supported this view of Mr. Brontë's eccentric personality, and he never denied most of the stories. Gaskell maintained that Charlotte told her the story about the silk gown and that it was verified by Nussey and another friend.

A fourth issue – the most controversial of all – did not surface until years after Gaskell's death. It concerned Gaskell's handling of Brontë's two years in Brussels and her affection for her tutor, Heger. Although as early as 1877 Brontë's next biographer, T. Wemyss Reid, implied that her novel

Villette (1853), with its story of love between a tutor and his pupil, held the answer as to why Brussels was the turning point in Brontë's life, it was not until Brontë's letters to Heger were turned over to the British Library by Heger's son in 1913 that biographers were made aware of the strength of Charlotte's love for her tutor. It appears that Gaskell knew of the circumstances, saw the letters, and chose to cover up the "affair" because she felt that it reflected badly on Brontë's character and because she wanted to protect Heger. Gaskell manipulated portions of two of the four letters to suggest only a pupil-teacher relationship. She had to explain, however, why Brontë was so depressed during her last months in Brussels and why she returned home so suddenly; she did so primarily by distorting the time sequence of Branwell's troubles. Although Gaskell emphasized Branwell's deterioration as the cause for Brontë's return, she did mention "various reasons" such as Mr. Brontë's failing eyesight, Brontë's homesickness, her growing disgust with the Catholic environment, and her estrangement from Madame Heger. While these explanations were not entirely falsifications (although Branwell's and Mr. Brontë's illnesses were exaggerated), by eliminating Brontë's growing attachment to Heger, Gaskell did not represent the whole truth as she knew it. The aims of truth, confidentiality, and honor clashed in this case, and Gaskell's sensitivity to the feelings of the Hegers and to Brontë's father and husband exacted some compromise.

The Life of Charlotte Brontë came at the midpoint of Gaskell's career. The works she wrote afterward – five novels and thirteen stories – were apolitical and unprovocative, unlike the social novels of her first period. The biography no doubt made her wary about dealing with topical events, but it also increased her understanding of the complexity of character. *Sylvia's Lovers* (1863) deals with unfulfilled love and martyrish suffering, and its sad, passionate tone seems to echo Brontë's life.

Gaskell considered writing a biography of Marquise de Sévigné, whose correspondence with her daughter during the period of Louis XIV charmed her, but it never materialized. She continued to be busy with her family and social duties, including the tireless relief work she and her daughters did for the impoverished cotton workers in 1862–1863. In this period Gaskell showed great maturity and control in her writing, and many judge *Wives and Daughters* (1866), her last

work, to be her finest. She used the earnings from this book to buy a retreat for her husband, whose health worried her. Gaskell died on Sunday, 12 November 1865, at her newly bought home, the Lawn, in Hampshire. She had gone there with some of her family (but not her husband, for whom the house was to be a present) to tend to the last of the refurnishing and to rest. She was buried in her favorite place, Knutsford, in a modest, private funeral.

In her lifetime her fiction was popular and well received, although she never achieved the intellectual brilliance of Eliot nor the passionate energy of the Brontës. As a classic of Victorian biography, *The Life of Charlotte Brontë* has been ranked alongside Lockhart's *Memoirs of the Life of Sir Walter Scott, Bart.* (1837–1838), Forster's *The Life of Dickens* (1872–1874), and James Anthony Froude's *Thomas Carlyle* (1884). Clement Shorter, an early Brontë critic, even wrote in 1896 that Gaskell's work "commands a place side by side with [James] Boswell's *The Life of Samuel Johnson* [LL.D., 1791]."

Generally speaking, though, Gaskell scholars such as Arthur Pollard, Coral Lansbury, and Angus Easson consider the biography more satisfactory than do Brontë scholars, who judge it primarily for its historical veracity. Although Brontë scholar Tom Winnifrith calls it "a classic of English biography," he blames Gaskell for being "the prime source of the fatal blurring of fiction and fact which has bedevilled Brontë studies." This comment points out the uneasy marriage between the literary and historical components of biography. Whatever their position, however, every biographer of Brontë acknowledges the force of Gaskell's work.

The Life of Charlotte Brontë, begun with such honorable intentions, ended in a "hornet's nest" of claims of defamation and threatened libel suits. At the height of the controversy Gaskell wrote to Nussey, "I *did so try* to *tell the truth,* & I believe *now* I hit as near the truth as any one *could* do. And I weighed every line with all my whole power & heart, so that every line should go to it's great purpose of making *her* known & valued, as one who had gone through such a terrible life with a brave & faithful heart." The subtle proviso in her statement is significant: she told the story as truthfully as anyone could – at that time, in that place, given the circumstances of living relatives and given the implicit Victorian code of ethics; for what is missing one has to look ahead 110 years to Gérin's biography. But the richness of incident and emotion that makes *The Life of Charlotte*

Brontë so enduring is a testament to Gaskell's sympathy with people, power of observation, and love of storytelling.

Letters:
The Letters of Mrs. Gaskell and Charles Eliot Norton: 1855–1865, edited by Jane Revere Whitehill (London: Humphrey Milford, Oxford University Press, 1932);

The Letters of Mrs. Gaskell, edited by J. A. V. Chapple and Arthur Pollard (Manchester, U.K.: Manchester University Press, 1966).

Bibliographies:
R. L. Selig, *Elizabeth Gaskell: A Reference Guide* (Boston: G. K. Hall, 1977);

Jeffrey Welch, *Elizabeth Gaskell: An Annotated Bibliography, 1929–75* (New York: Garland, 1977).

Biographies:
Mrs. Ellis H. Chadwick, *Mrs. Gaskell: Haunts, Homes and Stories* (London: Pitman, 1910);

Elizabeth Haldane, *Mrs. Gaskell and Her Friends* (London: Hodder & Stoughton, 1931);

Annette Brown Hopkins, *Elizabeth Gaskell: Her Life and Work* (London: Lehmann, 1952; New York: Octagon, 1971);

Arthur Pollard, *Mrs. Gaskell: Novelist and Biographer* (Manchester, U.K.: Manchester University Press, 1966);

Winifred Gérin, *Elizabeth Gaskell: A Biography* (Oxford: Clarendon Press, 1976);

Jenny Uglow, *Elizabeth Gaskell: A Habit of Stories* (London: Faber & Faber, 1993).

References:
James Donald Barry, "Elizabeth Cleghorn Gaskell," in *Victorian Fiction: A Second Guide to Research,* edited by George H. Ford (New York: MLA, 1978);

P. Beer, *Reader, I Married Him. . . .* (London: Macmillan, 1974);

W. A. Craik, *Elizabeth Gaskell and the English Provincial Novel* (London: Methuen, 1975);

Waldo Dunn, *English Biography* (London: Dent, 1916);

Angus Easson, *Elizabeth Gaskell* (London: Routledge & Kegan Paul, 1979);

George Eliot, *The George Eliot Letters,* 9 volumes, edited by Gordon S. Haight (New Haven: Yale University Press, 1954–1955, 1978);

Katharine Frank, "The Brontë Biographies," *biography,* 2 (Spring 1979): 141–156;

Margaret Ganz, *Elizabeth Gaskell: The Artist in Conflict* (New York: Twayne, 1969);

Margaret Lane, *The Brontë Story: A Reconsideration of Mrs. Gaskell's Life of Charlotte Brontë* (London: Heinemann, 1953);

Coral Lansbury, *Elizabeth Gaskell: The Novel of Social Crisis* (London: Elek, 1975; New York: Barnes & Noble, 1975);

J. Lucas, "Mrs. Gaskell and Brotherhood," in *Tradition and Tolerance in Nineteenth Century Fiction,* by D. Howard, J. Lucas, and J. Goode (London: Routledge & Kegan Paul, 1966);

Ira Bruce Nadel, *Biography: Fiction, Fact & Form* (London: Macmillan, 1984);

Margot Peters, "Biographies of Women," *biography,* 2 (Summer 1979): 201–217;

John Geoffrey Sharps, *Mrs. Gaskell's Observation and Invention: A Study of Her Non-Biographic Works* (London: Linden Press, 1970);

Edgar Wright, *Mrs. Gaskell, the Basis for Reassessment* (London: Oxford University Press, 1965).

Papers:
The Brotherton Collection at the Leeds University Library is a major repository of Elizabeth Cleghorn Gaskell's documents and letters. Other important collections are in Manchester, U.K., at the Manchester University Library, the Central Library, and the John Rylands Library. The Brontë Parsonage Museum at Haworth holds material relating to *The Life of Charlotte Brontë.* Harvard University Library holds important letters and annotated editions of *The Life of Charlotte Brontë.*

Alexander Gilchrist

(25 April 1828 – 30 November 1861)

Glyn Pursglove
University College of Swansea

BOOKS: *Life of William Etty, R.A.,* 2 volumes (London: Bogue, 1855);

Life of William Blake, "Pictor Ignotus": With Selections from His Poems and Other Writings, 2 volumes (London & Cambridge: Macmillan, 1863); enlarged as *Life of William Blake* (2 volumes, London & Cambridge: Macmillan, 1880; edited by Ruthven Todd, 1 volume, London: Lane / New York: Dutton, 1942).

Alexander Gilchrist's *Life of William Blake, "Pictor Ignotus"* (1863) effected a critical reassessment far beyond that which most biographies have ever occasioned. The book's subtitle, which means "unknown painter," was only a slight exaggeration. Blake may not have been completely unknown, but it was only with the publication of Gilchrist's biography that, as G. E. Bentley, Jr., says, "Blake at last took his place in literary and artistic history as one of the great figures of the Romantic movement." Gilchrist's *Life of William Blake* began the scholarly and critical interest in Blake that has continued unabated for more than a century. Naturally, there are aspects of the book that now appear inadequate and dated; yet those limitations have only become evident because of later work that Gilchrist himself inspired and made possible.

The sixth of seven children, Gilchrist was born on 25 April 1828 in London. His father, James Gilchrist, the posthumous son of a Scottish farmer, had been able, with the financial assistance of relatives, to study at the University of Edinburgh; he had become a minister in the Presbyterian sect known as the General Baptists, and his work as a missionary preacher had brought him to England. He was a deep and independent thinker on metaphysics and philology; his publications include *The Labyrinth Demolished; or, The Pioneer of Rational Philology* (1815) and *Philosophic Etymology: A Rational Grammar* (1816), as well as several works on theological matters; he also contributed to the *Encyclopædia Britannica.* He grew increasingly unhappy in his work as a minister, more and more uneasy at the dogmatism and ignorance that characterized many of his coreligionists. After a period of illness, which his widow was later to describe as "an attack of brain-fever," he resigned his ministry in 1829 and rented a water mill on a curve of the Thames in the village of Mapledurham, west of Reading. Alexander Gilchrist grew up in this quiet and beautiful country setting, a constant companion of his father as the latter went about his business. James Gilchrist was no businessman, and the enterprise failed. An unidentified wasting illness killed him at the age of fifty-two, and Alexander Gilchrist's brief country idyll was over. In straitened circumstances, the family returned to London.

Between the ages of twelve and sixteen Gilchrist went to London University College School. He then took up the study of law, entering the Middle Temple as a student in 1846. He was called to the bar in 1849; but by then he had conceived a desire for a literary career, and he never practiced law. His success was far from immediate; he was never a rapid or facile worker, and his early work cost him a great deal of effort. Only slowly did he develop a lucid manner of exposition.

His earliest patron was Thomas Price, the editor of the *Eclectic Review,* to which Gilchrist contributed many reviews of poetry, exhibitions, and books on art. In 1849 he contributed an essay on the painter William Etty; it was reprinted in pamphlet form and prompted a commission from the publisher David Bogue to write *Life of William Etty, R.A.* (1855). In February 1851 he married Anne Burrows, whom he had known for three years. They would have four children: Percy Carlyle, born on 27 December 1851; Beatrice Carwardine, born on 18 September 1854; Herbert Harlakenden, born on 18 March 1857; and Grace, born on 16 January 1859. Anne Gilchrist was herself an able scholar; her own later publications would include *A Woman's Estimate of Walt Whitman* (1870) and *Mary Lamb* (1883). Soon after their marriage the two went to Etty's native Yorkshire to undertake the research

Alexander Gilchrist; drawing by Herbert Gilchrist from an 1851 daguerreotype

for the biography; after collecting an abundance of letters and diaries, they retired to Lyme Regis and began sorting and digesting their research. In 1853 they moved to Guildford, Surrey. *Life of William Etty, R.A.* received little recognition in the press when it was published in 1855, but it acquired for Gilchrist a distinguished admirer: Gilchrist sent a copy to Thomas Carlyle, who responded in a letter dated 30 January 1855 that he found the book to have been "done in a vigorous, sympathetic, veracious spirit" and to offer "the delineation, actual and intelligible, of a man extremely well worth knowing." The biography is still of value as a discerning account of Etty as a man and an artist, and while evidently the result of much diligence, it achieves a readability that is spoiled only by the occasional mannerism — most often in instances where Carlyle's notions of hero worship and the "Great Man" exert too pronounced an influence. Gilchrist is occasionally prone to overly long digressions, but some of these are of interest for revealing his thoughts on biography. At one point he complains

of "the somewhat exaggerated theory which traces to the Mother the gifts of men of genius." Elsewhere he tells his reader that "Only for two reasons can any Life be really memorable; for the results achieved, results whereof others than the sower reap, — a test at once winnowing the few from the many; or, for the spirit in which it was fulfilled." Such reflections have an obvious relevance to the motives that led to the writing of *Life of William Blake*. So does his discussion of his conception of genius: "We *are* indeed all stupid, more or less; of our ownselves dull and blunt of sense and perception: opaque substances partially luminous; some, more utterly impervious to the light than others. What men call genius is but the partial exception, — *bonafide sight* of Nature, face to face, in one special direction: clear sight, which very few have in many directions; most, in none."

After completing *Life of William Etty, R.A.* Gilchrist planned a biography of Thomas Cochrane, tenth Earl of Dundonald, who was noted for his naval exploits and for his campaigns against corruption in the navy. Gilchrist perhaps contemplated writing the book more for its commercial possibilities than for any particular fascination with the man. Certainly, as Anne Gilchrist explains, "the enterprise was uncongenial, and relinquished without regret when it came to light that the Earl was preparing an autobiography."

Gilchrist's knowledge of Blake at this time was restricted to the brief and inadequate account in Allan Cunningham's *The Lives of the Most Eminent British Painters, Sculptors, and Architects* (1829–1833) and to Blake's illustrations for Robert Blair's *The Grave* (1803). During a visit to London he saw more of Blake's designs and was especially struck by the *Illustrations of the Book of Job* (1826). He became an enthusiastic admirer of Blake and determined to compile a biography of him. To undertake the necessary research he and his wife moved to London in 1856, becoming next-door neighbors of Carlyle's in Chelsea. Gilchrist's work on Blake suffered a lengthy interruption when one of his older brothers died and Gilchrist was obliged to attend to the brother's affairs. He also planned biographies of William Wordsworth; Marie Catherine La Mothe, Countess D'Aulnoy; Edward Herbert of Cherbury; and Sir Kenelm Digby. Gilchrist and his wife became friendly with several members of the Pre-Raphaelite circle, including Ford Madox Brown and the brothers William and Dante Gabriel Rossetti. In the autumn of 1861 two of Gilchrist's children caught scarlet fever and communicated the disease to him; the children recovered, but Gilchrist died on 30 November at the age of thirty-three.

At the time of Gilchrist's death the first eight chapters of *Life of William Blake* had already been printed. Many of the rest were, according to Anne Gilchrist's preface to the first edition, "substantially complete." The bulk of the biographical account in volume one is Gilchrist's, and the governing vision of that volume is certainly his. Some pages, notably on the Prophetic Books, were contributed by Anne Gilchrist. Dante Gabriel Rossetti wrote parts of chapter 32, "Inventions to the Book of Job," and the whole of chapter 39. Volume two is largely made up of a selection by Dante Gabriel Rossetti from Blake's writings and an "Annotated Catalogue of Blake's Pictorial Works," by William Rossetti; it was produced under the supervision of Anne Gilchrist. The text of the selections is unreliable, as Dante Gabriel Rossetti made "improvements" to the original in several places; nevertheless, many of Blake's works were, at least, being made publicly available for the first time. The catalogue is still useful. There were other collaborators: A. C. Swin-

burne contributed ideas and information, although he did not write any of the published work; chapter 33 closes with a long letter from Samuel Palmer written to Gilchrist in the early stages of his preparation of the book; and chapter 34, "Personal Details," gathers the testimony of many who had known Blake in his last years.

In the years since Blake's death there had been little public discussion of the man or his work. A few, such as Caroline Bowles, John Ruskin, and Dante Gabriel Rossetti, had taken an interest in him, but to the general public he was either unknown or regarded as an eccentric. Even an admirer such as Edward FitzGerald saw him largely as a madman. Against such a background, Gilchrist saw his purpose as essentially one of reclamation; his aim was to make known a life and a body of work that were unjustly neglected and to make possible fuller and deeper understanding of the work.

Gilchrist's commitment to the enthusiastic reclamation of Blake did not preclude meticulous attention to detail. He was well aware of the importance of accuracy, and in a letter to John Linnell of 25 April 1855 he remarked that "It is fullness of *detail* which to Biography imparts life & reality." The diligence of his inquiries among those who had known Blake enabled Gilchrist to incorporate a great deal of previously unknown information. For much of this information, indeed, Gilchrist is today the only source; it is a matter of regret, by the standards of modern scholarship, that Gilchrist did not normally provide adequate documentation of *his* sources. Often there is no means of checking Gilchrist's statements; it is reassuring, however, that where modern scholarship has been able to cross-check the material contained in the biography, Gilchrist has proved far more often than not to be accurate and to have been careful in his use of his sources. One of the most important modern Blake scholars, Bentley, notes in his magisterial *Blake Records* (1969): "When I have been able to trace Gilchrist's footsteps I have found that he is highly reliable, and I have therefore taken on trust those parts of his testimony that my own research into prior sources does not duplicate or controvert."

Central to Gilchrist's act of "reclamation" is his reassessment of Blake's character. In chapter 35, "Mad or Not Mad?," Gilchrist argues that what some observers took to be evidence of Blake's insanity was really testimony to the power of his imagination. He quotes with approval an analysis by James Smetham: "Blake never dreamed of questioning the correctness of his impressions. To him all thought came with the clearness and veracity of

*Gilchrist's father, James Gilchrist, circa 1827, artist unknown
(from Marion Walker Alcaro,* Walt Whitman's Mrs. G: A
Biography of Anne Gilchrist, *1991)*

vision. The conceptive faculty working with a perception of outward facts, singularly narrow and imperfect, projected every idea boldly into the sphere of the actual. What he thought, that he saw to all intents and purposes. It was this sudden and sharp crystallisation of inward notions into outward and visible signs which produced the impression, on many beholders, that reason was unseated." Gilchrist's Blake is, then, no madman. His reputation for insanity is seen as, in large part, the product of the presence of such a powerful imagination in a largely Augustan world. "Does not prophet or hero always seem 'mad' to the respectable mob, and to polished men of the world?" he asks rhetorically. Gilchrist's conception of Blake's age is of one in which "the supernatural world" had "removed itself further from civilised, cultivated humanity than it ever was before." The England in which Blake's imagination expressed itself was one in which there was "infinitely less practical belief in an invisible world, or even apprehension of it, than at any previous his-

torical era, whether Egyptian, classic, or mediæval." Gilchrist finds a kind of microcosmic image of Blake's relationship (or lack of it) to his times in his attendance in the early 1780s at the social gatherings hosted by the fashionable bluestocking Harriet Mathew. Gilchrist quotes an account by John Thomas Smith of the effect Blake created at such events: "There I have often heard him read and sing several of his poems. He was listened to by the company with profound silence, and allowed by most of the visitors to possess original and extraordinary merit." Gilchrist takes Smith's closing remarks to be ironic; he evidently presumes the company's "profound silence" to be no more than polite bewilderment, since he exclaims by way of comment on this account: "Phoenix amid an admiring circle of cocks and hens is alone a spectacle to compare mentally with this!"

Gilchrist's Blake is a "gentle yet fiery-hearted mystic" unfortunately placed in a world of prosaic rationality. In Gilchrist's account he is more saintly

Anne Burrows in 1851, the year of her marriage to Gilchrist

than mad. He is a faithful husband, temperate in his habits and appetites, diligent in his work, polite in social intercourse unless provoked, and kind to children. He has what Henry Crabb Robinson called a "natural gentility." The hallmarks of his behavior are his "great meekness and retirement of manner," his "simplicity and natural dignity." His temper is one of "equable gentleness." His profound inner happiness "communicated itself as a serene, benificent [*sic*] influence to others." His conversation was "copious and varied . . . full of mind, sagacity, and varied information": "In a walk with a sympathetic listener, it seldom flagged. He would have something pertinent to say about most objects they chanced to pass, were it but a bit of old wall. And such as had the privilege of accompanying him in a country walk felt their perception of natural beauty greatly enhanced. Nature herself seemed strangely more spiritual. Blake's mind warmed his listener's, kindled his imagination; almost creating in him a new sense." The simple surroundings, which to some eyes appeared squalid, of Blake's final home

at Number 3, Fountain Court, the Strand, were similarly transformed, Gilchrist avers, by Blake's personality. What might have been "mean and miserable" took on cheerfulness and dignity in his presence.

Gilchrist's conception of Blake's character was highly influenced by the accounts of those who had known him in his final years. From 1818 onward Blake found himself the center of a small circle of younger artists who admired his work, were fascinated by his personality, and loved and supported him. These so-called Ancients included Palmer, George Richmond, Edward Calvert, and Francis Oliver Finch. Much of their reverence for Blake was bound up with their sense of his absolute honesty. Gilchrist quotes Finch, for example, as saying that he found in Blake "*a new kind of man. . . .* Whereas most men are at the pains of softening down their extreme opinions, not to shock those of others, it was the contrary with him." Gilchrist says that Blake "frankly said, described, and drew everything as it arose to his mind." It was perhaps Palmer's view of Blake that most influenced Gilchrist's conception of Blake's character: Palmer, too, laid stress on Blake's absolute integrity, openness, and honesty. In a 23 August 1855 letter to Gilchrist from Palmer that is printed in chapter 33 of *Life of William Blake* can be seen the seeds of a great deal that informs the picture of Blake presented in the biography: "His knowledge was various and extensive . . . his conversation nervous and brilliant. . . . He was energy itself, and shed around him a kindling influence. . . . To walk with him in the country was to perceive the soul of beauty through the forms of matter; and the high, gloomy buildings between which, from his study window, a glimpse was caught of the Thames and the Surrey shore, assumed a kind of grandeur from the man dwelling near them. . . . He was a man without a mask; his aim, single, his path straightforwards, and his wants few; so he was free, noble, and happy. . . . He was one of the few to be met with in our passage through life, who are not in some way or other, 'double-minded' and inconsistent with themselves; one of the very few who cannot be depressed by neglect, and to whose name rank and station could add no lustre. Moving apart, in a sphere above the attraction of worldly honours, he did not accept greatness, but confer it. He ennobled poverty, and by his conversation and the influence of his genius, made two small rooms in Fountain Court more attractive than the threshold of princes." One must doubt whether an excited young artist's conception of his master's character, based only on experience of the last years of his hero's life, is an entirely satisfactory basis on which to build an account of the many earlier years of that life. Certainly one has the sense at times that Gilchrist's effort to project the Ancients' characterization of Blake back into events and attitudes of Blake's life before they knew him involves a degree of strain and awkwardness. It results in a portrayal of Blake as almost completely unworldly; in the process many of the contradictions and paradoxes inherent in Blake's life and work are simplified out of existence or at least smoothed into harmony with this dominant image. Gilchrist has much to say of Blake's ideas on art, and he discusses the designs and the shorter poems at length; of Blake's political and religious ideas, however, there is little or nothing of substance; and of the Prophetic Books there are only the most perfunctory, and mostly uncomprehending, accounts (most of which appear to have been the work of Anne Gilchrist). *America: A Prophecy* (1793), for example, is described as "verse hard to fathom; with far too little nature behind it, or back-bone; a redun-

dance of mere invention, — the fault of all this class of Blake's writings; too much wild tossing about of ideas and words." Of *Milton: A Poem in Two Books* (1804) the reader is told that just as the text "has no perceptible affinity with its title, so the designs it contains seem unconnected with the text." The bewilderment expressed here ensures that much that is most important and characteristic in Blake's work is dismissed in the most blandly general terms. As a result, a seriously unbalanced picture of Blake is produced. Gilchrist's Blake may not be mad, but he is a poet and artist who apparently wasted most of his creative energies on eccentric productions worthy of no more than condescending attention and even gentle mockery. That the Prophetic Books might be central to Blake's achievement was a discovery that had to await Gilchrist's successors.

Gilchrist's *Life of William Blake* scarcely begins to do justice to Blake's social and religious thought. Indeed, the presentation of his religious ideas involved something close to a kind of protective censorship. Palmer, in a letter of 24 July 1862, warned Anne Gilchrist against reproducing *The Marriage of Heaven and Hell* (1793?) in full, fearing that to do so "would at once exclude the work from every drawing-room table in England." In the text of *The Marriage of Heaven and Hell* that is quoted in volume one of the biography there are significant omissions (the work is entirely absent from the selections included in volume two). Several of the "Proverbs of Hell" are missing, such as "Prisons are built with Stones of Law, Brothels with bricks of Religion," "The nakedness of woman is the work of God," and "As the catterpillar chooses the fairest leaves to lay her eggs on, so the priest lays his curse on the fairest joys." While the Gilchrists clearly had Victorian sensibilities in mind in making such omissions, doing so also made it easier to sustain the image of Blake that they were concerned to promote. The question of Blake's religious heterodoxy is inadequately confronted; the radical nature of his political ideas is effectively ignored. That later ages could have produced works such as David Erdman's *Blake: Prophet against Empire. A Poet's Interpretation of the History of His Own Times* (1969) would, one suspects, have been entirely beyond the imagining of the Gilchrists, running almost wholly counter, as it does, to their sense of Blake as a man whose interests were too unworldly to possess any significant political dimension.

Given Gilchrist's prevailing stress on Blake's independence from the world around him, it is perhaps paradoxical that one of the most striking qualities of his biography should be the richness with

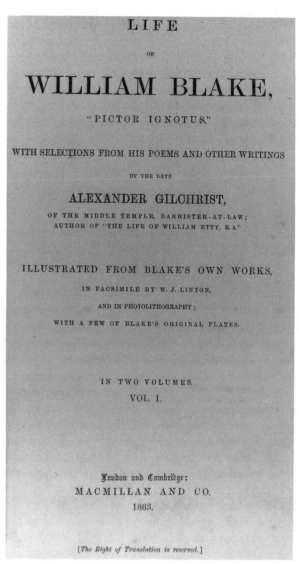

Frontispiece and title page for Gilchrist's posthumously published biography of the poet-artist-mystic

which it evokes the physical settings in which Blake lived out his days. The account of Blake's marriage, for example, concludes with a description of the "then newly rebuilt church of Battersea" in which the ceremony was performed, which ends with nice irony in pointing out that the church was adorned with works by the very clergyman, Joseph Gardner, who conducted the marriage. Gardner was an amateur artist, and the church contained, among other of his works, "two small 'paintings on glass' – *The Lamb* . . . and *The Dove* (descending) . . . paintings so 'natural' and familiarly 'like,' an innocent spectator forgets perhaps their sacred symbolism – as possibly did the artist too!" There is an apt wit in Gilchrist's closing question: "Did the future de-

signer of *The Gates of Paradise*, the *Jerusalem*, and the *Job*, kneel before these trophies of religious art?"

The houses in which Blake lived and worked are described, along with their surroundings. The newly married Blakes' first home, at 23 Green Street, Leicester Fields, is "located" both topographically and socially: "Green Street, then the abode of quiet private citizens, is now a nondescript street, given up to curiosity-shops, shabby lodging-houses and busy feet hastening to and from the Strand. No. 23, on the right-hand side going citywards, next to the house at the corner of the Square, is one – from the turn the narrow Street here takes – at right angles with and looking down the rest of it. At present, part tenanted by a shoemaker, the house is in

114

an abject plight of stucco, dirt, and dingy desolation." In chapter 34 the detailed description of the Blakes' last home in Fountain Court, down to the disposition of bed and cooking fire, is accompanied by a drawing by Herbert H. Gilchrist of Blake's "Work-Room and Death-Room."

In one case Gilchrist's topographical research let him down: in 1793 Blake moved from Poland Street to Number 13 Hercules Buildings, Lambeth, which, Gilchrist says, "was among the humbler, one-storied houses, on the right-hand side as you go from the Bridge [Westminster Bridge] to the palace." In fact, Number 13 was on the opposite side of the road, as Arthur Symons points out in his *William Blake* (1907). Such lapses are rare, though there are a few other errors or areas of ignorance. Gilchrist says, for example, that Catherine Blake was the only pupil her husband ever had. This claim is incorrect, since he had pupils during the years he spent at Felpham, and a record survives, dated 25 December 1805, of his being engaged to teach Thomas Butts, the son of one of his most enduring and generous patrons, "at 25 Guineas per Annum." Ruthven Todd points out in the notes to his 1942 edition of Gilchrist's biography that there are other small, but significant, errors where Butts is concerned. The beginning of Gilchrist's chapter 32, dealing with the years 1823 to 1825, paints a picture of the increasing neglect of Blake and says that "even his old friend Mr. Butts, a friend of more than thirty years' standing . . . grew cool" and took offense at the matter and manner of Blake's speaking to him. Todd notes that "There is no evidence for Gilchrist's statement that this friendship cooled; Blake mentions a visit from Butts in 1827, and it seems likely that the latter bought the posthumous copy of *Jerusalem* and a certain number of drawings from Catherine Blake. On the whole, Gilchrist seems to have known surprisingly little about Butts, calling him a 'wealthy merchant,' when he was Muster-Master General." There are other problems: in chapter 27, for example, Gilchrist confuses the two George Cumberlands, father and son. Such errors are, however, rare, and though later research has led to the discovery of information not known to Gilchrist, the factual outlines of his biography have not been challenged.

At times Gilchrist's narrative has a decided charm. Some of the biography's most enjoyable chapters are those devoted to Blake's years at Felpham. The portrait of William Hayley, as fussy and vain but well intentioned, and of the relationship between Hayley and Blake is often humorous. Gilchrist exactly articulates his sense of the differ-

Anne Gilchrist in 1874

ences between the two: "We can, for a moment, see the oddly assorted pair; both visionaries, but in how different a sense! the urbane amateur seeing nothing as it really was; the painter seeing only, so to speak, the unseen: the first with a mind full of literary conventions, swiftly writing without thought; the other, with a head just as full of originalities, – right or wrong – patiently busying his hands at his irksome craft, while his spirit wandered through the invisible world." Gilchrist's narrative manner is perhaps at its most effective in his account of Blake's dealings with the engraver Robert H. Cromek, who Blake thought had cheated him in regard to the drawings for *The Grave,* though his partiality toward Blake is such as to make the pages less than wholly just in their treatment of both Cromek and the painter and book illustrator Thomas Stothard, who received a commission from Cromek that Blake insisted had first been given to him.

In 1863 *Life of William Blake* was published in an edition of two thousand copies. A few reviewers felt that Gilchrist's enthusiasm for his "hero" was a fault; the *Westminster Review* (January 1864), for example, complained that the book was "conceived in a spirit of hero-worship which incapacitates the writer for a dispassionate statement of the few events which marked Blake's life, or for anything but an indiscriminate and vague laudation that partakes much more of rhetorical advocacy than critical judgement." Most readers and reviewers, however, responded favorably to Gilchrist's "advocacy." *Macmillan's Magazine* (November 1864) suspected that Gilchrist overrated Blake's abilities but readily conceded that Gilchrist and his "collaborators" had "done really a good work in rescuing from oblivion one of the most extraordinary men of our nation."

Fifteen hundred copies were printed of the 1880 edition. The 1863 edition has sixty-six plates; the 1880 edition has sixty-four. The selections from Blake's writings occupy pages 1–176 of volume two of the 1863 edition, which, in addition to the annotated list of Blake's paintings, drawings, writings, and engravings, also has an appendix reproducing ten of Blake's letters to Butts. In the 1880 edition these letters to Butts were incorporated into the main text of volume one; thirty-four letters from Blake to Hayley were also moved into the main text. The selections, occupying pages 1–200 of volume two of the 1880 edition, were revised and expanded. Several additions were made at the end of the second volume: "Descriptive Notes of the Designs to Young's 'Night Thoughts,' " by Frederick James Shields; a reprint with omissions of Smetham's review of the 1863 edition, under the title "Essay on Blake"; a note, "Francis Oliver Finch. In Memoriam," by Palmer; and Anne Gilchrist's "Memoir of Alexander Gilchrist." What had, in 1863, been a lonely piece of rediscovery today has an air of substantial Victorian solidity. Blake has been reclaimed — even if at some cost to his true originality.

The work of Gilchrist and his collaborators, including those whose contributions were chiefly made after Gilchrist's death, stood firmly as a base upon which a more comprehensive study of Blake could be built. The Blake they had created was, perhaps inevitably, a simplification. Carlyle, in "The Hero as Poet" (1841), had spoken of Dante and William Shakespeare as "Saints of Poetry," poets "if not deified, yet we may say beatified." Now Blake,

too, had undergone a process of beatification. Chapter 1 of *Life of William Blake* promises an account of a "Life and Character . . . romantic [and] pious – in the deepest natural sense," a life "animated by . . . unbroken simplicity . . . [and] high unity of sentiment." Chapter 37, "Last Days," gives an account of Blake's death that completes the process of beatification: "In that plain, back room, so dear to the memory of his friends, and to them beautiful from association with *him* – with his serene, cheerful converse, his high personal influence, so spiritual and rare – he lay chaunting Songs to Melodies, both the inspiration of the moment, but no longer, as of old to be noted down. To the pious Songs followed, about six in the summer evening, a calm and painless withdrawal of breath; the exact moment almost unperceived by his wife who sat by his side. A humble female neighbour, her only other companion, said afterwards: 'I have been at the death, not of a man, but of a blessed angel.' " It is quintessentially Victorian that this passage should be followed a few pages later by the information that "Blake left not a single debt behind." Gone is the madman of earlier accounts; Blake's piety and frugality have been well enough established for him to be accommodated within Victorian codes of acceptability.

References:

Marion Walker Alcaro, *Walt Whitman's Mrs. G: A Biography of Anne Gilchrist* (Rutherford, Madison & Teaneck, N. J.: Fairleigh Dickinson University Press / London & Toronto: Associated University Presses, 1991);

G. E. Bentley, Jr., *Blake Records* (Oxford: Clarendon Press, 1969);

Bentley, *Blake's Books,* revised edition (Oxford: Clarendon Press, 1977);

Deborah Dorfman, "Blake in 1863 and 1880: The Gilchrist *Life,*" *Bulletin of New York Public Library,* 71 (April 1967): 216–238;

Dorfman, *Blake in the Nineteenth Century: His Reputation as a Poet from Gilchrist to Yeats* (New Haven: Yale University Press, 1969);

Herbert H. Gilchrist, *Anne Gilchrist: Her Life and Writings* (London: Fisher Unwin, 1887);

Susanne Hoover, "The Public Reception of Gilchrist's *Life of Blake,*" *Blake Newsletter,* 8 (1974): 26–31;

Arthur Symons, *William Blake* (London: Constable, 1907).

George Gilfillan

(30 January 1813 – 13 August 1878)

Glyn Pursglove
University College of Swansea

BOOKS: *Hades, or the Unseen* (Dundee: Shaw, 1843);

A Gallery of Literary Portraits (Edinburgh: Tait, 1845); republished as *Sketches of Modern Literature, and Eminent Literary Men, (Being a Gallery of Literary Portraits)* (New York: D. Appleton; Philadelphia: George S. Appleton, 1846);

The Christian Bearings of Astronomy: A Lecture (London, 1848);

The Connection between Science, Literature and Religion: A Lecture (London, 1849);

A Second Gallery of Literary Portraits (Edinburgh: Hogg, 1850); republished as *Modern Literature and Literary Men: Being a Second Gallery of Literary Portraits* (New York: Appleton, 1850);

The Apocalypse of Jesus Christ: A Sermon (Aberdeen: Davidson, 1851);

The Bards of the Bible (New York: Appleton / Philadelphia: Appleton, 1851; Edinburgh: Hogg, 1851);

The Book of British Poesy, Ancient and Modern, Being Select Extracts from Our Best Poets, Arranged in Chronological Order. With an Essay on British Poetry (London: Tegg, 1851);

The Martyrs, Heroes, and Bards of the Scottish Covenant (London: Cockshaw, 1852; New York: Carter, 1853);

Lord Byron: A Lecture Delivered before the Young Men's Christian Association (London: Nisbet, 1852);

The Poets and Poetry of the Bible (Auburn, N.Y.: Derby & Miller / Buffalo: Derby, Orton & Mulligan, 1853);

The Grand Discovery; or, The Fatherhood of God (London: Blackader, 1854);

A Third Gallery of Portraits (Edinburgh: Hogg, 1854; New York: Sheldon, Lamport & Blakeman, 1855);

The History of a Man: Edited by George Gilfillan, as B. E. (London: Hall, Virtue, 1856);

Christian Missions: Their Divinity, Necessity, Past History, and Future Prospects. A Sermon (Edinburgh: Hogg, 1857);

Christianity and Our Era: A Book for the Times (Edinburgh: Hogg, 1857);

Alpha and Omega; or, A Series of Scripture Studies, 2 volumes (London: Hall, Virtue, 1860);

Night: A Poem (London: Jackson, Walford & Hodder, 1867);

Remoter Stars in the Church Sky: Being a Gallery of Uncelebrated Divines (London: Jackson, Walford & Hodder, 1867);

Modern Christian Heroes: A Gallery of Protesting and Reforming Men including Cromwell, Milton, the Puritans, Covenanters, First Seceders, Methodists, &c. (London: Stock, 1869);

Life of Sir Walter Scott, Baronet (Edinburgh: Oliphant, 1870);

Comrie and Its Environs, by Gilfillan and J. Bryce (Comrie: Brough, 1872);

Life of the Rev. William Anderson, LL.D. (London: Hodder & Stoughton, 1873);

Sketches, Literary and Theological: Being Selections from an Unpublished Manuscript of the Late Rev. George Gilfillan, edited by Frank Henderson (Edinburgh: Douglas, 1881);

The Massacre of Glencoe and the Campbells of Glenlyon, by Gilfillan, Duncan Campbell, and John Stuart Blackie (Stirling: Mackay, 1912).

Edition: *A Gallery of Literary Portraits,* edited by W. Robertson Nicoll (London: Dent / New York: Dutton, 1909).

OTHER: William Cullen Bryant, *Poems,* introductory essay by Gilfillan (Liverpool: Walker, 1850);

The Complete Poetical Works of Thomas Campbell: With a Memoir of His Life, and an Essay on His Genius and Writings, edited by Gilfillan (New York: Appleton, 1852);

John Milton, *Milton's Poetical Works,* 2 volumes, life, critical dissertation, and notes by Gilfillan (Edinburgh: Nichol, 1853);

James Thomson, *Thomson's Poetical Works,* life, critical dissertation, and notes by Gilfillan (Edinburgh: Nichol, 1853);

Edward Young, *Young's "Night Thoughts,"* life, critical dissertation, and notes by Gilfillan (Edinburgh: Nichol, 1853);

James Beattie, Robert Blair, and William Falconer, *The Poetical Works of Beattie, Blair and Falconer,* life, critical dissertation, and notes by Gilfillan (Edinburgh: Nichol, 1854);

The Complete Poetical Works of William Cullen Bryant, introductory essay by Gilfillan (London: Knight, 1854);

The Poetical Works of Samuel Butler, 2 volumes, life, critical dissertation, and notes by Gilfillan (Edinburgh: Nichol, 1854);

The Poetical Works of William Cowper, 2 volumes, life, critical dissertation, and notes by Gilfillan (Edinburgh: Nichol, 1854);

Oliver Goldsmith, William Collins, and Thomas Warton, *The Poetical Works of Goldsmith, Collins and T. Warton,* lives, critical dissertations, and notes by Gilfillan (Edinburgh: Nichol, 1854);

The Poetical Works of George Herbert, life, critical dissertation, and notes by Gilfillan (Edinburgh: Nichol, 1854);

The Poetical Works of William Shenstone, life, critical dissertation, and notes by Gilfillan (Edinburgh: Nichol, 1854);

The Poetical Works of William Lisle Bowles, 2 volumes, memoir, critical dissertation, and notes by Gilfillan (Edinburgh: Nichol, 1855);

The Poetical Works of Charles Churchill, memoir and notes by Gilfillan (Edinburgh: Nichol, 1855);

The Poetical Works of John Dryden, 2 volumes, life, critical dissertation, and notes by Gilfillan (Edinburgh: Nichol, 1855);

Samuel Johnson, Thomas Parnell, Thomas Gray, and Tobias Smollett, *The Poetical Works of Johnson, Parnell, Gray, and Smollett,* memoirs, critical dissertations, and notes by Gilfillan (Edinburgh: Nichol, 1855);

The Poetical Works of Robert Burns, 2 volumes, memoir and notes by Gilfillan (Edinburgh: Nichol, 1856);

Edward Howard, *The Genesis: A Poem,* introduction by Gilfillan (London: Longman, 1856);

The Poetical Works of Alexander Pope, 2 volumes, memoir and notes by Gilfillan (Edinburgh: Nichol, 1856);

William Shakespeare and Henry Howard, Earl of Surrey, *The Poetical Works of William Shakespeare and the Earl of Surrey,* memoirs, critical dissertations, and notes by Gilfillan (Edinburgh: Nichol, 1856);

The Poetical Works of Henry Kirke White and James Grahame, memoirs, critical dissertations, and notes by Gilfillan (Edinburgh: Nichol, 1856);

The Poetical Works of Mark Akenside, memoir and critical dissertation by Gilfillan (Edinburgh: Nichol, 1857);

Richard Crashaw and Francis Quarles, *The Poetical Works of Richard Crashaw and Quarles' Emblems,* memoirs and critical dissertations by Gilfillan (Edinburgh: Nichol, 1857);

The Poetical Works of Sir Walter Scott, 3 volumes, memoir and critical dissertation by Gilfillan (Edinburgh: Nichol, 1857);

The Poetical Works of Edmund Waller and Sir John Denham, memoir and critical dissertation by Gilfillan (Edinburgh: Nichol, 1857);

John Armstrong, John Dyer, and Matthew Green, *The Poetical Works of Armstrong, Dyer and Green,* memoirs and critical dissertations by Gilfillan (Edinburgh: Nichol, 1858);

William Johnston, *Nightshade,* preface by Gilfillan (London: Bentley, 1858);

Adolphus Pasquin, *The Age of Lead: A Satire,* introduction by Gilfillan (London: Judd & Glass, 1858);

Thomas Percy, ed., *Reliques of Ancient Poetry,* 3 volumes, memoir and critical dissertation by Gilfillan (Edinburgh: Nichol, 1858);

The Poetical Works of Sir Thomas Wyatt, memoir and critical dissertation by Gilfillan (Edinburgh: Nichol, 1858);

Joseph Addison, John Gay, and William Somerville, *The Poetical Works of Joseph Addison; Gay's Fables; and Somerville's Chase,* memoirs and critical dissertations by Gilfillan (Edinburgh: Nichol, 1859);

James Inches Hillocks, *Thoughts in Rhyme,* introductory sketch by Gilfillan (London: Tweedie, 1859);

The Poetical Works of Edmund Spenser, 5 volumes, memoir by Gilfillan (Edinburgh: Nichol, 1859);

Geoffrey Chaucer, *The Canterbury Tales,* 3 volumes, edited by Charles Cowden Clarke, memoir and critical dissertation by Gilfillan (Edinburgh: Nichol, 1860);

Specimens with Memoirs of the Less-Known British Poets, 3 volumes, edited by Gilfillan (Edinburgh: Nichol, 1860);

Hours of Quiet Thought, introduction by Gilfillan (London: Newby, 1865);

Janet Hamilton, *Poems and Ballads,* introduction by Gilfillan (Glasgow: Maclehose, 1868);

William Knight, *Auld Yule and Other Poems,* introduction by Gilfillan (Edinburgh: Menzies, 1869);

Alexander Anderson, *The Two Angels and Other Poems,* introduction by Gilfillan (London: Simpkin, 1875);

Alexander G. Murdoch, *The Laird's Lykewake and Other Poems,* preface by Gilfillan (London: Simpkin, 1877);

David Vedder, *Poems, Lyrics and Sketches,* essay on Vedder's life and writings by Gilfillan (London: Simpkin, 1878);

The National Burns: Including the Airs of All the Songs and an Original Life of Burns by the Editor, 4 volumes, edited by Gilfillan (Glasgow: Mackenzie, 1878);

John Malcolm, *Poems, Tales and Sketches,* essay by Gilfillan (Kirkwall: Peace, 1905).

On the occasion of George Gilfillan's funeral at Balgay Cemetery in Dundee, the coffin was followed by a procession some two miles in length. The tribute was primarily being paid to a clergyman who had been for many years a major influence in the United Presbyterian Church in Scotland and a distinguished member of the local community; Gilfillan's literary influence, however, was also considerable and not wholly incommensurate with such an occasion. He was the author of widely read biographies of Sir Walter Scott and Robert Burns. He was the editor of one of the Victorian age's most popular editions of the major and some minor British poets. He was largely responsible for bringing to public attention the work of two young poets who were to become immensely fashionable, Sydney Dobell and Alexander Smith. His series of essays, known as "Literary Portraits," ensured that, in the words of William Robertson Nicoll, "for about five years (1849–1854) George Gilfillan's position as a critic was one of very great influence. It may be doubted whether even [Thomas] Carlyle had more power over young minds." Gilfillan's fame was not to endure; but he was far more than the "obscure idiot" or "McGonagall of criticism" of John Gross's damning account in *The Rise and Fall of the Man of Letters* (1969). His style is frequently rhapsodic — at its worst, bombastic; his views are often dogmatic

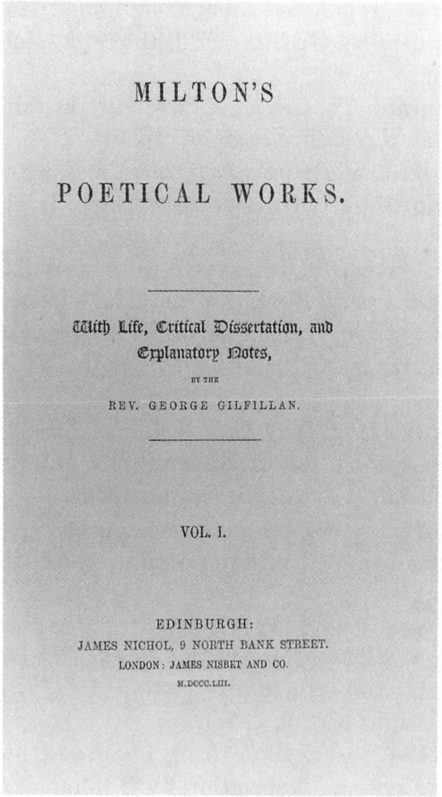

Title pages for three of the forty-eight volumes in the Library Edition of the British Poets for which Gilfillan wrote biographical and critical introductions and notes

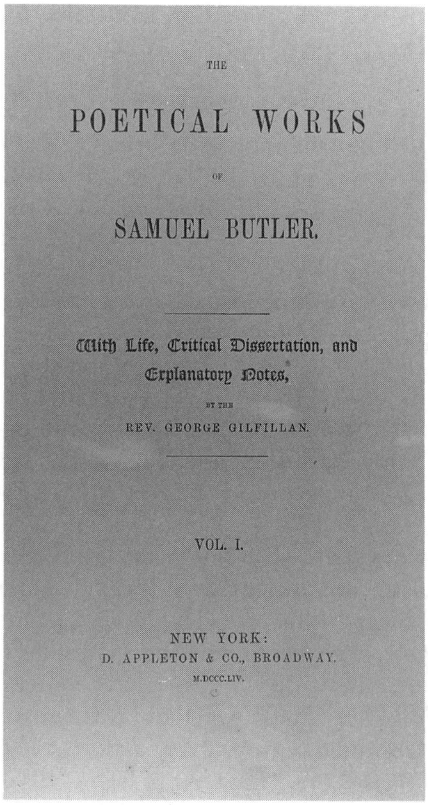

MILTON'S

POETICAL WORKS.

With Life, Critical Dissertation, and
Explanatory Notes,
BY THE
REV. GEORGE GILFILLAN.

VOL. I.

EDINBURGH:
JAMES NICHOL, 9 NORTH BANK STREET.
LONDON: JAMES NISBET AND CO.
M.DCCC.LIII.

THE

POETICAL WORKS

OF

SAMUEL BUTLER.

With Life, Critical Dissertation, and
Explanatory Notes,
BY THE
REV. GEORGE GILFILLAN.

VOL. I.

NEW YORK:
D. APPLETON & CO., BROADWAY.
M.DCCC.LIV.

THE

POETICAL WORKS

OF

ROBERT BURNS.

With Memoir, Critical Dissertation, and
Explanatory Notes,
BY THE
REV. GEORGE GILFILLAN.

VOL. I.

EDINBURGH:
JAMES NICHOL, 9 NORTH BANK STREET.
LONDON: JAMES NISBET AND CO.
DUBLIN: W. ROBERTSON.
M.DCCC.LVI.

but are often expressed with a vivacity that invites attention and, perhaps, refutation. He may strain after metaphor and simile, but in the process he sometimes lights on a memorable expression – describing William Wordsworth as "a mountain tarn – profundity without progress" or identifying Samuel Taylor Coleridge's plagiarism as "the kleptomania of a millionaire." His friends and correspondents included Carlyle, Ralph Waldo Emerson, and Henry Wadsworth Longfellow. He is the perfect exemplar of a particular aspect of Victorian taste.

Gilfillan was born on 30 January 1813 at Comrie in Perthshire, where his father, the Reverend Samuel Gilfillan, was a Secession minister. The elder Gilfillan was himself a figure of some importance in the church and merits an entry in the *Dictionary of National Biography*. His wife, Rachel Barlas Gilfillan, had been a young lady of famous beauty. George Gilfillan was the eleventh of twelve children born to the couple. Samuel Gilfillan died in 1826; the following year his son entered Glasgow College as a theological student. Among those who taught him were Robert Buchanan, historian of the Scottish church, and Sir Daniel Sandford, distinguished professor of Greek. He went on to study in the United Secession Hall of the United Presbyterian Church in Edinburgh. The move to Edinburgh increased Gilfillan's contacts with the literary world, and he made the acquaintance of Alexander Chalmers, Francis Jeffrey, and John Wilson ("Christopher North"). In 1835 he was licensed as a probationer by Edinburgh Presbytery, and in March 1836 he was ordained in Dundee as pastor of the School Wynd Congregation, with a manse and an annual stipend of £220. In November of the same year Gilfillan married Margaret Valentine; the marriage was childless. Dundee was to be his base for the rest of his life. His colorful and unorthodox manner as a preacher attracted large congregations, and he was soon established as one of the leading citizens of Dundee.

In 1837 Thomas Aird attended the funeral of one of his brothers at which Gilfillan was officiating. Now largely forgotten, Aird was a poet of some reputation in those years; he was a regular contributor to *Blackwood's Edinburgh Magazine* and the *Dumfriesshire and Galloway Herald*. Aird encouraged Gilfillan to write, without payment, a series of literary sketches to be published in the *Herald*. Gilfillan's miscellaneous essays on poets, novelists, critics, and thinkers attracted considerable attention, and a collection of them was published in Edinburgh in 1845 as *A Gallery of Literary Portraits* and in New York and Philadelphia in 1846 as *Sketches of Modern Literature*. It was well received on both sides of the Atlantic, and Gilfillan was launched on a literary career. Except for a certain amount of theological controversy, Gilfillan's was not a life of any great outward incident. He was a busy and respected clergyman; a prolific writer on literary and religious matters; an industrious editor and compiler; active in the antislavery movement; much in demand as a lecturer; and a hardworking supporter of free libraries and mechanics' institutes in his native Scotland.

A Gallery of Literary Portraits was succeeded by a second collection in 1850 and a third in 1854. These portraits, more than eighty in all, included studies of figures of great diversity: Romantics such as Coleridge, Wordsworth, Robert Southey, Percy Bysshe Shelley, and Leigh Hunt; Victorians such as Thomas Babington Macaulay, Elizabeth Barrett Browning, and Edward Bulwer-Lytton; William Shakespeare; Aeschylus; and various "sacred authors." For all the excesses of the author's style, there is much in these portraits to make them important documents in the history of taste, and they are not devoid of genuine critical perceptions. Each of Gilfillan's collections of literary portraits went into several editions. So did his *The Bards of the Bible* (1851), a colorful account of Hebrew poetry that appears to have been his most popular work. His *The History of a Man* (1856), a fictionalized autobiography, is worth reading for its lively accounts of some of Gilfillan's many literary acquaintances, including Carlyle, Wilson, and Thomas Campbell. Published posthumously was *Sketches, Literary and Theological* (1881), made up of extracts from an incomplete sequel to this work. Add to these works Gilfillan's published sermons, editions of the works of various poets, and the dull and lengthy verses of *Night: A Poem* (1867) and one has the picture of a prolific Victorian man of letters. By 1909, however, Nicoll, the editor of a collected edition of the literary portraits, could say that Gilfillan's books were almost wholly forgotten.

The limited familiarity of Gilfillan's name is in part due to his connection with the so-called Spasmodic school of poets. Gilfillan was the discoverer of the poetry of Dobell and Smith, in each of whom he found something of the mannerisms, something of the aspiration and intensity, of his hero Shelley. Shelley's grandeur has turned in the Spasmodics, however, to grandiosity, and the language of transcendence seems almost totally artificial. Dobell – and to a greater extent Smith, with the publication of his *A Life Drama* (1852) – achieved considerable popular and critical success, but there was an inher-

Gilfillan

ent absurdity in their work, a cultivation of excess in poetically shapeless and declamatory language, that could not remain popular and respected for long. In his parody *Firmilian* (1854) William Edmondstoune Aytoun effected a devastating exposure of the poetic poverty and pretentiousness of the Spasmodics, a name that seems to have been of Aytoun's coining. As their chief critical "begetter," Gilfillan could hardly escape his share in their downfall; indeed Aytoun includes him, under the pseudonym Apollodorus in *Firmilian,* where he is called "a vapouring blockhead" and "a charlatan." Though not destroyed by Aytoun's attack, Gilfillan was certainly damaged; the episode could hardly fail to throw doubt on the soundness of his taste and critical judgment.

As a literary biographer Gilfillan's main works are his lives of Scott and Burns and the biographical and critical introductions to the forty-eight volumes of the Library Edition of the British Poets, published by James Nichol of Edinburgh between 1853 and 1860. One volume was published every other month for as many as seven thousand subscribers, and individual volumes were sold to nonsubscribers. The books were attractively produced in demy octavo and in terms of appearance and readability are much superior to most of the similar series that preceded them. Dante Gabriel Rossetti said in a letter to Hall Caine (quoted in the introduction to W. Robertson Nicoll's edition of *A Gallery of Literary Portraits,* 1909) that the series was "the best of any to read, being such fine type and convenient bulk and weight (a great thing for an armchair reader)." Gilfillan's work in this series was one of popularization rather than scholarship; the nature of the project and the frequency of publication were not such as to encourage original biographical research, and, in any case, Gilfillan was at some distance from any large library. So, for example, Gilfillan's "Life of Oliver Goldsmith" (1854) opens with the declaration that since Goldsmith's life has previously been narrated "by various authors of distinguished name," he does not "profess . . . to add any new facts to those which have been laboriously collected by [James] Prior and [John] Forster, and gracefully narrated by Washington Irving." The texts provided are frequently of doubtful authority and accuracy, and bibliographical details are wholly absent. Gilfillan's biographical and critical introductions are, for the most part, lively and readable; Gilfillan is at his best as a communicator of enthusiasm. But they are quite without scholarly apparatus; rarely are references given, authorities cited, or sources identified. Many of Gilfillan's biographical essays begin with a rhapsodic or fanciful introductory paragraph followed by an imaginative chronological account of life and works (usually with frequent divagations into personal reminiscence or largely irrelevant generalization) before the whole is brought to an end with a rhetorical flourish. In the life prefaced to the works of John Milton (1853) he calls biography "a necessary article of public entertainment," and his brief biographies certainly have an air of public performance about them. For example, his account of William Cowper (1854) begins with a rhetorical playing with paradoxes that seeks to draw attention to its author: "It is with a singular emotion that we have jotted down the words, 'THE LIFE OF WILLIAM COWPER.' The terms seem almost a contradiction. The word 'life' usually suggests ideas of bustling energy, and gladness. But, as applied to an existence which was, on the whole, a long tissue of disappointment, misery, or despair, the word seems a misnomer. Shall we not rather call it 'The living death for seventy years of William Cowper?'" As he approaches the end of his narrative it is, again, to Gilfillan's own feelings that the reader's attention is drawn: "Shame, horror, and deep commiseration induce us to hurry over the remaining part of Cowper's life . . . Words are wanting to describe the sense of relief with which we close this saddest, most mysterious narrative." Gilfillan's final paragraph, characteristically, pulls out all the rhetorical stops: "Truly William Cowper was still more a marvellous, than he was a mild and gentle spirit, — stronger, even, than he was amiable — a very Prometheus chained to his rock, let us call him, — the rock being his rugged, deep-rooted woe; the chain his lengthened life; and himself the Titan, in his earnestness, lofty purpose, and poetic power."

Digression is of the essence of Gilfillan's performance in these brief lives. His "Life of [Mark] Akenside" (1857), for example, manages only three initial sentences of information — expressed in a form untypically free of stylistic pretension — before the fact that Akenside was the son of a butcher triggers a lengthy excursus on other distinguished sons of butchers and the ponderous affirmation that "genius has sprung up in stranger quarters than in butcher's shops." In "The Life and Writings of Henry Kirke White" (1856) the information that the poet spent a year of his adolescence working at

a stocking loom is enough to prompt Gilfillan's quite irrelevant memories of some time in his own youth spent with "a person who wrought at a stocking loom establishment" and who apparently introduced Gilfillan to the writings of Shakespeare. Gilfillan's "Life of Joseph Addison" (1859) has barely begun before the reader is treated to some silly and admittedly "fanciful" thoughts on the "correspondence between the particular months when celebrated men were born and the peculiar complexion of their genius." Elsewhere it is into irrelevant or overly lengthy generalizations that Gilfillan is readily seduced. Of the eighteen pages of his "Memoir and Criticism on the Works of the Rev. W. L. Bowles" (1855) the first twelve are devoted to a general and oversimplified account of the differences between the Augustan and Romantic (though Gilfillan uses neither word) schools of poetry. Only at the foot of page 12 does Bowles manage an initial appearance. Sometimes Gilfillan's prejudices are intrusive. This fault is particularly evident in "The Life of John Dryden" (1855). Dryden is presented as "a fickle, needy, and childish changeling" whose works are the products of "either a deliberate and systematic attempt to poison the sources of virtue, or, at least, an elaborate and incessant habit of conformity to the bad tastes of a bad age." One is not inclined to give much weight to Gilfillan's damning remarks on the morality of Dryden's plays (Gilfillan has a clear suspicion of most things theatrical, in any case) when he reveals that he has by no means read all of them. At the root of Gilfillan's judgment is, of course, the question of Dryden's conversion ("perversion" is Gilfillan's word) to Roman Catholicism — or "popery," as Gilfillan calls it.

Gilfillan's natural tastes in poetry were for the enthusiastic and the rapturous, the ardent and the yearning. He was capable, however, of taking an intelligent interest in the works of poets whose writings did not fulfill such demands. He displays a surprising sympathy for the verse of Charles Churchill (1855), which he calls "masculine and thoroughly English," and writes well of both Matthew Prior and Jonathan Swift in *Specimens with Memoirs of the Less-Known British Poets* (1860). Of Addison, too, he writes with some judiciousness and sympathy. William Shenstone (1854), however, stretches his patience beyond the breaking point. With a note of some exasperation Shenstone is dismissed as a man who, although talented, did little, a man whose "life was . . . in a great degree useless. He never understood, and therefore never did his work, as a man." The ruined state of Shenstone's garden at Leasowes is said to "preach the lesson of the weakness of this

*Title page for Gilfillan's edition of the works of Robert Burns,
which includes his biography of the poet*

honest but indolent man – this true but self-stunted Poet." Shenstone's crime, in Gilfillan's eyes, appears to have been to prefer comfort to ardency of aspiration. Gilfillan's natural sympathies, both aesthetic and nationalistic, were more readily evoked by the subjects of his two longer literary biographies: Scott and Burns.

Life of Sir Walter Scott, Baronet (1870) is avowedly an attempt to provide a biography less detailed and lengthy than John Gibson Lockhart's (1837–1838; revised, 1839), which Gilfillan acknowledges to be the standard life of Scott, but more comprehensive than the "meagre outlines" that, Gilfillan claims, are characteristic of the "many smaller lives." His purpose, he says, is to provide "an accurate summary of the leading events in Scott's life, and a candid, full, and general criticism on his principal works." Not for the first time, Gilfillan is essentially fulfilling the role of popularizer; his factual outline is essentially that of Lockhart's great biography, but he makes the fruits of that work available to the general audience that was attracted to Scott anew by the celebrations in 1871 of the centenary of Scott's birth. On occasion Gilfillan demurs from a judgment of Lockhart's. In discussing Scott's position as one of

the Principal Clerks of Session, for example, Gilfillan suggests that his predecessor has overestimated the labor required of the novelist: "Lockhart, indeed, tries to find a matter of marvel in reference to his hero, by magnifying the work he had to do at the clerk's table. But we have conversed with lawyers of experience, who have assured us that the situation was little other than a sinecure." The personal manner – "we have conversed . . ." – is a characteristic Gilfillan touch; not for him the citation of scholarly authorities. No sources of information are identified; no references are given; there are no footnotes, no bibliography, no index. By the time he came to write this biography, Gilfillan's style was a good deal less extravagant than it had been; rhetorical fireworks are not wholly absent, but there is more clear and expository prose than had often been the case in the lives contributed to the Library Edition of the British Poets or in "Literary Portraits."

The author's Romantic heritage is perhaps evident in the fervor with which he insists that in Scott ("as in many great men") the key to understanding character lies in recognition of the continuity between his infancy and his manhood. Gilfillan insists that in Scott's boyhood can be found vivid examples of the qualities that were to distinguish the man: an enthusiastic and affectionate nature, honesty, and perseverance. Gilfillan traces at some length the influence on Scott of the landscape of the Scottish Borders, and he seeks characters and incidents in Scott's family and upbringing that he believes to have found their way into the later novels. Some of the claims are less than convincing; his insistence that there was "nothing ... that ever flashed on the ear or vibrated on the eye of this extraordinary man but was in some form or other reproduced in his writings" leads to some tedious and highly speculative uncovering of sources. Gilfillan writes that "it is pleasant to think of each period of Scott's literary history as linked with some spot of special natural loveliness," but such thoughts too often turn away from the genuinely biographical and come closer to the autobiographical – Gilfillan is ever ready to reminisce (and rhapsodize) about his own visits to places associated with Scott.

Life of Sir Walter Scott, Baronet comprises twenty-seven chapters and a short concluding note, "The Coming Centenary." The first twenty-five chapters are a basically chronological account of Scott's life. The penultimate chapter offers reflections on Scott as man and poet, and the last chapter turns to his best-known works under the title "The Master of the Novel." Gilfillan is an enthusiastic admirer of Scott but is not altogether uncritical. Scott is "the master of the novel, the greatest by far that ever lived," but Gilfillan admits that *Woodstock* (1826) "is in many parts exceedingly tedious" and that *Redgauntlet* (1824) lacks unity of design and effect. Gilfillan admires Scott as a novelist for the breadth of his human sympathies and for his achievement of a prose manner that, while capable of elevation and eloquence, "pursues in general the tenor of its way as evenly as a common letter." The Waverley novels Gilfillan sees as "combining life-like reality with ideal beauty," and he has some interesting things to say about the principle of contrast as a recurrent device in Scott's fiction.

In the prefatory remarks to his biography Gilfillan tells his readers that they are not to expect gossip. His austerity in such matters, however, is not such as to preclude his narrating the occasional anecdote, one or two of which seem to be original: "One amusing little story we heard in Cumberland about him. Wordsworth and he were to climb Helvellyn, and on the way passed a small public-house, the proprietor of which, standing at the door, saluted Wordsworth as a neighbour but no customer; Scott, whose name he did not know, more warmly as a

stranger but a customer. It turned out that Wordsworth, being in his house as well as habits a very strict teetotaller, Scott had walked out on various occasions alone, and enjoyed his 'morning' at the little hostelry."

Gilfillan's is a lucid if unremarkable account of its subject's life and work. It communicates a vivid sense of Scott's contemporary popularity; it paints a plausible, if derivative and idealized, picture of Scott's character. The book is largely free of its author's worst habits; Gilfillan's fancifulness and digressiveness are mostly held in check. It is still eminently readable, though it is of limited value in the light of the absence of any serious attempt at scholarly exactitude or detail. It is for the larger view that it embodies that one might reasonably go to the book. Gilfillan certainly seeks to see a pattern in Scott's career; his concern is with the arc of Scott's life rather than with the minutiae of events. So, of Scott's financial crash he can unblushingly write that he has "neither inclination or sufficient knowledge of the ways of business" to offer any lengthy discussion of "the particular causes and circumstances of the well-known catastrophe." Whereas Lockhart's biography sees Scott's career as reaching its zenith with *The Heart of Mid-Lothian* (1818), Gilfillan prefers to "fix it a little later, when his illness had been mastered, and *Ivanhoe* [1819], his most brilliantly successful tale, was speedily succeeded by a baronetcy." The point, however, remains unargued.

Scott's meeting with Burns in 1786 occasions one of Gilfillan's more absurdly rhapsodic passages. The biographer initially exclaims, "Thus met Ovid with Virgil, and Milton with Galileo"; there is some unintended bathos in the subsequent confession that "Less singular in circumstances, and less august in aspect [was] the meeting of the two brightest geniuses of Caledonia." It was on a biographical study of the second of these "Caledonian geniuses" that Gilfillan was engaged in the closing years of his life.

The National Burns was published in four volumes in 1878; it was described as "Edited by George Gilfillan," with "an Original Life of Burns by the Editor." This life occupies some 120 pages of small type in double columns. Gilfillan had earlier contributed a brief biographical account of Burns to the volume of the poet's works (1856) included in the British Poets series. In the earlier sketch Gilfillan's tone is generally somewhat stern; he is unwilling to extend much sympathetic understanding to the difficulties of Burns's situation. Burns is seen as a man who "had no leading principle or guiding star: – not conscience, for that was often asleep; not benevolence, for his humane feelings, though sincere were fluctuating and uncertain; not religion, for although not an infidel, neither was he a firm believer; not a high ideal of art, for to this he had never risen; not even his boasted independence, for no man, at times, descended, although it was with reluctance, to more servile flatteries." When he wrote his longer biography of Burns, Gilfillan's attitude was generally more positive. The biography is, he says, "a favourable, friendly, enthusiastic history of Burns' life." He is more ready to catalogue Burns's achievements not only as a poet but also as "a painstaking ploughman, a diligent farmer, a pattern exciseman, a devoted father, a kind husband, a good neighbour." Burns's failure, despite his immense natural gifts, is accounted for in the light of Burns's chronic poverty and inadequate education, the weakness of his constitution, and his disparagement by "a haughty nobility." Gilfillan conceives of Burns as an essentially "noble being." Vitality was always likely to attract Gilfillan's excited admiration, and he finds Burns to have possessed such vitality in abundance: "Burns was the most intensely living man modern times have produced – had a perpetually active and seething brain; a heart beating in big and almost audible throbs; a 'pulse's maddening play'; the most living and eloquent lips that ever spoke in Scotland; a hand that if you touched it threatened to *burn* your's: from the sole of the foot to the crown of the head he was a Man." Gilfillan's emphasis is still on Burns's instability of character, but the interpretation of this "protean volatility" is more sympathetic. Gilfillan comes close to analyzing Burns as a quintessential manic-depressive, incorporating a characteristic poetic allusion in the process: "He was everything by turns, and nothing long. He yielded, as rule, to every impulse, good or bad, high or low, which assailed him. He was at the mercy of innumerable moods, as diverse from each other as heaven from hell." It is in Burns's volatility that Gilfillan finds an explanation for the various accounts given of the poet by those who knew or met him. The underlying and recurrent mood Gilfillan judges to be a "sombre melancholy."

Though the life of Burns is still largely devoid of scholarly apparatus, Gilfillan does, more frequently than in his earlier exercises in biography, quote from relevant source material, including Burns's journal of his travels around Scotland in 1787. In both manner and matter "The Life of Burns" is perhaps Gilfillan's most impressive and substantial achievement as a literary biographer. There is a fresh maturity of psychological perception, a broadening of moral sympathy, and a relative freedom from stylistic excess. It was to be his last biography; Gilfillan died on 13 August 1878.

Only modest claims can be made for Gilfillan's work in the field of literary biography; he contributes little that is new to the world's knowledge of his subjects, and he is too readily tempted into irrelevancy and empty rhetoric. Yet he was an effective popularizer and enthusiast; the biographical sketches of the British poets belong in a distinguished line that runs through Samuel Johnson and Robert Anderson, and as lively introductions to the lives and works of their subjects they have their limited merits and attractions. Gilfillan's critical insight, however, is not such as to give the sketches any great substance as considerations of literary merit, and they are now perhaps of greatest value as documents in the history of taste. Of his longer biographies, *Life of Sir Walter Scott, Baronet* is a readable popular account, with some judicious, if brief, observations on Scott's writings. "The Life of Burns" shows Gilfillan most fully liberated from the worst of his idiosyncratic mannerisms. Gilfillan is not a major figure, but he is by no means simply the absurd figure delineated by Gross. While his faults and failings may be obvious, they should not blind one to his virtues.

Letters:

George Gilfillan: Letters and Journals, with Memoir, edited by Robert A. Watson and Elizabeth S. Watson (London: Hodder & Stoughton, 1892).

Biography:

David Macrae, *George Gilfillan: Anecdotes and Reminiscences* (Glasgow: Morison, 1891).

References:

Francis Leroy Fennell, "George Gilfillan: A Biographical and Critical Study," Ph.D. dissertation, Northwestern University, 1968;

John Gross, *The Rise and Fall of the Man of Letters* (London: Weidenfeld & Nicolson, 1969);

Townsend Scudder, "Emerson in Dundee," *American Scholar,* 4 (1935): 331–344; revised as "A Harmless Stranger: Son of Genius," in his *The Lonely Wayfaring Man: Emerson and Some Englishmen* (London & New York: Oxford University Press, 1936).

Papers:

There are letters and papers of George Gilfillan in the National Library of Scotland and the University of Edinburgh Library.

Edmund Gosse

(21 September 1849 – 16 May 1928)

Phillip Mallett
University of St. Andrews

See also the Gosse entry in *DLB 57: Victorian Prose Writers After 1867*.

BOOKS: *Madrigals, Songs and Sonnets*, by Gosse and John A. Blaikie (London: Longmans, Green, 1870);

On Viol and Flute (London: King, 1873; New York: Holt, 1883; enlarged edition, London: Kegan Paul, Trench, Trübner, 1890);

The Ethical Condition of the Early Scandinavian Peoples (London: Hardwicke, 1875);

King Erik (London: Chatto & Windus, 1875);

The Unknown Lover: A Drama for Private Acting, With An Essay on the Chamber Drama in England (London: Chatto & Windus, 1878);

Studies in the Literature of Northern Europe (London: Kegan Paul, 1879); revised and enlarged as *Northern Studies* (London: Scott, 1890);

New Poems (London: Kegan Paul, 1879);

Memoir of Samuel Rowlands (N.p.: Privately printed, 1879);

Résumé of a Pamphlet on the Industry and Trade of Germany during the first year of the new Protective Policy (London: H.M.S.O., 1881);

Memoir of Thomas Lodge (N.p.: Privately printed, 1882);

Gray (London: Macmillan, 1882; New York: Harper, 1882);

Seventeenth-Century Studies: A Contribution to the History of English Poetry (London: Kegan Paul, Trench, 1883; New York: Dodd, Mead, 1897);

Cecil Lawson: A Memoir (London: Fine Art Society, 1883);

A Critical Essay on the Life and Works of George Tinworth (London: Fine Art Society, 1883);

An Epistle to Dr. Oliver Wendell Holmes on his Seventy-fifth Birthday, August 29, 1884 (London: Privately printed, 1884);

Six Lectures Written to be Delivered before the Lowell Institute in December, 1884 (London: Privately printed, 1884);

The Masque of Painters; as Performed by the Royal Institute of Painters in Water Colours, May 19, 1885 (London: Privately printed, 1885);

From Shakespeare to Pope: An Inquiry into the Causes and Phenomena of the Rise of Classical Poetry in England (Cambridge: The University Press, 1885; New York: Dodd, Mead, 1885);

Firdausi in Exile and Other Poems (London: Kegan Paul, Trench, 1885);

Raleigh (London: Longmans, Green, 1886; New York: Appleton, 1886);

A Letter to the Editor of the "Athenaeum" (London: Privately printed, 1886);

Life of William Congreve (London: Scott / New York: Whittaker, 1888; revised and enlarged edition, London: Heinemann, 1924; New York: Scribners, 1924);

A History of Eighteenth-Century Literature (1660–1780) (London & New York: Macmillan, 1889);

Robert Browning: Personalia (London: Unwin, 1890; Boston & New York: Houghton Mifflin, 1890);

The Life of Philip Henry Gosse, F.R.S. (London: Kegan Paul, Trench, Trübner, 1890); republished as *The Naturalist of the Sea-shore* (London: Heinemann, 1896);

Gossip in a Library (London: Heinemann, 1891; New York: Lovell, 1891);

Poetry (Philadelphia: Lippincott, 1891);

Shelley in 1892: Centenary Address at Horsham, August 11, 1892 (London: Privately printed, 1892);

The Secret of Narcisse: A Romance (London: Heinemann, 1892; New York: Tait, 1892);

Wolcott Balestier: A Portrait Sketch (Westminster: Privately printed, 1892);

Questions at Issue (London: Heinemann, 1893; New York: Appleton, 1893);

The Rose of Omar. Inscription for the Rose-Tree Brought by Mr W. Simpson from Omar's Tomb at Naishapur, and Planted To-day on the Grave of Edward Fitzgerald, at Boulge, 1893 (N.p.: Privately printed, 1893);

In Russet & Silver (London: Heinemann, 1894; Chicago: Stone & Kimball, 1894);

Edmund Gosse

The Jacobean Poets (London: Murray, 1894; New York: Scribners, 1894);

Critical Kit-Kats (London: Heinemann, 1896; New York: Dodd, Mead, 1896);

A Short History of Modern English Literature (London: Heinemann, 1897; New York: Appleton, 1897; revised and enlarged edition, London: Heinemann, 1924);

Henry Fielding: An Essay (Westminster: Constable / New York: Scribners, 1898);

The Life and Letters of John Donne, Dean of St Paul's, 2 volumes (New York: Dodd, Mead / London: Heinemann, 1899);

The Character of Queen Victoria (New York: Scott, 1901);

English Literature: Edmund Spenser (Philadelphia: Lippincott, 1901);

English Literature. Elizabethan and Jacobean (Philadelphia: Lippincott, 1901);

Hypolympia; or, The Gods in the Island: An Ironic Fantasy (London: Heinemann, 1901; New York: Dodd, Mead / London: Heinemann, 1901);

The Challenge of the Brontës (London: Privately printed, 1903);

English Literature: An Illustrated Record, 4 volumes: volume 2 by Gosse and Richard Garnett, volumes 3 and 4 by Gosse (London: Heinemann, 1903; New York: Macmillan, 1903);

Jeremy Taylor (London: Macmillan, 1904; New York: Macmillan / London: Macmillan, 1904);

French Profiles (London: Heinemann, 1905; New York: Dodd, Mead, 1905);

Coventry Patmore (London: Hodder & Stoughton, 1905; New York: Scribners, 1905);

Sir Thomas Browne (New York & London: Macmillan, 1905);

Ibsen (London: Hodder & Stoughton, 1907); republished as *Henrik Ibsen* (New York: Scribners, 1908);

Father and Son: A Study of Two Temperaments, anonymous (London: Heinemann, 1907); republished as *Father and Son: Biographical Recollections* (New York: Scribners, 1907);

Introduction to A History of the Library of the House of Lords (London: Privately printed, 1908);

Biographical Notes on the Writings of Robert Louis Stevenson (London: Privately printed, 1908);

The Autumn Garden (London: Heinemann, 1909);

Swinburne: Personal Recollections (London: Privately printed, 1909);

The Collected Poems of Edmund Gosse (London: Heinemann, 1911);

Two Visits to Denmark, 1872, 1874 (London: Smith, Elder, 1911; New York: Dutton, 1912);

The Life of Swinburne, with a Letter on Swinburne at Eton by Lord Redesdale (London: Privately printed, 1912);

Portraits and Sketches (London: Heinemann, 1912; New York: Scribners, 1912);

Lady Dorothy Nevill: An Open Letter (London: Privately printed, 1913);

The Future of English Poetry (Oxford: Printed for the University by H. Hart, 1913);

Two Pioneers of Romanticism: Joseph and Thomas Warton (London: Published by Oxford University Press for the British Academy, 1915);

Inter Arma: Being Essays Written in Time of War (London: Heinemann, 1916; New York: Scribners, 1916);

Reims Revisited (N.p.: Privately printed, 1916);

Lord Cromer as a Man of Letters (London: Privately printed, 1917);

The Life of Algernon Charles Swinburne (London: Macmillan, 1917; New York: Macmillan, 1917);

The Novels of Benjamin Disraeli (London: Privately printed, 1918);

France et Angleterre: L'Avenir de leurs relations intellectuelles (London: Hayman, Christy & Lilly, 1918);

Three French Moralists, and the Gallantry of France (London: Heinemann, 1918; New York: Scribners, 1918);

Some Literary Aspects of France in the War (London: Privately printed, 1919);

The First Draft of Swinburne's "Anactoria" (London: Privately printed, 1919);

Some Diversions of a Man of Letters (London: Heinemann, 1919; New York: Scribners, 1919);

A Catalogue of the Works of Algernon Charles Swinburne in the Library of Mr Edmund Gosse (London: Privately printed, 1919);

Malherbe and the Classical Reaction in the Seventeenth Century (Oxford: Clarendon Press, 1920);

Books on the Table (London: Heinemann, 1921; New York: Scribners, 1921);

Aspects and Impressions (London: Heinemann, 1922; New York: Scribners, 1922);

The Continuity of Literature (Oxford: Oxford University Press, 1922);

More Books on the Table (London: Heinemann, 1923; New York: Scribners, 1923);

Silhouettes (London: Heinemann, 1925; New York: Scribners, 1925);

Tallemant des Réaux; or, The Art of Miniature Biography: The Zaharoff Lecturer (Oxford: Clarendon Press, 1925);

Swinburne: An Essay First Written in 1875 and Now First Printed (Edinburgh: Privately printed, 1925);

Poems (London: Benn, 1926);

Leaves and Fruit (London: Heinemann, 1927; New York: Scribners, 1927);

Austin Dobson: Some Notes, by Gosse, Alban Dobson, and George Saintsbury (London: Oxford University Press, 1928);

Selected Essays, 2 volumes (London: Heinemann, 1928);

An Address to the Fountain Club, 1923 (Steyning: Privately printed, 1931);

America: The Diary of a Visit, Winter 1884–1885, edited by Robert L. Peters and David G. Halliburton (Lafayette, Ind.: English Literature in Transition, Purdue University, 1966);

A Norwegian Ghost Story, edited by W. M. Parker (St. Peter Port, Guernsey: Toucan Press, 1967);

Thomas Hardy, O.M., edited by Ronald Knight (Bulphan, Upminster: Knight & Knight, 1968);

Sir Henry Doulton: The Man of Business as a Man of Imagination, edited by Desmond Eyles (London: Hutchinson, 1970);

The Unequal Yoke (1886): A Novel (Delmar, N.Y.: Scholars' Facsimiles and Reprints, 1975).

OTHER: Peter Christen Asbjørnsen, *Round the Yule Log: Norwegian Folk and Fairy Tales,* translated by H. L. Bræstad, introduction by Gosse (London: Low, 1881);

English Odes, edited by Gosse (London: Kegan Paul, 1881; New York: Appleton, 1881);

Tarulatā Datta, *Ancient Ballads and Legends of Hindustan,* introductory memoir by Gosse (London: Kegan Paul, 1882);

Firdausī, *The Epic of Kings: Stories Retold from Firdausi,* translated and adapted by Helen Zimmern, prefatory poem by Gosse (London: Unwin, 1882);

The Discourses of Sir Joshua Reynolds, edited by Gosse (London: Kegan Paul, 1884);

The Works of Thomas Gray, 4 volumes, edited by Gosse (London: Macmillan, 1884);

Thomas Gray, *Selected Poems,* edited by Gosse (Oxford: Clarendon Press, 1885);

John Webster, *Love's Graduate: A Comedy,* adapted by Gosse, edited by Stephen Edward Spring Rice (Oxford: Private Press of Henry Daniel, 1885);

James Shirley, *James Shirley,* edited by Havelock Ellis, introduction by Gosse (London: Unwin / New York: Scribners, 1888);

Gosse during his early years in London

The Prose Dramas of Henrik Ibsen, volume 1, translated by William Archer and M. Carmichael, biographical and critical introduction by Gosse (New York: Lovell, 1890);

Henrik Ibsen, *The Master Builder: A Play in Three Acts,* translated by Gosse and Archer (London: Heinemann, 1890);

Ibsen, *The Lady from the Sea,* translated by Eleanor Marx-Aveling, critical introduction by Gosse (London: Unwin, 1890);

Henrik Jæger, *The Life of Henrik Ibsen,* translated by Clara Bell, verses translated by Gosse (London: Heinemann, 1890);

Ivan Vazov, *Under the Yoke: A Novel,* introduction by Gosse (London: Heinemann, 1890);

The Poetical Works of Thomas Lovell Beddoes, edited, with a memoir, by Gosse (London: Dent, 1890);

Ibsen, *Hedda Gabler,* translated by Gosse (London: Heinemann, 1891; New York: United States Book Co., 1891);

Thomas Nash, *The Unfortunate Traveller; or, The Life of Jack Wilton,* essay on the life and writings of Nash by Gosse (London: Whittingham, 1892);

Emile Zola, *The Attack on the Mill, and Three Sketches of War,* essay on the short stories of Zola by Gosse (London: Readers Library, 1892);

Louis Couperus, *Eline Vere,* translated by J. T. Grein, introduction by Gosse (New York: Appleton, 1892);

Elizabeth Barrett Browning, *Sonnets from the Portuguese,* introduction by Gosse (London: Dent, 1894; Portland, Maine: Mosher, 1901);

William Hazlitt, *Conversations of James Northcote,* edited by Gosse (London: Bentley, 1894);

John Thomas Smith, *Nollekens and His Times,* edited, with an essay on Georgian sculpture, by Gosse (London: Bentley, 1894);

The Letters of Thomas Lovell Beddoes, edited by Gosse (London: Elkin Mathews & John Lane / New York: Macmillan, 1894);

Edmund H. Garrett, ed., *Victorian Songs: Lyrics of the Affections and Nature,* introduction by Gosse (Boston: Little, Brown, 1895);

The Novels of Björnstjerne Björnson, 13 volumes, edited by Gosse (London & New York: Macmillan, 1895–1909);

Thomas Carlyle, *On Heroes and Hero-Worship,* introduction by Gosse (London: Ward, Lock & Bowdon, 1896);

Friedrich Heinrich Carl de La Motte Fouqué, *Undine: A Tale,* translated, with critical introduction, by Gosse (London: Lawrence & Bullen, 1896);

Saint-Juirs (pseudonym of René Delorme), *The Tavern of the Three Virtues,* critical essay on the art of Daniel Vierge by Gosse (London: Unwin, 1896);

The Works of Henry Fielding, 12 volumes, introduction by Gosse (London: Constable, 1898);

Hans Christian Andersen, *Fairy Tales,* translated by Brækstad, introduction by Gosse (London: Heinemann, 1900);

William Penn, *Some Fruits of Solitude,* introduction by Gosse (London: Freemantle, 1900);

Madison Julius Cawein, *Kentucky Poems,* introduction by Gosse (London: Richards, 1902);

Benjamin Disraeli, *Endymion,* introduction by Gosse (New York: Cambridge Society, 1905);

Richard Brinsley Sheridan, *The Plays of Sheridan,* introductions by Gosse (London: Heinemann, 1905);

William Shakespeare, *The Comedy of Errors,* volume 1 of *The Complete Works of William Shakespeare,* introduction by Gosse (London: Murray, 1906);

James Thomson, *The Seasons,* edited by Henry D. Roberts, biographical note and critical study by Gosse (London: Routledge / New York: Dutton, 1906);

The Works of Robert Louis Stevenson, Pentland Edition, 20 volumes, bibliographical notes by Gosse (London: Cassell, 1906–1907);

Letters of Thomas Carlyle Addressed to Mrs. Basil Montagu and B. W. Procter, edited by Anne Benson Procter, preface by Gosse (Lakeland, Mich.: E. B. Hill, 1907);

James Henry Leigh Hunt, *Imagination and Fancy,* introduction by Gosse (London: Blackie, 1907);

Eliza Brightwen, *The Life and Thoughts of a Naturalist,* edited by W. H. Chesson, introduction and epilogue by Gosse (London & Leipzig: Unwin, 1909);

Les petits poèmes de John Milton, translated by Fernand Henry, introduction by Gosse (Paris: Guilmoto, 1909);

Francis A. Judd, trans., *Under the Swedish Colours: A Short Anthology of Modern Swedish Poets,* preface by Gosse (London: Elkin Mathews, 1911);

The Poetical Works of John Milton, introduction by Gosse (London: Oxford University Press, 1911);

Percy Bysshe Shelley, *The Sensitive Plant,* introduction by Gosse (London: Heinemann, 1911; Philadelphia: Lippincott, 1911);

Sarojinī Nāyadu, *The Bird of Time: Songs of Love, Death and the Spring,* introduction by Gosse (London: Heinemann / New York: Lane, 1912);

Ernest Rhys, ed., *Restoration Plays from Dryden to Farquhar,* introduction by Gosse (London: Dent, 1912; New York: Dutton, 1953);

Elizabeth Barrett Browning, *Epistle to a Canary, 1837,* edited by Gosse (London: Printed for T. J. Wise, 1913);

Samuel Taylor Coleridge, *Two Addresses on Sir Robert Peel's Bill, April, 1818,* edited by Gosse (Hampstead: T. J. Wise, 1913);

Adam Gottlob Öhlenschläger, *The Gold Horns,* translated by George Borrow, edited by Gosse (London: Printed for Thomas J. Wise, 1913);

Memorial Exhibition of the Work of the Late Sir Alfred East, prefatory note by Gosse (London: Leicester Galleries, 1914);

Anton Kristen Nyström, *Before, during, and after 1914,* translated by H. G. de Walterstorff, introduction by Gosse (London: Heinemann, 1915);

G. Turquet-Milnes, *Some Modern Belgian Writers: A Critical Study,* prefatory note by Gosse (London: Muirhead, 1916);

Algernon Bertram Freeman Mitford, *Further Memories,* introduction by Gosse (London: Hutchinson, 1917);

Algernon Charles Swinburne, *Posthumous Poems,* edited by Gosse and Thomas J. Wise (London: Heinemann, 1917);

Robert Ernest Vernède, *War Poems and Other Verses,* introductory note by Gosse (London: Heinemann, 1917);

Georges Clemenceau, *Europe's Liberation: Speech,* translated by Gosse (London: Anglo-French Society, 1918);

Walter Hutchinson, *The Splendour of France: A Pictorial and Authoritative Account of Our Great and Glorious Ally and Her Country,* 2 volumes, introduction by Gosse (London: Hutchinson, 1918);

The Letters of Algernon Charles Swinburne, 2 volumes, edited by Gosse and Wise (London: Heinemann, 1918; New York: Lane, 1919);

Swinburne, *The Springtide of Life: Poems of Childhood,* edited by Gosse (Philadelphia: Lippincott / London: Heinemann, 1918);

Gosse's wife, Ellen Epps Gosse, at about the time of their marriage

Swinburne, *Contemporaries of Shakespeare,* edited by Gosse and Wise (London: Heinemann, 1919);

Selections from A. C. Swinburne, edited by Gosse and Wise (London: Heinemann, 1919; New York: Doran, 1920);

Robert Browning, *Letters from Le Croisic,* introduction by Gosse (London: Privately printed, 1919);

The Complete Works of Algernon Charles Swinburne, 20 volumes, edited by Gosse and Wise (London: Heinemann, 1925–1927; New York: Wells, 1925–1927);

The Oxford Book of Scandinavian Verse, XVIIth Century–XXth Century, edited by Gosse and W. A. Craigie (Oxford: Clarendon Press, 1925);

Sava Bocarić, *Twenty-five Caricatures by Sava,* introduction by Gosse (London: Elkin Mathews, 1926);

George Farquhar, *The Recruiting Officer,* note by Gosse (London: Davies, 1926);

Richard Lapthorne, *The Portledge Papers,* edited by Russell J. Kerr and Ida Coffin Duncan, preface by Gosse (London: Cape, 1928);

Alexandre Dumas the Younger, *Camille,* translated by Gosse (London: Printed for the Members of the Limited Editions Club at the Curwen Press, 1937).

SELECTED PERIODICAL PUBLICATIONS – UNCOLLECTED: "Ibsen, the Norwegian Satirist," *Fortnightly Review,* 19 (January 1873): 74–88;

"Renaissance in Italy," *Westminster Review,* 108 (October 1877): 351–374;

"Ibsen's Social Drama," *Fortnightly Review,* 51 (January 1889): 107–121;

"Robert Browning: In Memoriam," *New Review,* 2 (January 1890): 91–96;

"Ibsen's New Drama," *Fortnightly Review,* 55 (January 1891): 4–13;

"The Science of Criticism," *New Review,* 4 (May 1891): 408–411;

"A Note on Walt Whitman," *New Review,* 10 (April 1894): 447–457;

"Coventry Patmore," *Contemporary Review,* 71 (February 1897): 184–204;

"Charles Lamb," *Quarterly Review,* 192 (October 1900): 312–335.

RECORDING: "Thomas Hardy, O. M.," London, Columbia Gramophone Company for the International Educational Society, Record Nos. D40020–1, from the radio broadcast of 1928.

Edmund Gosse began his long literary career hoping to make his mark as a poet; but, although a small collection of poems, *On Viol and Flute* (1873), won the approval of some distinguished critics, it was as the first English translator of the plays and poems of Henrik Ibsen, then as an essayist and reviewer, that he earned his reputation. In 1882 his first full-length biography, a life of Thomas Gray, was published in the English Men of Letters series; thereafter he took as his specialty the period from William Shakespeare to Alexander Pope, with lives and studies of writers as diverse as Walter Ralegh (1886) and William Congreve (1888). He also wrote extensively about his contemporaries, including a controversial biography of Algernon Charles Swinburne (1917). But it is for *Father and Son* (1907), his autobiographical record of "the struggle between two temperaments," that he is now best known: it is his finest narrative and one of the great human documents of the Victorian age.

Edmund William Gosse was born in London on 21 September 1849, the only child of Philip Henry Gosse and Emily Bowes Gosse. Philip Gosse was a naturalist of some distinction, who became a fellow of the Royal Society in 1856; a successful author and lecturer, he is usually credited with inventing the aquarium and was certainly the first to popularize its use. Emily Bowes Gosse had been a governess before her marriage and was the author of two books of devotional poetry as well as many religious tracts. Both had known what it was to live on the lower edges of the genteel world, both were self-educated, and both were, above all, devout. They belonged to the Brethren, sometimes known as the Plymouth Brethren, one of the many fundamentalist groups that sprang up during the Evangelical revival of the early nineteenth century. The central doctrine of the Brethren was the unique efficacy for salvation of Christ's blood shed on the cross. They held to the absolute priority of faith over works, of Scripture over tradition, and of the Holy Ghost over the ministers of any church established on earth. Dancing, gambling, tobacco, and the theater were forbidden to those who wanted to join the "saints," since indulgence in any of these vices might impair one's ability to hear God's voice calling to the inner self. In later life Edmund Gosse was inclined to represent the Brethren as at best naive and at worst bigoted, but he also acknowledged that his parents, at least, were "always cheerful and often gay."

In 1857 Gosse's mother died of cancer after months of suffering during which Gosse was her daily companion. Almost her last words were an exhortation to her husband to hold himself and their son firm in their faith: "I shall walk with Him in white. Won't you take your lamb and walk with me?" The "poignant and irresistible insistence" of her final prayer was to add an extra sting to the conflict that gradually developed between Philip and Edmund Gosse.

In the same year as his wife's death Philip Gosse's *Omphalos* was published. The work was designed to resolve the quarrel between religion and science, which in the 1850s was focused on the short chronology demanded by a literal interpretation of the Scriptures and the much longer chronology proposed by the geologists. Philip Gosse argued that just as Adam had been created with a navel and Eden planted with full-grown trees, so, too, in every other respect – including fossils – the earth had been formed with the character of a planet on which life had long existed. The book was attacked by scientists and theologians alike; even Philip Gosse's close friend Charles Kingsley could not accept that God had "written on the rocks one enormous and superfluous lie." It was the second blow in a few months and perhaps did as much as the first to develop the severer and more difficult side of Philip Gosse's nature.

Father and son moved from London to Saint Marychurch, Devonshire, near Torquay. There Philip Gosse concentrated on his work on sea anemones – one new species, *Phellia murocincta,* was Edmund's discovery – and on Edmund's religious education. In 1859 Gosse was publicly baptized; it was, he recalled in *Father and Son,* "the central event of my whole childhood" and "dazzling beyond words." But, looking back fifty years later he was sure that, although he "wished extremely to be good and holy," there was "never . . . a moment in which my heart truly responded." He was aware instead of "a hard nut of individuality" that stood apart in resistance, not yet doubting his father's faith but unable to be swept along by it.

Gosse at age thirty

He started school in the summer of 1860, for the first time in regular contact with other children of his own age. At the end of the same year his father married Eliza Brightwen; though from a wealthy Quaker family, she, too, soon underwent public baptism and joined the "saints." Under her influence the Gosse household began to relax; Edmund was allowed to read the works of Charles Dickens, excitedly absorbing *The Pickwick Papers* (1836–1837), and at school he began to write poetry. In 1865 he achieved outstanding results in the Senior Cambridge Examinations; there was, however, no possibility of his going to Oxford or Cambridge, which would remain bound to the Church of England until the Universities Tests Act of 1871. Eventually his father's reputation, the support and patronage of Kingsley, and his knowledge of modern and classical languages and literature earned him a place as junior assistant at the British Museum, and in January 1867 he left for London to take up the post.

He took lodgings in Tottenham with Anne Buckham, an old friend of his father's. He joined in the local Brethren meetings and taught a Sunday school class, but he still had to endure the "torment of a postal inquisition" from his father, to whom anything less than absolute faith in the doctrines taught by the Brethren was the first step on the road to damnation. Gosse gradually drew away from his father's position, and in the mid 1870s he would arrive at that stance of sympathetic detachment that characterizes his treatment of their conflict in *Father and Son*. His love of literature, increasing social success, and – after his marriage – the happiness of his family life seem to have satisfied his emotional needs to the point where issues of belief and unbelief could be put aside. His published writings give no evidence of the struggle to reconstruct something in which to believe that one might have expected of a young man brought up as he had been.

The worst sin with which his father could charge him at this time seems to have been a letter he wrote to the distinctly heterodox Swinburne in 1867, asking for advice about his own poems. Gosse had become sure of his vocation as a poet. Among his colleagues at the British Museum were Richard

Garnett, later to write *The Twilight of the Gods, and Other Tales* (1888), and Arthur O'Shaughnessy, remembered now as the author of "Ode" (1874), which begins "We are the music-makers."

Early in 1870 Gosse told his father that he wished to marry Mary Jane Johnson, daughter of a churchwarden at Saint Paul's Cathedral. Philip Gosse consented to the proposed marriage, while pointing out that Gosse's salary of £105 a year would not be enough to marry on; but at the end of May 1870 Johnson died after an operation for cancer of the knee.

A collection of poems, *Madrigals, Songs and Sonnets,* by Gosse and his friend John Blaikie, was published at the end of 1870. Gosse bought 39 of the 150 copies printed, but the book provided him with an introduction to literary circles. In the 1870s he was tireless in making himself known to the painters and writers he admired. An admiring letter to William Bell Scott was answered with an invitation to visit. Through Scott he met the painter Ford Madox Brown, and through him Swinburne, Dante Gabriel Rossetti, and William Morris.

In 1871 Gosse took a vacation in Norway. An immediate product of his visit was an article for *Fraser's Magazine* on the Lofoden Islands, his first published essay; the long-term result was of much greater significance. In Norway Gosse had bought a recently published volume of poems by Ibsen, of whom he had never heard. He reviewed the poems in the *Spectator* in the spring of 1872; it was "the first time Ibsen's name was printed in any English publication," as Gosse was later to tell the Ibsen translator William Archer. In July 1872 he wrote an article about *Peer Gynt* (1867), again for the *Spectator,* and in January 1873 a longer essay, "Ibsen, The Norwegian Satirist," was published in the *Fortnightly Review.* Long before 1889, when Archer's translation of *A Doll's House* (1879) was first performed and Ibsen began to attract widespread attention in England, Gosse had made himself the foremost English authority on Scandinavian literature.

The time was right for someone to claim such a position. Morris was translating the Icelandic sagas, Hans Christian Andersen was still one of the best-known writers in Europe, and Ibsen was moving away from the earlier poetic dramas toward the problem plays that were to cause so much agitation in London in the 1890s. There was an intense rivalry between the supporters of the allegedly reactionary Ibsen (who seemed sufficiently liberal to Gosse) and those of the avowedly radical Björnstjerne Björnson; by insisting that he had no political agenda Gosse was able to remain on friendly terms with them all, and despite his admiration for Ibsen he was later invited to edit the English edition of Björnson's novels (1894). On visits to Norway and Denmark in 1872 and 1874 he was introduced to most of the significant Scandinavian literary figures of the time – though not to Ibsen, who was living in Dresden. In 1879 *Studies in the Literature of Northern Europe* established his reputation as a critic and scholar.

The early 1870s was the period of Gosse's closest friendship with Swinburne; it was a time when other friends, notably Rossetti, were backing away in alarm at Swinburne's increasingly difficult behavior. In 1875 Gosse wrote a long essay for a Danish journal in which he applauded his friend's readiness to defy the prejudices of a philistine public with his "thundering melodies of lust and cruelty and blasphemy" and to unfurl "the red flag" of his republican sympathies "in its most startling redness." The article was not published in English until 1925 and could hardly have been written at all if there was a chance that his father might read it. Gosse's own poetry was far from thunderous, still less blasphemous, nor were his politics ever "red." But Swinburne's influence over Gosse was powerful, and it is perhaps significant that when he married and moved away from his lodgings in Tottenham, he also abandoned his teaching in the Sunday school.

Through Ford Madox Brown, Gosse met Ellen Epps; the daughter of a homeopathic doctor, she had her own studio and was exhibiting her paintings regularly. She and Gosse were married in August 1875; they lived at first in the home of another artist, Lawrence Alma-Tadema, who had married Ellen's sister. Their financial position improved considerably when, not long after their marriage, Gosse received a lifetime appointment as translator to the Board of Trade. In 1876 Ellen gave birth to a stillborn child; a year later they had a daughter, Emily. A son, Philip, followed in 1879, and another daughter, Sylvia, in 1881. The marriage was a happy one; for most of the next fifty years the Gosses maintained the custom of keeping Sunday afternoons "at home," at the center of an ever-widening circle of friends and protégés.

By 1877 Gosse and Robert Louis Stevenson were members of the Savile Club, and whenever Stevenson was in London the two met as frequently as possible. Swinburne was a regular visitor to the Gosses until Theodore Watts (later Watts-Dunton) took him away to Putney in 1879. Around this time Gosse developed an intense affection for the sculptor Hamo Thornycroft. He spent the last half hour

Gosse in his library; etching by his daughter Sylvia

of 31 December 1879 writing to Thornycroft, describing him as "the inestimable treasure for which I was waiting nearly thirty years" and promising that "My last thoughts in this year and my first thoughts in next year will be of you." In an 1890 letter to John Addington Symonds, whom he knew to be homosexual, Gosse confessed that he, too, had known "the solitude, the rebellion, the despair" of which Symonds had written; it seems probable that the "obstinate twist" in his life to which this letter refers was his love for Thornycroft. But he was able to accommodate it, and the two remained close until Thornycroft's death in 1925.

Robert Browning was another friend of these years. In 1881 he allowed Gosse to question him about his life for an article for the *Century Magazine,* which was revised and published as a small book the year after Browning's death in 1889. Browning had charge of the papers and manuscripts of Thomas Lovell Beddoes, and he and Gosse went through them in 1883. Gosse would write the *Dictio-*

nary of National Biography (*DNB*) entries on Browning and Beddoes and edit Beddoes's *Poetical Works* (1890) as well as his letters (1894). During the autumn and winter of 1880–1881 Gosse strengthened his friendship with Thomas Hardy, who spent much of that winter in London ill and confined to bed. Another friend was Henry James, who settled permanently in England in 1883 and would, before his death in 1916, write more than four hundred letters to Gosse. Coventry Patmore was yet another friend acquired in the same period; Gosse wrote several articles on Patmore's poetry, in addition to a biography (1905). In later life Gosse was often to be accused of duplicity, of having one voice to his friends and another about them. The adjective most often attached to him was "feline"; even James, who enjoyed gossip as much as anyone, described him as a friend one would prefer to survive. But his friendships, if not deep, were genuine. His critical writing is at its strongest precisely when it is most relaxed, most thoroughly informed by the atmosphere of familiarity and understanding that he was able to establish with so many of his contemporaries. In 1879 Stevenson had written to Gosse about *Studies in the Literature of Northern Europe* that the "personal notes" were the best and had advised him to "See as many people as you can and make a book of them before you die. You have the touch required." It was advice that Gosse seems to have taken to heart.

In December 1881 Gosse set to work on a life of Thomas Gray for John Morley's English Men of Letters series, completing it four months later. It was an immediate success: Swinburne, Stevenson, and Matthew Arnold praised it, and Leslie Stephen used it as the basis for his *DNB* entry. Two years later Gosse's edition of *The Works of Thomas Gray* was similarly applauded. In fact, both the life and the edition reveal Gosse's extraordinary ability to be inaccurate. The errors in the biography are comparatively unimportant; for example, Gosse describes in elaborate detail a hoax played on Gray by two fellow commoners at Peterhouse College of Cambridge University. Afraid that rowdy behavior in the college might cause a fire, Gray had a rope ladder installed in his room; as Gosse tells the story, he was deceived one night by a false alarm into climbing down the ladder and into a tub of cold water prepared by his tormentors: "But the jest might easily have proved fatal; as it was, he shivered in the February air so excessively that he had to be wrapped in the coat of a passing watchman, and to be carried into the college by the friendly Stonehewer." The truth seems to be that Gray was fooled only to the extent of looking out of his window. But accuracy was not Gosse's first criterion. He wrote to Stevenson on 23 June 1882: "I want to know if you feel the *man* to have been a fine soul – if not, I have failed." On these terms, he had succeeded; his slips, though many and given unwarranted authority by Stephen's repetition of them in the *DNB,* hardly mattered to the popular audience the series was intended to attract. A more significant weakness is the blandness of the critical passages; of the *Elegy Written in a Country Churchyard* (1751), for example, Gosse has little to offer that had not already been said by Samuel Johnson, while the view that Gray's genius "pined away for want of movement in the atmosphere" merely reworks what Arnold had written in *Essays in Criticism* in 1865. The speed at which the book was written may account for its slightness as a work of criticism.

The problems in the edition are of a different order, including misdated letters, omissions, and mistranscriptions. Gosse claims in the preface that the text of Gray's letters to Thomas Warton was "scrupulously printed" from the Egerton Manuscripts in the British Museum; the task of transcription was in reality entrusted to a copyist who used an earlier printed edition, in the process adding to existing inaccuracies. Sustained criticism of Gosse's editing would not get under way, however, until the turn of the century. He tried to build on his success by putting his name forward for the newly established Clark Lectureship at Cambridge. Few candidates can ever have mustered better support: Browning, Arnold, and Alfred Tennyson wrote on his behalf. But the post went to Stephen, who was then beginning his work on the *DNB.* Their rivalry for the post had been inadvertent and did no harm to their friendship.

Gosse's disappointment was offset by a proposal that he give some lectures at the Lowell Institute in Boston and at Johns Hopkins University in Baltimore; he was also offered a professorship at Yale University. He was not seriously tempted by the offer of a chair, which would have required him to live in America, but the lecture tour was attractive. He was the London agent for the *Century Magazine,* and he had a genuine interest in American literature. In 1883 he had started a friendship with William Dean Howells, and it was Howells who set up the American trip. As Gosse was planning his lectures the news came that Stephen had resigned from the Clark Lectureship and that Gosse had been appointed as Stephen's successor. Almost at once, and with his usual exaggeration, he wrote Stevenson that he had become "Professor of English Literature at the University of Cambridge." He was given rooms in Trinity College, and in October 1884 he delivered his first lecture to an enthusiastic audience. In November he began his American tour, on which he was more popular than either Arnold or Oscar Wilde had been; his lectures were sold out, and people were turned away at the door. He visited Walt Whitman, to whom he had sent *On Viol and Flute* ten years earlier; Oliver Wendell Holmes came to each of the Boston lectures; President Chester A. Arthur showed Gosse and his wife around the White House.

On his return to England Gosse submitted to Macmillan, supposedly on behalf of a friend, the manuscript for a novel, *The Unequal Yoke,* which appeared in the *English Illustrated Magazine* from April to June 1886; it would not appear as a book until 1975, and Gosse never publicly acknowledged it. He was also beginning work on his next biography, a life of Ralegh for the English Worthies series; preparing for the press his next volume of poems, *Firdausi in Exile and Other Poems* (1885); and writing

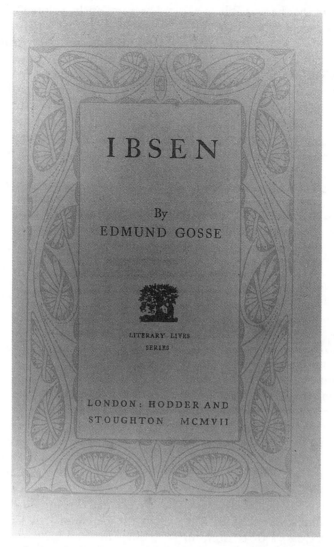

Title page for Gosse's biography of the Norwegian playwright. Gosse had been largely responsible for introducing Ibsen to English-speaking audiences in the 1870s.

up his lectures under the title *From Shakespeare to Pope: An Inquiry into the Causes and Phenomena of the Rise of Classical Poetry in England*. It was Gosse's most academic book, and its publication by the Cambridge University Press in the autumn of 1885 ought to have set the seal on his achievement. In fact, it marked the severest setback his career was ever to suffer.

The initial response was generally favorable, but in October 1886 John Churton Collins launched a fierce attack in the *Quarterly Review* under the title "English Literature at the Universities." Collins argued that men of letters had once formed an "intellectual aristocracy" and had been stimulated by their rivalry to produce work of the highest quality; but in the nineteenth century, an age of mass production and mass education, many books were written merely for the sake of establishing a "factitious reputation," and it had become the responsibility of the universities to maintain a standard of unquestioned excellence. But in publishing *From Shakespeare to Pope* Cambridge University had shirked this responsibility. Collins then demonstrated "the recklessness with which Mr. Gosse displays his ignorance of the very elements of literature": Gosse had written in a way that showed that he thought that Sir Philip Sidney's *Arcadia* (1590) was a poem, not a prose work; he had confused Sir John Harrington, the poet, with the later prose writer James Harrington; he had suggested that John Milton and Wentworth Dillon, Earl of Roscommon, were the only major poets to use blank verse between 1660 and 1760, apparently forgetting John Dryden's *All for Love* (1678), not to mention most of the work of James Thomson, Edward Young, and Mark Akenside. Gosse had written of "the value of dates and the paramount importance of a clear chronological sequence," but Collins showed that date after date was wrongly given. Worse, when Gosse had his facts right he was liable to boast of them, with "officious egotism," as discoveries of his own, whereas Collins was able to show that they were common knowledge.

Collins's article left Gosse devastated; but Collins was not a popular man, and Gosse was. James, Hardy, Symonds, and Stevenson all wrote to condole with Gosse and to reassure him that Collins's attack had so far overshot the mark that public opinion would come around in the end to Gosse's side. In an article in the *Athenaeum* in October 1886 Gosse tried, not very convincingly, to answer some of Collins's criticisms and concluded by referring to a period when Collins had been his friend and guest; the implication was that Collins had written out of malice and was not a gentleman. Others besides Gosse had suffered at Collins's hands and were ready to go along with this version of the affair. But Gosse would never entirely recover his reputation; the charge of inaccuracy was to be made against him with increasing frequency, and despite the blow he had suffered in 1886 it was a charge to which he continued to be vulnerable.

Gosse's biography *Raleigh* was published in 1886. There had been two recent studies for him to build on, by Edward Edwards and by James Augustus St. John, both in 1868, as well as an edition of Ralegh's correspondence. Gosse's aim was to portray Ralegh's personal career, as far as possible, "disengaged from the general history of the time." The emphasis is on personalities; on friendships made and broken or too much trusted to; on ambition, success, and failure. The analysis is correspondingly light; thus, Gosse notes "some excusable equivocation" in Ralegh's "great apology" from the scaffold but is more concerned to capture the drama of the scene – Ralegh's careful choice of clothes for the occasion, his hands thrust out as a signal to the executioner to strike, the executioner's hesitation – than to weigh the justice of what was said and done. And the narrative and drama are, as James wrote to assure him, "wondrous well done." The familiar stories are recounted with Carlylean verve, though with none of Carlyle's interest in the eternal verities underlying the human scene. Deservedly, within self-imposed limits, the book attracted friendly comment. Stevenson had "never

read anything more unaffected and effective"; Hardy wrote from Max Gate that his wife, Emma, was going to read it aloud to him. Such support was a welcome counterweight to the Collins scandal.

In 1887 Gosse was asked to write the *Life of William Congreve* for the Great Writers series, published by Walter Scott. Congreve's life had been largely uneventful, there was little interest in him or his work, and there were no competitors in the field. Nonetheless, Gosse approached his task with care and deserves credit for helping to prepare the way for the club performances of the plays in the early part of the twentieth century, as well as for the editorial work of Montague Summers in the 1920s. His account of the Collier controversy is balanced and detailed, and more intelligent about the stronger parts of Jeremy Collier's argument than most previous commentators had been. He also provides a good deal of information about the theater and actors of Congreve's day, and the critical discussion at the heart of the book is lively and informative enough to encourage a rereading of the plays. Gosse could occasionally sound priggish in his later years – E. M. Forster's *Howards End* (1910) struck him as "sensational and dirty and affected" – but in *Life of William Congreve* he declined to bend the knee to Mrs. Grundy, and in this respect his study was ahead of its time. Even so, he felt that because "a universal profligate coarseness" was part of the fabric of Restoration comedy and therefore "ineradicable," the plays could no longer be staged.

In 1888 Tennyson invited Gosse to Aldworth, where he was shown around by the Poet Laureate himself. Gosse later gave offense when, as a result of his carelessness, "The Throstle," a poem he had solicited from Tennyson for the *New Review,* was printed with two words missing. Gosse's father died in August 1888, and Gosse responded by beginning work on *The Life of Philip Henry Gosse, F.R.S.* (1890). Gosse was anxious to write something more objective than the routinely dutiful biography so often favored by the sons, daughters, and wives of the great Victorians. James considered it "singularly clever, skilful, vivid, . . . very happy in proportion, tact and talent," but several friends wrote that they missed the sense of Gosse's own life in the book. Symonds and George Moore urged him to write an autobiography: as Moore put it, "a great psychological work waits to be written." *Father and Son* was, however, not to appear for another seventeen years.

Gosse's *Gossip in a Library* (1891), based on articles he had written for the American *Independent* and other magazines, is a leisurely discussion of books in his own library; it set the pattern for his

THE LIFE

OF

ALGERNON CHARLES
SWINBURNE

BY

EDMUND GOSSE, C.B.

MACMILLAN AND CO., LIMITED
ST. MARTIN'S STREET, LONDON
1917

A. C. Swinburne and his sisters
from the painting by George Richmond R.A.
in the National Portrait Gallery

Frontispiece and title page for the biography in which Gosse omits mention of the scandalous aspects of his old friend's life

later work, much of which consisted of collections of previously published essays, articles, and introductions. He was increasingly drawn into the fashionable world: Sidney Colvin arranged for him to give a series of lectures in the drawing room of Almina Wombwell, Lady Carnarvon, and he became a friend of Lady Dorothy Nevill, to whom he dedicated his novel *The Secret of Narcisse* (1892). He was already on the committee of the London Library, and he began to be on every other literary committee as well: the Royal Literary Fund, the Royal Society of Literature, and the Society of Authors. He was becoming a member of the establishment and a man of influence in the world of letters.

Arthur Waugh in the *Fortnightly Review* (1932) noted that "Gosse loved to be a patron of the young, and he was a patron who did not patronise."

Others charged that Gosse was only enthusiastic about writers he could claim to have discovered. His long and often tetchy relationship with Arthur Christopher Benson, recorded in Benson's diary (1926), gives some support to the view that as he grew older Gosse became unduly demanding of the admiration of those around him. But he continued to associate himself with the new as well as the old. He was among the most enthusiastic of Rudyard Kipling's admirers – in part, perhaps, because he, like James and like Kipling himself, had fallen under the spell of Wolcott Balestier, who was in England to negotiate royalty contracts with English authors whose works were to be published in the United States. Gosse was also among the contributors to Aubrey Beardsley's *The Yellow Book* in 1894, and he remained an admirer of Beardsley's work (Beardsley's edition of Pope's *The Rape of the Lock* [1896] is dedicated to Gosse). He befriended Wilde's friend Robert Ross, though a letter to Ross after Wilde's trial, while supportive, makes it plain that Ross would be welcome to visit only "in future, calmer times." He urged William Heinemann to publish the poems of Arthur Symons and helped secure a Civil List pension for William Butler Yeats (though he was unwilling to do so for James Joyce, whom he considered a "charlatan"); around 1904 he began a friendship with André Gide and did a good deal to create an English audience for Gide's work.

In 1891 a misunderstanding set Gosse and Archer at odds over the right to translate Ibsen's *Hedda Gabler* (1890); the quarrel was soon patched up, but not before an article by Archer describing Gosse's translations as "inconceivably careless" and "fantastically inaccurate" had been published in the *Pall Mall Gazette* (23 January 1891). During the 1890s Gosse also came to know the forger Thomas J. Wise, and the claim has been made that he was implicated in some of Wise's dealings. The accusation is not well founded. It clearly served Wise's purpose to have his forgeries in Gosse's library; every reference to Wise in Gosse's works, and there are many, helped establish Wise's reputation as an authority. Gosse was an inveterate collector of rare editions, and he was persuaded that he was helping Wise to make available material that might, without their efforts, have lain undiscovered. Wise was not exposed until six years after Gosse's death, and before then he had imposed on many people, most of them less inclined to carelessness than Gosse. It seems almost certain that Gosse was Wise's dupe, not his ally; letters from Wise to Gosse that give a false provenance for forged editions are surely inconsistent with the idea that Gosse knew them to be forgeries.

Gosse's *A Short History of Modern English Literature* (1897) quickly established itself as a standard text, going through ten impressions by 1923 and being republished with new material in 1924. It is a polite and essentially unchallenging account of English writers from Geoffrey Chaucer to the end of the nineteenth century; most of its judgments would have been familiar to contemporary readers, though not all of those readers would have been quite so ready to relegate John Stuart Mill to the margins of intellectual history or as generous in tribute to Charles Darwin as "one of the great artificers of human thought." The few pages devoted to John Donne could have prepared nobody for the more substantial work Gosse was about to produce, the two volumes of *The Life and Letters of John Donne,*

Dean of St Paul's (1899). *A Short History of Modern English Literature* merely rehearses Johnson's objections to the metaphysical poets, though in a more florid prose and with no sign of Johnson's capacity for analysis and quotation, and concludes: "No one has injured English writing more than Donne, not even Carlyle." Nonetheless, it was the poetry above all that led Gosse to his work on Donne.

The materials with which he had to work were unpromising: mainly the letters published by John Donne the Younger in 1651 under the title *Letters to Severall Persons of Honour* and a few published elsewhere with scant regard for chronology and with many errors and omissions. *The Life and Letters of John Donne* was the first serious attempt to order this material; though Augustus Jessop had been working on a biography for some years, in 1897 he handed the responsibility over to Gosse. Subsequent biographers of Donne have corrected many of Gosse's suggestions while acknowledging the extreme complexity of the task that faced him, and he deserves some credit as a pioneer. Unfortunately, he was persuaded that many of the poems could be read as evidence of events in Donne's life, that "hardly a piece of his genuine verse" could not "be prevailed upon to deliver up some secret of his life and character." Inevitably, some of the secrets he uncovers, especially those relating to Donne's sexual life in the 1590s, are largely figments of his own imagination.

There are, too, the characteristic Gosse errors. He had bought the Westmoreland manuscript for the "Holy Sonnets" in 1892 and assured his readers that he had closely collated the manuscript with the earliest printed versions, but, even so, the text of "Since she whome I loved," for which the Westmoreland manuscript is the only authority, is wrongly given: Gosse's "early into heaven vanished" is an understandable misreading of the manuscript's "early into heaven ravished" but lame enough to have called for closer attention. It seems that Gosse could never be trusted to record a date or transcribe a manuscript correctly or to check that his amanuensis had done so. Nor is it clear why Gosse usually preferred the reading of the 1651 edition of the letters to the holograph, where the latter was available. Some other errors were quickly noticed by contemporary readers: for example, that the "Dr. Donne" who secured a divorce for the Countess of Essex so that she could remarry was Sir Daniel Dunn and not, as Gosse supposed, John Donne. Gosse also caused some offense by suggesting that Donne had not been converted until 1617, after he had taken Holy Orders, but what he had in mind was conversion as the Brethren would have

Gosse in the gardens of the château Malmaison, near Paris, about two weeks before his death

understood it: a sudden, overpowering sense of the need for God's grace. He was not intending to besmirch Donne's name, as one correspondent protested.

Herbert Grierson, in his edition of Donne's poems in 1912, paid tribute both to Gosse's biography and to the kindness Gosse had shown him when he began to work on the edition. Modern critical study of the poems, however, takes Grierson as a starting point, not Gosse; the remark by John Carey, that opposition to reading the poems autobiographically comes for the most part "from persons with literary gifts infinitely smaller than Gosse's," seems perverse when placed against some of the readings Gosse offers. But Gosse had done goundbreaking work on the biography. Whatever the local errors, his Donne is clearly recognizable in the figure who emerges from what is now the standard life, that by R. C. Bald, published in 1970. It seems appropriate that Gosse received his first hon-

orary degree, an LL.D. from the University of St. Andrews, in the year in which *The Life and Letters of John Donne* was published.

In 1901 the Gosses moved into a larger house overlooking Regent's Park, where Gosse lived until his death. His main literary work at this time was to write part of the second volume, and the whole of the third and fourth, of *English Literature: An Illustrated Record* (1903), a four-volume popular history mainly interesting for its pictures of writers, houses, autographs, and facsimiles that he produced with Garnett. In 1904 he left the Board of Trade to become librarian to the House of Lords at a salary of one thousand pounds a year. He would remain in the post until he was obliged to retire at the age of sixty-five in September 1914.

In 1904 and 1905 Gosse produced three biographies. Two of these, *Jeremy Taylor* (1904) and *Sir Thomas Browne* (1905), were for the English Men of Letters series. Taylor's work, especially *The Rule and Exercises of Holy Living* (1650), was widely admired throughout the nineteenth century. Perhaps with his own background in mind, Gosse praises Taylor's *The Liberty of Prophesying* (1647), a plea for freedom of conscience, or what Taylor calls, in a passage quoted by Gosse, "a mutual toleration and private liberty of persuasion." But Gosse was reluctant to become too deeply involved in the detail of Taylor's theological arguments; in keeping with the series title, he was concerned with his subject as a man of letters. The final chapter, "Taylor's Place in Literary History," shows Gosse's belletristic style of criticism in its most sympathetic light.

Sir Thomas Browne similarly, and perhaps with more justice, treats its subject as a literary craftsman, "interesting almost exclusively to the student and lover of style." Gosse is sympathetic to Browne's eagerness to gossip about himself, to reveal "the little secrets of his soul" with "exquisite skill," and he writes with admiration of Browne's tolerance, though he attributes it to "an easy-going temper" rather than to reason or principle. Only in his indignant account of Browne's role in the "judicial murder" of two women accused of witchcraft in 1664 does he seem seriously concerned with Browne's ideas and beliefs. But he is generally out of patience with the extravagance of Browne's literary manner and at times seems to be writing to complete a commissioned work rather than with commitment.

Between these two works came a quite different one, *Coventry Patmore* (1905). Patmore, who had died in 1896, at one time had wanted Gosse to act as his literary executor, but it had been agreed that this responsibility would better suit someone who, like Patmore, was a Roman Catholic. In 1900 Basil Champneys had published two volumes of Patmore's *Memoirs and Correspondence;* Gosse saw it as his task to round out these volumes with a critical estimate of Patmore's work and his own reminiscences of their friendship in the 1880s and 1890s, years in which his critical essays had helped to revive Patmore's flagging reputation. Benson was distressed by what he thought of as Gosse's "need of skipping and posturing before the people, of bowing them in to the show." There may be some oblique self-reference when Gosse reflects on the sudden renewal of creative energy that took place in Patmore's fifty-fifth year, an age when "a man has usually tasted all the dishes which make up the banquet of life, and has no great desire to begin the feast over again"; at the time of writing, Gosse was fifty-four. The final chapter of the book, on Patmore's personality toward the end of his life, is

for the most part unaffectedly moving; it is the kind of writing that Gosse did best.

Gosse wrote the long obituary notice in the London *Times* after Ibsen's death in May 1906, and his biography of the playwright appeared at the end of 1907. It had been thirty-five years since Gosse reviewed Ibsen's *Digte* (Poems, 1871) in the *Spectator* (16 March 1872); there is some irony in the fact that the two men had not met until 1899, the year in which a stroke put an end to Ibsen's career as a dramatist. While some of the Ibsen criticism Gosse had produced over the years was marked more by enthusiasm than insight, in the 1870s his had been almost a lone voice, and several of his essays – in particular "Ibsen's Social Dramas" in the *Fortnightly Review* (January 1889) – had been bold and intelligent. Gosse had long since said what he had to say, and his biography is a rather tired affair.

Gosse's other work of 1907 was *Father and Son.* It was first published anonymously, but within twelve months there were four further impressions, and Gosse put his name on the title page. In the preface Gosse describes the book "as a *document,* as a record of educational and religious conditions, which, having passed away, will never return." His ambition to write in a documentary manner is apparent throughout and perhaps explains the anonymous publication. Gosse proceeds as a naturalist of the human mind, seemingly committed to the inductive methods of the Victorian social scientist. In this way the account of "a struggle between two temperaments, two consciences and almost two epochs" can be presented dispassionately and the gradual rift between father and son seen as "inevitable": a matter of sorrow but not of blame or accusation.

Father and Son is, however, an autobiography as much as a documentary, concerned not only to record but also to defend the processes of development and individuation. The epilogue, which Gosse added at the request of his publisher, Heinemann, begins by insisting that the son should not occupy "the foreground of the piece" since ultimately the value of the work "consists in what light it may contrive to throw upon the unique and noble figure of the Father." But far more than the earlier chapters, the epilogue shows the father as an inquisitor and a barrier to the son's growth. The last paragraphs, in which the son resumes the central place in the narrative, are a manifesto on behalf of individual freedom as the father's yoke is broken and the son claims "a human being's privilege to fashion his inner life for himself." Throughout the book there is a tension between the documentary and the autobiographical elements: on the one hand, the patient submission of the narrative voice to the observable facts, and on the other, those moments of growth and resistance when the son is seen coming into possession of an experience uniquely his.

In 1912 Gosse wrote the entry on Swinburne for the *DNB* (he reprinted the entry the same year in his *The Life of Swinburne, with a Letter on Swinburne at Eton by Lord Redesdale*) and was caught in another characteristic error: the attribution to Swinburne of poems published over the initials A. C. S. but not written by him. But in *The Life of Algernon Charles Swinburne,* published in 1917, he was able to boast of "the checking and rechecking of eight years." What was at stake in this instance was not his accuracy but his timidity. Despite the closeness of their friendship in the 1870s and his access to the large number of manuscripts Wise bought after Swinburne's death, the biography makes no mention of the flogging block, and Swinburne's mistress Adah Isaacs Menken figures only as the author of a volume of poems titled *Infelicia* (1868). There were immense difficulties in Gosse's way, in particular a threat from members of the poet's family to denounce the book as a pack of falsehoods if he wrote anything "unpleasant." In addition, some reviewers had already attacked what they thought to be the indiscretions of the *DNB* article. Gosse's solution was to lodge Swinburne's confidential papers in the British Museum and to present in the biography what Ezra Pound derided as "a Swinburne coated with a veneer of British officialdom and decked out for a psalm-singing audience." Gosse himself was dissatisfied with the book, even though there was sufficient demand to justify a second impression within a month of the first publication. Yet *The Life of Algernon Charles Swinburne* remains of value. "There is," Gosse remarks at one point, "something very attractive in the accessibility of those who are difficult to approach," and the Swinburne of his study is, indeed, accessible: for example, in the account of him sitting on a sofa with Gosse's daughters on his knee, while young Philip Gosse stroked his bald cranium as though it were the egg of some enormous bird. If it is not the life that might have been looked for, that should not be allowed to obscure its real merits.

Gosse received a succession of honors that included the Légion d'Honneur in 1913 and culminated in knighthood in 1925. In January 1928 he attended the funeral of Hardy, his friend for nearly fifty years. In March his services to the literature of Norway were marked by the award of an honorary degree from the University of Oslo. He died on 16 May after an operation.

In 1931 T. S. Eliot, reviewing Evan Charteris's *The Life and Letters of Sir Edmund Gosse* in the *Criterion,* wrote that there would be no one to take the place filled by Gosse in the literary and social life of London "because it is, so to speak, an office that has been abolished." It was an accurate view of Gosse's role as a critic in the years between the end of World War I and his death in 1928. In the preface to *Leaves and Fruit* (1927), made up of pieces he had written for his regular column in the *Sunday Times* since 1919, Gosse claimed to have come "to regard with equal interest all forms of passionate expression, whether grave or gay, profound or superficial." At its best, this attitude could be seen as a generous openness, a readiness to take on the diversity of literature, and in his support for Ibsen, Swinburne, and Gide, as well as for postwar writers such as Siegfried Sassoon, Gosse exhibited such generosity. But his apparent evenhandedness can also be seen as a trivialized, and trivializing, version of the aestheticism that in his youth was being advanced as a radical and challenging position. Gosse's critical writing escapes this charge only intermittently, and hardly at all after the 1890s.

In his article on biography for the *Encyclopaedia Britannica* Gosse argued that the biographer's task was to provide "a faithful portrait of a soul in its adventures through life," not to offer a broader view of the individual in relation to the movement of history: "there is, perhaps, no greater literary mistake than to attempt what is called the 'Life and Times' of a man." This conception is at once the strength and the limitation of Gosse's work as a biographer. He delighted in the incidental detail, the revealing anecdote, the accidents as well as the substance of his subject's life; and however faulty his scholarship, his portraits are often illuminating, especially where he was able to draw on personal knowledge of those he was discussing. But his desire to separate the "Life" from the "Times" often proves frustrating.

On 13 March 1908 Gosse had written to Oscar Wilde's literary executor, Robert Ross, with Wilde's *De Profundis* (1905) in mind: "more and more personal liberty becomes a passion, almost a fanaticism, with me." But his biographical writing lacks this passion. After the death of John Addington Symonds in 1893 he had helped to burn a mass of Symonds's papers; Symonds's daughter, hearing the story from Gosse himself, was nauseated by the "smug gloating delight" with which he remembered it. Gosse's action was hardly unusual; there were any number of such bonfires in the later nineteenth century. But when the man who strikes the match is both a biographer and an avowed defender of personal freedom, it is easy to share her anger.

The critical debate about the genre to which *Father and Son* belongs, begun by Harold Nicolson in his *The Development of English Biography* (1927), shows no sign of abating; but few other books bring into the foreground with such subtlety the questions about compliance and reticence, authenticity and individuality, that confront the student of late-nineteenth- and early-twentieth-century biography. Even Gosse's most exasperated critics are drawn into describing it as a masterpiece: if not quite an indisputable one, at the least a text to which every critic and scholar is bound to refer.

Nevertheless, Gosse is, in many ways, a disappointing writer. He neither built up for himself a new faith to replace the one he had lost (as did "Mark Rutherford" [William Hale White], with whom he is often compared), nor did he make himself a place as a poet. Instead, he became that much less interesting creature, a man of letters – hence the biographies, both those that retold in more or less popular form the lives of past writers for such series as the English Men of Letters and those that traded on his personal acquaintance with the greater poets of his own time. Gosse was, then, a biographer by default. In *Father and Son,* and in the letter to Ross, he sees himself as a defender of the right of the individual to shape his or her own life and to have that right acknowledged and respected by others – by no means a view held by many Victorian biographers. In some of his work – as in his writing on Congreve and in his defense of Ibsen – he came close to acting on that view. But to burn papers, or to buy them in the British Museum, is not the act of a man prepared to stand up for his "passion, almost a fanaticism," for personal liberty. The nub of the problem is that Gosse lacked courage. A braver man would have faced up to his loss of faith with something other than Sunday afternoons at home, would have done more with his poetic talents than become a clubbable man of letters, would have reacted to his sense that he had come close to having his own life shaped by others by doing something more than produce discreet half-truths in his biographies.

Letters:

The Correspondence of André Gide and Edmund Gosse, 1904–1928, edited by Linette F. Brugmans (London: Owen, 1959; New York: New York University Press, 1959);

Sir Edmund Gosse's Correspondence with Scandinavian Writers, edited by Elias Bredsdorff (Copenhagen: Gyldendal, 1960);

Transatlantic Dialogue: Selected American Correspondence of Edmund Gosse, edited by Paul Mattheisen and Michael Millgate (Austin & London: University of Texas Press, 1965).

Bibliographies:

A Catalogue of the Gosse Correspondence in the Brotherton Collection (Leeds: University of Leeds Library Publications, 1950);

James D. Woolf, "Sir Edmund Gosse: An Annotated Bibliography of Writing About Him," *English Literature in Transition (1880–1920),* 11, no. 3 (1968): 126–172;

"Edmund Gosse," in *English Prose and Criticism, 1900–1950,* edited by Christopher C. Brown and William B. Thesing (Detroit: Gale Research, 1983), pp. 179–198.

Biographies:

Evan Charteris, *The Life and Letters of Sir Edmund Gosse* (London: Heinemann, 1931);

Ann Thwaite, *Edmund Gosse: A Literary Landscape, 1849–1928* (London: Secker & Warburg, 1984).

References:

Peter Abbs, Introduction to Gosse's *Father and Son* (Harmondsworth, U.K.: Penguin, 1983);

R. Victoria Arana, "Sir Edmund Gosse's *Father and Son:* Autobiography as Comedy," *Genre,* 10 (Spring 1977): 63–76;

Joseph O. Baylen, "Edmund Gosse, William Archer, and Ibsen in Victorian Britain," *Tennessee Studies in Literature,* 20 (1975): 124–137;

Max Beerbohm, "A Recollection by Edm*nd G*sse," in his *A Christmas Garland* (London: Heinemann, 1912), pp. 135–146;

Arthur Christopher Benson, *The Diary of Arthur Christopher Benson,* edited by Percy Lubbock (London: Hutchinson, 1926; New York: Longmans, Green, 1926);

Jerome Hamilton Buckley, *Season of Youth: The Bildungsroman from Dickens to Golding* (Cambridge: Harvard University Press, 1974), pp. 25, 116–119, 302;

Charles Burkhart, "George Moore and *Father and Son,*" *Nineteenth-Century Fiction,* 15 (June 1960): 71–77;

John Carey, *John Donne: Life, Mind and Art* (New York: Oxford University Press, 1981);

John Churton Collins, "English Literature at the Universities," *Quarterly Review,* 163 (October 1886): 289–329;

David J. DeLaura, ed., *Victorian Prose: A Guide to Research* (New York: Modern Language Association, 1973), pp. 457–459;

Philip Dodd, "The Nature of Edmund Gosse's *Father and Son,*" *English Literature in Transition (1880–1920),* 22, no. 4 (1979): 270–280;

William J. Gracie, Jr., "Truth of Form in Edmund Gosse's *Father and Son,*" *Journal of Narrative Technique,* 4 (September 1974): 176–187;

John Gross, *The Rise and Fall of the Man of Letters: Aspects of English Literary Life since 1800* (London: Weidenfeld & Nicolson, 1969);

David Grylls, *Guardians and Angels* (London & Boston: Faber & Faber, 1978);

Howard Helsinger, "Credence and Credibility: The Concern for Honesty in Victorian Autobiography," in *Approaches to Victorian Autobiography,* edited by George P. Landow (Athens: Ohio University Press, 1979), pp. 56–63;

James Hepburn, Introduction to Gosse's *Father and Son: A Study of Two Temperaments* (London: Oxford University Press, 1974), pp. xi–xvii;

William Irvine, Introduction to Gosse's *Father and Son* (Boston: Houghton Mifflin, 1965), pp. v–xlii;

Leslie Marchand, "The Symington Collection," *Journal of the Rutgers University Library,* 12 (1948): 1–15;

George Moore, *Avowals* (London: Heinemann, 1919), pp. 1–96;

Harold Nicolson, *The Development of English Biography* (London: Hogarth Press, 1927);

E. Pearlman, "Father and Mother in *Father and Son,*" *Victorian Newsletter,* no. 55 (Spring 1979): 19–23;

Linda H. Peterson, "Gosse's *Father and Son:* The Evolution of Scientific Apology," in her *Victorian Autobiography: The Tradition of Self-Interpretation* (New Haven & London: Yale University Press, 1986), pp. 156–191;

Roger J. Porter, "Edmund Gosse's *Father and Son:* Between Form and Flexibility," *Journal of Narrative Technique,* 5 (September 1975): 174–195;

James K. Robinson, "A Neglected Phase of the Aesthetic Movement: English Parnassianism," *PMLA,* 67 (September 1953): 733–754;

Fredric R. Ross, "Philip Gosse's *Omphalos,* Edmund Gosse's *Father and Son,* and Darwin's Theory of Natural Selection," *ISIS,* 68 (March 1977): 85–96;

Ruth Z. Temple, "Sir Edmund Gosse," in her *The Critic's Alchemy* (New York: Twayne, 1953), pp. 185–228;

Arthur Waugh, "The Book of Gosse," *Fortnightly Review,* new series 132 (1 September 1932): 284–302;

Douglas Wertheimer, "The Identification of Some Characters and Incidents in Gosse's *Father and Son,*" *Notes and Queries,* new series 23 (January 1976): 4–11;

Howard R. Wolf, "British Fathers and Sons, 1773–1913: From Filial Submissiveness to Creativity," *Psychoanalytical Review,* 52 (Summer 1965): 53–70;

James D. Woolf, "The Benevolent Christ in Gosse's *Father and Son,*" *Prose Studies,* 3 (September 1980): 160–175;

Woolf, "'In the Seventh Heaven of Delight': The Aesthetic Sense in Gosse's *Father and Son,*" in *Interspace and the Inward Sphere: Essays on Romantic and Victorian Self,* edited by Norman A. Anderson and Margene E. Weiss (Macomb: Western Illinois University Press, 1978), pp. 134–144;

Woolf, *Sir Edmund Gosse* (New York: Twayne, 1972);

Virginia Woolf, "The Art of Biography," in her *The Death of the Moth and Other Essays* (London: Hogarth Press, 1942), pp. 119–126;

Clement H. Wyke, "Edmund Gosse as Biographer and Critic of Donne: His Fallible Role in the Poet's Rediscovery," *Texas Studies in Literature and Language,* 17 (Winter 1976): 805–819.

Papers:

There are three major Edmund Gosse archives: in the Brotherton Collection at the University of Leeds; in the manuscript section of the Cambridge University Library; and at the Alexander Library at Rutgers University, New Brunswick, New Jersey. There is also a significant holding at the British Library, mainly among the Ashley Manuscripts.

Leigh Hunt

(19 October 1784 – 28 August 1859)

Dennis Paoli
Hunter College of the City University of New York

See also the Hunt entries in *DLB 96: British Romantic Poets, 1789–1832, Second Series* and *DLB 110: British Romantic Prose Writers, 1789–1832, Second Series.*

BOOKS: *Juvenilia* (London: Printed by J. Whiting, 1801; Philadelphia: Printed & published by H. Maxwell, 1804);

Critical Essays on the Performers of the London Theatres (London: Printed by & for John Hunt, 1807);

An Attempt to Shew the Folly and Danger of Methodism (London: Printed for & sold by John Hunt, 1809);

The Prince of Wales v. the Examiner: A Full Report of the Trial of John and Leigh Hunt (London: Printed by & for John Hunt, 1812);

The Feast of the Poets, with Notes, and Other Pieces in Verse (London: Printed for James Cawthorn, 1814; New York: Printed & published by Van Winkle & Wiley, 1814; enlarged edition, London: Gale & Fenner, 1815);

The Descent of Liberty, a Mask (London: Printed for Gale, Curtis & Fenner, 1815; Philadelphia: Printed for Harrison Hall, 1816);

The Story of Rimini (London: Printed by T. Davison for J. Murray; W. Blackwood, Edinburgh; and Cummings, Dublin, 1816; Boston: Published by Wells & Lilly and M. Carey, Philadelphia, 1816);

Foliage; or, Poems Original and Translated (London: Printed for C. & J. Ollier, 1818; Philadelphia: Published by Littell & Henry and Edward Earle, printed by W. Brown, 1818);

Hero and Leander, and Bacchus and Ariadne (London: Printed for C. & J. Ollier, 1819);

The Poetical Works of Leigh Hunt, 3 volumes (London: C. & J. Ollier, 1819);

The Months, Descriptive of the Successive Beauties of the Year (London: C. & J. Ollier, 1821);

Ultra-Crepidarius: A Satire on William Gifford (London: Printed for John Hunt, 1823);

Lord Byron and Some of His Contemporaries (London: Colburn, 1828; Philadelphia: Carey, Lea & Carey, 1828);

Christianism; or, Belief and Unbelief Reconciled (London: Bradbury, 1832); revised and enlarged as *The Religion of the Heart: a Manual of Faith and Duty* (London: Chapman, 1853; New York: Printed by J. J. Reed, 1857);

The Poetical Works of Leigh Hunt (London: Moxon, 1832);

Sir Ralph Esher: or Adventures of a Gentleman of the Court of Charles II, 3 volumes (London: Colburn & Bentley, 1830–1832 [i.e., 1832]);

The Indicator and the Companion: A Miscellany for the Fields and for the Fireside, 2 volumes (London: Published for Henry Colburn by R. Bentley, 1834); republished as *The Indicator: A Miscellany for the Fields and for the Fireside,* 1 volume (New York: Wiley & Putnam, 1845);

Captain Sword and Captain Pen: A Poem, With some Remarks on War and Military Statesmen (London: Knight, 1835);

A Legend of Florence, A Play in Five Acts (London: Moxon, 1840);

The Seer; or, Common-places Refreshed, 2 parts (London: Moxon, 1840; Boston: Roberts, 1864);

Essays by Leigh Hunt: The Indicator, The Seer (London: Moxon, 1841);

The Palfrey: A Love Story of Old Times (London: How & Parsons, 1842);

The Poetical Works of Leigh Hunt (London: Moxon, 1844);

Rimini and Other Poems (Boston: Ticknor, 1844);

Stories from the Italian Poets: With Lives of the Writers, 2 volumes (London: Chapman & Hall, 1845; New York: Wiley & Putnam, 1846);

Men, Women, and Books: A Selection of Sketches, Essays and Critical Memoirs, 2 volumes (London: Smith, Elder, 1847; New York: Harper, 1847);

A Jar of Honey from Mount Hybla (London: Smith, Elder, 1848);

The Town: Its Memorable Characters and Events: St. Paul's to St. James's, 2 volumes (London: Smith, Elder, 1848);

The Autobiography of Leigh Hunt, with Reminiscences of Friends and Contemporaries (3 volumes, London: Smith, Elder, 1850; 2 volumes, New York: Harper, 1850; revised edition, 1 volume, London: Smith, Elder, 1860);

Table-Talk (London: Smith, Elder, 1851; New York: Appleton, 1879);

The Works of Leigh Hunt, 4 volumes (Philadelphia: Hazard, 1854);

Stories in Verse; Now First Collected (London & New York: Routledge, 1855);

The Old Court Suburb; or, Memorials of Kensington, Regal, Critical, and Anecdotical, 2 volumes (London: Hurst & Blackett, 1855; enlarged, 1855);

The Poetical Works of Leigh Hunt: Now First Entirely Collected, Revised by Himself, edited by S. Adams Lee (Boston: Ticknor & Fields, 1857);

The Poetical Works of Leigh Hunt, Now Finally Collected, Revised by Himself, edited by Thornton Hunt (London & New York: Routledge, Warne & Routledge, 1860);

A Saunter through the West End (London: Hurst & Blackett, 1861);

A Day by the Fire; and Other Papers Hitherto Uncollected, edited by Joseph Edward Babson (London: Sampson Low, Son & Marston, 1870; Boston: Roberts, 1870);

The Wishing-Cap Papers, edited by Babson (Boston: Lee & Shepard, 1873; London: Sampson Low, Marston, Low & Searle, 1874);

Tales by Leigh Hunt, Now First Collected, edited by William Knight (London: W. Paterson, 1891);

Musical Evenings, or Selections, Vocal and Instrumental, edited by David R. Cheney (Columbia: University of Missouri Press, 1964);

Hunt on Eight Sonnets of Dante, edited by Rhodes Dunlap (Iowa City: University of Iowa School of Journalism, 1965).

Editions: *The Works of Leigh Hunt,* 7 volumes (London: Smith, Elder, 1870–1872);

Leigh Hunt as Poet and Essayist, edited by Charles Kent (London & New York: Warne, 1889);

The Poetical Works of Leigh Hunt, edited by H. S. Milford (London & New York: Oxford University Press, 1923).

PLAY PRODUCTIONS: *A Legend of Florence,* London, Theatre Royal, Covent Garden, 7 February 1840;

Lovers' Amazements, London, Lyceum Theatre, 20 January 1858.

OTHER: *Classic Tales, Serious and Lively on the Merits and Reputations of the Authors,* 5 volumes (London: J. Hunt & C. Reynell, 1807) – includes critical essays by Hunt on five of the authors;

William Hazlitt, *The Round Table: A Collection of Essays on Literature, Men, and Manners,* 2 volumes (Edinburgh: Printed for Archibald Constable and Longman, Hurst, Rees, Orme & Brown, London, 1817) – includes twelve essays by Hunt;

Amyntas, a Tale of the Woods: From the Italian of Torquato Tasso, translated, with notes, by Hunt (London: T. & J. Allman, 1820);

Bacchus in Tuscany, a Dithyramic Poem from the Italian of Francesco Redi, translated by Hunt (London: Printed for John & H. L. Hunt, 1825);

The Masque of Anarchy, a Poem by Percy Bysshe Shelley, Now First Published with a Preface by Leigh Hunt (London: Moxon, 1832);

The Dramatic Works of Wycherley, Congreve, Vanbrugh, and Farquhar (London: Moxon, 1840) – includes biographical and critical notices by Hunt;

The Dramatic Works of Richard Brinsley Sheridan, edited, with a biographical and critical sketch, by Hunt (London: Moxon, 1840);

One Hundred Romances of Real Life, edited and annotated by Hunt (London: Whittaker, 1843);

Imagination and Fancy: or, Selections from the English Poets with an Essay in Answer to the Question What is Poetry?, edited, with commentary and an introductory essay, by Hunt (London: Smith, Elder, 1844; New York: Wiley & Putnam, 1845);

Wit and Humour, Selected from the English Poets with an Illustrative Essay, edited, with an introductory essay, by Hunt (London: Smith, Elder, 1846; New York: Wiley & Putnam, 1847);

A Book for a Corner, or Selections in Prose and Verse from Authors the Best Suited to That Mode of Enjoyment, edited, with an introduction and comments, by Hunt (2 volumes, London: Chapman & Hall, 1849; 1 volume, New York: Putnam, 1852);

Readings for Railways; or, Anecdotes and Other Short Stories, Reflections, Maxims, Characteristics, Passages of Wit, Humour and Poetry, etc., selected by Hunt (London: Gilpin, 1849);

Beaumont and Fletcher, or The Finest Scenes, Lyrics, and Other Beauties of Those Two Poets, preface by Hunt (London: Bohn, 1855);

The Book of the Sonnet, 2 volumes, edited by Hunt and S. Adams Lee, with an essay by Hunt (Boston: Roberts, 1867; London: S. Low, Son & Marston, 1867).

SELECTED PERIODICAL PUBLICATIONS – UNCOLLECTED: "Memoir of James Henry Leigh Hunt written by himself," *Monthly Mirror,* 7 (April 1810): 243–248;

"The Works of Henry Howard, Earl of Surrey, and of Sir Thomas Wyatt the Elder," edited by George Frederick Nott, *Edinburgh Review,* 27 (December 1816): 390–422;

"The Family Journal," *New Monthly Magazine and Literary Journal,* 13 (January 1825): 17–28; (February 1825): 166–176; (March 1825): 276–282; (April 1825): 353–369, 419–423; (May 1825): 457–466; (June 1825): 548–555; 14 (July 1825): 41–45; (September 1825): 199–206; (October 1825): 323–332; (November 1825): 429–431; (December 1825): 514–518;

"The Wishing Cap," *Tait's Edinburgh Magazine,* 2 (January 1833): 435–442; (March 1833): 689–693; 3 (April 1833): 141–148; (June 1833): 275–280; (July 1833): 417–421; (September 1833): 695–701;

"Lady Mary Wortley Montagu, Letters and Works, edited by Lord Wharncliffe," *London and Westminster Review,* 37 (April 1837): 130–164;

"Memoirs of the Colman Family, by R. B. Peake," *Edinburgh Review,* 73 (July 1841): 389–424;

"The Life, Journal and Correspondence of Samuel Pepys, Esq. by the Rev. John Smith," *Edinburgh Review,* 74 (October 1841): 105–125;

"Madame Sevigne and her Contemporaries," *Edinburgh Review,* 76 (October 1842): 203–236;

"George Selwyn and his Contemporaries, by John H. Jesse," *Edinburgh Review,* 80 (July 1844): 1–42.

Leigh Hunt's *Lord Byron and Some of His Contemporaries* (1828) is the only biography he produced in a literary career extraordinary for its length and breadth. He outlived most of his Romantic colleagues and presided over the movement's assumption into Victorian sensibility. Hunt had works published in every recognized genre and brought to publication works by many representative writers of the time, including its greatest geniuses. One of the most important of the minor Romantics, Hunt was the editor of and a major contributor to the *Examiner,* the most influential liberal magazine of the period. His political commentary made his reputation, but he is also credited with inventing serious, analytical drama criticism and with adapting and personalizing the periodical essay, setting a new tone and creating a taste for the next generation of practitioners, including his friend Charles Dickens. He "discovered" Percy Bysshe Shelley and John Keats, seeing their earliest and some of their finest work into publication and defending them, in a well-known essay, against the attacks of conservative reviewers. Through Hunt's efforts his friends Charles Lamb and William Hazlitt were afforded the opportunity to find their authorial voices and audience.

It could also be argued that Hunt was the most pathetic failure of all the Romantics. With a handful of exceptions, his poetic oeuvre, on which he planned to found his fame, is negligible. His aesthetics were fatuous – the cause of his falling out with Keats – and his liberalism decidedly bourgeois, which alienated Hazlitt. Few of his journalistic efforts were popular enough to be profitable, and his incessant struggles with poverty and illness dictated a slapdash, under-the-gun style. In the end he presided over the bathetic apotheosis of Shelley and Keats to effete giants in the Victorian canon.

Hunt was born the year Samuel Johnson died, amid great revolutions in political and aesthetic sensibilities. Mary Shewell Hunt, his sickly mother, never fully recovered from seeing her husband, Issac Hunt, carried through the streets of Philadelphia by an angry mob of republicans for publishing a pamphlet of loyalist sentiments. Ironically, after immigrating to England, Isaac proved too liberal to be successful in his new profession as an itinerant preacher, though his oratorical skill fitfully sustained the family. On 19 October 1784 Mary Hunt gave birth to the family's first English-born child, James Henry Leigh, named in a propitiary and wishful act after the son of the duke of Chandos, whom Isaac was tutoring. That opportunity was squandered, too, and later Leigh Hunt wrote that "the first room I have any recollection of, is a prison."

As a child Hunt suffered from a succession of illnesses, including measles and smallpox, with his mother his constant nurse. At seven he entered Christ's Hospital, the venerable London school for impoverished scholars. A stammering mama's boy who chafed at the rigid regimen and rote pedagogy, he was a favorite of neither the fellows nor the masters. The Reverend James Boyer, an imposing but revered figure in the memoirs of former bluecoat boys Lamb and Samuel Taylor Coleridge, once knocked a tooth from Hunt's mouth with a well-aimed volume of Homer. A convalescence from an accidental scalding gave him leisure to study without supervision, which became his favorite pastime. He learned to loathe the classics and love those authors he discovered for himself, primarily William Collins, Thomas Gray, and Edmund Spenser. He also started to write poetry.

Hunt's *Juvenilia* was published in 1801 to good reviews, with an impressive subscription list accumulated by his father. It went through two editions and decided his future as a writer. The poetry, however, is not very good. Coleridge recalled of his own youth: "Thank Heaven, it was not the age nor the fashion of getting up prodigies! but at twelve or fourteen I should have made as pretty a juvenile prodigy as was ever emasculated and ruined by fond and idle wonderment. Thank Heaven, I was flogged instead of flattered!," and the flattery of reviewers, family, and friends did not serve Hunt well. His verse would always be precocious, precious, clever; if Keats strove, as he said in a letter to Shelley of 16 August 1820, to "fill every rift with ore," Hunt labored to fill every nook with a figurine. He had little poetic vision, and while he brought taste and intuition to his reading of others' works he had no critical perspective on his own.

He found his form when, at age twenty, he became the theater critic for his brother John's *News*. "We saw that independence in theatrical criticism would be a great novelty," Hunt later recalled of the editorial decision that made him both a popular and respected journalist. He revealed and righteously reviled "the system of the day," which saw critics dining at actors' tables, puffery rewarded by free tickets rewarded by puffery, and little serious writing: "the etiquette was, to write as short and favourable a paragraph on the new piece as could be." In 1807 Hunt's collected *Critical Essays on the Performers of the London Theatres* was published; the next year John Hunt began the journalistic enterprise that would make the Hunt brothers' reputations, the *Examiner*.

On 3 July 1809 Hunt married Mary Anne Kent after an eight-year courtship. Hunt was finely featured, and his deep color and the Barbadian background of his father's family led to rumors of African heritage, while Mary Anne was plain and pale. He was mercurial in speech and on the page, while she was barely literate when they met. Her ink-blotched, inarticulate letters annoyed him; his lecturing, hectoring letters must have hurt her. When he became insufferable, she broke off the relationship. He determined to marry her prettier and brighter sister Bess, whom many thought the better match, then won his first love back.

The accepted biographical wisdom is that Hunt compromised his ideal of a prospective mate and came to appreciate Mary Anne's maternal gifts; but if he did bargain down his implausible ideal, it was not without effort on her part to attain it. She labored to improve her verbal skills, and witticisms attributed to her pepper Hunt's memoirs. It has been suggested that she finally settled on signing her name as "Marianne," over the more prosaic "Mary Anne" and "Marian," which she also used, to please him. She was a hard worker, a trait they shared; when Hunt first came to woo her she was a seamstress, pitching in to help defray the family debts after her draper father died. Her familiarity with debt was another quality that recommended her to him, for she was unafraid of and unaffronted by it. A bailiff residing in their house for a few weeks in 1832 to assure that they did not sell off assets would not unduly upset her, and she would prove a tireless, shameless beggar in their behalf. They also shared fragile health and the attendant relief and pride in recovery. At a critical point in their courtship Hunt had a serious neurasthenic episode, probably set off by sexual tension, and she nursed him back to health. From then on they were mates for life.

Besides contributing theatrical criticism, Hunt edited and provided political commentary for the *Examiner*. He claimed that writing about politics was "against the grain" of his literary sensibility, but he was soon a popular pundit who attracted the attention of liberal wits, radical activists, and government prosecutors. He met William Godwin and, in 1811, Shelley, who had just been expelled from Oxford for writing and publishing *The Necessity of Atheism*. Then, after several trials in which the brothers successfully defended their right to publish politically provocative articles, including an exposé of army flogging practices, they were convicted in 1812 of seditious libel for attacking the Prince Regent (the future King George IV) as a hypocrite for abandoning his Whig principles, a liar, a libertine, and a fat "Adonis" of fifty. The sentence was two years imprisonment and a fine of five hundred pounds each.

Leigh Hunt's reputation as professional journalist and liberal touchstone was increased by his imprisonment. His cell became a fashionable salon visited by such contemporary lights as Hazlitt, Jeremy Bentham, James Mill, Maria Edgeworth, Benjamin Robert Haydon, Charles Cowden Clark, and Charles and Mary Lamb. Thomas Moore brought George Gordon, Lord Byron, who returned with books and encouragement for Hunt's reawakened poetic aspirations. In jail Hunt continued working on the *Examiner* so that when he had served his term his editorial organ would be intact.

Hunt never had money or any idea of economy, but the libel fine left him in serious debt. Principle kept him from accepting donations toward paying the damages, though through the years he would accept — indeed, beg — loans and monetary gifts from friends to discharge domestic debts. He raised a large family, was host to several generations of writers, and started many personal publishing projects — unwise but characteristic behavior for a habitual spendthrift. He often made terrible deals for his written work and writing services, and no budget was safe around Hunt or his wife. Since intellectual capital was his only asset, he poured out paragraphs and stanzas, pages and volumes in a prodigious effort to get out of debt, necessitating a fluent style with a pleasing surface but little depth.

During his incarceration his interest in politics, always secondary, waned. In the privation of prison, listening to the construction of gallows and feeling his already uncertain health deteriorate, Hunt escaped into the verbal play and liberating introspection of verse composition. After his release the *Examiner*, once the liberal standard-bearer, broke out in poetry; the most vigorous editorial to appear in it was Hunt's defense of Keats, Shelley, and John Hamilton Reynolds against the attacks in the *Quarterly Review* and *Blackwood's Edinburgh Magazine* on the Cockney school poets.

The burdens of unremitting debt unrelieved by unremitting labor, recurring illness, growing family responsibilities, and professional disappointments could easily have ground him down, but Hunt was a man of extraordinary good humor and an eternal optimist; and he was sustained by his Christian faith and his faith in history, which was turning more liberal and more accepting of his heroes, especially Shelley, as the century progressed. He was like a less-serious Thomas Carlyle, articulating, instead of an "Everlasting Yea," what his biographer Ann Blainey calls a "philosophy of cheer." He had a good word for almost everyone, a smiling stoicism bordering on simplicity, a carefree appreciation that charmed its objects, and a genuine love of life. He was part of the bourgeois mainstream of the age; he avoided the great crises of identity and imagination that informed the decisive works of his peers. Sentiment served him in every instance.

With the possible exception of his marriage, Hunt's friendship with Shelley was the most significant relationship of his life. When they reestablished contact in 1816 Shelley had recently returned

Hunt at age thirty-six (engraving by J. C. Armitage after an unfinished miniature by Joseph Severn)

from Europe, where he had spent the summer with Byron; within months Shelley's first wife, Harriet, would commit suicide and he would marry Mary Godwin. Shelley was twenty-four years old, his life was in turmoil, and he was estranged from his own father and from William Godwin, his intellectual father. At thirty-two Hunt was just old enough and, as editor of a magazine, just established enough, to be, according to Shelley's biographer Richard Holmes, a "mentor and father figure." They were also close enough in age and opinion to be great friends.

It was a friendship spiced with mutual benefit: Shelley craved a public, and Hunt had pages of periodicals to fill; Hunt was chronically indebted, and Shelley, for all his own financial vicissitudes, was generous and a gentleman about it. Not that there was a quid pro quo – Hunt's editing was always professional. Discovering fine poetry was a calling realized in his school days, and putting it before the public was a genuine pleasure for him. His nickname among fellow journalists was "the Indicator," after the dingbat that identified his columns – a closed fist with pointing finger, which catches the

character of his critical craft: he could point at a passage of fine poetry and give an indication of a poet's mind in an anecdote. He had, however, no genius for analysis, no patience for synthesis, and an easily satisfied curiosity. He read the German Romantics, argued with Coleridge and Hazlitt, and corresponded with Keats and Shelley, but he never followed them to the heights or to the depths. His virtues as a critic were enthusiasm and generosity.

Hunt's friendship with Shelley was, however, founded on mutual delusion. Shelley, impressed with Hunt's publishing credentials, imprisonment, and table talk, took Hunt and his wife for atheists and radical advocates of free love, like himself. Hunt, for his part, would always swear to Shelley's Christian nature; and while he extolled nonexclusive love relationships, his marriage lasted forty-eight years and produced eleven children.

One of the most troubling questions in the biographies of both Hunt and Shelley is why, in 1819, the former refused to publish the latter's *The Masque of Anarchy*. It is one of Shelley's finest poems, a white-hot response to the Peterloo massacre, and the poet was anxious to see it published while the blood was still fresh on the government's hands. But Hunt, his great friend and defender, while never openly rejecting the submission, neglected it issue after issue, frustrating Shelley, who felt voiceless and helpless in exile. It seems likely that Hunt feared prosecution. Such self-censoring not only dulled his editorial decisions but deprived his own poetry of an essential source of power. Hunt would finally edit and publish the poem in book form in 1832, ten years after Shelley's death.

In 1821 Hunt and Marianne were sick, one or two of the six children were always sick, John Hunt was back in prison, and the *Examiner* was suffering. Hunt's own periodical, the *Indicator,* which he had started in 1819 and in which he wrote almost every entry, failed; Hazlitt was estranged; Keats had recently died; the Hunts were in debt and with shrinking prospects. In these straits Hunt's attachment to British soil wavered when Shelley proposed a journal to be published in Italy with Hunt as editor and Shelley and Byron as major contributors.

Hunt needed the job, so he and his family made the journey. The winter voyage was a disaster: historic storms battered their vessel, their little cabin was filled with retching children, and Marianne became dangerously ill. When the ship put in at an English port to wait out the weather, the Hunts forfeited their passage and wintered at Portsmouth. Shelley sent money and encouragement, and the following May the family set sail again.

When the ship docked at Livorno – "Leghorn" to the expatriate English community – the Hunts were met by the strapping, swashbuckling Edward John Trelawny, who awaited them on Byron's yacht, the *Bolivar.* He escorted them to Byron's villa outside of town, where they walked into a domestic dispute among servants that had escalated into pistol waving and a knife fight in which Byron's mistress's brother had been stabbed for interceding. Byron introduced the new arrivals to the Contessa Teresa Guiccioli, the married woman who was his mistress, and her wounded sibling, the Conte Pietro of the Gamba clan, who were known sympathizers with the secret revolutionary society, the Carbonari. Hunt later wrote that he felt as if he had entered an Anne Radcliffe novel, full of foreigners and menace.

Shelley finally arrived in Leghorn and proceeded to lie, flatter, coax, and tease Hunt and Byron in the service of their shared enterprise. John Hunt was designated publisher of the new journal, a choice that scandalized Byron's Tory and moderate Whig friends. The collaborators argued about a name for the publication; Byron's suggestion, the *Liberal* – the first recorded use of the adjective as a noun – was inspired.

When Byron moved back to Pisa and took up residence in the Palazzo Lanfranchi, the Hunts moved in downstairs. Things progressively fell apart. Hunt's children were left largely to themselves; their boisterous behavior was, to their parents, heartwarming evidence of healthy and "self-possessed" natures, but Byron set his bulldog on the staircase to keep the brood away from his rooms. Furthermore, when the great Italian physician Andrea Vacca, called in by Shelley, pronounced that Marianne Hunt had less than a year to live, it was difficult for Byron to be sympathetic: housing a failing consumptive was a burden, but enduring her insults, especially when they were devilishly clever, was insupportable. " 'Trelawny has been speaking against my morals,' " Byron once complained to her in jest; " 'What do you think of that?' " " 'It is the first time I ever heard of them,' " retorted Marianne. When Byron made tasteless remarks about the appearance of some of the Hunts' friends, Hunt asked if he had heard of Marianne's comment on seeing G. H. Harlow's drawing of him; when Byron replied that he had not, Hunt repeated her observation, originally made to the Shelleys, that the portrait "resembled a great schoolboy, who had had a plain bun given him, instead of a plum one." Byron did not find her remarks funny.

In retrospect, the *Liberal* can be seen as a monumentally bad idea, representative of Romanticism at its worst. It was an arena for clamoring egos. Considering the talents involved, though, there was a chance that it could have succeeded. But the one shock the project could not possibly withstand befell it. On 8 July 1822 Shelley and his friend Edward Williams boarded their boat, the *Ariel,* to sail from Leghorn to the villa they shared on the shore at Lerici. Trelawny was to accompany them in Byron's yacht but was prevented from doing so by the harbor authorities for lack of proper authorization to leave port. Shelley was an intrepid, instinctive sailor with more courage than skill; a body of water would inspire him to abandon, and he would float downstream or run downwind with little regard for weather, destination, or the fact that he could not swim. When a violent squall hit them their deckless craft foundered. Shelley had intimated several times that he intended not to struggle against a drowning death; thirteen days later his decomposing body washed up on the shore at Viareggio, recognizable by the clothes and the books in the pockets – including Keats's latest volume, borrowed from Hunt, which was opened to "Lamia." On 15 August Hunt,

Byron, Trelawny, and local officials dug up the body, which had been limed and buried in the sand, and cremated it. Hunt, overcome, could not leave the carriage; Byron swam out to the *Bolivar,* anchored offshore; Trelawny, according to his own account, braved the flames and retrieved Shelley's heart. Sharing the carriage on the journey back to Pisa, Hunt and Byron drank, sang, and laughed together in a binge of release. When their hysterics subsided, their relationship unraveled, and all hope for the *Liberal* was lost.

Hunt and Byron tried to make a go of it, more in memory of Shelley than with the prospect of success. Hunt wrote in the mornings, through which Byron and the countess regularly slept; Hunt and Byron rode together in the afternoons; Byron settled down to work and drink after the Hunts went to bed. Byron told Hunt to consider him "as standing in Mr. Shelley's place" and to "find him the same friend that the other had been"; but this remark only angered Hunt, who took it as an insult to both himself and Shelley, with whom the comparison of any mortal, much less Byron, could only inspire invidious pathos and woeful disappointment. Hunt had always perceived Shelley "the best of friends and of men," as saintly, and now that he was dead he qualified in the most definitive respect. His death seems to have unhinged Hunt; there is a story that he begged the poet's disembodied heart from Trelawny and then refused Mary Shelley's requests for it until Byron intervened. Hunt did keep a piece of his dead friend's jawbone in a small box, a precious relic, for the rest of his life. Marianne, at death's threshold herself, saw Shelley's image several times. The half-mad Hunt and his idolatry made Byron nostalgic for Shelley in the flesh. The two men were divided by their common loss.

Before the first issue of the *Liberal* appeared Byron moved to Genoa, in effect fleeing the Hunts. They followed, moving in with Mary Shelley a mile from Byron, in Albaro. Mary Shelley and Hunt were on frosty terms, and at first the forty-room villa was hardly large enough. But Marianne was pregnant, an often fatal condition at the time in consumptives, and Mary, her strength and maturity called upon, responded. Relations thawed, grew warm, and resolved into lifelong friendship. In June 1823 Marianne Hunt was better and gave birth to a son. In July, though, Mary Shelley and her only child, Percy Florence, left for England. The Hunts missed her and her English manner terribly.

Somehow the first issue of the *Liberal,* published on 15 October 1821, succeeded, a testament to Shelley's efforts and inspiration on its behalf. It featured one of Byron's finest, most biting satires, "The Vision of Judgment," taking its title from Robert Southey's panegyric to George III (1821). This attack on the then-laureate, "apostate jacobin" Southey (who had been Shelley's first poet-surrogate-father, until they met and promptly appalled each other) and its pathetic, patronizing portrait of the late king struck an old, familiar chord in Hunt and set the editorial tone for the magazine: "The object of our work," wrote Hunt in the preface, "is not political, except inasmuch as all writing now-a-days must involve something to that effect, the connection between politics and all other subjects of interest to mankind having been discovered, never again to be done away." Hunt achieved in his editing of the *Liberal* a combination of political commentary and literary quality that had been approached in the best issues of the *Examiner.*

Shelley's major contribution to the first issue was an able translation of several passages from Johann Wolfgang von Goethe's *Faust* (1808). At the time of his death he had been in a fallow period, probably caused by his troubles with Mary, who had recently had a miscarriage and had been exhibiting distressing signs of bourgeois conformity ("Mary is under the dominion," he had complained, "of the mythical monster 'Everybody'"), and by his poetic rivalry with Byron. Having been around Byron had spurred Shelley to some of his major creations, such as the poetic depiction of their relationship in "Julian and Maddalo" (1824); *being* around Byron had seemed to stifle him. He had had aspirations to be the poet of his age, but to all appearances Byron had beaten him to it. (When his and Williams's schooner was delivered and he found *Don Juan* painted on the mainsail, he had labored for hours trying to expunge the large black letters, finally having them cut out and the hole patched over; according to Holmes, he "absolutely refused to sail under the title of Byron's greatest work.") There is some question, then, whether his survival would have had much effect on the magazine's. There can be no question, however, that his greatest contribution to the *Liberal,* which some critics consider one of the most important literary journals of the first half of the nineteenth century, was its coming into being at all.

Though conservative journals, such as the *Literary Gazette,* saw in "The Triumvirate" a rogues' gallery – Byron impious and wicked, Shelley a fool, Hunt a flouncing imbecile – the first issue even delivered a profit; Byron turned his share over to Hunt, and Hunt gave his to his creditors. Flush with success, Hunt set to work on the second issue. Published on New Year's Day 1823, it was half again as big as the first, and with a pay rate of a pound a page (a Byronic gesture of largesse), it lost money. Among the contributors were Hazlitt, Mary Shelley, and Thomas Jefferson Hogg, but Hunt, as in the first issue, wrote most of the items — including one of his most ambitious verse satires, "The Dogs," which fritters away in Byron-influenced ottava rima a fine premise taken from the diary of a starving soldier in the Peninsular Campaign assigned to the dog-feeding detail. Shelley was materially missed, however, and Byron chose to cut his losses. He offered some poems and translations for the second issue, but he pulled *The Age of Bronze* from the third issue and asked John Hunt to print it and *The Island,* another project for the magazine, as individual works. Reluctantly, John did so; and when they made money while the third and fourth issues of the *Liberal* sold poorly, Hunt felt betrayed.

The fourth and final number of the *Liberal* came out in July 1823; the Hunt brothers had already begun a backup publication, the *Literary Examiner.* For publishing "The Vision of Judgment" John Hunt was again under indictment; he suspected mischief on the part of Byron's former publisher John Murray, who had sent him the manuscript but neglected to include the explanatory preface that might have insulated the satire by providing a context. Byron paid the legal fees, but as with all his financial assistance, his help was sneered at as a crass attempt to buy the admiration that accrued so naturally to — the comparison was impossible to avoid — Shelley. For Hunt, sunny, rustic rides with Byron had given way to mournful winter walks alone. The two former friends could not even find a comfortable manner in which to address each other. Hunt, at Shelley's suggestion, had been carefully formal, for which he was chided by Byron, who responded with "dear lord Hunt." Hunt then affected an informality that was offensive to Byron, who was never forgiven for arrogating Shelley's pet name, "Leontius," for Hunt. When Byron departed for Greece in July 1823, he offered to pay the Hunts' way back to England; but, fearing debtor's prison on his return, Hunt settled for Florence.

The Hunts came to hate Italy; as literary associations wore off, the dusty roads, glaring sun, and cold marble became unbearable. Hunt professed to love Florence but said that "Italy had a certain hard taste in the mouth." Marianne refused even to try to learn Italian, and they made few friends (one was Walter Savage Landor) and had few visitors (one was Hazlitt). They pined for the wooded green expanse of Hampstead Heath, the snug rooms and warming hearths of English homes. Hunt read avidly to fill the empty hours and wrote urgently to feed his family and pay his debts. He labored over poems, translations, and intimate letters to Bess Kent, and he contributed personal essays on English topics to the *Examiner* under the heading "Wishing Cap Papers." But he made little headway against his debts.

While raising and training an armed force to fight for Greek independence from Turkey, Byron was stricken with swamp fever at Missolonghi; he died on 19 April 1824. On his death many biographies appeared, most of them groveling efforts to cash in on his fame. Extolled as the European poet of his age, he was exalted as an exemplary nobleman, gentleman, and Christian; the wickedness his critics once delighted in detailing was explained, excused, or expunged. This blatant whitewashing, while Shelley went unmourned by the English establishment, outraged Hunt. Still, he had no plan to publish his resentment until the publisher Henry Colburn, to whose *New Monthly* he was contributing, offered him an advance of two hundred pounds to expand some autobiographical sketches, which he had been compiling as an introduction to an anthology of his own work, to include and feature his recollections of Byron. Hunt was, at the time, in a worse way than usual: he was estranged from his brother, who had asserted his claim according to a prior agreement and against Hunt's debt to take over the *Examiner,* and from his mother-in-law, who was quarreling with his sister-in-law; he was also bereaved by his eleven-year-old son Swinburne's death. The Hunts used the advance from Colburn to return to England in September 1825. There Hunt toiled on the prospective anthology and a historical novel about a nobleman in the time of Charles II, but Colburn, who had already published several Byron books, pressed Hunt for another. Hunt, who still owed Colburn for the fare home, at last agreed.

Lord Byron and Some of His Contemporaries appeared in 1828. It is a biographical oddity, perverse in almost every important respect. Hunt's biographical method is memoir, recording his remembrance of shared experience or hearsay. His recollections are literally that: re-collected memories, letters, manuscripts, dinner conversations from the clutter of his hectic life. It is primary research with the occasional editorial bent — Keats was a great poet, Shelley was a great man, Byron was a fraud — and a structuring principle of roughly chronological wandering, browsing, rummaging. Hunt is at the reader's elbow, at the reader's ear, recalling images,

Frontispiece for Hunt's Lord Byron and Some of
His Contemporaries

bons mots, exchanges from his interaction with whomever. The narrative presence and impressionistic style suggest fiction, but Hunt was a journalist and respected fact. As a journalist, though, he could also editorialize around an unpromising truth.

The preface is brisk; with bracing honesty, it prepares the reader for disaster. What had been meant to be a memoir is now the collected lives of several poets with special reference to a particular one, leaving the material misshapen and refractory. "Time . . . as well as place, is violated," Hunt complains in the preface. Though he would never show much facility in organizing long-form literature, and though he shoulders the blame for having to abandon the original arrangement – confessing to procrastination and to "bad habits of business and the

sorriest arithmetic," which made monetary motives more persuasive than considerations of quality – he is direct in attributing the editorial decision that, while "adding to the attractions of the title-page" by featuring Byron, to the implied detriment of the rest of the poets treated, gave "altogether a different look to the publication from what was contemplated at first": "my publisher thought it best." Hence, the work is a farrago of brief bits and unseemly bloat because it was conceived not as a serious study of an interesting, revelatory life, or even as providing a context for some collected works, but as a commodity, with name recognition and opinion valued over complexity and insight.

Besides, Hunt had no love for the genre of biography. He pleaded poverty and illness, as he does in the preface, most of his life, but this economic decision was particularly distasteful: "such is my dislike of these personal histories ... that had I been rich enough ... my first impulse on finishing the work would have been to put it in the fire." At the core of his "dislike" was a conflict of principles. On the positive side, his account "should put an end to a great deal of false biography," which must have appealed to the crusading journalist in him. Byron had become the object of the kind of obsequious political mythmaking that Leigh and John Hunt had attacked in the heyday of the *Examiner* and that Byron himself had skewered in "The Vision of Judgment." To demystify the myth, however, was at cross purposes to Hunt's philosophy of cheer: "it has long ceased to be within my notions of what is necessary for society, to give an unpleasant account of any man." This dialectic of truth and cheer, of dark-corner reporting and bright-side rationalizing, was sorely tested and nearly exhausted by the subject. "What was to be told of the Noble Poet, involved of necessity a painful retrospect; and humanize as I may, and as I trust I do, upon him as well as every thing else ... in renewing my intercourse with him in imagination, I had involuntarily felt a re-access of the spleen and indignation which I experienced, as a man who thought himself ill-treated. With this, to a certain extent, the account is coloured, though never with a shadow of untruth." For Hunt, the biographer's job was a difficult one.

Once he warmed to the task, though, Hunt struck with a will. Rationalizing swung all to the side of "truth," and, as he could blame his publisher for anomalies of form, he could impute responsibility for noisome content to his principles. "O Truth! what scrapes of portraiture have you not got me into!" he frets, after several pages parading instances of Byron's professional and pecuniary meanness to fellow poets, schoolfellows, his mistress, the Greeks, and Hunt himself, culminating with a recollection of how when "the Noble Poet" lent a book, he made much of its condition, "though he did not scruple to make marks and dogs'-ears in yours." Against anticipated charges that he speaks ill of the dead, he again appeals to principle: "never to give others to understand any thing against an acquaintance, not only which I would not give, but which I *have* not given himself to understand; a principle, to which this book will have furnished no exception." He proclaims "how little I have been in the habit of speaking against any body" and complains: "what a nuisance it is to me to do it now."

Truth ultimately tramples cheer; the author's proclivity to "humanize" is overcome by "the contamination of these personal histories." Hunt explores the limits of biography for his age: "I have not told all," he admits, "for I have no right to do so." "I would not say any thing about [Byron's "want of generosity in money-matters"], nor about twenty other matters, but that they hang together more or less, and are connected with the truth of a portrait which it has become necessary to me to paint. It is fortunate that there are some which I can omit." This disclaimer suggests a shaping principle of "hanging together," of biography not as encyclopedic but as aesthetic. At times Hunt deliberates with himself on the truth-teller's responsibility to the subject, the readers, and the publisher of a biography. Modern academic biography, while more thorough, objective, and critically sophisticated, is the lesser for its lack of the biographer as participant.

Whether its truth merits respect or not, Hunt's biography has been a primary source for all of Byron's later biographers, and perhaps, excepting Byron's letters, the most important. It demands attention, therefore; not just the incidents but the attitude must be accounted for. If Hunt is overheated in some passages, Byron must in some way be implicated: one morning, "not in good humour," he heard Hunt "dabbling on a piano-forte" and "said that all lovers of music were effeminate. ... He, the objector to effeminacy, was sitting in health and wealth, with rings on his fingers, and baby-work to his shirt; and he had just issued, like a sultan, out of his bath." The portrait is so lively that there must be some truth in it. The exuberance in the accumulation of Byron's failures and venalities is also persuasive: "His failure in the House of Lords is well known"; "His Lordship was one of a management that governed Drury-lane Theatre ... and made a sad business of their direction"; he was one of those "who only seek personal importance in their generosity"; one whose "superstition was remarkable ... because it was petty and old-womanish"; one whose "nose, though handsome in itself, had the appearance when you saw it closely in front, of being grafted on the face, rather than growing properly out of it"; whose "love of notoriety was superior even to his love of money; which is giving the highest idea that can be entertained of it." And worse: "He did not care for the truth"; "he felt jealous of the smallest accomplishments"; "Christian he certainly was not."

In piling on the "truths" Hunt gives the lie to his aesthetic intentions, working himself into an encyclopedic frenzy to leave no wrong unnoticed, no fault undiscovered. There are recognizable themes, such as that of the "spoiled child of fame" and

Byron's effeminate affectations, but much of the work reads like a rant. When Hunt does attempt — and at times attain — insight into his subject's character, the effect is rationalizing (pressing a sensitive discussion of Byron's lameness into service as an apologia: "nor could any thing have induced me to give a portrait of Lord Byron and his infirmities if I had not been able to say at the end of it, that his faults were not his own, and that we must seek the causes of them in mistakes common to us all"), sad (his host was "by far the pleasantest when he had got wine in his head"), or savage ("I doubt greatly whether he was a man of courage. . . . I suspect, that personal anxiety, coming upon a constitution unwisely treated, had no small hand in hastening his death in Greece"). Toward the end of his extended sketch he takes issue with several of Byron's posthumous biographers, disputing their praise of the late lord in practically every particular and revealing the source of his inclusive method as a response to their flattery. "It is only a pity," he writes tongue in cheek of one of these "compilations," "that in addition to the list of Lord Byron's accomplishments, [the anonymous author] did not mention, that besides being 'a scholar,' and 'a rock,' and 'a reed shaken by the wind,' he was a rat-catcher and the Pope's grandson." Hunt refuses to concede even the simplest virtues — Byron rode well, he was a strong swimmer, he did not fear big dogs — without compromise. It is hard not to conclude that Hunt's biography itself is a perverse example, turned against its subject, of what he criticizes as "the predominant feature in [Byron's] character, – which was an indulgence of his self-will and self-love united, denying himself no pleasure that could add to the intensity of his consciousness, and the means of his being powerful and effective, with a particular satisfaction in contributing as little as possible to the same end in others."

Nowhere else in his works does Hunt perform such a hatchet job; he is usually among the most generous of writers. The exceptions are his political journalism and his theatrical criticism, and here he applies both. As the history of the *Liberal* suggests, Byron was committed to make a show of his political principles, not necessarily to make a stand on them. To Hunt this attitude was hypocrisy, as bad or worse than the arrant Toryism he had been contending against since early in his career. Hunt's tone, though, is less attacking than patronizing irony: "He was a warm politician, and thought himself earnest in the cause of liberty." In a verse epistle on the eve of Byron's first trip to Greece, Hunt had commended him "for a rank worn simply, and the

scorn / Of those who trifle with an age free-born"; but in retrospect it was obvious that he "had as little real regard for liberty as . . . any other proud man of rank" and "an impatience for any despotism not his own." Basing his judgment on firsthand experience, Hunt mocks another biography that glorifies Byron, returning to Greece, as an "apostle of liberty"; according to Hunt he "would have been a very unwilling apostle, had he known he was also to be a martyr."

In applying the rhetoric of theatrical criticism to Byron's life Hunt makes a contribution to the means of biography that, recognizing his credentials as a drama critic, must be deemed seminal. "The first time I saw Lord Byron," Hunt writes in the first sentence of the text proper, "he was rehearsing the part of Leander," an innocent choice of verb that, however, suggests calculating, self-conscious image-making, a self-serving talent for pomp and presentation and for self-representation at the expense of "truth." "Lord Byron was always acting, even when he capriciously spoke the truth." Yet Hunt is inconsistent in his application of the idiom, likening the lord to a "stage-tyrant" at one point but later ridiculing "the vulgar melodramatic idea entertained of Lord Byron" in other biographies.

From his wife's witticisms to his own one-liners ("Mr. Hobhouse," alarmed at the *Liberal*, "rushed over the alps, not knowing which was more awful, the mountains, or the Magazine"), Hunt's sense of humor demonstrates an ear, eye, and timing that anticipate Dickens and, in a deflating phrase, ridiculous detail, or clever reversal, annihilates Byron. "He enabled this adoring sex to discover," Hunt writes of Byron's relationships with women, "that a great man may be a very small one." Refuting Thomas Medwin, who found that Byron "shone" in conversation, Hunt comments that the lord lacked "address," "hummed and hawed," and – in one of the awful puns for which Hunt was famous – "had no conversation, properly speaking" (though Hunt himself suffered from a stammer that cost him becoming a Grecian at school, and though he admits elsewhere in the biography that even Swift and Johnson "no doubt oftener produced awkward retaliations" in their repartee "than biographers have thought fit to record"). No joke is too low or fleeting for the purposes of Byron-bashing; but no predilection is more poisonous to biography than humor, no voice more vicious in a biographer than a humorist's. The subject should be treated seriously and fairly, without any irony except that discovered in the life. Hunt is a natural ironist, and he turns his talent to the denigration of Byron – "no man in Italy, certainly no Englishman, ever contrived to practise more rakery and economy at one and the same time" – instead of probing the ironies of the life to the purpose of appreciation or, at least, understanding.

Hunt makes fun of Byron but does not allow Byron to make fun of himself. When "in one of his most agreeable, off-hand couplets" of *Don Juan* (1819–1824) Byron writes, "for a good old gentlemanly vice, / I think I shall take up avarice," Hunt makes him out a hypocrite for practicing a vice he satirizes. Yet he has just characterized the poem's hero as "a picture of the better part" of the poet's nature, an interpretation that could allow a self-mocking reading of the passage. But no – when "the author speaks in his own person," he abandons his character and his "better part," "endeavouring to bully himself into a satisfaction with the worse." Though no less "a connoisseur in the spirit of contradiction" than Hazlitt may claim that Byron would argue a contrary for wit's sake, Hazlitt was suspect because he liked Byron. Hunt, who disliked him, was better situated to recognize the "perversity of his spoiled nature" in his composition and banter and could marshal evidence to support the interpretation, though there is little to indicate that Hunt had the patience to listen or explore for any more complex tone or tenor.

Still Hunt's considerable talents for observation and appreciation push some of his judgments beyond the double bind he uses to trap his subject so that they achieve an independence of his self-justification and tap his self-knowledge. His defense of Byron against charges of madness is made in the main to justify his own charges of "perversity and self-will"; but when he identifies Byron, in his writing, "not as the madman witty, but as the wit, injured by circumstance considered to be rational," he could just as well be defending himself against Tory critics and their dismissal of his "imbecility." He agrees with Byron's self-assessment that he was prey to the "very painful attribute" of "mobility," a restlessness and slavery to fashion expressive of a disquietude of soul and "incontinence of will" central to a strain of nineteenth- and twentieth-century literature and observable in Hunt's own chronic financial desperation, though he refuses to recognize Byron's self-awareness. And when Hunt claims, "I do not believe that he ever had the good fortune of knowing what real love is," Byron's defenders must answer the charge, because there is no more serious criticism of a Romantic poet.

Hunt's biography of his former friend is graceless, at times tasteless, and must have been thankless to write, because there is something crucial missing at its core. Ultimately, it is not about Byron but about what Byron was not; and to Hunt, in every important respect, what Byron was not was Shelley. Shelley was a real friend, a real poet, a real liberal, and with a little adjustment of definition, a real Christian; he was really generous, really brave; he knew real love. If Hunt knew real love, it was for Shelley, and his loss shadows every sentence and embitters every anecdote in the life of Byron.

It follows that Hunt's sketch of Shelley, the longest among those of the contemporaries, should be an example of real biography; instead, it recapitulates the sycophantic mythmaking of the worst of the Byron biographies he railed against in his own. "He was like a spirit," Hunt gushes, "that had darted out of its orb, and found itself in another planet." Shelley's effect on Hunt is apparent in the prose, as is Byron's, and the biography of Shelley is most authentic as an impressionistic sketch, as is that of Byron. The collected quotes, verse passages, and correspondence add more to the effect than to the knowledge of Shelley; they indicate rather than inform. Hunt makes his least contribution where he intends to make his greatest: in the rationalizations that clog the text. He is tireless and nearly persuasive in the pains he takes to make Shelley out a Christian, despite the prevailing opinion of reviewers, friends, and Shelley himself: "An impatience in contradicting worldly and pernicious notions of a supernatural power, led his own aspirations to be misconstrued; for though, in the severity of his dialectics, and particularly in moments of despondency, he sometimes appeared to be hopeless of what he most desired, – and though he justly thought, that a Divine being would prefer the increase of benevolence and good before any praise, or even recognition of himself, (a reflection worth thinking of by the intolerant,) yet there was in reality no belief to which he clung with more fondness than that of some great pervading 'Spirit of Intellectual Beauty.'" Hunt arrays quotation and anecdote to support his claim that Shelley practiced a "practical Christianity" that valued charity over faith and appreciated Christ as reformer as opposed to Redeemer. Shelley, however, framed neither his poetry nor his philosophy in Christian terms, whether revolutionary, like William Blake's, or reasonable, like Hunt's. He advertised his atheism as a basic element in his character, as when he followed his signature in the register at several Alpine hotels with "Δημοκρατικος, Φιλανθρωποτος, και 'αθεος" (Democrat, Philanthropist, and Atheist) in the occupation column. It makes for compelling irony to

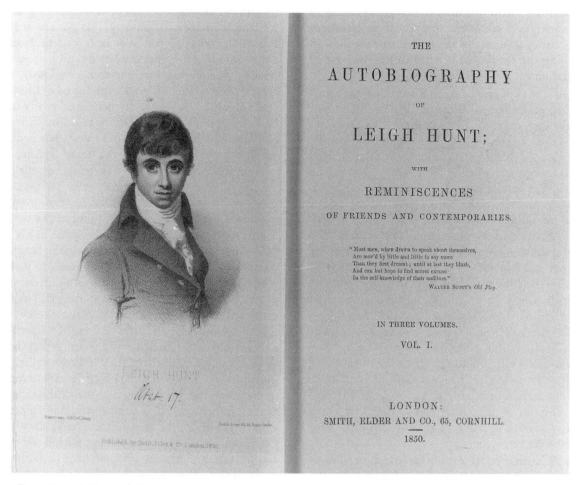

Frontispiece and title page for Hunt's autobiography, in which he tempered the portrait of Byron he had presented in Lord Byron and Some of His Contemporaries

hold Shelley up next to worldly and pompous critics who bruit their faith for moral leverage, but it does not make him a Christian. The imaginative rigor necessary to apprehend the "Spirit of Intellectual Beauty" demands that it be distinguished from Christianity, though it may appear within Christianity; to rationalize that rigor away is a violence to Shelley's views that he would in all probability have resented at least as much as the critics' cant.

He probably would have agreed, though, with Hunt's expounding of Harriet Shelley's suicide by drowning in the Serpentine canal in Hyde Park in 1816. Shelley had married Harriet Westbrook in 1811, when she was sixteen and he had just turned nineteen, but within three years he had left her with a child and pregnant with a second. Shelley told Hunt that they "had separated by mutual consent" and blamed her and her sister Eliza, who had lived and traveled with them, for deserting the radical cause and using the marriage to attach the Westbrook family to his prospects of property. Hunt swallowed this account whole and took on his exculpatory duty like a protective parent: "The fact, as we have seen, is, that they had been living apart for some time, during which the lady was accountable to no one but herself . . . he was not without remorse for having no better exercised his judgment with regard to the degree of intellect he had allied himself with, and for having given rise to a premature independence of conduct in one unequal to the task. The lady was greatly to be pitied; so was the survivor." The fact is that, having compromised his nonconformist principles to marry Harriet, he refused to compromise them to stay with her and his children. A few weeks after learning of her death he compromised his "unconventional spirit" again and married Mary, for whom he had abandoned Harriet. Harriet's last word, in a letter to Eliza, apostrophizes to "dear Bysshe": "if you had never left me I might have lived." A Chancery suit put the children in fosterage, and Shelley came out of the melodrama feeling like a martyr. Following his lead,

Hunt's defense is not very gallant: Harriet was, no doubt, growing bourgeois; in the Shelleyan scheme, she was responsible for herself; and Mary, more his match in most ways, better served his posterity and literary history – but the pathos of Harriet's fall (she was pregnant when she drowned) and death is unappreciated in Hunt's account, as the questions of Shelley's guilt are unanswered.

Hunt's sketch of Shelley is, finally, as unfair as his biography of Byron, his portrait of Shelley's "seraphical character" as static as that of the "spoiled child" Byron, its argument as unrelieved by objectivity. Shelley, whom Hazlitt described as "a man in knowledge" and "a child in feeling," never gets a chance to mature – to the extent that he did – and the reader never sees Byron actually "spoil." Hunt misses entirely the vital and vigorous interchange between the men; when there is change it is all one way, Shelley's influence drawing Byron out of his fashionable circle, out of himself, evoking the only instances of true generosity and honest talk in the lord's life in Italy.

These memoirs are celebrity biographies, polishing Shelley's image and dishing the dirt on Byron; as such, they were a success, scandalizing Byron's apologists and public and doing the stoop labor for the Shelley legend that Lady Jane Shelley, Percy Florence's wife, would tend so assiduously that Victorians would read Hunt's account as gospel. To give Hunt his due, he was first in the field, as he was a lone voice in the crowd of sycophants eulogizing Byron. From his school days Hunt, who suffered fagging and flogging and indignities of all sorts with chipper stoicism, showed courage when defending friends against bullies and arbitrary orthodoxies, so standing up for Shelley was a reflex as well as a sacred obligation. Piling abuse on Byron, or anyone, was not so natural for Hunt, but casting him among the bullies made Hunt honor bound to attack. There was the problem of Byron's friendship with Shelley, but Hunt subverts that inconvenience with recurrent references to instances of betrayal, such as Byron leaving Shelley off "a list of Englishmen he had seen since he left England" that he "told the public . . . was complete," and his lack of public praise for, or even acknowledgment of, Shelley's poetry: "Shelley he did not dare to acknowledge, even as a visitor." Byron's denial of Shelley demanded a response in kind.

The rest of the recollections in the volume are practically negligible. Keats rates a page of personal history followed by an extended appreciation of his poetry, with some of Hunt's most insightful commentary expressed in several of his more memora-

ble phrases. He quotes the sonnet "On First Looking into Chapman's Homer" in its entirety and recognizes it as a small masterpiece "which terminates with so energetic a calmness, and which completely announced the new poet taking possession." Moore comes off rather well for someone who had demonstrated dubious commitment to principle; descriptions of Lamb's "sensibility" are diverting and definitive; Coleridge was "very metaphysical and very corporeal." The other contemporaries, including Henry Fuseli, the painter of the sublime, appear as if at random as their anecdotes occur to the ruminating author, his musings winding down to silence.

By far the better part of the book is taken up by the "Recollections of the Author's Life," comprising what is left of the introduction to the abandoned anthology. "My own reminiscences, I fear," he demurs in his preface, "coming after [his reminiscences of Byron], will be like bringing back the Moselle, after devils [spiced meats] and Burgundy." They are more like champagne, palate-clearing and full of fizz. The autobiographies of the period, such as William Wordsworth's *The Prelude* (1850) or Thomas De Quincey's *Confessions of an English Opium Eater* (1822), were penetrating and intimate, but the genre also accommodates a lighter touch, like Hunt's, and his deflating irony appears in the "Recollections" as refreshing modesty. He is less confessional than self-deprecating; the reader does not penetrate Hunt's soul so much as watch individuals and events parade through his life. Chronology repeatedly gives way to association, and Hunt "runs on to the public," in Hazlitt's description, "as he does at his own fire-side." Critics might wish that he had addressed his personal struggles more extensively and had investigated the anomalies of his own character, but he would have had to step out of character to do so. In conversation he would never be Coleridge, who, sitting by his fireside, could see in an ash fluttering on the grate or frost crystallizing on his window a significance Hunt found only in a great friend's poetry or a great friend's death. One comes to know Coleridge, though, primarily through his conversation poems, *Biographia Literaria* (1817) and *Specimens of the Table Talk of the Late Samuel Taylor Coleridge* (1835), in the same way one learns about Hunt in his personal essays and recollections: not in scenes from his life but in the movements of his mind.

Two decades later Hunt edited and updated the biographical sketches and incorporated them into the text of his *The Autobiography of Leigh Hunt, with Reminiscences of Friends and Contemporaries* (1850). The later-life additions, which comprise only three of the fifteen chapters, are of minor interest compared with the editions of the original material. As elements in a memoir, the portraits seem less sketchy; their deficiencies of evidence or perspective are less important now, since the subject is no longer the figure portrayed but the author, whose life the biographies fill out. A major edit is done on Hunt's representation of Byron: the material is much the same, and the opinion is still disparaging; but the tone is much less mean-spirited, and the attitude is far less intrusive. Hunt had alarmed even his friends with the biography, and he seems genuinely relieved to temper it. "I was far more alive to other people's defects than to my own," he writes in a framing apology to his chapter on the fateful days of 1822; "I am now sufficiently sensible of my own to show to others the charity which I need myself." There was still little cheer in recalling the episodes of his life that involved Byron – prison, failed poetry, the end of Shelley – but he can take a longer view and render the truth with less coloring: "I was agitated by grief and anger. . . . I am now free from anger."

He was free because Byron was no longer the central, featured presence; the book turns on Shelley's death. Byron has been reduced to a functionary, providing a contrast that throws Shelley into high relief and affording Hunt, now the sentimental apostle as opposed to the petty complainer, a more liberal perspective. After Shelley is gone, chronology is depleted of purpose; it leads nowhere special, only to more of the same – more children, more debts, more magazines, more literary friendships – and less: lost zest, lost opportunities, lost loved ones.

Times changed more than Hunt did. His faith in progress was vindicated as English politics slouched toward liberalism and Keats and Shelley rose in reputation. As he outlived his peers he, too, rose in reputation, gaining a government pension and, when Wordsworth died in 1850, entertaining the once-absurd notion of becoming poet laureate. The autobiography may have been published as part of his campaign for the position, but his reflected fame as a living literary curiosity who quipped with Byron, wove a laurel wreath for Keats's brow, and received a bequest from Shelley's estate was a threadbare qualification. He had produced little memorable work since the biography he had written for Colburn. He tried new genres – a play was a success, a labored novel a long-winded failure – but his most successful efforts were anthologies of poetry, humor, or stories. His brother John had died, but Marianne had recovered to outlive

Vacca and "many another physician who had augured her a brief existence." She suffered, though, from "a lifelong spitting of blood" and from rheumatism and its "consolation," alcoholism. Hunt himself endured incessant pain and illness, nursing his sinking wife and tubercular children, churning out all or the larger part of failing journal after failed journal, clinging fiercely to his own consolation: cheer. "I have, myself," he wrote in a letter more dramatic than anything he wrote about himself in his autobiography, "a world of troubles to go through, daily, and my brain, partly by anxiety and partly by work, is kept in such a constant state of ultra-sensitiveness, that where any additional strain upon it can do no good, I am thankful at having it spared me." Cheer here is a state of desperate denial, the stress reaction of a precarious sanity. In sparing the reader that strain, Hunt's autobiography, while it is generally considered to be one of the best autobiographies of the nineteenth century – certainly of its first fifty years – is another missed chance.

He wrote another chapter on the next decade for the next edition (1860). It is a sad one: his son Vincent had died after a long decline, followed soon by Marianne at age sixty-nine in 1857. Like much of Hunt's work, the chapter is intriguing in what it leaves out. In 1853 Dickens's *Bleak House* had been published; among its multitude of characters is the comically corrupt Harold Skimpole, a scathing caricature of Hunt. Dickens had been a friend since the late 1830s and had organized one of his amateur theatricals for the benefit of the impoverished Hunt. He must also have been an admirer, for he asked Hunt to contribute to his periodical *Household Words,* and, as many said at the time and more have said since, he adopted and developed Hunt's familiar style and ironic flair and was among the first to benefit from the change in popular literary taste Hunt helped bring into being. That the successful novelist should publicly mock his friend's least attractive characteristics – his shallow aesthetic, childish posturing, irresponsible beggary, and sophistic cheerfulness – galled Hunt's other friends and admirers and must have wounded Hunt. Dickens bragged about the likeness in his correspondence, while denying to Hunt's face that he had any such thing in mind. The literary set anticipated that Hunt might address the affair in his autobiography; but it never arises, and Dickens appears as an "admirable friend." The incident points to several complexities of the artistic temperament: Dickens's cold calculation and imperious imagination, Hunt's peculiar forbearance when he is the injured party, and his gift for annoying his friends (Carlyle, when he was a neighbor in Chelsea, would on each visit leave coins on the Hunts' mantelpiece as a sort of ritual offering to ward off their suppliant and incessant cadging). But most provocative in the context of Hunt's biographical craft is the ironic parallel of Dickens's Skimpole and Hunt's Byron: each is an unflattering, scandalous portrait in print of an avowed friend and collaborator on a magazine.

In the last paragraph of the autobiography Hunt muses on immortality; on 28 August 1859 he died. His oldest son, Thornton, saw the 1860 edition into print. It was a great success and secured Hunt's reputation. His epitaph is taken from one of his few but enduring anthology pieces, the poem "Abou Ben Adhem" (first published in C. S. Hall's *Book of Gems,* 1838), which presents, with a directness worthy of Blake or James Stephens, the most profound principle of Hunt's philosophical "Christianism." Abou awakes from a dream, sees a seraph writing the names of the elect – "those who love the lord" – "in a book of gold," and asks if his name is among them. Told curtly that it is not, he modestly protests, saying to the angel, in a low voice but "cheerly still," the line that serves as the inscription on Hunt's memorial bust in Kensal Green cemetery: "Write me as one that loves his fellow-men." When the angel returns the next night and reveals the list of those "whom love of God had blessed," Hunt's humanist vision of Christianity is vindicated, as "Ben Adhem's name led all the rest." For such moments Hunt makes the list of authentic Romantic writers, as his biography of Byron, abusive and unhappy as it is, hurtling headlong into as yet undiscovered pitfalls in the genre, but somehow in the process tweaking life from a subject that had become a Romantic monument, assures Hunt's inclusion in the list of biography's pioneers.

Letters:

The Correspondence of Leigh Hunt, 2 volumes, edited by Thornton Hunt (London: Smith, Elder, 1862);

My Leigh Hunt Library: The Holograph Letters, edited by Luther A. Brewer (Iowa City: University of Iowa Press, 1938);

Charles Richard Sanders, "The Correspondence and Friendship of Thomas Carlyle and Leigh Hunt," *Bulletin of the John Rylands Library,* 45 (March 1963): 439–485; 46 (September 1963): 179–216;

David R. Cheney, *The Correspondence of Leigh Hunt and Charles Ollier in the Winter of 1853–54* (Lon-

don: Keats-Shelley Memorial Association, 1976);

Charles E. Robinson, "The Shelleys to Leigh Hunt: A New Letter of 5 April 1821," *Keats Shelley Review,* 31 (1980): 52–56;

Robinson, "Shelley to the Editor of the Morning Chronicle: A Second New Letter of 5 April 1821," *Keats Shelley Review,* 32 (1981): 55–58;

Anne Kaier, "John Hamilton Reynolds: Four New Letters," *Keats Shelley Journal,* 30 (1981): 182–190;

Marcia Allentuck, "Leigh Hunt and Shelley: A New Letter," *Keats Shelley Journal,* 33 (1984): 50.

Bibliographies:

Alexander Ireland, *List of the Writings of William Hazlitt and Leigh Hunt* (London: John Russell Smith, 1868);

Alexander Mitchell, "A Bibliography of the Writings of Hunt," *Bookman's Journal,* 15 (1927): 3–19;

Luther A. Brewer, *My Leigh Hunt Library* (Cedar Rapids, Iowa: Privately printed by the Torch Press, 1932);

Louis Landré, *Leigh Hunt (1784–1859): Contribution à l'histoire du romantisme anglais,* 2 volumes (Paris: Société d'Edition "Les Belles Lettres," 1936), II: 483–595;

David Bonnell Green and Edwin Graves Wilson, *Keats, Shelley, Byron, Hunt, and Their Circles: A Bibliography* (Lincoln: University of Nebraska Press, 1964);

Carolyn Washburn Houtchens and Lawrence Huston Houtchens, *The English Romantic Poets and Essayists: A Review of Research and Criticism,* revised edition (New York: Published for the Modern Language Association of America by New York University Press, 1966), pp. 255–288;

O. M. Brack and D. H. Stefanson, *A Catalogue of the Leigh Hunt Manuscripts in the University of Iowa Libraries* (Iowa City: Friends of the University of Iowa Libraries, 1973);

Robert A. Hartley, ed., *Keats, Shelley, Byron, Hunt, and Their Circles: A Bibliography. July 1, 1962–December 31, 1974* (Lincoln: University of Nebraska Press, 1978);

Clement Dunbar, "Current Bibliography," *Keats Shelley Journal,* 30 (1981): 221–265;

Timothy J. Lulofs and Hans Ostrom, *Leigh Hunt: A Reference Guide* (Boston: G. K. Hall, 1985);

John L. Waltman and Gerald G. McDaniel, *Leigh Hunt: A Comprehensive Bibliography* (New York & London: Garland, 1985).

Biographies:

Charles and Mary Cowden Clarke, *Recollections of Writers* (London: Sampson, Low, Marston, Searle & Rivington, 1878), pp. 190–272;

Cosmo Monkhouse, *Life of Leigh Hunt* (London: Walter Scott, 1893);

Edmund Blunden, *Leigh Hunt: A Biography* (London: Cobden-Sanderson, 1930);

Louis Landré, *Leigh Hunt (1784–1859): Contribution à l'histoire du romantisme anglais,* volume 1 (Paris: Société d'Edition "Les Belles Lettres," 1936);

Molly Tatchell, *Leigh Hunt and His Family in Hammersmith* (London: Hammersmith Local History Group, 1969);

Richard Russell, *Leigh Hunt and Some of His Contemporaries* (London: Creed, 1984);

Ann Blainey, *Immortal Boy: A Portrait of Leigh Hunt* (London & Sydney: Croom, Helm, 1985).

References:

H. Allingham and D. Radford, eds., *William Allingham: A Diary* (London: Macmillan, 1907);

William Baker, "Leigh Hunt, George Henry Lewes and Henry Hallam's *Introduction to the Literature of Europe,*" *Studies in Bibliography,* 32 (1979): 252–273;

Ernest Bernbaum, *Guide through the Romantic Movement,* revised and enlarged edition (New York: Ronald, 1949);

Edmund Blunden, *Leigh Hunt's "Examiner" Examined* (London: Cobden-Sanderson, 1928);

Kenneth Neill Cameron, "Leigh Hunt (19 October 1784–28 August 1859)," in *Romantic Rebels: Essays on Shelley and His Circle,* edited by Cameron (Cambridge, Mass.: Harvard University Press, 1973), pp. 146–160;

David R. Cheney, "Leigh Hunt Sued for Debt by a Friend," *Books at Iowa,* 27 (November 1977): 30–56;

Paul M. Clogan, "Chaucer and Leigh Hunt," *Medievalia et Humanistica,* new series 9 (1979): 163–174;

Paul M. S. Dawson, "Byron, Shelley, and the 'New School,' " in *Shelley Revalued: Essays from the Gregynog Conference,* edited by Kelvin Everest (Totowa, N. J.: Barnes & Noble, 1983), pp. 89–108;

Donald H. Ericksen, "Harold Skimpole: Dickens and the Early 'Art for Art's Sake' Movement," *Journal of English and Germanic Philology,* 72 (January 1973): 48–59;

Theodore Fenner, "Ballet in Early Nineteenth Century London as Seen by Leigh Hunt and Henry Robertson," *Dance Chronicle,* 2 (1977–1978): 75–95;

Fenner, *Leigh Hunt and Opera Criticism: The "Examiner" Years (1808–1821)* (Lawrence: University Press of Kansas, 1972);

Walt Fisher, "Leigh Hunt as Friend and Critic of Keats: 1816–1859," *Lock Haven Review,* no. 5 (1963): 27–42;

Stephen F. Fogle, "Leigh Hunt and the End of Romantic Criticism," in *Some British Romantics: A Collection of Essays,* edited by James V. Logan, John E. Jordan, and Northrop Frye (Columbus: Ohio State University Press, 1966), pp. 119–139;

Eleanor M. Gates, "Leigh Hunt, Lord Byron, and Mary Shelley: The Long Goodbye," *Keats Shelley Journal,* 35 (1986): 149–167;

William Hazlitt, *The Spirit of the Age* (London: Colburn, 1825);

Richard Holmes, *Shelley: The Pursuit* (New York: Viking Penguin, 1987);

R. H. Horne, *A New Spirit of the Age* (London: Smith, Elder, 1844);

[Thornton L. Hunt], "A Man of Letters of the Last Generation," *Cornhill Magazine,* 1 (January 1860): 85–95;

Ian Jack, *English Literature 1815–1832* (London: Oxford University Press, 1963);

Reginald Brimley Johnson, *Leigh Hunt* (London: Swan Sonnenschein, 1896);

Johnson, ed., *Shelley-Leigh Hunt: How Friendship Made History: and Extended the Bounds of Human Freedom and Thought* (London: Ingpen & Grant, 1928);

Kenneth E. Kendall, *Leigh Hunt's "Reflector"* (The Hague: Mouton, 1971);

Louis Landré, *Leigh Hunt (1784–1859): Contribution à l'histoire du romantisme anglais,* 2 volumes (Paris: Société d'Edition "Les Belles-Lettres," 1936);

Marie Hamilton Law, *The English Familiar Essay in the Early Nineteenth Century: The Elements, Old and New, Which Went into Its Making as Exemplified in the Writings of Hunt, Hazlitt, and Lamb* (Philadelphia: University of Pennsylvania Press, 1934);

William Maginn, "Leigh Hunt," in *The Maclise Portrait Gallery of "Illustrious Literary Characters,"* with Memoirs, edited by William Bates (London: Chatto & Windus, 1883), pp. 242–256;

William Marshall, *Byron, Shelley, Hunt, and "The Liberal"* (Philadelphia: University of Pennsylvania Press, 1960);

Robert A. McCown, ed., *The Life and Times of Leigh Hunt; Papers Delivered at Symposium at the Univer-*

sity of Iowa April 13, 1984, Commemorating the
200th Anniversary of Leigh Hunt's Birth (Iowa
City: Friends of the University of Iowa Libraries, 1985);

Barnette Miller, *Leigh Hunt's Relations with Byron,
Shelley, and Keats* (New York: Columbia University Press, 1910);

Ernest Pereira, "Sonnet Contests and Verse Compliments in the Keats-Hunt Circle," *Unisa English Studies,* 25 (May 1987): 13–23;

Bryan Waller Procter, *An Autobiographical Fragment
and Biographical Notes* (Boston: Roberts, 1877);

Peter Quennell, *Byron in Italy* (New York: Viking,
1957);

H. E. Rollins, *The Keats Circle: Letters and Papers and
More Letters and Poems of the Keats Circle,* 2 vol-
umes (Cambridge, Mass.: Harvard University
Press, 1948);

David H. Stam, "Leigh Hunt and *The True Sun:* A
List of Reviews, August 1833 to February
1834," *Bulletin of the New York Public Library,* 77
(Summer 1974): 436–453;

George Dumas Stout, "Leigh Hunt's Money Troubles: Some New Light," *Washington University
Studies,* 12 (April 1925): 221–232;

James R. Thompson, *Leigh Hunt* (Boston: Twayne,
1977);

Clarence Dewitt Thorpe, "An Essay in Evaluation:
Leigh Hunt as Man of Letters," in *Leigh Hunt's
Literary Criticism,* edited by Lawrence Huston
Houtchens and Carolyn Washburn Houtch-
ens (New York: Columbia University Press,
1956), pp. 3–73;

Lisa Vargo, "Unmasking Shelley's Mask of Anarchy," *English Studies in Canada,* 13 (March
1987): 49–64;

Jack Welch, "The Leigh Hunt-William Moxon Dispute of 1836," *West Virginia University Philological Papers,* 18 (September 1971): 30–41;

Stanley Wells, "Shakespeare in Leigh Hunt's Theatre Criticism," *Essays and Studies,* 33 (1980):
119–138;

Carl R. Woodring, "Leigh Hunt as Political Essayist," in *Leigh Hunt's Political and Occasional Essays,* edited by Houtchens and Houtchens
(New York: Columbia University Press,
1962), pp. 3–71.

Papers:

The largest collection of Leigh Hunt's correspon-
dence and manuscripts is in the Luther A. Brewer
Collection, University of Iowa Libraries. Among
other important collections are those at the British
Library; the University of Leeds Library; the Carl
H. Pforzheimer Collection and the Berg Collection
of the New York Public Library; the Houghton
Library at Harvard University; and the Huntington
Library, San Marino, California.

George Henry Lewes

(18 April 1817 – 30 November 1878)

Natalie J. McKnight
Boston University

See also the Lewes entry in *DLB 55: Victorian Prose Writers Before 1867.*

BOOKS: *A Biographical History of Philosophy,* 4 volumes (London: Knight, 1845–1846); revised and enlarged as *The Biographical History of Philosophy from Its Origin in Greece down to the Present Day,* 1 volume (London: Parker, 1857; New York: Appleton, 1857); republished as *The History of Philosophy from Thales to Comte,* 2 volumes (London: Longmans, Green, 1867; revised, 1871);

The Spanish Drama: Lope de Vega and Calderón (London: Knight, 1846);

Ranthorpe (London: Chapman & Hall, 1847; New York: Gottsberger, 1881);

Rose, Blanche, and Violet, 3 volumes (London: Smith, Elder, 1848); republished as *Three Sisters and Three Fortunes; or, Rose, Blanche, and Violet,* 1 volume (New York: Harper, 1848);

The Life of Maximilien Robespierre: With Extracts from His Unpublished Correspondence (London: Chapman & Hall, 1849; Philadelphia: Carey & Hart, 1849);

The Noble Heart: A Tragedy, in Three Acts (London: Chapman & Hall, 1850); republished as *The Noble Heart: A Play. In Three Acts* (New York: French, 1855?);

A Cozy Couple: A Farce in One Act, as Slingsby Lawrence (London: Lacy, 1850);

A Strange History: A Dramatic Tale, in Eight Chapters, by Lewes, as Lawrence, and Charles Mathews (London: Lacy, 1850);

The Game of Speculation: A Comedy in Three Acts, as Lawrence (London: Lacy, 1851);

A Chain of Events: A Dramatic Story in Eight Acts. Correctly Printed from the Prompt Book, with Exits, Entrances, &c. First Performed at the Royal Lyceum Theatre, on Easter Monday, April 12th, 1852, by Lewes, as Lawrence, and Mathews (London: Fairbrother, 1852);

Comte's Philosophy of the Sciences: Being an Exposition of the Principles of the Cours de Philosophie Positive of Auguste Comte, Bohn's Scientific Library, volume 20 (London: Bohn, 1853);

The Lawyers: A Comedy. In Three Acts, as Lawrence (London: Lacy, 1853?; New York & London: French, 1873);

Give a Dog a Bad Name: A Farce in One Act, as Lawrence (London: Lacy, 1854);

Sunshine through the Clouds: A Drama in One Act. Adapted from "La joie fait peur" by Madame de Girardin, as Lawrence (London: Lacy, 1854; New York: French, 1854?);

Buckstone's Adventure with a Polish Princess: An Original Farce in One Act, as Lawrence (London: Lacy, 1855);

The Life and Works of Goethe: With Sketches of His Age and Contemporaries, from Published and Unpublished Sources, 2 volumes (London: Nutt, 1855; Boston: Ticknor & Fields, 1856); revised as *The Life of Goethe,* 2 volumes (London: Smith, Elder, 1864; New York: Dutton, 1864);

Sea-Side Studies at Ilfracombe, Tenby, the Scilly Isles & Jersey (Edinburgh & London: Blackwood, 1858);

The Physiology of Common Life, 2 volumes (Edinburgh: Blackwood, 1859, 1860; New York: Appleton, 1860);

Studies in Animal Life (New York: Harper, 1860; London: Smith, Elder, 1862);

Aristotle: A Chapter from the History of Science, Including Analyses of Aristotle's Scientific Writings (London: Smith, Elder, 1864);

Problems of Life and Mind. First Series: The Foundations of a Creed, 2 volumes (London: Trübner, 1874, 1875; Boston: Osgood, 1874, 1875);

On Actors and the Art of Acting (London: Smith, Elder, 1875; New York: Holt, 1878);

The Physical Basis of Mind: Being the Second Series of Problems of Life and Mind (London: Trübner, 1877; Boston: Osgood, 1877);

George Henry Lewes

Problems of Life and Mind: Third Series, 2 volumes
(London: Trübner, 1879; Boston: Osgood,
1879–1880) – comprises volume 1, *The Study
of Psychology: Its Object, Scope, and Method;* volume 2, *Mind as a Function of the Organism; The
Sphere of Sense and Logic of Feeling; The Sphere of
Intellect and Logic of Signs;*

The Principles of Success in Literature (San Francisco:
Printed for Albert S. Cook, 1885); edited by
T. Sharper Knowlson (London: Scott, 1898?);

*Dramatic Essays: Reprinted from the "Examiner" and the
"Leader,"* by Lewes and John Forster, edited
by William Archer and Robert W. Lowe (London: Scott, 1896);

Literary Criticism of George Henry Lewes, edited by
Alice R. Kaminsky (Lincoln: University of Nebraska Press, 1964).

PLAY PRODUCTIONS: *The Noble Heart,* Manchester, Theatre Royal, 18 February 1849; London, Olympic Theatre, 18 February 1850;
New York, Bowery Theatre, 5 February 1851;

The Game of Speculation, as Slingsby Lawrence, adapted
from *Mercadet,* an abridgment by Adolphe-
Philippe d'Ennery of Honoré de Balzac's *Le
Faiseur,* London, Royal Lyceum Theatre, 2 October 1851;

A Chain of Events, by Lewes, as Lawrence, and
Charles Mathews, adapted from *La Dame de la
Halle,* by Anicet-Bourgeois and Auguste-
Michel Masson, London, Royal Lyceum The-
atre, 12 April 1852;

Taking by Storm!, as Frank Churchill, adapted from
Tambour battant, by Pierre-Henri-Adrien
Decourcelle, Theodore Barrière, and Jules
Lorin, London, Royal Lyceum Theatre, 3
June 1852;

A Strange History, by Lewes, as Lawrence, and
Mathews, adapted from *Marianne,* by Anicet-
Bourgeois and Masson, London, Royal Ly-
ceum Theatre, 29 March 1853;

The Lawyers, as Lawrence, adapted from *Les Avocats,*
by Philippe Dumanoir and L. F. Nicolai, Lon-

don, Royal Lyceum Theatre, 19 May 1853;
New York, Burton's Theatre, 19 August 1853;

Give a Dog a Bad Name, as Lawrence, adapted from *Quand on veut tuer son chien,* London, Royal Lyceum Theatre, 18 April 1854;

Sunshine through the Clouds, as Lawrence, adapted from *La Joie fait peur,* by Emile de Girardin, London, Royal Lyceum Theatre, 15 June 1854;

A Cozy Couple, by Lewes, as Lawrence, and Mathews, adapted from *Le Village,* by Octave Feuillet, London, Royal Lyceum Theatre, 15 March 1855;

Buckstone's Adventures with a Polish Princess, as Lawrence, London, Royal Lyceum Theatre, 29 June 1855;

Stay at Home, adapted from *Un Mari qui se derange,* London, Olympic Theatre, 11 February 1856;

Captain Bland, New York, Wallack's Theatre, 30 May 1864.

OTHER: James Finlay Weir Johnston, *The Chemistry of Common Life,* 2 volumes, revised by Lewes (Edinburgh, 1859);

Selections from the Modern British Dramatists, 2 volumes, introductions and biographical notices by Lewes (Leipzig: Brockhaus, 1867);

Female Characters of Goethe: From the Original Drawings of William Kaulbach, explanatory text by Lewes (New York: Stroefer / Munich: Bruckmann, 1868);

Alexander Main, *Life and Conversations of Dr. Samuel Johnson: Founded Chiefly on Boswell,* preface by Lewes (London: Chapman & Hall, 1874);

The Ethics of Aristotle, translated by D. P. Chase, introductory essay by Lewes (London: Scott, 1890).

SELECTED PERIODICAL PUBLICATIONS – UNCOLLECTED: "Hints towards an Essay on the Sufferings of Truth," *Monthly Repository,* new enlarged series 1 (July–December 1837): 374–376;

"A Companion for the Fragment of Simonides," *Monthly Repository,* new enlarged series 1 (July–December 1837): 401–402;

"Percy Bysshe Shelley," *Westminster Review,* 35 (April 1841): 303–344;

"Percy Bysshe Shelley," *Penny Cyclopaedia,* 21 (1841): 374–376;

"Errors and Abuses of English Criticism," *Westminster Review,* 38 (October 1842): 446–486;

"The Life and Works of Goethe," *British and Foreign Review,* 14 (March 1843): 78–135;

"Augustus Wilhelm Schlegel," *Foreign Quarterly Review,* 32 (October 1843): 160–181;

"Balzac and George Sand," *Foreign Quarterly Review,* 33 (July 1844): 145–162;

"The Rise and Fall of the European Drama," *Foreign Quarterly Review,* 35 (July 1845): 290–334;

"Recent Novels: French and English," *Fraser's Magazine,* 36 (December 1847): 686–695;

"Charles Lamb – His Genius and Writings," *British Quarterly Review,* 7 (May 1848): 306;

Review of *Vanity Fair,* by William Makepeace Thackeray, *Athenaeum,* no. 1085 (12 August 1848): 794–797;

"Charles Lamb and His Friends," *British Quarterly Review,* 8 (November 1848): 382;

"Shakespeare's Critics: English and Foreign," *Edinburgh Review,* 90 (July 1849): 40–47;

"Currer Bell's *Shirley,*" *Edinburgh Review,* 91 (January 1850): 151–173;

"The Lady Novelists," *Westminster Review,* 58 (July 1852): 129–141;

Review of *Poems,* by Matthew Arnold, *Leader,* 4 (26 November 1853): 1146–1147; 4 (3 December 1853): 1170–1171;

"Realism in Art: Recent German Fiction," *Westminster Review,* 70 (October 1858): 493–496;

"Novels of Jane Austen," *Blackwood's Edinburgh Magazine,* 86 (July 1859): 99–113;

"Criticism in Relation to Novels," *Fortnightly Review,* 3 (15 December 1865): 352–361;

"Mr. Darwin's Hypotheses," *Fortnightly Review,* new series 3 (1 April 1868): 353–373; (1 June 1868): 611–628; new series 4 (1 July 1868): 61–80; (1 November 1868): 492–509;

"Dickens in Relation to Criticism," *Fortnightly Review,* new series 17 (1 February 1872): 141–154;

"On the Dread and Dislike of Science," *Fortnightly Review,* new series 29 (1 June 1878): 805–815.

A man of remarkable intellectual versatility, George Henry Lewes wrote biographies of Johann Wolfgang von Goethe and Maximilien Robespierre, a multivolume biographical history of a wide range of philosophers, and biographical articles on Percy Bysshe Shelley and Charles Lamb, while also making significant contributions to the fields of philosophy, literature, science, and psychology. His biography of Goethe was the first to cover the author's entire life, and it was an immediate success, winning the praises of Thomas Carlyle and many German critics. His lucid and engaging prose enlivened his biographies while making diverse and complex subjects such as positivism, marine biology, literary

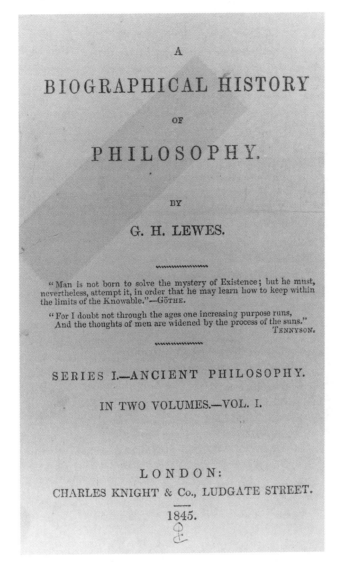

A

BIOGRAPHICAL HISTORY

OF

PHILOSOPHY.

BY

G. H. LEWES.

"Man is not born to solve the mystery of Existence; but he must,
nevertheless, attempt it, in order that he may learn how to keep within
the limits of the Knowable."—GÖTHE.

"For I doubt not through the ages one increasing purpose runs,
And the thoughts of men are widened by the process of the suns."
TENNYSON.

SERIES I.—ANCIENT PHILOSOPHY.

IN TWO VOLUMES.—VOL. I.

LONDON:
CHARLES KNIGHT & Co., LUDGATE STREET.
1845.

Title page for the work that established Lewes's reputation

criticism, and the relation between psychology and physiology accessible to the general reading public. As a biographer, Lewes chose not to idealize his subjects but to present the truth of their lives as objectively as possible. He did not moralize or judge, as did many of his Victorian colleagues. Lewes also turned his hand to novels, but, although they were fairly well received in his time, they never earned him as much praise as his nonfictional works. Lewes is chiefly remembered now, however, for his unorthodox relationship with the novelist George Eliot (Mary Ann Evans), with whom he lived from 1854 until his death in 1878. Still, several of his works have attracted the attention of twentieth-century scholars, particularly *A Biographical History of Philosophy* (1845–1846), *The Life and Works of Goethe* (1855), and his miscellaneous literary criticism.

Lewes was born in London on 18 April 1817 to John Lee Lewes and Elizabeth Ashweek. He was their third illegitimate son; John Lewes had had four other children by his legal wife, Elizabeth Pownall Lewes, and he abandoned both his legitimate and illegitimate families when he immigrated to Bermuda when George Henry was still a baby. When Lewes was six his mother married Capt. John Gurens Willim, an irascible man whom the entire family came to dislike.

Lewes's education was erratic. He attended boarding school in London from ages nine to eleven. From 1828 to 1830 he attended school in Jersey, where he mastered French. In 1830 the family moved to Gloucestershire, where Lewes attended Dr. Charles Parr Burney's school until 1832; he then studied medicine briefly at University College,

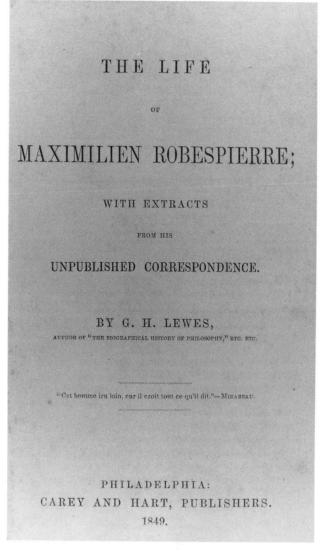

THE LIFE

OF

MAXIMILIEN ROBESPIERRE;

WITH EXTRACTS

FROM HIS

UNPUBLISHED CORRESPONDENCE.

BY G. H. LEWES,

AUTHOR OF "THE BIOGRAPHICAL HISTORY OF PHILOSOPHY," ETC. ETC.

"Cet homme ira loin, car il croit tout ce qu'il dit."—MIRABEAU.

PHILADELPHIA:
CAREY AND HART, PUBLISHERS.
1849.

Title page for Lewes's first full-length biography

London, although no records exist to show whether he ever formally enrolled. Lewes abandoned his medical studies when he realized that he could not bear watching patients in pain; but his interest in biology would grow throughout his life and would influence some of his most successful books. Always sensitive about his lack of a formal classical education, Lewes tried to make up for the deficiency through self-teaching, and few classically trained Victorians could have been as knowledgeable on such a vast array of topics as Lewes would prove to be in his varied writings.

At age seventeen Lewes wrote to Leigh Hunt, a radical magazine editor and onetime friend of Shelley and George Gordon, Lord Byron, asking Hunt to publish one of his stories. Hunt did not print the tale, but he accepted Lewes into a circle of young men who were admirers of Hunt and worshipers of Shelley. Planning to write a biography of Shelley, Lewes recorded Hunt's reminiscences of the poet. Hunt warned him that Shelley's widow, Mary, might not encourage his attempt since she was being supported by Shelley's father on the condition that she not help in the production of any biographies of his son; and when Lewes sent the manuscript, via Hunt, to Mary Shelley in 1839 she returned it, politely declining to read it. Lewes abandoned the project but put his research to use in his review in the *Westminster Review* (April 1841) of Mary Shelley's edition of her husband's poetry and in the Shelley entry he wrote for the *Penny Cyclopaedia* (1841). Later he was to claim that he was glad that the biography was never published, "for though I have not altered my opinion of Shelley, I have considerably altered my views of composition; and the m.s. of the Life makes me shudder when I look at it. I was so young when it was written; and though only six years older now these six years have been twelve in point of development." The *Westminster Review* essay demonstrates the nonjudgmental approach Lewes tends to take toward his biographical subjects; his intent, he says, is to look at Shelley "not from *our* central point of view, but rather from *his*."

During 1837–1838 Lewes wrote miscellaneous criticism; his first piece was for Hunt's *Monthly Repository* (July–December 1837). Along with other Hunt devotees – William Bell Scott, Egertton Webbe, and Hunt's son Thornton – Lewes edited the *National Magazine and Monthly Critic;* the magazine was short-lived, but it is worth noting as the place where Lewes first published criticism of Charles Dickens's early work. In December 1837 he favorably reviewed Dickens's *Sketches by Boz* (1836), *Pickwick Papers* (1836–1837), and *Oliver Twist* (1838), claiming that "no one has ever combined the nicety of observation, the fineness of tact, the exquisite humour, the wit, heartiness, sympathy with all things good and beautiful in human nature, the perception of character and accuracy of description, with the same force that he has done." By July 1838 the magazine was defunct.

From August 1838 to April 1839 Lewes studied German in Berlin. He began studying the works of Goethe while attending lectures at Berlin University and supporting himself by giving lessons in English and French. In a letter 15 November 1838 to Hunt, Lewes described his life at this time: "My days are spent in study – my evenings in society – at Concerts or Theatre. Touching the former I am reading 'Faust' in the original – no easy task – & translating Goethe's 'Torquato Tasso.' " His was not the conventional university education, but it prepared him well for his life as a man of letters. "Not many young men coming down from Oxford or Cambridge in 1840–1 had a width of well digested reading comparable to Lewes's," his biographer David Williams asserts. In his novel *Ranthorpe* (1847) Lewes would place his hero in Berlin, "preparing himself for the great combat with the world," much as Lewes himself had.

In 1839 Lewes returned to England, where he continued writing miscellaneous criticism for minor journals; his first *Westminster Review* article, an essay on French drama, was published in September 1840. He also worked as a tutor to the children of Swynfen Jervis, a member of Parliament from Straffordshire, and in February 1841 he married Jervis's

eighteen-year-old daughter, Agnes. In the early years of their marriage Agnes helped Lewes with his work and contributed some translations of her own to *Fraser's Magazine*. The first two of their four sons, Charles and Thornton, were born in 1842 and 1844, respectively.

In the first few years after his marriage Lewes had articles published on Georg Wilhelm Friedrich Hegel's aesthetics, August Wilhelm von Schlegel, Benedict de Spinoza, Honoré de Balzac, George Sand, English drama and criticism, and French philosophy and science, the latter influenced by a visit to France, where he met with Auguste Comte. In 1842 he began corresponding to Karl August Varnhagen von Ense, a former friend of Goethe with whom Lewes had become acquainted in Berlin; Varnhagen's firsthand accounts of Goethe would enable Lewes to bring his subject to life in his biography. A long article Lewes wrote on Goethe for the *British and Foreign Review* (March 1843) combines biography and criticism. As he would continue to do in his full-length biography of Goethe, Lewes defends the artist against charges of immorality in his life and works. In art, Lewes claims, "ethics became subordinate in fact to aesthetics." As Lewes's biographer Rosemary Ashton points out, this idea would become the thesis of his *The Life and Works of Goethe*.

In 1845 and 1846 appeared the work that was to make Lewes's reputation: *A Biographical History of Philosophy*, a four-volume survey of Western philosophy from Thales to Comte. It is a clear, energetic, accessible, and relatively brief work that makes complex philosophical subjects accessible to the layperson. Lewes praises Francis Bacon's scientific approach to knowledge as an advance over the abstract philosophizing of earlier thinkers; he criticizes René Descartes's deductive reasoning, which makes the mistake of beginning with concepts and then moving to observable phenomena. Lewes calls Comte "the Bacon of the nineteenth century"; he admires Comte's empiricism and avoidance of theology.

Although a few scholars criticized the book's lack of depth and Lewes's insufficient background in the area, ten thousand copies had been sold by 1846. Comte wrote to thank Lewes for his praise; Lewes wrote back on 10 July 1846 that "My book is read at Oxford and Cambridge as well as by artisans and even women." The book inspired Harriet Martineau to translate Comte's works; it also sparked Herbert Spencer's interest in psychology, which was to be his primary area of study for the next fifty years. Lewes enlarged the book for a one-volume second edition in 1857; a two-volume edi-

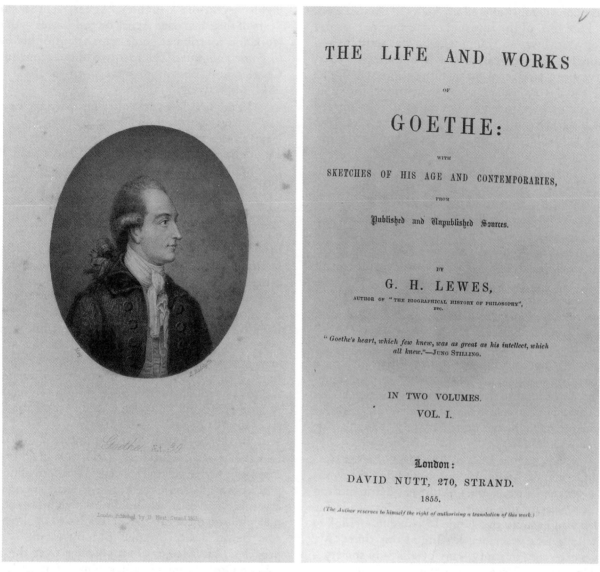

Frontispiece and title page for Lewes's biography of the German writer, the first study to attempt a comprehensive view of Goethe rather than concentrating on isolated aspects of his life and work

tion appeared in 1867 under the title *The History of Philosophy from Thales to Comte* and was revised in 1871. In the later editions Lewes added more scholarly apparatus; but the academic elite was still not impressed, and the general reading public preferred the original work for its brevity and accessibility.

In a letter dated June 1846 to his friend W. B. Scott, Lewes summed up his activities by saying that he was "buried full five fathoms deep in work . . . [working on] a Life of Goethe; finishing a book for Knight on the Spanish Dramatists; revising a novel to appear in Chapman & Hall's series; & writing Review articles by way of variety." The book on Spanish dramatists was *The Spanish Drama: Lope de Vega and Calderón* (1846), and the novel was *Ranthorpe;* a

second novel, *Rose, Blanche, and Violet,* appeared in 1848. *Ranthorpe* particularly interests Lewes scholars today because of its autobiographical elements. The review articles included one in *Fraser's Magazine* (December 1847) on Charlotte Brontë's *Jane Eyre* (1847), which led to a regular correspondence between the two writers, and one in the *Athenaeum* (12 August 1848) on William Makepeace Thackeray's *Vanity Fair* (1847–1848). His sons Herbert and St. Vincent Arthy were born in 1846 and 1848, respectively. During these same years Lewes began acting in Dickens's amateur theatrical company, which played in London, Manchester, Liverpool, Birmingham, Edinburgh, and Glasgow. Lewes and Dickens, with their boundless energy and staggering writing

*Mary Ann Evans (George Eliot), who lived with Lewes from 1854
until his death in 1878 (photograph by John Edwin Mayall, 1858)*

commitments, must have been a fascinating combination on stage and behind the scenes. Although tension existed in the relationship between the two men, they remained friendly for the rest of Dickens's life.

Lewes's next biography was *The Life of Maximilien Robespierre* (1849). The French socialist Louis Blanc, who had left Europe during the multiple failed revolutions of 1848, aided Lewes in composing the work. Edgar W. Hirshberg faults *The Life of Maximilien Robespierre* for its prolix passages concerning liberal thought, which revealed ideological similarities between Lewes and his subject, but in general Hirshberg assesses the book as "objective and capably conceived." Though written rapidly in the midst of many other projects, the work received favorable reviews. The reviewer in the *Spectator* (24 February 1849) wrote that "All that is known [of Robespierre] Mr. Lewes has collected, and pre-

sented in a manner which not only brings out the biographical character of the facts, but helps the reader to a biographical conclusion, from the picture it suggests of France at the time." The reviewer applauded Lewes's inclusion of Robespierre's poetry, speeches, and correspondence, for helping to provide a fuller picture of the man. While acknowledging that Lewes did not try to be original in the biography, the reviewer commends him for bringing together "sometimes from out-of-the-way sources, all that is known upon the subject" and taking "a distinct and rational view of Robespierre's conduct and character, which preserves the lineaments of the man without sinking those of the criminal."

The Life of Maximilien Robespierre also received an enthusiastic review from George Jacob Holyoake in the *Reasoner* (July 1849). Lewes was pleased by the review but could not agree, in spite of his own liberal views, with Holyoake's wholehearted support of the French Revolution. Lewes wrote to Holyoake, thanking him for the review and beginning a friendship that would last the rest of his life. In the same year Holyoake began assisting Lewes and Thornton Hunt in their preparations for publishing a new radical periodical, the *Leader*.

During this busy year Lewes found time to act in a tragedy he wrote, *The Noble Heart* (1850), and to perform as Shylock in a professional production of William Shakespeare's *The Merchant of Venice* (1600). Perhaps his excessive activity contributed to the estrangement from his wife that Jane Welsh Carlyle noticed in April 1849. "I used to think these Leweses a perfect pair of lovebirds always cuddling together on the same perch – to speak figuratively – but the female lovebird appears to have hopped off to some distance and to be now taking a somewhat critical view of her shaggy little mate." The distance between the two was exacerbated by Lewes's effusive praises of other women; according to Jane Carlyle, Agnes grew annoyed and jealous at these outbursts, which he made in public in front of her. Lewes had a reputation as a womanizer in spite of his notorious ugliness: his face was marked by smallpox, his features were course, his hair wild, and his head too big for his diminutive body, yet his wit and intensity attracted women. But Agnes did her share of philandering as well. Sometime during 1849 she began an affair with Thornton Hunt; on 16 April 1850, less than a month after her fourth son by Lewes died of measles, she gave birth to a son by Hunt. Lewes, who had always been a free-love advocate, accepted the situation calmly and claimed the child as his own. But the next year Agnes bore Hunt another child, and Lewes grew increasingly discontented with the situation. According to Lewes's biographer Rosemary Ashton, Lewes probably moved out in 1852; but he continued to use his wife's address for correspondence until 1854.

That Lewes was able to accomplish anything during such personally tumultuous times is remarkable; that he accomplished much is impressive. The *Leader* was a success, attracting much attention and selling almost three thousand copies a week in its first year. For the literature section Lewes created the character of Vivian, a bachelor–bon vivant who reviewed with wit and sarcasm the literature and theater of the day. The character was a hit; Bernard Shaw acknowledged that his own theater reviews were influenced by Lewes's. By mid 1854 Hunt and Lewes had relinquished their control of the *Leader* due to financial difficulties and changing interests.

In October 1852 Lewes had an article published in the *Westminster Review* on Goethe as a man of science; Lewes had consulted with Richard Owen, a leading comparative anatomist, to assess Goethe's contribution to that field. Lewes argues that Goethe never received his due respect from scientists because of their perception of him as a poet, even though he had done noteworthy work in biology and botany. (Lewes's own scientific writings often met with a similar cool reception from the scientific community, and for similar reasons.) Lewes would incorporate the essay into his biography of Goethe.

To continue his research on Goethe, Lewes traveled to Germany in July 1854. Evans, to whom he had been introduced by Spencer, went with him, scandalizing their friends and London society in general. German society, particularly that in Weimar, accepted the relationship without a fuss; what did cause a stir was Lewes's plan to write a complete biography of the complex and prolific Goethe. No one had as yet attempted to tell Goethe's full story; writers had instead concentrated on specific periods of his life or aspects of his work. It took someone of Lewes's self-confidence, ambition, energy, and determination to grapple with such an undertaking. The Germans were in awe of Lewes and somewhat jealous that a German writer had not been the first to embark on the project.

In Weimar, Lewes met some of the few remaining people who had known Goethe. Johann Peter Eckermann, Goethe's secretary, and Ottilie von Goethe, the poet's daughter-in-law, supplied him with reminiscences; Gustav Adolf Scholl, director of the Art Institute, showed Lewes some of the poet's letters, which Scholl had edited. Lewes also went to see Goethe's study and bedroom, which he describes in the biography.

In Berlin, Lewes became reacquainted with Varnhagen, who lent him books, read his manuscript, and discussed Goethe with him. Evans contributed by translating Goethe's prose. In March 1855 they returned to England, and with remarkable rapidity *The Life and Works of Goethe,* which was dedicated to Carlyle, was published by David Nutt in November.

The book achieved immediate success. In the first three months it sold more than one thousand copies; it went into many editions, was translated into several languages, and has been reprinted as recently as 1965. As an anonymous critic for the *Times* (3 December 1878) quipped, the biography received "the highest tributes of respect which can be paid to a book of the kind: in Germany it has been translated and admired, and in France it has been plagiarized." Carlyle, never quick with his praise, lauded

Lewes in 1867; drawing by Rudolph Lehmann (British Museum)

the book as "a very good bit of Biography; far, far beyond the kind of stuff that usually bears that name in this country and in others." A critic in the *Westminster Review* (January 1856) called Lewes "a clear, strong, resolute, unflinching person, with great analytical and discriminating faculty" and noted that he had "allowed his judgment to mature itself for many years upon the subject before he began to write"; as a result, "we have before us an account of Goethe which is natural and intelligible, in many respects very different from any of which we were before in possession, in all respects more simple, more loveable, and human." *Fraser's Magazine* (December 1855) also praised the work but felt that Lewes should not have defended the immorality of Goethe's life and writings.

As Lewes's biographer Ashton indicates, Lewes was well suited to be the first to write a full-length biography of Goethe. Both men were eclectic in their intellectual interests, both gave up medical studies because they could not tolerate the sight of people in pain, both wrote on science and liter-

ature, both were mainly self-educated, and both were liberal in their sexual relationships. These similarities led Lewes to write an honest, sympathetic account of Goethe without idealizing him, as many German scholars did, or judging him, as some English critics did. In addition, Lewes's own literary criticism and fiction writing enabled him to critique Goethe's prose and translate his poetry effectively throughout the biography. Many critics, however, such as the one in *Fraser's Magazine,* felt that Lewes had been too frank and sympathetic about Goethe's character faults, particularly those involving his treatment of women. Conversely, some German critics objected to any adverse criticism Lewes offered of Goethe or his works, while others charged that Lewes had not been sufficiently accurate about details. Still, the German translation of the biography went into several editions, and Lewes was received as a hero on his subsequent visits to Germany.

After completing *The Life and Works of Goethe,* Lewes turned his attention increasingly to science.

In the next ten years he published *Sea-Side Studies at Ilfracombe, Tenby, the Scilly Isles & Jersey* (1858), *The Physiology of Common Life* (1859, 1860), *Studies in Animal Life* (1860), and *Aristotle: A Chapter from the History of Science, Including Analyses of Aristotle's Scientific Writings* (1864). In the same period Evans, under the name George Eliot, wrote *Scenes of Clerical Life* (1858), *Adam Bede* (1859), *The Mill on the Floss* (1860), *Silas Marner* (1861), and *Romola* (1863). Lewes never seemed to mind that she quickly became much more successful than he was. He selflessly promoted her career, and she, in turn, was always the most enthusiastic supporter of his many projects.

The last twelve years of Lewes's life were spent working on the ambitious *Problems of Life and Mind* (1874–1879), in which he tried to relate biology, psychology, and philosophy in a coherent analysis of human behavior. Reviewing the first two volumes of the series, *The Foundations of a Creed* (1874, 1875), in the *Atlantic Monthly* (September 1875), the American philosopher and psychologist William James claimed that the work would cause "a most important ferment in the philosophic thought of the immediate future." In general, however, critics found the work too obscure, abstract, and wordy. While working on *Problems of Life and Mind* Lewes was also revising earlier works for republication; writing miscellaneous articles; caring for his son Thornton, who died a painful and protracted death in 1869; and encouraging and supporting Eliot in her writing. Their social lives were also busy, including visits with Spencer, Alfred Tennyson, Richard Wagner, and Queen Victoria's daughter Princess Louise.

Lewes's final essay to be published in his lifetime, "On the Dread and Dislike of Science," appeared in the *Fortnightly Review* in June 1878; around that time Lewes's health began to decline, and he died on 30 November of enteritis. He was buried in the dissenters' section of Highgate Cemetery on 4 December. Lewes's friends wrote tributes that give the modern reader a glimpse of what Lewes must have been like as a friend and scholar. Edward Robert Bulwer Lytton wrote to Eliot, "I am terribly cut up by the death of my dear old friend. . . . I have known and loved him since childhood. He had the most omnivorous intellectual appetite of any man I ever knew; a rare freedom from prejudice; soundness of judgment in criticism, and a singularly wide and quick sympathy in all departments of science and literature." Anthony Trollope said in his *Fortnightly Review* (1 January 1879) obituary of Lewes that "there was no form of literary expression in which [Lewes] did not delight and instruct" and singled out for praise *A Biographical History of Philosophy, Sea-Side Studies, The Physiology of Common Life,* and *The Life and Works of Goethe.* On a personal note Trollope recalled at the end of the obituary: "There was never a man so pleasant as he with whom to sit and talk vague literary gossip over a cup of coffee and a cigar . . . he has left behind him here in London no pleasanter companion with whom to while away an hour." The final two volumes of *Problems of Life and Mind – The Study of Psychology* and *Mind as a Function of the Organism –* came out posthumously in 1879 under Eliot's supervision.

There has been a resurgence of interest in Lewes's contributions to biography, literary and dramatic criticism, philosophy, and science; *A Biographical History of Philosophy, The Life and Works of Goethe, The Spanish Drama, Problems of Life and Mind, On Actors and the Art of Acting* (1875), *The Principles of Success in Literature* (1885), and *Literary Criticism of George Henry Lewes* (1964) were all in print in 1994. Prolific and eclectic, Lewes well represents the industrious nineteenth-century man of letters, while his unorthodox lifestyle reminds twentieth-century readers that not all Victorians fit the stereotyped image of the prude. He was both a typical and an atypical Victorian author – typical in his energy, astonishing productivity, and high-mindedness, atypical in his openly unconventional sexual relations. A skillful, thoughtful, and objective biographer, Lewes might have hoped that his own life would be viewed as he depicted Goethe's – with sympathy and understanding, not judgment or idealization.

Letters:

The George Eliot Letters, 9 volumes, edited by Gordon S. Haight (New Haven: Yale University Press, 1954–1955, 1978; London: Oxford University Press, 1954–1956; London: Yale University Press, 1978).

Bibliographies:

William Baker, "G. H. Lewes and the *Penny Cyclopaedia,*" *Victorian Periodicals Newsletter,* 7 (September 1974): 15–18;

Baker, *The George Eliot–George Henry Lewes Library: An Annotated Bibliography of Their Books at Dr. Williams's Library* (New York & London: Garland, 1977);

Baker, "Some Additions to George Henry Lewes's Bibliography," *Victorian Periodicals Review,* 12 (Fall 1979): 117–118.

Biographies:

Anna Theresa Kitchell, *George Lewes and George Eliot: A Review of Records* (New York: Day, 1933);

Lewes's grave in Highgate Cemetery

David Williams, *Mr. George Eliot: A Biography of George Henry Lewes* (London: Hodder & Stoughton, 1983; New York: Watts, 1983);

Rosemary Ashton, *G. H. Lewes: A Life* (Oxford: Clarendon Press, 1991).

References:

Rosemary Ashton, "George Eliot's 'Husband': Writing the Life of G. H. Lewes," *George Eliot Fellowship Review,* 22 (1991): 32–37;

Ashton, *The German Idea: Four English Writers and the Reception of German Thought, 1800–1860* (Cambridge, London & New York: Cambridge University Press, 1980);

R. L. Brett, "George Henry Lewes: Dramatist, Novelist, and Critic," *Essays and Studies,* new series 11 (1958): 101–120;

K. K. Collins, "G. H. Lewes Revised: George Eliot and the Moral Sense," *Victorian Studies,* 21 (Summer 1978): 463–492;

Collins, "Sources of Remaining Unidentified Serial Offprints in the George Eliot–George Henry Lewes Library," *Papers of the Bibliographical Society of America,* 77, no. 4 (1983): 486–489;

Patrick Creevy, "The Victorian Goethe Critics: Notions of Greatness and Development," *Victorians Institute Journal,* 13 (1985): 31–57;

Peter Allan Dale, "George Lewes' Scientific Aesthetic: Restructuring the Ideology of the Symbol," in *One Culture: Essays in Science and Literature,* edited by George Levine and Alan Rauch (Madison: University of Wisconsin Press, 1987), pp. 92–116;

Franklin Gary, "Charlotte Brontë and George Henry Lewes," *PMLA,* 51 (June 1936): 518–542;

Morris Greenhut, "George Henry Lewes and the Classical Tradition in English Criticism," *Review of English Studies,* 24 (April 1948): 126–137;

Greenhut, "George Henry Lewes as a Critic of the Novel," *Studies in Philology,* 45 (July 1948): 491–511;

Greenhut, "G. H. Lewes's Criticism of the Drama," *PMLA,* 64 (June 1949): 350–368;

John Gross, *The Rise and Fall of the Man of Letters: Aspects of English Literary Life since 1800* (London: Weidenfeld & Nicolson, 1969);

Gordon S. Haight, *George Eliot: A Biography* (New York: Oxford University Press, 1968);

Edgar W. Hirshberg, *George Henry Lewes* (New York: Twayne, 1970);

John Hill Hopkin, "George Henry Lewes' Contributions to the *National Magazine and Monthly Critic,* and to the *Foreign Monthly Review* and *Continental Literary Journal,*" *George Eliot–George Henry Lewes Newsletter,* 11 (September 1987): 1–7;

Alice R. Kaminsky, *George Henry Lewes as Literary Critic* (Syracuse, N.Y.: Syracuse University Press, 1968);

Jack Kaminsky, "The Empirical Metaphysics of George Henry Lewes," *Journal of the History of Ideas,* 13 (June 1952): 314–332;

Harold Orel, *Victorian Literary Critics* (London: Macmillan, 1984);

T. H. Pickett, "George Henry Lewes's Letters to K. A. Varnhagen von Ense," *Modern Language Review,* 80 (July 1985): 513–532;

Joseph R. Roach, Jr., "G. H. Lewes and Performance Theory: Towards a 'Science of Acting,'" *Theatre Journal,* 42 (October 1980): 312–328;

Daniel N. Robinson, Preface to *Significant Contributions to the History of Psychology, 1750–1920,* series A, volume 6, edited by Robinson (Washington, D.C.: University Publications of America, 1977);

Diderik Roll-Hansen, "George Henry Lewes and His Critics," *English Studies,* 60 (April 1979): 159–165;

Marie U. Secor, "The Legacy of Nineteenth Century Style Theory," *Rhetoric Society Quarterly,* 12 (Spring 1982): 76–94;

W. M. Simon, *European Positivism in the Nineteenth Century: An Essay in Intellectual History* (Port Washington, N.Y. & London: Kennikat Press, 1972);

Barbara Smalley, Introduction to Lewes's *Ranthorpe* (Athens: Ohio University Press, 1980);

[James Sully], "George Henry Lewes," *New Quarterly Magazine,* 2 (October 1879): 356–376;

Hock Guan Tjoa, *George Henry Lewes: A Victorian Mind* (Cambridge, Mass. & London: Harvard University Press, 1979);

Anthony Trollope, "George Henry Lewes," *Fortnightly Review,* new series 31 (1 January 1879): 15–24.

Papers:

The Beinecke Rare Book and Manuscript Library at Yale University holds the most substantial collection of George Henry Lewes materials, including some letters, his manuscript journals from 1856 to 1870, diaries from 1869 to 1876, manuscripts of some plays, a literary-receipts book, and a notebook. The British Library has other letters.

John Gibson Lockhart

(14? July 1794 – 25 November 1854)

Sondra Miley Cooney
Kent State University

See also the Lockhart entries in *DLB 110: British Romantic Prose Writers, 1789–1832: Second Series* and *DLB 116: British Romantic Novelists, 1789–1832.*

BOOKS: *Peter's Letters to His Kinsfolk,* as Dr. Peter Morris the Odontist (3 volumes, Edinburgh: Printed for William Blackwood / London: T. Cadell & W. Davies / Glasgow: Smith, 1819; 1 volume, New York: Printed by C. S. Van Winkle for A. T. Goodrich, Kirk & Mercein, C. Wiley, W. B. Gilley, and James Olmstead, 1820);

Valerius: A Roman Story (3 volumes, Edinburgh: W. Blackwood / London: T. Cadell, 1821; 2 volumes, Boston: Wells & Lilly, 1821; revised edition, 1 volume, Edinburgh & London: W. Blackwood & Sons, 1842);

Letter to the Right Hon. Lord Byron: By John Bull, sometimes attributed to Lockhart (London: Printed by & for William Wright, 1821);

Some Passages in the Life of Mr. Adam Blair, Minister of the Gospel at Cross-Meikle: A Novel (Edinburgh: W. Blackwood / London: T. Cadell, 1822; Boston: Wells & Lilly, 1822);

Reginald Dalton (3 volumes, Edinburgh: W. Blackwood / London: T. Cadell, 1823; 2 volumes, New York: E. Duyckinck, 1823);

The History of Matthew Wald (Edinburgh: W. Blackwood / London: T. Cadell, 1824; New York: E. Duyckinck, Collins & Hannay, 1824);

Janus; or, The Edinburgh Literary Almanack, by Lockhart and John Wilson (Edinburgh: Oliver & Boyd, 1826);

Life of Robert Burns (Edinburgh: Constable / London: Hurst, Chance, 1828; revised and enlarged edition, Edinburgh: Constable / London: Hurst, Robinson, 1830; New York: W. Stodart, 1831);

The History of Napoleon Buonaparte, 2 volumes (London: Murray, 1829; New York: Harper, 1830);

The History of the Late War; Including Sketches of Bonaparte, Nelson, and Wellington for Children (London, 1832);

Memoirs of the Life of Sir Walter Scott, Bart. (7 volumes, Edinburgh: R. Cadell / London: Murray & Whittaker, 1837–1838; 2 volumes, Philadelphia: Carey, Lea & Blanchard, 1837, 1838; revised edition, 10 volumes, Edinburgh: Cadell / London: Murray & Whittaker, 1839); revised and abridged as *Narrative of the Life of Sir Walter Scott, Bart.,* 2 volumes (Edinburgh: R. Cadell / London: Houlston & Stoneman, 1848);

The Ballantyne-Humbug Handled in a Letter to Sir Adam Ferguson (Edinburgh: R. Cadell / London: Murray & Whittaker, 1839);

Theodore Hook: A Sketch (London, 1852).

Editions: *Some Passages in the Life of Mr. Adam Blair; and the History of Matthew Wald* (Edinburgh & London: W. Blackwood & Sons, 1843);

Lockhart's Literary Criticism, edited by M. Clive Hildyard (Oxford: Blackwell, 1931);

John Bull's Letter to Lord Byron, edited by Alan Lang Strout (Norman: University of Oklahoma Press, 1947).

OTHER: *Lectures on the History of Literature, Ancient and Modern: From the German of Frederick Schlegel,* 2 volumes, translated by Lockhart (Edinburgh: W. Blackwood / London: Baldwin, 1818; Philadelphia: Thomas Dobson & Son, 1818);

The History of the Ingenious Gentleman, Don Quixote of La Mancha; translated from the Spanish of Cervantes by Motteux: A New Edition with Copious Notes; and an Essay on the Life and Writings of Cervantes, 5 volumes, introduction and notes by Lockhart (Edinburgh: A. Constable / London: Hurst, Robinson, 1822);

Ancient Spanish Ballads: Historical and Romantic, translated by Lockhart (Edinburgh: W. Blackwood / London: T. Cadell, 1823; revised edition,

*John Gibson Lockhart (portrait by Sir Francis Grant, Scottish
National Portrait Gallery)*

London: Murray, 1841; New York: Wiley &
Putnam, 1842);
Poetical Works of Sir Walter Scott, Bart., 12 volumes,
edited by Lockhart (Edinburgh: Robert
Cadell, 1833–1834).

"Lockhart . . . is the second greatest . . . of all
British biographers," claimed Harold Nicolson in
The Development of English Biography (1928). John Gibson Lockhart and his biography of Sir Walter Scott
may not be so highly esteemed today. Nevertheless,
his qualities of mind and characteristics of personality, combined with his unique literary talent, made
him a biographer who was unequaled for more than
a century.

Lockhart was born in Cambusnethan, Lanark-
shire, on 12 July 1794, according to the parish register, or 14 July, according to the presbytery's record
of births, to the Reverend Dr. John Lockhart and
his second wife, Elizabeth Gibson Lockhart. Both
families had long Scottish histories. The Lockhart
name reached back to the eleventh century in the
west of Scotland; Mrs. Lockhart, daughter of the
Reverend John Gibson, minister of Saint Cuth-

bert's, Edinburgh, came from old Border families.
At the time of Lockhart's birth Dr. Lockhart was in-
cumbent at Cambusnethan – then predominantly
an agricultural and coal-mining area of the Clyde
valley – but two years later the family moved to
Glasgow when Dr. Lockhart became minister of the
College Kirk of Blackfriars. Lockhart's early education was typically Scottish. He attended an "English" school as a three- and four-year-old, then
moved to a writing school to study writing, geography, and arithmetic. At six he began studying
Greek and Latin at Glasgow High School. He was
usually *dux* (head) of his class, despite not seeming
to work hard; George Robert Gleig, Lockhart's
friend and biographer, attributed his success to his
strength of memory. Possessing high spirits and a
keen sense of mockery, he often amused his classmates by drawing caricatures of teachers. He matriculated at Glasgow University when he was
eleven. Glasgow was still essentially medieval in discipline and curriculum; Lockhart studied Humanity
(as Latin was known in Scotland), Greek, and logic.
Besides regularly winning prizes in his classes, he
received two prizes for Latin in 1808–1809, one for

the best translation of the seventh book of Lucan into verse and the other for the best Latin verses. The same year he won the Blackstone prize in Greek for his performance in the viva voce examination. As a result he was awarded a Snell Exhibition to Balliol, the Scots College of Oxford.

Just fourteen when he left Glasgow for Oxford, Lockhart spent his university years characteristically mixing work and play. He read classics, receiving his First Class degree in Greats in 1813. He also read the works of English writers, especially the Elizabethans, as well as those of French authors and of Italians such as Dante, Torquato Tasso, Giovanni Boccaccio, and Niccolò Machiavelli. He also learned Spanish and Portuguese. At Oxford he made friendships that, with one exception, were to last his lifetime: Gleig, William Hamilton, Jonathan Christie, John Williams, Henry Hart Milman, James Traill, and Alexander Nicoll; Hamilton and Lockhart became estranged over a small matter. Despite shyness and a tendency to reclusiveness, which his biographer Andrew Lang attributed to partial deafness from a childhood illness, Lockhart was still full of high spirits. He belonged to a boat club, hunted, and visited the local pubs. Christie recalled Lockhart's "incessant" caricaturing: his papers, his books, and the walls of his room were covered with his drawings, and he even had the audacity to caricature the examination masters while sitting for his graduation examinations.

On leaving Oxford, Lockhart had no real sense of his future. He considered taking holy orders in the Church of England if his father would approve his joining the army of Arthur Wellesley, first Duke of Wellington, as a chaplain. Dr. Lockhart did not approve, so Lockhart returned to Glasgow and spent the next two years with his family. He occupied his time reading, primarily the works of English writers such as Scott, William Wordsworth, and George Gordon, Lord Byron. He planned a novel to be based on his observations of Scotland and the Scots, particularly the clergy, because he thought writers had neglected the Scottish character. He corresponded regularly with Christie, describing people, places, and events. But he needed to prepare himself for the future, and Glasgow bored him. "I think a man may tolerate even Glasgow for half the year, with the prospect of spending the other half in company of his own choice," he wrote Christie on 25 November 1814. Studying law, he decided, was his only recourse.

His move to Edinburgh in the autumn of 1815 introduced Lockhart to the people and the work that would shape the rest of his life; and he would acquire a reputation there that he would try to explain and excuse for the rest of his life. At the end of 1816 he was admitted to the bar. His letters recount much social activity, the doings of old friends, and meetings with new personalities such as John Wilson (Christopher North), Thomas De Quincey, and the publisher William Blackwood. So many young women asked for locks of his hair, he reported to his sister, that he feared he would go bald. In 1817 he agreed to translate Friedrich Schlegel's *Geschichte der alten und neuen Litteratur* (1815) for Blackwood as *Lectures on the History of Literature, Ancient and Modern* (1818). He used the three-hundred-pound payment to travel to Germany, where he visited Johann Wolfgang von Goethe in Weimar, sketched Johann Gottlieb Fichte lecturing to his class, and absorbed German language and culture.

After returning to Edinburgh, Lockhart began to contribute regularly to *Blackwood's Edinburgh Magazine*. Essentially a Tory rival to the *Edinburgh Review*, *Blackwood's* was less serious and less highbrow; it even published fiction. Writing pseudonymously along with Wilson and the poet James Hogg, the "Ettrick Shepherd" – both of whom were older than he and were well-established writers – Lockhart helped give *Blackwood's* its reputation for shamelessness. To the first issue (October 1817) they contributed the infamous "Translation from an Ancient Chaldee MS." Purporting to be a recently discovered treasure of scholarship, it satirized in biblical language and imagery the Edinburgh literary and social scene. Not excluding its creators from ridicule, the piece gave nicknames to all – Blackwood was Ebony, Wilson was "the beautiful leopard from the valley of the Palm Trees," and Hogg was "the great wild boar from the forest of Lebanon." Perhaps most apropos was Lockhart's nickname – "Scorpion which delightest to sting the faces of men." Eventually damaging to Lockhart's reputation were several articles appearing from October 1817 to August 1818 that he had a hand in writing – of which, indeed, he was perhaps the sole writer. Beginning with a review of Leigh Hunt's *The Story of Rimini* (1816), the series "On the Cockney School of Poetry" also included a review of John Keats's *Endymion* (1818). Whether or not Lockhart was responsible for it, Keats thought he was; and although the review may not have hastened Keats's death in 1821, as some have claimed, it made Lockhart notorious. Two other targets for the Scorpion's sting were the eminent Scotsmen Dr. Thomas Chalmers and Prof. John Playfair, both of whom were contributors to the *Edinburgh Review*. Because Chalmers and Playfair were esteemed in Scotland, Lock-

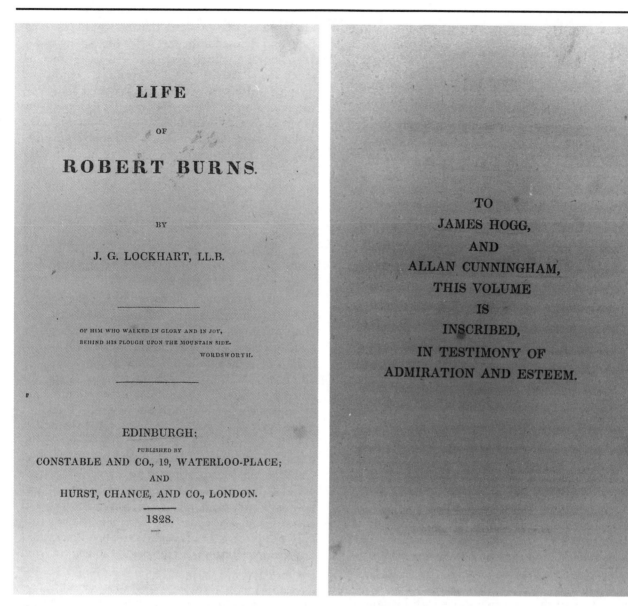

LIFE

OF

ROBERT BURNS.

BY

J. G. LOCKHART, LL.B.

OF HIM WHO WALKED IN GLORY AND IN JOY,
BEHIND HIS PLOUGH UPON THE MOUNTAIN SIDE.
WORDSWORTH.

EDINBURGH:
PUBLISHED BY
CONSTABLE AND CO., 19, WATERLOO-PLACE;
AND
HURST, CHANCE, AND CO., LONDON.
1828.

TO
JAMES HOGG,
AND
ALLAN CUNNINGHAM,
THIS VOLUME
IS
INSCRIBED,
IN TESTIMONY OF
ADMIRATION AND ESTEEM.

Title page and dedication for Lockhart's biography of the Scottish poet, which presents little new factual information but shows sympathy for Burns's position as a social outsider

hart and Wilson were castigated in an anonymous pamphlet, *Hypocrisy Unveiled,* and received anonymous challenges through the *Scotsman* newspaper. More mildly expressed, yet no less critical, was Scott's comment in a letter to Lockhart of 29 October 1818 that "it is one consequence of such hostility that men of inferior literary consideration endeavour to distinguish themselves in an alleged vindication of others when in fact they only seek to gratify their own envy and malignity or to enhance their no-importance."

Although Scott, whom Lockhart met in June 1818, and Christie urged Lockhart to disassociate himself from Blackwood and the "Maga," as it was known, Lockhart continued to write for it through-

out his life. He excused himself to Benjamin Haydon, Keats's friend, on the grounds that he had been a raw boy, writing without any malice. He would claim to have spent the rest of his life making reparation to the victims of his attacks. And he knew himself to have been cut off from all advancement and political preferment because of his early writing.

Not all of Lockhart's contributions to *Blackwood's* were so professionally detrimental. He wrote several articles on German literature; another on Greek tragedy; "Sketches of Foreign Scenes and Manners," a by-product of his German tour; and humorous poems under such pseudonyms as William Wastle and The Odontist. Another of his alter egos, Dr. Peter Morris, was born in late 1818. Lockhart had proposed to the publisher James Ballantyne a three-volume "collection" of the letters of Dr. Morris to be titled *Peter's Letters to His Kinsfolk* (1819). The first volume was to describe the social and literary culture of Edinburgh; the second would treat Glasgow, the west country, and the Scottish clergy and church; the third volume, to be written by Wilson, would follow the doctor touring through the Highlands and Tweeddale and along the Clyde. When the work was published, the subject matter for volume one became volumes one and two, the proposed volume two became the third, and the planned volume three was abandoned. The format gave Lockhart the opportunity to do what he did so well – write sketches of people and places and descriptions of social gatherings and natural settings. Some of the descriptions verged on caricature, and the Scorpion could still sting, but Lockhart used the opportunity to redress some of his own earlier *Blackwood's* criticisms, apologizing for the young men who had acted foolishly at the beginning of their careers. Dr. Morris also attacked the *Edinburgh Review* for its mistreatment of writers whom Lockhart admired, among them Wordsworth, Charles Lamb, and Robert Burns. *Peter's Letters to His Kinsfolk* is undeniably autobiographical, because it deals with the west of Scotland – the world of Lockhart's childhood and youth – and the Edinburgh of his young manhood. According to Francis Russell Hart's *Lockhart as a Romantic Biographer* (1971), "The future biographer is present ... in narrative and anecdotal style, in the power of significant description, in a sense of epistolary tact and of characterizing tone and manner in individual speech," and "he is present in architectonic power – the ability to organize the multiple details of Peter Morris's experience into a thematic unity. . . ." The book was a sensation. There were those who were offended, although Gleig thought that there was "no single expression which ought to have rankled in the most sensitive minds." Scott liked it even though its tone was "perhaps too favourable both to the state of our public society and of individual character"; Scott's daughter Sophia described it as "one of the most clever, and at the same time rather severe books that has been written for ages."

Lockhart and Scott were formally introduced in June 1818, at which time Scott invited Lockhart to visit him at his estate, Abbotsford. Shortly thereafter Scott offered Lockhart, through Ballantyne, the assignment of compiling the historical portion of the *Edinburgh Annual Register,* a job Scott had handled before. Throughout the summer of 1818 Lock-

hart regularly visited Scott's Edinburgh home, and Scott invited Lockhart and Wilson to Abbotsford in October. It may have been at an earlier visit in Edinburgh or during the two-day visit at Abbotsford in October that Lockhart and Sophia Scott met for the first time. By January 1820 Scott was reporting to his son Walter that Lockhart had formally asked for Sophia's hand, and they were married on 29 April 1820. They spent their winters in Edinburgh and the summers at Chiefswood, a cottage close to Abbotsford.

At the end of 1820 and the beginning of 1821 John Scott (no relation to Sir Walter Scott) published in his *London Magazine* a series of articles accusing Lockhart of being the secret editor of *Blackwood's* and of having written defamatory reviews of works by Samuel Taylor Coleridge. Lockhart denied the allegations. They exchanged charges; then Lockhart's friend Christie became involved in the contretemps. Scott challenged Christie to a duel, which took place on 16 February 1821 – two days after the birth of Lockhart's first child, John Hugh. Scott fired first, missing Christie, who then fired into the air. Both seconds forced him to fire again, this time taking aim at Scott; Scott died of his wound on 27 February. Christie and the seconds, Joseph Traill and P. G. Patmore, were charged with murder by a coroner's inquest; Christie then escaped to France but returned to stand trial with Traill. Verdicts of not guilty were handed down. (At his later trial, Patmore, too, was found not guilty.) Sir Walter Scott wrote to Lockhart, assuring him that he would not be affected "as a man of honor," and again urged him to break with *Blackwood's:* "Do not *promise,*" he wrote, "but *act* and act at once."

During this period Lockhart, like many other young writers, tried writing novels; four were published between 1821 and 1824. Each was, to some degree, innovative. *Valerius: A Roman Story* (1821) reads "like a translation from the Latin," in the estimation of Lang. *Some Passages in the Life of Mr. Adam Blair, Minister of the Gospel at Cross-Meikle* (1822), the only novel of interest to twentieth-century readers, is based on a story told by his father; often compared to Nathaniel Hawthorne's *The Scarlet Letter* (1850), it tells of a fallen clergyman who, having confessed his waywardness, is reinstated in his position and regains the esteem of his congregation and fellow clergy. The first Oxford novel written in English, *Reginald Dalton* (1823) is based on Lockhart's university days. *The History of Matthew Wald* (1824) is a psychological study of a man driven mad by hate; Scott complained that it was "full of power but disagreeable and ends vilely ill."

MEMOIRS

OF THE LIFE

OF

SIR WALTER SCOTT, BART.

VOLUME THE SECOND.

MDCCCXXXVII.

ROBERT CADELL, EDINBURGH.

JOHN MURRAY AND WHITTAKER AND CO., LONDON.

Title page for Lockhart's monumental biography of his father-in-law

Simultaneously, Lockhart was preparing for publication some translations of Spanish works. In 1822 an edition of Peter Anthony Motteux's translation of Miguel de Cervantes' *Don Quixote* (1605–1615) appeared with an introduction and notes by Lockhart. A year later the collection *Ancient Spanish Ballads: Historical and Romantic,* translated by Lockhart, was published; some of the selections had originally appeared in *Blackwood's.* Lockhart provided a critical and historical introduction discussing the Spanish language and people.

In the summer of 1825 Lockhart received a letter from John Murray, the Scots-born London-based publisher, saying that "Mr. Disraeli," as Murray's emissary, wanted to meet with Lockhart to discuss Lockhart's becoming editor of, or at least adviser to, a newspaper Murray was planning to start. To Lockhart's surprise the visitor was Benjamin Disraeli, not his father Isaac D'Israeli. It was Benjamin Disraeli himself who had convinced Murray to undertake a new daily newspaper, to be called the *Representative.* After consulting with Murray and Scott, Lockhart refused the offer: being a newspaper editor would be beneath the dignity of a lawyer.

Murray, however, had other plans for Lockhart. The *Quarterly Review,* which Murray had founded in 1809, had not been in good condition for at least three years. John Croker had served in an interim capacity as editor but had too many other responsibilities to continue full-time; John

Taylor Coleridge had succeeded Croker. On 20 October 1825 negotiations between Lockhart and Murray were completed: Lockhart was to receive £250 per quarter for editing the *Quarterly* and assisting in the publishing business; if five numbers were published, he would be paid £1,250; for advice and occasional articles in the *Representative* he would be paid £1,500. Because someone raised objections to his appointment, Lockhart did not assume his new position immediately; once again his *Blackwood's* past was haunting him. In December 1825 Lockhart became editor of the *Quarterly,* a position he was to hold for more than twenty-five years. Lockhart and Scott expected that the *Quarterly* editorship would enable Lockhart to obtain political advancement.

Lockhart had been present at Abbotsford in May 1825 when the publisher Archibald Constable and the printers James and John Ballantyne called on Scott to present a new business scheme: "printing and bookselling," Constable told Scott and Lockhart, "as instruments for enlightening and entertaining mankind, and, of course, for making money, are as yet in mere infancy." He proposed to publish a volume a month in a series to be called Constable's Miscellany; each volume would sell for either three shillings or half a crown. In January 1826, before the project was started, Constable went into bankruptcy, dragging Scott with him. Constable's Miscellany was eventually rescued, and its first volume appeared in January 1827.

Constable had asked Lockhart to write a biography of Burns for the series. Lockhart's preface to his *Life of Robert Burns* (1828) describes some of the strictures under which it was to be written: it was to be a single volume, and it was to be a biography only, not a collection of Burns's works. Previous works about Burns included Robert Heron's *A Memoir of the Life of the Late Robert Burns* (1797), James Currie's *The Works of Robert Burns; with an Account of his Life, and a Criticism on his Writings* (1800), David Irving's *The Lives of the Scottish Poets* (1804), R. H. Cromek's *Reliques of Robert Burns* (1808), Francis Jeffrey's review of Cromek's book in the *Edinburgh Review* (January 1809), Scott's review of Cromek's book in the *Quarterly Review* (February 1809), Josiah Walker's *Poems by Robert Burns: With an Account of His Life* (1811), and Allan Cunningham's essay in the *London Magazine* (1824). Lockhart's extensive references to these works in his own biography of Burns show that he depended on them. He divides Burns's life into four stages: his education and life on the farm; the writing of his first poems to the publication of his first book of poetry; the first and second Edinburgh periods, with the intervening Highland tours; and his return to the country, including his marriage to Jean Armour, song writing, government employment, and ill health culminating in his death.

Lockhart presents the events of Burns's life according to a design that may have been influenced by his legal training. First, in an introductory passage he identifies the event or period of time, providing, whenever possible, Burns's own account of what transpired. He then supports or supplements Burns's testimony with information from corroborating witnesses – Burns's brother Gilbert, correspondents, friends and associates, and other biographers. When appropriate, he incorporates poems or portions of poems that he thinks grew out of the events in question. Usually he closes with a comment on or evaluation of the episode. This discussion leads, in turn, to the introduction to the next event.

The factual material Lockhart used was not significantly different from that used by his predecessors. In 1825 Cunningham had given Lockhart unpublished information he had collected; but Lockhart had left the material behind when he moved to London, assuming that Constable's bankruptcy meant the end of Constable's Miscellany. He was well into writing his manuscript by the time he did receive new material from Cunningham and others, which he incorporated into the revised and enlarged edition of 1830. Not only did Lockhart not have new, firsthand information for his biography of Burns, his interpretation of the data offered little that was new. He did make some effort to clarify puzzling sequences and straighten out dates, as at the beginning of chapter 5, where he questions Currie's account of Burns's trip to Edinburgh and Burns's delay in presenting himself to Dr. Thomas Blacklock, for whose critical support he had hoped, once he arrived. Because so many associates of Burns, including his wife, children, and brother, were still alive, assessment of Burns's behavior had to be circumspect. His excessive drinking, for instance, was explained as an aberration, not habitual. Usually, not being close to either the events or the person (as he would be with Scott), Lockhart withholds judgment about them.

What is unique about Lockhart's perspective on Burns is his understanding of Burns as a social outsider – not unlike Lockhart himself. "It is," he says, "but a melancholy business to trace among the records of literary history, the manner in which most great original geniuses have been greeted on their first appeals to the world." Because of his genius, the poet is different from other men. The rustic Burns's "conversational habits" were "far too bitter not to produce deep resentment." When his "new arrogance in conversation" was added to his democratic political views – at a time when the establishment's enthusiasm for the French Revolution had been replaced by fear – tension between poet and society was inevitable. Yet Burns and his poetry made a significant contribution. He was a public figure when there were no significant English poets writing and when there had been no Scottish poets of note for generations. Moreover, by writing in dialect Burns interpreted "the inmost soul of the Scottish peasant in all its moods, and in verse exquisitely and intensely Scottish." By using the people's language, he gave them an identity.

Of the responses to the *Life of Robert Burns,* two of particular note came from fellow Scots. Thomas Carlyle, reviewing in the *Edinburgh Review* (December 1828), accepted the biographical information and appreciated Lockhart's interpretations of the poetry; on the other hand, he thought that the biography was "too cautious and derivative" and lacked a sense of focus. In 1851 Robert Chambers, who had supplied Lockhart with some anecdotes about Burns, edited *The Life and Works of Robert Burns.* He acknowledged Lockhart's *Life of Robert Burns* as a "graceful treatment of the subject" but said that it added "little to the details previously known, and certainly any effort made by the author to attain correctness in the statement and arrangement of facts, was far from what would appear to have been necessary in the case." Chambers was the first biographer of Burns to do extensive research into primary sources. Franklyn Bliss Snyder, a twentieth-century biographer of Burns, considered Lockhart a liar who, working in association with Cunningham, was responsible for everything bad about Burns biography. Hart provides a detailed study of Lockhart's biographical technique and of his sources; he admits that Lockhart frequently was not fastidious in regard to names of correspondents, dates, and the handling of texts, but he says that Lockhart was not responsible for the myth of Burns: "so varied were Burns's masks as a social, political, and cultural phenomenon that one doubts there is recoverable a nucleus of indubitable fact which was *the* life of Burns."

Lockhart's second son, Walter, had been born in April 1826; a daughter, Charlotte Harriet Jane, was born on 1 January 1828. In April 1831 Scott suffered a stroke. In the hope of restoring his health, Scott and his daughter Anne left for southern Europe in October. Before returning home he suffered another stroke. In December Lockhart's son John Hugh died of a spinal disease.

Scott returned to Abbotsford in July 1832; he died on 21 September 1832. His daughter Anne, in ill health and worn out from caring for her father, died on 25 June 1833. Sophia Lockhart survived her father and sister by just a few years; she died 17 May 1837.

Lockhart had been named literary executor in Scott's will; and, since Scott was in debt when he died, Lockhart felt it his duty to help pay off some of the debt by editing Scott's poetry and writing a biography of him. *Poetical Works of Sir Walter Scott, Bart.* appeared in twelve volumes in 1833–1834. By 1836 Lockhart had "fairly begun" writing the biography. His plan was to let Scott largely speak for himself by drawing from the correspondence and diaries and only then recalling what he himself remembered. The correspondence, autobiographical fragments, diary, and journal comprise half of the seven-volume *Memoirs of the Life of Sir Walter Scott, Bart.* (1837–1838); the letters make up a bit more than a fourth; biographical reminiscences by others constitute the remainder.

As in the Burns biography, Lockhart presents Scott's life in stages. The first stage, the period up to Scott's becoming a lawyer, is predominantly autobiographical; it is based on the Ashetiel fragment written by Scott and found after his death. Subsequent stages include Scott's early years as a lawyer, poet, soldier, and collector; Scott as the "Great Unknown"; Scott as failed businessman and desperate writer; Scott as creator of myth and living legend. The burden of the story is mainly carried by the letters; interspersed among them are scenes showing Scott in action. Many are re-creations of events at which Lockhart was present. Although there is some interpolated evaluation, as in the *Life of Robert Burns,* the most significant evaluation makes up the last chapter of the work. Always present, providing critical distance throughout, is the commenting "I," Lockhart himself.

Lockhart received much praise for the work, particularly from friends and associates of Scott, but attacks were made. In a review that appeared in the *Westminster Review* before the seventh volume was published, Carlyle complained that the work was essentially a compilation, that it had no form. Many, including Carlyle and James Fenimore Cooper, felt that Lockhart had been disloyal to Scott, revealing faults that should have been concealed. Also, as in the case of the Burns biography, Lockhart was accused of combining parts of letters, autobiographical fragments, and diary and journal material to suit his own ends; his "manipulations" allegedly ranged from correcting Scotticisms to toning down descriptions of Scott's condition after his strokes, protecting people who were still alive, and omitting, without any indication of having done so, material repeated in letters to various correspondents.

Whatever its shortcomings, Lockhart's life of Scott is remarkable for its forceful presentation of persons, places, and scenes; it communicates an intensity that more-accurate modern accounts of Scott cannot have. The primary reason is Lockhart's talent for dramatic presentation, developed through his years of corresponding with friends. His letters are full of people in action, observed by his clear eye and reported by his witty pen. Harold Nicolson observed that the selecting of anecdote and the cumulative method were Lockhart's strengths. And although Carlyle thought that the work had no form or focus, it does: Lockhart is the focus. He uses himself, says Hart, as a novelist uses a central consciousness – hence, the "inaccuracies" and "lies." In Nicolson's judgment Lockhart worked impressionistically, using the letters, diaries, and journals illustratively. Scott's faults are part of the impression. However close to his subjects Lockhart may have been, he always viewed them critically – whether drawing caricatures or writing about them.

Regularly peeved at Murray and frustrated with the *Quarterly*, Lockhart tried again for a government post in 1841; through the offices of Croker he was appointed to the sinecure of auditor of the duchy of Lancaster at a salary of four hundred pounds a year. He had no illusions about his work at the *Quarterly Review:* "the Editor gets no credit at all," he told one contributor. At one time he had had "fond dreams of doing something permanently worthy in letters. But with less idle dreams these too have flown," he wrote Croker in 1843.

He was often ill; Murray and Croker frequently wondered if he could continue his work. He increasingly took time off for travel and rest after each number of the *Quarterly* was published; he would dictate plans to Croker, who would oversee the work while Lockhart was gone. His son Walter was always a problem for his father; although he matriculated at Cambridge in 1844, he left to join the army. Although he inherited Abbotsford in 1847, he got into serious financial problems. From 1850 to 1852 he and his father were totally estranged. Walter died a derelict in Versailles, France, in January 1853.

Charlotte had always been closer to her father than Walter was and a great source of satisfaction to him. She married James Robert Hope on 19 October 1847; Lockhart's granddaughter, Mary Monica, was born on 4 October 1852. After Walter's death Charlotte inherited Abbotsford, and her husband changed his name to Hope-Scott.

Lockhart retired from the *Quarterly* in April 1853. In October he took a final trip to Rome. Returning to England in March 1854, he resigned his sinecure in the duchy of Lancaster and was granted a pension equal to his salary. After spending some time in London he visited relatives in Glasgow, then traveled to Abbotsford. He collapsed there on 19 November 1854 and died on 25 November. He was buried at the feet of Sir Walter Scott in Dryburgh Abbey.

Biographies:

George Robert Gleig, [untitled article], *Quarterly Review,* 116 (October 1864): 439–482;

Andrew Lang, *The Life and Letters of John Gibson Lockhart,* 2 volumes (London: Nimmo / New York: Scribners, 1897);

Marion Lochhead, *John Gibson Lockhart* (London: Murray, 1954).

References:

Richard D. Altick, *Lives and Letters: A History of Literary Biography in England and America* (New York: Knopf, 1965);

Myron F. Brightfield, *John Wilson Croker* (London: Allen & Unwin, 1940);

Robert Chambers, ed., *The Life and Works of Robert Burns,* 4 volumes (New York: Harper, 1851);

Francis Russell Hart, *Lockhart as Romantic Biographer* (Edinburgh: Edinburgh University Press, 1971);

Hart, "Proof-reading Lockhart's *Scott:* The Dynamics of Biographical Reticence," *Studies in Bibliography: Papers of the Bibliographical Society of the University of Virginia,* 14 (1961): 3–22;

Harold Nicolson, *The Development of English Biography* (New York: Harcourt, Brace, 1928);

Franklyn Bliss Snyder, "Burns and His Biographers," *Studies in Philology,* 25 (October 1928): 401–415;

Snyder, *The Life of Robert Burns* (New York: Macmillan, 1932).

Papers:

The largest collection of John Gibson Lockhart's papers is at the National Library of Scotland. His correspondence with John Croker is in the Croker papers at the William L. Clements Library, University of Michigan. Correspondence with John Murray is held by the Murray firm, London.

David Masson

(2 December 1822 – 6 October 1907)

Hugh Wilson
Texas Tech University

BOOKS: *History of Greece: Its Literature, Philosophy and Arts* (Edinburgh: Chambers, 1845);

Ancient History, attributed to Masson (Edinburgh: Chambers, 1848);

The British Museum, Historical and Descriptive, attributed to Masson (Edinburgh: Chambers, 1848);

History of Rome, attributed to Masson (Edinburgh: Chambers, 1848);

Medieval History, attributed to Masson (London & Edinburgh: Chambers, 1855);

Modern History from the Reformation to the Present Time, attributed to Masson (London & Edinburgh: Chambers, 1856);

Essays Biographical and Critical: Chiefly on English Poets (Cambridge: Macmillan, 1856);

British Novelists and Their Styles: Being a Critical Sketch of the History of British Prose Fiction (Cambridge & London: Macmillan, 1859; Boston: Gould & Lincoln / New York: Sheldon, 1859);

The Life of John Milton, Narrated in Connexion with the Political, Ecclesiastical, and Literary History of His Time, 7 volumes (Cambridge & London: Macmillan, 1859–1880; revised edition, London & New York: Macmillan, 1881–1894);

Life of Milton, with an Estimate of His Genius and Character by Lord Macaulay (New York: Delisser & Proctor, 1860);

Recent British Philosophy: A Review, with Criticisms; Including Some Comments on Mr. Mill's Answer to Sir William Hamilton (London & Cambridge: Macmillan, 1865; New York: Appleton, 1866; enlarged edition, London: Macmillan, 1867; enlarged, 1877);

The State of Learning in Scotland: A Lecture (Edinburgh: Edmondston & Douglas, 1866);

Drummond of Hawthornden: The Story of His Life and Writings (London: Macmillan, 1873);

The Three Devils: Luther's, Milton's, and Goethe's. With Other Essays (London: Macmillan, 1874; Folcroft, Pa.: Folcroft Press, 1969);

Chatterton: A Story of the Year 1770 (London: Macmillan, 1874); revised as *Chatterton: A Biography* (London: Hodder & Stoughton, 1899; New York: Dodd, Mead, 1899);

Wordsworth, Shelley, Keats and Other Essays (London: Macmillan, 1874; revised, London: Macmillan, 1875; Folcroft, Pa.: Folcroft Press, 1969);

De Quincey (London: Macmillan, 1878; New York: Harper, 1878);

Carlyle, Personally and in His Writings: Two Edinburgh Lectures (London: Macmillan, 1885);

In the Footsteps of the Poets, by Masson and others (New York: Whittaker, 1890; London: Isbister, 1893);

Carlyle: The Address Delivered by David Masson . . . on Unveiling a Bust of Thomas Carlyle, in the Wallace Monument (Glasgow, 1891);

Edinburgh Sketches and Memories (London & Edinburgh: Black, 1892);

James Melvin: Rector of the Grammar School of Aberdeen: A Sketch (Aberdeen: Printed for the Centenary Committee, 1895);

Chapters from the Sixth Volume of The Life of John Milton: Narrated in Connexion with the Political, Ecclesiastical and Literary History of His Time (London: Macmillan, 1898);

Memories of London in the 'Forties, edited by Flora Masson (Edinburgh & London: Blackwood, 1908);

Memories of Two Cities, Edinburgh and Aberdeen, edited by Flora Masson (Edinburgh & London: Oliphant, Anderson & Ferrier, 1911);

Shakespeare Personally, edited by Rosaline Masson (London: Smith, Elder, 1914).

OTHER: *Banner* (Aberdeen, Scotland), edited by Masson (1842–1844);

Thomas De Quincey, *Confessions of an English Opium Eater,* edited by Masson (New York: Dutton, 1856);

Macmillan's Magazine, edited by Masson, 1–17 (November 1859–April 1868);

Reader: A Review of Literature, Science and Art, 1–5 edited by Masson (January 1863–January 1867);

The Poetical Works of John Milton, edited by Masson (3 volumes, Boston: Little, Brown, 1864; 2 volumes, London: Macmillan, 1874);

The Miscellaneous Works of Oliver Goldsmith, Globe Edition, biographical introduction by Masson (Philadelphia: Lippincott, 1869);

Report of a Meeting of the London National Society for Women's Suffrage, Held at the Gallery of the Architextural Society in Conduit Street, Saturday, July 17th, 1869, includes remarks by Masson (London: Printed by Spottiswoode & Co., 1869);

Women's Suffrage at the Great Meeting in Edinburgh, in the Music Hall on 12th January 1871, under the Auspices of the Edinburgh Branch of the National Society for Women's Suffrage, includes transcriptions of speeches by Masson (Edinburgh: Grieg, 1871);

The Quarrel between the Earl of Manchester and Oliver Cromwell: An Episode of the English Civil War. Unpublished Documents Relating Thereto, Collected by the Late John Bruce, edited by Masson (Westminster: Printed for the Camden Society, 1875; New York: Johnson Reprint, 1965);

Rosaline Orme Masson, ed., *Three Centuries of English Poetry: Being Selections from Chaucer to Herrick,* preface by Masson (London: Macmillan, 1876);

Paradise Lost as Originally Published by John Milton, Being a Facsimile Reproduction of the First Edition, edited by Masson (London: Stock, 1877);

The Register of the Privy Council of Scotland, first series, volumes 3–14, second series, volume 1, edited and abridged by Masson (Edinburgh: General Register House, 1880–1899);

Oliver Goldsmith, *The Vicar of Wakefield,* edited by Masson (London: Macmillan, 1883);

Select Essays of De Quincey: Narrative and Imaginative, 2 volumes, edited by Masson (Edinburgh: Black, 1888);

The Collected Writings of Thomas De Quincey, 14 volumes, edited by Masson (Edinburgh: Black, 1889–1890);

Familiar Letters of John Milton, edited by Donald L. Clark, translated by Masson, volume 12 of *The Works of John Milton,* edited by Frank Allen

David Masson.

Patterson (New York: Columbia University Press, 1936).

SELECTED PERIODICAL PUBLICATIONS – UNCOLLECTED: "On Emotional Culture," anonymous, *Fraser's Magazine,* 29 (May 1844): 528–535;

"The Pulpit in the Nineteenth Century," anonymous, *Fraser's Magazine,* 30 (September 1844): 287–294;

"Milton's Blindness," anonymous, *Chambers's Edinburgh Journal,* 3 (1845): 392–394;

"Female Characters of Goethe and Shakespeare," attributed to Masson and to James Lorimer, *North British Review,* 8 (February 1848): 265–296; reprinted, *Eclectic Magazine,* 14 (1848): 1–18;

"Recent French Social Philosophy – Organization of Labour," anonymous, *North British Review,* 9 (May 1848): 213–251;

"The Socialist Party in France," anonymous, *North British Review,* 10 (February 1849): 261–292;

"The Slavonians and Eastern Europe," anonymous, *North British Review,* 11 (August 1849): 528–568;

"Douglas Jerrold," anonymous, *British Quarterly Review,* 10 (August 1849): 192–208;

"Vincent Gioberti," anonymous, *North British Review,* 11 (August 1849): 369–405;

"German Socialism," attributed to Masson, *North British Review,* 11 (August 1849): 406–435;

"Rabelais – His Life, Genius," anonymous, *British Quarterly Review,* 10 (November 1849): 502–525;

"Recent Aspects of Socialism," anonymous, *British Quarterly Review,* 11 (May 1850): 467–499;

"Edwin Chadwick," anonymous, *North British Review,* 13 (May 1850): 40–84;

"Mahomet and the Koran," anonymous, *North British Review,* 13 (May 1850): 189–224;

"Ledru-Rollin on England," anonymous, *British Quarterly Review,* 12 (August 1850): 262–291;

"Wordsworth," anonymous, *North British Review,* 12 (August 1850): 262–291;

"Wordsworth's Autobiographical Poem," anonymous, *British Quarterly Review,* 12 (November 1850): 549–579;

"Carlyle's *Latter-Day Pamphlets*," anonymous, *North British Review,* 14 (November 1850): 1–40;

"Italy, Germany, and England," anonymous, *British Quarterly Review,* 13 (February 1851): 190–216;

"William and Robert Chambers," anonymous, *Dublin University Magazine,* 37 (February 1851): 177–190;

"Literature and the Labour Question," anonymous, *North British Review,* 14 (February 1851): 382–420;

"*Pendennis* and *Copperfield*," anonymous, *North British Review,* 15 (May 1851): 57–89;

"The Story of Thomas Chatterton," anonymous, *Dublin University Magazine,* 38 (July 1851): 1–17; (August 1851): 178–192; (October 1851): 420–435;

"The Social Science: History and Prospects," anonymous, *North British Review,* 15 (August 1851): 291–330;

"To the Editor of the *Times*," *Times* (London), 19 September 1851, p. 5F;

"English Statesmanship with Regard to Italy," attributed to Masson, *British Quarterly Review,* 14 (November 1851): 488–510;

"Translations from the Classics: Aeschylus," anonymous, *North British Review,* 16 (November 1851): 259–278;

"The Doctrine of Non-Intervention," anonymous, *British Quarterly Review,* 15 (February 1852): 240–253;

"The Works of John Milton," anonymous, *North British Review,* 16 (February 1852): 295–335;

reprinted as "Milton," anonymous, *Eclectic Magazine,* 25 (April 1852): 433–447;

"Thomas Moore," anonymous, *British Quarterly Review,* 15 (May 1852): 486–508;

"Shakespeare and Goethe," anonymous, *British Quarterly Review,* 16 (November 1852): 512–543;

"Pre-Raphaelitism in Art and Literature," attributed to Masson, *British Quarterly Review,* 16 (August 1852): 197–220;

"Lord Cockburn's *Life of Jeffrey*," anonymous, *North British Review,* 17 (August 1852): 283–326;

"Guizot on Corneille and Shakespeare," anonymous, *North British Review,* 18 (November 1852): 106–137;

"America, from a Cosmopolitical Point of View," anonymous, *British Quarterly Review,* 17 (May 1853): 565–591;

"*Lorenzo Benoni*," anonymous, *North British Review,* 19 (May 1853): 185–208;

"Theories of Poetry and a New Poet," anonymous, *North British Review,* 19 (August 1853): 297–344;

"Horace," anonymous, *British Quarterly Review,* 18 (August 1853): 202–227;

"Portrait-painting in History," anonymous, *British Quarterly Review,* 18 (November 1853): 484–512;

"Wycliffe," anonymous, *North British Review,* 20 (November 1853): 110–134;

"Dante's Beatrice," anonymous, *British Quarterly Review,* 19 (January 1854): 205–233;

"Union with England and Scottish Nationality," anonymous, *North British Review,* 21 (May 1854): 69–100;

"De Quincey and Prose-Writing," anonymous, *British Quarterly Review,* 20 (July 1854): 163–188;

"The Literature of the Restoration: Dryden," anonymous, *British Quarterly Review,* 20 (1 July 1854): 3–44;

"Hugh Miller of Cromarty," anonymous, *North British Review,* 21 (August 1854): 329–374;

"Swift: His Life and Genius," anonymous, *British Quarterly Review,* 20 (October 1854): 528–560;

"Kaye's *Life of Lord Metcalfe*," anonymous, *North British Review,* 22 (November 1854): 145–178;

"Present Aspects and Tendencies of Literature," anonymous, *British Quarterly Review,* 21 (January 1855): 157–181;

"Old English Songs," anonymous, *North British Review,* 22 (February 1855): 485–504;

"Reform of the Civil Service," anonymous, *North British Review,* 23 (May 1855): 137–192;

"Administrative Reform 'Movement,' " anonymous, *Fraser's Magazine,* 51 (June 1855): 602–627;

"*Maud, and Other Poems,*" anonymous, *British Quarterly Review,* 22 (October 1855): 467–498;

"Samuel Butler," anonymous, *North British Review,* 24 (November 1855): 50–90;

"Browning's *Men and Women,*" anonymous, *British Quarterly Review,* 23 (January 1856): 151–180;

"Bain, on the Senses and the Intellect," anonymous, *Fraser's Magazine,* 53 (February 1856): 212–230; reprinted, *Anthropological Review,* 2 (1864): 250–262;

"Ben Jonson," anonymous, *North British Review,* 24 (February 1856): 447–478;

"Peace, and Its Political Duties," anonymous, *North British Review,* 25 (May 1856): 257–280;

"Aubrey, Antiquary and Gossip," anonymous, *British Quarterly Review,* 26 (July 1856): 159–209;

"The *Noctes Ambrosiae,*" anonymous, *National Review,* 3 (July 1856): 175–200;

"Samuel Rogers," anonymous, *North British Review,* 25 (August 1856): 399–436;

"Edinburgh Fifty Years Ago," anonymous, *Westminster Review,* new series 10 (October 1856): 224–243;

"Lord Cockburn's Memorials of His Time," attributed to Masson, *British Quarterly Review,* 24 (October 1856): 343–364;

"Sir Thomas Browne of Norwich," anonymous, *British Quarterly Review,* 25 (January 1857): 143–176;

"Contemporary Notices of Shakespeare," anonymous, *British Quarterly Review,* 26 (July 1857): 159–209;

"Beranger," anonymous, *British Quarterly Review,* 26 (October 1857): 449–475;

"Tobias Smollett," anonymous, *Quarterly Review,* 103 (January 1858): 66–108;

"Sylvester's *Du Bartas,*" anonymous, *Fraser's Magazine,* 58 (October 1858): 480–491;

"Politics, Home and Foreign," anonymous, *Fraser's Magazine,* 59 (28 April 1859): 629–634;

"Politics of the Present, Foreign and Domestic," anonymous, *Macmillan's Magazine,* 1 (November 1859): 1–10;

"Colloquy of the Round Table," anonymous, *Macmillan's Magazine,* 1 (December 1859): 148–160;

"The Vice of Our Current Literature," anonymous, *Dublin University Magazine,* 56 (January 1860): 515–528; revised as "Three Vices of Current Literature," anonymous, *Macmillan's Magazine,*

Masson at age nineteen; engraving after a daguerreotype

2 (May 1860): 1–13; reprinted, *Eclectic Magazine,* 52 (January 1861): 103–115;

"Writings of Louis-Napoleon," anonymous, *Macmillan's Magazine,* 1 (January 1860): 161–173;

"Whewell's *Platonic Dialogues,*" anonymous, *Macmillan's Magazine,* 1 (January 1860): 225–229;

"Meeting of Parliament," anonymous, *Macmillan's Magazine,* 1 (February 1860): 318–320;

"Thomas Hood," *Macmillan's Magazine,* 2 (August 1860): 315–324;

"Life and Poetry of Shelley," anonymous, *Macmillan's Magazine,* 2 (September 1860): 338–350;

"Life and Poetry of Keats," anonymous, *Macmillan's Magazine,* 3 (November 1860): 1–16;

"Chinese Capital, Pekin," anonymous, *Macmillan's Magazine,* 3 (January 1861): 248–256;

"Gaelic and Norse Popular Tales," *Macmillan's Magazine,* 3 (January 1861): 213–224; reprinted, *Living Age,* 68 (1861): 387–396;

"Vacation Tourists," anonymous, *Macmillan's Magazine,* 4 (May 1861): 92–96;

"Mr. Buckle's Doctrine as to the Scotch and Their History: Part I," anonymous, *Macmillan's Magazine,* 4 (July 1861): 177–189;

"Mr. Buckle's Doctrine as to the Scotch and Their History. Part II: The Weasel-Wars of Scotland and the Scottish Reformation," *Macmillan's Magazine*, 4 (August 1861): 309–322;

"Mr. Buckle's Doctrine as to the Scotch and Their History. Part III: Scotland in the Seventeenth Century," *Macmillan's Magazine* 4 (September 1861): 370–383;

"Mr. Alexander Smith's Poems and His New One," anonymous, *Macmillan's Magazine*, 4 (September 1861): 404–413;

"From London to Ballachulish and Back," anonymous, *Macmillan's Magazine*, 4 (October 1861): 481–494;

"Death of the Prince Consort," anonymous, *Macmillan's Magazine*, 5 (January 1862): 273–276;

"Universal Information and *The English Cyclopedia*," anonymous, *Macmillan's Magazine*, 5 (March 1862): 357–370;

"Rifle-shooting and Drill: The Crisis of Volunteering," anonymous, *Macmillan's Magazine*, 5 (March 1862): 427–432;

"The Poems of Arthur Hugh Clough," anonymous, *Macmillan's Magazine*, 6 (August 1862): 318–331;

"The Highlands and the Hebrides," anonymous, *Macmillan's Magazine*, 5 (September 1862): 421–432;

"Anagrams and All Their Kin," anonymous, *Macmillan's Magazine*, 7 (November 1862): 13–26;

"The Prussian Contest," anonymous, *Macmillan's Magazine*, 7 (November 1862): 75–80;

"Genius and Discipline in Literature," *Macmillan's Magazine*, 7 (December 1862): 81–94;

"The Pines of Hampstead: A Dream of Christmas Eve," anonymous, *Macmillan's Magazine*, 7 (January 1863): 161–173;

"Dead Men Whom I Have Known; or, Recollections of Three Cities," *Macmillan's Magazine*, 9 (November 1863): 52–67;

"The Rev. Dr. James Kidd," *Macmillan's Magazine*, 9 (December 1863): 143–159;

"The Aberdeen Grammar-School – Dr. James Melvin," *Macmillan's Magazine*, 9 (January 1864): 225–239;

"Old Marischal College – Dr. William Knight – Local Miscellanea – William Thom of Inverbury," *Macmillan's Magazine*, 9 (February 1864): 325–343;

"Thackeray: 'Come children, let us shut up the box and the puppets, for our play is played out,' "

as D. M., *Macmillan's Magazine*, 10 (February 1864): 356–368;

"Edina, Scotia's Darling Seat," *Macmillan's Magazine*, 10 (May 1864): 32–49;

"Mr. Matthew Arnold and the Great Public Schools: Eton," anonymous, *Macmillan's Magazine*, 10 (June 1864): 175–176;

"Dr. Chalmers – Part I: His Youth," *Macmillan's Magazine*, 10 (July 1864): 203–218;

"Dr. Chalmers – Part II: His Middle Life," *Macmillan's Magazine*, 10 (September 1864): 365–382;

"Dr. Chalmers – Part III: His Studies, Opinions, and Schemes," *Macmillan's Magazine*, 10 (October 1864): 458–475;

"Reminiscences of Edinburgh University – Professors and Debating Societies," *Macmillan's Magazine*, 11 (December 1864): 123–140; reprinted, *Eclectic Magazine*, 64 (1865): 572–588;

"An Edinburgh Brotherhood – Agostino Ruffini," *Macmillan's Magazine*, 11 (February 1865): 323–336;

"Dr. Samuel Brown – Hugh Miller – De Quincey," *Macmillan's Magazine*, 12 (May 1865): 74–90;

"London from the Top of St. Paul's. Part I," *Macmillan's Magazine*, 12 (July 1865): 275–288;

"Professor Masson on Edinburgh Literature," *Times* (London), 16 November 1865, p. 10C;

"Mrs. Gaskell," anonymous, *Macmillan's Magazine*, 13 (December 1865): 153–156;

"From the Lip of Loch Etive," anonymous, *Macmillan's Magazine*, 14 (September 1866): 395–400;

"Alexander Smith," attributed to Masson, *Macmillan's Magazine*, 15 (February 1867): 342–352;

"Long Holidays," attributed to Masson, *Macmillan's Magazine*, 16 (July 1867): 250–256;

"London University and London Colleges and Schools of Science," *Macmillan's Magazine*, 16 (October 1867): 417–432;

"The Poem Supposed to Be Milton's: To the Editor of the *Times*," *Times* (London), 21 July 1868, p. 5E;

"The Poem Supposed to Be Milton's: To the Editor of the *Times*," *Times* (London), 25 July 1868, p. 12F;

"How Literature May Illustrate History," anonymous, *Macmillan's Magazine*, 24 (1871): 200–208;

"A Memoir of Mazzini," anonymous, *Macmillan's Magazine*, 25 (April 1872): 509–520;

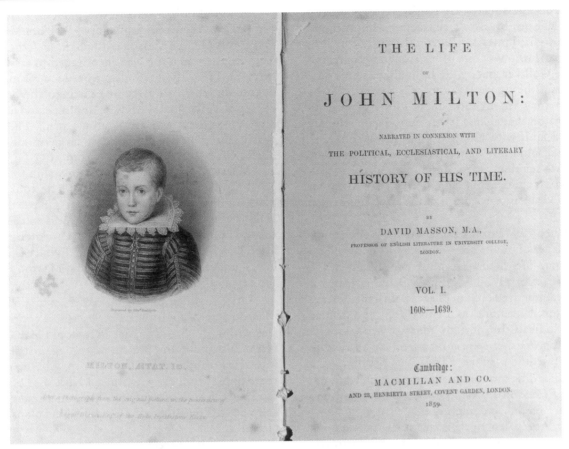

Frontispiece and title page for the massive biography that took Masson more than twenty years to complete

"The Three Interests in Old English Literature," as D. M., *Contemporary Review,* 21 (January 1872–1873): 199–225;

"The Traditions of Sterne and Bunyan," anonymous, *Macmillan's Magazine,* 28 (July 1873): 238–242;

"Milton's House: To the Editor of the *Times,*" *Times* (London), 22 October 1875, p. 4F;

"Carlyle's Edinburgh Life: Part I," anonymous, *Macmillan's Magazine,* 45 (November 1881): 64–80;

"Carlyle's Edinburgh Life: Part II," anonymous, 45 (1882): 145–163;

"*The Haigs of Bemersyde,*" anonymous, *Edinburgh Review,* 155 (April 1882): 502–532;

"Carlyle's Edinburgh Life: Part III," 45 (November 1882): 234–256;

"Dr. John Brown of Edinburgh," anonymous, *Macmillan's Magazine,* 47 (February 1883): 281–295; reprinted, *Eclectic Magazine,* 100 (April 1883): 547–560;

"The Story of Gifford and Keats," *Living Age,* 193 (1892): 719–731;

"Local Memories of Milton," anonymous, *Good Words,* 34 (1893): 41–44; 232–234;

"Ben Jonson in Edinburgh," anonymous, *Blackwood's Edinburgh Magazine,* 154 (December 1893): 790–804.

David Masson is one of the great literary figures of the Victorian era: his corpus is large, rich in erudition, generously conceived, and finely executed. Aside from his imposing biography of John Milton (1859–1880), Masson composed book-length studies of Thomas Chatterton (serialized in the *Dublin University Magazine,* 1851; published in book form, 1874) William Drummond of Hawthornden (1873), Thomas De Quincey (1878), Thomas Carlyle (1885), and William Shakespeare (1914). In addition, he portrayed the lives and writings of scores of literary figures and historical characters, both major and minor, renowned and previously obscure.

Stanley Kunitz and Howard Haycraft describe Masson as a "standard authority on Milton, [Oliver] Goldsmith, and De Quincey," and one might add the names of Carlyle, Chatteron, and Drummond.

Aside from the sheer scale of his masterly biography of Milton, Masson's character is imposing in its own right; James M. Barrie, the author of *Peter Pan* (1904), who was one of his students, compared him to a Gulliver among the Lilliputians of his day. To amend the figure, Masson was something of a Brobdingnagian, a gentle giant with a generosity and a vision that shame lesser men. Later scholars can find fault with him just as Gulliver could see blemishes and other imperfections in Brobdingnag, but few scholars can stand comparison with Masson's achievement any better than Gulliver withstood the interrogation of the Brobdingnagian king.

Much of Masson's known work is filed away in the pages of out-of-print nineteenth-century journals, some of which were quite prestigious at the time. No existing bibliography of his writings is complete; hundreds of uncollected, unsigned essays lie scattered in more than two dozen newspapers and periodicals. In addition, Masson wrote articles for the *English Cyclopedia of Biography* and the eighth and ninth editions of the *Encyclopædia Britannica*.

Hazarding attributions can be treacherous, but many of Masson's probable periodical essays are miniature literary biographies that deserve to be recovered. Article-length character sketches and briefer cameos are scattered throughout his historical narratives and memoirs. His footnotes are often short essays that sketch unfamiliar characters and arouse interest in forgotten figures. Although his portrayals are nuanced and subtle rather than indelible or striking, they have an unself-conscious authority that makes it easy to ignore their hard-earned artistry.

Although several of his books have been reprinted repeatedly, Masson's achievement has yet to receive the attention it merits. His work seems only to have attracted the attention of a few reprint houses, graduate students, and topical specialists. Indeed, much of his work is daunting in nature, scope, or scale. Few purely "literary" scholars have had occasion to peruse the imposing volumes of his edition of the papers of the Scottish Privy Council (1880–1899), and few casual students or scholars have read all the way through his monumental biography of Milton. At the same time, many of his insights seem to have been assimilated without acknowledgment. Nonetheless, the impress of an admirable character with an amiable personality and a vigorous style pervades his writings. In addition, much of his anonymous writing is as good, as interesting, and as well written as any of his openly acknowledged work; some of his fugitive essays are among the best of his era.

David Mather Masson was born on 2 December 1822 in Aberdeen, Scotland, to William Masson and Sarah Mather Masson. Although his father was a stonecutter, Masson was encouraged to strive for learning. He attended the Aberdeen Grammar School under the tutelage of a distinguished classical scholar, Dr. James Melvin, and received a thorough grounding in "Latin, Latin, Latin." The University of Aberdeen offered a large number of places for promising students from poor families, and Masson won a competitive scholarship to Marischal College. Graduating in 1839, he took first place among the masters candidates. Characteristically, he modestly credited his success to the bursary (scholarship) system of Aberdeen. After graduation he spent three years studying divinity at Edinburgh under Dr. Thomas Chalmers; Masson found the experience exciting.

After contemplating a career as a minister, Masson was swept into the ecclesiastical controversies within the Scottish Kirk that would lead to the Great Disruption of 1843. In protest against secular interference in ecclesiastical affairs, Chalmers led the exodus from the established Kirk that became the Free Church of Scotland. Masson aligned himself with his teacher and abandoned his plans for a clerical career.

In 1842 Masson returned to Aberdeen to support the Free Church movement by assuming the editorship of a weekly newspaper, the *Banner*. On a vacation during the summer of 1843 Masson visited London for the first time; there he was introduced to Carlyle's wife, Jane Welsh Carlyle, who described the meeting in a letter of 24 July 1843 to her husband: "[John] Robertson brought here last night to tea a youth from Aberdeen of the name of Mason [*sic*] – A newspaper Editor poor thing, and only twenty! – he is one of your most ardent admirers and immitators [*sic*] – Robertson said, 'he had come up to town to see the "lions" and so he had brought him to "me . . . " ' He is a better 'speciment' of Aberdeen than ever I saw before – an innocent intelligent modest affectionate-looking creature – I quite took to him – when he went away, which he seemed to do very unwillingly, I said that he must come and see us when he returned to London and I hoped to make up then for his present disappointment by introducing him to you – to which he answered with a cordial grasp of my hand 'Eh! What a real shame in ye to say "that!" ' He told me 'if I would come to Aberdeen they would get up a mob for me in the fish-market Place, and give me a grand hurrah – and a paragrap[h] "of course." ' "

Frontispiece and title page for Masson's biography of the seventeenth-century Scottish poet

Carlyle's own description of Masson was quoted some ten years later in a contemporary biographical dictionary. Just as cordial, Carlyle's comments are less humorous and more ardent than those of his wife: "Nobody can know him without feeling that he is a man of truly superior qualities, calculated at once to secure success in his undertakings, and the love of his fellow-creatures by the way. A man of many attainments in scholarship and literature; and with a natural fund of intelligence, delicate, strong, and deep, such as belongs to very few, even among scholars and men of letters. A man of beautiful and manly character withal; ardent, vivid, veracious, and yet altogether quiet, discreet, and harmonious. . . . Masson is likely to be distinguished, I should expect, at once by love of peace, and by felicity and steadiness in doing work. For he is full of what one might call central fire, which is singularly well covered in and tempered into genial warmth, of many useful and beautiful kinds."

After two years with the *Banner,* Masson resigned and moved to Edinburgh. In August 1844 George Lillie Craik introduced him to William and Robert Chambers, who persuaded him to become a staff writer for their publishing firm. Masson also began submitting articles to outside periodicals. His maiden article in a prestigious national periodical was an impassioned rhapsody in *Fraser's Magazine* (May 1844), "On Emotional Culture." The essay is idealistic but immature; as the philosopher John Stuart Mill said of Masson in a letter to John Kemble of 22 August 1844: "Masson is I think a young man of great promise & even the faults of his stile are not of a discouraging kind – but he is not yet out of his apprenticeship."

In 1847 Masson moved to London, supporting himself by submitting anonymous articles to periodicals. He came to London to make his mark – as he put it, "to set the Thames on fire" – but much of his time was spent in the reading room of the British Museum, where he could see, as he says in his *The British Museum, Historical and Descriptive* (1848), "the young student reading professionally, the humble copyist driving his pen mechanically over the paper, and so earning his scanty and laborious livelihood; or, lastly, the conscientious writer of history, deep in the business of research." These characters and the "reader who annoys you with his 'bassoon nose'; another with his whisperings to himself; a third with his clanking heels; a fourth with his wo-

worn look" were his daily companions. After working hours he frequently visited with Jane and Thomas Carlyle.

In February 1848 Masson noticed a placard outside a newspaper office: "Revolution in Paris – Abdication of King Louis Philippe." He began to read voraciously about contemporary events and recent political theory. The events of 1848 in Europe helped him to understand those of 1648 in England. As he explained in an interview in 1901, the year 1848

> has always marked for me the beginning of a new era in the history of the stretch of time that lies within my own recollection. You know what followed in the political world – how thrones tottered and toppled all over Europe. But the revolution seems to have been intellectual as much as political. There was the coming into the air of all sorts of new speculative notions. One is sometimes inclined to wonder whether at such a period the earth may not have sailed into some new region of space, so that the air had become impregnated with new principles. That, of course, is mere whimsy but who can say that the transition from one spiritual period to another may not be marked by some actual change in the telluric conditions, rendering men's nerves more responsive to one set of stimuli, more insensible to another? At any rate, one remembers the effects of the 1848 revolution as not incomparable with those of the first French Revolution, sixty years earlier, of which we are told:

> > Bliss was it in that dawn to be alive,
> > But to be young was very heaven.

> That is scarcely too much to say of the exaltation of mind throughout Europe during the years that followed 1848 ... the flush of confidence in the high destinies of mankind, and the approaching solution of the great problems of social well-being, which then suffused the whole atmosphere of thought.

The revolutions failed, but the possibilities they revealed were not forgotten. Masson's flurry of periodical articles reflects that burgeoning, urgent speculation. During this period Masson became more closely associated with Mill. He involved himself in the movements of the day; he argued for domestic social reforms and offered active sympathy and support to oppressed nations abroad, laboring all the while in anonymity. An unnamed admirer describes him in *Men of the Time* (1857) as "one of the great workers in the world, who work anonymously in the profession of Journalism, where so many labour almost unknown to those whom they delight and instruct, and so few can build up a fame commensurate with their powers. There are many thus toiling, of whom the world seldom hears by name, who possess brilliant and solid intellectual capacities, such as would win a wide renown could they converse and concentrate them on some public work. In the first rank of these unpublished writers and teachers is David Masson."

Masson also found time for scholarship. In 1851 his "The Story of Thomas Chatterton," one of his finest works, was serialized in the *Dublin University Magazine*. His sense of history vivifies bits of evidence such as scrapes of paper strewn about the floor of Chatterton's abandoned apartment; legend and hearsay leaven the work without eclipsing the demonstrable. Masson's manner is freer and more emotive than that of the modern academician; he sometimes resorts to platitudes or fumbles on details. Still, when he is at his best, Masson's imagination sweeps over an era and peers into the hearts of his characters. Aware of the ambiguities of evidence – "allowing for uncertainties in our construction of these documents," he will say – he goes over all the ground himself, "weaving the facts together," and his painstaking and imaginative historical research (even into data about the weather) bears him out of difficulty. Even some of his most audacious speculations about fugitive motives or states of mind are patiently substantiated and finally convincing.

In 1852 Masson was appointed to succeed Arthur Hugh Clough as Professor of English Language and Literature at University College, London. In 1853 he married Rosaline Orme and eventually fathered four children: David Orme, Flora, Helen, and Rosaline.

In 1855 and 1856, respectively, Chambers published anonymously Masson's *Medieval History* and *Modern History from the Reformation to the Present*. In 1856 the Macmillan firm published under Masson's name *Essays Biographical and Critical: Chiefly on the English Poets,* a selection of revised periodical pieces.

In 1858 Masson agreed to undertake the editorship of a newly founded "shilling monthly," *Macmillan's Magazine*. During its day it was among the best of the literary magazines. According to the editors of the *Wellesley Index* (1966), the serious articles of *Macmillan's* "seem more impressive than those of its rivals." Although his editorship ended in 1868, Masson appears to have had some association with the magazine for some time afterward.

In 1859 appeared *British Novelists and Their Styles,* a pioneering early history of the novel that went through several reprintings. Michael Adams and Richard Stang refer to it as "one of the best early histories of the novel." Masson's survey is synoptic, broad-minded, and virtually canonical; it demonstrates a mastery of most of the relevant literature. He recognizes and accords respect to the potential of both the realist and the Romantic traditions.

Also during 1859 the first volume of Masson's biography of Milton appeared. His publisher, Alexander Macmillan, had expressed his elation about the work in a letter of 27 October 1858 to James Maclehose: "Masson's *Milton* you know about. It is going to be a gigantic book – three vols., 700 pages each. But every page is solid, genuine stuff. It will be the best history of the time, spiritual and literary, that exists." Masson's biography of Milton took more than twenty years to complete and grew to more than twice the size Macmillan had imagined; the work was capped by a 242-page index, which appeared in 1894 as part of the second edition. The anonymous author of Masson's memorial notice in the *Scotsman* of 5 October 1907 remarks, "the work is not only a remarkable appreciation of Milton, but it is a political and literary history of the time. It is marked by a thoroughness and earnestness, and by a deep insight into character, and by a strong grasp of the inner meaning of events." In 1911 A. W. Ward would call Masson's work the "most important English biography produced in the mid-Victorian age." Although Ward admits that Carlyle is a more powerful writer, he claims that Masson equals him in "candour and sincerity" and excels him in the "assiduity of his research" and the "simplicity of his attitude towards the facts."

For more than a hundred years after the first edition, Masson's life of Milton was routinely cited as "the standard authority" or the "standard biography." Perhaps not until J. M. French's compilation of *The Life Records of John Milton* (1949–1958) or William Riley Parker's *Milton: A Biography* (1968) did any single scholar register a comparable achievement in Milton studies, and Masson's biography has still not been entirely superseded; Galbraith Crump, for example, warns that Parker's work "does not replace David Masson's monumental seven-volume *Life of John Milton*." Although some scholars, such as John Smart and Joseph Wittreich, have spoken of a need to "De-Massonize" Milton, familiarity with Masson's work is still necessary. Although modern scholars tend to reject Masson's romantic reading of *Paradise Lost* (1667) and his reading and dating of *Samson Agonistes* (1671) are contested, Masson's work is invaluable. Parker, the most authoritative modern biographer of Milton, says, "The greatest Life of Milton has long been, and long will continue to be, the six-volume labour of David Masson. Since my own work is no presumptuous attempt to supersede so stately a memo-

Masson in his study in 1884 (sketch by William Hole; Edinburgh University Library)

rial, comparisons can only be pointless. I have chosen a smaller canvas. In common with all who view Milton today, I have perched like a pygmy on Masson's noble shoulders." Christopher Hill, perhaps the preeminent twentieth-century scholar of seventeenth-century England, lists Masson first among "the great Miltonists": "For many years I have known that, whenever I think I have had an original idea about seventeenth-century England, I am apt to find it tucked away in one of S. R. Gardiner's footnotes. So it is with Masson." For A. N. Wilson, a more recent biographer of Milton, Masson's learning is nothing less than proverbial.

Masson's work opens up a broad and vivid panorama of one of the most dramatic periods of English or world history. Masson was an admirer of the novels of Tobias Smollett, Sir Walter Scott, Charles Dickens, Elizabeth Cleghorn Gaskell, and William Makepeace Thackeray, and at his best his history has the ample scope and leisurely flow of a vast Victorian novel.

In 1863 Masson initiated the *Reader*, an encyclopedic weekly paper of literature, science, and the arts. He almost certainly wrote the anonymous "leaders" and much else besides. Masson's venture into periodical publication lapsed after three years, but his weekly was lively and gives dissident insights into the development of literature and the currents of opinion.

Masson's edition of Milton's poetry was published in 1864. Revised several times and frequently reprinted, it would hold the field as a standard text well into the next century.

In 1865 Masson accepted an invitation to succeed William Edmonstoune Aytoun as Professor of Rhetoric and English Literature at the University of Edinburgh. The same year he published a survey of the development of recent British philosophy. In the years immediately after his appointment Masson campaigned for the admission of women into Scottish universities; his full contribution to this cause has yet to be adequately appraised and appreciated. In addition, Masson was active, along with Mill and Mill's stepdaughter Helen Taylor, in the movement to attain the vote for women. He was an important speaker at some of the annual public meetings of the Edinburgh Branch of the National Society for Women's Suffrage. In 1869 Masson published selections from Goldsmith with a biographical introduction.

In 1873 Macmillan published Masson's nearly five-hundred-page biography of Drummond. The anonymous reviewer in the *Spectator* (21 February 1874) saw the volume as new proof of Masson's "untiring industry and radiant geniality" but doubted whether Masson's "fervid enthusiasm" for Drummond would be appreciated outside of Scotland. The reviewer thought that "the literary and other biographies grouped around Drummond are very interesting, and generally done in Mr. Masson's best style; but the history is tedious, and Drummond, with all his merits — a good minor poet, and a highly cultivated Scotch laird, quietly, though keenly watching political events, and occasionally entering into them — is not the man round whom to write the history of Scotland." In the reviewer's opinion "Professor Masson, naturally bent on doing his best for his hero, evidently finds it uphill work to carry him even so high as mediocrity, and gives up the attempt to carry him further."

Subsequent comments, however, were generally favorable. Some forty years after the publication of Masson's biography L. E. Kastner, the editor of Drummond's poetry, described Masson's study as "the standard biography" and quoted Masson's critical remarks on Drummond's poetry with appreciation. Almost forty years after Kastner, French Fogle regarded Masson as one of the two "most reliable biographers of Drummond" —

along with Ward — and credited him with writing "an imaginative and learned study of Drummond and his times." Fogle, like Kastner, echoes Masson's criticism of Hawthornden with approval.

The opening pages of the biography are characterized by a leisurely and informed nostalgia as Masson casually introduces his subject by surveying the remains of Drummond's country estate. The main narrative is drier, only episodically romantic, and occasionally spiced by a refreshing candor. Masson places Drummond's literary achievements in the context of his life, and his life in the context of contemporary history. Masson rehearses the main events and developments that led to the English Civil War and culminated with the execution of the king in 1649, the year of Drummond's death. Writing of the meeting of Drummond and Ben Jonson, Masson gives his imagination free rein so that "if you know anything of the two men, you can see the scene as distinctly as if you had been peeping through the window." When Masson reads a document, he tries to submerge his sensibility into it and revive the life of the inert words. Sometimes his readings are astute, as when he restores Drummond's "Irene" (written, 1638; published, 1656) to its historical context; sometimes his critical faculty lapses as his imagination wanders. The close of one of Drummond's letters quotes a melancholy passage from the Vulgate, and Masson remarks, with slightly melodramatic emphasis: "were they not written with a sigh, and an arrest of the pen, that the writer might lift his eyes, mutter a moment to himself, and look round his solitary room?" Occasionally Masson revels in sentiment; for example: "Four years had passed since his love-bereavement; but the image of his dead betrothed [*sic*] was continually before him, and his heart still haunted the grass that waved above her grave." This passage is not sufficently relieved by the drier objectivity of the immediately following footnote citing his source in Drummond's letters. At other times Masson's sense of humor adds a lighter touch. Describing Drummond and Michael Drayton making up after a lapse in correspondence occasioned by a friend's misplacing a letter, Masson says that they decided to "excuse themselves for their long mutual silence, and, like Adam and Eve, agree to lay blame on a third party."

Masson includes ample extracts from relevant documents; but since much of Drummond's literary achievement came relatively early in his career, there seems to be a waning of interest and material as the end approaches. An undertone of impatience mutters through the concluding chapters and occasionally erupts in critical outbursts: Masson's initial patriotic sympathy struggles against his disgruntle-

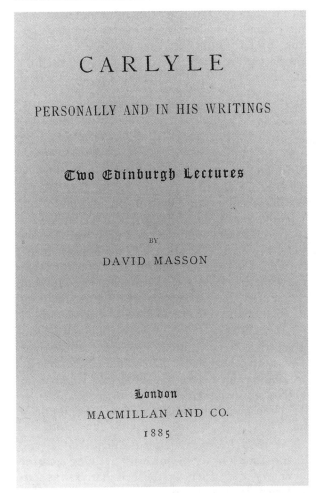

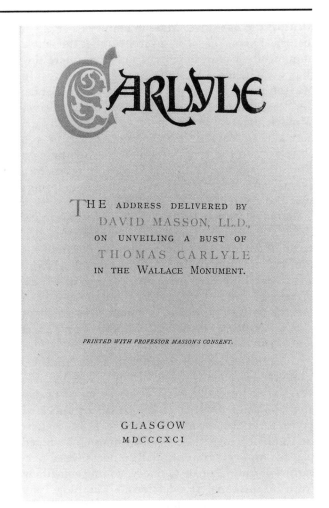

Title pages for the published versions of three talks Masson gave about his old friend

ment with the rigid aristocratic assumptions, narrow social horizons, and relative inactivity of his protagonist. Sometimes the man of letters suffers by comparison with the man of action: in the immediacy of events, perhaps nothing Drummond or Milton did had an impact comparable to the exploits of James Graham, first Marquess of Montrose, the militant struggles of John Lilburne, or the dominating presence of Oliver Cromwell, but nevertheless, in retrospect, the man of letters leaves a more intelligible legacy. The nuances of literature became legible in the light of history, and, in turn, past history is illuminated by literature and current history, by the light thrown on the past by events and contemporaneous struggles. Like Thomas Babington Macauley, Carlyle, Gardiner, or G. M. Trevelyan, Masson could see the English revolution in light of recent French revolutions, Chartism, feminism, and the emergence of the labor movement. In contrast with his friend and coconspirator Montrose, Drummond played a relatively minor role in the civil war. Nev-

ertheless, Masson's biography of Drummond is an act of Scottish patriotism; as he remarks of Drummond, "He was a Scot, we shall find, to the last, with a keen and even studious fondness for Scottish History and Traditions, including the traditions of old Scottish Literature; and I have no doubt that he could talk, and did talk, the Scottish vernacular to the last, in ordinary intercourse, as racily as his neighbours." What Masson says of Drummond often applies to Masson himself. Still, Masson has more sympathy with the revolutionary Englishman Milton than the conservative Scotsman Drummond. Masson's biography is consistently intelligent and sometimes exciting, but an aphorism of Drummond's seems to apply: "*Materiam superabat opus*" (The workmanship is more valuable than the material).

In his best biographies, such as those on Milton and Drummond, Masson depicts his subjects in their social landscape: biography is embedded in history. Although the man and his work are the focus of the narrative, Masson conveys a sense of historical perspective, an awareness that the whole of humanity is more important and more interesting than even its most outstanding representatives. In Masson's work, as in the paintings of his friends, the Pre-Raphaelites, the background often receives as much attention as the subject. In a biography undertaken on Masson's principles, each person is to be related to the significant struggles of the day. The subject's works have to be seen in relation to events, and these events will sometimes upstage even the greatest individual; the reader's interest in the protagonist may be swallowed up by the spectacle of the history. Ironically, however, this rich sense of history makes Masson's accounts of his subjects more convincing. At the same time, laborious research licenses an unusual degree of self-expression: Masson's exemplary scholarship earned him the right to express or insinuate his sometimes liberal, sometimes dissident opinions without being simply dismissed by hostile reviewers.

In 1865 Masson had said that the materials for a biography of De Quincey did not exist, but five years after the publication of his study of Drummond he made the attempt: his *De Quincey* appeared in 1878. In the *Academy* (7 January 1882) Robert Leighton depreciated De Quincey himself but noted that Masson "gives us in small compass what is regarded as known of De Quincey, adding something from his personal recollections." The biography proved to be popular, and at least twenty editions were published in the following century.

Nevertheless, Masson's biography of De Quincey is less serious, less substantial, and less memorable than that of Drummond. It omits the historical background; De Quincey lived through a momentous period of world history, but from Masson's narrative one would hardly know it. Depressions, rebellions, revolutions, mass movements, wars, famines, political struggles, social upheavals, changes of ministries, and struggles over policies and power are passed over without mention. Historical context is assumed, perhaps on the grounds that De Quincey is a recent contemporary, but as a consequence modern readers are likely to feel that De Quincey floats in a historical void.

Not only is history largely omitted but, in addition, biography and literary criticism are segregated rather than merged in a seamless whole. Although the biographical narrative is curiously gripping, nothing of consequence happens to De Quincey or because of him. Interest is sustained by a breathless style, anecdotes, revelations of eccentricity, and the anticipation that something of significance is coming. Trust in Masson's reputation sustains suspense, but the great events and developments of De Quincey's era, and De Quincey's attitude toward them, pass without remark. Personal friendship or political prudence – the political issues in contention were and still are bitterly debated – may have deterred candid appraisal of contemporary figures or events. By publishing his memories and editing De Quincey's scattered works, Mason may have been doing the last offices of a friend. The last quarter of the book provides a review of De Quincey's writings, but they are organized topically rather than chronologically. Consequently, one does not develop an adequate idea of how De Quincey's writing evolved. Masson is more inclined to stress De Quincey's generosity to the poor than the imperial pride or gleeful malice that he is sometimes obliged to concede. For Masson, the essential De Quincey was the ever-enchanting conversationalist and the spellbinding prose poet.

In 1879 Masson began editing the registers of the Scottish Privy Council; before he turned over the work to others in 1899 he would edit and write introductions for twelve of the fourteen volumes. In 1893, in acknowledgment of his yeoman labors, he would be appointed Royal Historiographer for Scotland.

In 1885, four years after the death of Carlyle, Masson gave a brace of powerful, moving lectures in memory of his friend; published that year as *Carlyle, Personally and in His Writings,* they are among the most striking of Masson's surviving orations. Ten years after Carlyle's death Masson was chosen to deliver an oration at the unveiling of the bust of Carlyle at the Wallace Monument at Stirling on 25 July 1891. In 1889–1890 Masson's fourteen-volume edition of *The Collected Writings of Thomas De Quincey* was published. Although Stuart Tave has discovered several additions to the De Quincey canon and prefers different texts of some of De Quincey's works, he acknowledges that "Masson's edition . . . has many virtues, is the best we have, and is certainly necessary for convenience." Masson's is still the standard edition of De Quincey's works.

As the end of his seventieth year approached, Masson revised several of his periodical essays as *Edinburgh Sketches and Memories* (1892). In 1895 he retired from teaching but continued to edit the Privy Council records. In 1896 he was elected an honorary member of the Royal Scottish Academy and nominated professor of ancient literature. As early as 1867 he had helped found the precursor of the Edinburgh Association for the University Education of Women; on 24 November 1897 a subcommittee of the association, having raised funds to erect a residence for undergraduate women, named the new dormitory Masson Hall.

In his 1901 *Pall Mall Magazine* interview with William Archer, Masson refers to the present as "a period of reaction." Nonetheless, he anticipates a moral and political revival that would include "a return to the older Muses, with the reappearance of a poetry as worthy as has ever been in the world, but strangely reinvigorated and refreshed." He quotes John Keats, ranging himself among those "Other spirits there are, standing apart / Upon the forehead of the age to come."

Dying on 6 October 1907, Masson was mourned as a great scholar, a master of British literature and history, an esteemed teacher, and a "grand old man." Shortly before his death he had revised some of his articles, manuscripts, and memoirs; his daughter Flora published her father's elegiac *Memories of London in the 'Forties* in 1908 and his *Memories of Two Cities, Edinburgh and Aberdeen* in 1911. Finally, his daughter Rosaline published some of her father's lectures on Shakespeare as *Shakespeare Personally* in 1914. The lectures defend intuitive literary biography as a legitimate method of scholarly research. Masson's study was intended as a rebuttal of the fashionable positivistic dismissal of interest in the man who was Shakespeare. Masson imputes no particular theological or political views to Shakespeare, but he was convinced that the visage of the author is sometimes discernible in the work and that these glimpses of the writer are illuminating and worthwhile. Far from being a mere subjectivist, Masson defends the value of both external and internal, objective and subjective evidence.

In his own time Masson earned the friendship and respect of distinguished men and women as diverse as Mill, the Carlyles, Thackeray, Gaskell, Charles Kingsley, Robert Browning, Robert Louis Stevenson, Alfred Tennyson, Giuseppe Mazzini, and Ralph Waldo Emerson. Distinguished as a journalist, editor, literary critic, historian, essayist, orator, and activist, Masson occupies a rank only slightly below that of the greatest Victorians.

Masson was convinced of the capacity of history and literature to illuminate one another. He saw the past in light of contemporary struggles. Even where his research is not comprehensive, his judgments are usually sound; though occasionally florid, his style is, even in some of his most apparently unstudied sketches, distinctive and engaging. He has a vivid sense of historical perspective and an eye for the telling detail. Above and beyond his sensitive appreciation of literature, Masson was a fine academic histo-

Masson at the time of his retirement as Professor of Rhetoric and English Literature at the University of Edinburgh (portrait by Sir George Reid; Scottish National Portrait Gallery)

rian. As a nineteenth-century historian of the English Civil War, Masson ranks just after Gardiner; of twentieth-century British historians perhaps only R. H. Tawney and Hill have held comparable authority. Masson tried to make literature and history accessible; his footnotes carry the paraphernalia of a scholar, but his text is as accessible as the conversation of a friend, as open as his detailed outlines in front of every volume and at the head of each chapter. Like a patient teacher, he shares his knowledge with the reader.

Masson had some of the typical limitations of the best British intellectuals of his age. While he was untouched by the racism of Thomas Carlyle, the hauteur of John Ruskin, or the hostility to the working class of Matthew Arnold, Masson, like Mill, combined a genuine humanism with an apparent reluctance to confront the evils of British imperialism. Masson held progressive views on most issues: he supported equal rights for women and the extension of the suffrage to the working class, and he spoke out against slavery and the slave trade.

Although omissions and failings vitiate his work, they do not negate his wide-ranging services to scholarship or obliterate his splendid achievement. With all its ponderous scale and sometimes appalling detail, *The Life of John Milton* can still enchant a willing reader. For the scholar Masson scatters hints with a generous hand and an open, if not entirely informed, heart. His life of Milton commemorates the generosity and humanity of the scholar as well as the genius and grandeur of the poet.

Finally, one should not ignore the possibility that duress constrained his utterances. Masson had a family to support, and he lived in a country and time in which academic freedom was at worst nominal and at best tenuous. In Victorian Scotland and England scholars were rather routinely dismissed or passed over for promotion because of controversial views. The year before Masson assumed his first professorship one of his associates, Frederick Denison Maurice, had been forced to resign from Oxford. Once the midcentury ferment subsided and the opening for progressive social change seemed to recede, Masson withdrew into scholarship and teaching, trying to enlighten the next generation.

After World War I Masson was left behind in undeserved oblivion. Fashionable biographical writers took the more cynical stance epitomized by Lytton Strachey; some critics and academicians turned away from history in the name of "art for art's sake" while others turned toward social and economic history. In literary criticism, the fashionable conservative aestheticism of Henry James and T. S. Eliot, the despairing apolitical nihilism of James Joyce, and the positivism of I. A. Richards fostered a disengagement of writers and scholars from literary history and the kind of ethical concerns that animated Masson.

Overall, one might say the keynote of his work is a certain largeness, a certain grandeur of scope and scale of conception, a largeness of imagination and sympathy, a largeness of heart far beyond carping comments of smaller men. Like his fellow countryman Robert Burns, Masson never forgot his antecedents. Aberdeen has a venerable Masonic tradition, and Masson was the son of the stonecutter who never forgot his working-class heritage. Long before he joined "the majority," Masson earned his initiation in the perpetual freemasonry of all men of good will. His best work shows the hand of a master.

Bibliographies:

Frederick William Poole and William Fletcher, eds., *Poole's Index to Periodical Literature,* revised edition, 6 volumes (Gloucester, Mass.: Peter Smith, 1963);

Walter E. Houghton, Josef L. Altholz, Eileen Curran, Harold E. Dailey, Esther Rhoads Houghton, and John A. Lester, Jr., eds., *The Wellesley Index to Victorian Periodicals, 1824–1900,* 5 volumes (Toronto: University of Toronto Press / London: Routledge & Kegan Paul, 1966);

C. Edward Wall, Edward Przebienda, and Wayne Somers, eds., *Cumulative Author Index for Poole's Index to Periodical Literature, 1802–1906* (Ann Arbor, Mich.: Pieran, 1971).

References:

Rhoda Abramowitz, "The Nature of Autobiography: The Sonnet of the Self. An Annotated Critical Edition of 'Autobiography of Shakespeare from His Thirty-fourth to His Thirty-ninth Year, Delivered from His Sonnets – Together with the Sonnets Themselves Arranged and Elucidated' by David Masson, with Analysis and Discussion of the Sonnet as a Literary Form and Autobiography as a Literary Genre," Ph.D. dissertation, City University of New York, 1993;

Michael Wayne Adams, "David Masson: A Study of His Literary Criticism," Ph.D. dissertation, University of Texas at Austin, 1973;

Adams, "David Masson's Theory of Imagination and Matthew Arnold's 1853 'Preface,'" *Studies in Scottish Literature,* 11 (January 1974): 141–155;

William Archer, "Real Conversations, Recorded by William Archer; Conversation VII: – With Professor Masson," *Pall Mall Magazine,* 25 (September–December 1901): 378–386;

James M. Barrie, *An Edinburgh Eleven: Pencil Portraits from College Life* (New York: Lovell, Coryell, 1889);

Galbraith Crump, ed., *Approaches to Teaching Milton's "Paradise Lost"* (New York: Modern Language Association, 1986);

David Masson Scholarship Scheme, 1972 (Edinburgh: H.M.S.O., 1972);

"Death of Professor Masson," *Times* (London), 8 October 1907;

French Fogle, *A Critical Study of William Drummond of Hawthornden* (New York: Columbia University Press, 1952);

J. M. French, *The Life Records of John Milton,* 5 volumes (New Brunswick, N. J.: Rutgers University Press, 1949–1958);

Charles L. Graves, *Life and Letters of Alexander Macmillan* (London: Macmillan, 1910);

Christopher Hill, *Milton and the English Revolution* (Harmondsworth, U.K.: Penguin, 1977);

William Hole, *Quasi Cursores: Portraits of the High Officers and Professors of the University of Edinburgh at Its Tercentenary Festival* (Edinburgh: Tercentenary Committee, 1884);

L. E. Kastner, ed., *The Poetical Works of William Drummond of Hawthornden,* 2 volumes (Manchester, U.K.: Manchester University Press, 1913);

Stanley Kunitz and Howard Haycraft, eds., *British Authors of the Nineteenth Century* (New York: Wilson, 1936);

"The Late Emeritus Professor Masson: A Distinguished Literary Career," *Scotsman,* 8 October 1907, p. 5;

Flora Masson, *Victorians All* (London: Chambers, 1931);

F. O. Matthiessen, "The Responsibilities of the Critic," in *The Responsibilities of the Critic,* edited by John Rackliffe (New York: Oxford University Press, 1952), pp. 3–18;

Jo McMurty, "David Masson," in her *English Language, English Literature* (Hamden, Conn.: Archon, 1985), pp. 111–135;

Men of the Time: Biographical Sketches of Eminent Living Characters . . . Also Biographical Sketches of Women of the Time (London: Kent, 1857), pp. 517–519;

William Riley Parker, *Milton: A Biography,* 2 volumes (Oxford: Clarendon Press, 1968);

Donald A. Roberts, "Masson," in *A Milton Encyclopedia,* edited by William B. Hunter, John T. Shawcross, John M. Steadman, Purvis E. Boyette, and Leonard Nathanson, volume 5 (Lewisburg, Pa.: Bucknell University Press / London: Associated University Presses, 1979), pp. 100–101;

Clyde de L. Ryals, Kenneth Fielding, Ian Campbell, Aileen Christianson, and Hilary J. Smith, eds., *The Collected Letters of Thomas and Jane Welsh Carlyle,* volume 16 (Durham, N.C. & London: Duke University Press, 1990), pp. 311–313;

George Saintsbury, "An Appreciation," *Scotsman,* 8 October 1907, p. 5;

John S. Smart, ed., *The Sonnets of John Milton* (Oxford: Clarendon, 1966);

George Barnett Smith, "Masson's Life of Milton," *Macmillan's Magazine,* 28 (1873): 536–547;

Stuart Tave, ed., *New Essays by De Quincey: His Contributions to the Edinburgh Saturday Post and the Edinburgh Evening Post 1827–1828* (Princeton: Princeton University Press, 1966);

Paul Turner, *English Literature: 1832–1890, Excluding the Novel* (Oxford: Clarendon Press, 1989);

A. W. Ward, "Biographers and Memoir-Writers," in *The Cambridge History of English Literature,* edited by Ward and A. R. Waller, volume 7 (New York: Putnam / Cambridge: Cambridge University Press, 1911), pp. 123–124;

A. N. Wilson, *The Life of John Milton* (Harmondsworth, U.K.: Penguin, 1984);

Joseph Wittreich, *Feminist Milton* (Ithaca, N.Y.: Cornell University Press, 1987).

Papers:

The Folger Shakespeare Library, Washington, D.C., has the manuscript for David Masson's "Autobiography of Shakespeare from his Thirty-fourth to his Thirty-ninth Year, Derived from His Sonnets: together with the Sonnets Themselves Arranged & Elucidated," written circa 1846. Edinburgh University Library has records of the master's examinations Masson composed and administered, student notebooks from classes Masson taught, and testimonials for Masson (presumably those submitted when he was nominated for the professorship around 1865). The Univeristy of London has the testimonials submitted on behalf of Masson when he was nominated as professor there. The University of Virginia also has some manuscripts.

Thomas Moore
(28 May 1779 – 25 February 1852)

Gert Ronberg
University of Aberdeen

See also the Moore entry in *DLB 96: British Romantic Poets, 1789–1832, Second Series.*

BOOKS: *Poetical Works of the Late Thomas Little Esq.* (London: J. & T. Carpenter, 1801; Philadelphia: Printed & published by Hugh Maxwell, 1804);

Epistles, Odes, and Other Poems (London: Printed for James Carpenter, 1806; Philadelphia: Published by John Watts, 1806);

A Selection of Irish Melodies, parts 1–7, lyrics by Moore, musical arrangements by Sir John Stevenson (London: James Power / Dublin: William Power, 1808–1818); parts 8–10 and supplement, lyrics by Moore, musical arrangements by Sir Henry R. Bishop (London: James Power, 1821–1834);

Corruption and Intolerance, Two Poems, anonymous (London: Printed for J. Carpenter, 1808);

The Sceptic: A Philosophical Satire (London: Carpenter, 1809);

A Letter to the Roman Catholics of Dublin (London: Printed for J. Carpenter, 1810);

M. P.; or, The Blue-Stocking: A Comic Opera, in Three Acts first performed at the English Opera, Theatre Royal, Lyceum, on Monday, Sept. 9, 1811 (London: J. Power, 1811; New York: Published by the Longworths, 1812);

Intercepted Letters; or, The Two-Penny Post-Bag, as Thomas Brown the Younger (London: J. Carr, 1813; Baltimore: Published by E. J. Coale, Wm. Warner, Joseph Robinson, J. & T. Vance, and P. Mauro; A. Finlay, & P. H. Nicklin, Philadelphia; A. T. Goodrich, New York; Bradford & Read and C. Williams, Boston; Printed by P. Mauro, 1813; Philadelphia: Published by Moses Thomas, printed by J. Maxwell, 1813);

A Series of Sacred Songs, Duetts and Trios, The Words by Thomas Moore, Esqr. The Music, Composed and Selected by Sir John Stevenson, part 1 (London: J. Power / Dublin: William Power, 1816; Philadelphia: Published by Geo. E. Blake, 1817?); part 2 (London: J. Power, 1824);

Lalla Rookh, An Oriental Romance (London: Longman, Hurst, Rees, Orme & Brown, 1817; New York: Published by Kirk & Mercein, 1817; New York: Published by Van Winkle & Wiley, 1817; Philadelphia: Published by M. Thomas, printed by J. Maxwell, 1817);

A Selection of Popular National Airs, part 1, lyrics by Moore and musical arrangements by Stevenson (London: James Power / Dublin: William Power, 1818); part 2, lyrics by Moore and musical arrangements by Bishop (London: James Power / Dublin: William Power, 1820); parts 3–6 (London: James Power, 1822–1827);

The Fudge Family in Paris, as Thomas Brown the Younger (London: Printed for Longman, Hurst, Rees, Orme & Brown, 1818; New York: Published by W. B. Gilley, 1821);

Tom Crib's Memorial to Congress (London: Longman, Hurst, Rees, Orme & Brown, 1819; New York: Kirk & Mercein, 1819);

The Works of Thomas Moore (6 volumes, Paris: Galignani et Cie, 1819; 5 volumes, New York: Gilley, 1821);

Irish Melodies, Moore's lyrics only (unauthorized edition, Dublin: William Power, 1820; authorized edition, London: Printed for James Power and Longman, Hurst, Rees, Orme, & Brown, 1821; Philadelphia: Jekyll, 1821);

The Loves of the Angels: A Poem (London: Longman, Hurst, Rees, Orme & Brown, 1823; revised, 1823; New York: James & John Harper, 1823; Philadelphia: E. Littell / New York: Henry, 1823);

Fables for the Holy Alliance, as Thomas Brown the Younger (London: Printed for Longman, Hurst, Rees, Orme & Brown, 1823; Philadelphia: Littell, 1823);

Memoirs of Captain Rock, The Celebrated Irish Chieftain, With Some Account of His Ancestors (London: Hurst, Rees, Orme, Brown & Green, 1824; New York: M'Laughlin, 1824);

Thomas Moore; portrait by Sir Martin Shee (from L. A. G. Strong,
Minstrel Boy: A Portrait of Tom Moore, *1937)*

Memoirs of the Life of the Right Honourable Richard Brinsley Sheridan (London: Longman, Hurst, Rees, Orme, Brown & Green, 1825; Philadelphia: Carey & Lea, 1825);

Evenings in Greece: First Evening, lyrics by Moore and musical arrangements by Bishop (London: Published by J. Power, 1826);

The Epicurean: A Tale (London: Longman, Rees, Orme, Brown & Green, 1827; Boston: Wells & Lilly, 1827; revised and enlarged edition, London: Macrone, 1839; New York: C. S. Francis / Boston: J. H. Francis, 1841);

Odes upon Cash, Corn, Catholics, and Other Matters (London: Longman, Rees, Orme, Brown & Green, 1828; Philadelphia: Carey, Lea & Carey, 1828);

Legendary Ballads, lyrics by Moore and musical arrangements by Bishop (London: Published by J. Power, 1828);

The Summer Fête; A Poem with Songs; The Music Composed and Selected by Henry R. Bishop and Mr. Moore (London: J. Power, 1831; Philadelphia: Carey, Lea & Blanchard, 1833);

Evenings in Greece: The Second Evening, lyrics by Moore and musical arrangements by Bishop (London: J. Power, 1831);

The Life and Death of Lord Edward Fitzgerald (London: Longman, Rees, Orme, Brown & Green, 1831; New York: Harper, 1831);

Travels of an Irish Gentleman in Search of a Religion (2 volumes, London: Longman, Rees, Orme, Brown, Green & Longmans, 1833; 1 volume, Baltimore: J. Murphy, 1833; New York: Printed for M. Carey, 1833; Philadelphia: Carey, Lea & Blanchard, 1833);

The Fudges in England, as Thomas Brown the Younger (London: Longman, Rees, Orme, Brown, Green & Longmans, 1835; Philadelphia: Carey, Lea & Blanchard, 1835);

The History of Ireland (41 volumes, London: Printed for Longman, Brown, Green & Longmans and John Taylor, 1835–1846; 2 volumes, Philadelphia: Lea & Blanchard, 1843, 1846);

Alciphron: A Poem (London: Macrone, 1839; Philadelphia: Carey & Hart, 1840);

The Poetical Works of Thomas Moore, Collected by Himself, 10 volumes (London: Longman, Orme, Brown, Green & Longmans, 1840–1841);

Memoirs, Journal, and Correspondence of Thomas Moore, 8 volumes, edited by Lord John Russell (London: Longman, Brown, Green & Longmans, 1853–1856);

Prose and Verse, Humorous, Satirical and Sentimental, with Suppressed Passages from the Memoirs of Lord Byron, and Including Contributions to the Edinburgh Review between 1814 and 1834, edited by R. H. Shepherd (London: Chatto & Windus, 1878; New York: Scribner, Armstrong, 1878);

Tom Moore's Diary, edited by J. B. Priestley (Cambridge: Cambridge University Press, 1925);

The Journal of Thomas Moore, 4 volumes, edited by Wilfred S. Dowden (Newark: University of Delaware Press / London & Toronto: Associated University Press, 1983–1987).

OTHER: *Odes of Anacreon,* freely translated by Moore (London: Printed for John Stockdale, 1800; Philadelphia: Printed & published by Hugh Maxwell, 1804);

Letters and Journals of Lord Byron: With Notices of His Life, 2 volumes, edited, with biography, by Moore (London: Murray, 1830; New York: Harper, 1830).

Although he came to be regarded as the national lyricist of Ireland, Thomas Moore was also a musician, novelist, satirist, historian, and the biographer of Richard Brinsley Sheridan; George Gordon, Lord Byron; and the Irish revolutionary Lord Edward Fitzgerald. He was born on 28 May 1779 in Dublin. His mother, Anastasia Codd Moore, was a devout Catholic, an ambitious woman, and had an interest in the arts. His father, John Moore, from Kerry, was a wine grocer with a quiet sense of humor and was decidedly less religiously inclined than his wife. Catholic births were not registered, owing to the power of the Protestant Anglo-Irish minority, but Moore's mother had a one-crown coin cast to commemorate the date. (The coin is in the British Museum in London.)

Most of the Irish at the time were tenant farmers, almost all of whom were Catholics forced, despite considerable hardship, to pay tithes to the Anglican church. They were not allowed to vote, to hold government offices or professional posts, or to serve on juries. There were also severe restrictions on the education of Catholics, although these re-

strictions were eased during Moore's early years. There was a strong movement aimed at establishing an independent Irish republic; such revolutionary views were given added impetus by the American and French revolutions and were in full spate by the time Moore entered his teens.

In spite of this divisive social picture, Moore had a fairly untroubled childhood. His parents were not poor, and Aungier Street, where he was born, was situated in a fairly prosperous area of Dublin and was home to several members of the Parliament. Two younger sisters completed the family (three children had died in infancy). Moore's mother encouraged him to develop his musical talents, and he soon learned to sing and to play the piano and the harpsichord.

At the age of five Moore began his formal education at the Classical English School on Aungier Street, run by Thomas S. Malone. He won a silver medal in history and a book prize before moving to the English Grammar School on Grafton Street: its headmaster, Samuel Whyte, was a famed teacher whose pupils had included Sheridan. Moore won another silver medal there, and he soon moved ahead of his fellow students in French and Italian — and ahead even of some of his teachers in Latin and Greek. Whyte had written two books on poetry and encouraged his pupils to write verse; Moore was exercising his writing talent by the age of eleven, and at fourteen he contributed to the *Anthologia Hibernica,* a Dublin periodical, the poem "To Zelia, on Her Charging the Author with Writing too Much on Love," which was followed by many others in the same publication. Whyte made a deep impression on Moore, who pays warm tribute to his teacher in his book on Sheridan.

In 1793 Catholics were allowed admission to Trinity College, Dublin; in 1794 Moore's parents sent their gifted son there, although his religion prevented him from receiving a scholarship. He was a law student, but his penchant for the classics distracted him from his main subject of study.

It was at Trinity College that Moore first gave any public indication of his politically rebellious inclinations by writing, under a pseudonym that did not fool everybody, a letter exhorting his fellow students to oppose the union with England that was about to be effected; it was published in December 1797 in the *Press,* an anti-English revolutionary newspaper. Moore's friendship with the Irish rebel Robert Emmet, who was expelled from the college, nearly got him involved with the plots of a revolutionary group known as the United Irishmen. Other pro-Irish activities, including a second outspoken article in the *Press,* almost cost him expul-

Moore, circa 1819

sion from the college, but his integrity and the support of influential friends allowed him to graduate with a B.A. in 1799.

While at Trinity he had produced a free translation of Greek imitations of Anacreon's odes, although these were regarded as Anacreon's own at the time. Moore went to London a month after his graduation, supposedly to read for the bar but actually spending his time finishing the translation. When *Odes of Anacreon* was published the following year, Moore was back in Ireland after spending three months in London.

This publication brought Moore immediate attention. He was introduced by a friend, Joseph Atkinson, to Francis Rawson-Hastings, second Earl of Moira (later the marquis of Hastings), an advocate of the Irish cause who admitted Moore to a highly select circle that included the Prince of Wales (the future King George IV); Lord John Russell, sixth Duke of Bedford; Henry Petty-Fitzmaurice, third Marquess of Lansdowne; and Lady Georgiana Spencer Cavendish, Duchess of Devonshire, all of whom became subscribers to his work. Cultured, witty, and a fine raconteur, Moore was much sought after at social gatherings; despite his short stature – he was barely five feet tall – he commanded attention wherever he went. He was considered something of a snob by some, and it was said that he dearly loved a lord. Unkind tongues suggested that it was this aspect of Moore's nature that made him decide to write a biography of Fitzgerald, a relatively minor figure.

Atkinson and Moira tried to create an Irish poet laureateship for Moore; but he declined the honor, considering himself too young and inexperienced. He was probably right in his estimation, judging by *Poetical Works of the Late Thomas Little Esq.*, which appeared in 1801. (The pseudonym "Little" may be a self-mocking reference to his height.) The poems contained a considerable amount, for their time, of sexual explicitness (Samuel Taylor Coleridge and some other prominent critics were not amused, though others were enthusiastic), which was later to embarrass the author; and although *Odes of Anacreon* was good enough to remain the standard translation throughout the nineteenth century, it showed some weaknesses, mainly in trite word collocations and occasionally hackneyed diction.

Lord Moira's sponsorship resulted in the offer of the post of admiralty registrar in Bermuda. Moore accepted, perhaps because he considered it the first step on the ladder leading to more remunerative government posts. He began his voyage on 25 September 1803, stopping for two months at Norfolk, Virginia, since there was no direct route to Bermuda. On the way, and in Bermuda, he wrote several poems about the places he saw. It was in this year that Emmet, Moore's friend since his Trinity days, was hanged for being the ringleader of an Irish rebellion. Emmet's words to his judges, "Let no man write my epitaph," are enshrined in Moore's song "Oh, breathe not his name" in the 1808 installment of his *A Selection of Irish Melodies* (1808–1834).

Moore found his bureaucratic duties tedious; after a few months he put a deputy in charge of the post and went on a tour of the United States and Canada. Niagara Falls made a deep impression on him. "We must have new combinations of language to describe the Falls of Niagara," he wrote in a 24 July 1804 letter. The social life he observed during his tour impressed him less: he found that it lacked polish compared to the society in which he had come to feel comfortable in Ireland and England.

The tour lasted nine months, after which he returned to London and to his wonted life in high society. He continued to write poetry, and in 1806 his *Epistles, Odes, and Other Poems*, dedicated to Lord Moira, was published. Like the *Poetical Works of the Late Thomas Little Esq.*, the new collection contained many of the risqué expressions and subjects of dubious morality that "society" loved. The *Edinburgh Review*, however, did not: its editor, Francis Jeffrey, gave the poems such a savage review that Moore challenged him to a duel. As they stood with pistols in hand, the police put a stop to the proceedings. The would-be combatants made peace with one another, each admitting to having gone too far. Moore, however, remained sensitive about the affair, especially since it had resulted in a good deal of public ridicule. Byron referred scathingly to the incident in his *English Bards, and Scotch Reviewers* (1809); when Moore found out who had written the anonymous poem, he wrote a furious letter to its author in which he hinted at another duel. Byron was abroad at the time and never received the letter. When he returned, much later, Moore wrote to him again, but this time in a much milder vein, and received a courteous and conciliatory reply. So no sec-

ond duel was attempted, and Byron, like Jeffrey, eventually became a close friend. When the American edition of *Epistles, Odes, and Other Poems* appeared in 1806 the writer of the preface (possibly Joseph Dennie) found some worth in the poems but went on to attack Moore's *Odes of Anacreon* at considerable length and to criticize sharply Moore's attitude to the United States.

Around this time the publisher brothers James and William Power asked Moore to write words to old Irish folk-song melodies. The opportunity suited the highly musical poet to perfection, and he poured into his verses his love of Ireland and its history. The first of the ten volumes of *A Selection of Irish Melodies* appeared in 1808, the last in 1834. Musically arranged by Moore's friend Sir John Stevenson, the songs were an instant success not just in Ireland but also in England. When the third edition appeared, James Power said in the preface that these songs "will do more . . . towards liberalizing the feelings of society, and producing that brotherhood of sentiment which it is so much our interest to cherish, than could ever be effected by the arguments of wise, but uninteresting politicians." Hoover H. Jordan says in *Bolt Upright: The Life of Thomas Moore* (1975): "Today it is almost impossible to find first editions of Moore's songs for the simple reason that the bindings gave way and the paper wore out from the constant use in thousands of homes." One of the best loved of the songs, "Tis the last rose of summer," was used by Friedrich von Flotow in his opera *Martha* (1847). The songs were translated into several languages, including Russian. Byron was enthusiastic about them; James Joyce was fascinated by the rhythms in relation to the words. In his time Moore's works were far more extensively read than those of Coleridge, William Wordsworth, John Keats, or Percy Bysshe Shelley.

While composing the Irish melodies, Moore also turned to satire; in 1808 a volume of poems in the Juvenalian style, *Corruption and Intolerance, Two Poems*, was published. The following year *The Sceptic: A Philosophical Satire* appeared. Neither book was very successful, perhaps because Moore had tried too hard to imitate the manner of Alexander Pope. Although he was a highly skilled metrist, his forte was not the heroic couplet.

Moore had gone back to Dublin toward the end of 1806. He had tried his hand at acting in theatricals when he was younger, and he belonged to a dramatic society in Kilkenny. Actresses from Dublin were hired for the performances that were put on by the group to raise money for charity; one of these actresses was Elizabeth (Bessy) Dyke, the daughter of an English dance teacher working in Cork. On 25 March 1811

THE AUTHOR OF "LALLA ROOKH"

Portrait by Daniel Maclise in the Fraser's Magazine *"Gallery of Illustrious Literary Characters" (1830–1838)*

Moore and Dyke were married at St. Martin's-in-the-Fields, London; he was thirty-two, she sixteen. The couple at first stayed in London but soon left for Kegworth, then settled in Mayfield Cottage near Ashbourne in Derbyshire. Moore had to spend a great deal of his time in London because he had agreed with his publisher to promote his songs by singing them at social gatherings. The Moores had five children: Barbara, born in 1812; Anastasia, born the following year; Olivia, who was born in 1814 and died at the age of seven months; Thomas, born in 1818; and John Russell, born in 1823.

Moore wrote a conventional "mixed-identities" comedy with songs, *M.P.; or, The Blue-Stocking* (1811); the play was a slight and trite affair, and Moore resolved never again to dabble in drama. He continued his satiric writings, chiefly aimed at the prince regent (the Prince of Wales had become prince regent in 1810), whose love for cutlets,

curaçao, and aging mistresses was mercilessly exposed, thereby provoking the wrath of Tory politicians. The satires were collected in *Intercepted Letters; or, The Two-Penny Post-Bag* (by "Thomas Brown the Younger"), which appeared in 1813 and was so popular that fourteen editions came out within a year. Around this time Moore debuted as a literary reviewer with pieces for the *Edinburgh Review* on minor poems and prose treatises.

In 1816 appeared Moore's *A Series of Sacred Songs, Duetts and Trios;* the biblical passages in the songs are liberally interspersed with Homeric ones. Complaints at the time were generally about Moore's lack of grandeur in treating such sublime subjects. Among the composers whose music was used for the songs were Joseph Haydn, Wolfgang Amadeus Mozart, and Ludwig van Beethoven. A second volume would be published in 1824. Moore studied oriental literature in preparation for his next important publication, *Lalla Rookh, An Oriental Romance* (1817), comprising four poetic tales connected by brief prose narratives. The "Fire-Worshippers," Byron's favorite tale in the book, contains semiconcealed references to the cause of the United Irishmen; and the love of Hafed and Hinda and their tragic end in the same episode were inspired by the fate of Emmet and Sarah Curran, daughter of the celebrated barrister John Philpot Curran. *Lalla Rookh* is rich in exotic imagery and descriptions of Eastern life and thought and shows Moore's command of a variety of meters; its weakness lies chiefly in its characterizations. It was reviewed favorably in most British journals, and Moore would receive a letter in which Prince Friedrich Wilhelm of Prussia said that he slept with *Lalla Rookh* under his pillow and had taken part in a court performance of the poem at the Château Royal in Berlin on the occasion of a state visit by Grand Duke Nicholas of Russia in 1821.

Later in 1817 the Moores' daughter Barbara sustained fatal injuries in a fall. The following year the Moores moved, at the urging of their friend the marquess of Lansdowne, from Hornsey to the idyllic Sloperton Cottage in the grounds of the Spye Park estate in Bromham, Wiltshire. Moore began a new song series, *A Selection of Popular National Airs,* the first installment of which was published in April 1818; later numbers appeared in 1820, 1822, 1826, and 1827. A satiric poem, *The Fudge Family in Paris,* was also published in 1818, under the pseudonym Thomas Brown the Younger; within two weeks five editions had appeared. At the end of the year Moore began work on a biography of Sheridan, who had died in 1816 and whom Moore had known, though not as a close friend, for many years.

Moore's satiric writings continued with *Tom Crib's Memorial to Congress* (1819), which, in the guise of a comparison of boxing in ancient times with the bouts of his own day, lampoons contemporary political issues; the book also discusses slang and argot, of which Moore had made a detailed study. The work was a failure; Moore was ashamed of it and refused to include it in the edition of his collected works that appeared the same year, but it is of considerable interest to linguists for its information on Regency cant.

Moore, who still retained his post in Bermuda in absentia, had appointed a new deputy, John William Goodrich, in 1810. Goodrich turned out to be an embezzler, apparently absconding with the then huge sum of six thousand pounds; that was the amount that was charged to Moore by a court decision in 1819. Moore's friends offered financial assis-

tance, but Moore was too proud to accept it. A friend advised him to leave the country for France to avoid debtor's prison. Moore departed from Dover in September 1819; he stayed in Paris for ten days before setting off for Italy with Lord John Russell as his companion. He visited Byron in Venice for four days, finding that the poet had lost what Moore called his spiritualized look.

On 11 December Moore returned to Paris; he remained in exile until November 1822, apart from a brief, furtive trip to England and Ireland with a couple of false mustaches at the ready in his suitcase. (It is because of Moore's sojourn in France that his collected works up to that time were published in Paris.) On his return to England he was able to discharge his Bermuda debt, which had been considerably reduced.

The Loves of the Angels: A Poem (1823) comprises the confessions of three seraphim expelled from heaven for loving a mortal woman; Moore's praise of womankind in this context did not go over well in religiously orthodox circles, and the reviews were unfavorable. So he turned once more to satire: *Fables for the Holy Alliance* (1823) was published under the pseudonym Moore had used for *The Fudge Family of Paris.* The eight fables boldly satirize royalty, the church, and the state; not unexpectedly, several reviews were hostile, although some praised Moore for speaking for the poor and the powerless. The following year his *Memoirs of Captain Rock, The Celebrated Irish Chieftan, With Some Account of His Ancestors* came out; the first considerable prose volume (376 pages) from Moore's hand, it deals with the oppression of the Irish by the English from the time of Pope Adrian in the twelfth century. Not being a historian, Moore was attacked for failing to appreciate the reasons for Ireland's plight.

Byron died on 19 April 1824. He had given his memoirs to Moore during Moore's visit with him in Venice; Moore had left them with the publisher John Murray against a loan of two thousand guineas to pay off his Bermuda debt. William Gifford of the *Quarterly Review* had read the memoirs and found them so distasteful that he felt sure they would ruin Byron's reputation. Murray, who had not read them, believed Gifford and burned the memoirs. Although Moore was angry, he claimed that most of the content could be found in other of Byron's writings.

Moore's biography of Sheridan had been interrupted while he was in exile, but *Memoirs of the Life of the Right Honourable Richard Brinsley Sheridan* finally appeared in 1825. It is a conscientious work, with extremely detailed documentation of the pub-

Sloperton Cottage in Wiltshire, where Moore moved in 1818

lic Sheridan; of the private person, however, the reader learns little. To those of his time Sheridan was regarded primarily as a political orator rather than as a playwright, and Moore's biography is crammed with details of political affairs and causes that are likely to overwhelm the average reader today. To a historian of the period, however, Moore offers valuable observations on the issues of his day, and he does so with honesty and fairness. Moore comes into his own when discussing Sheridan's theatrical career; he provides thorough analyses of Sheridan's plays in terms of style and structure, paying particular attention to *The School for Scandal* (1777). Whig journals gave the work good reviews, whereas those with Tory sympathies were less sympathetic; the *Quarterly Review* (March 1826) said, "When you can't talk sense, talk metaphor."

In 1826 appeared Moore's song series *Evenings in Greece: First Evening*, which was set to music by Sir Henry Bishop. This rather flaccid series is far from being one of Moore's better efforts. Much more suc-

cessful was his only novel, *The Epicurean* (1827); it was favorably reviewed, went into five editions within six months, and was soon translated into Italian, French, German, and Dutch. The book is not about Epicurean philosophy but deals with religious bigotry and its tragic results; it is partly set in Egypt. The rich imagery often interferes with the action, and once again Moore shows his weakness in characterization. The novel was followed the next year by the political satire *Odes upon Cash, Corn, Catholics, and Other Matters,* a collection of fifty-two poems, and by *Legendary Ballads,* twelve songs that deal with classical characters such as Cupid and Psyche and that are largely without merit. In 1829 Moore's daughter Anastasia died shortly before her sixteenth birthday.

In 1830 Moore's *Letters and Journals of Lord Byron: With Notices of His Life* appeared in two volumes totaling fifteen hundred pages. The writer and his subject were the two most celebrated poets of the day, and Moore knew Byron well enough to have been entrusted with his memoirs. The biogra-

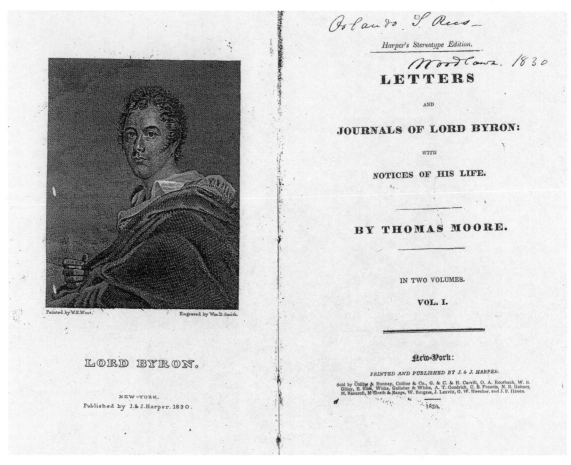

Frontispiece and title page for Moore's edition of Byron's letters and journals, which includes Moore's masterly biography of the poet

phy was a far greater work than the one he had written of Sheridan; it remains one of the finest biographies in English, and every subsequent Byron biographer has had to return to it for information on and elucidation of one of the most complex of human beings. A principal reason for its success is its language: Moore wisely avoided his customary florid, decorative style. In this biography, which was obviously a labor of love, Byron comes vividly to life. Any vanity on the part of the author is absent, partly because Moore lets Byron speak for himself to a large extent through his letters and journals. A modern biographer, Howard Mumford Jones, says that because Moore did not "do" Byron as he had "done" Sheridan, "the result was the one book by which Moore really lives today."

Moore was, however, faced with questions of morality that were considerably more sensitive then than they are now. He destroyed Byron's letters after he had used them and omitted any material having to do with Byron's homosexual tendencies or his incestuous relationship with his half sister, Augusta Leigh. Had he included such material

the book would have been suppressed; but even if such had not been the case, it is doubtful whether Moore would have revealed such aspects of Byron's nature. Although not regarded as a prude by his contemporaries – rather, indeed, the opposite – Moore thought, and had told Byron, that *Don Juan* (1819–1823) was unfit for publication. However much one may regret Moore's suppressions, they are understandable. It is harder to condone Moore's editorial procedure: he sometimes transferred sections of one letter to another, omitted passages referring to people still alive, and occasionally merged two letters into one. But today's editorial standards are much more rigorous than those of Moore's time. The *British Critic, Fraser's,* and especially the *Westminster Review* were hostile, mainly to what they considered profane, licentious, and immoral in Byron's letters; the *Athenaeum,* the *Monthly Review,* and the *Quarterly Review* praised the style and Moore's fairness. Thomas Babington Macaulay, one of the greatest writers of English prose, provided the most positive review in the *Edinburgh Review* (June 1831):

We have read this book with the greatest pleasure. Considered merely as composition, it deserves to be classed among the best specimens of English prose which our age has produced. It contains, indeed, no single passage equal to two or three, which we could select from the Life of Sheridan. But, as a whole, it is immeasurably superior to that. The style is agreeable, clear, and manly; and, when it rises into eloquence, rises without effort or ostentation. Nor is the matter inferior to the manner.

It would be difficult to name a book which exhibits more of kindness, fairness, and modesty. It has evidently been written, not for the purpose of showing, what, however, it often shows, how well its author can write; but for the purpose of vindicating, as far as truth will permit, the memory of a celebrated man who can no longer vindicate himself. Mr. Moore never thrusts himself between Lord Byron and the public. With the strongest temptations to egotism, he has said no more about himself than the subject absolutely required .... When we consider the life which Lord Byron had led, his petulance, his irritability, and his communicativeness, we cannot but admire the dexterity with which Mr. Moore has contrived to exhibit so much of the character and opinions of his friend, with so little pain to the feelings of the living.

The Irish question still occupied Moore, and he had hardly written the last words of his Byron biography when he addressed himself to a biography of the Irish revolutionary leader Fitzgerald. Moore's advocacy of the Irish cause had made him immensely popular with the Irish, especially in Dublin, where he attended, in September 1830, a huge gathering to celebrate the French Revolution. Although Moore was not one of the scheduled speakers, he was forced to speak by the crowd. Uncharacteristically, he was suddenly at a loss for words; but an incident indicative of Moore's sense of humor and quickness of mind defused the tension: a dog began to bark loudly, and Moore responded: "Never mind, it is only the member for *Bark*shire."

The Life and Death of Lord Edward Fitzgerald was published in 1831. As in the Byron biography Moore uses his subject's letters combined with eyewitness accounts, and his prose remains clear and vivid. Moore's politically rebellious nature had softened; in the preface he pleads for a settlement to the Irish question that is not based on violence, and in the last chapter he says, with typical eloquence: "Of the right of the oppressed to resist, few, in these days, would venture to express a doubt. . . . To be able to fix, however, with any precision, the point at which obedience may cease, and resistance to the undue stretches of authority begin, is a difficulty which must for ever leave vague and undirected the application of the principle."

The book will be hard to read for those not intimately acquainted with both Irish and English history, and it would not be inappropriate to say that the work is as much a political history as a biography. Moore does not give a clear picture of Fitzgerald's career, and the book received only lukewarm reviews. It remains, however, the standard life of Fitzgerald.

In 1832 Moore was asked to stand for Parliament for Limerick, but although he had been told that his election would be a certainty, he declined. His next work, *Travels of An Irish Gentleman in Search of a Religion*, was published in two volumes in 1833. A work on religious controversy from the beginning of the Christian era, it is divided into two parts: one devoted to Catholicism and the other to Protestantism. In the latter part Moore reprehends the Protestants for their attacks on Catholicism and takes issue with German rationalism, which he saw as a threat to religion. The often lively narrative is occasionally weighted down by a too-heavy-handed scholarly manner; the work was not extensively reviewed.

The final volume of *A Selection of Irish Melodies* appeared in 1834. In 1835 the first volume of *The History of Ireland* appeared. It was to grow into three further volumes (twelve hundred pages in all), published in 1837, 1840, and 1846 and impressively spanning the period from the first records to the seventeenth century although, because of his lack of Gaelic, Moore's faulty knowledge of the early epochs in Irish history mars his work. Moore may not have been a professional historian, but he does display a healthy skepticism with little prejudice. His prose, with few embellishments, is suitable for a work of this kind. *The History of Ireland* was translated into several European languages and went through three editions in Germany within two years. The *News* (24 July 1836) said that Moore's work gave dignity to being Irish, and the *Spectator* (20 May 1837) thought that for an Irishman Moore was surprisingly impartial. The *Christian Examiner* (1836), on the other hand, used the first volume as a justification for English rule. Jones remarks that "It is probable that no living person has read through this dull work." The Reverend Mortimer O'Sullivan had not been amused by Moore's *Travels of an Irish Gentleman* and had replied to it with the utmost gravity in his *A Guide to an Irish Gentleman in His Search for a Religion* (1833). Moore got revenge in *The Fudges in England* (1835) by turning him into a character named O'Mulligan who is enamored of the

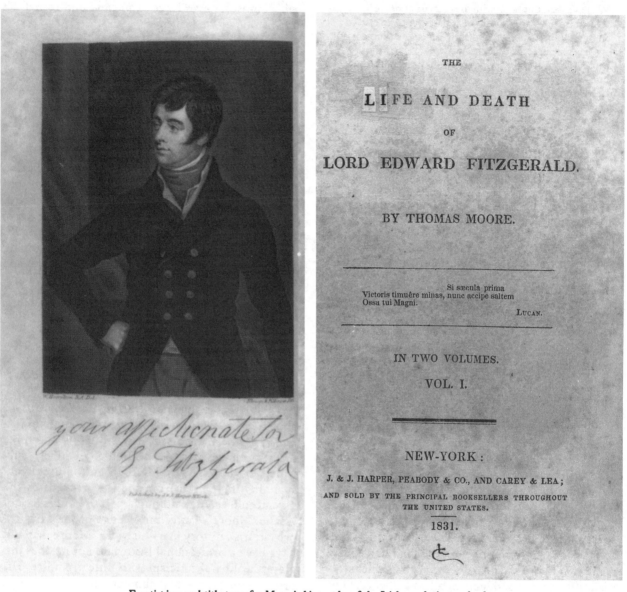

THE

LIFE AND DEATH

OF

LORD EDWARD FITZGERALD.

BY THOMAS MOORE.

Si sæcula prima
Victoris timuêre minas, nunc accipe saltem
Ossa tui Magni.

LUCAN.

IN TWO VOLUMES.

VOL. I.

NEW-YORK:

J. & J. HARPER, PEABODY & CO., AND CAREY & LEA;

AND SOLD BY THE PRINCIPAL BOOKSELLERS THROUGHOUT
THE UNITED STATES.

1831.

Frontispiece and title page for Moore's biography of the Irish revolutionary leader

silly Biddy Fudge. This sequel does not have the sparkle of its predecessor.

In 1839 Moore's novel *The Epicurean* came out in a new edition with illustrations by J. M. W. Turner and with the addition of *Alciphron,* a fragmentary poem from which the novel had originally evolved; *Alciphron* was published separately the same year. *The Poetical Works of Thomas Moore, Collected by Himself* appeared in 1840–1841; each of the ten volumes is prefaced by an autobiographical account. A year later Moore's son John died of tuberculosis; and in March 1846 his last child, Thomas, died in Algeria, where he was serving in the French Foreign Legion.

Moore's memory began to fail, and by 1850 senile dementia had set in. He died on 25 February 1852 and was buried in Bromham Churchyard. Moore's friend Russell, who was then foreign secretary, edited the writer's memoirs; he drew extensively on diaries that Moore had kept until 1845. *Memoirs, Journal, and Correspondence of Thomas Moore,* published in eight volumes from 1853 to 1856, includes an autobiography that stops at 1799, the journal, and about four hundred letters. Although the journal contains some intimately personal entries, such as that describing the death of his daughter Anastasia, Moore tends to avoid self-revelation — no doubt because he expected posthumous publication of his diaries.

Moore, Byron, and Sir Walter Scott were the most celebrated writers of their day. Moore's poetry

Statue of Moore by Christopher Moore in College Green, Dublin

was exceedingly popular, and he was one of the last poets to capture the reading public that was soon to turn to novels. According to modern standards, Moore frequently lacks depth; the density of his imagery too often does not reflect a proportionate profundity of thought or emotion, and posterity has come out in favor of Romantic poets such as Wordsworth, Coleridge, Shelley, and Keats, all of whom commanded much less attention during the first half of the nineteenth century. To the modern reader Moore's masterpiece remains his biography of Byron.

Letters:

Memoirs, Journal, and Correspondence of Thomas Moore, 8 volumes, edited by Lord John Russell (London: Longman, Brown, Green & Longmans, 1853–1856);

Notes from the Letters of T. Moore to His Music Publisher, J. Power, edited by T. C. Croker (New York: Redfield, 1854);

"Moore to Hobhouse: An Unpublished Letter," edited by Bradford A. Booth, in *Modern Language Notes,* 55 (1940): 42–45;

The Letters of Thomas Moore, 2 volumes, edited by Wilfred S. Dowden (Oxford: Clarendon Press, 1964).

Bibliography:

M. J. MacManus, "A Bibliography of Thomas Moore," *Dublin Magazine,* 8 (1833): 55–61.

Biographies:

H. R. Montgomery, *Thomas Moore, His Life, Writings, and Contemporaries* (London: Newby, 1860);

Andrew J. Symington, *Thomas Moore the Poet: His Life and Works* (New York: Harper, 1880);

Stephen L. Gwynn, *Thomas Moore* (London: Macmillan, 1905);

Seamus MacCall, *Thomas Moore* (Dublin: Talbot, 1935);

Howard Mumford Jones, *The Harp That Once — A Chronicle of the Life of Thomas Moore* (New York: Holt, 1937);

L. A. G. Strong, *The Minstrel Boy: A Portrait of Tom Moore* (New York: Knopf, 1937);

Hoover H. Jordan, *Bolt Upright: The Life of Thomas Moore,* 2 volumes, Salzburg Studies in English

Literature, no. 38 (Salzburg: Institut für Englische Sprache und Literatur, 1975);

Terence de Vere White, *Tom Moore The Irish Poet* (London: Hamilton, 1977).

References:

Daniel Ambrose, "Thomas Moore: The Religion in Which He Died," *Irish Ecclesiastical Record,* 15 (1895): 18–26;

William Bates, *The Maclise Portrait-Gallery of Illustrious Literary Characters, with Memoirs* (London: Chatto & Windus, 1898), pp. 22–30;

Howard O. Brogan, "Thomas Moore, Irish Satirist and Keeper of the English Conscience," *Philological Quarterly,* 24 (July 1945): 255–275;

Wallace C. Brown, "Thomas Moore and English Interest in the East," *Studies in Philology,* 34 (1937): 576–588;

James Burke, *Memoir of Thomas Moore* (Dublin: Duffy, 1852);

J. C. L. Clark, *Tom Moore in Bermuda* (Boston: Smith, McCanse, 1909);

Miriam Allen DeFord, *Thomas Moore* (New York: Twayne, 1967);

Wilfred S. Dowden, " 'Let Erin Remember': A Re-Examination of the Journal of Thomas Moore," *Rice University Studies,* 61 (Winter 1975): 39–50;

William Dumbleton, "Angels, Women, and Thomas Moore," *Eire,* 19, no. 1 (1977): 52–66;

Herbert G. Eldridge, "The American Republication of Thomas Moore's *Epistles, Odes, and Other Poems:* An Early Version of the Reprinting 'Game,' " *Papers of the Bibliographical Society of America,* 62 (1968): 199–205;

Eldridge, "Anacreon Moore and America," *PMLA,* 83 (March 1968): 54–62;

Paula R. Feldman, "Mary Shelley and the Genesis of Moore's *Life* of Byron," *Studies in English Literature,* 20 (Autumn 1980): 611–620;

John Hennig, "Thomas Moore as Theologian," *Irish Monthly,* 75 (1947): 114–123;

Hennig, "Thomas Moore and the Holy Alliance," *Irish Monthly,* 74 (1946): 282–294;

Raymond Mortimer, "Thomas Moore," *London Mercury,* 5 (1922): 476–486;

Patrick Murray, *The Poetical Genius of Thomas Moore* (Cork: Mulcahy, 1856);

J. A. Strahan, "Byron's Biographer," *Blackwood's Edinburgh Magazine,* 215 (1924): 574–582;

Allen B. Thomas, *Moore en France* (Paris: Champion, 1911);

W. F. Trench, *Tom Moore: A Lecture* (Dublin: At the Sign of the Three Candles, 1934);

W. P. Trent, "Paradise and the Peri," *Year Book,* 9 (Boston: Bibliophile Society, 1910): 109–127.

Papers:

Thomas Moore's letters are in collections throughout Britain and the United States, and a few can be found in Scandinavia. The most important collections are in the British Library; the University of Edinburgh; the National Libraries of Ireland and Scotland; the John Rylands Library, Manchester; Trinity College, Dublin; the Victoria and Albert Museum, London; the Firestone Library, Princeton University; the Quaker Collection, Haverford College; the Widener and Houghton Libraries, Harvard University; the Sterling Memorial Library, Yale University; the Clements Library, University of Michigan; the New York Public Library; the Historical Societies of Maine and Pennsylvania; Lund University, Sweden; Bergen University, Norway; and the National Library of Denmark, Copenhagen. Moore's journals are in the manuscript and rare-book room of the London publishing firm Longman Group Limited.

John Morley

(24 December 1838 – 23 September 1923)

David Hopkinson

See also the Morley entry in *DLB 57: Victorian Prose Writers After 1867.*

BOOKS: *Modern Characteristics,* anonymous (London: Tinsley, 1865);

Studies in Conduct, anonymous (London: Chapman & Hall, 1867);

Edmund Burke: A Historical Study (London: Macmillan, 1867; New York: Knopf, 1924);

Critical Miscellanies, 4 series (volumes 1–2, London: Chapman & Hall, 1871, 1877; volume 1 republished, New York: Scribner & Welford, 1879; volumes 1–2 revised and republished with volume 3, London & New York: Macmillan, 1886; volume 4, London & New York: Macmillan, 1908); volume 4 also published as *Miscellanies Fourth Series* (London: Macmillan, 1908);

Voltaire (London: Chapman & Hall, 1872; revised, 1872; New York: Appleton, 1872);

Rousseau, 2 volumes (London: Chapman & Hall, 1873; New York: Scribner & Welford, 1878);

The Struggle for National Education (London: Chapman & Hall, 1873);

On Compromise (London: Chapman & Hall, 1874; London & New York: Macmillan, 1903);

Diderot and the Encyclopaedists (2 volumes, London: Chapman & Hall, 1878; 1 volume, New York: Scribner & Welford, 1878);

Burke (London: Macmillan, 1879; New York: Harper, 1879);

Life of Richard Cobden (2 volumes, London: Chapman & Hall, 1881; 1 volume, Boston: Roberts Brothers, 1881);

Ralph Waldo Emerson: An Essay (New York: Macmillan, 1884);

Walpole (London & New York: Macmillan, 1889);

Studies in Literature (London & New York: Macmillan, 1891);

Machiavelli: The Romanes Lectures Delivered in the Sheldonian Theatre, June 2, 1897 (London: Macmillan / New York: Macmillan, 1897);

Oliver Cromwell (London: Macmillan, 1900; New York: Century, 1900);

The Life of William Ewart Gladstone, 3 volumes (New York & London: Macmillan, 1903);

Literary Essays (London: Humphreys, 1906);

Speeches on Indian Affairs (Madras: Natesan, 1908; revised and enlarged, 1917);

Indian Speeches (London: Macmillan, 1909);

Science and Literature (Oxford: Privately printed, 1911);

Notes on Politics and History (London: Macmillan, 1913; New York: Macmillan, 1914);

Recollections, 2 volumes (London: Macmillan, 1917; New York: Macmillan, 1917);

Memorandum on Resignation, August 1914 (London: Macmillan, 1928; New York: Macmillan, 1928).

Editions and collection: *The Life of William Ewart Gladstone,* 2 volumes (London: Macmillan, 1905, 1907; London & New York: Macmillan, 1905, 1911);

The Works of Lord Morley (15 volumes, London: Macmillan, 1921; revised, 12 volumes, London: Macmillan, 1923);

The Life of Gladstone: Popular Edition, Abridged (London: Hodder & Stoughton, 1927).

John Morley had two distinguished careers — first, as a journalist, editor, biographer, and critic, and second, as a politician. In his first role he is now best known as the writer of a monumental life of William Ewart Gladstone (1903), but he was also the author of other biographies and biographical essays. As a politician he was elected to Parliament as a Liberal and held ministerial office as chief secretary for Ireland and later as secretary of state for India. He was the recipient of many honors, including a peerage and the Order of Merit, initiated in 1902 by Edward VII as the most exclusive of all civilian honors.

Morley was born on 24 December 1838 to Jonathan and Priscilla Donkin Morley in Blackburn, a Lancashire town where the early stages of industrialization had produced poverty and unrest. Morley's father was a surgeon and had a love of books. Morley received a sound classical education at

John Morley

Hoole's Academy, University College School, and Cheltenham College, and he won a scholarship to Lincoln College, Oxford, in 1856. Later he came to regard the influence of an older, more sophisticated fellow student, J. Cotter Morison, as more potent than that of his tutors in extending his intellectual horizons. The new ideas acquired at Oxford provoked a quarrel with his father, who cut off his allowance; this action forced Morley to leave the university with an ordinary degree at the end of his third year. The difference between father and son arose from Morley's religious doubts and consequent determination not to study for the church. What Oxford did for Morley's thought is summed up in the first chapter of his *Recollections* (1917): "traditional thought, devotion, dogma, were brought from their place of inaccessible constellations in the spacious firmament on high, down into the rationalist arena of earth."

Though he found that he had no liking and little aptitude for teaching, Morley earned his living and improved his knowledge of French literature by some months of tutoring in Paris. Returning to En-

gland, he began to read for the bar in London while supporting himself through journalism. His long review articles, chiefly on historical subjects, which often extended over two or more numbers of the journals to which he contributed, were published anonymously, as was then the custom. In his own estimation the two most formative influences at this stage of his life were those of the novelist and poet George Meredith, whom he met in 1863, and the liberal philosopher John Stuart Mill, whose *On Liberty* (1859) he had read at Oxford and whom he met in 1865. "It would be hard," he writes in *Recollections,* "to imagine finer personal inspiration for a beginner with a strong feel for letters in their broadest sense — letters in terms of life and in relation to life — than was Meredith in his early prime." Morley was already a voracious reader, but Meredith's inspiration served to give "new life, inner meaning, vivacity, surprise, to lessons from wholesome books and teachers and to inspire a heartening cataract of freshness on them all." *Austere* is an adjective that was frequently applied to Morley, but in early and middle life he responded to nature with an enthusiasm inspired by Meredith. He regarded Mill as a prime source of wisdom and a beacon of virtue. For many years Morley lived and wrote under the shadow of Mill; while Meredith lured him toward fresh horizons, Morley held himself firmly attached to the ideals and beliefs of the liberal Enlightenment that Mill, together with Ralph Waldo Emerson and John Ruskin, carried a stage further as the nineteenth century proceeded.

After writing for the *Saturday Review* for three years, in late 1866 Morley succeeded George Henry Lewes as editor of the *Fortnightly Review,* which had been started by Morison, Anthony Trollope, and Frederick Chapman the previous year. Thus began Morley's great period of success as an editor and essayist; his authority in the world of literature and ideas was to flourish for the next twenty years as he built up a circle of talented contributors. Morley believed that his mission as editor was to combat prejudice and to assist in modernizing the opinions of educated people. Controversy on all important subjects should become earnest and direct; in serious journalism the practice of anonymity should be abandoned, as it had been in the *Fortnightly Review* under Lewes. Morley's agnosticism became firmly established in this period. He was attracted by the ideas of Auguste Comte, but he did not adopt Comte's positivism as a creed despite the enthusiasm of his friend and associate editor, Frederic Harrison; he attributed his resistance to positivism to the influence of Mill and the scientific rationalism of Thomas Henry Huxley, whose article "The Physical Basis of Life" he published in February 1869. Natural science and political philosophy were prominent in the pages of the *Fortnightly Review,* but in his own writing Morley was more concerned with the quest for a science of history and a theory of ethics that could be supported by history. He defended Mill's modified utilitarianism against William Edward Hartpole Lecky's beliefs and his own moderately determinist view of history against James Anthony Froude's satirical realism, in which no faith in any principle could be discerned. According to Morley, while no fixed law of retribution for evil could be found in history, there was much evidence that certain results have always followed on identifiable causes or conditions.

In old age Morley asserted that he had always written slowly, but his output was so extensive that this claim is difficult to accept. Certainly he never wrote carelessly, but always with solidity and a well-balanced breadth of vision. He had a flair for choosing provocative themes and writers. His first book to be published under his name (two earlier ones were published anonymously) was a short study of the eighteenth-century statesman and essayist Edmund Burke (1867); not a biography but a criticism of his subject's contribution to the issues of his time, most of it had already appeared in the *Fortnightly Review.* Burke is held to be the precursor of "the modern spirit" that was destined to govern the best minds in Britain and America. Though Burke lacked democratic fervor, his strength lay in his sense of realism and in the nobility of his style.

Morley's main writings in the 1870s took the form of biographical essays and full-scale biographies dealing with leaders of thought whom he judged to have inspired the modern spirit. As he says in *Recollections,* "I tried to do justice to truths presented and services rendered by men in various schools with whom in important respects I could not in the least bring myself to agree." It struck Morley that the ideas of French writers had been surprisingly neglected by radical activists in England, where Voltaire and Jean-Jacques Rousseau, in particular, were still regarded as disreputable. The time seemed to have arrived for rationalism and natural science to "blow defiant bugles" against outworn traditions. Morley and his two principal friends, Harrison and Leslie Stephen, devoted themselves with youthful zest to emerging as prophets of liberalism, radiating a confidence that, when freed from superstition, humanity and society could be improved.

In the *Fortnightly Review* during 1870 Morley published his own essays on Marie-Jean-Antoine-Nicolas de Caritat, Marquis de Condorcet, in the January and February numbers; on Luc de Clapiers de Vauvenargues in April; and on Anne-Robert Jacques Turgot in August. In each case he lays emphasis on the debt owed to these men by socially committed intellectuals of the nineteenth century. Turgot had a particular appeal for Morley because he undertook important political responsibilities as well as being a philosopher.

During the 1870s Morley also wrote three full-length biographies of French thinkers: *Voltaire* (1872), *Rousseau* (1873), and *Diderot and the Encyclopaedists* (1878). Their lively, enthusiastic, at times rather rhetorical style pleased the taste of contemporary readers, but today these biographies are almost forgotten. Morley finds much to disapprove of in his subjects — for example, Voltaire's irreverence and Rousseau's indecency and moral failings — but his purpose is to understand, not to condemn. He was unable to resolve the contradictions in Rousseau's personality, such as the combination of courage and cowardice he displayed. "Pity is the right mind in which to think of the miserable wretch" was his revealing outburst in a let-

Sir John Gladstone
from a painting by William Bradley.

THE LIFE OF

WILLIAM EWART

GLADSTONE

BY

JOHN MORLEY

IN THREE VOLUMES — VOL. I
(1809–1859)

New York
THE MACMILLAN COMPANY
LONDON: MACMILLAN & CO., LTD.
1903

All rights reserved

Frontispiece and title page for Morley's biography of the prime minister in whose government he served

ter to Harrison. Nevertheless, he judged Rousseau to be one of the most daring, original thinkers of his age, who exposed ancient errors and prejudice in every aspect of life.

On 16 June 1871 Morley wrote to Harrison, "I was seized, after the manner of poets, with a phrenetic and wholly invincible oestus — to write a monograph — VOLTAIRE. Everything else has vanished from my mind. Night and day I am possessed with him, and I stick to my table like a slave. What a subject!!!" The critics praised *Voltaire* when it appeared in 1872; in the opinion of Morley's friend and biographer, F. W. Hirst, it was "perhaps the most finished of his masterpieces." In *Recollections* all he has to say about the book is that it was a summary and amounted to little more than "a suggestion for people with unfounded pretensions to literary education that he was a writer on whom they ought to leave a card." The book, though well received in its day, has not subsequently been highly valued. Its anticlericalism is

not shocking in itself, but its mocking tone seems misplaced, even offensive.

With the passage of time Morley moderated the polemical tone of his writing. Increasingly he adopted the stance of a teacher, aiming rather to inform than to denounce. He came to recognize that in *Rousseau* his argumentative tone had carried him far from the detached standpoint of the historian that he had intended to adopt, and when it was republished in his collected works (1921), he cut the book severely. In his book on Denis Diderot and the *encyclopédistes* he trimmed his style, on Meredith's advice, and avoided the temptation to plead a case. It was enough to outline the wide-ranging account to be found in the *Encyclopédie* (1751–1780) of the scientific and social ideas of the eighteenth century and that century's faith that the world could be made a better place, that the evil in it was the fruit of bad institutions and general ignorance, and that it was possible to achieve reform.

In politics Morley worked with Joseph Chamberlain and a group of other radicals opposed to the Education Bill that Gladstone's government had introduced: in the new system of elementary education that was to be instituted, a place was to be retained for state aid to church schools. Morley, Chamberlain, and their allies demanded that schools be purely secular and that admission be free for all. Morley argued this point in *The Struggle for National Education* (1873), in which Gladstone is heavily criticized.

Morley had married Rose Mary Ayling in May 1870; when she fell ill, they moved, on medical advice, closer to London from a home in the country near Guildford, Surrey, that had happy associations for them. Mill's death in Avignon, France, on 7 May 1873 was a severe blow, especially as it followed closely on a visit to the Morleys when the two friends had, as Morley says in *Reflections,* "sauntered aimlessly together for nearly four hours, talking and botanising." The posthumous publication of Mill's essay "Theism" (1874) distressed Morley because its author appeared to relax his own rules of reasoning to achieve a compromise with orthodoxy. The essay wrung from Morley a critical review in the *Fortnightly Review* and an essay of his own, *On Compromise* (1874), a plea for courage and independent judgment and a polemic against unthinking acceptance of orthodoxy. The essence of Morley is to be found in this short book. Its influence on the younger generation of Liberal leaders could be ranked with that of Ruskin's *Unto This Last* (1860) and Matthew Arnold's *Culture and Anarchy* (1869). Herbert Henry Asquith, who was to become prime minister, paid tribute to the formative influence of the book; Edward Grey, Asquith's foreign secretary, did the same. Herbert Samuel, who became home secretary in 1917 and later led the Liberal party, wrote in his *Memoirs* (1945), "If I was asked to name one book which had affected my life more than any other I should choose John Morley – *On Compromise.*"

Morley's *Burke* (1879) is still seen as a just estimate of one who was a major influence on the development of parliamentary democracy. In Burke, Morley looked up to a man of genius who taught his own and subsequent generations how to think about politics, the very thing that Morley himself was attempting. Like Burke, Morley worked his way into an honored position in the political world of his day, but he lacked Burke's exceptional literary and oratorical gifts; he was thus denied the power to erect any landmark in the field of political thought comparable to the achievements of Burke.

Of all the midcentury radicals, Richard Cobden was the one whose achievements in politics seemed to Morley the clearest reflection of Mill's ideas. Cobden, who had died in 1865, had done more than anyone else to promote free trade. Morley's two-volume *Life of Richard Cobden* (1881) and his even-more-voluminous life of Gladstone were his most important political biographies. In Cobden he was focusing on a politician of whose entire life he could express unqualified approval, which was not to be the case with Gladstone. Also, as compared with Gladstone, Cobden's greater simplicity of mind and more restricted range of activity reduced the biographer's problems. Morley's book was well received, but his enthusiasm for his subject seems to have required the introduction of excessive detail. Modern historians, while giving credit to Cobden for the success of his Anti–Corn Law League in the early 1840s, have tended to regard him as achieving no more than a slight reduction in the supremacy of the aristocratic social elite in British politics.

In 1880 Morley accepted the editorship of a daily newspaper, the *Pall Mall Gazette*. This position afforded him enlarged influence within the Liberal party. He resigned from the *Fortnightly Review* in 1882. He had attempted to win a seat in Parliament in 1869 and 1880, and in 1883 he was elected as a member for Newcastle upon Tyne. That year he resigned from the editorship of the *Pall Mall Gazette* and assumed that of *Macmillan's Magazine.* He had served less than three years in the House of Commons when, in January 1886, Gladstone brought him into the government as chief secretary for Ireland. Gladstone's call for Ireland to have a parliament of its own in Dublin split the Liberal party; when the Irish Home Rule Bill was presented to Parliament in June 1886, Morley was at the prime minister's side while other radicals, such as Chamberlain, John Bright, and George Otto Trevelyan, deserted Gladstone. The bill was defeated. The Liberal government fell in July, and Robert Cecil, third Marquis of Salisbury, then presided over six years of Conservative rule with the support of those Liberals who had opposed Gladstone's Irish policy.

Out of the government but still in Parliament, Morley had time to resume his literary work. He had been associated since the 1860s with the publisher Macmillan as literary adviser and as editor from 1883 to 1885 of *Macmillan's Magazine,* and in 1877 he had created the successful English Men of Letters series, which he edited and to which he and many of his friends contributed (his 1879 book on Burke was written for the series). He acted as adviser for a second English Men of Letters series and prepared a study of the eighteenth-century prime minister Sir Robert Walpole for a new series, Twelve British Statesmen, which he also edited. The lucid, well-balanced, and unpretentiously straightforward *Walpole* (1889) shows Morley at his wise and patient best. In little more than two hundred pages he steers a course through the many political and diplomatic complications of Walpole's long tenure in office. Walpole had his faults, but Morley is with Burke in his contention that they were superficial. He defends Walpole as a pragmatic politician, cool and tenacious, who did good service to his country and to Europe.

A sensational divorce case in which Charles Stewart Parnell, the leader of the Irish members, was involved contributed to Gladstone's resignation as leader of the divided Liberal party; but by general acclamation he became prime minister for a fourth term in 1892. Morley returned to the post of chief secretary for Ireland and held it until the defeat of the government in 1895.

In a lecture delivered at Oxford in June 1897 Morley discussed Niccolò Machiavelli's supreme secular state, with policies based on self-interest and with force as its chief means of realizing them. Published later the same year, the speech attracted much attention at home and abroad. It asserted its author's central belief that political questions must be approached with moral principles in mind.

The genesis of Morley's next biography seems to have occurred when a proposal for the erection of a statue of Oliver Cromwell in the precincts of Parliament was introduced by the Liberal government. The Irish members were incensed; the Conservatives greeted the proposal with satirical gibes, demanding to know whether Cromwell was to be honored as a regicide, an imperialist, or the armed destroyer of the House of Commons. It fell to Morley to withdraw the motion, to the disgust of many English Liberals.

Morley's *Oliver Cromwell* (1900) may also have been the outcome of the intense thought he had been giving to the intractable Anglo-Irish problem. He also alludes in *Recollections* to the militaristic imperialism that was invading both the main parties in British politics, with Cromwell seen "as a name on an Imperialist flag." Perhaps, too, he remembered a student debate at Oxford in 1858 in which he had proposed that the execution of Charles I was a necessary step for the preservation of liberty; only three votes had supported him. His opinion of the regicides was no longer enthusiastic, but, as with Voltaire and Rousseau, Morley was fascinated by

men who in his judgment had contributed to human progress. It may have appeared unlikely that a rationalist and an agnostic should achieve insight into the character of a man spurred to action by his Calvinistic faith, but Morley's portrait of Cromwell is lifelike, sympathetic, and judicious. Morley regarded Thomas Carlyle's hyperbole in defense of Cromwell not merely as nonsense but as repulsive nonsense. Cromwell's revolution seemed to Morley to signal the end of the medieval era rather than the beginning of the modern era, for the latter was inspired by a faith in human progress that was lacking in Cromwell. Cromwell's conviction that God would provide and that only the godly elect knew what was good for the people and how to procure it had nothing to offer the modern democrat. The voluminous researches of an immensely industrious historian, Samuel Gardiner, were available to Morley, but in the same year that his book appeared a life of Cromwell by an Oxford professor, Sir Charles Harding Firth, was published; it, rather than Morley's biography, became the accepted authority for a considerable time.

Soon after Gladstone's death in 1898 his family proposed that Morley write the official biography. His qualifications were obvious: he had enjoyed close friendship with Gladstone and his family for years and had been the great man's most loyal associate in government. He had to deal with vast quantities of documentary evidence: in his own estimate Gladstone's private papers comprised between two and three hundred thousand items and forty volumes of diaries. He had the assistance of Hirst, but when the diaries were eventually published, misquotations, misdatings, and even amendments to Gladstone's sentences were discovered in Morley's biography. But in 1903, when *The Life of William Ewart Gladstone* was published, Morley was held to have triumphed. One hundred thousand copies of the original three-volume edition were sold before it went out of print in 1942; a two-volume edition in small print, published in 1905 and 1907, strained the eyes of history students for the next half century; a popular abridged edition with illustrations was published in 1927 (even that ran to 559 pages). Morley includes long passages from Gladstone's letters and speeches, but while the great man's power over an audience was unrivaled, on paper his orotund style and remorseless flow of words make for heavy going; his verbiage is often obscure. Morley wanted the reading public to know not only what Gladstone had done for his country but also what kind of a man he was, what sort of inner life he lived. In the early pages of his work

Morley makes it clear that religion was his subject's central motivating force, but, because Gladstone's family had asked him to steer clear of Gladstone's religious life, he was unable to isolate and identify the operation of this element in the great decisions of Gladstone's career. Some of what he might have said on this theme had been spoken, before the biography was completed, at the unveiling of Gladstone's statue in Manchester: "The thought with which he rose in the morning and went to rest at night was of the universe as a supreme moral theatre, in which an omnipotent Dramaturgist uses kingdoms and rulers, laws and policies, to exhibit sovereign purposes for good. This was the thought that lighted up the prose of politics with a ray from the diviner mind, and exalted his ephemeral discourse into a sort of visible relation with the counsels of all time." In Morley's book it is rarely apparent that Gladstone was ruled by the sense that a mystical authority was calling on him to serve humanity. As a young man he had joined with a small group of friends, all on the threshold of professional or political careers, in a vow of service to those who were in distress through weakness or poverty. This vow led him into the strangest and bravest of all his undertakings – a personal campaign for the rescue and redemption of London prostitutes, which he carried on for many years. Morley makes scant and, in fact, misleading reference to this activity; in dealing with such matters Morley was not a man to take risks with the conventions of his time, nor could he grasp the depth of conviction that inspired Gladstone.

When writing *Life of Richard Cobden* Morley had expressed doubts about introducing into a political biography anything of his subject's private life; he could only justify a small step in that direction by referring to the malicious gossip about Cobden that had been in circulation. In Gladstone's case the work suffers from the neglect of this side of his life. Little attention is paid to his childlike love of his spirited, sometimes eccentric, but always devoted wife. Morley's own childlessness may explain why he failed to capture Gladstone's relationship with his children, particularly his eldest son, who predeceased him, and his two younger daughters, one so weak and one so strong. To cut Gladstone off from his religion and his attachment to his family is to miss the deeper sources of his endurance.

After the Liberal electoral triumph of 1906 Morley may have hoped to become Chancellor of the Exchequer, but he was content to accept office as secretary of state for India. The reforms he initiated were first steps toward establishing Indian participation at the highest level in the government of India. In 1908 he was made Viscount Morley of Blackburn. He resigned as secretary of state in 1910 but stayed in the cabinet and, being then in the House of Lords, took the lead in arguing the government's case for the reduction of the Lords' legislative powers. In 1914 he resigned from the cabinet rather than serve in a government that was leading the country into war. He died on 23 September 1923.

Morley's principal aims as a writer were to seek out the truth and point out the lessons to be learned from great writers, thinkers, and statesmen. Eloquence came naturally to him; he heeded advice to simplify his style but was not fearful of fine writing when the occasion for it arose. As a statesman, a writer, and a man of conscience, Morley is representative of many of his age's best qualities.

Biographies:

Saiyad Sadar Ali Khan, *The Life of Lord Morley* (London: Pitman, 1923);

F. W. Hirst, *Early Life and Letters of John Morley,* 2 volumes (London: Macmillan, 1927).

References:

Edward Alexander, *John Morley* (New York: Twayne, 1972);

Edwin M. Everett, *The Party of Humanity* (Chapel Hill: University of North Carolina Press, 1939);

John Gross, *The Rise and Fall of the Man of Letters* (London: Weidenfeld & Nicolson, 1969), pp. 99–112;

D. A. Hamer, *John Morley: Liberal Intellectual in Politics* (Oxford: Clarendon Press, 1968);

Frances W. Knickerbocker, *Free Minds: John Morley and His Friends* (Cambridge: Harvard University Press, 1943);

John Hartman Morgan, *John, Viscount Morley: An Appreciation and Some Reminiscences* (Boston & New York: Houghton Mifflin, 1924);

Herbert Samuel, *Memoirs* (London: Cresset, 1945);

Warren Staebler, *The Liberal Mind of John Morley* (Princeton: Princeton University Press, 1943);

Lytton Strachey, *Characters and Commentaries* (London: Chatto & Windus, 1933; New York: Harcourt Brace, 1933);

Basil Willey, "John Morley," in his *More Nineteenth Century Studies: A Group of Honest Doubters* (London: Chatto & Windus, 1956), pp. 248–301.

Papers:

Collections of John Morley's papers and letters are at the India Office Library, Wadham College, Oxford; the London School of Economics; Imperial College; and the Library of Congress.

Bryan Waller Procter
(Barry Cornwall)
(21 November 1787? – 4 October 1874)

Meredith B. Raymond
University of Massachusetts — Amherst

See also the Procter entry in *DLB 96: British Romantic Poets, 1789–1832.*

BOOKS: *Dramatic Scenes, and Other Poems* (London: Ollier, 1819); revised and enlarged as *Dramatic Scenes: With Other Poems, Now First Printed* (London: Chapman & Hall, 1857; Boston: Ticknor & Fields, 1857; New York: Appleton, 1857);

A Sicilian Story, with Diego de Montilla, and Other Poems (London: Ollier, 1820);

Marcian Colonna, an Italian Tale; with Three Dramatic Scenes, and Other Poems (London: Warren/Ollier, 1820; Philadelphia: Carey & Son, 1821);

Mirandola: A Tragedy (London: Warren, 1821; Philadelphia: Carey, 1821);

The Poetical Works of Barry Cornwall, 3 volumes (London: Colburn, 1822);

The Flood of Thessaly, The Girl of Provence, and Other Poems (London: Colburn, 1823);

Effigies Poeticae; or, The Portraits of the British Poets (London: Carpenter, 1824);

The Poetical Works of Milman, Bowles, Wilson, and Barry Cornwall (Paris: Galignani, 1829);

English Songs, and Other Small Poems (London: Moxon, 1832; Boston: W. D. Ticknor, 1844; enlarged edition, London: Chapman & Hall, 1851; Boston: Ticknor, Reed & Fields, 1851); republished as *English Songs* (London: Bell & Daldy, 1870);

The Life of Edmund Kean (2 volumes, London: Moxon, 1835; 1 volume, New York: Harper, 1835);

The Songs and Miscellaneous Poems of Barry Cornwall, edited by Nathaniel Parker Willis (New York, 1844);

Essays and Tales in Prose, 2 volumes (Boston: Ticknor, Reed & Fields, 1853);

Charles Lamb: A Memoir (London: Moxon, 1866; Boston: Roberts, 1866);

An Autobiographical Fragment and Biographical Notes, with Personal Sketches of Contemporaries, Unpublished Lyrics, and Letters of Literary Friends, edited by Coventry Patmore (London: Bell, 1877; Boston: Roberts, 1877);

The Literary Recollections of Barry Cornwall, edited by Richard Willard Armour (Boston: Meador, 1936).

Editions: *The Life of Edmund Kean* (New York: Bloom, 1969);

A Sicilian Story and Mirandola, edited by Donald H. Reiman (New York & London: Garland, 1977);

Dramatic Scenes and Marcian Colonna, edited by Reiman (New York & London: Garland, 1978);

The Flood of Thessalay, edited by Reiman (New York & London: Garland, 1978).

PLAY PRODUCTION: *Mirandola: A Tragedy,* London, Theatre Royal, Covent Garden, 9 January 1821.

OTHER: Nathaniel Parker Willis, *Melanie and Other Poems,* edited by Procter (London: Saunders & Otley, 1835);

Ben Jonson, *The Works of Ben Jonson,* edited, with a biography, by Procter (London: Moxon, 1838);

William Shakespeare, *The Works of Shakespeare, Revised from the Best Authorities, with a Memoir and Essay on His Genius, by Barry Cornwall,* 3 volumes (London: Tyas, 1843; Cleveland: Jewett, 1857);

Robert Browning, *Selections from the Poetical Works of Robert Browning,* edited by Procter and John Forster (London: Chapman & Hall, 1863).

Bryan Waller Procter was an aspiring writer of moderate abilities who was accepted into London

literary circles. His career in the legal profession provided him with an income sufficient to support his chosen lifestyle. William Hazlitt, Leigh Hunt, and Charles Lamb were Procter's friends of an earlier generation; Lamb provided him with a subject for a biography that is, perhaps, the work by which Procter's place in literature is primarily established. John Forster, Charles Dickens, and Robert Browning were members of a later generation with whom he enjoyed personal friendships and shared literary interests. Although such well-known contemporaries obscure his visibility today, his experiments in a variety of genres – drama, lyric poetry, biography, the familiar essay, articles, and reviews – indicate the scope of his talent. Possessing a congenial disposition, an open mind, and a substantial, if self-schooled, knowledge of William Shakespeare and other Elizabethan dramatists, he had a secure position among the London literary lions.

Procter was the first son of Nicholas and Amelia Procter, whose forebears came from Yorkshire and Cumberland. The place and date of his birth cannot be determined with certainty, although evidence points to London and 21 November 1787. He was named after his father's wealthy great-uncle; but this relative's estate went to his younger brother Nicholas, who legally changed his name from Proc-

ter to Waller in 1816. His father, who was engaged in commerce, possibly as a wine merchant, received a bequest that enabled his family to live in comfortable circumstances and to send Bryan to a boarding school and, in 1801, to Harrow. There he received the standard instruction of the day with emphasis on the classics. George Gordon, Lord Byron; Robert Peel; Aubrey de Vere; and William Harness were among his schoolmates.

In 1804 Procter's father sent him to Calne in Wiltshire to serve as clerk to a solicitor, Nathaniel Atherton. There he became acquainted with William Lisle Bowles, the rector of nearby Bremhill, whose *Fourteen Sonnets, Elegiac and Descriptive, Written During a Tour* (1789) had received praise from Samuel Taylor Coleridge and William Wordsworth and who, in 1806, published what became a controversial edition of the works of Alexander Pope. Although Procter says in the posthumously published "Autobiographical Fragment" (1877) that this friendship was confined to duets with "my flute and his violoncello," he must have been exposed to the rector's literary enthusiasm. The circulating library at Calne provided nourishment for Procter's insatiable appetite for literature and history. Hence, his training at Calne represented a balance between law and letters.

In 1811 Procter moved to London and enrolled in Chancery as a solicitor. From 1812 to 1819 he was a partner in a law firm with offices in Brunswick Square. His autobiography reveals a lifestyle during this period that was quite different from that of any other period in his life: that of a dandy indulging in hunting and boxing (for boxing he engaged the services of one Tom Cribb, a "Champion of England"). He also became known for his generous hospitality, a reputation that was subsequently maintained. He frequently attended the theater and developed acquaintances with such actors as members of the Kemble family, William Charles Macready, Edmund Kean, and also John Howard Payne, the American actor-playwright; with the Reverend George Croly, the drama critic for the *New Times*; and with the poet, critic, journalist, and literary biographer Hunt. Through Hunt he met Hazlitt and Lamb. In 1817 some of Procter's poems were published in William Jerdan's *Literary Gazette*. The first work bearing the pseudonym Barry Cornwall (a partial anagram of his real name) was *Dramatic Scenes, and Other Poems* (1819), a collection that reveals the influence of the "old poets." In 1820 Procter met Anne Benson Skepper, the stepdaughter of Basil Montagu, a prominent lawyer and a champion of the literati. This household, presided over by Mrs. Montagu, whose reputation as a hostess and conversationalist was an established one, provided an additional entrée to the society into which Procter had already been initiated.

Procter's second book, *A Sicilian Story, with Diego de Montilla, and Other Poems* (1820), which, with the exception of *The Falcon*, abandoned dramatic scenes for poetry, was soon followed by *Marcian Colonna, an Italian Tale; with Three Dramatic Scenes, and Other Poems* (1820), both published under his pseudonym. "A Sicilian Story," based on the fifth story of the fourth day of Giovanni Boccaccio's *Decameron* (1353), about the Pot of Basil, invites comparison with John Keats's "Isabella; or, The Pot of Basil"; although Keats had composed his poem between February and April 1818, Procter's was published some months before Keats's appeared in 1820. They are of comparable length, but Procter's stanza length and rhyme scheme vary, in contrast to Keats's patterned ottava rima. The most substantive difference is that the Voice in the vision scene in "A Sicilian Story" announces that his body is unburied and directs his bride to bury his heart beneath a basil tree, an act she performs after washing the heart. This action replaces the digging and decapitation scenes in Boccaccio's and Keats's versions of the story. *Blackwood's Edinburgh Magazine* (March 1820) called "A Sicilian Story" "great as a work of art" and said, "We know of no young poet in our day who stands in a more enviable state than Barry Cornwall." At the time, Procter's version was more enthusiastically received than Keats's.

"Diego de Montilla, a Spanish Tale," a poem of eighty-six stanzas in ottava rima, concerns Don Diego's divided attraction to two sisters. In "Gyges," another poem in the volume, also in ottava rima and in the Byronic style, Procter develops his treatment of the myth from Herodotus via William Painter's *The Palace of Pleasure* (1566) because, according to his headnote, it was a better source than Plato's *Republic* to illustrate the moral pronounced in the concluding stanza: "Namely that women of the present day / Are not so bad, nor half, as those of old." Percy Bysshe Shelley, in a letter to Hunt's wife, Marianne, dated 29 October 1820, called "A Sicilian Story" pretty enough but denounced the vulgarity of the "wretched imitations of Lord Byron." Oddly enough, however, he respected Procter's critical judgment. In a letter of 16 June 1821 he advised Charles Ollier to show his [Shelley's] verses to Procter, "who is far better qualified to judge than I am." Byron, in a letter to his publisher John Murray dated 4 J[anuary] 1821, said that he liked *Dramatic Sketches* but regarded *A Sicilian Story* and *Marcian Colonna* as an affectation "of Wordsworth, and Hunt, and [Thomas] Moore, and Myself, all mixed up into a kind of Chaos." He added that Procter could produce a good tragedy if he would keep to his natural style.

Procter's biographer Richard Willard Armour calls "Marcian Colonna, an Italian Tale" "Procter's most ambitious effort at the writing of what we may call an epic" as well as the "most original in story and in style" and says that it has "the stuff of poetry." The poem of some two thousand lines traces, as Procter's "Advertisement" states, "the fluctuations of a fatalist's mind, – touched with insanity." It is a serious attempt to study inherited madness, guilt, and hallucination within a romantic narrative. In spite of an abundance of melodrama, Procter arouses sympathy for his characters and creates a sense of authenticity; such factors contributed to the work's immediate popularity. Hunt, reviewing "Marcian Colonna" in the *Examiner* (17 September 1820), spoke of Cornwall's "exquisite taste" and talent in the dramatic part of his writing and wished that he "would give us a whole play." But the *Edinburgh Monthly Review* (August 1820) expressed dismay at the poem's "worst kind of *cockneyism*." (More than a decade after writing the poem, Procter was appointed a Commissioner of Lunacy.)

[Song.]

Within the chambers of her breast
Love lives, and makes his spicy nest,
'Midst downy blooms and fragrant flowers,
And there he dreems away the hours;—
— There let him rest!
Some'time hence, when the cuckoo sings,
I'll come by night and bind his wings,—
Bind him, That he shall not roam
From his warm, white, virgin home.

Maiden of the Summer season,—
Angel of the rosy time,,—
Come, unless some graver reason
Bid thee scorn my rhyme;
Come, from thy serener height
On a golden cloud descending,—
Come, ere Love hath taken flight,—
And let thy stay be like the light,
When its glory hath no ending
In the Northern night!

Yours very truly B. W. Procter.

Manuscript of a poem by Procter (from James T. Fields, Yesterdays with Authors, 1900)

The tragedy *Mirandola* (1821), the "whole play" for which Hunt was waiting, is filled with conventional devices; its conclusion, for example, depends on tardy delivery of letters containing clarifying information. Nevertheless, it was a success; Byron called it the "new tragedy of great expectation." The role of the remorseful Duke was played by Macready, who claimed that it was almost written under his inspection. The drama ran for sixteen nights at Covent Garden.

The Flood of Thessaly, The Girl of Provence, and Other Poems was published in 1823. "The Flood of Thessaly," written in blank verse, gave Procter the opportunity to use the currently popular subject of the Flood in a classical rather than a biblical setting. Part 1 describes the devastation brought on Thessaly for its wicked ways and the particular plight of Deucalion and Pyrrha, the amorous and innocent pair who are caught up in the catastrophe and escape in a raft. In part 2 the world is re-created as Deucalion and Pyrrha cast stones that are metamorphosed into forms of life, including human beings. *Blackwood's* (May 1823) called the entire volume "dull" and took strong exception to the idea of the world's being peopled by the characters' casting stones "over their left shoulders"; the reviewer accused Procter of clothing "the simple sublimity of the great catastrophe of the world – the deluge" with the fancy of heathenism.

A critical piece, "English Tragedy," appeared in the *Edinburgh Review* in February 1823; it would be republished as "On English Tragedy" in Procter's *Essays and Tales in Prose* (1853). Procter takes issue with August Wilhelm Schlegel's insistence that in drama the dialogue must reveal "a change in the minds of the persons represented"; to Procter, this contention was almost equivalent to saying "that argument is not sound . . . unless it shall produce conviction." He prefers to define a play as "a succession and change of *events,* and not a change of sentiment" in the characters.

In the essay "Poetry – English Poetry," which appeared in the *Edinburgh Review* in April 1825 and is republished as "On English Poetry" in *Essays and Tales in Prose,* Procter begins by regretting that no successful attempts to show the general characteristics of poetry have been made. Surprisingly, he ignores Wordsworth's and other well-known remarks on the subject. After deciding what poetry is not – for example, versification – he notes poetry's opposition to the reasoning and analytical powers of prose and emphasizes its complicated nature. Like Shelley in *A Defense of Poetry,* which would not be published until 1840, he stresses the vatic and rec-

onciling power of poetry. After presenting his theory, he adds a survey of British poets from Geoffrey Chaucer to Robert Burns. The essay is a standard Romantic document.

Procter and Skepper had become engaged in 1821, but, because of health and financial problems, they were not married until October 1824. The Procters had six children, the eldest of whom, the future poet Adelaide Anne Procter, was born in October 1825. Procter, determined to become a good provider for his growing family, worked as a conveyancer and studied law with the intention of becoming a barrister. He limited his writing to short pieces suitable for annuals such as the *Keepsake.* Another theoretical essay, "Poetry – Cunningham's Songs," was published in the *Edinburgh Review* in January 1828; it appears in *Essays and Tales in Prose* as "A Defence of Poetry." It is addressed to the utilitarians, who decry poetry on the grounds of its uselessness. Procter answers them by pointing out that poetry provides pleasure and reminding them of their own motto, "the greatest happiness of the greatest number." He also refers to Sir Francis Bacon's advocacy of poetry as commending "*the dictates of Reason to the Imagination, for the better moving of the Appetite and the Will.*"

Procter was admitted to the bar in 1831. In 1832 he received a renewable appointment as a Metropolitan Commissioner of Lunacy, a position that provided him with additional income but minimal duties. The same year brought the publication of *English Songs, and Other Small Poems,* which initiated an arrangement with a German composer, Sigismund Neukomm, to set to music many of Procter's lyrics. In his introduction Procter laments the dearth of "Song-writers" in England, noting that most of them are actually Scottish. He cites Burns and the Scottish poets of the last half-century as "scattering among us the seeds of a better taste." The poems in *English Songs, and Other Small Poems* were compared favorably with Elizabethan lyrics and with those of Burns and Moore. Henry Chorley, writing in the *Athenaeum* (16 June 1832), said that Procter had "in a great measure restored the poetic grace, richness of fancy, and not a little of the simplicity and the quiet quaint elegance of the elder lyrists." A. C. Swinburne, in his elegiac poem "In Memory of Barry Cornwall" (1874), recalls especially Procter's songs. Half a dozen editions of the volume were published during the next fifty years; it is considered his most original, albeit sentimental, poetry.

During the 1830s, which period marked the deaths of Lamb and Hazlitt, Procter added Forster,

Browning, Dickens, Thomas Talfourd, Mary Russell Mitford, Richard Henry Horne, and John Kenyon to his circle. *The Life of Edmund Kean* (1835) was his most important work of the period. The book has provided a source for later biographers of Kean; it was written by one who frequented the theater during the height and decline of Kean's fame, who was familiar with the theatrical scene, and who, as a student of Shakespeare, was able to offer criticism grounded in familiarity with the tragic characters Kean portrayed.

Procter's introduction states a simple purpose: "to touch lightly, (agreeably if we can) and impartially, upon the principal events of our hero's life." He does so all too lightly, but also informatively. Harold Newcomb Hillebrand's thoroughly documented *Edmund Kean* (1933), the standard biography, indicates posterity's indebtedness to Procter. Hillebrand accepts Procter's theories that Edmund Kean and Nancy Carey were Kean's parents, in spite of reports that Miss Charlotte Tidswell, who cared for Kean as a child, was his real mother, and that 4 November 1789 is the most probable date for his birth. Procter's story of a deformity requiring leg irons as a corrective measure – if not the precise condition – is perpetuated by Hillebrand.

The period to 1814 saw Kean acting in the Shearness, Watson, and Cherry companies; his marriage to the actress Mary Chambers in 1808; and the birth of their two sons. Procter sympathetically portrays the Kean family wandering about England in search of employment, their suffering accentuated by the death of the older son in the autumn of 1813. He describes the complicated and precarious arrangements that autumn that led climactically to Kean's acceptance at Drury Lane and his first performance as Shylock on 26 January 1814, initiating his career as a Shakespearean actor. Although Procter is prone to digress by giving his analyses of the characters Kean portrayed, Hillebrand believes that the best comment on Kean's representation of Zanga in Edward Young's *The Revenge* (1721) is Procter's eyewitness account.

Procter has been accused of emphasizing the more colorful episodes in the life of his subject. He is, however, careful to place such accounts in an explanatory framework, and he holds to a firm chronology of events. Kean's first trip to the United States in 1820–1821 receives short shrift, but Procter's claim that "Kean's progress through the United States of America, was one continued march of triumph" is a fair one and notes exceptions. He gives too many pages to Kean's reinterment of the body of the British actor George Frederick Cooke

and the macabre report of his carrying off Cooke's toe bone as a relic, but the sensational story is true. Introducing his account of Kean's affair with Frances Cox and the trial in 1825 at which he was ordered to pay Mr. Robert Cox eight hundred pounds, Procter says that he will "touch upon it as slightly as possible" and justifies discussing the scandal by making the point that Kean never completely reinstated himself after the incident. Kean's second visit to the United States in 1825 receives a single sentence in the text and a footnote describing Kean's reception as a chief by a tribe of Huron Indians in Quebec. (Kean prized this distinction and enjoyed wearing and acting in his Indian dress.)

The biography hastens to a close, noting the decline in Kean's health and his increasing dependence on alcohol. Procter fails to write of the mild renewal of Kean's popularity during the last half-dozen years of his life or of his Paris excursion in 1827–1828, but he renders a vivid and apparently accurate account of Kean's final performance on 25 March 1833, two months before his death. With his son Charles as Iago, Kean played his usual role of Othello until the "farewell" speech, when he collapsed and had to be carried from the stage. Procter suggests a reconciliation between Kean and his wife at the end but does not say that she actually returned to him.

Despite Procter's propensity for anecdote and his somewhat superficial account of Kean's later years, he provides a reliable record of the principal events of the actor's life and projects a sense of the suffering and privation, the joy and rewards that Kean experienced. Along with his deep admiration for Kean as a master of histrionics, he recognizes the contradictory qualities of tenacity and frailty that possessed the actor.

John Wilson, writing in *Blackwood's Edinburgh Magazine* (July 1835), considered the work "the silliest book of the season"; the *Quarterly Review* (July 1835) declared Procter to be "perpetually hesitating between airs of hilarity and hints of reprehension." In contrast, the *Athenaeum* commended the biography in two successive issues (30 May and 6 June 1835), congratulating Procter for showing "no common quickness of apprehension, and justness of taste, in separating the fragments of personal interest concerning his hero, from the stage gossip in which they were entangled." The review notes "above all" the author's "fine spirit of humanity ... which makes him regard the extravagances and errors of an actor's precarious life with a kindly and forgiving eye." The second article concludes by declaring the reviewer "so well pleased with the manner in which [Procter] has acquitted himself

Bust of Procter by John Henry Foley (National Portrait Gallery)

of a task at the best unpromising and delicate" that he hopes to see him again "in the character of a biographer." Armour calls the work "less a biography than a novel . . . after the manner of [Henry] Fielding or [Laurence] Sterne" with Kean as the adventurous hero; while considering *silly* too strong a term, he regards *biography* as hardly an appropriate label for the work.

Procter contributed introductions to editions of the works of Ben Jonson (1838) and Shakespeare (1843). The latter, according to Armour, was the most popular of all the works with which Procter was in any way associated – some eighteen editions or reprintings appeared by 1891. His essay "Memoir and Essay on the Genius of Shakespeare" includes a biographical sketch and commentaries on the history and state of the drama and on Shakespeare's relation to his predecessors; it concludes with remarks on some of the plays, all reflecting his enthusiasm for "the greatest genius . . . that ever the world produced." The essay is a concise and informative introduction to the study of Shakespeare.

During the 1840s and 1850s Procter continued writing reviews and poems, but they did not match those of the earlier decades in number or quality. In 1845 Procter became a permanent Commissioner of Lunacy; the post then required more attention to his duties. The conversion of their daughters to Roman Catholicism was a source of disappointment to the Procters, and anxiety about their son, Montagu, who served in the Bengal army during the Indian revolts in the 1850s (he survived as a hero) added to their distress during this period.

The 1853 American edition of Procter's prose includes, in addition to the essays from the *Edinburgh Review,* several short stories. "The Story of the Back-Room Window," written in 1838, imagines a house unroofed to disclose the lives and deaths of various unfortunate tenants. "The Usher," written in 1841, traces the rise, fall, and premature death of a lowly schoolmaster with plaintive realism. The undated farce "The Happy Day" focuses on the activities of London literary lions and aristocrats, ridiculing the British devotion to sport and dogs, feminism, and the relations between master and servant with wit and humor. These pieces may indicate a road Procter should have traveled more often.

As Armour says, "Old age was with Procter a long time," and the society that frequented health resorts and spas, especially Brighton, replaced that of his accustomed confederates at the London literary meetings. He and Forster, a fellow Commissioner of Lunacy, coedited *Selections from the Poetical Works of Robert Browning* (1863). Procter's daughter Adelaide Anne died of consumption in 1864.

Unlike his earlier work on Kean, Procter's *Charles Lamb: A Memoir* (1866), written some thirty-two years after its subject's death, has earned general commendation. Procter's account is based on close friendship and familiarity with virtually all of his subject's publications. In his preface he declares that he knew Lamb "more intimately than any other existing person, during the last seventeen or eighteen years of his life." In addition, Talfourd's 1837 and 1848 editions of Lamb's letters and sketches of his life and companions were available to jog Procter's memory, as his acknowledgments of Talfourd indicate.

In the opening words of the biography Procter says that his study "lies within a narrow compass. It comprehends only few events." The compass is London and its environs; up to the point of Procter's introduction to Lamb in 1817 or 1818, the "few events" comprise Lamb's humble origin, his education at Christ's Hospital (where his schoolfellow Coleridge became his friend), his employment at the South Sea Company in 1791 and at India House in 1792, his early poetry and the famous *Tales from Shakespear* (1807) in collaboration with his sister Mary, his early essays in Hunt's *Reflector* (1811), and his later contributions to periodicals. These events, and subsequent ones, were dominated by Lamb's "devotion to one grand and tender purpose" to which "everything was made subservient": to bear willingly the burden of acting as custodian and companion to his sister Mary, who, in a sudden outburst of madness on 23 September 1796, fatally stabbed their mother. Her sanity was restored, but not without intermittent attacks that required the vigilant attendance her brother provided until his death — and beyond, if financial provisions are considered.

Procter relentlessly tracks the many residences of Lamb and his sister as he recollects domestic scenes suggesting the close companionship they enjoyed; he describes the evening parties in their homes; he intersperses such vignettes as Lamb in worn black clothing and gaitered legs making his habitual walks in and out of town; he recalls Lamb's diffidence, his stammer, his excesses of drink and tobacco, and his pithy way of speaking. As a regular participant in the "Wednesday evenings" and supper parties Lamb hosted, Procter, as had Talfourd, gives the reader insights into the personalities of the guests and friends. The reader learns that Hazlitt and Hunt were, like Lamb, Unitarians; reads of the quarrel and reconciliation between Lamb and Robert Southey; gets glimpses of Wordsworth, of the absent-minded George Dyer as he walks obliviously into the New River to be rescued by Lamb, and of the unkempt Martin Burney, about whom Lamb's remark — "if dirt were trumps, what a hand you would hold" — has become a legend. More attention is given to Coleridge, whom Procter calls "the great friend and Mentor" of Lamb's youth. An anecdote gives a sense of Lamb's wit: " 'Charles,' said Coleridge to Lamb, 'I think you have had heard me preach?' 'I n-n-never heard you do anything else,' replied Lamb."

While George L. Barnett labels Procter's biography "Pleasant reminiscence rather than accurate scholarship by a close friend," E. V. Lucas's standard biography, *The Life of Charles Lamb* (1921), refers to Procter's work more than fifty times as a source of information and quotes him, often at length.

Procter calls attention to his subject's "essentially English" humor, his combination of prudence with generosity and of tenderness of heart with a firm will, and his simplicity and natural sensibility. He appreciates Lamb's tendency to respect writers of the past more than his contemporaries (except for Coleridge, Wordsworth, and Burns) and says that *Specimens of Dramatic Poets, Who Lived About the Time of Shakespeare* (1808) "made Lamb known as a man conversant with our old English literature, and helped mainly to direct the taste of the public to those fine writers." He describes the *Elia* essays (1823) as "genial, delicate, terse, full of thought and full of humor" and praises their variety of subject matter and "witty melancholy." He applauds phrases "brought back from the land of shadows, and made denizens of England, in modern times" and calls Lamb "the last true lover of Antiquity."

The final event, precipitated by a fall in 1834, followed the death of Coleridge by a few months — months during which, says Procter, "Charles's sorrow was unceasing." This response, like his devotion to his sister, epitomizes Lamb's loyalty.

The reviewer in the *Athenaeum* (18 August 1866) described the book as "full of grace and sweet-thought, and grave, glad memories, and deep earnestness" but noted some errors. Thomas Carlyle, in an undated letter to Procter that is included in Procter's *An Autobiographical Fragment and Biographical Notes, with Personal Sketches of Contemporaries, Unpublished Lyrics, and Letters of Literary Friends* (1877), praised the biography for its "brevity, perspicuity, graceful clearness; then also perfect veracity, gentleness, lovingness, justness, peaceable candour throughout ... all the qualities, in short, which such a book could have, I find visible in this, now dating, it appears, in your seventy-seventh year."

During the final decades of his life Procter struggled with the infirmities of old age and depended on his younger friend Forster for contacts with the society from which he was becoming isolated. Yet even after his retirement in 1861, Procter continued to attend meetings of the Lunacy Commission.

His death on 4 October 1874 prompted Swinburne to compose "In Memory of Barry Cornwall," which includes the lines:

> Beloved of men, whose words on our lips were
> honey,
> Whose name in our ears and our fathers' ears was
> sweet,
> Like summer gone forth of the land his songs made
> sunny,
> To the beautiful veiled bright world where the glad
> ghosts meet,
> Child, father, bridegroom and bride, and anguish and
> rest,
> No soul shall pass of a singer than this more blest.

Procter's popularity as a writer reached its zenith in the 1820s. His literary reputation is slight, but his biographies of Kean and Lamb cannot be ignored. Interest in him has remained primarily historical, as a figure who may enhance portraits of the great and near-great of his contemporaries. Modern editions of his publications, such as the Garland facsimiles edited by Donald H. Reiman, may induce a new appreciation of his work. Whatever his literary achievements, his charity, modesty, and amiability have earned him a lasting reputation.

Biographies:

James T. Fields, *Old Acquaintance: Barry Cornwall and Some of His Friends* (Boston: Osgood, 1876);

Franz Becker, *Bryan Waller Procter* (Vienna & Leipzig: Braumüller, 1911);

Richard Willard Armour, *Barry Cornwall: A Biography of Bryan Waller Procter, with a Selected Collec-*

tion of Hitherto Unpublished Letters (Boston: Meador, 1935).

References:

George L. Barnett, *Charles Lamb* (Boston: Twayne, 1976);

"Bryan Waller Procter," *British Quarterly Review,* 68 (July 1878): 33–44;

"Bryan Waller Procter (Barry Cornwall)," *Appleton's Journal of Popular Literature, Science, and Art,* 4 (17 September 1870): 348–351;

James T. Fields, *Yesterdays with Authors* (Boston: Houghton, Mifflin, 1882), pp. 353–419;

George H. Ford, "Keats and Procter: A Misdated Acquaintance," *Modern Language Notes,* 66 (December 1951): 532–536;

Edmund H. Garrett, "B. W. Procter," in *Victorian Songs: Lyrics of the Affections and Nature* (Boston: Little, Brown, 1895), pp. 165–171;

Henry G. Hewlett, "Barry Cornwall," *Nineteenth Century,* 4 (October 1878): 643–652;

Hewlett, "Barry Cornwall's Life and Poems," *Edinburgh Review,* 147 (April 1878): 333–353;

Harold Newcomb Hillebrand, *Edmund Kean* (New York: Columbia University Press, 1933);

William Howitt, "Waller Bryan Procter," in his *Homes and Haunts of the Most Eminent British Poets,* 2 volumes (London: Bentley, 1847), II: 447–451;

E. V. Lucas, *The Life of Charles Lamb,* 2 volumes (London: Methuen, 1921);

Charles Mackay, *Through the Long Day; or, Memorials of a Literary Life During a Half Century* (London: Allen, 1887);

Harriet Martineau, "Barry Cornwall," in her *Biographical Sketches, 1852–1875,* fourth edition (London: Macmillan, 1876), pp. 475–487;

S. R. Townshend Mayer, " 'Barry Cornwall': Unpublished Letters, Personal Recollections, and Contemporary Notes," *Gentleman's Magazine,* new series 13 (November 1874): 555–568;

D. M. Moir, "Barry Cornwall," in his *Sketches of the Poetical Literature of the Past Half-Century,* third edition (Edinburgh & London: Blackwood, 1856), pp. 232–238;

George Saintsbury, *A History of Nineteenth Century Literature* (New York: Macmillan, 1906);

G. A. Simcox, "Barry Cornwall," *Fortnightly Review,* 27 (May 1877): 708–718;

E. C. Stedman, "Bryan Waller Procter," in his *Victorian Poets* (Boston & New York: Houghton, Mifflin, 1900), pp. 100–113;

Stedman, "A Representative Triad: Hood, Arnold, Procter," *Scribner's Monthly,* 7 (February 1874): 463–478;

Arthur Symons, "Bryan Waller Procter: Barry Cornwall (1787–1874)," in his *The Romantic Movement in English Poetry* (London: Constable, 1909), pp. 236–238;

Thomas Noon Talfourd, *Memoirs of Charles Lamb,* edited and annotated by Percy Fitzgerald (London: Gibbings, 1892);

Henry T. Tuckerman, "Barry Cornwall," in his *Thoughts on the Poets,* third edition (New York: C. S. Francis / Boston: J. H. Francis, 1848), pp. 251–261;

Edwin Percy Whipple, "Barry Cornwall and Some of His Contemporaries," in his *Recollections of Eminent Men, with Other Papers* (Boston: Ticknor, 1886), pp. 305–343;

Whipple, "English Poets of the Nineteenth Century," in his *Essays and Reviews,* second edition, 2 volumes (Boston: Ticknor, Reed & Fields, 1851), I: 347–350;

P. M. Zall, "The Memory of Barry Cornwall," *Charles Lamb Bulletin,* 10–11 (1974): 61–64.

Papers:

The largest collection of Procter correspondence and poetry manuscripts is at the University of Iowa, Iowa City; it includes documents by not only Bryan Waller but also by his wife and their daughter Adelaide Anne. The Houghton Library at Harvard University and the Huntington Library in San Marino, California, each hold collections of some thirty letters; and the Huntington collection also includes some verse items and the manuscript of Procter's biography of Lamb. The University of Chicago Library has correspondence from Procter to Robert and Elizabeth Barrett Browning, and the University of Edinburgh and the Lilly Library at Indiana University each hold one letter from Procter.

Sir Walter Scott

(15 August 1771 – 21 September 1832)

Ian Duncan
Yale University

See also the Scott entries in *DLB 93: British Romantic Poets, 1789–1832: First Series; DLB 107: British Romantic Prose Writers, 1789–1832: First Series;* and *DLB 116: British Romantic Novelists, 1789–1832.*

BOOKS: *The Eve of Saint John. A Border Ballad* (Kelso: Printed by James Ballantyne, 1800);

The Lay of the Last Minstrel (London: Printed for Longman, Hurst, Rees & Orme and A. Constable, Edinburgh, by James Ballantyne, Edinburgh, 1805; Philadelphia: Printed for I. Riley, New York, 1806);

Ballads and Lyrical Pieces (Edinburgh: Printed by James Ballantyne for Longman, Hurst, Rees & Orme, London, and Archibald Constable, Edinburgh, 1806; Boston: Published & sold by Etheridge & Bliss and by B. & B. Hopkins, Philadelphia, 1807);

Marmion: A Tale of Flodden Field (Edinburgh: Printed by J. Ballantyne for Archibald Constable, Edinburgh, and William Miller & John Murray, London, 1808; Philadelphia: Hopkins & Earle, 1808);

The Lady of the Lake: A Poem (Edinburgh: Printed for John Ballantyne, Edinburgh, and Longman, Hurst, Rees & Orme and William Miller, London, by James Ballantyne, 1810; Boston: Published by W. Wells & T. B. Wait, printed by T. B. Wait, 1810; New York: E. Sargeant, 1810; Philadelphia: E. Earle, 1810);

The Vision of Don Roderick: A Poem (Edinburgh: Printed by James Ballantyne for John Ballantyne, Edinburgh, and Longman, Hurst, Rees, Orme & Brown, London, 1811; Boston: Published by T. B. Wait, 1811);

Rokeby: A Poem (Edinburgh: Printed for John Ballantyne, Edinburgh, and Longman, Hurst, Rees, Orme & Brown, London, by James Ballantyne, Edinburgh, 1813; Baltimore: J. Cushing, 1813);

The Bridal of Triermain, or The Vale of St. John. In Three Cantos (Edinburgh: Printed by James Bal-lantyne for John Ballantyne and for Longman, Hurst, Rees, Orme & Brown and Gale, Curtis & Fenner, London, 1813; Philadelphia: Published by M. Thomas, printed by W. Fry, 1813);

Waverley; or, 'Tis Sixty Years Since (3 volumes, Edinburgh: Printed by James Ballantyne for Archibald Constable, Edinburgh, and Longman, Hurst, Rees, Orme & Brown, London, 1814; 1 volume, Boston: Published by Wells & Lilly and Bradford & Read, 1815; 2 volumes, New York: Van Winkle & Wiley, 1815);

Guy Mannering; or, The Astrologer. By the Author of "Waverley" (3 volumes, Edinburgh: Printed by James Ballantyne for Longman, Hurst, Rees, Orme & Brown, London, and Archibald Constable, Edinburgh, 1815; 2 volumes, Boston: Published by West & Richardson and Eastburn, Kirk, New York, printed by T. W. White, 1815);

The Lord of the Isles: A Poem (Edinburgh: Printed for Archibald Constable, Edinburgh, and Longman, Hurst, Rees, Orme & Brown, London, by James Ballantyne, 1815; New York: R. Scott, 1815; Philadelphia: Published by Moses Thomas, 1815);

The Field of Waterloo: A Poem (Edinburgh: Printed by James Ballantyne for Archibald Constable, Edinburgh, and Longman, Hurst, Rees, Orme & Brown and John Murray, London, 1815; Boston: T. B. Wait, 1815; New York: Van Winkle & Wiley, 1815; Philadelphia: Published by Moses Thomas, printed by Van Winkle & Wiley, 1815);

The Ettricke Garland; Being Two Excellent New Songs on The Lifting of the Banner of the House of Buccleuch, At the Great Foot-Ball Match on Carterhaugh, Dec. 4, 1815, by Scott and James Hogg (Edinburgh: Printed by James Ballantyne, 1815);

Paul's Letters To His Kinsfolk (Edinburgh: Printed by James Ballantyne for Archibald Constable, Edinburgh, and Longman, Hurst, Rees, Orme &

234

Sir Walter Scott (portrait by Sir Henry Raeburn; Scottish National Portrait Gallery)

Brown and John Murray, London, 1816; Philadelphia: Republished by M. Thomas, 1816);

The Antiquary. By the Author of "Waverley" and "Guy Mannering" (3 volumes, Edinburgh: Printed by James Ballantyne for Archibald Constable, Edinburgh, and Longman, Hurst, Rees, Orme & Brown, London, 1816; 2 volumes, New York: Van Winkle & Wiley, 1816);

Tales of My Landlord, Collected and Arranged by Jedediah Cleishbotham, Schoolmaster and Parish-Clerk of Gandercleugh (4 volumes, Edinburgh: Printed for William Blackwood and John Murray, London, 1816; 1 volume, Philadelphia: Published by M. Thomas, 1817) — comprises *The Black Dwarf* and *Old Mortality*;

Harold the Dauntless: A Poem (Edinburgh: Printed by James Ballantyne for Longman, Hurst, Rees, Orme & Brown, London, and Archibald Constable, Edinburgh, 1817; New York: Published by James Eastburn, printed by Van Winkle & Wiley, 1817);

Rob Roy; by the Author of "Waverley," "Guy Mannering," and "The Antiquary" (3 volumes, Edinburgh: Printed by James Ballantyne for Archibald Constable, Edinburgh, and Longman, Hurst, Rees, Orme & Brown, London, 1818 [i.e., 1817]; 2 volumes, New York: J. Eastburn, 1818; New York: Published by Kirk & Mercein, printed by E. & E. Hosford, Albany, 1818; Philadelphia: Published by M. Thomas, printed by J. Maxwell, 1818);

Tales of My Landlord, Second Series, Collected and Arranged by Jedediah Cleishbotham, Schoolmaster and Parish-Clerk of Gandercleugh, 4 volumes (Edinburgh: Printed for Archibald Constable, 1818; Philadelphia: Carey, 1818) — comprises *The Heart of Mid-Lothian*;

Tales of My Landlord, Third Series, Collected and Arranged by Jedediah Cleishbotham, Schoolmaster and Parish-Clerk of Gandercleugh (4 volumes, Edinburgh: Printed for Archibald Constable, Edinburgh, and Longman, Hurst, Rees, Orme &

Brown and Hurst, Robinson, London, 1819; New York: Published by Charles Wiley, W. B. Gilley & A. T. Goodrich, printed by Clayton & Kingsland, 1819; Philadelphia: Thomas, 1819) — comprises *The Bride of Lammermoor* and *A Legend of Montrose*;

Provincial Antiquities and Picturesque Scenery of Scotland, text by Scott with plates by J. M. W. Turner and others (10 parts, Edinburgh: Printed by James Ballantyne, 1819–1826; 2 volumes, London: Arch, 1826);

Miscellaneous Poems (Edinburgh: Printed for Archibald Constable, Edinburgh, and Hurst, Robinson, London, 1820);

Ivanhoe: A Romance; By "the Author of Waverley" &c. (3 volumes, Edinburgh: Printed for Archibald Constable, Edinburgh, and Hurst, Robinson, London, 1820 [i.e., 1819]; 2 volumes, Philadelphia: Carey, 1820);

The Monastery: A Romance; By the Author of "Waverley" (3 volumes, Edinburgh: Printed for Longman, Hurst, Rees, Orme & Brown, London, and for Archibald Constable and John Ballantyne, Edinburgh, 1820; 1 volume, Philadelphia: Carey, 1820);

The Abbot; By the Author of "Waverley" (3 volumes, Edinburgh: Printed for Longman, Hurst, Rees, Orme & Brown, London, and for Archibald Constable and John Ballantyne, Edinburgh, 1820; 2 volumes, New York: J. & J. Harper, 1820; 1 volume, Philadelphia: Carey, 1820);

Kenilworth: A Romance; By the Author of "Waverley," "Ivanhoe," &c. (3 volumes, Edinburgh: Printed for Archibald Constable and John Ballantyne, Edinburgh, and Hurst, Robinson, London, 1821; Hartford: S. G. Goodrich, 1821; Philadelphia: Carey, 1821);

The Pirate; By the Author of "Waverley," "Kenilworth," &c. (3 volumes, Edinburgh: Printed for Archibald Constable and Hurst, Robinson, London, 1822 [i.e., 1821]; 2 volumes, Boston: Wells & Lilly, 1822; 1 volume, Hartford: S. G. Goodrich and Huntington & Hopkins, 1822; 2 volumes, New York: E. Duyckinck, 1822; 1 volume, Philadelphia: Carey & Lea, 1822);

The Fortunes of Nigel; By the Author of "Waverley," "Kenilworth," &c. (3 volumes, Edinburgh: Printed for Archibald Constable, Edinburgh, and Hurst, Robinson, London, 1822; 2 volumes, New York: T. Longworth, 1822; Philadelphia: Carey & Lea, 1822);

Halidon Hill: A Dramatic Sketch (Edinburgh: Printed for Archibald Constable and Hurst, Robinson, London, 1822; New York: S. Campbell, printed by E. B. Clayton, 1822; Philadelphia: Carey & Lea, 1822);

Peveril of the Peak, By the Author of "Waverley, Kenilworth," &c. (4 volumes, Edinburgh: Printed for Archibald Constable, Edinburgh, and Hurst, Robinson, London, 1822 [i.e. 1823]; 3 volumes, Philadelphia: Carey & Lea, 1823);

Quentin Durward; By the Author of "Waverley, Peveril of the Peak," &c. (3 volumes, Edinburgh: Printed for Archibald Constable, Edinburgh, and Hurst, Robinson, London, 1823; 1 volume, Philadelphia: Carey & Lea, 1823);

St. Ronan's Well; By the Author of "Waverley, Quentin Durward," &c. (3 volumes, Edinburgh: Printed for Archibald Constable, Edinburgh, and Hurst, Robinson, London, 1824 [i.e., 1823]; Philadelphia: Carey & Lea, 1824);

Redgauntlet: A Tale of the Eighteenth Century; By the Author of "Waverley" (3 volumes, Edinburgh: Printed for Archibald Constable, Edinburgh, and Hurst, Robinson, London, 1824; 2 volumes, Philadelphia: Carey & Lea, 1824);

Tales of the Crusaders; By the Author of Waverley (4 volumes, Edinburgh: Printed for Archibald Constable, Edinburgh, and Hurst, Robinson, London, 1825; New York: Published by E. Duyckinck, Collins & Hannay, Collins, E. Bliss & E. White, and W. B. Gilley, printed by J. & J. Harper, 1825; 2 volumes, Philadelphia: Carey & Lea, 1825) — comprises *The Betrothed* and *The Talisman*;

Letter to the Editor of the Edinburgh Weekly Journal from Malachi Malagrowther, Esq. on the Proposed Change of Currency and Other Late Alterations, As They Affect, or Are Intended to Affect, the Kingdom of Scotland (Edinburgh: Printed by James Ballantyne for William Blackwood, 1826);

A Second Letter to the Editor of the Edinburgh Weekly Journal, from Malachi Malagrowther, Esq.: On the Proposed Change of Currency, and Other Late Alterations, As They Affect, or Are Intended to Affect, the Kingdom of Scotland (Edinburgh: Printed by James Ballantyne for William Blackwood, 1826);

A Third Letter to the Editor of the Edinburgh Weekly Journal, from Malachi Malagrowther, Esq.: On the Proposed Change of Currency, and Other Late Alterations, As They Affect, or Are Intended to Affect, the Kingdom of Scotland (Edinburgh: Printed by James Ballantyne for William Blackwood, Edinburgh, and T. Cadell, London, 1826);

Woodstock; or, the Cavalier: A Tale of the Year Sixteen Hundred and Fifty-One; By the Author of "Waverley, Tales of the Crusaders," &c. (3 volumes, Edinburgh: Printed for Archibald Constable, Edinburgh, and Longman, Rees, Orme, Brown & Green, London, 1826; 2 volumes, Philadelphia: Carey & Lea, 1826);

The Life of Napoleon Buonaparte, Emperor of the French: With a Preliminary View of the French Revolution, 9 volumes (Edinburgh: Printed by Ballantyne, for Longman, Rees, Orme, Brown & Green, London, 1827; Philadelphia: Carey, Lea & Carey, 1827);

The Miscellaneous Prose Works of Sir Walter Scott, Bart., 6 volumes (Edinburgh: Cadell, 1827; Boston: Wells & Lilly, 1829);

Chronicles of the Canongate. By the Author of "Waverley," &c. (2 volumes, Edinburgh: Printed for Cadell, Edinburgh, and Simpkin & Marshall, London, 1827; 1 volume, Philadelphia: Carey, Lea & Carey, 1827) — comprises "The Highland Widow"; "The Two Drovers"; "The Surgeon's Daughter";

Religious Discourses. By a Layman (London: Henry Colburn, 1828; New York: Printed by J. & J. Harper, sold by Collins & Hannay, 1828);

Chronicles of the Canongate: Second Series; By the Author of "Waverley" &c. [The Fair Maid of Perth] (3 volumes, Edinburgh: Printed for Cadell, Edinburgh, and Simpkin & Marshall, London, 1828; 1 volume, Philadelphia: Carey, Lea & Carey, 1828);

Tales of a Grandfather: Being Stories Taken from Scottish History, first-third series (9 volumes, Edinburgh: Printed for Cadell, 1828-1830 [i.e., 1827-1830]; 8 volumes, Philadelphia: Carey, Lea & Carey, 1828-1830);

Anne of Geierstein; or, The Maiden of the Mist; By the Author of "Waverley," &c. (3 volumes, Edinburgh: Printed for Cadell, Edinburgh, and Simpkin & Marshall, London, 1829; 2 volumes, Philadelphia: Carey, Lea & Carey, 1829);

The History of Scotland, 2 volumes, in *The Cabinet Cyclopædia, Conducted by Rev. Dionysus Lardner* (London: Printed for Longman, Rees, Orme, Brown & Green and John Taylor, 1830);

The Doom of Devorgoil: A Melo-drama. Auchindrane; or, the Ayrshire Tragedy (Edinburgh: Printed for Cadell, Edinburgh, and Simpkin & Marshall, London, 1830; New York: Printed by J. & J. Harper, 1830);

Letters on Demonology and Witchcraft (London: J. Murray, 1830; New York: Harper, 1830);

Tales of a Grandfather: Being Stories Taken from the History of France (3 volumes, Edinburgh: Cadell, 1831; 2 volumes, Philadelphia: Carey & Lea, 1831);

Tales of My Landlord: Fourth and Last Series, Collected and Arranged by Jedediah Cleishbotham, Schoolmaster and Parish-Clerk of Gandercleugh [Count Robert of Paris and *Castle Dangerous]* (4 volumes, Edinburgh: Printed for Robert Cadell, Edinburgh, and Whitaker, London, 1832; 3 volumes, Philadelphia: Carey & Lea, 1832);

The Journal of Sir Walter Scott, 3 volumes, edited by John Guthrie Tait and W. M. Parker (Edinburgh: Oliver & Boyd, 1939-1949).

Editions: *Waverley Novels,* Magnum Opus Edition, 48 volumes, with Scott's prefaces and final revisions (Edinburgh: Cadell, 1829-1833);

Miscellaneous Prose Works, 30 volumes, edited by John Gibson Lockhart (Edinburgh: Cadell, 1834-1846);

The Miscellaneous Works of Sir Walter Scott, 30 volumes (Edinburgh: Black, 1870-1871);

The Waverley Novels, Centenary Edition, 25 volumes (Edinburgh: Black, 1870-1871);

The Waverley Novels, Dryburgh Edition, 25 volumes (London & Edinburgh: Black, 1892-1894);

The Waverley Novels, Border Edition, 48 volumes, edited by Andrew Lang (London: Nimmo, 1892-1894; Boston: Estes & Lauriat, 1893-1894);

The Poetical Works of Sir Walter Scott, with the Author's Introductions and Notes, edited by J. Logie Robertson (London: Frowde, 1894);

Lives of the Novelists (London, New York & Toronto: Oxford University Press, 1906);

Minstrelsy of the Scottish Border, edited by Thomas Henderson (London: Harrap, 1931);

Private Letters of the Seventeenth Century, edited by Douglas Grant (Oxford: Clarendon Press, 1947);

The Life of John Dryden, edited by Bernard Kreissman (Lincoln: University of Nebraska Press, 1963);

Sir Walter Scott on Novelists and Fiction, edited by Ioan Williams (New York: Barnes & Noble, 1968);

The Journal of Sir Walter Scott, edited by W. E. K. Anderson (Oxford: Clarendon Press, 1972);

The Prefaces to the Waverley Novels, edited by Mark A. Weinstein (Lincoln: University of Nebraska Press, 1978);

The Letters of Malachi Malagrowther, edited by P. H. Scott (Edinburgh: Blackwood, 1981);

Scott on Himself: A Collection of the Autobiographical Writings of Sir Walter Scott, edited by David

The entrance hall (top) and Scott's study at his estate, Abbotsford

Hewitt (Edinburgh: Scottish Academic Press, 1981);

The Edinburgh Edition of the Waverley Novels, 30 volumes projected, 3 volumes published; Hewitt, editor in chief (Edinburgh: Edinburgh University Press / New York: Columbia University Press, 1993–).

OTHER: *The Chase, and William and Helen: Two Ballads from the German of Gottfried Augustus Bürger,* translated by Scott (Edinburgh: Printed by Mundell & Son for Manners & Miller and sold by T. Cadell, Jun. & W. Davies, 1796);

Goetz of Berlichingen, With the Iron Hand: A Tragedy. Translated from the German of Goethe, translated by Scott (London: Printed for J. Bell, 1799);

"The Fire King," "Glenfinlas," "The Eve of Saint John," "Frederick and Alice," and "The Wild Huntsmen," in *Tales of Wonder; Written and Collected by M. G. Lewis, Esq., M.P.,* 2 volumes (London: Printed by W. Bulmer for the author & sold by J. Bell, 1801), I: 62–69, 122–136, 137–147, 148–152, 153–163;

Minstrelsy of the Scottish Border, 2 volumes, edited by Scott (Kelso: Printed by James Ballantyne for T. Cadell, Jun. & W. Davies, London, and sold by Manners & Miller and A. Constable, Edinburgh, 1802); enlarged edition, 3 volumes (Edinburgh: Printed by James Ballantyne for Longman & Rees, London, and sold by Manners & Miller and A. Constable, Edinburgh, 1803; revised, 1810; Philadelphia: Carey, 1813);

Sir Tristrem: A Metrical Romance of the Thirteenth Century; by Thomas of Ercildoune, edited and completed by Scott (Edinburgh: Printed by James Ballantyne for Archibald Constable, Edinburgh, and Longman & Rees, London, 1804);

Original Memoirs, Written during the Great Civil War: Being the Life of Sir Henry Slingsby, and Memoirs of Capt. Hodgson, edited by Scott (Edinburgh: Printed by J. Ballantyne for A. Constable, 1806);

The Works of John Dryden, 18 volumes, edited, with a biography, by Scott (London: Miller, 1808);

Joseph Strutt, *Queenhoo-Hall: A Romance; and Ancient Times: A Drama,* 4 volumes, edited by Scott (Edinburgh: Printed by J. Ballantyne for J. Murray, London, and A. Constable, Edinburgh, 1808);

Memoirs of Capt. George Carleton, An English Officer.... Written by Himself, edited by Scott (Edinburgh: Printed by J. Ballantyne for A. Constable and J. Murray, London, 1808);

Memoirs of Robert Carey, Earl of Monmouth, edited by Scott (Edinburgh: Constable, 1808);

The State Papers and Letters of Sir Ralph Sadler, Knight-Banneret, edited, with an introductory essay, by Scott (Edinburgh: Printed for Archibald Constable and for T. Cadell & W. Davies, William Miller, and John Murray, London, 1809);

A Collection of Scarce and Valuable Tracts [The Somers Tracts], second edition, 13 volumes, edited by Scott (London: Printed for T. Cadell & W. Davies, 1809–1815);

English Minstrelsy: Being a Selection of Fugitive Poetry from the Best English Authors, 2 volumes, edited by Scott (Edinburgh: Ballantyne, 1810);

The Poetical Works of Anna Seward; with Extracts from Her Literary Correspondence, 3 volumes, edited by Scott (Edinburgh: Ballantyne, 1810);

Secret History of the Court of James the First, 2 volumes, edited by Scott (Edinburgh: Printed for J. Ballantyne, 1811);

The Works of Jonathan Swift, 19 volumes, edited, with a biography and notes, by Scott (Edinburgh: Constable, 1814);

The Border Antiquities of England and Scotland, 2 volumes, includes an introduction by Scott (London: Printed for Longman, Hurst, Rees, Orme & Brown, 1814, 1817);

James, eleventh Baron Somerville, *Memorie of the Somervilles,* 2 volumes, edited by Scott (Edinburgh: Constable, 1815);

Ballantyne's Novelist's Library, 10 volumes, edited, with biographical prefaces, by Scott (London: Hurst, Robinson, 1821–1824);

Memorials of the Haliburtons, edited by Scott (Edinburgh: Printed by J. Ballantyne, 1824).

In addition to being the most celebrated European poet and novelist of the early nineteenth century, Sir Walter Scott was an antiquarian and literary scholar of some distinction. The most notable of his contributions to the developing genre of literary biography are the lives of John Dryden and Jonathan Swift that he wrote to accompany his important editions of their works and the biographical prefaces he composed for a reprint series of British novels. With these works Scott helped to establish biography as a formal component of modern textual scholarship and, in deliberate extension of Samuel Johnson's work on behalf of the English poets, dignified the novelist as a fit subject for the genre. More subtly, Scott's novels provided a narrative model for biography as well as for the writing of history. It might be said that Scott's greatest contribution to literary biography turned out to be as subject rather than author: the monumental *Memoirs of the Life of Sir Walter Scott, Bart.* (1837–1838), by his son-in-law and literary executor, John Gibson Lockhart, redefined the form for the Victorians.

The first chapter of Lockhart's biography is occupied with a memoir that Scott began writing in 1808, at the height of his reputation as a poet, and resumed in 1810–1811 and again in 1826 but never completed. With characteristic anxiety about his identity as Romantic poet, Scott undertakes the memoir as a defense against modern biography: "The present age has discovered a desire, or rather a rage, for literary anecdote and private history that may be well permitted to alarm one who has engaged in a certain degree the attention of the public." Citing the unhappy cases of Robert Burns, Thomas Chatterton, and Richard Savage, Scott refuses to stake his identity on anything so risky as poetical character and appeals instead to the Scotsman's "national prerogative" of "pedigree." Scott claims that his own life has been "very quiet and uniform" and boasts of his descent from the wild Border barons whose exploits inspire the traditional ballads he has edited and the modern verse romances with which he has won his present fame. In short, the self is a product of history: poetical identity is an effect not of alienated genius but of culture and lineage. In this conservative critique of Romantic ideology from within it, Scott affirms the intellectual principles of his Scottish Enlightenment education, as he did throughout his career.

Scott was actually born into the thriving eighteenth-century Edinburgh professional class. His father, Walter Scott, was a lawyer, a Writer to the Signet (equivalent to the English solicitor), in politics a Whig, and in religion a devout Presbyterian. In the absence of a political aristocracy after the union of Scotland and England in 1707, the legal profession constituted one of the elite classes of Edinburgh society along with the high dignitaries of the Church of Scotland and the professors at the university. Scott's mother, Anne Rutherford Scott, was the daughter of a professor of medicine.

Scott was born on 15 August 1771 in one of the noisome medieval alleys of the Edinburgh Old Town, where five infant siblings had died before him, and he narrowly escaped contracting tuberculosis from a nurse. Largely for his sake the family moved to the more salubrious neighborhood of George Square, on the southern fringe of the city's modern development, but not before an attack of polio when he was eighteen months old had left him lame in his right leg. Although he would grow up to be a robust young man, Scott spent much of his childhood in convalescence on his grandfather's farm in the Borders. In properly Romantic vein, Scott would locate the origins of his aesthetic imagination in these spells of enforced retirement, set in an ancestral countryside and occupied in the consumption of tales and ballads. The essential part of Scott's education, or so he would later suggest, consisted of this illicit literature ("the Delilahs of my imagination"), first recited to him by his female relatives and then devoured on his own in insatiable reading. Scott's formal education began in Bath, England, in 1775–1776, then followed the traditional upward path of the Edinburgh middle-class elite through the High School from 1779 to 1783 and the university (where he attended the lectures of the distinguished moral philosopher Dugald Stewart) to the study of law. Scott rather neglected his classical schooling and, while dutifully fulfilling its requirements, played imaginative truant from "the dry and barren wilderness" of the law in reading and imitating "works of fiction of every kind."

Apprenticed to his father while still a student in 1786, in 1792 Scott was admitted to the Faculty of Advocates. This was a thoroughly satisfactory achievement for the son of a Writer to the Signet, since the advocates were the superior rank in the Scottish legal profession and provided much of the city's political and cultural leadership.

The third element of Scott's education, besides the official college curriculum and his private reading of romances and histories, was provided by the circles of friendship and future patronage in which he moved. British reaction to the French Revolution determined the politics of Scott's generation, and Edinburgh was the seat of a particularly violent anti-Jacobitism throughout and beyond the 1790s. In common with those of his friends who would constitute the city's ruling elite, Scott acquired solid Tory principles, enhanced by an aesthetic interest in feudalism, Catholicism, and Jacobitism that was rather contrary to his Whig and Presbyterian upbringing. The anti-French, anti-Enlightenment spirit of the literary societies and debating clubs that flourished around the university encouraged a fashion for Gothic and Germanic literature, and in 1792 Scott joined a German reading group. His first book, published four years later, would consist of verse translations of two supernatural ballads by Gottfried August Bürger.

Meanwhile, Scott was a young advocate with some well-placed friends but uncertain prospects and little enthusiasm for the legal career upon which he was embarking. After being rejected in

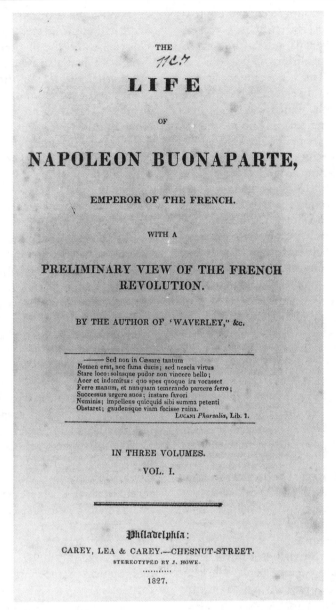

THE

LIFE

OF

NAPOLEON BUONAPARTE,

EMPEROR OF THE FRENCH.

WITH A

PRELIMINARY VIEW OF THE FRENCH
REVOLUTION.

BY THE AUTHOR OF 'WAVERLEY,' &c.

——— Sed non in Cæsare tantum
Nomen erat, nec fama ducis; sed nescia virtus
Stare loco: solusque pudor non vincere bello;
Acer et indomitus: quo spes quoque ira vocasset
Ferre manum, et nunquam temerando parcere ferro;
Successus urgere suos; instare favori
Numinis; impellens quicquid sibi summa petenti
Obstaret; gaudensque viam fecisse ruina.
LUCANI *Pharsalia*, Lib. 1.

IN THREE VOLUMES.

VOL. I.

Philadelphia:

CAREY, LEA & CAREY.—CHESNUT-STREET.
STEREOTYPED BY J. HOWE.
....
1827.

Title page for Scott's nine-volume biography of Napoleon I

1796 by Williamina Belsches, the daughter of a wealthy baronet, on 24 December 1797 Scott married Charlotte Margaret Carpenter, a ward of Arthur Hill, second Marquis of Downshire, and supposedly the daughter of a French Royalist refugee named Jean Charpentier. Her origins were the object of speculation and controversy after Scott's death – she was rumored to have been Downshire's illegitimate daughter – and remain mysterious today. She bore him four children: Charlotte Sophia in 1799, Walter in 1801, Anne in 1803, and Charles in 1805. In 1799 Scott was appointed Sheriff-Depute of Selkirkshire through his connections with Henry Dundas, first Viscount Melville (Prime Minister William Pitt's "Scotch manager"), and Henry Scott, third Duke of Buccleuch (whom Scott regarded as his "clan chief"). Their patronage would also ensure Scott's appointment as Clerk of the Court of Session in 1806. Throughout the decades of literary fame that followed, Scott would continue to occupy both his official jobs, dividing his residence between Edinburgh for the legal terms of winter and summer and the Borders for the rest of the year.

In 1799 Scott met Matthew Gregory Lewis, author of the sensational Gothic romance *The Monk* (1796), who helped him find a publisher for his translation (1799) of Goethe's tragedy *Götz von*

Berlichingen (1773) and asked him to contribute to a miscellany, *Tales of Wonder* (1801). Scott's verses, imitations of old Scottish ballads, reflect the turn of his interests to a native tradition of popular romance. His job as sheriff and his residence in the country meant that he could seriously pursue the collection of Border ballads, which until then had been a hobby. Scott rode energetically about the remote hills and glens to gather materials, assisted by native informants and collectors as well as by correspondence with fellow antiquarians. The result, *Minstrelsy of the Scottish Border* (1802), is the last of the great Enlightenment collections of British oral poetry. It marks Scott's establishment in Edinburgh literary society, which was undergoing a revival after the collapse of Scottish Enlightenment culture in the reaction to the French Revolution.

One of the Edinburgh booksellers who was involved in the publication of *Minstrelsy of the Scottish Border* was Archibald Constable. In 1802 Constable began publishing the *Edinburgh Review,* which soon became the most authoritative vehicle of criticism in the country; it was edited by a set of brilliant young Whig lawyers who could not get preferment under the Melville regime. Scott became a contributor despite his party differences with the editors, for in its early years the *Edinburgh Review* was able to reproduce a moderate, gentlemanly, Enlightenment ideological consensus. The political pressures of war with France would not allow that consensus to last, however, and in 1809 Scott would break with the *Edinburgh Review* and collaborate with establishment friends in London to instigate the rival, progovernment *Quarterly Review.* The founding of the *Quarterly Review* announced a political division of Edinburgh literary culture that would become violent in the years following the defeat of France; Scott's part in it is evidence of the enormous prestige and influence he had acquired by the end of the decade.

Scott was by then the most famous poet in Europe. From collecting ancient Border ballads he had turned to imitating them in a "goblin tale," *The Lay of the Last Minstrel* (1805). With this work Scott had invented that distinctively nineteenth-century phenomenon, the popular verse romance or ballad-epic. *The Lay of the Last Minstrel* was followed by the still more extravagantly successful *Marmion: A Tale of Flodden Field* (1808), a story of corrupted chivalry for which Constable paid Scott one thousand pounds, and *The Lady of the Lake* (1810), a romance of the Highlands. By this time Scott's fans included the prince regent, and in 1813 he would turn down the office of poet laureate in favor of his needy friend Robert Southey.

With the triumph of *The Lay of the Last Minstrel* Scott had consolidated a business relationship with Constable and the printers John and James Ballantyne, who had also been involved in the production of *Minstrelsy of the Scottish Border*. In March 1805 Scott purchased a one-third share in the Ballantyne firm in a secret arrangement. The Ballantynes became not only his printers and partners but trusted advisers, critics, and business agents; Scott insisted that his publishers engage the firm for the production not only of his own works but of the host of miscellaneous literary speculations he undertook over the next nine years. Among the more distinguished of these projects were editions of the works of Dryden (1808) and Swift (1814), for which Scott wrote biographical memoirs.

In preparing his editions Scott did extensive reading in documents of the period, and he provides the texts with elaborate historical annotations. At the end of the nineteenth century George Saintsbury would call the eighteen-volume Dryden edition "one of the best-edited books on a great scale in English" and praise the accuracy and thoroughness of Scott's notes, while Leslie Stephen would pay similar tribute to the nineteen-volume Swift edition. They have been surpassed only by the resources of modern academic research. In applying the standards of historical scholarship to his introductory memoirs of the authors, Scott did much to establish literary biography within the formal discipline of textual criticism. He drew on the systematic antiquarianism of the late Enlightenment exemplified by Edmond Malone's research into Dryden's life for his edition of *The Critical and Miscellaneous Works of John Dryden* (1800), to expand the genre of the biographical preface into a full-volume scientific history.

Contemporary readers expressed the keenest interest in the biographical component of these works. "That a poet should write the life of a poet," Henry Hallam began his *Edinburgh Review* essay on the Dryden edition (October 1808), "is both a natural and pleasing species of biography." It was not poetic enough for Hallam, however; he goes on to complain of Scott's copiousness in retailing so much contextual material, although he recognizes Scott's intention of enabling "the reader to estimate, how far the age was indebted to the poet, and how far the poet was influenced by the taste and manners of the age." These are the terms, according to Scott's modern biographer Edgar Johnson, of Scott's "characteristic achievement": "relating Dryden's work to his character and showing how his writings both molded and were molded by the climate of the age."

Johnson admits that while the memoir might lack the brilliance of Johnson's critical essay on Dryden in *Prefaces, Biographical and Critical, to the Works of the English Poets* (1779–1781), it is always lucid and judicious; and while it adds little new information to Malone's compilation of the facts of Dryden's life, it is far superior in narrative coherence and circumstantial texture.

The memoir of Swift was reviewed by the formidable editor of the *Edinburgh Review* (September 1816), Francis Jeffrey, who praised Scott for the worldly tolerance, good sense, and moderation with which he represented the personalities and politics of the age but blamed him for being "too favourable to the personal character of his author." Jeffrey's attack on Swift's character, according to Lockhart, was sufficient to depress the sale of the edition, which did not repeat the extraordinary success of the Dryden edition. Johnson calls Scott's work on Swift "a valuable pioneer job," all the more impressive for the absence of prior scholarly research. Johnson finds "the great contours" of Scott's portrayal to be "illuminating and true," despite deficiencies in detail and a tendency to make Swift "more consistent, less ambiguous and contradictory" than he would appear to modern critics. Like the life of Dryden, it is composed in the sober and judicious register of Enlightenment scholarship. In her article "Sir Walter Scott as Literary Biographer," in *Scott and His Influence* (1983), Jill Rubenstein claims that the memoirs are most interesting to modern readers as "essays in conjectural aesthetics" through which Scott is able to reflect on his own relationship to the politics and literary market of his day.

The year 1814 marked a crossroads in Scott's career. In 1809 he had quarreled with Constable over the conduct of a partner who had criticized his progress on the Swift edition. With the advice of John Murray, the London publisher of the *Quarterly Review,* Scott set up an independent publishing firm with the Ballantyne brothers. Once again his financial interest – a controlling share – remained secret. Despite the immense success of *The Lady of the Lake* the business was soon in financial disarray, not least through some of the bad speculations to which Scott committed the firm. In 1811 Scott bought a farm by the river Tweed; soon his enormous literary earnings were pouring into the construction of Abbotsford, a manor house designed in an elaborately Gothic style but fitted with modern conveniences such as gaslight. Just as the family was moving into Abbotsford, Scott's reputation as a poet was beginning to decline; *The Vision of Don Roderick* (1811) and

Rokeby (1813) did not reap anything like the acclaim of their predecessors, and with the publication in 1812 of George Gordon, Lord Byron's *Childe Harold's Pilgrimage* it was clear that another poet had risen to public favor.

Scott liked to claim that Byron's superiority turned him from verse to prose romance and that in a leisurely search for fishing tackle in the autumn of 1813 he had happened upon a forgotten manuscript, begun in 1805, that became the opening chapters of *Waverley; or, 'Tis Sixty Years Since* (1814). It seems likely, however, that Scott had been at work on the novel as recent as 1810 and that he resumed it in response to the same exigency that drove him and the Ballantynes back to Constable in the summer of 1813. In a year of economic turbulence the firm's failure seemed certain, and Constable's terms were liberal. When Scott went to Edinburgh at the beginning of 1814 he took with him the manuscript for the first volume of the novel, and in July *Waverley* was published anonymously. In September Scott returned from a voyage around the northern coasts and islands to find that Constable had sold out two editions and wanted to contract for a third. At the age of forty-three Scott was launched on his spectacular career as a novelist.

With *Waverley,* the tale of a young man's involvement in the Jacobite rebellion of 1745, Scott raised the novel to the dignity of a canonical literary form and redefined the scope of narrative for the nineteenth century. Scott's reviewers praised him for invigorating the decadent, "feminine" genre of prose romance – even though Scott was indebted to prototypes by female novelists, such as Ann Radcliffe's Gothic romance and the national tale of Sydney Owenson and Maria Edgeworth. Here was a work of fiction in which national history and personal identity, public sphere and private interest, cultural transformation and individual desire were articulated together. To the novelistic narrative of personal destiny Scott brought the collective narrative of cultural stages and modes of production he had learned from the philosophical historians and political economists of the Scottish Enlightenment: Adam Ferguson, Adam Smith, and John Millar. Scott's political sympathies were closer, however, to those promoted by David Hume in his great *History of England* (1754–1762), and from Hume, Scott derived the technique of embedding set-piece, essayistic "characters" of historical protagonists within the diachronic flow of the narrative. The technique is less characteristic of *Waverley* and the two novels following it – in which conventional literary types alternate with vividly realized representations of com-

Scott's tomb

mon folk who reveal themselves in their speech — than it is of the first three series of the great *Tales of My Landlord* (1816–1819), in which Scott undertakes a more rigorously historical representation, and of some of the later romances, in which historical individuals feature prominently: one thinks of the portraits of John Graham of Claverhouse and John Balfour of "Burley" (that is, John Balfour, third Baron Balfour of Burleigh) in *Old Mortality* (1816), or of Elizabeth I in *Kenilworth* (1821), or Oliver Cromwell in *Woodstock; or, the Cavalier* (1826). *Old Mortality,* which forms part of the first series of *Tales of My Landlord,* is a particularly fine example of the mixed mode of Scott's characterization — the range of techniques by which he represents individual lives in relation to larger historical forces and cultural contexts — and his major contribution to biographical practice may be found here rather than in his less interesting and innovative formal exercises in the genre.

The success of *Waverley* was repeated with *Guy Mannering; or, the Astrologer* (1815) and *The Antiquary* (1816), romances of eighteenth-century Scotland that established "the Author of *Waverley*" as a major force in the representation of a national and historical cultural identity. With *Tales of My Landlord* Scott once more turned away from Constable and struck a deal with Murray's Edinburgh agent, the rising publisher

William Blackwood. The new direction was signaled by the adoption of an elaborate apparatus of pseudonymous editorial masks, as though a singular anonymity were not enough to baffle the public. Appearing in the multiple guise of the shadowy landlord of a country inn, two village schoolmasters (one a dead Romantic youth, the other a veteran pedant), and a series of narrators and informants, Scott wrote a series of historical tales of national life, three of which — *Old Mortality, The Heart of Mid-Lothian* (1818), and *The Bride of Lammermoor* (1819) — have generally been praised as his finest. Blackwood, however, offended Scott by criticizing the first of the series, the unsuccessful *The Black Dwarf* (1816), and haggling over a later edition of *Old Mortality,* and once again Scott went back to Constable. "The Author of *Waverley*" remained active alongside the "editors" of *Tales of My Landlord,* producing in 1818 the wildly popular Highland romance *Rob Roy* — as, for that matter, did Scott the poet, with *The Lord of the Isles* (1815) and *Harold the Dauntless* (1817). Scott maintained his astonishing rate of production by relying on assistants and collaborators, such as the Ballantynes and his estate manager and amanuensis William Laidlaw, in addition to his own prodigious energies.

Scott was earning unprecedented sums for his novels; but his expenditure on his estate continued to outrun his income, and he remained burdened by debts and unsold stock from his ill-advised publishing venture with the Ballantynes. In 1815 the terms of James Ballantyne's marriage settlement obliged Scott to assume sole partnership and liability in the printing business and to retain Ballantyne as a salaried employee. Meanwhile, an ambition to recover the ancestral territories of his own romances was driving Scott to buy up tracts of land around Abbotsford, often at inflated prices, and he was soon mortgaging his literary production several books ahead of the one he was completing. Between 1817 and 1819 Scott was afflicted with gallstones so severely that his friends feared for his life, and at the crisis of the illness, in June 1819, rumors of his death circulated in Edinburgh.

Yet Scott maintained the pace and quality of his literary production; Lockhart's account of Scott dictating *The Bride of Lammermoor* in a delirious trance is true to the spirit if not the letter of the occasion. On his recovery Scott changed direction yet again, forsaking his great topic of the modernization of Scotland for a new historical setting in *Ivanhoe,* a romance of medieval England published at the end of 1819. With its greenwood and Gothic scenery and a cast of characters including Robin Hood and Richard Coeur de Lion, *Ivanhoe* quickly became the most popular of all Scott's works. The novels that followed ranged widely across early modern British and Continental history: the Scottish Reformation in *The Monastery* (1820) and its sequel, *The Abbot* (1820); the court of Elizabeth I in *Kenilworth;* the Shetland Islands in the seventeenth century in *The Pirate* (1821); Jacobean and Restoration London in *The Fortunes of Nigel* (1822) and *Peveril of the Peak* (1823); and fifteenth-century France in *Quentin Durward* (1823). Two novels returned to Scott's native Scotland: *St. Ronan's Well* (1823) was an attempt to write a satiric melodrama of contemporary manners, while *Redgauntlet* (1824), one of his finest works, constitutes a complex reflection on the "Scotch novels" of his earlier career. With *Tales of the Crusaders* (1825) – comprising *The Betrothed* and *The Talisman* – Scott turned again to the fantastic medieval romance exemplified by *Ivanhoe.*

The reception of these works was relatively uneven, although if *The Betrothed* disappointed readers in comparison with the sensational *The Talisman,* it remained true that even a weaker Waverley novel enjoyed better sales and reviews than any other novel of the time. Scott stood at the pinnacle of his reputation in the early 1820s. A powerful local industry of "Scotch novel-writing" responded to his example, and such talents (some of them consider-

able) as Lockhart, James Hogg, John Galt, Susan Ferrier, and John Wilson competed with Scott and one another to produce imitations, revisions, and critical refutations of the model of national historical narrative represented by the Waverley novels. The author of those novels might officially be anonymous, but there was no doubt that Scott was the leading force in Edinburgh cultural life, a sort of viceroy of letters. He was a patron of the city's theatrical revival, the founder or president of literary clubs and scientific and antiquarian societies, and the expert commander of networks of patronage. At Abbotsford he played with gusto the role of Border laird, generous in hospitality and indefatigable in improvement of his estate. As Scott's "romance in limestone" took form he stocked it with antiques and curiosities from the worlds of his own novels, including the great door of "the Heart of Mid-Lothian" (the old Edinburgh prison) and a live Highland piper.

Nor was the highest official recognition wanting. In 1818 the prince regent had communicated his intention to grant Scott a baronetcy, and the honor was duly published on the prince's accession to the throne as George IV in 1820. Scott's association with a pageantry of royalist revival, exemplified by his discovery of the Scottish regalia in 1818 and his newspaper account of the coronation ceremony in 1821, culminated in his orchestration of George IV's visit to Scotland in 1822 as an extravagant spectacle of nationalist loyalty.

Such pageantry must be understood in the context of the dire economic recession and social unrest that followed the Napoleonic Wars. In these years of mass unemployment, rick burning, machine breaking, reform agitation, and savage government repression, Scott was among those who feared a revolutionary outbreak, and he played his part in organizing a loyalist militia in his district and composing antiradical pamphlets. Scott viewed reform as a reckless ploy by the Whig gentry to get back into power by countenancing radicals and flattering the mob, a tactic that could only result in the destruction of the British constitution. He held that the solution to the country's troubles lay in a revival of the wartime income tax and a paternalistic, community-based program of public works and self-help projects run by the government and men of property – a program such as he himself was organizing on his estate to provide employment for neighborhood families. Some commentators have described a growing political pessimism on Scott's part after 1820 and have argued that he began to lose his faith in an Enlightenment historiographical model of economic progress and social consent.

The period's political turbulence overtook Edinburgh literary life, which became the stage for a fierce struggle between the Whig cultural establishment of the *Edinburgh Review,* as their party began at last to gain political ground in the south, and a Tory backlash led by a group of young lawyers and intellectuals. Notable among the latter were Lockhart and Wilson, prime movers of *Blackwood's Edinburgh Magazine,* which scandalized the public with its personal scurrilities when it first appeared in 1817. Ferocious in its assault on Whigs and "Cockneys," *Blackwood's* was soon provoking duels, brawls, and litigation. Scott's role in these culture wars is somewhat equivocal. Careful to maintain a public neutrality, and always on friendly terms with Whig literati such as Jeffrey and Henry Cockburn, Scott was, nevertheless, increasingly active behind the scenes on behalf of his party's interests. He deplored the excesses of the satire in *Blackwood's* but supported the magazine through a proxy, Laidlaw. Wilson and Lockhart soon became his protégés; in 1820 Scott lobbied for Wilson's election as professor of moral philosophy at the University of Edinburgh over a vastly better-qualified Whig candidate, and in the same year Lockhart married Scott's elder daughter, Sophia. In 1821 Scott was exposed as one of a cabal of establishment sponsors that had financed a libelous Tory paper, the *Beacon,* and until it was proven that he bore no editorial responsibility for the contents, it seemed as though Scott might have to fight a duel. It was a bleak season for the civic tradition of moderation to which Scott had been bred.

Meanwhile, financial pressures remained heavy. In addition to the continuing expenses at Abbotsford, Scott was outfitting his elder son Walter to become a cornet in the Hussars. He remained as busy as ever with a variety of literary projects besides the major fiction. One of these projects, a popular reprint series of works by British novelists with biographical prefaces, had been suggested to Scott by Murray as early as 1808. Scott did not take up the idea until 1819, when he did so as a benefit for the ill and insolvent John Ballantyne. Ballantyne died in 1821, shortly after publication of the first volume, devoted to Henry Fielding; the clumsy format – bulky tomes with double columns of small type – made Ballantyne's Novelist's Library unattractive to the public, and Constable discontinued publication in 1824, after the appearance of the tenth volume, on Radcliffe. Lockhart, in an anonymous review in *Blackwood's* (April 1824), however, noted the treasure buried in these awkward volumes – critical biographies of the British novelists

by "the Author of *Waverley.*" In Paris in 1825 Galignani published Scott's prefaces in a pirated edition under the title *Lives of the Novelists,* and they were included in *The Miscellaneous Prose Works of Sir Walter Scott, Bart.* in 1827.

Although Anna Laetitia Barbauld had prefaced her fifty-volume series *The British Novelists* (1810) with a fairly extensive account of Samuel Richardson and brief notes on her other selections, no such canon of novelists' biographies had been compiled before, and Scott's prefaces are part of his important achievement in raising the cultural status of prose fiction. They are notable for their narrative sobriety, typical rather than merely anecdotal focus, and moderation of judgment: "We did not think it proper to reject the works of so eminent an author from the collections of the British Novelists, merely on account of speculative errors," Scott declares of the radical Robert Bage. In format the prefaces are divided between life narrative and critical essay. Their most recent editor, Ioan Williams, describes their ethos as "a combination of neo-classic respect for restraint with a pre-Victorian desire for the evidently moral." Nineteenth-century readers thought highly of them. "Scott combines all the graces of his easy narrative," wrote Lockhart, "with a perpetual stream of deep and gentle wisdom in commenting on the tempers and fortunes of his best predecessors in novel literature." Cultural consensus, rather than originality or idiosyncrasy, was, as usual, Scott's rhetorical aim.

In 1821 James Ballantyne was readmitted as a partner in the printing business, but Scott remained liable for all current debts, which amounted to some twenty-seven thousand pounds. Cash income tended to be swallowed up by such pressing expenses as Abbotsford; meanwhile, Scott and Constable went on drawing and renewing bills of accommodation against one another, extending a precarious network of credit that would unravel all at once should misfortune strike either party. The year 1825 was full of financial uncertainty. A frenzy of stockjobbing had strained the London money market, and in the autumn the major banks were beginning to restrict credit. The Ballantyne debt then stood at around forty thousand pounds. Scott had married off his son, Walter, to an heiress, and in addition to buying him a captain's commission he settled Abbotsford on him, thus securing the estate against any reversal to which he himself might be prone. Young Walter was posted to unsettled Ireland, where Scott visited him in the summer before going on to visit his literary friends Edgeworth and William and Dorothy Wordsworth. The family cir-

The Scott Memorial in Edinburgh

cle was dispersing: Lockhart was off with Sophia and their son to London to be the new editor of the *Quarterly,* while Scott's younger son Charles was a student at Oxford. In November, amid growing anxieties about the London money market, Scott — as if he sensed what was coming — began to keep a journal.

Soon Lockhart passed on some disturbing rumors about rash speculation on the part of Constable's London partners, Hurst and Robinson. By mid December banks were stopping payment, and news came of the London firm's failure. Constable's ruin, and therefore Scott's and Ballantyne's, became inevitable, and by mid January 1826 the worst was clear. Scott's debts amounted to nearly £130,000. Instead of declaring bankruptcy Scott proposed a trust conveyance of his property to his creditors; they accepted. Scott got to reside at Abbotsford, keep his library and furniture, and stay on in his salaried posts, but he had to give up his townhouse on North Castle Street. He would pay off the immense debt with his literary labor.

So began the honorable drudgery that consumed the remainder of Scott's life. "I see before me a long tedious and dark path," he wrote in his journal, "but it leads to true fame and spotless reputa-

tion. If I die in the harrows, as is very likely, I shall die with honour." Praise of Scott's character, and of the journal as its authentic expression, has become commonplace even on the part of those who dismiss the novels, but it is important to recognize that the journal is an artful rhetorical construct in which Scott fashions himself as a tragic hero, noble in his fall and suffering. It was the major literary work of Scott's last years, the one he wrote for himself even as he was grinding out volumes of public prose to pay his debts. Lockhart used this immensely moving document to form the last volume of his *Memoirs of the Life of Sir Walter Scott, Bart.* as Scott no doubt intended that he should, and its importance for subsequent literary biography is considerable. Here Scott staged for himself and for his biographer the tragic drama of the inner life stoically meeting its suffering that he had been unable to represent in his official exercises in the genre. The young Charles Dickens, obsessed with his own fortunes, copied extracts from the journal as it appeared in Lockhart's biography, and Scott's example both inspired and admonished Dickens and other Victorian novelists.

The fashioning of literary identity had become a crucial matter with the ruin, for now Scott stood revealed in public as "the Author of *Waverley.*" One of the major projects of these years involved the full-scale reassembly and marketing of that identity in the Magnum Opus Edition of the Waverley novels, published between 1829 and 1833 by Constable's surviving partner, Robert Cadell, in fine but – thanks to new printing technologies – inexpensive volumes, with revisions, notes, and prefaces by the author. As Jane Millgate has pointed out, the Magnum Opus Edition is historically important in its construction of the novelist as a coherent cultural figure, a unity of life and literary production signified by the presence of the author, as editor, informing his own collected works. Where "the Author of *Waverley*" had been a ghostly figure separate from Sir Walter Scott, now Scott's notes – specifying the circumstances of a novel's production, identifying autobiographical references secreted in a text – insisted that they were one. It was the necessary precondition for a monumental biography, committed to the union of life and works such as Lockhart would provide.

In May 1826 Lady Scott died, leaving Scott's daughter Anne to nurse her father through his decline. He completed *Woodstock* and the enormous *The Life of Napoleon Buonaparte, Emperor of the French* (1827); upset his friends in the government by writing a series of pamphlets under the pseudonym Malachi Malagrowther (1826) attacking a measure to reform the Scottish currency; and began the series *Chronicles of the Canongate* (1827–1828), which is remarkable for the disillusioned persona of its "editor," the ruined Crystal Croftangry. In 1829 Scott's health began to break down, and in the following year, after suffering a stroke, he retired from his clerkship at the Court of Session. But he would not abate his literary labors: *Anne of Geierstein; or, The Maiden of the Mist* (1829) was followed by *Letters on Demonology and Witchcraft* (1830) and a fourth series of *Tales of My Landlord,* comprising *Count Robert of Paris* (1832) and *Castle Dangerous* (1832).

Despite his growing infirmity Scott canvased for the Tory cause in the parliamentary elections of the spring of 1831. The ministry of Arthur Wellesley, first Duke of Wellington, had fallen, and the ascendancy of a Whig party committed to reform seemed certain. When Scott attempted to address a public meeting in Jedburgh he was shouted down by the hostile crowd, and on election day his carriage was stoned. According to his old friend Hogg, these events precipitated his death.

After two more severe strokes Scott's doctors advised him to spend the next winter in a warmer climate. The new Whig administration and the new monarch, William IV, arranged free passage for Scott and his daughter on a Royal Navy frigate bound for Malta. They sailed in October and made their way from Malta to Naples. But Scott grew weary and listless, and on the return journey through Germany in June 1832 he collapsed with a fourth apoplectic seizure. He was rushed back to London, where he lay for three weeks in a paralytic coma; he revived slightly on the return to Abbotsford, then relapsed into stupor and delirium, dying peacefully on 21 September. On 26 September, a day of national mourning, Scott was buried in the rose-brown ruins of Dryburgh Abbey. The following year his creditors dissolved the trust on payment of the principal of the debt by the family, who borrowed money from Cadell in exchange for the rights to Scott's literary properties.

Scott was the most important European literary figure of his generation, and his authority and influence remained preeminent throughout the first half of the century. His historical novels redefined both history and the novel, making them the dominant narrative genres of nineteenth-century literary culture, and became the model for the developing national literatures of Europe and its colonies. As well as learning their technique from Scott, the Victorian novelists were haunted by his example. Kind in private life, honorable in public, and breathtakingly prolific, Scott set the pattern for the author's career: heroic production maintained by the power of an individual. His end warned that such heroism might be tragic.

By the last decades of the century subsequent developments had appeared to supersede the Waverley novels, much as Byron had eclipsed Scott's poems, and there began what Stephen called the descent "from the library to the schoolroom." Modernist taste seemed to have relegated Scott to the category of the subliterary, and since 1945 even Scott's status as a popular writer has declined as many of the Waverley novels have fallen out of print. More-recent years have brought signs of a revival of critical and scholarly interest in the novels, although the poems remain, for now, beyond the pale. Modern scholars continue to respect Scott's work on Dryden and Swift, and literary historians are beginning to recognize the importance of his promotion of the novelist to the dignity of biography. Nevertheless, Scott's greatest influence on the development of the genre must be found in the technical innovations of his novels and in the example set by his own career.

Letters:

The Letters of Sir Walter Scott, 12 volumes, edited by Sir Herbert J. C. Grierson, assisted by Davidson Cook, W. M. Parker, and others (London: Constable, 1932–1937).

Bibliographies:

Greville Worthington, *A Bibliography of the Waverley Novels* (London: Constable, 1931);

William Ruff, *A Bibliography of the Poetical Works of Sir Walter Scott, 1796–1832* (Edinburgh: Edinburgh Bibliographical Society, 1938);

James Clarkson Corson, *A Bibliography of Sir Walter Scott: A Classified and Annotated List of Books and Articles Relating to His Life and Works, 1797–1940* (Edinburgh & London: Oliver & Boyd, 1943);

Jill Rubenstein, *Sir Walter Scott: A Reference Guide* (Boston: G. K. Hall, 1978).

Biographies:

John Gibson Lockhart, *Memoirs of the Life of Sir Walter Scott, Bart.* (7 volumes, Edinburgh: Cadell, 1837–1838; revised, 10 volumes, 1839);

Sir Herbert Grierson, *Sir Walter Scott, Bart.: A New Life Supplementary to and Corrective of Lockhart's Biography* (London: Constable, 1938);

Edgar Johnson, *Sir Walter Scott: The Great Unknown,* 2 volumes (New York: Macmillan, 1970).

References:

J. H. Alexander and David Hewitt, eds., *Scott and His Influence: The Papers of the Aberdeen Scott Conference, 1982* (Aberdeen: Association for Scottish Literary Studies, 1983);

Alexander and Hewitt, eds., *Scott in Carnival: Selected Papers from the Fourth International Scott Conference, Edinburgh, 1991* (Aberdeen: Association for Scottish Literary Studies, 1993);

James Anderson, *Sir Walter Scott and History; With Other Papers* (Edinburgh: Edina, 1981);

Bruce Beiderwell, *Power and Punishment in Scott's Novels* (Athens: University of Georgia Press, 1991);

Alan Bell, ed., *Scott Bicentenary Essays: Selected Papers Read at the Sir Walter Scott Bicentenary Conference* (Edinburgh & London: Scottish Academic Press, 1973);

Alan Bold, ed., *Sir Walter Scott: The Long-forgotten Melody* (London: Vision Press, 1983);

David Brown, *Walter Scott and the Historical Imagination* (London & Boston: Routledge & Kegan Paul, 1979);

Alice Chandler, *A Dream of Order: The Medieval Ideal in Nineteenth-Century Literature* (Lincoln: University of Nebraska Press, 1970);

A. O. J. Cockshut, *The Achievement of Sir Walter Scott* (London: Collins, 1969);

Daniel Cottom, *The Civilized Imagination: A Study of Ann Radcliffe, Jane Austen, and Sir Walter Scott* (Cambridge & New York: Cambridge University Press, 1985);

Robert Crawford, *Devolving English Literature* (Oxford: Clarendon Press, 1992);

Thomas Crawford, *Scott,* revised and enlarged edition, Scottish Writers Series (Edinburgh: Scottish Academic Press, 1982);

David Daiches, *Sir Walter Scott and His World* (New York: Viking, 1971);

Donald Davie, *The Heyday of Sir Walter Scott* (London: Routledge & Kegan Paul, 1961);

D. D. Devlin, *The Author of Waverley: A Critical Study of Walter Scott* (London: Macmillan, 1971);

Ian Duncan, *Modern Romance and Transformations of the Novel: The Gothic, Scott, Dickens* (Cambridge: Cambridge University Press, 1992);

John P. Farrell, *Revolution as Tragedy: The Dilemma of the Moderate from Scott to Arnold* (Ithaca, N.Y.: Cornell University Press, 1980);

Ina Ferris, *The Making of Literary Authority: Gender, History and the Waverley Novels* (Ithaca, N.Y.: Cornell University Press, 1991);

Avrom Fleishman, *The English Historical Novel: Walter Scott to Virginia Woolf* (Baltimore: Johns Hopkins University Press, 1971);

Duncan Forbes, "The Rationalism of Sir Walter Scott," *Cambridge Journal,* 7 (October 1953): 20–35;

Peter Garside, "Popular Fiction and National Tale: The Hidden Origins of Scott's *Waverley,*" *Nineteenth-Century Literature,* 46 (June 1991): 30–53;

Garside, "Scott and the Philosophical Historians," *Journal of the History of Ideas,* 36 (July–September 1975): 497–512;

Douglas Gifford, ed., *The History of Scottish Literature,* volume 3: *The Nineteenth Century* (Aberdeen: Aberdeen University Press, 1988);

Mark Girouard, *The Return to Camelot: Chivalry and the English Gentleman* (New Haven & London: Yale University Press, 1981);

Robert C. Gordon, *Under Which King? A Study of the Scottish Waverley Novels* (Edinburgh: Oliver & Boyd, 1969);

Francis R. Hart, *Scott's Novels: The Plotting of Historic Survival* (Charlottesville: University Press of Virginia, 1966);

John O. Hayden, ed., *Scott: The Critical Heritage* (London: Routledge & Kegan Paul, 1970);

James T. Hillhouse, *The Waverley Novels and Their Critics* (Minneapolis: University of Minnesota Press, 1936);

Andrew D. Hook, "Jane Porter, Sir Walter Scott and the Historical Novel," *Clio,* 2 (Winter 1976): 181–192;

Gary Kelly, *English Fiction of the Romantic Period 1789–1830* (London & New York: Longman, 1989);

James Kerr, *Fiction against History: Scott as Storyteller* (Cambridge: Cambridge University Press, 1989);

Mary Lascelles, *The Story-Teller Retrieves the Past: Historical Fiction and Fictitious History in the Art of Scott, Stevenson, Kipling, and Some Others* (Oxford: Clarendon Press, 1980);

George Levine, *The Realistic Imagination: English Fiction from Frankenstein to Lady Chatterley* (Chicago: University of Chicago Press, 1981);

Georg Lukàcs, *The Historical Novel,* translated by Hannah Mitchell and Stanley Mitchell (London: Merlin, 1962);

James MacQueen, *The Enlightenment and Scottish Literature,* volume 2: *The Rise of the Historical Novel* (Edinburgh: Scottish Academic Press, 1989);

Susan Manning, *The Puritan-Provincial Vision: Scottish and American Literature in the Nineteenth Century* (Cambridge: Cambridge University Press, 1990);

David Marshall, *Sir Walter Scott and Scots Law* (Edinburgh: Hodge, 1932);

Graham McMaster, *Scott and Society* (Cambridge: Cambridge University Press, 1981);

Jane Millgate, *Scott's Last Edition: A Study in Publishing History* (Edinburgh: Edinburgh University Press, 1987);

Millgate, *Walter Scott: The Making of the Novelist* (Toronto: University of Toronto Press, 1984);

Jerome Mitchell, *Scott, Chaucer, and Medieval Romance: A Study in Sir Walter Scott's Indebtedness to the Literature of the Middle Ages* (Lexington: University Press of Kentucky, 1987);

Coleman O. Parsons, *Witchcraft and Demonology in Scott's Fiction: With Chapters on the Supernatural in Scottish Literature* (Edinburgh & London: Oliver & Boyd / New York: Clarke Irwin, 1964);

Murray J. Pittock, *The Invention of Scotland: The Stuart Myth and the Scottish Identity, 1638 to the Present* (London: Routledge, 1991);

James Reed, *Sir Walter Scott: Landscape and Locality* (London: Athlone, 1980);

Harry E. Shaw, *The Forms of Historical Fiction: Sir Walter Scott and His Successors* (Ithaca, N.Y.: Cornell University Press, 1983);

Kathryn Sutherland, "Fictional Economies: Adam Smith, Walter Scott and the Nineteenth Century Novel," *ELH,* 54 (Spring 1987): 97–127;

Katie Trumpener, "National Character, Nationalistic Plots: National Tale and Historical Novel in the Age of *Waverley,* 1806–1830," *ELH,* 60 (Fall 1993): 685–731;

Graham Tulloch, *The Language of Walter Scott* (London: Deutsch, 1980);

Joseph Valente, "Upon the Braes: History and Hermeneutics in *Waverley,*" *Studies in Romanticism,* 25 (Summer 1986): 251–276;

Alexander Welsh, *The Hero of the Waverley Novels* (New Haven, Conn. & London: Yale University Press, 1963);

Judith Wilt, *Secret Leaves: The Novels of Sir Walter Scott* (Chicago & London: University of Chicago Press, 1985).

Papers:

Collections of Sir Walter Scott's manuscripts, letters, documents, and memorabilia are in the Henry W. and Albert A. Berg Collection and the Carl H. Pforzheimer Collection of the New York Public Library; the Boston Public Library; the British Museum; the Folger Shakespeare Library, Washington, D.C.; the Forster Collection in the Victoria and Albert Museum; the Houghton Library and the Harry E. Widener Library of Harvard University; the Henry E. Huntington Library; the Pierpont Morgan Library; the National Library of Scotland; the library of Princeton University; and the library of the University of Rochester.

James Spedding

(26 June 1808 – 9 March 1881)

W. A. Sessions
Georgia State University

BOOKS: *Evenings with a Reviewer; or, A Free and Particular Examination of Mr. Macaulay's Article on Lord Bacon, in a Series of Dialogues,* 2 volumes (London: Printed by Richard & John E. Taylor, 1848); republished as *Evenings with a Reviewer; or, Macaulay and Bacon: With a Prefatory Notice by G. S. Venables,* 2 volumes (Boston: Houghton, Mifflin, 1882);

Companion to the Railway Edition of Lord Campbell's Life of Bacon, as "a Railway Reader" (London: Chapman, 1853);

Publishers and Authors (London: John Russell Smith, 1867);

Reviews and Discussions, Literary, Political, and Historical, not Relating to Bacon (London: Kegan Paul, 1879);

Studies in English History, by Spedding and James Gairdner (Edinburgh: Douglas, 1881);

Prefaces and Prologues to Famous Books, with Introductions, Notes and Illustrations (New York: Collier, 1910).

OTHER: *The Works of Francis Bacon,* 14 volumes, edited by Spedding, Robert Leslie Ellis, and Douglas Denon Heath (London: Longman; Simpkin; Hamilton; Whittaker; J. Bain; E. Hodgson; Washbourne; Richardson Brothers; Houlston; Bickers & Bush; Willis & Sotheran; J. Cornish; L. Booth; J. Snow; Aylott, 1858–1874) – includes as volumes 8–14 *The Letters and the Life of Francis Bacon, Including All His Occasional Works, Namely Letters, Speeches, Tracts, State Papers, Memorials, Devices and All Authentic Writings Not Already Printed among His Philosophical, Literary, or Professional Works, Newly Collected and Set Forth in Chronological Order with a Commentary Biographical and Historical;* edited, with biographical commentary, by Spedding (1861–1874); biographical commentary republished as *An Account of the Life and Times of Francis Bacon,* 2 volumes (London: Trübner, 1878; Boston: Houghton, Mifflin, 1880);

A Conference of Pleasure, Composed for Some Festive Occasion about the Year 1592 by Francis Bacon: Edited from a Manuscript Belonging to the Duke of Northumberland, edited by Spedding (London: Longmans, Green, Reader & Dyer, 1870);

Charles Tennyson Turner, *Collected Sonnets, Old and New,* edited by Hallam, Lord Tennyson, introductory essay by Spedding (London: Kegan Paul, 1880; New York: Macmillan, 1898);

The Philosophical Works of Francis Bacon, Baron of Verulam, Viscount of St. Albans, translated, with notes and prefaces, by Spedding and Ellis, edited by John M. Robinson (London: Routledge / New York: Dutton, 1905).

Victorian culture dominated the world by the end of the nineteenth century, and James Spedding participated in the intellectual development of that culture as did few others. His contribution is, however, hardly recognized today. The mammoth edition of the works of Francis Bacon (1858–1874), including Bacon's biography – one of the central scholarly projects of his time, to which Spedding devoted thirty years of his life – is generally ignored. Spedding's recovery of Bacon for his own time, however, brought praise from Thomas Carlyle, Alfred Tennyson, Edward FitzGerald, Leslie Stephen, and other Victorian intellectuals and helped in the actualization of the Baconian method in the work of Victorian scientists, including Charles Darwin. But the Bacon edition was only one of Spedding's achievements. He developed a powerful control of the English sentence, with a manipulation of syntax that came from a combination of knowledge of Latin and Greek and an inherited eighteenth-century prose style. Spedding's magnificently understated style can be seen in a passage from his preface to Bacon's *De Interpretatione Naturae Proemium* that could also be descriptive of Spedding himself: "After considering what was the best thing to be done, he proceeds to consider what he was himself best fitted to do. He finds

James Spedding

in himself a mind at once discursive enough to seize resemblances, and steady enough to distinguish differences; a mind eager in search, patient of doubt, fond of meditation, slow to assert, ready to reconsider, careful to dispose and set in order; not carried away either by love of novelty or by admiration of antiquity, and hating every kind of imposture; a mind therefore especially framed for the study and pursuit of truth." While this passage sounds suitably Victorian in its idealism, it is in actuality an adaptation of a Latin passage from Bacon, but it has the rhetorical ease and controlled understatement that mark almost everything Spedding wrote. It describes Spedding's own work, which exemplifies the kind of practical industry and energy that the great Victorians combined with their idealism and developing ideologies. Carlyle wrote to Spedding's close friend FitzGerald that the second half of Spedding's Bacon project – *The Letters and the Life of Francis Bacon* (1861–1874), written and edited entirely by Spedding was "the hugest and faithfullest bit of literary navvy work I have ever met with in this gen-

eration" and said that "Bacon is washed clean down to the natural skin." No doubt Carlyle was surprised at the grandeur of what Spedding attempted: "There is a grim strength," writes Carlyle to Fitz-Gerald, the translator of the *Rubáiyát of Omar Khayyám* (1859), "in Spedding, quietly, very quietly, invincible, which I did not quite know of before this book."

Spedding, the third son of John and Sarah Gibson Spedding, was born in Cumberland, on 26 June 1808 in Mirehouse; he attended the East Anglian grammar school of Bury St. Edmunds and, from 1827 to 1831, nearby Trinity College, Cambridge, where he and Tennyson became lifelong friends. From 1835 to 1841 he worked in the Colonial Office. He spent most of 1842 in the United States as secretary to the Ashburton commission, which was negotiating a settlement of a boundary dispute between that country and Canada. In 1847 he was offered the position of permanent undersecretary of state for the colonies at a salary of two thousand pounds per annum, but Spedding, as Stephen wrote in the *Dic-*

Drawing of Alfred Tennyson, attributed to Spedding (from Philip Henderson, Tennyson: Poet and Prophet, *1978)*

tionary of National Biography, "could not be persuaded to abandon Bacon." He did serve briefly on the Civil Service Commission in 1855, however. A lifelong bachelor, Spedding lived from 1835 until around 1864 at 60 Lincoln's Inn Fields, near the Public Record Office; after that he moved in with a niece in Westbourne Grove. He was a good swimmer and walker and relaxed with archery and billiards, "though," adds Stephen, he was "a brilliant performer at neither." Physically, he was noteworthy for his high-domed, bald head. On the resignation of Charles Kingsley in 1869, Spedding was offered the Professorship of Modern History at Cambridge; in 1874 the university offered him an honorary degree. He refused both, accepting only an honorary fellowship at his beloved Trinity College.

For the Victorians, Bacon was not only a masterful prose stylist and the leading jurist and political authority of his day but, most of all, the innovator of a modern conception of science and learning that had revolutionized Europe. It is likely this Bacon of heroic intellect and his "truth" most attracted Spedding and not, as has been suggested, the putative homosexual Bacon, although such an attraction cannot be ruled out for one of Tennyson's "Apostles."

Certainly the thirty years Spedding spent on the texts and life of Bacon point toward some larger concept. For Spedding, Bacon was an example of the highest form of intellect European civilization might produce, and the Baconian methods and imagery could still provide a vision for the future.

Spedding organized the stages of his project meticulously and on enunciated principles. No detail is included that does not act within a larger system and for a definite purpose.

The first result of Spedding's work on Bacon, *Evenings with a Reviewer; or, A Free and Particular Ex-*

amination of Mr. Macaulay's Article on Lord Bacon, written in 1845 and published in 1848, shows how this precise method contrasted with that of the work he is attacking: Thomas Babington Macaulay's own attack on Bacon in the *Edinburgh Review* (July 1837). Spedding's two-volume work, written in dialogue form, exposes Macaulay's misrepresentations of Bacon with what Stephen calls "a quiet humor and a shrewd critical faculty which, to a careful reader, make the book more interesting than its rival."

Sensing that the time for a Bacon edition was ripe, Spedding agreed in 1847 to organize the project into two main divisions: the editing of the major texts was to be shared with Robert Leslie Ellis, a young scientist and historian of science, and Douglas Denon Heath, a prominent jurist; the remaining texts would be edited, and a biography of Bacon written, by Spedding. Spedding would also supervise the entire work.

His method in the biography is to arrange Bacon's texts "strictly according to the order of time" — the very inductive opposite of the abstract deduction and personal monologism of a Victorian such as Macaulay. Spedding's method is, thus, essentially Baconian, avoiding the techniques both of the exemplum — that is, he would let the texts, not some predetermined moral, move the narrative — and that of unabashed skewing of the evidence motivated by prejudice. His method clearly adumbrates the one that Stephen would use in creating the *Dictionary of National Biography:* the conjunction of sociology and literature, with the former used as a means of understanding the latter.

Spedding explains his approach to editing Bacon's writings in his first preface — that to the philosophical works of Bacon. He stresses Bacon's various audiences: "He now addresses a new set of readers, differently prepared, knowing much which the others were ignorant of, ignorant of much which the others knew, and on both accounts requiring explanations and elucidations of many things which to the original audience were sufficiently intelligible. These it is the proper business of an editor to supply." The problem is to determine "the different classes of readers whose requirements [the author] had in view when he composed them." Spedding divides Bacon's writings into three groups: first, works in philosophy, science, and general literature, which were "addressed to mankind at large, and meant to be intelligible to educated men of all generations"; second, the legal works, addressed to lawyers or readers with technical legal knowledge; third, all occasional texts, letters, speeches, charges, tracts, state papers, and business reports — the vari

ety here is such that it cannot be classified except as occasional, "addressed to particular persons and bodies" or with "reference to particular occasions," and its readers should know and understand these circumstances or have them so outlined in accompanying text that even the general reader can follow a narrative.

This kind of empirical framing meant the unearthing and contextualizing of manuscripts and texts from the late Elizabethan and Jacobean periods, work to be done either at the British Museum and Library, a short walk from his home at Lincoln's Inn Fields, or the Public Record Office, just around the corner. The method of biography entails reproducing the texts with, Spedding says in the preface, "an explanatory narrative running between, in which the reader will be supplied to the best of my skill and knowledge with all the information necessary to the right understanding of them." Such particulars, "when finished will in fact contain a complete biography of the man, — a biography the most copious, the most minute, and by the very necessity of the case the fairest, that I can produce; for any material misinterpretation in the commentary will be at once confronted and corrected by the text." In this innovative method, "the new matter which I shall be able to produce is neither little nor unimportant; but more important than the new matter is the new aspect which (if I may judge of other minds by my own) will be imparted to the old matter by this manner of setting it forth."

Two years after the launching of the project Ellis, the editor of the philosophical works, came down with rheumatic fever. Spedding recalls in the preface: "it was long before he [Ellis] could finally resolve to abandon his task. As soon as he had done so, he handed all his papers over to me, with permission to do with them whatever I thought best," and so, "in all matters which lay within my compass I promised to do my best to complete the illustration and explanation of the text; adding where I had anything to add, objecting where I had anything to object, but always distinguishing as my own whatever was not his."

This kind of sensitivity was to mark the entire fourteen volumes that would appear from 1858 to 1874. Spedding's remarkable command of the scientific material can be seen throughout the philosophical texts but especially in his notes B and C to Ellis's preface to the *Novum Organum* (1620) — Spedding had to finish the preface, picking up in midsentence. The first of these notes is a precise compilation of Latin and English passages in which Bacon declares his intention "to keep his system secret."

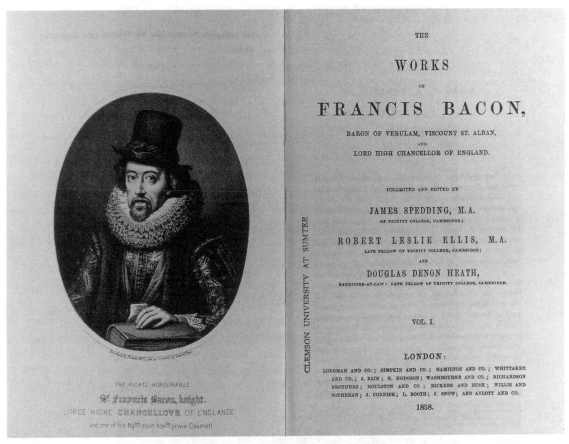

Frontispiece and title page for the first volume of the fourteen-volume Bacon edition, edited by Spedding and others, which includes Spedding's biography of Bacon

The second explicates the changes in Bacon's treatment of his doctrine of the Idols, from earlier texts to their grand statement in the *Novum Organum.* Yet even in these sections, and especially as Spedding turns to works that take on aspects of the prophetic, he remarks on the human being behind the process, Bacon's own sense of experimentation or "what may be called the *personal* history of his great philosophical scheme, — the practical enterprise in which it engaged him, and its effects on his inner and outer life." In his note to Ellis's preface to the early *Valerius Terminus,* Spedding combines the best editorial skills, especially of manuscript analysis, with a vivid sense of the author behind the text and of the evolution of Bacon's ideas. He can especially blend the two worlds of objective text and subjective shaping in his analysis in the preface to Bacon's utopia, the *New Atlantis,* and all in a style so clear and logical that the arguments carry a sense of inevitability.

This sense of the human being behind the text presents Spedding with the dilemma that confronts all such heroic life studies: whether to admit weakness and failure in the hero. Throughout the four-teen volumes Spedding makes it clear that Bacon's ideas in science and philosophy were not profound and were not developed sufficiently; Bacon actually denigrates the very method that Darwin, in 1859, would acknowledge as his own in the most dramatic scientific project of the century. Although Spedding also remarks on the reasons behind Bacon's fall as lord chancellor in 1521, attributing the disaster to too many preoccupations in a politically uneven time, he is less concerned with personal failures than with intellectual ones. Spedding is especially concerned with Bacon's failure to understand the great scientific and mathematical achievements of his time, a failure that hindered all Bacon's endeavors and vitiated all his conclusions: "He would soon have arrived at a point where the phenomena of nature could not be separated accurately enough for the purposes of the enquiry without instruments more delicate and exact, or modes of calculation more subtle and complicated, than any which he could have devised or used."

Spedding confronts this problem directly in his preface to the philosophical work *De Interpre-*

Photograph of Spedding by Julia Margaret Cameron

tatione Naturae Proemium, particularly as he analyzes an autobiographical passage where the middle-aged Bacon casts a clear eye on himself and his prospects. In his analysis, Spedding says: "Bacon's deficiency lay in the intellect itself." He lacked development of "the faculty of *distinguishing differences,*" although "in his large, discursive faculty which detects analogies and resemblances between different and distant things, it would be difficult probably to name his equal." The problem, Spedding says, arose from Bacon's personal sense of his endeavor: "Bacon failed to devise a practicable method for the discovery of the Forms of Nature, because he misconceived the conditions of the case; he expected to find the phenomena of nature more easily separable and distinguishable than they really are; a misconception into which a discursive intellect, an enterprising spirit, and a hopeful nature, would most naturally fall."

The heart of the problem was something that, perhaps, Spedding himself had been tempted toward: involvement in society and its transforma-

tions, quite natural for a Lord Chancellor, and too little time for reading and research. And the temptation could work both ways, as Spedding describes with the detail of a Victorian novelist when he looks at the causes of Bacon's trial and fall from power: "That an absorbing interest in one thing should induce negligence of others not less important, is an accident only too natural and familiar; and if he did not allow the *Novum Organum* to interfere with his attention to the causes which came before him in the Chancery, it did probably prevent him from attending as carefully as he should and otherwise would have done to the proceedings of his servants and the state of his accounts."

This kind of understanding of human character is found in all fourteen volumes of the edition of Bacon. Spedding's method was derived from the concern with personalities and relationships that marked his own life and that made him one of the endearing figures of Victorian England. If both his life and work have hardly survived with the assurance and vitality of many of his contemporaries, Spedding nevertheless remains a true exemplar of his time. His contribution to intellectual history, scholarship, and biography is an untapped but quite fruitful model for both scholars and writers.

Spedding had literary interests that extended beyond Bacon – he always held a private ardor for the novels of Jane Austen, for example, and his *Reviews and Discussions, Literary, Political, and Historical, not Relating to Bacon* (1879) includes an essay on the authorship of William Shakespeare's plays. In the last year of his life he published two key studies of British history in a volume co-authored by the historian James Gairdner. On 1 March 1881 Spedding was struck by a hansom cab. Tennyson tried to visit him in St. George's Hospital but was denied admission. Even at the point of death, writes Stephen, "he was characteristically anxious to make it clear that he considered the accident to have been due not to the driver, but to his own carelessness." Spedding died of his injuries on 9 March.

References:

Doris Alexander, "Benevolent Sage or Blundering Booby?," *Dickens Quarterly,* 8 (September 1991): 120–127;

Catherine Brinker Bowen, *Francis Bacon: The Temper of a Man* (Boston: Little, Brown, 1966);

Richard Dellamora, *Masculine Desire: The Sexual Politics of Victorian Aestheticism* (Chapel Hill & London: University of North Carolina Press, 1990);

Daphne du Maurier, *The Winding Stair: Francis Bacon, His Rise and Fall* (New York: Doubleday, 1977);

Joel J. Epstein, *Francis Bacon: A Political Biography* (Athens: Ohio University Press, 1977);

K. J. Fielding, "Carlyle and the Speddings: New Letters," *Carlyle Newsletter,* 7 (Spring 1986): 12–20;

Fielding, "Carlyle and the Speddings – New Letters II," *Carlyle Newsletter,* 8 (Spring 1987): 51–66;

Christopher Ricks, "Spedding's Annotations of the Trinity MS of In Memoriam," *Tennyson Research Bulletin,* 4 (November 1984): 110–113;

Charles Tennyson, "James Spedding and Alfred Tennyson," *Tennyson Research Bulletin,* 2 (November 1974): 96–105.

Leslie Stephen

(28 November 1832 – 22 February 1904)

Steve Ferebee
North Carolina Wesleyan College

See also the Stephen entry in *DLB 57: Victorian Prose Writers After 1867.*

BOOKS: *The Poll Degree from a Third Point of View* (Cambridge & London: Macmillan, 1863);

Sketches from Cambridge: By a Don (London & Cambridge: Macmillan, 1865);

The "Times" on the American War: A Historical Study, as L. S. (London: Ridgeway, 1865; New York: Abbatt, 1915);

The Playground of Europe (London: Longmans, Green, 1871; London & New York: Longmans, Green, 1894);

Essays on Freethinking and Plainspeaking (London: Longmans, Green, 1873; New York: Putnam, 1877);

Hours in a Library (3 volumes, London: Smith, Elder, 1874–1879; volume 1 republished, New York: Scribner, Armstrong, 1875; enlarged, 3 volumes, London: Smith, Elder, 1892; New York: Putnam, 1894; enlarged again, 4 volumes, New York & London: Putnam, 1904);

History of English Thought in the Eighteenth Century, 2 volumes (London: Smith, Elder, 1876; New York: Putnam, 1876);

Samuel Johnson (London: Macmillan, 1878; New York: Harper, 1878);

Alexander Pope (London: Macmillan, 1880; New York: Harper, 1880);

Swift (London: Macmillan, 1882; New York: Harper, 1882);

The Science of Ethics (London: Smith, Elder, 1882; New York: Putnam, 1882);

Life of Henry Fawcett (London: Smith, Elder, 1885; New York: Putnam, 1886);

An Agnostic's Apology, and Other Essays (London: Smith, Elder, 1893; New York: Putnam, 1893);

The Life of Sir James Fitzjames Stephen, Bart., K.C.S.I., a Judge of the High Court of Justice, by His Brother (London: Smith, Elder, 1895; New York: Putnam, 1895);

Social Rights and Duties: Addresses to Ethical Societies, 2 volumes (London: Sonnenschein / New York: Macmillan, 1896);

Studies of a Biographer, 4 volumes (London: Duckworth, 1898–1902; New York: Putnam, 1898–1902);

The English Utilitarians, 3 volumes (London: Duckworth, 1900; New York: Putnam, 1900);

George Eliot (London: Macmillan, 1902; New York: Macmillan, 1902);

Robert Louis Stevenson: An Essay (New York & London: Putnam, 1902);

English Literature and Society in the Eighteenth Century (London: Duckworth, 1904; New York & London: Putnam, 1907);

Hobbes (New York & London: Macmillan, 1904);

Some Early Impressions (London: Hogarth Press, 1924);

Men, Books, and Mountains: Essays, edited by S. O. A. Ullman (London: Hogarth Press, 1956; Minneapolis: University of Minnesota Press, 1956);

Sir Leslie Stephen's Mausoleum Book, edited by Alan Bell (London: Oxford University Press, 1977).

OTHER: Hermann von Alexander Berlepsch, *The Alps; or, Sketches of Life and Nature in the Mountains,* translated by Stephen (London: Longmans, Green, Longman & Roberts, 1861);

"The Allelein-Horn," in *Vacation Tourists and Notes of Travel in 1860,* 3 volumes, edited by Francis Galton (London: Macmillan, 1861-1864), I: 264–281;

Leslie Stephen in 1860

"The Ascent of the Schreckhorn" and "The Eiger Joch," in *Peaks, Passes and Glaciers,* second series, 2 volumes, edited by E. S. Kennedy (London: Longmans, Green, 1862), II: 3–32;

"On the Choice of Representatives by Popular Constituencies," in *Essays on Reform* (London: Macmillan, 1867), pp. 85–125;

"The Writings of W. M. Thackeray," in *The Works of William Makepeace Thackeray,* 24 volumes (London: Smith, Elder, 1878–1879), XXIV: 313–378;

William Kingdon Clifford, *Lectures and Essays,* 2 volumes, edited by Stephen and Frederick Pollock (London: Macmillan, 1879; London & New York: Macmillan, 1886);

The Works of Henry Fielding, Esq., 10 volumes, edited, with a biographical essay, by Stephen (London: Smith, Elder, 1882);

"Richardson's Novels: Introduction," in *The Works of Samuel Richardson,* 12 volumes (London: Sotheran, 1883–1884), I: ix–lv;

The Dictionary of National Biography, 66 volumes, volumes 1–21 edited by Stephen; volumes 22–26 edited by Stephen and Sidney Lee (London:

Smith, Elder, 1885–1901) – includes 386 contributions by Stephen;

Margaret Veley, *A Marriage of Shadows and Other Poems,* biographical preface by Stephen (London: Smith, Elder, 1888; Philadelphia: Lippincott, 1889);

"James Dykes Campbell," in *Samuel Taylor Coleridge,* by Campbell (London: Macmillan, 1896; New York: Macmillan, 1896);

Emile Legouis, *The Early Life of William Wordsworth, 1770–1798,* translated by J. W. Matthews, prefatory note by Stephen (London: Dent, 1897);

James Payn, *The Backwater of Life; or, Essays of a Literary Veteran,* introduction by Stephen (London: Smith, Elder, 1899);

"Evolution and Religious Conceptions," in *The 19th Century: A Review of Progress* (London & New York: Putnam, 1901), pp. 370–383;

Letters of John Richard Green, edited by Stephen (London & New York: Macmillan, 1901);

"Robert Browning" and "Thomas Carlyle," in *Encyclopædia Britannica,* eleventh edition, 29 volumes (Cambridge & New York: Cambridge University Press, 1910), IV: 670–674; V: 349–354.

SELECTED PERIODICAL PUBLICATIONS –
UNCOLLECTED: "The Political Situation in England," *North American Review,* 107 (October 1868): 543–567;

"The Comtist Utopia," *Fraser's Magazine,* 80 (July 1869): 1–21;

"Mr. Matthew Arnold and the Church of England," *Fraser's Magazine,* 82 (October 1870): 414–431;

"Sidgwick's Methods of Ethics," *Fraser's Magazine,* 91 (March 1875): 306–325;

"Art and Morality," *Cornhill Magazine,* 32 (July 1875): 91–101;

"Order and Progress," *Fortnightly Review,* 23 (1875): 820–834;

"An Attempted Philosophy of History," *Fortnightly Review,* 33 (May 1880): 672–695;

"The Moral Element in Literature," *Cornhill Magazine,* 43 (January 1881): 34–50;

"In Memoriam: Thomas Woodbine Hinchliff," *Alpine Journal,* 11 (1882): 41–44;

"In Memoriam: John Birkbeck," *Alpine Journal,* 15 (1890): 277–281;

"John Ormsby," *Alpine Journal,* 18 (1896): 33–36;

"James Payn," *Cornhill Magazine,* 78 (1898): 590–594;

"In Memoriam: George Smith," *Cornhill Magazine,* 84 (1901): 577–580;

"James Spedding," *National Review,* 39 (1902): 241–257.

As Virginia Woolf says in her 1932 centenary *Times* article, when she heard her father, Leslie Stephen, dropping books to the floor of his study in the 1890s, he had already lived a full life. Stephen was prolific in that nonchalant way the Victorians had about hard work. He wrote voluminously: philosophy, literary essays, reminiscences, and letters. As a biographer he wrote five books in the English Men of Letters series and three full-length biographies; he edited twenty-one volumes of *The Dictionary of National Biography* (1885–1901), coedited five volumes, and contributed a total of 386 entries to all but three of the original sixty-six volumes. Stephen set a standard for biography as clear, concise scholarly analysis of the subject's life, character, work, and influences.

Stephen's interest in writing was an inherited trait. His great-grandfather James Stephen, after leaving Scotland, surviving a shipwreck, and being arrested for debt, wrote an indictment of the penal system. His grandfather James Stephen, outraged at the treatment of slaves in the West Indies, wrote a pamphlet of some importance in the parliamentary debates about abolition. His father, Sir James Stephen, wrote about the evangelical, abolitionist Clapham sect. Leslie Stephen's mother, Jane Catherine, was the daughter of the rector of Clapham, John Venn. The Venns were a more lively and less austere family than the Stephens: Stephen described his father as an undemonstrative man who suffered nervous breakdowns, refused himself cigars because he liked them, and would not have a mirror in his room; he also sacrificed his comfort for his children and often dictated ten pages of an *Edinburgh Review* essay before breakfast.

Stephen was born at Kensington Gore on 28 November 1832 and was the fourth of five children. His childhood was congenial, though he was plagued by his nerves and illnesses. In 1840 the family moved to Brighton, hoping to improve his health. In her diary his mother describes her son as sensitive to criticism and overly susceptible to the emotional appeal of poetry. A lifelong habit of blurting out lines from poetry (immortalized in Woolf's portrayal of Mr. Ramsay in *To the Lighthouse* [1927]) began early, and Jane Stephen records that he would "play the band" – hum lines of poems – long after being put to bed. Beginning on 15 April 1842 Stephen spent four miserable years as a day boy at Eton College, where the regulars bullied him and his older brother Fitzjames protected him. In March 1848 he went to King's College, London, but he spent that summer battling asthma in a dark bedroom and having leeches periodically applied.

In 1850 he matriculated at his father's college, Trinity Hall, Cambridge, where he studied mathematics and quickly received a scholarship, earning his B.A. in January 1854. On 23 September 1854 he was appointed to a fellowship, on 21 December 1855 he was made deacon, and on 29 April 1856 he was given a tutorship. He received his M.A. in 1857, and on Trinity Sunday 1859 he was ordained a clergyman.

As a student and later a don at Cambridge Stephen changed into a respectable athlete and a famous rowing coach. In a later essay about these years he described himself standing in frozen mud, his nose a bright purple, cheering for his Cambridge boys. Though his contemporaries remembered him at this time for his athletic feats, quiet habits, and the bullfinch he kept in his room to talk to, he was also quietly teaching himself German, French, economics, and modern literature. He read the books of John Locke, John Stuart Mill, Auguste Comte, Immanuel Kant, David Hume, George Berkeley, Jeremy Bentham, David Ricardo, Charles Darwin, Herbert Spencer, and Thomas Hobbes. In Mill's *A System of Logic* (1843) Stephen found a view of his-

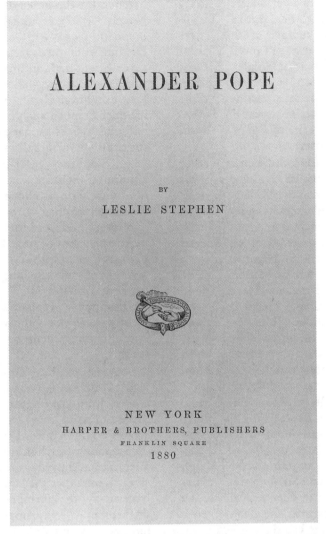

ALEXANDER POPE

BY

LESLIE STEPHEN

NEW YORK
HARPER & BROTHERS, PUBLISHERS
FRANKLIN SQUARE
1880

*Title page for Stephen's biography of the eighteenth-century poet for
the English Men of Letters series*

tory as the product of natural laws; in Comte's works he found the theme that humanity is progressing toward a control of social conditions. His reading convinced him to reject the historical evidence for Christianity; he wrote later that he did not so much change his mind about Christianity as he simply uncovered what he had thought all along.

In the tradition of his grandfather and father Stephen took fierce thirty-mile walks. In 1857 he made the first of twenty-five climbs in the Alps, and in 1858 he joined the Alpine Club, becoming president in 1865 and editor of the *Alpine Journal* in 1868. Some of his earliest publications were his vividly descriptive essays about mountain climbing, collected in *The Playground of Europe* in 1871. Mountain climbing, as well as walking with the group of London men who called themselves the Sunday

Tramps – organized by Stephen in 1879 – represented more than attempts to keep fit. Testing his physical strength was important to a man who had had a sickly childhood, but the rules of sports and the discipline necessary for climbing represented an exemplary and necessary structure for living as well. His affection for the mountains and for the men with whom he climbed and walked are obvious in his writings about them.

As a Cambridge don in the early 1860s Stephen was a radical reformer who tried, but failed, to broaden the curriculum and break down the walls between disciplines; much of his program was finally accomplished twenty years later. He became a vehement champion of the North in the American Civil War, even though this position contradicted the view of his own social class. Before leaving

Cambridge in 1864 – some two years after realizing that he could not fulfill his clerical duties – he visited the United States in the summer of 1863. There he made friends with James Russell Lowell, Charles Eliot Norton, and Oliver Wendell Holmes. His first notable publication, *The "Times" on the American War: A Historical Study* (1865), was an indictment of the newspaper's pro-South stance. That year his *Sketches from Cambridge: By a Don,* a series of *Pall Mall Gazette* essays, appeared in book form.

When he left Cambridge, Stephen moved to London to become a journalist. He wrote in his notebook, "I mean to live and die like a gentleman if possible." With Fitzjames's help he quickly began contributing to major magazines and newspapers. Between 1865 and 1871 he wrote about four articles a week, often completing six thousand words at a sitting. He also read the works of Benedict de Spinoza, Georg Wilhelm Friedrich Hegel, David Strauss, Ernst Renan, and George Henry Lewes. He became friendly with the editor John Morley and the publisher George Smith, and his articles appeared alongside those of major writers such as Anthony Trollope, Matthew Arnold, George Eliot, Thomas Babington Macaulay, and John Ruskin.

Stephen married William Makepeace Thackeray's daughter Harriet Marian early in the morning of 19 June 1867; they honeymooned in the Alps. They visited the United States in 1868, where Stephen met but was relatively unimpressed by Ralph Waldo Emerson. By this time Stephen was writing for the *Fortnightly Review,* the *Saturday Review,* the *Pall Mall Gazette, Fraser's Magazine,* the *Nation* in New York, and the *Alpine Journal.* His daughter, Laura, was born in 1870. In 1871 he became the editor of Thackeray's former magazine, the *Cornhill Magazine.* Stephen wrote seventy-five essays for the magazine, collecting many of them in his *Hours in a Library* (1874–1904). In 1873 Stephen collected a series of his articles on religious topics into *Essays on Freethinking and Plainspeaking.* By this time he was a chief spokesman for agnosticism and a public challenger of popular beliefs.

Stephen assumed that his duty as a writer was to enlighten his upper-middle-class readers, who would respond to his good sense with their own. On 23 December 1869 he had written to Holmes that if a journalist is "an honest man . . . and speaks the truth with some vigour, he may help things a bit." But by 1873 he was discouraged with politics and gave up writing political essays for the *Nation.*

In the 1870s Stephen made his name as a literary essayist. Though not yet writing biographies, Stephen said that when he read a literary work he listened for the voice of the author. In "Fielding's Novels" (1877), republished in his *Hours in a Library,* Stephen, faced with a lack of anecdotes about Fielding's life, turns to his novels for what they will reveal about their author. *Hours in a Library* includes thirty-two essays, such as "De Foe's Novels," "The First Edinburgh Reviewers," and "Country Books," in which Stephen analyzes writers' lives, their times, and their works as inseparable units. In "Crabbe," for example, originally published in the *Cornhill* in 1874, Stephen's description of George Crabbe's childhood includes a long passage on the family's old house with its slippery back staircase and old-fashioned kitchen. After meals the family would nap for an hour and then entertain neighbors with large quantities of brandy. From this lifestyle, Stephen argues, Crabbe derived his rough literary style, in which "the language seldom soars above the style which would be intelligible to the merest clodhopper." Stephen's literary essays written during these years show a wide reading and a desire to connect writers with their works and their times.

As editor of the *Cornhill* he published works by writers such as Robert Louis Stevenson, Edmund Gosse, John Addington Symonds, Henry James, Thomas Hardy, and George Meredith (whose character Vernon Whitford in *The Egoist* [1879] is based on Stephen). Stephen offered what he thought his Victorian middle-class readers would find unoffensive. "Remember the country parson's daughters. *I* have always to remember them!" he wrote to Hardy in October 1875, probably remembering his own mother. His blue penciling of Hardy's manuscripts (for example, substituting *sentimental* for *amorous*) would lead to a professional break between the two; but it was Hardy whom, in March 1875, Stephen asked to witness his renunciation of Holy Orders. Hardy would always remember Stephen, in his long, flowing dressing gown, pacing the dimly lit room and then solemnly signing his renunciation. Gosse recalled that as a young contributor for the *Cornhill* he, along with Stevenson, dined with the Stephens in 1875. Neither Stephen, with his bright blue "melancholy eyes" and fan-shaped red beard, nor his wife said much, though both young men felt welcome.

Stephen's mother died early in 1875; he wrote to Norton on 3 March that an uncle hoped that her death would make Stephen into a Christian. "It won't do that," he wrote, "but I hope that it may help to make me a better man in some sense. This is the only good one can get out of such losses." Stephen's wife died suddenly on 28 November of

*Two of Stephen's children, Virginia (the future Virginia Woolf)
and Adrian, in 1886*

the same year — his birthday, which he never celebrated again.

In 1876 appeared what some consider to be Stephen's major work, a two-volume study of the eighteenth-century Deist controversies titled *History of English Thought in the Eighteenth Century.* (In 1900 he was to extend this study into the nineteenth century, with less success, in *The English Utilitarians.*) Stephen packed *History of English Thought* with astute analyses of political, moral, and economic theories. His attempt to establish continuities in the history of ideas and his critique of eighteenth-century contributions to intellectual history quickly made him a major philosopher, and he was elected to both the Athenaeum Club and the Metaphysical Society. Stephen's biographer Noël Annan believes that the book may never be superseded.

In June 1876 Stephen moved from Southwell Gardens to Hyde Park Gate, where he lived for the rest of his life. His neighbor Julia Duckworth, also widowed, provided emotional support for him. Stephen realized that he was in love with her one day when he was out walking. He proposed to her, but she was reluctant. He courted her quietly but intensely. She finally relented, and they were married on 26 March 1878. Julia brought three children from her first marriage, and they were to have four of their own. They were frequently separated while he climbed mountains or she nursed sick friends. During such periods Stephen wrote more than four hundred letters to her that show the intimacy and happiness of their life together.

When the publisher Alexander Macmillan chose Morley as editor in chief of a new series of critical biographies of great writers, Morley involved Stephen from the beginning. After some debate they settled on the title English Men of Letters. The thirty-nine volumes of the first series (1878–1892) began with Stephen's *Samuel Johnson,* and the twenty-eight volumes in the second series (1902–1919) began with his *George Eliot.* The brief (about forty-five thousand words) anecdotal biographies combine biography and history with literary analysis, and the experience of working on the series would help Stephen when he began to oversee *The Dictionary of National Biography.*

Stephen's fellow walker and biographer Frederic William Maitland calls *Samuel Johnson* "a model among models"; contemporary reviews were favorable, and Stephen wrote Morley on 16 February 1879 that the book "has been the cause of more compliments to me than anything, perhaps everything, that I have ever done before. My vanity has been tickled." Stephen portrays the youthful Johnson as a popular boy who became a plainspoken and practical professional writer. He condemns an early attempt at playwriting except for the money it made Johnson. He recoils from the image of Johnson sweating into his food but praises his witty conversation. Stephen had a lifelong awe of James Boswell, and when he reaches the part of Johnson's life that Boswell recorded he backs away, quoting and paraphrasing from anecdotes in Boswell's portrait. What Stephen admires in Johnson's *Prefaces, Biographical and Critical, to the Works of the English Poets* (1779–1781) is what he strives for in his own biographies: "A vigorous summary of the main facts," a "pithy analysis" of the subject's "character," and a "short criticism" of the subject's works.

In the English Men of Letters volume *Alexander Pope* (1880) Stephen sympathizes with Pope's ill health, "crooked figure," and "humble social position." He also admires Pope for using his pen to rise above his problems, as, for example, in *An Epistle from Mr. Pope, to Dr. Arbuthnot* (1735), where Pope analyzes his own relationships with people who are hostile to him. Stephen is less forgiving about Pope's dishonest machinations to publish his letters to Jonathan Swift without seeming to be responsible: "It is a relief to turn from this miserable record of Pope's petty or malicious deceptions to the history of his legitimate career." Carefully researched and conscientiously detailed, Stephen's biography of Pope did not meet with the critical approval that *Samuel Johnson* garnered, but it is still a readable, insightful portrayal of a man Stephen obviously found to be a moral conundrum.

Stephen also wrote *Swift* (1882) for the English Men of Letters series. He claims in the preface that without a Boswell, Swift's biographies have been inaccurate, useless, and dull. Stephen's life is lively, concrete, and filled with researched information. To unravel Swift's involvement with "Vanessa" and Stella, Stephen considers Swift's mood at this time in his life, Swift's treatment of women in general, his treatment of servants, the playful language in his writings to and about the women, and the reports of other people. In all his English Men of Letters monographs and in his later *Dictionary of National Biography* entries, Stephen returns to the impossibility of separating the person from the work: "No writer has ever been more thoroughly original than Swift, for his writings are simply himself." By the time he wrote *Swift,* Stephen's experiences as an essayist, editor, and biographer had prepared him for his next project.

When Stephen had begun editing the *Cornhill Magazine* in 1871, the circulation was twenty-five thousand; by 1882 it was down to twelve thousand, and Stephen resigned, admitting that he might not understand the public's changing tastes. But George Smith quickly moved to make Stephen the editor of a new biographical dictionary that he wanted to finance even though it was sure to lose money. Stephen was just finishing what was, he later told his daughter Virginia (who was born this year), his favorite book, *The Science of Ethics* (1882), which, although it was quickly and repeatedly adopted as a textbook, was never received as well by the critics as Stephen had hoped. He was also finishing *Swift,* he was about to be elected the first Clark Lecturer in English Literature, he was writing essays for several magazines and newspapers, and he was taking fifty-mile Sunday walks with the Tramps. But he launched himself on another project, one that would almost kill him – *The Dictionary of National Biography,* his greatest contribution to the history of biography.

Smith wanted a universal dictionary, but Stephen convinced him to restrict it to Britain and its colonies. On 10 January 1883 Stephen advertised in the *Times,* and in June he began issuing twice-annual appeals in the *Athenaeum* for suggestions for subjects (rejecting one for fourteen hundred hymn composers). He built up a group of about 100 regular contributors and constantly searched for others; they eventually totaled 653. The first volume appeared on 1 January 1885; then one volume appeared regularly every quarter until the summer of 1890.

Stephen's contribution to *The Dictionary of National Biography* is difficult to exaggerate. He established the standards, the professional tone, and the rules. He edited copy and wrote detailed letters to contributors. He nurtured Sidney Lee, his coeditor, who would take over when Stephen resigned in 1891. From 1885 to 1900 the volume chronicled 29,120 lives. Stephen himself wrote 386 entries in his calm but forceful, erudite but witty style, providing no-nonsense portraits of his subjects' families, careers, works, influence, and characters and listing the main secondary sources. He took for himself most of the major literary figures of the eighteenth and nineteenth centuries, most of the economic leaders, and many of the lesser-known religious di-

Stephen and his wife Julia in 1892

vines. His entries range from twenty-six pages on John Churchill, first Duke of Marlborough, to one page on his friend Croom Robertson, the philosopher and editor of *Mind.*

Stephen's view of history as a progressive series of events leading to a discernible outcome led him to see *The Dictionary of National Biography* as a place where readers could watch the development of an individual's life and era. Stephen was to write in 1896, in the essay "National Biography" (republished in his *Studies of a Biographer* [1898–1902]), that he hoped that the dictionary provided readers with "an indispensable guide" through the "hopelessly intricate jungle" of history because "every individual life is to some extent an indication of the historical conditions of his time." But, above all, he wrote in 1893, in "Biography" (collected in *Men, Books, and Mountains* [1956]), "the aim should be revelation . . . of a character." To reveal character, the biographer must show the good with the bad. Stephen said in an 1888 lecture that telling the story of Samuel Taylor Coleridge without revealing his addiction to opium perverts the whole story; and in his *Dictionary of National Biography* entry on Coleridge, Stephen re-

counts the information known about the poet's experiences with the drug. He disliked James Anthony Froude's revelations about Thomas Carlyle's marriage, but in his entry on Carlyle he reported what he knew about the explosive and unsatisfactory alliance.

Though Stephen believed that methodological and relatively exhaustive research in all available sources was necessary, he doubted that such data would, by itself, reveal the subject's character. He held that a condensation of the facts must tell most of the story in a biographical dictionary entry, though he knew that some speculation, based on incomplete or suspect information, would also be necessary. He is, for example, uncertain whether or not Coleridge's opium addiction seriously harmed the poet, but he says that it probably did not. In another entry he speculates that Adam Smith led a solitary life at Oxford on the grounds that Scottish students there were generally disliked and that Smith mentions only one friend in his many letters to his mother. But in his Swift entry Stephen records at length the verifiable information as well as the rumors (and their sources) about Swift's possible marriage before admitting that the truth will never be known. The biographer, he believed, must gather as much material, and present the story as fully, as possible.

In November 1884 Stephen's friend Henry Fawcett died, and his widow asked Stephen to write a biography of him; though he was just beginning his work on the dictionary, he never hesitated. *Life of Henry Fawcett* (1885) is a lively, sympathetic book in which Stephen analyzes Fawcett's career and social milieu. He describes an inquisitive and precocious child keeping a diary and giving lectures on the uses of steam, a student who chose his college for its academic successes rather than its athletic trophies, a young man blinded by his father in a hunting accident, a young teacher who did not think students needed anything but the classics, a commonsensical politician, and a man with a little dog named Oddo that he had rescued from the pound. *Life of Henry Fawcett* went through five editions in two years.

Stephen's emotional and physical health began to fail soon after he took on the dictionary. He was unprepared for what he later called the "great quantity of wearisome and petty detail" that is necessary in editing, yet he would not slow down. Inundated with work, he took no holiday in 1885, and Maitland thinks he never really recovered from that year. He could not sleep, waking with what he called "the horrors." In January 1887 he followed his doctor's orders and took a trip to the Alps – without Julia, who was nursing her father – but began writing back immediately that he was bored and wanted to come home.

His health continued to deteriorate; in early 1889, after Julia found him lying unconscious, they went to Switzerland. (Maitland comments that though Stephen's own feelings about the dictionary were mixed, Julia's were not.) Finally his health broke down severely, and he had to begin transferring duties to Lee, whose name he added as coeditor in March 1890. He went to the United States later in 1890 to see his dying friend Lowell and to receive an honorary doctorate from Harvard. On 7 April 1891 Julia wrote to Smith that her husband's health would not permit him to continue with the dictionary; he did not know how sick he had been, she said. Lee is listed alone as editor of volume twenty-seven, published in 1891. In June, Stephen wrote to Norton that a great weight had been taken off his shoulders; even so, he was revising some of his periodical articles for *An Agnostic's Apology, and Other Essays* (1893) and beginning *The English Utilitarians*. He also continued writing entries for the

supplements to the dictionary. In fact, he was as productive as ever.

Stephen wrote a second full-length biography, *The Life of Sir James Fitzjames Stephen* (1895), after his brother died on 11 March 1894; he completed the book between November 1894 and January 1895. This biography provided Stephen the chance to explore his own family history, and for the first sixty pages he chronicles his ancestors. He traces his brother's life from Fitzjames's methodical notes about which career to choose through his years as a lawyer, journalist, diplomat in India, legislator, and legal writer. "I have sought to show my brother as he was," Stephen concludes. The portrait that emerges from the book is of a man with profound intellectual strengths though perhaps too blunt a manner, a Victorian gentleman who tried to leave the world a better place – in other words, a Stephen.

In his two full-length biographies Stephen is present as a judicious narrator who is honest about his own shortcomings. For example, he jokes about the poorly written newspaper he edited during one of Fawcett's elections; and as he approaches his brother's legal career, he confesses that he knows little about the law. This narrative presence becomes a voice that the reader comes to recognize and trust. The books are richer for this autobiographical dimension: it does not obscure his subject; indeed, he uses it to reveal details or nuances about the subject that might otherwise not be apparent.

Julia Stephen died on 5 May 1895. Stephen turned to writing to express his grief in what the children called "The Mausoleum Book" (published in 1977 as *Sir Leslie Stephen's Mausoleum Book*). The death of Stephen's second wife left him with four children from their marriage: the sixteen-year-old Vanessa, fifteen-year-old Thoby, thirteen-year-old Virginia, and twelve-year-old Adrian; as well as the retarded twenty-five-year-old Laura from his first marriage. There were also three young adult children from Julia's first marriage: George, age twenty-seven; Stella, twenty-six; and Gerald, twenty-five. Like her husband, Julia had spread herself thin; Virginia wondered whether or not she had ever spent any time alone with her mother. Julia had nursed her dying parents, had given birth to four children in five years, had taken care of her husband, and had rushed from one house to another, offering her services as a nurse wherever she saw the need. She died at forty-nine, exhausted.

The death of Julia began the final period of Stephen's life, the one Woolf recalls in her mem-

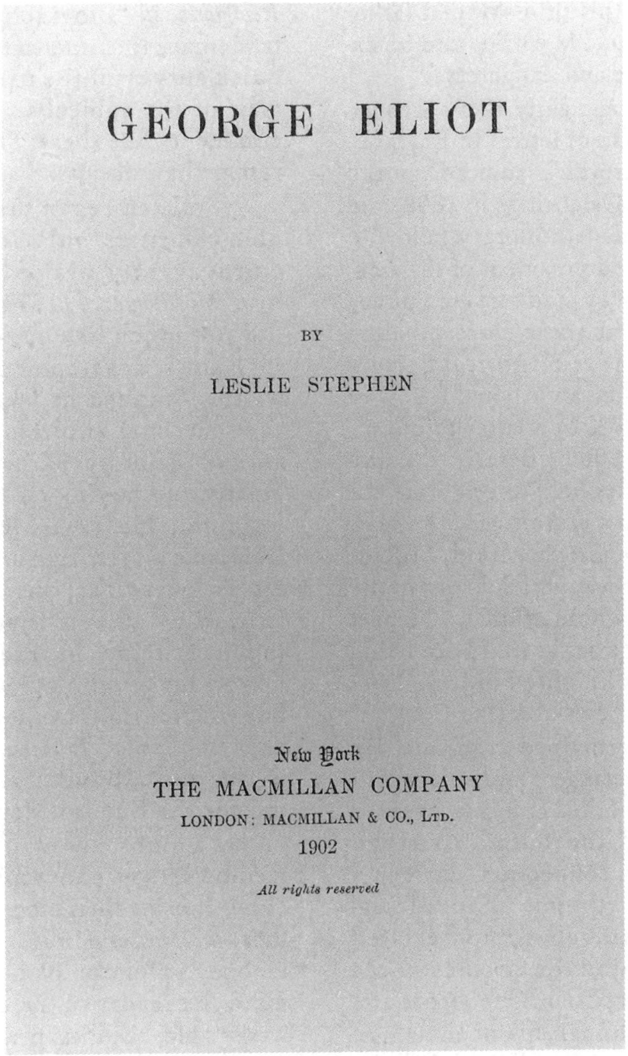

GEORGE ELIOT

BY

LESLIE STEPHEN

New York
THE MACMILLAN COMPANY
LONDON: MACMILLAN & CO., LTD.
1902

All rights reserved

Title page for the volume that launched the second series of English Men of Letters, in which Stephen made use of his personal acquaintance with Eliot

oirs. She describes Stephen stumbling past her as she went to view the still-warm body of her mother; she criticizes his emotional demands on his stepdaughter Stella, who died soon after her marriage in 1897, and then on Vanessa. His dramatic groaning about how much money Vanessa was spending on household expenses made Virginia hate him. But the freedom he allowed her in his library, the efforts he made to teach his children, and the fantastic animals he often drew for them made her love him.

No one who looks into this part of Stephen's life story can avoid the contradictory portraits of, on the one hand, the kindly, honest man Morley describes in his *Recollections* (1917) and the wise, erudite man of letters in the Maitland biography and Lee memorials (1912 and 1917) and, on the other

hand, the emotionally and professionally insecure family man who needed petting and who thought nothing of abruptly leaving the room or moaning aloud when he did not want to see a visitor. The men who walked, climbed, conversed, or worked with Stephen remembered his grave silences, clearheaded advice, and affectionate friendship. His letters to Lowell are genuinely moving, and he made him godfather of – or, as Stephen put it, asked him to stand in quasi-sponsorial relation to – Virginia. The children remembered a man driven to distraction by nonexistent money problems, a father demanding unreasonable emotional succor. As he aged, Stephen withdrew more and more from public life, grew deafer, and demanded more and more from his women. Stephen praised his mother for providing a sanctuary for his thin-skinned father from the troubles of the outside world, and he expected no less from his wife and daughters.

During the late 1890s and early 1900s Stephen was the most important man of letters in England. He received honorary doctorates from Edinburgh in 1885, Harvard in 1890, Cambridge in 1892, and Oxford in 1901. He was made honorary fellow of Trinity Hall. He was elected president of the London Library in 1892; he was made trustee of the National Portrait Gallery; he was a corresponding member of the Massachusetts Historical Society from 1895. He was appointed an original fellow of the British Academy in 1902. In a letter to his sister-in-law dated 27 May 1900 he described a dinner with the Prince of Wales held to celebrate the completion of the *Dictionary of National Biography*. As soon as the prince left, Stephen said, "I fled, and got upon the top of a bus, which brought me home, wondering at the whole affair.... I part with [the dictionary] with a sense that I am being laid on the shelf." He was knighted in June 1902 at the coronation of King Edward VII.

His literary output remained vigorous. He edited and wrote a connecting narrative for *Letters of John Richard Green* (1901); in his preface he says that he wanted the letters to stand alone, but his belief in the connection between a life and its times prevented him: "The full significance of the letters can only be appreciated by readers who bear in mind the circumstances under which they were written." He wrote the Ford Lectures for 1903, though his nephew had to deliver them. They were published (on the day of his death) as *English Literature and Society in the Eighteenth Century* (1904). He wrote four autobiographical essays for the *National Review* in 1903 that were published by his daughter Virginia and her husband, Leonard Woolf, as *Some Early Impressions* in 1924.

Two series of *Studies of a Biographer* came out in four volumes in 1898 and 1902, collecting essays Stephen had written for the *National Review* during the 1890s. In essays such as "Johnsoniana," "The Browning Letters," and "Shakespeare as a Man" Stephen continues to combine biography, history, and literary analysis. He says that a biography of Johnson is successful because it is a "study of human life," showing its subject in the "foreground of a group of living and moving human beings."

Curiously enough for a philosopher, Stephen did not theorize about biography. In "National Biography," which opens the first volume of *Studies of a Biographer,* and in the 1893 *National Review* essay "Biography," Stephen articulates his trademarks: condensation, restrained rhetoric, a quick survey of the useful references, and a portrait of the subject's character. But he left few comments like these; Stephen wrote examples of, rather than discussions about, biography.

Stephen began the second series of English Men of Letters with *George Eliot* in 1902. Morley extravagantly praised Stephen for his insight into *Middlemarch* (1871–1872), a novel Stephen did not much like but that he intelligibly places in Eliot's development as a person and as a writer. Stephen had known Eliot, and he used that personal knowledge when he could: he describes Eliot speaking with enthusiasm about Hardy and paying close attention to Lewes, for example. He treats Eliot's relationship with Lewes as a marriage and refuses to condemn it. He is aware that his literary analyses are informed by who he is and what his opinions are (about religion, for example). He praises Eliot's novels for psychologically believable characters but worries that the later novels are didactic. Except for *Samuel Johnson,* Stephen's book on Eliot is the most thoughtful and insightful work he did for the English Men of Letters series.

As a precursor to Stephen's beloved eighteenth-century philosophers, Hobbes was an apt choice for his final biography. Much of the second half of *Hobbes* (1904) is a lengthy analysis of Hobbes's philosophy, but Stephen continues to remind the reader of the close connections among a writer's life, historical period, and works. "As Hobbes condemned their principles," Stephen writes about a dispute with Parliament, "we must remind ourselves how things appeared at the time." Maitland wrote a note at the end of *Hobbes* describing the conditions under which the dying Stephen wrote it. Stephen asked for help in finishing the book, but it needed, according to Maitland, no revision.

The doctors had found stomach cancer in April 1902, and for the remaining two years of his life Stephen had lain in the bed in which the children had been born and Julia had died. By all accounts he showed much the same courage and acceptance of death that he noted about many of his *Dictionary of National Biography* subjects. He died at 22 Hyde Park Gate on 22 February 1904. He was cremated, and his ashes were buried in Highgate Cemetery. A memorial lectureship was started at Cambridge in 1905 for a biennial talk about literary and biographical topics.

Leslie Stephen's book-length biographies, however readable, may become outdated by new methodologies and discoveries, but the *Dictionary of National Biography* will remain. As editor and writer Stephen helped change biography from an impressionistic memorial to a scholarly analysis. Lytton Strachey's ironic, condensed biographical portraits certainly show Stephen's influence in the early twentieth century, and in 1989 Reed Whittemore recognized that Stephen "brought a kind of order to the least orderly genre we have."

Biographies:

Frederic William Maitland, *The Life and Letters of Leslie Stephen* (London: Duckworth, 1906);

Noël Annan, *Leslie Stephen: The Godless Victorian* (New York: Random House, 1984).

References:

Noël Annan, "The Intellectual Aristocracy," in *Studies in Social History: A Tribute to G. M. Trevelyan,* edited by J. H. Plumb (London: Longmans, Green, 1955), pp. 241–287;

Jeffrey von Arx, *Progress and Pessimism: Religion, Politics, and History in Late Nineteenth-Century Britain* (Cambridge, Mass.: Harvard University Press, 1985);

Quentin Bell, "The Mausoleum Book," *Review of English Literature,* 6 (January 1965): 9–18;

Bell, *Virginia Woolf: A Biography,* 2 volumes (New York: Harcourt Brace Jovanovich, 1972);

John W. Bicknell, "Mr. Ramsay Was Young Once," in *Virginia Woolf and Bloomsbury: A Centenary Celebration,* edited by Jane Marcus (Bloomington: Indiana University Press, 1987);

Laurel Brake, "Problems in Victorian Biography: The *DNB* and the *DNB* 'Walter Pater,'" *Modern Language Review,* 70 (1975): 731–742;

Ronald William Clark, *The Victorian Mountaineers* (London: Batsford, 1953);

Charles Crawley, *Trinity Hall: The History of a Cambridge College, 1350–1975* (Cambridge: Cambridge University Press, 1976);

Edwin Everett, *The Party of Humanity: The Fortnightly Review and its Contributions, 1865–1874* (Chapel Hill: University of North Carolina Press, 1939);

Gillian Fenwick, "Leslie Stephen at Trinity Hall, Cambridge," *Notes and Queries,* 235 (March 1990): 40–42;

Jane Elizabeth Fisher, "The Seduction of the Father: Virginia Woolf and Leslie Stephen," *Women's Studies,* 18, no. 1 (1990): 31–48;

Edmund Gosse, "Sir Leslie Stephen," in *Encyclopædia Britannica,* eleventh edition (Cambridge: Cam-

bridge University Press, 1910), XXV: 885–886;

John Gross, *The Rise and Fall of the Man of Letters* (London: Weidenfeld & Nicolson, 1969);

Phyllis Grosskurth, *Leslie Stephen* (London: Longmans, Green, 1968);

Katherine Hill, "Virginia Woolf and Leslie Stephen: History and Literary Revolution," *PMLA,* 96 (May 1981): 351–362;

Gertrude Himmelfarb, "Leslie Stephen: The Victorian as Intellectual," in her *Victorian Minds* (New York: Knopf, 1968), pp. 198–219;

Virginia Hyman, "Concealment and Disclosure in Sir Leslie Stephen's *Mausoleum Book,*" *Biography,* 3 (Spring 1980): 121–131;

Hyman, "Late Victorian and Early Modern: Continuities in Criticism of Leslie Stephen and Virginia Woolf," *English Literature in Transition,* 23, no. 3 (1980): 44–54;

Hyman, "Reflections in the Looking Glass: Leslie Stephen and Virginia Woolf," *Journal of Modern Literature,* 10 (July 1983): 197–216;

Q. D. Leavis, "Leslie Stephen: Cambridge Critic," in *A Selection from Scrutiny,* edited by F. R. Leavis (Cambridge: Cambridge University Press, 1968);

Sidney Lee, "Postscript to 'Statistical Account,'" in *Dictionary of National Biography,* volume 1, edited by Lee and Stephen (Oxford: Oxford University Press, 1917), pp. lxxix–lxxxiv;

Lee, "Sir Leslie Stephen," in *Dictionary of National Biography: Supplement, January 1901–December 1911,* volume 1, edited by Lee (Oxford: Oxford University Press, 1912), pp. 398–405;

Jean Love, *Virginia Woolf: Sources of Madness and Art* (Berkeley: University of California Press, 1977);

Desmond MacCarthy, *Leslie Stephen* (Cambridge: Cambridge University Press, 1937);

Oscar Maurer, Jr., "Leslie Stephen and the *Cornhill Magazine,*" *University of Texas Studies in English,* 32 (1953): 67–95;

John Morley, *Recollections* (New York: Macmillan, 1917);

Ira Bruce Nadel, *Biography: Fiction, Fact and Form* (New York: St. Martin's Press, 1984);

C. W. F. Noyce, *Scholar Mountaineers: Pioneers of Parnassus* (London: Dobson, 1950);

S. P. Rosenbaum, "An Educated Man's Daughter: Leslie Stephen, Virginia Woolf and the Bloomsbury Group," in *Virginia Woolf: New Critical Essays,* edited by Patricia Clements and Isobel Grundy (Totowa, N. J.: Barnes & Noble, 1983), pp. 32–51;

Barbara Ann Schmidt, "In the Shadow of Thackeray: Leslie Stephen as the Editor of the *Cornhill Magazine*," in *Innovators and Preachers: The Role of the Editor in Victorian England,* edited by Joel Wiener (Westport, Conn.: Greenwood Press, 1985), pp. 77–96;

John W. Robertson Scott, *The Story of the Pall Mall Gazette, of Its First Editor Frederick Greenwood and of Its Founder George Murray Smith* (London & New York: Oxford University Press, 1950);

Martin Stemerick, "From Stephen to Woolf: The Victorian Family and Modern Rebellion," Ph.D. dissertation, University of Texas at Austin, 1982;

Reed Whittemore, *Whole Lives: Shapers of Modern Biography* (Baltimore & London: Johns Hopkins Press, 1989);

Virginia Woolf, "Leslie Stephen, the Philosopher at Home," in her *The Captain's Deathbed and Other Essays* (New York: Harcourt, Brace, 1950), pp. 69–75;

Woolf, "Reminiscences" and "A Sketch of the Past," in her *Moments of Being,* edited by Jeanne Schulkind, revised edition (New York & London: Harcourt Brace Jovanovich, 1985), pp. 25–60; 61–137;

David D. Zink, *Leslie Stephen* (New York: Twayne, 1972).

Papers:

Collections of Leslie Stephen's letters are at the Houghton Library, Harvard University; the Perkins Library, Duke University; the Henry W. and Albert Berg Collection, New York Public Library; the National Library of Scotland; the Pierpont Morgan Library, New York; the Bodleian Library, Oxford; the Brotherton Library, University of Leeds; and the Macmillan Archives, British Library. Manuscripts are scattered: the Perkins Library has forty manuscripts for articles from Stephen's *Cornhill Magazine* essays; the Pierpont Morgan Library has the manuscript for *History of English Thought in the Eighteenth Century*; the Berg Collection has the manuscript for *The Science of Ethics;* the British Library has the manuscript for the *Mausoleum Book* and others. The Rose Memorial Library at Drew University has two notebooks with reading notes. Trinity Hall, Cambridge, retains various records such as the letter announcing Stephen's intention to resign his fellowship on 31 December 1862 and folios of his handwritten accounts of college elections in 1864–1865.

John Addington Symonds

(5 October 1840 – 19 April 1893)

Paul R. Johnson
Conception Seminary College

See also the Symonds entry in *DLB 57: Victorian Prose Writers After 1867.*

BOOKS: *The Escorial: A Prize Poem, Recited in the Theatre, Oxford, June 20, 1860* (Oxford: Shrimpton, 1860);

The Renaissance: An Essay Read in the Theatre, Oxford, June 17, 1863 (Oxford: Hammans, 1863);

An Introduction to the Study of Dante (London: Smith, Elder, 1872; London: Black / New York: Macmillan, 1899);

The Renaissance of Modern Europe: A Review of the Scientific, Artistic, Rationalistic, Revolutionary Revival, Dating from the 15th Century. Being a Lecture Delivered before the Sunday Lecture Society, the 24th November, 1872 (London: Scott, 1872);

Studies of the Greek Poets, 2 volumes (London: Smith, Elder, 1873, 1876; New York: Harper, 1880);

Sketches in Italy and Greece (London: Smith, Elder, 1874); republished in *Sketches and Studies in Southern Europe,* 2 volumes (New York: Harper, 1880);

Renaissance in Italy, 7 volumes (London: Smith, Elder, 1875–1886; New York: Holt, 1881–1887);

Callicrates, Bianca, Imelda, Passio Amoris Secunda, A Rhapsody, Liber Temporis Perditi (Bristol: Privately printed, circa 1875–1880);

Crocuses and Soldanellas (Bristol: Privately printed, circa 1875–1880);

Genius Amoris Amari Visio (Bristol: Privately printed, circa 1875–1880);

The Lotos Garland of Antinous [and *Diego*] (Bristol: Privately printed, circa 1875–1880);

Love and Death: A Symphony (Bristol: Privately printed, circa 1875–1880);

The Love Tale of Odatis and Prince Zariadres (Bristol: Privately printed, circa 1875–1880);

Old and New (Bristol: Privately printed, circa 1875–1880);

[*Pantarkes (and Other Poems)*] (Bristol: Privately printed, circa 1875–1880);

Rhaetica (Bristol: Privately printed, circa 1875–1880);

Tales of Ancient Greece, No. 1: Eudiades, and A Cretan Idyll (Bristol: Privately printed, circa 1875–1880);

Tales of Ancient Greece, No. 2 (Bristol: Privately printed, circa 1875–1880);

Many Moods: A Volume of Verse (London: Smith, Elder, 1878);

Shelley (London: Macmillan, 1878; New York: Harper, 1879);

Sketches and Studies in Italy (London: Smith, Elder, 1879); republished in *Sketches and Studies in Southern Europe,* 2 volumes (New York: Harper, 1880);

New and Old: A Volume of Verse (London: Smith, Elder, 1880; Boston: Osgood, 1880);

Animi Figura (London: Smith, Elder, 1882);

Italian Byways (London: Smith, Elder, 1883; New York: Holt, 1883);

A Problem in Greek Ethics (N.p.: Privately printed, 1883);

Fragilia Labilia (N.p.: Privately printed, 1884; Portland, Maine: Mosher, 1902);

Shakespeare's Predecessors in the English Drama (London: Smith, Elder, 1884; London: Smith, Elder / New York: Scribners, 1900);

Vagabunduli Libellus (London: Kegan Paul, Trench, 1884);

Sir Philip Sidney (London & New York: Macmillan, 1886);

Ben Jonson (London: Longmans, Green, 1886; New York: Appleton, 1886);

Essays Speculative and Suggestive (2 volumes, London: Chapman & Hall, 1890; 1 volume, New York: Scribners, 1894);

A Problem in Modern Ethics: Being an Enquiry into the Phenomenon of Sexual Inversion. Addressed Especially to Medical Psychologists and Jurists (N.p.: Privately printed, 1891?);

Our Life in the Swiss Highlands, by Symonds and Margaret Symonds (London & Edinburgh: Black, 1892);

The Life of Michelangelo Buonarroti: Based on Studies in the Archives of the Buonarroti Family at Florence, 2 volumes (London: Nimmo, 1893 [i.e., 1892]; London: Macmillan / New York: Scribners, 1900);

In the Key of Blue and Other Prose Essays (London: Mathews & Lane / New York: Macmillan, 1893);

Walt Whitman: A Study (London: Nimmo, 1893; London: Routledge / New York: Dutton, 1906?);

On the English Family of Symonds (Oxford: Privately printed, 1894);

Blank Verse (London: Nimmo, 1895; New York: Scribners, 1895);

Giovanni Boccaccio as Man and Author (London: Nimmo, 1895);

Das Konträre Geschlechtsgefühl, by Symonds and Havelock Ellis, edited by Hans Kurella (Leipzig: Wingard, 1896); English version revised as *Sexual Inversion,* by Symonds and Ellis (London: Wilson & Macmillan, 1897; republished, omitting appendixes by Symonds and without

Symonds's name on the title page, Philadelphia: Davis, 1901);

Last and First; Being Two Essays (New York: Brown, 1919);

Gabriel: A Poem, edited by Robert L. Peters and Timothy D'Arch Smith (London: De Hartington, 1974);

Memoirs of John Addington Symonds, edited by Phyllis Grosskurth (London: Hutchinson, 1984; New York: Random House, 1984).

OTHER: John Addington Symonds, M.D., *Verses,* edited by Symonds (Bristol: Privately printed, 1871);

The Sonnets of Michael Angelo Buonarroti and Tommaso Campanella, translated by Symonds (London: Smith, Elder, 1878; Portland, Maine: Mosher, 1895);

Wine, Women, and Song: Mediaeval Latin Students' Songs, translated, with an essay, by Symonds (London: Chatto & Windus, 1884; Portland, Maine: Mosher, 1899);

Christopher Marlowe, edited by Havelock Ellis, general introduction by Symonds (London: Vizetelly, 1887);

Thomas Heywood, edited by A. Wilson Verity, introduction by Symonds (London: Vizetelly, 1888);

Webster and Tourneur, introduction and notes by Symonds (London: Vizetelly, 1888);

The Life of Benvenuto Cellini: Written by Himself, edited and translated, with a biographical sketch, by Symonds (London: Nimmo, 1888; New York: Scribner & Welford, 1888);

The Memoirs of Count Carlo Gozzi, translated, with an introduction, by Symonds (London: Nimmo, 1890).

In his 1878 biography of the English Romantic poet, John Addington Symonds wrote that the young Percy Bysshe Shelley's intellect and aesthetic sensibilities "sustained him at a perilous height above the . . . race of man." The same could well be written of Symonds's own career. Though he is today a relatively obscure figure, especially in comparison to contemporaries such as Robert Browning, Alfred Tennyson, John Ruskin, and Oscar Wilde, he is, nevertheless, important for understanding the intellectual and moral climate of the later Victorian age. His biographies and other writings provide a window on nineteenth-century canons of taste; but, even more significantly, they tell much about Symonds's own struggle as a homosexual and religious skeptic at a time when neither was socially acceptable. His substantial body of public writing and his popular success mask considerable emotional turmoil as he, like Shelley, sought to reconcile his dreams and desires with the often-uncompromising social world of his day. This constant perilous tension continually emerges in his writing, especially in his literary biographies, and makes him a worthy figure of study.

Symonds was born on 5 October 1840 in Bristol into a conventional yet intellectually and culturally stimulating middle-class Victorian household. His father, Dr. John Addington Symonds, was a physician and lecturer at the General Hospital and British Medical School; his mother was Harriet Sykes Symonds. The sixth of seven children, Symonds was a sickly child. His mother died of scarlet fever when Symonds was four; his one clear memory of her was an incident when the horses drawing their carriage suddenly bolted on a steep incline. More than forty years later Symonds could vividly recall the scene: "I can still see a pale face, a pink silk bonnet and beautiful yellow hair," he wrote in his memoirs, published in 1984.

Symonds grew up with his father's typical Victorian attitudes, including a reverence for work and a strong sense of duty. Yet Symonds was never able to fulfill his father's expectations for him "to be made a man"; he was a nervous, sensitive, and isolated boy with fragile health and a taste for intense aesthetic experiences: "Simplicity and purity and wayward grace in natural things, strength and solidity and decent form in things of art, were what my temperament unconsciously demanded." He had an active imagination; nightmares would frequently compel him to run out of his room, leading his father to order him tied to his bed. Though Symonds wrote in his memoirs that he was fundamentally different from his father in sensibility and moral inclination, Dr. Symonds's influence remained a controlling psychological force throughout his son's life, exhibited in a continual struggle between Symonds's conventional public expressions and his private homoerotic dreams and desires.

In 1851 the family moved to Clifton Hill House, a mansion overlooking Bristol; the house became for Symonds an emotional haven as well as a formative aesthetic influence, its good prospect, exquisite garden, and rich odors objectifying beauty for him as a child. He would always consider his years at Clifton Hill House the happiest of his life – in sharp contrast to his time at Harrow, where he was sent in 1854. He hated the school, with its rough physical games and what Symonds considered its thoroughly impoverished and corrupt aesthetic and moral atmosphere. In 1858 he revealed to his father that the headmaster, Charles Vaughan – a seeming paragon of piety and moral rigor – had made sexual overtures to one of Symonds's friends, Alfred Pretor. Under pressure from the elder Symonds, Vaughan resigned to avoid public exposure. Symonds always felt ambivalent about what he had done; he also had homoerotic tendencies, but at this age he was still attempting to conform to his father's expectations of proper moral behavior.

The counterpoint to the sordid and unhappy state of affairs at Harrow was the sanctuary of Symonds's aesthetic life, to which he withdrew through reading and indolent daydreams. During a visit home in the spring of 1858 what he came to regard as "one of the most important nights of my life" came when he read Plato's *Phaedrus* and *Symposium;* there he found a coherent philosophical sanction and idealization of his own love of male beauty. This ideal was realized for Symonds in Willie Dyer, a chorister at Bristol Cathedral, with whom he had a clandestine and chaste affair in the spring of 1858. Symonds later described their first intimate meeting

Clifton Hill House, the mansion overlooking Bristol, where the young Symonds spent the happiest years of his life, from 1851 to 1854. After his father's death in 1871 he moved his own wife and children into the house.

in the cloisters as "the birth of my real self"; he had begun to acknowledge his homosexuality.

Symonds went up to Balliol College, Oxford, in the autumn of 1858 and achieved some success once he decided to apply himself to his studies. His initial indifference and withdrawn indolence gave way to a more confident manner, though he was still tormented by his homosexual longings. His most important mentor during this time was Benjamin Jowett, the master of Balliol and one of the leading lights of Oxford, under whose tutelage he learned the value of clear thinking and writing.

Symonds continued to be torn between the voice of duty, responsibility, and Victorian conventionality represented by his father, on the one hand, and, on the other, what he termed "seelensehnsucht" (longing of the soul) — his homoerotic longings, which had taken the form of what he describes in his memoirs as a "quest of ideal beauty, incarnated in breathing male beings, or eternalized in everduring works of art." This supreme tension, which was leading him toward a "precipice," or emotional crisis, was exacerbated by his passionate love for another Bristol chorister, Alfred Brooke, whom he met in 1862. Though he resisted involvement with Brooke, Symonds came to realize that his homosexual desires were an irradicable part of his nature.

After receiving his B.A. in 1862 he was elected a fellow of Magdalen College and was anticipating a modest happiness as an Oxford don when his prospects were shattered by attacks on his character by his former college friend G. H. Shorting. Though he was formally cleared of the charges, the other faculty shunned him, and he was compelled to leave Oxford. This incident, along with his abiding emotional self-division, caused an emotional breakdown.

After leaving Oxford in 1863 Symonds settled in London, studying law unenthusiastically and writing unsigned reviews for the *Saturday Review* as well as a good deal of poetry. He vowed at this time to seek a more conventional sexual life in marriage, and on a visit to Switzerland in the summer of 1864 he proposed to Catherine North. They were married on 10 November. His hopes that marriage would resolve his sexual tensions and emotional unrest were not realized, although he and Catherine had four daughters. The first, Janet, was born in 1865.

With his interests increasingly moving in the direction of literary criticism, Symonds abandoned his plans for a law career in early 1866. Always physically fragile, he had begun developing symptoms of tuberculosis, and his father prescribed

Symonds as a student at Oxford

travel to the Riviera. Symonds had by this time had pieces on the Elizabethan dramatists published in the *Cornhill Magazine* and the *Pall Mall Gazette;* he was attracted to the Elizabethans' seemingly uninhibited vitality, and through them he began to develop an interest in Italian literature. Yet this time was a difficult one for Symonds, who suffered not only from lung disease but also from the emotional tensions connected with his repressed homosexuality. While staying in Cannes with his family, he had another breakdown. His second daughter, Lotta, was born in July 1867. Symonds gave up their London home for one near his father's house in Clifton in the late autumn of 1868. His third daughter, Margaret, was born early the next year. He and Catherine remained married until his death, but by 1869 he had requested to be allowed to pursue his homosexual relationships. Though she assented to this arrangement, she developed a depression that deepened throughout their remaining years.

Symonds's love of Greece and the Greek ideals of beauty was lifelong and superseded even the Renaissance, which he valued because it had inherited, in part, the liberating, more permissive spirit of Hellas. He was able to focus his ideas on Greek literature through the preparation of a series of lectures for Dr. John Percival's sixth form class at Clifton College in 1869. These lectures were published as *Studies of the Greek Poets* (1873, 1876) and are important for understanding Symonds's attitude toward Hellenic ideals of beauty and sexual liberty and his views about their application in Victorian society. He was especially enamored of the lyric poets of Lesbos and the vital life of the island's society: "Nowhere in any age of Greek history, or in any part of Hellas, did the love of physical beauty, the sensibility to radiant scenes of nature, the consuming fervor of personal feeling, assume such grand proportions and receive so illustrious an expression as they did on Lesbos." Above all, it is the ideal of freedom that Symonds valued in Greek civilization, and that ideal became his standard for measuring the progressive development of culture. For the termination of this ideal of freedom Symonds blames medieval Christianity and its division of body and spirit, and he calls on his own society to "imitate the Greeks . . . by approximating to their free and fearless attitude of mind."

Symonds's move into Clifton Hill House following the death of his father on 25 February 1871 marks the end of his apprenticeship as a writer. He continued writing essays and reviews for various periodicals but devoted most of his energy to lengthier biographies, translations, and historical and critical studies, and he rapidly emerged as a recognized literary critic. Even at this early period in his career a characteristic tone and approach are evident in Symonds's work. His motivation for writing biography was an intense sympathy with his subject. Moreover, for Symonds biography was intimately tied to history because of their similar concern with depicting an organic whole infused with the spirit of a personality – in an individual and in a collective, respectively. Thus a period such as the Renaissance in a particular country such as Italy or England takes on a representative personality that is expressed most characteristically in its works of art. This same focus is found in Symonds's literary criticism. For Symonds a work of literature was essentially an expression of a writer's personality – of his or her deepest values and beliefs – and, thus, Symonds's "biographies" are usually merged with "criticism." The result can be a vital and intensely human contact with the author and his work, but in many cases it becomes a sketchy amalgam of biographical fact and highly personalized impressions. As Edmund Gosse wrote in his unsigned obituary of Symonds in the *Saturday Review* (29 April 1893), Symonds was "one who aimed at the highest things and came a little short."

Symonds's first major work of biographical criticism to appear in print was *An Introduction to the Study of Dante* (1872), written in the summer of 1870 in Heiligenblut, Switzerland, as a series of lectures to make Dante more accessible to the English public. Symonds was to continue to be a popularizer and arbiter of culture for the rest of his career. Besides a relatively brief sketch of Dante's life against the background of Italian history, the work offers a close examination of the *Divine Comedy* (1321), celebrating its concrete detail, moral sublimity, and realistic humanism. It made Symonds a more visible public figure, and he was offered many reviewing jobs; among these offers was one with the *Academy*, a review of European scientific and literary activity.

Symonds's efforts to understand and sympathize with the religion of Dante's time left him depressed; it underscored his own "hopeless and abysmal state of skepticism," as he wrote to Henry Dakyns. Skepticism was a constant theme of Symonds's early life, though its source was more complex than simply a loss of faith. Certainly he felt alienated from the suffocating Nonconformist piety of his father's family, and he undertook to purge himself of the past when he burned the family letters in 1881. But Symonds's skepticism and alienation were rooted in his sexuality. His celebrated ennui and laments over the "waste" in things came out of the tension between his inner life of aesthetic dreams and idealized homoerotic desire and the often frustrating conventionality and material and biological necessity of his life in the world. As he had expressed it to Dakyns in 1866: "My soul is stagnant, and I see no God, no reason for the world, no vigour in myself, no content in the things around me. . . ." Symonds's quest for meaning was contingent on reconciling his homosexuality with a world that denied it.

If there is a constant in Symonds's career as a writer of critical biographies, it is his abiding love of the Renaissance, both in Italy and in England. His major study of this period is *Renaissance in Italy*, published in seven volumes from 1875 to 1886. Symonds's view of the Renaissance as the springtime of civilized freedom following the cramped winter of medieval oppression reflects the historicism of his own century, with its penchant for periodizing history and its valuation of the "modern" world over the "Dark Ages" of medievalism.

The first volume, *The Age of the Despots*, defines the Renaissance as a "new birth to liberty – the spirit of mankind recovering consciousness and the power of self-determination, recognizing the beauty of the outer world, and of the body through art, liberating the reason in science and the conscience in religion, restoring culture to the intelligence, and establishing the principle of political freedom." Freedom and cultural superiority were attained, Symonds argues, despite the political fragmentation of Italy, and "even the wildest and most perfidious of tyrants felt the ennobling influences and the sacred thirst of knowledge." Symonds took a personal approach to his study of the Renaissance, identifying with its impulses of enlightenment and freedom.

The second and third volumes of *Renaissance in Italy* came out two years later. In *The Revival of Learning* Symonds says that he is writing the "Biography of a nation" whose history and culture mani-

Symonds with peasants at Davos Platz, Switzerland, where he lived from 1877 until his death

fest themselves in "men greater than their race." Symonds sees the Renaissance values of intellectual emancipation, toleration, and liberty as lacking in Victorian society: "Men were, and dared to be, themselves for good or evil without too much regard for what their neighbors thought of them." *The Fine Arts* expresses Symonds's belief that one could comprehend the Italians of the Renaissance only through their art, above all their painting and sculpture. With its reconciliation of body and soul, its expression of ideal beauty incarnate, Renaissance art stands on the threshold of the modern world. Symonds considered these volumes to show a marked improvement in his expertise and professionalism as a writer.

Following an unsuccessful campaign for the Professorship of Poetry at Oxford in the spring of 1877, Symonds was advised to leave England for more hospitable climes when his tuberculosis flared up. The family — which by this time included the fourth daughter, Katharine, born in 1875 — left in August for the Nile River by way of the Alps, but Symonds decided to winter in Davos Platz, near the Tirol in eastern Switzerland, because of the health-giving air. Davos Platz became his home for the remainder of his days; in 1881 he had a house

built in Davos Platz that he called Am Hof, which became a favored stopping place for the literati of England. It was there, in comfortably furnished rooms papered in Morris prints, that he wrote his remaining works.

In the Romantic poet Shelley, Symonds found a kindred idealist and nonconformist. His 1878 biography of the poet attempts to create the image of an exemplary life of unselfish benevolence cut off before its time, while ignoring or explaining away some of the less savory aspects of Shelley's life, such as his treatment of his first wife, Harriet. Despite his youth and immaturity, Symonds argues, Shelley earnestly tried to live out his theories. He "invested the commonplaces of reality with dark hues borrowed from his own imagination" and gave to English literature new qualities of "ideality, freedom, and spiritual audacity." Clearly, Symonds projected his own desires for a marriage of thought and practice into his biography of Shelley; but his enthusiastic portrait is thin as either biography or criticism, and it received mixed reviews.

Symonds returned to the Italian Renaissance series with the fourth and fifth volumes, collectively titled *Italian Literature* (1881). He illustrates the process by which "vernacular literature absorbed into

Symonds with his wife, Catherine; their youngest daughter,
Katherine; and their dog, Ciò, circa 1886

itself the elements of scholarship, and gave form to the predominating thoughts and feelings of the people" through a close study of writers such as Dante, Giovanni Boccaccio, Ludovico Ariosto, and Niccolò Machiavelli. Despite its political fragmentation during this period, Italy retained an organic unity of spirit corresponding to evolutionary development in living creatures. This unity was part of a cohesive chain of development in the history of civilization from antiquity to the present. This theory of cultural history, indebted to the theory of evolution as well as Romantic organicism, became a key element in the rest of Symonds's works of history and biographical criticism.

Symonds was becoming more deeply involved in life at Davos Platz; he organized the first international toboggan race there in the late autumn of 1883. He relished the company of the local peasants, idealizing their "primitive" culture of manly simplicity and falling in love with one of them, Christian Buol. Yet he also yearned for the more luxurious climes of the south, and he began making regular trips to Venice each spring. Because of his tuberculosis the city was a dangerous attraction, and Symonds was usually grateful to return to

Davos Platz; but he found Venice a sanctuary of the wayward soul, as he had written in his study of Dante in 1872: "Venice, unconquered by the Lombards, and fenced within the solitudes of her lagoons, became the resort of all exiles and daring persons." Part of its attraction for Symonds was Angelo Fusato, a young gondolier with whom he had become infatuated in May 1881. He described their relationship in his memoirs as "an affair not merely of desire and instinct but also of imagination" that evolved into a sustaining friendship.

Symonds returned to the historical-biographical issue of "organic development" in aesthetic culture in *Shakespeare's Predecessors in the English Drama*. He had drafted this work twenty years earlier as a series of essays but had put it away; he decided to bring it to life again as a full-length study, and it was published in 1884. This decision turned out to be a misstep in an otherwise scintillating career; the book was savaged by the critics, especially Churton Collins, who described it in the *Quarterly Review* (October 1885) as "a narrative clogged with endless repetitions, without symmetry, without proportion" and thought it dangerous in its middling competence. One of the problems lay in Symonds's forced application of Herbert Spencer's evolutionary hypothesis to the literature of the sixteenth century to demonstrate that Shakespeare was the apex of a long process of development.

Symonds had regained his momentum by 1886, the year his studies of Sir Philip Sidney and Ben Jonson and the final volumes of *Renaissance in Italy* were published. There is in these works a more confident, less encumbered tone that marks Symonds's maturation as a stylistic craftsman.

Sidney, wrote Symonds, "shines with a pure lustre," and his biography of the English Renaissance courtier and poet vibrates with sympathetic admiration for a fellow humanist. Unlike the Shelley biography, there is more specific criticism of the poet's work here – particularly of the sonnet sequence *Astrophel and Stella* (1591), which takes up nearly a quarter of the volume. Symonds is most interested in Sidney's sincere expression of personal emotion in these sonnets. Symonds finds in Sidney a kindred spirit in his love of learning; his career as a critic and poet; and his humanity, cultivation, and loyalty. Most important for Symonds, Sidney was a "Renaissance man" – an exemplar of that all-important transition to the modern world. Sidney had clashed with the sordid affairs of earth, had died, and was raised to ideality "for ever living and for ever admirable."

Symonds's sometimes-cloying tone of adulation in the Sidney book is modulated in his *Ben Jonson,* a volume for Andrew Lang's English Worthies series that demonstrates Symonds's competence as both a critic and prose stylist. He emphasizes Jonson's erudition and common sense as the key features of his dramatic and poetic work, admiring him as a teacher of "world-wisdom" and a rebel against mere public taste. For Symonds, Jonson was a classicist in intellectual training but a Romantic genius in his visionary imagination – a "Titan" of Renaissance literature whose work is marked by his "untiring energy and giant strength of intellectual muscle." *Ben Jonson* was praised by H. C. Beeching in the *Academy* (16 October 1886) as a good, readable analysis, "remarkably well done," but Wilde, in the *Pall Mall Gazette* (20 September 1886), criticized Symonds's oversimplifying rhetoric, his avoidance of Jonson's literary criticism, and his sometimes "strained" style: "Mr. Symonds has written some charming poetry, but his prose, unfortunately, is always poetical prose, never the prose of a poet."

The Catholic Reaction, comprising the final two volumes of Symonds's study of the Renaissance, was published in 1886. As one might expect from Symonds's hostility to organized religion, he recounts the stultifying effect of the Counter-Reformation on Italian culture and manners: "The frank audacity of the Renaissance is superseded by cringing timidity, lumbering dulness, somnolent and stagnant acquiescence in accepted formulae." This work, like the other volumes of the series, was generally a critical success. The *Dial* obituary for Symonds (1 May 1893) would emphasize that the Renaissance "period as a whole, its political and domestic life, its literature and art, received at his hands a treatment that . . . is distinctly the best and most attractive in English literature."

Symonds followed the completion of his seven-volume work on the Renaissance by writing a biography of Boccaccio in 1887. Published posthumously in 1895, the volume is of a piece with Symonds's other work on the Renaissance in focusing on a particular literary figure who embodies the modern aesthetic ideals that make the period valuable for Symonds's own quest for identity and belonging. Like Dante and Petrarch, Boccaccio, for Symonds, anticipated modern literature with his "self-conscious" use of formal innovation, projection of personality, and vivid realism. His work, according to Symonds, was the precursor of the novel in its handling of "the complex stuff of daily life," and he dominated Italian taste for three centuries because he anticipated the future preoccupation with the earthly and the immediate.

Symonds's oldest daughter, Janet, died of tuberculosis on 7 April 1887. Symonds began to reconsider old questions about God and existence, and his skepticism evolved into what he termed "Cosmic Enthusiasm," a positive acceptance of the order of the universe and his place in it.

Whereas in his public expressions Symonds could not divulge his inner tensions and sometimes overpowering homoerotic desires, he did so in his memoirs, which were not published until 1984. *Memoirs of John Addington Symonds* is a captivating and thoroughly honest look into the heart of a man at odds with the conventional mores of his day. Symonds began writing his memoirs in 1889, although already in 1863 he had written to his friend A. O. Rutson that he thought of his life as a kind of training for the writing of his confessions. Completed in 1893, the work is really an emotional history rather than a memoir and leaves out a good deal of information about his children, friends, and the events of his life. Symonds's intent is, he says, to "describe the evolution of a somewhat abnormally constituted individual." The work tells much about the experience of a homosexual in the Victorian age; it reveals a great deal about the often-

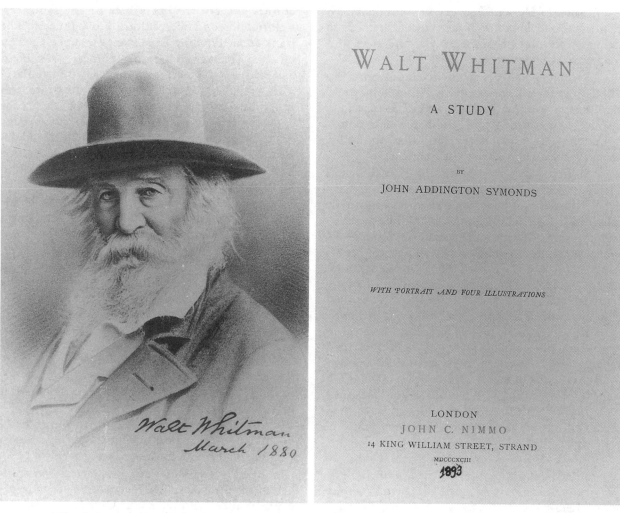

WALT WHITMAN

A STUDY

BY

JOHN ADDINGTON SYMONDS

WITH PORTRAIT AND FOUR ILLUSTRATIONS

LONDON
JOHN C. NIMMO
14 KING WILLIAM STREET, STRAND
MDCCCXCIII
1893

Frontispiece and title page for Symonds's study of the American poet with whom he had corresponded since 1871

unreconcilable tensions in Symonds's life, especially between his idealizing temperament and his often purely carnal proclivities; finally, it helps to modify one's view of Symonds's agnosticism, or search for God, which Horatio F. Brown's biography (1895) identifies as "his dominating pursuit." His memoirs make plain that Symonds's skeptical anxiety about the uncertainties of the modern age were due in part to his struggles to understand his own identity as a homosexual in nineteenth-century European society.

Symonds's *Essays Speculative and Suggestive* (1890) is a collection of essays dealing with the themes of idealism and evolution in the arts. Several of the essays attempt to explain his evolutionary, or "organic," theory of aesthetic development, derived in part from Spencer; others are devoted to questions of style or to specific writers such as Walt Whitman. While interesting today as an explication of Symonds's ideas, the essays were characterized

by contemporary critics as unremarkable and derivative. A later collection, *In the Key of Blue* (1893), is a more aesthetic series of writings typical of the 1890s — especially the title essay, a languorously impressionistic word painting of the color blue.

J. C. Nimmo, the publisher of Symonds's translations of the autobiography of Benvenuto Cellini (1888) and the memoirs of Carlo Gozzi (1890), as well as of the Boccaccio volume, offered Symonds five hundred pounds in 1890 to write a life of Michelangelo. He threw himself into the task with tremendous energy, traveling all over Italy to study Michelangelo's works and gaining access to the previously closed archives of Casa Buonarroti in Florence, where he spent two months poring over the artist's unedited letters. *The Life of Michelangelo Buonarroti* (1892) is his most detailed biography, though his final assessment of the man is that he "eludes our insight." Symonds used Thomas Carlyle's phrase, the "Hero as Artist," to describe

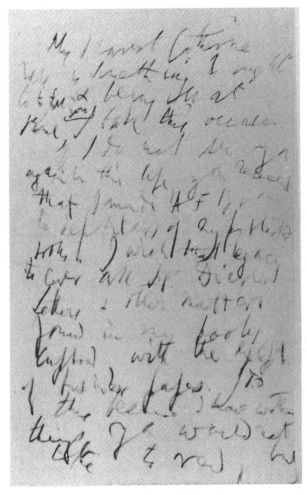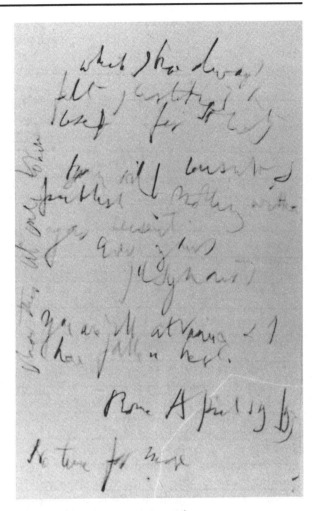

Symonds's last letter, written to his wife on the day of his death (University of Bristol)

this exemplar of the incomprehensible artistic genius. Although at times Michelangelo reaches the status of a demigod "beyond humanity," his tormented personal life also emerges – especially Symonds's important discovery that some of the artist's impassioned letters were written to a young Roman, Tommaso Cavalieri. The volume appeared in the year of Symonds's death and was favorably received by the public and critics.

After completing the Michelangelo study Symonds devoted his efforts to a public examination of homosexuality. He had been writing about his sexual longings and frustrations in his poetry from an early age, and, like his memoirs, the poems are significant for what they reveal of the man beneath the conventional public mask. He had had several books of poetry privately printed in the 1870s and early 1880s, but after his *Vagabunduli Libellus* (1884) was severely attacked by the critics he never had any more of his verse published. *A Problem in Greek Ethics*, privately printed in 1883 but adapted from

the final chapter of his *Studies of the Greek Poets*, looks at homosexual love in the context of the culture of ancient Greece; its companion volume, *A Problem in Modern Ethics* (1891?), examines homosexuality in modern times. Symonds was barraged by letters from other homosexuals, confiding their life histories to him. In 1891 he began a collaboration with the psychologist Havelock Ellis on a clinical study of homosexuality in an effort to debunk the assumption that it was a degenerative perversion. First published in 1896 in German, and in English in 1897 as *Sexual Inversion*, it argues for the legal and social liberation of homosexuality.

Symonds's ideal of life lived in robust and enlightened moral and sexual freedom was most closely represented by the poetry of Whitman. Symonds's biographical study of Whitman was the consummation of a devotion to the American poet's works dating from the beginning of his correspondence with the poet in 1871. Written after Whitman's death in 1892, it is as much an account of Whitman's impact on Symonds as it is a comprehensive study. Symonds praises Whitman's poetry unabashedly, finding in the "Calamus" sequence in the 1860 edition of *Leaves of Grass,* for example, a poetic expression of his own homoerotic ideals, though Whitman himself refused to confirm Symonds's reading of the poem as a personal statement. Symonds deals with Whitman's life in the opening "Notice," then examines a series of themes in *Leaves of Grass.* Symonds finds "courage" and "candor" to be the preeminent values expressed in Whitman's poetry and bears witness to the consolation he found in Whitman's work: "During my darkest hours, it comforted me with the conviction that I too played my part in the illimitable symphony of cosmic life." One can see here the dominant emotional theme in Symonds's life: to feel at one with the cosmos, to belong to it and not feel himself to be an outsider because of his sexual orientation. As he writes in *Walt Whitman: A Study* (1893), "it is my simple desire to live in the whole, and to see things, so far as may be possible, in their relation to the whole."

Symonds traveled to England and then, with his daughter Margaret, to southern Italy in the spring of 1893. In Rome he contracted influenza, which developed into pneumonia; he died in Rome on 19 April and was laid to rest in the Protestant cemetery, not far from Shelley's grave.

Contemporary critics consistently praised Symonds's readability despite their reservations over his somewhat florid style, but they often attacked his lack of technical knowledge. Yet in his day he was a popular success and was often compared favorably to Ruskin. After two biographical studies, by Brown in 1895 and Van Wyck Brooks in 1914, Symonds lapsed into relative critical obscurity. But a renaissance of sorts came in 1964 with Phyllis Grosskurth's excellent biography, followed by an edition of his letters in 1967–1969 and, finally, the publication of his memoirs in 1984. His self-portrait in the memoirs may lead readers back to his other works, which present a remarkable portrait of an emotionally complex person as well as an indispensable view of the late nineteenth century.

Letters:

The Letters and Papers of John Addington Symonds, edited by Horatio F. Brown (London: John Murray, 1923);

The Letters of John Addington Symonds, 3 volumes, edited by Herbert M. Schueller and Robert L. Peters (Detroit: Wayne State University Press, 1967–1969).

Bibliographies:

Percy L. Babington, *Bibliography of the Writings of John Addington Symonds* (London: Castle, 1925);

Carl Markgraf, "John Addington Symonds: An Annotated Bibliography of Writings about Him," *English Literature in Transition,* 18, no. 2 (1975): 79–138.

Biographies:

Horatio F. Brown, *John Addington Symonds: A Biography,* 2 volumes (London: Nimmo, 1895);

Van Wyck Brooks, *John Addington Symonds: A Biographical Study* (New York: Kennerley, 1914; London: Richards, 1914);

Phyllis Grosskurth, *John Addington Symonds* (London: Longmans, Green, 1964; New York: Holt, Rinehart & Winston, 1964).

References:

Katherine Furse, *Hearts and Pomegranates* (London: Davies, 1940);

Margaret Symonds, *Out of the Past* (London: John Murray, 1925);

Arthur Symons, *Studies in Prose and Verse* (London: Dent, 1904), pp. 85–90.

Papers:

Some of John Addington Symonds's papers are at the University of Bristol.

Edward John Trelawny

(13 November 1792 – 13 August 1881)

Fiona Stafford
Somerville College, Oxford

See also the Trelawny entries in *DLB 110: British Romantic Prose Writers, 1789–1832: Second Series* and *DLB 116: British Romantic Novelists, 1789–1832.*

BOOKS: *Adventures of a Younger Son,* anonymous, 3 volumes (London: Henry Colburn & Richard Bentley, 1831; New York: Harper, 1832);

Recollections of the Last Days of Shelley and Byron (London: Moxon, 1858; Boston: Ticknor & Fields, 1858); revised and enlarged as *Records of Shelley, Byron, and the Author,* 2 volumes (London: Pickering, 1878; New York: Scribners, 1887; edited by David Wright, Harmondsworth: Penguin, 1973);

The Relations of Lord Byron and Augusta Leigh: With a Comparison of the Characters of Byron and Shelley, and a Rebuke to Jane Clairmont on Her Hatred of the Former. (Four Letters) (London: Privately printed for T. J. Wise, 1920);

The Relations of Percy Bysshe Shelley with His Two Wives Harriet and Mary (in three letters . . . to Clara Jane Clairmont), and a Comment on the Character of Lady Byron (London: Privately printed for T. J. Wise, 1920).

OTHER: "Sahib Tulwar (Master of the Sword)," in *Heath's Book of Beauty,* edited by Marguerite, Countess of Blessingham (London: Longman, Orme, Brown, Green & Longmans, 1839), pp. 196–206.

SELECTED PERIODICAL PUBLICATIONS – UNCOLLECTED: "A Description of the Cavern Fortress of Mount Parnassus," *Examiner,* 14 November 1825, pp. 719–720;

"Trelawny's Journal," *London Literary Gazette,* 12 February 1831, pp. 97–98.

Edward John Trelawny is remembered today as the "friend" of Percy Bysshe Shelley and George Gordon, Lord Byron. His work as a biographer consists of personal memories of and anecdotes about the two poets, with whom he was connected briefly in the 1820s. He was present at Shelley's cremation in Italy in 1822 and attended to Byron's body in Greece in 1824, but more than thirty years elapsed before Trelawny composed his *Recollections of the Last Days of Shelley and Byron* (1858). In the interval the poets and their deaths had been magnified by the vivid imagination of a man whose hopes of immortality rested on their reputations. Trelawny is now seen more as an image maker than a biographer and his *Recollections of the Last Days of Shelley and Byron* as a creative rather than scholarly memorial. Harold Nicolson refers to Trelawny as "a liar and a cad" in his *Byron: The Last Journey* (1924), while David Wright describes him as "an imaginative manipulator of reality"; but if the degree of moral censure has varied from critic to critic, there is a widespread consensus that *Recollections of the Last Days of Shelley and Byron,* later enlarged as *Records of Shelley, Byron, and the Author* (1878), forms essential reading for anyone interested in the Romantic period. While Trelawny cannot be relied on for factual information, he nevertheless offers a gripping narrative, full of details that are all the more fascinating because of the uncertainty as to their provenance.

Trelawny was born on 13 November 1792 and was the second son among the six children of Charles and Maria Hawkins Trelawny. During his youth the family home was in Soho Square, London, but Trelawny's parents were descended from old Cornish families, and he may have been born in Cornwall. His mother's elder brother, Sir Christopher Hawkins, Bart., owned a country house and estate at Trewithen in Cornwall. His father, though in reduced circumstances during Trelawny's infancy, had attained the rank of lieutenant colonel in the British army; in 1798 he inherited a substantial legacy from his cousin Owen Salusbery Brereton and

Edward John Trelawny; portrait by J. Severn (from H. J. Massingham, The Friend of Shelley: A Memoir of Edward John Trelawny, *1930)*

moved his family to London. The bequest entailed the adoption of Brereton as a surname, but the children remained Trelawnys, and Edward John always referred to southwest England as his "native country."

Facts about Trelawny's early years have been notoriously difficult to ascertain, largely as a result of the extravagant self-image he developed as a young man. When the Shelleys met him in 1822, the mask of exotic adventurer was already firmly in place. Mary Shelley wrote to Maria Gisborne on 9 February 1822: "he is six feet high – raven black hair which curls thickly & shortly like a Moors, dark, grey – expressive eyes – overhanging brows upturned lips & a smile which expresses good nature & kindheartedness – his shoulders are high like an Orientalist – his voice is monotonous yet emphatic & his language as he relates the events of his life energetic and simple – whether the tale be one of blood & horror or of irresistable comedy." A few days earlier she had recorded in her diary: "he tells strange stories of himself, horrific ones, so that they harrow one up, while with his emphatic but unmodulated voice, his simple yet strong language, he pourtrays the most frightful situations; then all these adventures took place between the age of thirteen & twenty. I believe them now I see the man." These were the stories that would eventually appear as *Adventures of a Younger Son* (1831), a work published anonymously in the form of a novel but claimed in a 19 January 1831 letter to Mary Shelley by Trelawny as "my true story."

The myth of the Romantic adventurer was to prove remarkably enduring, and as late as 1950 Rosalie Glynn Grylls's *Trelawny* would rely heavily on *Adventures of a Younger Son* for biographical detail. In 1956, however, the results of Lady Anne Hill's research among the Hawkins family papers and nineteenth-century naval records were published in an article that was devastating to the Trelawny myth. It is now clear that although *Adventures of a Younger Son* drew on Trelawny's own experiences, the more exuberant parts of the narrative – his desertion from the Royal Navy, his exploits with the wild privateer De Ruyter, his marriage to the beau-

Part of a letter from Trelawny to Claire Clairmont (from H. J. Massingham, The Friend of Shelley: A Memoir of Edward John Trelawny, 1930)

tiful Arab girl he had rescued – derived instead from an imagination nourished by the works of Byron and Sir Walter Scott.

That Trelawny spent his formative years at sea is beyond doubt. After an unhappy experience at the Royal Fort Boarding School in Bristol, he joined the navy as a midshipman in 1805. Over the next seven years he served on twelve ships and was present at the British capture of Mauritius in 1810 and of Java in 1811. The general course followed by the hero of *Adventures of a Younger Son* – to India, Mauritius, Penang, Borneo, and Java – is based on his career in the navy, as are the details of life aboard ship. The vividness of firsthand experience gives an air of authenticity to highly improbable events.

The novel also offers important psychological insight into its author, whose awareness of the social disadvantages of primogeniture for those unlucky enough to be younger siblings is plain from the first paragraph: "My birth was unpropitious. I came into the world, branded and denounced as a vagrant; for I was a younger son of a family, so proud of their antiquity, that even gout and mortgaged estates were traced, many generations back, on the genealogical tree, as ancient heir-looms of aristocratic origin, and therefore reverenced." The tale of the Younger Son, who compensates for the deficiencies of birth and fortune by joining the forces of a pirate chief, is a telling paradigm for the Romantic biographer whose fame was to rest on his acquaintance with the great.

What *Adventures of a Younger Son* avoids is any confession of failure. Expulsion from school is

presented as the triumph of the oppressed over the oppressor, as the narrator describes himself – in scenes strikingly reminiscent of Tobias Smollett's *The Adventures of Roderick Random* (1748) – driven to physical violence against his tyrannical masters. The relationship with the Arab girl Zela is passionate, idealized, and brief; Trelawny's own first marriage was brief but ended in a humiliating divorce rather than death through poisoning. Indeed, Trelawny's creation of a fictional past appears to have been closely connected with the failure of his personal relationships. After his discharge from the navy in 1812 he met and married Caroline Addison, incurring the disapproval of his family. Their first daughter was born in 1814, but less than two years later, when Caroline was expecting their second child, she eloped with a Captain Coleman, who was lodging in the same building. Trelawny challenged his wife's lover to a duel but was forced instead to proceed with expensive and public litigation, which resulted in divorce from his wife and disownment by his father.

During this period it seems that Trelawny devoted much of his time to reading, especially the poetry of Byron. When his divorce finally came through in 1819 Trelawny, like Childe Harold, left his native land to wander the Continent in search of a future. The following year found him in Geneva, where he became acquainted with Shelley's second cousin Thomas Medwin and Medwin's friend Edward Williams. Their conversations turned frequently on Shelley, whose atheistic views and liaison with the young Mary Godwin had given him a notoriety that was shocking to many but fascinating to Trelawny. When Medwin received a copy of Shelley's *The Cenci* (1819, 1821), he allowed his friends to read it, and shortly afterward they decided to go to Pisa in search of the poet and his entourage.

From the perspective of literary history the early months of 1822 were the most significant of Trelawny's long life. In Pisa he became a close associate of the Shelleys, visiting them almost daily and accompanying them on outings in the countryside. Nor was he merely a starry-eyed acolyte: when an amateur production of William Shakespeare's *Othello* (1604) was planned, Trelawny was to take the leading role opposite Mary's Desdemona, with Byron as Iago.

Trelawny made a huge impact on the Shelley circle with his exotic appearance and thrilling tales of derring-do. Even Byron, though less susceptible than the others to Trelawny's romancing, was still deeply intrigued by "the personification of my Corsair." It was not merely Trelawny's personality or conversation that impressed Shelley and Byron, however, but also his practical knowledge of the sea.

Trelawny's arrival in Italy did much to stimulate Shelley's long-standing obsession with water and, in particular, his desire to own a boat. In January Trelawny showed Shelley a model of an American schooner and, within weeks, plans for building a small, fast-moving vessel were underway. Trelawny also made arrangements for a larger boat – the *Bolivar* – to be built for Byron, and Trelawney later became its captain.

By the summer both boats were ready to put to sea. On 8 July Shelley set sail from Leghorn, on the west coast of Italy, with Williams in the newly painted *Don Juan*. Trelawny was to follow in the *Bolivar,* but he was prevented from embarking by the port authorities. Ten days later he had the unenviable tasks of identifying the mutilated bodies that had been washed ashore and of communicating the news to the widowed Mary Shelley and Jane Williams.

Arrangements for cremating the bodies also fell to Trelawny, whose letters of the period include many of the vivid details that were to color the climax of his *Recollections of the Last Days of Shelley and Byron*. Shelley's body had to be disinterred from its temporary grave in the sand and was already "in a state of putridity": "Both the legs were separated at the knee joint – the thigh bones bared and the flesh hanging loosely about them – the hands were off and the arm bones protruding – the skull black and

no flesh or features of the face remaining." The length of time taken to burn the body is recorded with the same matter-of-fact tone. Shelley's heart resisted the flames; after more than three hours Trelawny drew the heart from the fire, burning his hand in the process. The ashes were taken to the Protestant cemetery in Rome, where plans were under discussion for a memorial to John Keats, who had died the previous year. Trelawny planted a row of cypress trees by Shelley's grave and had part of Ariel's song from Shakespeare's *The Tempest* (1611) engraved on the tombstone:

> Nothing of him that doth fade
> But doth suffer a sea-change
> Into something rich and strange.

He also purchased the adjacent plot to ensure that his own remains would be laid by those of his idol.

In the year following the traumatic events at Pisa the circle of friends dispersed, and Trelawny followed Byron to Greece to join the forces fighting for independence from the Ottoman Empire. There Trelawny's imagination was captured by the exploits of the Greek warlord Odysseus Androutzos. Operating from a fortified cave on the northern side of Mount Parnassus, Odysseus led a band of freedom fighters in attacks on Greek towns occupied by the Turks, and Trelawny rapidly became an important member of the force. He was with Odysseus's men when the news of Byron's death at Missalonghi reached him in the spring of 1824.

Trelawny hurried to the scene and, according to his own account, saw that the embalmed body was "more beautiful in death than in life." Once again Trelawny was put in charge of the funeral arrangements, and as the body was prepared for dispatch to Britain, he sorted through Byron's papers. Although he sent the manuscripts to Byron's close friend John Cam Hobhouse, Trelawny copied out the unfinished stanzas of canto 17 of *Don Juan* (1819–1824), from which he subsequently quoted in his *Adventures of a Younger Son* (the lines were not published as part of Byron's great poem until 1903). He also transcribed Byron's last letter to his half sister, Augusta Leigh, and included it in *Recollections of the Last Days of Shelley and Byron*.

After Byron's affairs had been settled, Trelawny returned to Odysseus, for whom he had developed a passionate attachment: "I have had the merit of discovering and bringing out a noble fellow, a gallant soldier, and a man of most wonderful mind, with as little bigotry as Shelley, and nearly as much imagination; he is a glorious being. I have

RECOLLECTIONS

OF THE

LAST DAYS OF

SHELLEY AND BYRON.

BY

E. J. TRELAWNY.

"No living poet ever arrived at the fulness of his fame ; the jury
which sits in judgment upon a poet, belonging as he does to all time,
must be composed of his peers : it must be impannelled by Time
from the selectest of the wise of many generations."
SHELLEY's *Defence of Poetry*.

LONDON :
EDWARD MOXON, DOVER STREET.
1858.

J. A. Vinter, lith.　　　　　　　　　　　　　　Day & Son Lith's to The Queen.

PERCY BYSSHE SHELLEY.

FROM THE ORIGINAL PICTURE BY CLINT

Frontispiece and title page for Trelawny's self-centered account of the final years of his friends

lived with him — he calls me brother — wants to connect me with his family." The connection took the form of marriage to Odysseus's half sister, the thirteen-year-old Tersitsa, as Trelawny's life at last began to match his romantic self-image. William St. Clair has commented that "Trelawny achieved the impossible. He had taken Byron's fictions and turned them into facts. He had made a reality of Shelley's romantic dreams."

The idyll came to an abrupt, if romantic, conclusion when Trelawny was seriously wounded by two British visitors sent by Prince Aléxandros Mavrokordátos to undermine the power of Odys-

seus, who had allied himself with the Turks. Although Trelawny survived the attack, his brother-in-law was murdered shortly afterward, and the life on Mount Parnassus was over. So was Trelawny's second marriage, despite the arrival of a daughter, Zela, and another pregnancy. Tersitsa entered a convent, and when the baby arrived she sent her to her estranged husband. The child died, and when Trelawny returned the body to Tersitsa he was suspected of infanticide. Although he was cleared of the charge, his behavior facilitated Tersitsa's petition for divorce, and in 1828 Trelawny found himself single again.

When he returned to England, Trelawny paid suit to both Mary Shelley and her stepsister, Claire Clairmont; his proposals of marriage met with firm refusals, and he left for Italy but continued to correspond with both women. Trelawny intended to write his memoirs, including the period at Pisa and the death of Shelley; when Mary Shelley refused to supply biographical details, however, he decided to focus on his early years at sea. The autobiography turned into *Adventures of a Younger Son,* though the title was not Trelawny's original choice. Indeed, the entire book was altered considerably through the influence of Mary Shelley, who felt that contemporary readers would be offended by certain passages, including a brothel scene in India. She also assisted with the selection of suitable quotations from the poetry of Shelley, Byron, and Keats as epigrams for each chapter, giving the work a more literary atmosphere than the narrative might otherwise convey.

The year after the publication of *Adventures of a Younger Son,* Trelawny visited the United States and Canada. Determined to live up to the reputation he had acquired through his "autobiography," he swam the Niagara River close to the falls and nearly drowned. When he returned to London, he channeled his energies into politics, becoming involved with a group committed to reform, the Philosophical Radicals. He also began to move in elevated social circles. In 1839 he dropped abruptly from the public eye and began a relationship with a married woman, Augusta Goring. When her divorce was final in 1841, they were married and moved to Wales. In the mid 1850s they had financial and marital difficulties, and when Trelawny brought home a mistress, his wife left him. The farm was sold, and Trelawny returned to London with his new companion.

In 1858 Trelawny's third marriage came to an end, and his most successful book was published. In *Recollections of the Last Days of Shelley and Byron* Trelawny draws together his memories of the 1820s, offering firsthand accounts of Shelley's funeral pyre and of the physical deformity that was revealed when Trelawny drew back the shroud that covered Byron's clubfoot. Although it is full of inaccuracies and inventions, Trelawny's use of sensational effects made his work irresistible to his Victorian readers even as they expressed shock and disapproval.

Although Trelawny's work became famous for its sensationalism, its real interest lies in its careful unfolding of the personalities of its subjects. Rather than adopt a traditional biographical structure, Trelawny begins his account of Shelley and Byron in medias res and includes material about their earlier years through reported conversations and anecdotes. The reader shares the gradual process of uncovering the past and thus becomes imaginatively involved in the narrative and made to feel privy to the secret lives of Shelley and Byron. Much of the text is dialogue, so the personalities appear to be revealed as much through their own words as through authorial comment; it is clear from Trelawny's revisions of various scenes known from other sources, however, that the conversations were largely his creations.

Many of the literary devices are employed not only to increase the imaginative power of the writing but also to emphasize the central importance of Trelawny himself. The dialogues show him in a favorable light while avoiding direct self-congratulation, as in this scene from the enlarged version of 1878:

> A short time after I knew Byron I said to Shelley, "How very unlike Byron is to what people say of him. I see no mystery about him – he is too free; he says things better not said. I shall take care what I say to him. He reads parts of letters from his London correspondents." (Mrs Shelley smiled; she knew they cautioned Byron not to risk his popularity by coupling his name with Shelley's.) "He is as impulsive and jealous as a woman, and may be as changeable."
>
> At a subsequent conversation Shelley called Mrs Shelley and said,
> "Mary, Trelawny has found out Byron already. How stupid we were – how long it took us."
> "That," she observed, "is because he lives with the living, and we with the dead."

The portraits of Shelley and Byron are full of contradictory impressions, but Trelawny is always the man of the world, adding the realistic observation or acting with practical good sense when all around are in mental disarray. His assertion that "Autobiography was the kind of reading [Byron] preferred to all others" is a typical example of Trelawny's submerged self-justification. *Recollections of the Last Days of Shelley and Byron* can, thus, be seen as the continuation of *Adventures of a Younger Son* that he had originally thought of writing in the late 1820s.

But if *Recollections of the Last Days of Shelley and Byron* is as much autobiography as biography, Trelawny's approach was by no means unique. The mixture of memoir, anecdote, documentation, literary criticism, narrative, and essay has close affinities to works such as Thomas De Quincey's "Recollections of Grasmere" and "Southey, Wordsworth,

Trelawny circa 1871

and Coleridge," which had appeared first in 1839 and were revised for republication in the 1850s. As biography such works fall short of modern academic standards, but they are full of interest and artistic merit.

Nor was Trelawny naive about his own practice. His work contains many disparaging references to other biographies, such as Thomas Moore's life of Byron (1830): "a lifeless life, giving no notion of the author, nothing told as Byron told it, and, excepting the letters it contains, unreadable and unread." His criticism of fellow biographers is an implicit manifesto for Trelawny's own work, which claims to create living characters rather than to eulogize the dead. His biographical principles are, thus, reminiscent of those of James Boswell and resulted in a similarly mythic representation of his subjects. Doubts about the authenticity of Trelawny's tales nevertheless influenced the format of the new edition of his work, *Records of Shelley, Byron, and the Author,* a greatly enlarged version that included alterations of the original text and many more letters.

By 1878, when the revised edition appeared, Trelawny was living in Sompting, Surrey, with Emma Taylor. When Sidney Colvin visited the eighty-eight-year-old writer in 1880, he was struck by this extraordinary relic from the Romantic age; Colvin is quoted in the biography of Trelawny by St. Clair (1977): "He wore an embroidered red cap, of the unbecoming shape in use in Byron's day, with a stiff projecting peak. His head thus appeared to no advantage: nevertheless in the ashen colour of the face, the rough grey hair and beard and firmly modelled mouth set slightly awry, in the hard, clear, handsome aquiline profile, (for the nose, though not long, was of a marked aquiline shape) and in the masterful, scowling grey eye, there were traces of something both more distinguished and more formidable than is seen in Sir John Millais's well-known likeness of him as an old seaman in his picture 'The North-West Passage' – a likeness with which the sitter was much dissatisfied."

Trelawny died on 13 August 1881. His body was taken to Germany for cremation, and the ashes

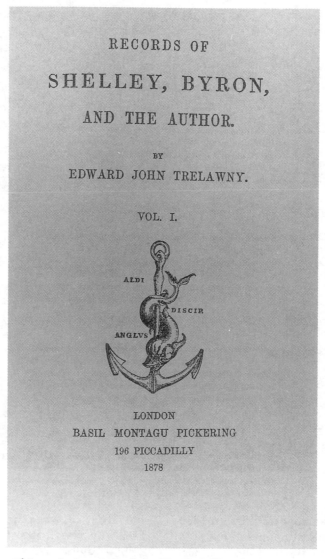

RECORDS OF

SHELLEY, BYRON,

AND THE AUTHOR.

BY

EDWARD JOHN TRELAWNY.

VOL. I.

LONDON
BASIL MONTAGU PICKERING
196 PICCADILLY
1878

Title page for the revised and enlarged version of Recollections of the
Last Days of Shelley and Byron

were buried in the grave he had purchased in Rome almost sixty years before.

Letters:

Letters of Edward John Trelawny, edited by H. Buxton Forman (London & New York: Henry Frowde, Oxford University Press, 1910);

The Collected Letters of Edward John Trelawny, edited by Paula R. Feldman (Kent, Ohio: Kent State University Press, 1992).

Biographies:

Margaret Armstrong, *Trelawny: A Man's Life* (New York: Macmillan, 1940);

Rosalie Glynn Grylls, *Trelawny* (London: Constable, 1950);

Lady Anne Hill, *Trelawny's Strange Relations* (Stanford, Dingley: Mill House Press, 1956);

William St. Clair, *Trelawny: The Incurable Romancer* (London: John Murray, 1977; New York: Vanguard, 1977).

References:

Betty T. Bennett, ed., *The Letters of Mary Wollstonecraft Shelley,* 3 volumes (Baltimore: Johns Hopkins University Press, 1980–1987);

Richard Edgcumbe, "Talks with Trelawny," *Temple Bar,* 89 (May 1890): 29–42;

Paula R. Feldman, "Letters Unravel the Mystery of Trelawny's American Years," *Manuscripts,* 32 (Summer 1980): 168–185;

Feldman and Diana Scott-Kilvert, eds., *The Journals of Mary Shelley,* 2 volumes (Oxford: Clarendon Press, 1987);

Lady Anne Hill, "Trelawny's Family Background and Naval Career," *Keats-Shelley Journal,* 5 (Winter 1956): 11–32;

Frederick L. Jones, "Trelawny and the Sinking of Shelley's Boat," *Keats-Shelley Memorial Bulletin,* 16 (1965): 42–44;

Samuel J. Looker, *The Worthing Cavalcade, Shelley, Trelawny and Henley: A Study of Three Titans* (Worthing, Sussex: Aldridge, 1950);

Leslie A. Marchand, "Trelawny on the Death of Shelley," *Keats-Shelley Memorial Bulletin,* no. 4 (1952): 9–34;

Marchand, ed., *Byron's Letters and Journals,* 12 volumes (London: John Murray, 1973–1982; Cambridge, Mass.: Harvard University Press, 1973–1982);

H. J. Massingham, *The Friend of Shelley: A Memoir of Edward John Trelawny* (London: Cobden-Sanderson, 1930);

Joaquin Miller, *Trelawny with Shelley and Byron* (Pompton Lakes, N. J.: Biblio Co., 1922);

Harold Nicolson, *Byron: The Last Journey* (London: Constable, 1924);

Donald H. Reiman, ed., *Shelley and His Circle: 1773–1822,* volumes 5, 6, and 8 (Cambridge, Mass.: Harvard University Press, 1973–1986);

Cecil Roberts, "And Did Trelawny Lie?," *Books and Bookmen,* 19 (October 1973): 62–66;

William Michael Rossetti, "Talks with Trelawny," *Athenæum,* no. 2855 (15 July 1882): 78–79; no. 2857 (29 July 1882): 144–145; no. 2858 (5 August 1882): 176–177.

Papers:

The manuscripts for *Adventures of a Younger Son* and *Records of Shelley, Byron, and the Author* are in the Houghton Library, Harvard University. Major collections of letters and other related documents are in the British Library; the Bodleian Library, Oxford; the Keats-Shelley Memorial Library, Rome; the Carl H. Pforzheimer Collection at the New York Public Library; Archives of the London Greek Committee, National Library, Athens; collection of Mr. John Murray, London; collection of Lord Abinger, on deposit at the Bodleian Library.

Sir George Otto Trevelyan

(20 July 1838 – 17 August 1928)

John Henry Raleigh
University of California, Berkeley

BOOKS: *The Cambridge Dionysia, a Classic Dream: By the Editor of "The Bear"* (Cambridge: Privately printed, 1858);

Horace at the University of Athens (Cambridge: Palmer, 1861);

The Pope and His Patron (London: Longman, Green, Longman & Roberts, 1862);

The Competition Wallah: With Omissions and Corrections (London & Cambridge: Macmillan, 1864; revised and enlarged, 1866);

Cawnpore (London & Cambridge: Macmillan, 1865; London & New York: Macmillan, 1886);

The Ladies in Parliament and Other Pieces (Cambridge: Deighton, Bell, 1869);

Speeches on Army Reform, Delivered since the Session (London: Longmans, Green, 1870);

Speech Delivered on the Second Reading of the Army Regulation Bill (London: Longmans, Green, 1871);

Five Speeches on the Liquor Traffic, Delivered since the Session (London: Partridge, 1872);

The Life and Letters of Lord Macaulay, 2 volumes (London: Longmans, Green, 1876; New York: Harper, 1876; enlarged, London & New York: Longmans, Green, 1881);

The American Revolution, 14 volumes (London: Longmans, Green, 1880–1914); volumes 1 and 2 republished as *The Early History of Charles James Fox,* 1 volume (New York: Harper, 1880); volumes 5–10 republished as *The American Revolution,* 4 volumes (New York: Longmans, Green, 1899–1912); volumes 13–14 republished as *George the Third and Charles Fox, the Concluding Part of The American Revolution,* 2 volumes (New York: Longmans, Green, 1912, 1914);

The Unveiling of the Memorial Portrait of the Late Lord Frederick Cavendish by the Right Hon. G. O. Trevelyan, in Keighley Institute, May 16th, 1888 (Keighley: Borough Printing Works, 1888);

Interludes in Verse and Prose (London: Bell, 1905).

OTHER: Thomas Babington Macaulay, *Selections from the Writings of Lord Macauley,* edited by Trevelyan (New York: Harper, 1877);

Macauley, *Marginal Notes by Lord Macaulay,* edited by Trevelyan (New York: Longmans, Green, 1907).

George Otto Trevelyan was born on 20 July 1838 to Sir Charles Trevelyan and Hannah Macaulay Trevelyan; his mother was the sister of Thomas Babington Macaulay. Macaulay lived in bachelor lodgings but was an almost daily visitor to his sister's household during Trevelyan's childhood and youth. Trevelyan attended Harrow and Trinity College, Cambridge. Failing to obtain a fellowship, in 1862 he accompanied his father, who had been appointed governor of Madras, to India as his private secretary. Returning to London in 1864, he entered Parliament as member from Tynemouth the following year. He served in several of William Ewart Gladstone's cabinets, resigning twice on matters of principle. In 1869 he married Caroline Phillips; they had three sons.

The writing of *The Life and Letters of Lord Macaulay* (1876) occupied Trevelyan during the years 1874 to 1876. Trevelyan knew his subject well and loved, admired, and respected him. Macaulay was a superb companion for children and had been such for the young Trevelyans: he delighted in them and gave them delight, playing hide-and-seek with them; teaching them poems, stories, and jokes; and taking them on sight-seeing tours of cathedrals and museums, with never-failing historical explanations for everything. As Trevelyan says in his biography of his uncle: "His influence over us was so unbounded – there was something so impressive in the displeasure of one whose affection for us was so deep, and whose kindness was so unfailing – that no punishment could be devised one half so formidable as the knowledge that we vexed our uncle."

When Trevelyan studied classics at Trinity College, Cambridge, Macaulay was his unofficial

292

George Otto Trevelyan

and indefatigable classics tutor, not only by way of visits to Cambridge but also through long letters filled with classical lore. After 1852 Macaulay was in declining health with heart disease and withdrew somewhat from society, but his attention to his nieces and nephew did not decline. On 28 December 1859 Trevelyan stopped at Macaulay's lodging and found that his uncle, though sitting upright, was barely conscious. Trevelyan went home to tell his mother, and when they returned they found Macaulay had died, still sitting upright in his chair, in his fifty-ninth year.

The records at Trevelyan's disposal were enormous, as he says in the biography. Macaulay had preserved almost everything he had written since childhood. Trevelyan was given access to thousands of letters from Macaulay to his family and friends, as well as to Macaulay's diaries and journals. Trevelyan's mother composed a memoir of her brother for her son, and others had kept journals, printed or in manuscript, in which Macaulay's name and doings appeared. There were also people still living who had known Macaulay – Gladstone was one of many – whose memories Trevelyan tapped for information.

Trevelyan's life had in several respects recapitulated that of his uncle and had, thus, given him invaluable insights into his uncle's career. Both had been outstanding classical scholars and social successes at Cambridge. Both had been to India and been involved in the British administration there. Both had been members of Parliament and served in the cabinet. Both had worked for the passage of reform bills, Macaulay for that of 1832 and Trevelyan for that of 1867. And both believed that politics and public affairs were at the center of the history of nations and of the world.

Macaulay had been fortunate in many ways in his life; in death he was fortunate to have such a nephew to compose the story of his life, which was to be generally acclaimed as one of the classic English biographies. The opportunity for Trevelyan to devote himself to the life of his uncle came in 1874 when Benjamin Disraeli triumphed in the general election. Being in the opposition party gave Trevelyan a great deal more leisure than he would have had if Gladstone had remained in power.

In the opening chapter of *The Life and Letters of Lord Macaulay* Trevelyan spells out the reasons he

Trevelyan's mother, the former Hannah More Macaulay, circa 1870

undertook the work. Trevelyan believed that the public would be interested in the biography of a man who produced works that were universally known but that tell nothing of his private life. Many people had known him as a politician, an orator, an administrator, and a social lion, but little of the private man could be gleaned from these activities. Meanwhile, many of his personal acquaintances had died or would soon die, while his readership was continually increasing. In addition, Macaulay had created a public persona that, especially since he was often involved in controversy, was not a wholly pleasant one: he was known as a slashing reviewer; a vehement controversialist and orator (his politics were sometimes said to be the opposite of those of whomever he happened to be talking); an extremist who did not know the virtues of restraint and moderation; and a ceaseless talker who was once called "Thomas Babbletongue Macaulay." Trevelyan wanted to reveal the private man, who was so different from the public persona.

Trevelyan shows that Macaulay was a child prodigy, noted from the age of three for his omnivorous consumption of books and for his prodigious memory. At seven he composed a universal history of the world from creation to his own time ("not a bad performance," says Trevelyan). At Trinity College, Cambridge, he proved to be an outstanding classical scholar but was poor in mathematics. Politics and literature were his first and last loves, and in August 1825 he made himself famous in literary circles with his essay on John Milton in the *Edinburgh Review*. In 1826 he was called to the bar but never practiced law. In 1830 he was elected to Parliament from a pocket borough; he soon made his mark by his powerful oratory and was notable for his support of the Reform Bill of 1832. He continued to contribute essays to the *Edinburgh Review,* and his combined literary and political fame made him a lion in high Whig society. The formidable Elizabeth Vassall Fox, Lady Holland, wined and dined him, and he became well known

Trevelyan and his younger sister, Alice; drawing by H. B. Ziegier (from George
Macaulay Trevelyan, Sir George Otto Trevelyan: A Memoir, *1932)*

for a third gift, his conversation: he appeared to know everything and was willing to share it, nonstop, with everybody, leading to Sydney Smith's witticism about how "delightful" were Macaulay's "occasional flashes of silence."

He was appointed to the Supreme Council of India in 1834 and was a driving force in bringing freedom of the press to Indian newspapers, establishing an educational system with English as the basic language (for the debate on this matter he wrote his famous minute about the incomparable riches of the English language and literature), and writing a uniform penal code for the country. (The code was supposed to have been written by a commission, but because of the illness of several commissioners it was written almost solely by Macaulay and constituted his most lasting achievement in India.) He returned to England in 1838, financially self-sufficient because of savings from his handsome salary. He embarked on the writ-

ing of his history of England in March 1839. From that time onward the history was to be his main occupation, although he continued to serve in Parliament and held cabinet posts.

On 5 November 1841, in a letter quoted by Trevelyan, Macaulay announced: "I have at last begun my historical labors; I can hardly say with how much interest and delight. I really do not think that there is in our literature so great a void as that which I am trying to supply. English history, from 1688 to the French Revolution, is, even to educated people, almost a *terra incognita*." In the same letter Macaulay expresses his hope – subsequently realized – for the reception of his work: "I shall not be satisfied unless I produce something which shall for a few days supercede the last fashionable novel on the table of young ladies."

Trevelyan stresses the extraordinary scope of Macaulay's research and his attention to the most minute details, documenting William Makepeace Thackeray's encomium that Macaulay read twenty books to write a sentence and traveled a hundred miles to produce a line of description; the actual writing of the history; the scrupulous attention Macaulay paid to seeing the book through the press and to such matters as the composition of the index; and his unsparing criticism of his own work, wherein he proved to be quite other than the cocksure and overconfident spouter of his own opinions of popular legend. He would at times allow himself a modest bit of self-praise: "My third chapter, which is the most difficult part of my task, is done, and I think, not ill done."

On 8 February 1849, the year after the publication of the first two volumes, Macaulay wrote in his journal: "I have now made up my mind to change my plan about my 'History.'" The nature of the change is not stated, but the context appears to indicate that he will do much more extensive research on William III than he had originally contemplated: "I will first set myself to know the whole subject, to get, by reading and traveling, a full acquaintance with William's reign." He estimates that it will take him eighteen months to accomplish this aim: he must visit Holland, Belgium, Scotland, Ireland, and France; the Dutch and French archives must be ransacked, and he will see what he can get from other diplomatic collections; he must see Londonderry, the Boyne, Aghrim, Limerick, Kinsale, Namur (again), Landen, and Steinkirk; he estimates that he will look at thousands of pamphlets; he will visit Lambeth, the Bodleian and other Oxford libraries, and inspect the Devonshire Papers and the British Museum's resources. Trevelyan provides, as footnotes, generous extracts from Macaulay's journal to illustrate the care and scope of his research: "June 29th [1849] – To the British Museum, and read and extracted there till near five. I find a glowing pleasure in this employment. The reign of William III, so mysterious to me a few weeks ago, is beginning to take a clear form. I begin to see the men, and to understand all their difficulties and jealousies." He spent 2–3 October 1854 in the library of All Souls, Oxford, examining Narcissus Luttrell's diary – seven thick volumes in cramped writing. After such a day's work he would walk for an hour and then dine at his inn, reading James Fenimore Cooper's *The Pathfinder* (1840). Besides the larger picture, Macaulay cherished the odd and curious facts that he came across. Thus in reading Luttrell's diary he found out why the Jacobites would drink treasonable toasts while limping about the room with their glasses at their lips:

To limp meant L. Lewis XIV
I. James
M. Mary of Modena
P. Prince of Wales

On 4 October he went to the Bodleian, where he got out the Tanner Manuscripts, the Wharton Manuscripts, and the "far more remarkable" Nairne Manuscripts. And so it went, month after month.

The geography – the physical scene of the event he was writing – was also of great importance to Macaulay. The site of the Glencoe massacre had to be seen both in rain and in sunshine. At another place in Scotland he walked the trail an English army once trod. On such occasions he would make rapid notes on the spot that were translated into standard Macaulayese in the final text – Trevelyan gives examples of this transformation from brief and hasty notes to the measured prose of history. Macaulay spent two days in Londonderry, making the most of each minute of daylight, penetrating every corner where there still lurked a vestige of the past, and questioning any inhabitant who was acquainted with any tradition worth hearing. He visited the suburbs, sketched a plan of the streets, and walked four times around the walls of the city for which he was to do what Thucydides (Macaulay's model as a historian) had done for Plataea.

Describing the actual composition of the history, Trevelyan says that Macaulay's success lay in his uniting extraordinary fluency and facility to patient, minute, and persistent diligence. Trevelyan adds that if Macaulay's method of composition ever came into fashion, books would be better and shorter.

As soon as Macaulay thought that he had in his head all the necessary information on a particular historical episode he would dash off the whole story at a headlong pace as it flowed "straight from his busy brain to his rapid fingers." At this stage the manuscript was intelligible only to himself, since he used a self-invented shorthand in which a straight line, with a half-formed letter at each end and another in the middle did duty for a word; he also used simple abbreviations such as *cle* for *castle*. After finishing his rough draft he began to fill it in at the rate of six sides of foolscap every morning. He wrote in a large hand and was constantly erasing, so that the six pages were compressed into the two pages of print that he called his "daily task." The mark of any Macaulay manuscript, from the minute on education in India to the history, was erasures and corrections. Trevelyan remarks that his uncle deserved the compliment that William Cecil paid to

Drawing of Trevelyan, circa 1864, by George Howard (The National Trust, Wallington)

Sir Walter Ralegh: "I know that he can labor terribly." When he felt that a passage was as good as he could make it, he would read it aloud to his family or to his close friend Thomas Flower Ellis. Once, after reading from his manuscript to the Trevelyans, he noted with some satisfaction, "Hannah cried and Trevelyan kept awake."

When his book was in press Macaulay was looking over the shoulder of the publisher at all times: lines had to be leveled to a hair's breadth and the punctuation correct to the last comma; every paragraph must conclude with a telling sentence; and every sentence must flow like running water. He gave express directions as to how the index was to be compiled: mostly proper names, with a few other entries such as *Convocation* or *Non-jurors* or *Bank of England.* Through the whole process he remained his own most severe critic: "yet I see every day more and more clearly how far my performance is below excellence."

Volumes three and four of *The History of England from the Accession of James II* were published in 1855. In 1856 Macaulay retired from politics. He

began volume five but did not live to finish it; it was edited and published in 1861, after his death, by his sister Hannah.

Macaulay was already quite well known as a writer for his *Lays of Ancient Rome* (1842) and eight volumes of essays; but the crown of his lifetime was *The History of England.* He had planned to treat English history from 1685 to 1789, but volume four had gotten only to 1697, and volume five stopped at the death of William III in 1702. Yet because of backward and forward glimpses beyond the dates encompassed, Macaulay provides a rather substantial picture of English history as a whole. Furthermore, although the work focuses on political history, conceived of as a unifying process or reconciliation of Crown, Parliament, and people, it is also a commentary on and illustration of the unparalleled material progress that Macaulay thought had occurred between the late seventeenth century and his own period. It is also the history of the rise and fall of religious sects and literary tastes and of changes in dress, furniture, diet, and public amusements.

The work was an immense success not only in England but also in the United States and on the Continent; it was translated into Polish, Danish, Swedish, Italian, French, German, Dutch, Spanish, Hungarian, the Bohemian languages, and Persian. It was praised by the great German historian Leopold von Ranke. The commercial success was equally overwhelming: Macaulay established a literary record when, in February 1856, he received from his publisher a check for twenty thousand pounds. But through it all he was conscious of his inferiority to Thucydides, in Macaulay's eyes the greatest of all historians.

Trevelyan's most powerful impulse in portraying his uncle was to give a picture of the Macaulay of private life, who was completely different from the figure of public perception and legend. Macaulay was considered physically unattractive by many; but he was quite otherwise in the eyes of his nephew, who provides a graphic picture of Macaulay talking – the endless preoccupation of his life: "Sitting bolt upright, his hands resting on the arms of his chair or folded over the handle of his walking-stick; knitting his great eyebrows if the subject was one which he thought out as he went along, or brightening from the forehead downward when a burst of humor was coming; his massive features and honest glance suited well with the manly, sagacious sentiments which he set forth in his sonorous voice." Trevelyan goes on to point out that he was truly considerate of others, his courtesy never failing. He was eminently capable of brief and witty retorts and of succinct, often humorous, epigrams. He was always ready to accept a friendly challenge to a feat of memory: he could recite a full list of senior wranglers at Trinity, with their dates and colleges, for a hundred years past. " 'But can you say your Archbishops of Canterbury?' 'Any fool,' said Macaulay, 'could say his Archbishops of Canterbury backward.' " And he proceeded to do so. He talked rapidly but, according to his nephew, quite clearly. He was said to have been the despair of the reporters trying to take down verbatim accounts of his speeches in the House of Commons, not only because of the flow of his language but also because of the multiplicity of references to literature and the historical parallels and analogies – many of them obscure – that his capacious memory ceaselessly provided.

Trevelyan emphasizes three aspects of his uncle's private life: his powerful domestic impulses, at first satisfied by his parents' home and later by the home of his sister and brother-in-law;

the great emotional crises when his passionately beloved sisters, Hannah and Margaret, "deserted" him by getting married; and finally, his daily existence – buying books, entertaining, managing his money, helping the needy, and so on. By the time Macaulay was fourteen he had three brothers and five sisters, but all agreed that the young and ceaselessly vocal genius was the star of the show. One of the odd things about Trevelyan's biography – and the same is true of John Clive's *Macaulay: The Shaping of the Historian* (1973) – is that almost no sense is provided of any of Macaulay's siblings save the two youngest sisters, Margaret and Hannah, who were Macaulay's favorites. The only tension in the household was between father and son: Zachary Macaulay was neat, self-disciplined, and careful; his first son was loud and vehement in expression, eager, impetuous, wrote an execrable hand, grew fat, and was careless of dress. Further, though the father was a Tory the son became a Whig at Cambridge. Thus throughout the considerable correspondence between the two the father is often admonishing his son, although there was never a real quarrel or break. Trevelyan quotes his mother, who called Macaulay the "sunshine" of their home: "To us [the siblings] he was an object of passionate love and devotion. To us, he could do no wrong. His unruffled sweetness of temper, his unfailing flow of spirits, his amusing talk, all made his presence so delightful that his wishes and tastes were our law."

Although Zachary Macaulay disapproved of novels and once forbade their reading during the day, his children devoured them; in the evenings they read history and poetry aloud. Jane Austen was the great favorite and remained so for Macaulay all his life. The children often answered questions or made assertions by quoting from a fictional dialogue, and they played games such as "Name the people who attended Clarissa Harlowe's funeral." Macaulay cherished bad novels and loved to quote from particularly awful ones. At intervals in 1831–1832 Margaret Macaulay kept a journal of her brother's home life, from which Trevelyan quotes extensively: one night they had a wager, her *Mysteries of Udolpho* against his *German Theatre,* that he could not make two hundred puns in an evening; he did it in two hours. One morning he came by for a walk with Hannah and with sparkling eyes gave her a blow-by-blow account of the previous evening in Parliament, when the second reading of the Reform Bill had occurred. On 8 January 1832 Macaulay dined with his family, stayed late,

Trevelyan at his estate, Wallington, in Northumberland

talked almost uninterruptedly for six hours, and made many charades in verse. Through these visits and conversations the Macaulay sisters got vivid pictures of such figures as Sir Robert Peel, Lord and Lady Holland, Lord Jeffries, and Lord Brougham (a quite negative picture here). When he did not come in person he sent long and detailed letters describing a night in Parliament or a dinner at Holland House, where he once met the French statesman Charles-Maurice de Talleyrand-Périgord, by then a hideous old man but full of charm and good conversation.

But this paradise of mutual domestic affection could not last, although Macaulay appears to have thought it would. Margaret's engagement to Edward Cropper in 1832 was a blow to Macaulay, and, according to Trevelyan, he never again recovered the boyishness that had been produced by intimacy with those younger than himself. On 12 December 1832 he wrote to Hannah: "And it is all I can do to hide my tears, and to command my voice, when it is necessary to reply to their congratulations [for a political triumph]. Dearest, dearest sister, you alone are now left to me. Whom have I on earth but thee? But for you, in the midst of all these successes, I should wish that I were lying by poor Hyde Villiers [recently deceased]." Letters still came thick and fast to Hannah. The one of 17 August 1833 was one of the

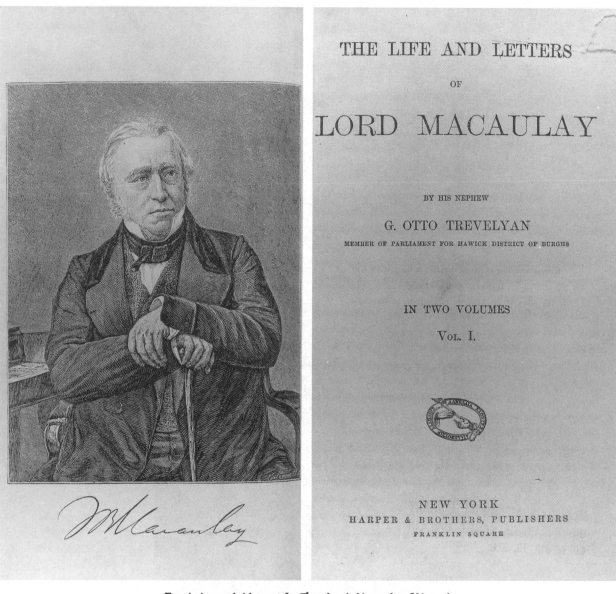

THE LIFE AND LETTERS

OF

LORD MACAULAY

BY HIS NEPHEW

G. OTTO TREVELYAN

MEMBER OF PARLIAMENT FOR HAWICK DISTRICT OF BURGHS

IN TWO VOLUMES

VOL. I.

NEW YORK

HARPER & BROTHERS, PUBLISHERS

FRANKLIN SQUARE

Frontispiece and title page for Trevelyan's biography of his uncle

most important letters of his life, Trevelyan suggests. He was about to be appointed to the Supreme Council of India; he asked that she go with him, knowing what a sacrifice he asked of her: at that time India was regarded as an obscure and distant region of disease and death. She agreed to accompany him; both Trevelyan and Clive say that he would not have gone without her. Within six months of their arrival she was engaged to Charles Trevelyan, an energetic and reforming administrator. Macaulay did nothing to discourage the marriage, but privately he was devastated once more, as he explained in a letter to Margaret that concluded with a sad little nursery rhyme:

These foolish lines contain the history of my life
There were two birds that sat on a stone:

One flew away, and there was but one.
The other flew away, and there was none;
And the poor stone was left all alone.

In 1835 he learned of Margaret's death and was crushed once more, even fearing for his life and reason. At this nadir he turned to books: "Literature has saved my life and reason," he said. The Trevelyans were posted back to London soon after Macaulay returned from India in 1838; they insisted that he live with them, and with the arrival of their first child he settled into the domestic role he played for the rest of his life: that of the beloved uncle of the Trevelyan children. In February 1859 Sir Charles Trevelyan returned to India, and in October Macaulay learned that Han-

*Trevelyan with Theodore Roosevelt at Welcombe, the estate
near Stratford-upon-Avon inherited by Trevelyan's wife,
on 4 June 1910*

nah was to join him. The pain of the impending separation may have contributed to his death.

Victorian brother/sister relationships were often intense, but Macaulay's affection for his sisters was unusual even by those standards. And although Trevelyan promises the reader that he will suppress nothing, it appears that in regard to this matter he did not keep his word. Clive reports that a friend suggested to Trevelyan's son George Macaulay Trevelyan that he publish the full text of Macaulay's diary; Trevelyan vehemently said that he would not have Bloomsbury laughing at his great-uncle – referring, presumably, to passages describing Macaulay's passion for Margaret and Hannah. In the letters that George Otto Trevelyan cites in *The Life and Letters of Lord Macaulay* the word *marriage* occurs only twice, and then to be dismissed as a nonpossibility for Macaulay. Clive's thesis is that he was "married" to Margaret and Hannah.

Trevelyan's penultimate chapter, covering the years 1856 to 1858, provides many details of Ma-

caulay's daily existence. He liked to entertain at breakfast, with the talk lasting until noon; he also maintained an excellent wine cellar. He was a good manager of money; was an investor, not a speculator; paid all bills within twenty-four hours; and was exceedingly generous, dealing out what must have been hundreds of pounds to those in need. He treated his servants with great courtesy and delicacy. He was the acknowledged head of his family, immensely concerned with their welfare, crushed by any illness suffered by any of them; but he never obtruded himself on them or interfered in their lives. He detested dogs. After his retirement from Parliament he took an interest in small everyday matters, such as arrangements in the home and the state of the garden, that he had previously neglected. In books he liked most those he had been brought up with, annotated all his favorites, and considered his books his best friends in his years of seclusion: "He positively lived upon the associations of his own past," according to Trevelyan.

Macaulay's greatest gifts as a historian, says Trevelyan, were his literary power, his historical learning, and his practical familiarity with the conduct of great affairs. Just as Edward Gibbon thought that his experience in Parliament contributed to his understanding of Roman politics and history, so Macaulay thought his careers as politician and historian were mutually reinforcing. Trevelyan concludes that Macaulay's was "one of the happiest lives that it has ever fallen to the lot of a biographer to record."

In 1882 Lord Frederick Cavendish, the newly appointed chief secretary for Ireland, was assassinated while walking in Phoenix Park in Dublin, and Gladstone appointed Trevelyan to take his place. During his two years in the post he had to deal on the floor of the House of Commons with the barbed queries of Charles Stewart Parnell and his Irish political associates about the "Irish Question." Trevelyan became a baronet on his father's death in 1886. His last position under Gladstone was as secretary for Scotland from 1892 to 1895. He retired from Parliament in 1897.

His fourteen-volume history, *The American Revolution* (1899–1914), occupied seventeen of his later years. It was written from a Whig point of view and is quite sympathetic to the colonists and censorious of George III and the ministry of Lord Frederick North. Accordingly, it was more popular in the United States than in England and earned tributes from such eminent Americans as Theodore Roosevelt, Henry James, Henry Cabot Lodge, Henry and Brooks Adams, John Hay, and Elihu Root. Roosevelt informed Trevelyan that during intervals of his 1904 presidential campaign he reread *The American Revolution* and *The Life and Letters of Lord Macaulay*, and Macaulay's *History of England*. Trevelyan died in 1928 at his ancestral home, Wallington, Northumberland, at the age of ninety.

Letters:
Cowboys and Kings: Three Great Letters, by Trevelyan and others, edited by Elting E. Morison (Cambridge, Mass.: Harvard University Press, 1954).

Biography:
George Macaulay Trevelyan, *Sir George Otto Trevelyan* (London: Longmans, Green, 1932).

References:
Herman Ausubel, ed., *Some Modern Historians of Britain* (New York: Dryden, 1951);

Joseph Bucklin Bishop, *Theodore Roosevelt and His Time Shown in His Own Letters* (New York: Scribners, 1920);

George Carver, "Trevelyan and Macaulay," in his *Alms for Oblivion* (Milwaukee: Bruce, 1946), pp. 243–253;

John Clive, *Macaulay: The Shaping of the Historian* (New York: Knopf, 1973);

H. A. L. Fisher, *Pages from the Past* (Oxford: Oxford University Press, 1931).

The Dictionary of National Biography

Pat Rogers
University of South Florida

Leslie Stephen is best known today as the first editor of *The Dictionary of National Biography* (*DNB*, 1885–) and as the father of Virginia Woolf. Both achievements date from 1882: Virginia Stephen was born that year, and it was during the same year that the publisher George Smith conceived what Stephen called "the general scheme" of the dictionary.

Smith, the "prince of publishers" of his era, represents a characteristic Victorian success story. The son of a bookseller of Scottish origin who had helped to found the firm of Smith, Elder in 1816, Smith was born above the shop in Fenchurch Street, in the City of London, in 1824. He entered the firm at the age of fourteen; after his father died in 1846 he took responsibility for the publishing side of the business and took the house to the pinnacle of Victorian publishing. His first great success came with Charlotte Brontë's *Jane Eyre* (1847); after that the firm dealt with almost all the great writers of the time, including William Makepeace Thackeray, Robert and Elizabeth Barrett Browning, Anthony Trollope, Wilkie Collins, George Eliot, George Henry Lewes, George Meredith, Thomas Hardy, Matthew Arnold, Henry James, and Mrs. Humphry Ward. Smith also published an important literary monthly, the *Cornhill Magazine,* which began in 1860 under the editorship of Thackeray. Stephen, who had married Thackeray's daughter Harriet Marian in 1867, became editor of the magazine in 1871.

The *Cornhill* was never particularly profitable, and it lost money steadily during Stephen's tenure as editor. When he took the job Stephen asked, "What can one make of a magazine which excludes the only subjects in which reasonable men take any interest: politics and religion?" One tends to think of Stephen as he appeared at the end of his career: the grand Victorian patriarch and Knight of the Bath, the Autocrat of the Breakfast Table of Woolf's recollection, the author of many standard biographies who had been able to spend leisured hours in a library. But his honors came late, and it was the *DNB* that effected the alteration. For most of his life Stephen was a hardworking professional writer and journalist. When he took on the *Cornhill*

he was probably known as much as anything as a mountaineer, a former president of the Alpine Club, and editor of the *Alpine Journal.*

Smith's original idea was for a dictionary of "universal" biography; but Stephen convinced him that such an undertaking would be impracticable, and it was agreed that the dictionary would be limited to the British Isles and the colonies. Smith went into the dictionary enterprise expecting to lose money; he was to put £150,000 into it, derived mainly from a successful line in German mineral waters he had acquired, and anticipated losing £50,000; as it turned out, he lost almost half of his risk capital. Yet an even greater contribution was made by Stephen at the outset, when he charted the course of the volumes and laid out the working methods of the contributors. By the end of the year Stephen – who was paid £800 annually but never had a formal contract – had drafted a set of guidelines for the work that was published in the *Athenaeum* on 23 December. The article is a request for assistance but also a manifesto, laying emphasis on the need for selectivity and on the prime requisite of conciseness. A "businesslike" approach would be necessary, although Stephen was a sworn foe to a "dry-as-dust" pedantry and sheer antiquarianism. Lists of proposed subjects, running to almost a thousand names, were published at six-month intervals in the *Athenaeum* so that the public could suggest additions and deletions. During his period as editor Stephen continued to receive suggestions for subjects, including on one occasion a proposal for entries on fourteen hundred hymn writers. He was firm on such matters: it was not enough simply to have lived and to have reached print. In practice, however, several country clergymen who had each produced one slim volume of verse would slip through the net.

Stephen at first supposed that fifty volumes would be enough; but as the dictionary moved through the alphabet, entries tended to get longer, and sixty-six volumes ultimately would be required. The first volume, covering names from *Abbadie* to *Anne,* appeared on 1 January 1885; succeeding volumes followed on the first day of each quarter of the

George Smith, the publisher who conceived the idea for The Dictionary of
National Biography *(painting by G. F. Watts; from* The Dictionary of
National Biography, *volume 1, reprinted 1949)*

year, with meticulous precision, until 29 September 1901. Such obsessive punctuality is something an enterprise on this scale would be hard-pressed to match today, even with modern technology. There is something heroic about the accomplishment of such a large task with military attention to the schedule, and it reminds one of the great Victorian engineers carving out railroads across continents and building bridges between previously unconnected parts of the landscape. The price per volume in standard binding was set at twelve shillings sixpence, later raised to fifteen shillings as Smith's losses began to mount. Stephen edited the first twenty-one volumes, up to 1890, single-handedly; volumes twenty-two to twenty-six (1890–1891) were jointly edited with Sidney Lee; while Lee took sole responsibility for the remaining forty. The alphabet was completed with volume sixty-three, *Whichcord* to *Zuylenstein,* in 1900. A grand banquet, hosted by the lord mayor of London, was held at

the Mansion House on 30 June 1900. The principal speaker was John Morley, general editor of Macmillan's English Men of Letters series, who said that Smith had "not merely inspired a famous literary achievement, but had done an act of good citizenship of no ordinary quality or magnitude." Three supplementary volumes appeared the following year, covering figures accidentally excluded and those who had died during the production of the dictionary. The most important addendum was an entry on Queen Victoria, whose death occurred in January 1901. In 1903 Lee brought out the *Index and Epitome,* which was later retitled *A Concise Dictionary of National Biography: From the Beginnings to 1900.*

   In an essay written for the *National Review* in 1903 and collected in the volume *Some Early Impressions* (1924), Stephen calls the *DNB* "the most troublesome undertaking in which I was ever involved." He says that he recognized immediately that, without an official subsidy, he had to get on with the job: "As it was, after all, done by private enterprise, I had to take care that the self-imposed sacrifice should not be much greater than even a generous proprietor could be expected to stand. I made up my mind in the first place that the book should be finished therefore, if possible, within the lifetime of Smith and myself." He succeeded in this aim, but only narrowly: the *DNB* was completed in 1901; Smith died in 1902 and Stephen in 1904. By that time the work was already a national institution. In 1903 the sixty-six volumes were reprinted on thinner paper and consolidated into twenty-two volumes.

Lee was already planning the first of the regular supplements, which have continued until the present day. He edited the first supplement, covering those who died between 1901 and 1911; it was published in 1912 and was the last Smith, Elder contribution to the series. The ultimate canonization of the enterprise came when the dictionary was formally offered to the University of Oxford in 1917, after the death of Smith's son-in-law Reginald Smith. In 1920 Oxford University Press began reprinting the twenty-two volumes of the "main" *DNB,* and starting in 1927 Oxford has also published the ten-year supplementary volumes covering persons who have died in the previous decade. The decade-by-decade pattern was not broken until 1990, when a volume covering figures who had died from 1981 to 1985 was published. A *Missing Persons* volume appeared in 1993, filling in omissions from the original volumes. Those volumes have never been updated, despite a regular series of revisionary notes in the *Bulletin of Historical Research,* but a full-scale revision of the entire project is now underway, edited by H. C. G. Matthew. The second part of *A Concise Dictionary of National Biography,* covering twentieth-century figures, was most recently updated in 1982, carrying the entries forward to 1970. *The Compact Edition of the Dictionary of National Biography,* comprising the twenty-two volumes of the "main" *DNB* plus the decennial supplements through 1960, was published in two volumes, in a reduced type size for use with a magnifying glass, in 1975.

Lee wrote a "Statistical Account" as a preface to volume sixty-three; it leaves out the three supplementary volumes, since they were then in preparation, and, as Gillian Fenwick has shown, it is not reliable: the counts are inaccurate, names and initials are sometimes mistranscribed, and much is left out. Stephen is credited with writing 378 entries, whereas he signed only 281. Fenwick assumes that Lee had private knowledge of 97 unsigned entries for which Stephen was responsible. Lee allots himself 820; his signed entries account for only 757, suggesting 63 unsigned

ones. The total number of unsigned contributions, according to Fenwick, is about 320 out of 28,201 biographies in the original sixty-six volumes. Lee gives the total number of entries for the first sixty-three volumes (without supplements) as 29,120, which Fenwick corrects to 27,236. There was a team of regular editorial assistants, paid on the order of twenty-one pounds a month, who helped revise and correct entries submitted by outside contributors. Some of these assistants were also contributors themselves; the forgotten Thompson Cooper leads the way with 1,415 signed entries. Some sixty individuals wrote 100 or more entries; among them the best known, aside from Lee and Stephen themselves, are A. F. Pollard, T. F. Tout, Sir Charles Firth, and A. W. Ward.

Entries written by Stephen include Joseph Addison; Robert Burns; George Gordon, Lord Byron; Thomas Carlyle; Samuel Taylor Coleridge; Daniel Defoe; Charles Dickens; John Dryden; Oliver Goldsmith; David Hume; Walter Savage Landor; Thomas Babington Macaulay; John Stuart Mill; John Milton; Alexander Pope; Sir Walter Scott; Jonathan Swift; Thackeray; and William Wordsworth — certainly the most significant writers, and almost certainly the most eminent group of figures, undertaken by any contributor. But he also compiled articles on many less eminent persons, consistent with his belief that it was in its coverage of "second-rate" figures that the dictionary would excel all competitors. Thus, he wrote on John Balguy, the murderess Mary Blandy, John Copington Bampfylde, Thomas Amory, and a host of lesser-known individuals, chiefly of the later seventeenth and the eighteenth centuries. Stephen's participation was reduced after his health started to fail, and he was forced to resign as editor, but even then, according to Lee, he supplied entries for almost every volume. Late in the alphabet he can still be found treating John Rickman, Henry Thornton, and Abraham Tucker, but he allowed himself fewer of the less important figures in the later portions of the dictionary.

Lee was responsible for a large number of entries on minor figures, as his tally of more than 750 signed articles suggests. He achieved prominence, however, with his longer pieces, above all with a 49-page entry on William Shakespeare — by far the longest item in the original sixty-three volumes. This preeminence was comfortably supplanted by the entry on Queen Victoria in the supplementary volumes: for her Lee compiled an entry of 111 pages, as long as many separately published biographies. It was garnished, uniquely, with marginal subheadings to facilitate the reader's progress through the lengthy text. Among Lee's other entries were those on figures as diverse as Philip Dormer Stanhope, fourth Earl of Chesterfield; Eliza Haywood; and Samuel Ireland. His main area of concentration was Elizabethan writers, with entries on Raphael Holinshed, Thomas Kyd, John Lyly, Christopher Marlowe, Thomas Nashe, Sir Philip Sidney, and Edmund Spenser, among many others. Lee's practice in adapting his entry on Shakespeare into a book was followed by other contributors, though few achieved as much success: Lee's *Life of William Shakespeare* (1898) was standard for a generation or more, and even today it is seen by scholars as a far-from-contemptible survey of the knowledge then available.

The "Statistical Account" supplies a list of the longest entries in the original sixty-three volumes. The Shakespeare entry is followed in length by the entries on Arthur Wellesley, first Duke of Wellington, with 34 pages; Francis Bacon, 31; Oliver Cromwell, 31; Queen Elizabeth I, 28; Robert Walpole, 28; John Churchill, first Duke of Marlborough, 26; Scott, 25; King Edward I, 24; Byron, 24; King Charles II, 24; Isaac Newton, 23; and Swift, also 23 pages. It is unlikely that these proportions would be maintained if the dictionary were being compiled today: Victoria would not receive nearly four times as much space as Elizabeth I; Henry VIII is a striking omission from the list of longest entries; and revaluation of English literary history would almost certainly cause Scott to be allotted a lower position in the hierarchy. But for the most part the ranking is not eccentric by the standards of its day.

From the start fault was found with the dictionary. Some of the critical responses during the years of its original appearance drew attention to a measure of ponderous and ill-digested annalizing, which Stephen had tried to eliminate at the outset. But the work gradually achieved recognition as the most comprehensive, accurate, and useful compendium of its kind. Firth, in a memoir of Lee (who died in 1926) published in the 1912–1921 decennial volume (1927), put this success down to the differing inputs of the three founding fathers: "Smith's bold plan for a comprehensive national record, Stephen's desire to summarize lucidly and concisely whatever of importance was already known, Lee's zeal for adding to knowledge." The lasting value of the dictionary may be contrasted with the fate of a series planned and executed around the same time: the English Men of Letters series, edited by Morley, with such distinguished contributors as Stephen, Thomas Henry Huxley, Edmund Gosse, George

Saintsbury, Austin Dobson, R. C. Jebb, and Mark Pattison, many of whom also wrote for the dictionary. Yet the *DNB* has remained a vital resource while the English Men of Letters series has become relatively obsolete. This power of survival, when literary and historical scholarship have moved so far and so fast, is partly a matter of the continuing publication of supplementary volumes, which has prolonged the active life of the *DNB* into modern times and made it a sort of "Who Was Who" for recent decades. More important, perhaps, is the sheer scale of the enterprise. Individual entries may be based on outdated and, as it now seems, incomplete evidence, but the *DNB* represented a massive advance on its rather puny forebears. Among the benefits of its scale is the facility for cross-reference that such an Olympian scheme allows. The *DNB* has been the model for parallel ventures in other English-speaking countries; these ventures embody more-up-to-date scholarship, and their principles of selection may be more in accord with contemporary notions of who counts historically and who does not. But their basic plan is, in each case, close to that of the *DNB,* and without its inspiration such time-consuming and expensive operations might never have gotten underway. Like the Victorian sewer system, the *DNB* is obsolete in design, flawed in construction, and defective in materials, but it is still a basic part of the infrastructure, unreplaced and, in the near future, pretty well irreplaceable.

Some of the more common charges leveled against the dictionary relate to shifts of emphasis within historical studies. Not many of the original contributors were historians; in any case, they had been trained and had formed their intellectual allegiances in the mid-Victorian era, sometimes earlier. They lived before the era of cliometrics, at a time when economic history was still a poor relation. Many contributors were antiquarians pure and simple, nearer in outlook to Scott's comically misguided fictional archaeologist Jonathan Oldbuck than to Leopold von Ranke, let alone Karl Marx. They would not all have accepted the full Carlylean doctrine of heroism, but most of them probably felt at ease with the notion of history as the narrative of great individual lives than would professional historians today.

Then there is the vexed question of which subjects were included and which were not. The 1901 supplement was chiefly designed to record those who had died during the production of the original volumes. But there is also evidence of some rethinking, with several personages from earlier periods now deemed worthy of a place. Since that time there has been no opportunity to plug gaps from past epochs; the *DNB,* though it makes contempo-

Leslie Stephen, the first editor of The Dictionary of National Biography
(photograph by Julia Margaret Cameron)

rary judgments on those who have recently died, has not been able to perform any further catching-up operation. Thus, the principles for admission to the main series are those, at the latest, of the first decade of the twentieth century. Among the omissions that now look most peculiar are three diarists: Celia Fiennes, James Woodforde, and Francis Kilvert. There are others in this category, and one cannot blame the original compilers for their absence. It is only by chance that Samuel Pepys, John Evelyn, and John Aubrey were fully covered: they would probably have earned only short entries if their private jottings had not been published. The *Missing Persons* volume has rectified these omissions.

Certain other gaps cannot be explained away so easily. It is obvious that some groups are badly underrepresented according to present-day values. There are far too few working-class figures, but equally too few businessmen, merchants, and capitalists. A good example might be Sir John Blunt

(1667–1733), a significant power at the time of the "financial revolution" and the chief promoter of the South Sea Bubble. An equally regrettable absentee is Peter Walter (1664?–1746), attorney, usurer, marriage broker, land agent, and crook. It happens that both men had important links with Pope, but they would be worthy of entries independently of that connection. Associates of Samuel Johnson are less often conspicuous by their absence: James Boswell had been so fully internalized by late-Victorian authors that even minor figures from his *The Life of Samuel Johnson, LL.D.* (1791) tend to be present.

Another group that is plainly underrepresented is women. It is difficult to determine the proportion of female entrants in the dictionary. The "Statistical Account" does not give a breakdown of subjects by sex, although it does mention such details as that there are 195 entrants with the surname Smith, and that *P* and *W* rank almost equal as the first letter of surnames (1,807 and 1,797 entries, respectively); there is a table showing numbers of subjects century by century, and it is noted that one in five thousand of those believed to have reached adult age has earned a place, and that there is a gradual decrease in the ratio until it arrives at one in four thousand for the 1800s. A dip in proportion to the adult population in the 1700s is put down to some leveling off in "total of men and women of the Dictionary's level of distinction." Lee suggests that "the stagnation of the ratio" of inclusions related to the general population "may be attributable to the absence of such stupendous crises in our national history" as occurred in earlier or later centuries. The great leap in coverage for the Victorian era is explained in Benthamite terms: "Improvements in educational machinery may . . . have enlarged the volume of the nation's intellectual capacity." Lee notes a large surge in inclusions occurring in the sixteenth and nineteenth centuries but little awareness that unconscious biases, hidden assumptions, and ideological factors may help to explain these surges. (Chronologically from the ninth century, the figures listed are 57, 76, 186, 377, 515, 678, and 659; then the sixteenth century with 2,138, followed by 5,674 for the seventeenth, 5,789 for the eighteenth, and 12,608 for the nineteenth). Lee mentions "a well marked decline in the fifteenth century for which it is difficult to account"; the drop from 678 to 659 is not all that "marked," were it not for the Whig expectation of steady increase.

But there are internal signs that women were not regarded as likely to score high in the total spread of entries. One is a prefatory note – possibly by Lee – to the supplementary volume covering those who died between 1901 and 1911 that says "The names of eighteen women are included on account of services rendered to art, literature, science, and social or educational reform." This number was out of a total of 578 entries in that volume. Which important services were rendered by some of the male biographees it would be hard to say today. Second, there is Stephen's own account in *Some Early Impressions,* where he observes, "We were to treat of all manner of people – statesmen, divines, philosophers, poets, soldiers, sailors, artists, musicians, men of scientific and literary mark; and not only men of mark, but every one about whom the question might arise in the course of general reading, Who was he? Some one thought eminent murderers unworthy of record; but surely to the social inquirer the crime of any period is full of instruction." It is instructive to note how easily "people" gets elided into "men," and how, while "eminent murderers" are not "unworthy of record," women

are implicitly sidelined with the question, "Who was *he?*"

A random sample in the middle of the alphabet suggests that women account for no more than three percent of the entries in the original series. Of these a fair number are members of royal or noble families born to a position of eminence. Also, wives can sometimes be found under their husbands' names: for example, Dorothy Osborne has a paragraph in an eighteen-column entry for Sir William Temple, and Jane Welsh Carlyle is discussed in the entry on Thomas. A casual check of the letter *L* in the supplementary volume covering deaths from 1961 to 1970 shows only three women out of forty-five, a proportion still ridiculously low at under seven percent. This may be an unreliable sample, but the editor does not disclose such figures for the volume.

The original editors do not seem to have been unduly concerned about the gender imbalance, though they did worry about the number of scientists (which today appears to be adequate). Clergymen seem to be well represented, including – possibly because of Stephen's influence – a good sprinkling of Dissenters. There are some surprisingly unpuritanical choices – gamblers such as Tregonwell Frampton, ne'er-do-wells such as Dennis O'Kelly, and jockeys such as John Scott. Early cricket is quite well covered, from the Nyrens to Fuller Pilch and Alfred Mynn, though one looks in vain for Silver Billy Beldham and Lumpy Stevens. A nice touch appears in the life of Henry Montagu Butler, of Harrow and Trinity fame: "Despite delicate health he played in the school cricket eleven."

Laurel Brake points out silent revisions of entries in the early editions of the *DNB* and goes on to discuss the making and possible remaking of the entry on Walter Pater. The entry was written by Gosse and originally appeared in volume forty-four, a year after Pater's death in 1894. In the 1909 edition an amended version appeared. Brake notes the suppression of passages that indicated that Johann Joachim Winckelmann served as Pater's "true prototype" not just as a critic but also as a homosexual. Brake observes: "Whoever the censor was, he merely honoured one of the great taboos of Victorian biography. The *DNB* editors encouraged frankness on many subjects, but homosexuality proved an exception." As recently as 1981 the outgoing director of the *DNB* noted that, finally, "less reticence" was possible about homosexuality, which would make more intelligible the career of E. M. Forster or W. Somerset Maugham. While certain varieties of heterosexual activity were equally beyond the pale when the *DNB* first appeared, the work was, if anything, rather unprudish by the standards of the age.

Brake refers to one account of the *DNB* as "a shamefaced defense of the work as a minimal authority," and she quotes what seems to her a "sad claim for a great dictionary." This claim ends with the passage: "Obviously its value diminishes as the years pass, but I think that it will remain an essential work of reference, not only to the ordinary enquirer, but even to the historian and specialist for many years to come." This claim is surely justified, and it is not too shameful to have to make reservations on points of detail. Brake is right to draw attention to the errors and to the little-known corrections. But in practice the dictionary is used principally as a first port of call rather than a court of final appeal. One has to make allowances for its biases, limitations, and gaps; but one would have to do the same for any work composed so long ago, and, after all, posterity will need to perform the same task in respect to today's contributions to knowledge.

The main achievement of the dictionary was in its declared role as a work of national reference. But it may also have had a role in developing a taste in the public for succinct and unflowery biography. Scarcely any brief lives of literary distinction were written during the Victorian heyday of the ponderous three-volume biography (which was often, to swell things further, a "Life and Times"). Even the businesslike Samuel Smiles moved from the comparatively snappy treatment of individuals in *Self-Help* (1859) to the more-voluminous *Lives of the Engineers* (1861–1862). A public figure who did not receive twelve hundred pages of commemoration was not much of a success to be emulated. The *DNB* provided an example of a more concise way of reading about human actions. Stephen was adamant about excluding the long-winded and the irrelevant (though he did not always manage to eliminate qualities he disliked just as much: the antiquarian for its own sake and the piously reverential). It can perhaps be argued that the ground was prepared for Lytton Strachey's deadly miniatures in *Eminent Victorians* (1918) by the unaccustomed brevity and sharpness of focus found in the *DNB*. Reed Whittemore has gone further and suggested that Woolf, oppressed in her girlhood by the mammoth undertaking of her overbearing father, took her revenge by recasting the nature of biography; on this showing, Woolf's *Orlando* (1928) and *Flush* (1933) are modernist revisions of biographic narrative, where the author has "managed to move beyond the chronological . . . in her understanding of herself and others."

This is an intriguing speculation, but it moves well beyond established facts. What can safely be said is that the dictionary helped to codify the practice of biography in the direction of comparative brevity, of solidly documented factual narrative, and of the avoidance of "fine writing" – that is, of inert commendation and woolly "imaginative" recreation of the past. After a few generations the *DNB* manner came to seem too stiff and limited to a new generation of biographers who were anxious to explore their subjects' private psychic histories. The dictionary belongs to a pre-Freudian era, and even the contributors to the latest supplements are cautious about delving into their subjects' unconscious minds. Still, the *DNB* remains a monument to an age of generally confident national reassessment and to the heroic industry of its creators. Literary biographies are no longer composed in that way, but many people still need to consult the great dictionary at times, and scarcely any biography of an English writer has been written without recourse to its pages. In that sense, the *DNB* continues to exert its influence.

References:

Noël Annan, *Leslie Stephen: the Godless Victorian* (London: Weidenfeld & Nicolson, 1984);

Alan Bell, "Leslie Stephen and the *DNB*," *Times Literary Supplement,* 16 December 1977, p. 1478;

Laurel Brake, "Problems in Victorian Biography: The *DNB* and the *DNB* 'Walter Pater,' " *Modern Language Review,* 70 (October 1975): 731–742;

Gillian Fenwick, *The Contributors' Index to the Dictionary of National Biography 1885–1901* (Winchester: St. Paul's Bibliographies, 1989);

Jenifer Glynn, *Prince of Publishers: A Biography of George Smith* (London: Allison & Busby, 1986);

Ira Bruce Nadel, *Biography: Fiction, Fact and Form* (New York: St. Martin's Press, 1984);

Pat Rogers, "Diversions of the *DNB*," *Essays & Studies,* new series 37 (1984): pp. 75–86;

Reed Whittemore, *Whole Lives: Shapers of Modern Biographers* (Baltimore: Johns Hopkins University Press, 1989).

Papers:

The original dictionary records were destroyed after the completion of the first edition in 1901. Some of Leslie Stephen's correspondence concerning the *DNB* survives in various archives: that with George Smith in the National Library of Scotland, Edinburgh; that with Sidney Lee in the Bodleian Library, Oxford; and that with Edmund Gosse in the Brotherton Library, University of Leeds.

Macmillan's English Men of Letters, First Series

(1878 - 1892)

John L. Kijinski
Idaho State University

VOLUMES: James Cotter Morison, *Gibbon* (London: Macmillan, 1878; New York: Harper, 1879);

William Black, *Goldsmith* (London: Macmillan, 1878; New York: Harper, 1879);

Leslie Stephen, *Samuel Johnson* (London: Macmillan, 1878; New York: Harper, 1878);

Richard Holt Hutton, *Sir Walter Scott* (London: Macmillan, 1878; New York: Harper, 1878);

John Addington Symonds, *Shelley* (London: Macmillan, 1878; New York: Harper, 1878);

John Morley, *Burke* (London: Macmillan, 1879; New York: Harper, 1879);

John Campbell Shairp, *Burns* (London: Macmillan, 1879; New York: Harper, 1879);

A. W. Ward, *Chaucer* (London: Macmillan, 1879; New York: Harper, 1880);

William Minto, *Defoe* (London: Macmillan, 1879; New York: Harper, 1879);

Thomas Henry Huxley, *Hume* (London: Macmillan, 1879; New York: Harper, 1879);

Mark Pattison, *Milton* (London: Macmillan, 1879; New York: Harper, 1880);

Edward Dowden, *Southey* (London: Macmillan, 1879; New York: Harper, 1880);

Anthony Trollope, *Thackeray* (London: Macmillan, 1879; New York: Harper, 1879);

Henry James, *Hawthorne* (London: Macmillan, 1879; New York: Harper, 1880);

Richard William Church, *Spenser* (London: Macmillan, 1879; New York: Harper, 1879);

James Anthony Froude, *Bunyan* (London: Macmillan, 1880; New York: Harper, 1880);

John Nichol, *Byron* (London: Macmillan, 1880; New York: Harper, 1880);

Goldwin Smith, *Cowper* (London: Macmillan, 1880; New York: Harper, 1880);

Thomas Fowler, *Locke* (London: Macmillan, 1880; New York: Harper, 1880);

Stephen, *Alexander Pope* (London: Macmillan, 1880; New York: Harper, 1880);

F. W. H. Myers, *Wordsworth* (London: Macmillan, 1881; New York: Harper, 1881);

David Masson, *De Quincey* (London: Macmillan, 1881; New York: Harper, 1882);

George Saintsbury, *Dryden* (London: Macmillan, 1881; New York: Harper, 1881);

Sidney Colvin, *Landor* (London: Macmillan, 1881; New York: Harper, 1881);

Ward, *Dickens* (London: Macmillan, 1882; New York: Harper, 1882);

Edmund Gosse, *Gray* (London: Macmillan, 1882; New York: Harper, 1882);

Alfred Ainger, *Lamb* (London: Macmillan, 1882; New York: 1882);

H. D. Traill, *Sterne* (London: Macmillan, 1882; New York: Harper, 1882);

Stephen, *Swift* (London: Macmillan, 1882; New York: Harper, 1882);

Richard Jebb, *Bentley* (London: Macmillan, 1882; New York: Harper, 1882);

Morison, *Macaulay* (London: Macmillan, 1882; New York: Harper, 1882);

Austin Dobson, *Fielding* (London: Macmillan, 1883; New York: Harper, 1883);

Margaret Oliphant, *Sheridan* (London: Macmillan, 1883; New York: Harper, 1883);

W. J. Courthope, *Addison* (London: Macmillan, 1884; New York: Harper, 1884);

Church, *Bacon* (London: Macmillan, 1884; New York: Harper, 1884);

Traill, *Coleridge* (London: Macmillan, 1884; New York: Harper, 1884);

Symonds, *Sir Philip Sidney* (London: Macmillan, 1886; New York: Harper, 1886);

Colvin, *Keats* (London: Macmillan, 1887; New York: Harper, 1887);

Nichol, *Carlyle* (London: Macmillan, 1892; New York: Harper, 1892).

In 1877, early in his long association with the House of Macmillan, John Morley suggested to Alexander Macmillan that the firm establish, under

Alexander Macmillan, publisher of the English Men of Letters series (portrait by
Sir Hubert von Herkomer, R.A., 1887; from Charles L. Graves, The Life
and Letters of Alexander Macmillan, *1910)*

Morley's editorship, a series of biographical-critical volumes on great British writers. An indefatigable presence in British culture until his death in 1923, Morley was clearly the man to take on the task of putting together a series that would become a standard introduction to the lives and works of great writers of the English tradition. He had already established himself as a cultural arbiter through his editorship of the *Fortnightly Review;* in 1880 he would also take on the editorship of the *Pall Mall Gazette.* Such positions placed him in daily contact with the leading writers and scholars of the day — the people he would commission to write the volumes of the proposed series. Macmillan received Morley's suggestion enthusiastically. In a letter dated 2 October 1877 he wrote: "Morley has projected a series of *Short Books on Great Writers* ["English Men of Letters" had not yet been selected as the title for the series]. . . . The idea is a sort of Essay — biographical and critical — on each of the authors about twice as long as a *Quarterly* article, in

a little volume to sell at about half-a-crown. I think the series should do and do good." Thus began a project that would result in the publication of thirty-nine volumes between 1878 and 1892.

Morley says in his *Recollections* (1917) that he hoped to direct the series toward a popular audience, those too busy to devote large amounts of time to the acquisition of "knowledge, criticism, and reflection"; the goal would be to bring "all these three good things within reach of an extensive, busy, and preoccupied world." But popular appeal would in no way suggest a compromise in the quality of the volumes. In a 5 October 1877 letter to Macmillan, Morley expressed his resolve to follow the most demanding criteria for the selection of contemporary men and women of letters to be contributors to the series: each must possess, he said, the "highest respectability and the highest capacity." Morley testified that he had given a great deal of thought to the selection of contributors, and he compared his job as editor of the series to that of a conductor who wields the baton over a particularly accomplished orchestra.

A question that naturally arose as the series was being developed was who would write the volume on William Shakespeare, the supreme voice of the English tradition. By the late 1870s Matthew Arnold and George Eliot stood at the top of the world of English letters, and Morley hoped to recruit one of them for the Shakespeare volume. Arnold declined, claiming that his time was already overtaxed with various literary and official duties. Macmillan's great desire was to have Eliot write the volume; he hoped to make her, he said, "the *Prima Donna*" of the series, and he authorized Morley to offer her three to five times the one-hundred-pound-per-volume commission that was being paid to other writers for the series. In a letter of 9 November 1877 Macmillan told Morley: "I have just come back from a very pleasant interview with George Eliot. She did not say *no,* and promised to think it over and write to us. She repeated what [her lover, George Henry] Lewes had told us was her feeling, that she has a dread of coming forward in her own person and passing judgment on authors, and spoke as you, or even I, might speak with aversion of the habit of mind that leads people to pass off as sort of *final utterances* the feelings and thought which come to you in reading an author." Macmillan continued to hope that she might relent, but Eliot finally wrote to him on 10 November: "I feel obligated to decline your proposal, though your kindness has given me many reasons for wishing to meet your views. I like to think that you will not be at a loss to find a writer who will treat that supreme subject in literature at once reverently and with independence." No one, however, was found, and the series, under Morley's editorship, never did include a volume on Shakespeare. Although references to Shakespeare abound in the series, and his works are often used as the ultimate touchstone for determining literary worth, it was not until 1907, in the second English Men of Letters series, that Walter Raleigh would finally write a volume on Shakespeare.

Although he failed with Arnold and Eliot, Morley was able to recruit some of the most distinguished critics of his time. He was convinced that his series, because of the caliber of the contributors he selected, made a substantial contribution to the quality of professional criticism of his day. He writes in *Recollections,* "It has been unkindly observed that our age, 'though largely occupied in talking about literature, has produced little criticism of the first order.' I am much inclined to demur when I recall a dozen volumes of [the English Men of Letters] series, and add to them a half-dozen names of critics who are not in that list."

Henry James and Anthony Trollope are perhaps the best known of the contributors. James, at the time a new Macmillan author and eager to have his name before the British public, was commissioned to write the one volume in the series about an American: *Hawthorne* (1879). This monograph continues to be of particular interest because of the light it sheds on James's estimation of his predecessor; it also offers insights into James's views on the relationship between British and American culture. James considers American literature a subgenre of English literature; he attempts to estimate how seriously Nathaniel Hawthorne can be taken within the larger domain of the British, rather than the specifically American, tradition. Trollope, long an admirer of William Makepeace Thackeray, was willing to take on the volume (1879) on a writer who, because of his unconventional domestic situation, was considered a risky subject. Trollope was willing to pay homage to Thackeray as a novelist without inquiring too deeply into his private life.

Another contributor was Leslie Stephen, the father of Virginia Woolf, future first editor of the monumental *Dictionary of National Biography* (1885–   ), and the man who was generally assumed to be his generation's prime authority on eighteenth-century literature. Morley commissioned him to write the important volume on Samuel Johnson (1878) during the series' first year. No one but Stephen contributed more than two volumes to Morley's series; besides the volume on Johnson, Stephen also wrote *Alexander Pope* (1880) and *Swift* (1882). The other most widely recognized contemporary authority on eighteenth-century English literature, Austin Dobson, wrote the volume on Henry Fielding (1883). Thus the series offers a valuable index of the state of eighteenth-century studies at the end of the nineteenth century.

Other contributors, who may not be widely remembered today, had considerable influence within the official high culture of the late Victorian period. Morley was particularly pleased by the respectability that Richard William Church, Dean of St. Paul's Cathedral and noted as perhaps the most impressive preacher of his time, brought to the series with his volumes on Edmund Spenser (1879) and Francis Bacon (1884). James Anthony Froude, who contributed the volume on John Bunyan (1880) and later wrote a highly regarded biography of Thomas Carlyle (1882–1884), was considered one of the finest prose stylists of his time; his work was published regularly in the *Westminster Review* and *Fraser's Maga-*

John Morley, editor of the first series of English Men of Letters

zine. John Addington Symonds, who contributed the volumes on Percy Bysshe Shelley (1878) and Sir Philip Sidney (1886), earned recognition as the greatest Italianist of his time with the publication of his *Renaissance in Italy* (1875–1886). Thomas Henry Huxley, author of the volume on David Hume (1879), was famous – or, perhaps, infamous – as the great defender of both the theory of evolution and agnosticism. Morley, in fact, worried about Huxley's volume, writing to Macmillan, "I am a *trifle* unhappy about *Hume.* It hath a savour of heresy in every page." Morley himself, along with his editorial duties, contributed the volume on Edmund Burke (1879).

Other contributors were connected with respectable periodicals of the time. Richard Holt Hutton, author of *Sir Walter Scott* (1878), along with having held the post of professor of mathematics at Bedford College, London, was a founder of the *National Review* and an editor of the *Spectator.* Margaret Oliphant, the author of *Sheridan* (1883) – the only woman to write for the series – was an important contributor of fiction and historical pieces to

Blackwood's Edinburgh Magazine. James Cotter Morison, who wrote the two volumes in the series devoted to historians – *Gibbon* (1878) and *Macaulay* (1882) – was himself a noted historian, an advocate of positivism, and an important contributor to the *Saturday Review.* H. D. Traill, the author of *Sterne* (1882) and *Coleridge* (1884), a champion of the traditional British novel, and a foe of realist innovations in the genre, was the first editor of *Literature,* which would become the *Times Literary Supplement.* W. J. Courthope, the author of *Addison* (1884) was an assistant editor of the *National Review;* as a civil-service commissioner he worked to incorporate knowledge of the humanities into the examinations that were required for appointments to governmental posts.

Morley also drew on the talents of academics – and not just those at Oxford and Cambridge. Several of his contributors were early professors of English literature, a discipline that was late in coming to the ancient universities. Edward Dowden, the author of *Southey* (1879) and of one of the first academic studies of Shakespeare (1875), was the holder of the chair of English literature at Trinity College in Dublin. John Nichol, who wrote *Byron* (1880) and *Carlyle* (1892), was chair of English language and literature at the University of Glasgow. David Masson, the author of *De Quincey* (1881), was professor of English both at University College, London, and at Edinburgh University, and he was, as Franklin E. Court has demonstrated, "the first in the network of nineteenth-century English Professors who initiated the mainstream tradition of academic English as we recognize it today." Goldwin Smith, the contributor of *Cowper* (1880), who had been a tireless worker for reform at Oxford, had accepted an appointment in 1868 as the first professor of English and constitutional history at the newly founded Cornell University in the United States. A. W. Ward, the author of *Chaucer* (1879) and *Dickens* (1882), was professor of history and English language and literature at Owens College, Manchester. George Saintsbury, who wrote *Dryden* (1881) and whose *History of Criticism* (1900–1904) made him the premier academic critic of the late nineteenth and early twentieth centuries, held the Regius Chair of English at Edinburgh.

Other contributors were affiliated with more-traditional education at Cambridge and Oxford. John Campbell Shairp, the author of *Burns* (1879), was principal of the United College at Saint Andrews in Scotland and also held the professorship of poetry at Oxford. When Richard Jebb wrote *Bentley* (1882) he was a lecturer in classics at Trinity College, Cambridge; later he would be appointed professor of Greek at Glasgow. Mark Pattison, the author of *Milton* (1879), was rector of Lincoln College, Oxford. F. W. H. Myers was a school inspector when he wrote *Wordsworth* (1881); he had been a lecturer in classics at Trinity College, Cambridge. Sidney Colvin, the author of *Landor* (1881) and *Keats* (1887), held the Slade Professorship of Fine Arts at Cambridge. And Edmund Gosse, the author of *Gray* (1882), although not a professional academic, would be Clark Lecturer at Trinity College, Cambridge, from 1884 to 1889 and would become the librarian of the House of Lords in 1904.

The English Men of Letters series was one of the many successful books and series on English culture that the Macmillan firm launched during the years when its editorial policy was influenced by Morley. Others were Stopford Brooke's *English Literature* (1876), which would become part of a series of primers on literature and history edited by J. R. Green; Green's own *Short History of the English People* (1874) and *The Making of England* (1882); Thomas Humphry Ward's four-volume anthology *The English Poets* (1880); and what would become the Twelve English Statesmen series, which Morley proposed in the same year that he developed the plan for the English Men of Letters series. All of these projects were aimed at providing a broad readership with information about topics that had previously only been within the domain of the educated elite. That Macmillan was the publisher gave the general reader an assurance that these books would present serious and enduring – rather than fashionable – treatments of their subjects. These books and series helped to establish the notion of a shared English culture that united all citizens of the nation, regardless of their class or region. Green's claim in a December 1869 letter to Macmillan about the purpose of his *Short History of the English People* is representative: he said that his history will trace the "growth, political, social, religious, intellectual, of the people itself," not of a particular class or party.

Morley and other prominent figures associated with his venture believed that the reading public needed professional guidance in their choice and reading of literature. In "The Choice of Books," which originally appeared in the *Fortnightly Review* in 1879, Morley's friend Frederic Harrison addresses the issue of how one should read in a society inundated with printed matter. He wonders whether recent innovations in printing are beneficial or detrimental to the culture (that same year a writer in *Blackwood's* compared the mixed blessing of printing to the mixed blessing of innovations in explosives). The basic question of what to read, "which comes home to all of us at times, presses hardest upon those who have lost the opportunity of systematic education, who have to educate themselves, or who seek to guide the education of their young people." This problem can only be solved, Harrison says, if professional cultural arbiters become actively involved in improving the reading tastes of the public.

Two of Morley's contributors took the same position on the public's need for guidance. Gosse, writing in 1891, calls on professional men of letters to provide light to a public "groping their way through the darkness of the book-market." Dowden, in an 1889 article in the *Fortnightly Review*, offers perhaps the most striking comment, comparing the professional man of letters who makes knowledge about literature available to "the multitudes of imperfectly educated readers" with the engineer whose work provides clean water to a city.

Morley's own comments on culture and the general public are also revealing. In "On Popular Culture," a lecture he presented in Birmingham in 1876 as the president of the Midland Institute, he declared his commitment to developing projects through which the fruits of high culture can be made to serve even the "roughest-handed man or woman in Birmingham." In "On the Study of Literature," a lecture delivered in 1887, he said: "Our object is – and it is that which in my opinion raises us infinitely above the Athenian level – to bring the Periclean ideals of beauty and simplicity and cultivation of the mind within the reach of those who do the drudgery and service and rude work of the world. And it can be done – do not let us be afraid – it can be done without in the least degree impairing the skill of our handicraftsmen or the manliness of our national life." This faith permeates the volumes of Morley's series.

Each volume in the series was to be between 160 and 200 pages in length. In *Recollections* Morley says: "Editorial supervision was no child's play. Harsh were the binding necessities of time and space, and heart-breaking was it to present an editorial demand for sacrifice of slice upon slice of admirable work, where limits were inexorable." Each volume was to provide an overview of the life of the subject; an estimation of his historical significance; and an overview and interpretation of the major works written by the subject, along with an estimation of their value. A variety of approaches are taken toward achieving these biographical and critical goals. In some volumes one continuous narrative deals with both the life and the work: for example, in Symonds's *Shelley* and Gosse's *Gray* each chapter covers a portion of the life and also treats the literature the subject wrote during those years. Other volumes, such as Colvin's *Keats* and Hutton's *Sir Walter Scott,* alternate chapters that are mainly biographical with chapters that are mainly critical. Huxley divides his volume into "Part I. – Hume's Life" and "Part II. – Hume's Philosophy." Some contributors reserve the last chapter for an overall estimate of the lasting importance of the subject's contributions to letters.

The entire series embodies the Victorian desire – expressed definitively by Carlyle – to view the important writer as a kind of hero. Morley, in his essay "The Man of Letters as Hero" (1884), argues that when approaching the works of a writer who sets himself up as a teacher of conduct one must look at the life of the writer before judging the worth of his works. Myers, for example, praises Wordsworth for his service to the English people as an instructor in national honor. Dowden argues that although Southey's poetry may not be the most accomplished, he is an exemplary person whose voice must be preserved in the national tradition: "But he who has once come to know Southey's

voice as the voice of a friend, so clear, so brave, so honest, so full of boyish glee, so full of manly tenderness, feels that if he heard that voice no more a portion of his life were gone." Southey is to be admired as a man who all his life "was actively at work accumulating, arranging, and distributing knowledge." Even those volumes of the series that are devoted to writers who lived less than traditionally respectable lives – as in the cases of Shelley, Samuel Taylor Coleridge, and George Gordon, Lord Byron – still attempt to advocate a literature of respectability. In these cases the life is treated as a negative exemplar, a warning about what happens when weakness or artistic excess gets the best of prudence.

Closely related to the notion of the true man of letters as a hero of respectability is the series' commitment to defining a classical literary tradition that would embody all of the prime virtues of the English nation. Literature, although often seen as the antithesis of all that is utilitarian, is awarded a crucial social function by the series: the right kind of literature, when properly understood, gives a people a unified and stable sense of its cultural past. A theme that runs throughout the series is the need to identify and privilege one particular "classical" tradition in English letters. Writers in the series are consistently concerned about what books and authors should be a part of this tradition and what rank within this tradition various works and authors should hold. The series, thus, has a canon-creating mission: it proposes to determine what works and writers will continue to be read and valued in England and in the British colonies. Implicit is the message that the culturally informed reader has a personal stake in the preservation and reading of texts that permanently bind him or her to other people – past and present – who belong to what the writers of the series often refer to as the "English race."

Although the literary professionals writing for the series were eager to establish a national tradition, they insisted that the canonical works of English letters embody universal values that transcend national and historical limits; the great works of the past teach lessons that apply to the human condition. The great writing of the past is also thought to serve as a permanent record of the best possible use of the English language, an antidote to the contemporary corruption of the language that was being caused by the proliferation of cheap, popular writing. The best language is the appropriate vehicle for conveying the best cultural values of the English tradition; high standards of language preserve high standards of thought and taste.

The series was well received. In a letter of 30 August 1878 Macmillan commented to his friend the Reverend J. H. Budden, who was residing in India: "Also, I have put in three volumes of a series which we have recently commenced under the editorial care of Mr. John Morley. We have a really distinguished staff. You will see that Dean Church is to do the Spenser for it. We have had much praise for it." The series was so well received that a second series, with Morley as an adviser but not as editor, was begun in 1902. The original thirty-nine volumes went through many editions and continued to be reprinted into the twentieth century both in Britain and in the United States, where they were published under an agreement with Macmillan by Harper and Brothers. Morley's biographer, F. W. Hirst, calls the series "the most successful venture of the kind since Johnson's *Lives of the Poets* [1779–1781]," and Patrick Parrinder, in his history of the cultural role of English criticism, refers to it as "monumental." John Gross points out that it achieved a distinctive place in British literary education: "Right from the start, it was accorded semiofficial status, and for a couple of generations it remained an unfailing standard for harassed teachers and conscientious students. No comparable series has ever come so close to attaining the rank of a traditional British institution."

References:

Noel Annan, *Leslie Stephen: The Godless Victorian* (Chicago: University of Chicago Press, 1984);

"Contemporary Literature: Readers," *Blackwood's Edinburgh Magazine,* 8 (1879): 235–256;

Franklin E. Court, *Institutionalizing English Literature: The Culture and Politics of Literary Study, 1750–1900* (Stanford, Cal.: Stanford University Press, 1992);

Edward Dowden, "Hopes and Fears for Literature," *Fortnightly Review,* 45 (1889): 166–183;

Edmund Gosse, "The Influence of Democracy on Literature," *Contemporary Review,* 59 (1891): 523–536;

Charles L. Graves, *The Life and Letters of Alexander Macmillan* (London: Macmillan, 1910);

J. R. Green, *A Short History of the English People* (New York: American Book Company, 1874);

John Gross, *The Rise and Fall of the Man of Letters: Aspects of English Literary Life Since 1800* (London: Weidenfeld, 1969);

Frederic Harrison, "The Choice of Books," in his *The Choice of Books and Other Literary Pieces* (London: Macmillan, 1886), pp. 1–93;

F. W. Hirst, *Early Life and Letters of John Morley,* 2 volumes (London: Macmillan, 1927);

John L. Kijinski, "John Morley's 'English Men of Letters' Series and the Politics of Reading," *Victorian Studies,* 34 (1991): 204–225;

F. J. M. Korsten, "The 'English Men of Letters' Series: A Moment in Late-Victorian Criticism," *English Studies,* 73 (December 1992): 503–516;

Charles Morgan, *The House of Macmillan (1843–1943)* (New York: Macmillan, 1944);

John Morley, "The Man of Letters as Hero," *Macmillan's Magazine,* 51 (November 1884): 62–70; reprinted in *Nineteenth-Century Essays,* edited by Peter Stansky (Chicago: University of Chicago Press, 1970);

Morley, "On Popular Culture," in his *Critical Miscellanies,* 4 volumes (London: Macmillan, 1886–1908), III: 1–36;

Morley, "On the Study of Literature," in his *Literary Essays* (London: Humphreys, 1906), pp. 335–384;

Morley, *Recollections,* 2 volumes (London: Macmillan, 1917; New York: Macmillan, 1917);

Simon Nowell-Smith, ed., *Letters to Macmillan* (London: Macmillan, 1967);

Patrick Parrinder, *Authors and Authority: A Study of English Literary Criticism and Its Relations to Culture 1750–1900* (London: Routledge, 1977).

Checklist of Further Readings

Aaron, Daniel, ed. *Studies in Biography*. Cambridge, Mass.: Harvard University Press, 1978.

Alter, Robert. *Motives for Fiction*. Cambridge, Mass.: Harvard University Press, 1984.

Altick, Richard Daniel. *The Art of Literary Research*. New York: Norton, 1963.

Altick. *Lives and Letters: A History of Literary Biography in England and America*. New York: Knopf, 1965.

Altick. *The Scholar Adventurers*. New York: Macmillan, 1950.

Anderson, James William. "The Methodology of Psychological Biography," *Journal of Interdisciplinary History*, 11 (Winter 1981): 455–475.

Atlas, James. "Literary Biography," *American Scholar*, 45 (Summer 1976): 448–460.

Barzun, Jacques. "Biography and Criticism – a Misalliance Disputed," *Critical Inquiry*, 1 (March 1975): 479–496.

Bell, Susan Groag, and Marilyn Yalom, eds. *Revealing Lives: Autobiography, Biography, and Gender*. Albany: State University of New York Press, 1990.

Berry, Thomas Elliott, ed. *The Biographer's Craft*. New York: Odyssey Press, 1967.

Birkets, Sven. *An Artificial Wilderness: Essays on 20th-Century Literature*. New York: Morrow, 1987.

Bloom, Harold, ed. *Dr. Samuel Johnson and James Boswell*. New York: Chelsea House, 1986.

Bloom, ed. *James Boswell's Life of Johnson*. New York: Chelsea House, 1986.

Bowen, Catherine Drinker. *Adventures of a Biographer*. Boston: Little, Brown, 1959.

Bowen. *Biography: The Craft and the Calling*. Boston: Little, Brown, 1969.

Brady, Frank, John Palmer, and Martin Price, eds. *Literary Theory and Structure: Essays in Honor of William K. Wimsatt*. New Haven: Yale University Press, 1973.

Britt, Albert. *The Great Biographers*. New York: McGraw-Hill, 1936; London: Whittlesey House, 1936.

Bromwich, David. *Choice of Inheritance: Self and Community from Edmund Burke to Robert Frost*. Cambridge, Mass.: Harvard University Press, 1989.

Browning, J. D., ed. *Biography in the 18th Century*. New York & London: Garland, 1980.

Cafarelli, Annette. *Prose in the Age of Poets: Romanticism and Biographical Narrative from Johnson to De Quincey*. Philadelphia: University of Pennsylvania Press, 1990.

Clifford, James Lowry. *From Puzzles to Portraits: Problems of a Literary Biographer*. Chapel Hill: University of North Carolina Press, 1970.

Clifford, ed. *Biography as an Art: Selected Criticism, 1560–1960*. New York: Oxford University Press, 1962.

Clingham, Greg. *James Boswell: The Life of Johnson*. New York & Cambridge: Cambridge University Press, 1992.

Clingham, ed. *New Light on Boswell: Critical and Historical Essays on the Occasion of the Bicentenary of* The Life of Johnson. New York & Cambridge: Cambridge University Press, 1991.

Cockshut, A. O. J. *Truth to Life: The Art of Biography in the Nineteenth Century*. London: Collins, 1974; New York: Harcourt Brace Jovanovich, 1974.

Connely, Willard. *Adventures in Biography: A Chronicle of Encounters and Findings*. London: W. Laurie, 1956; New York: Horizon, 1960.

Daghlian, Philip B., ed. *Essays in Eighteenth-Century Biography*. Bloomington: Indiana University Press, 1968.

Daiches, David. *Critical Approaches to Literature*. Englewood Cliffs, N.J.: Prentice-Hall, 1956.

Davenport, William H., and Ben Siegel, eds. *Biography Past and Present*. New York: Scribners, 1965.

Denzin, Norman K. *Interpretive Biography*. Newbury Park, Cal.: Sage, 1989.

Dowling, William C. *Language and Logos in Boswell's Life of Johnson*. Princeton: Princeton University Press, 1981.

Dunn, Waldo H. *English Biography*. London: Dent, 1916; New York: Dutton, 1916.

Durling, Dwight, and William Watt, eds. *Biography: Varieties and Parallels*. New York: Dryden, 1941.

Edel, Leon. *Literary Biography*. Toronto: University of Toronto Press, 1957; London: Hart-Davis, 1957; revised edition, Garden City, N.Y.: Doubleday, 1959; revised again, Bloomington: Indiana University Press, 1973; revised and enlarged as *Writing Lives: Principia Biographica*. New York & London: Norton, 1984.

Edel. *Stuff of Sleep and Dreams: Experiments in Literary Psychology*. New York: Harper & Row, 1982.

Ellmann, Richard. *Golden Codgers: Biographical Speculations*. New York & London: Oxford University Press, 1973.

Ellmann. *Literary Biography: An Inaugural Lecture Delivered Before the University of Oxford on 4 May 1971*. Oxford: Clarendon Press, 1971.

Epstein, William H., ed. *Contesting the Subject: Essays in the Postmodern Theory and Practice of Biography and Biographical Criticism*. West Lafayette, Ind.: Purdue University Press, 1991.

Epstein, *Recognizing Biography*. Philadelphia: University of Pennsylvania Press, 1987.

Flanagan, Thomas. "Problems of Psychobiography," *Queen's Quarterly*, 89 (Autumn 1982): 596–610.

Folkenflik, Robert. *Samuel Johnson, Biographer*. Ithaca, N.Y.: Cornell University Press, 1978.

Fowler, Alastair. *Kinds of Literature: An Introduction to the Theory of Genres and Modes*. Cambridge, Mass.: Harvard University Press, 1982.

Frank, Katherine. "Writing Lives: Theory and Practice of Literary Biography," *Genre,* 13 (Winter 1980): 499–516.

Friedson, Anthony M., ed. *New Directions in Biography: Essays.* Honolulu: Published for the Biographical Research Center by the University of Hawaii Press, 1981.

Fromm, Gloria G., ed. *Essaying Biography: A Celebration for Leon Edel.* Honolulu: Published for the Biographical Research Center by the University of Hawaii Press, 1986.

Frye, Northrop. *Anatomy of Criticism: Four Essays.* Princeton: Princeton University Press, 1957.

Frye. *The Well-Tempered Critic.* Bloomington: Indiana University Press, 1963.

Gardner, Helen Louise, Dame. *In Defence of the Imagination.* Cambridge, Mass.: Harvard University Press, 1982.

Garraty, John Arthur. *The Nature of Biography.* New York: Knopf, 1957.

Gittings, Robert. *The Nature of Biography.* London: Heinemann, 1978; Seattle: University of Washington Press, 1978.

Greene, Donald. " 'Tis a Pretty Book, Mr. Boswell, But – , " *Georgia Review,* 32 (Spring 1978): 17–43.

Hamilton, Ian. *Keepers of the Flame: The Making and Unmaking of Literary Reputations from John Donne to Sylvia Plath.* New York: Paragon House, 1993.

Hampshire, Stuart N. *Modern Writers and Other Essays.* London: Chatto & Windus, 1969; New York: Knopf, 1970.

Havlice, Patricia Pate. *Index to Literary Biography,* 2 volumes. Metuchen, N.J.: Scarecrow Press, 1975.

Heilbrun, Carolyn G. *Hamlet's Mother and Other Women.* New York: Columbia University Press, 1990.

Heilbrun. *Writing a Woman's Life.* New York: Norton, 1988.

Hoberman, Ruth. *Modernizing Lives: Experiments in English Biography, 1918–1939.* Carbondale: Southern Illinois University Press, 1987.

Holland, Norman Norwood. *The Dynamics of Literary Response.* New York: Oxford University Press, 1968.

Holland. *Poems in Persons: An Introduction to the Psychoanalysis of Literature.* New York: Norton, 1973.

Holmes, Richard. *Footsteps: Adventures of a Romantic Biographer.* New York: Viking, 1985.

Homberger, Eric, and John Charmley, eds. *The Troubled Face of Biography.* New York: St. Martin's Press, 1988.

Honan, Park. *Authors' Lives: On Literary Biography and the Arts of Language.* New York: St. Martin's Press, 1990.

Honan. "The Theory of Biography," *Novel,* 13 (Fall 1979): 109–120.

Horden, Peregrine, ed. *Freud and the Humanities.* New York: St. Martin's Press, 1985; London: Duckworth, 1985.

Hough, Graham. *Style and Stylistics*. London: Routledge & Kegan Paul, 1969; New York: Humanities, 1969.

Hyde, Marietta Adelaide, ed. *Modern Biography*. New York: Harcourt, Brace, 1926.

Johnson, Edgar. *One Mighty Torrent: The Drama of Biography*. New York: Stackpole, 1937.

Johnson, ed. *A Treasury of Biography*. New York: Howell, Soskin, 1941.

Kaplan, Justin. "In Pursuit of the Ultimate Fiction," *New York Times Book Review*, 19 April 1987, pp. 1, 24–25.

Kazin, Alfred. *The Inmost Leaf: A Selection of Essays*. New York: Harcourt Brace, 1955.

Kendall, Paul Murray. *The Art of Biography*. New York: Norton, 1965.

Kenner, Hugh. *Historical Fictions: Essays*. San Francisco: North Point, 1990.

Kermode, Frank. *The Art of Telling: Essays on Fiction*. Cambridge, Mass.: Harvard University Press, 1983.

Kermode. *The Genesis of Secrecy. On the Interpretation of Narrative*. Cambridge, Mass.: Harvard University Press, 1979.

Kermode. *The Sense of an Ending: Studies in the Theory of Fiction*. New York: Oxford University Press, 1967.

Krupnick, Mark L. "The Sanctuary of Imagination," *Nation*, 209 (14 July 1969): 55–56.

Levin, David. *In Defense of Historical Literature: Essays on American History, Autobiography, Drama, and Fiction*. New York: Hill & Wang, 1967.

Levin, Harry. *Contexts of Criticism*. Cambridge, Mass.: Harvard University Press, 1957.

Lomask, Milton. *The Biographer's Craft*. New York: Harper & Row, 1986.

Longaker, Mark. *English Biography in the Eighteenth Century*. Philadelphia: University of Pennsylvania Press, 1931.

Mandell, Gail Porter. *Life into Art: Conversations with Seven Contemporary Biographers*. Fayetteville: University of Arkansas Press, 1991.

Maner, Martin. *The Philosophical Biographer: Doubt and Dialectic in Johnson's Lives of the Poets*. Athens: University of Georgia Press, 1988.

Mariani, Paul L. *A Usable Past: Essays on Modern and Contemporary Poetry*. Amherst: University of Massachusetts Press, 1984.

Marquess, William Henry. *Lives of the Poet: The First Century of Keats Biography*. University Park: Pennsylvania State University Press, 1985.

Maurois, Andre. *Aspects of Biography*. New York: D. Appleton, 1929.

Meyers, Jeffrey. *The Spirit of Biography*. Ann Arbor, Mich.: UMI Research Press, 1989.

Meyers, ed. *The Biographer's Art: New Essays*. New York: New Amsterdam, 1989.

Meyers, ed. *The Craft of Literary Biography*. New York: Schocken, 1985.

Mintz, Samuel T., Alica Chandler, and Christopher Mulvey, eds. *From Smollett to James: Studies in the Novel and Other Essays Presented to Edgar Johnson.* Charlottesville: University Press of Virginia, 1981.

Nadel, Ira Bruce. *Biography: Fiction, Fact and Form.* New York: St. Martin's Press, 1984.

Nagourney, Peter. "The Basic Assumptions of Literary Biography," *Biography,* 1 (Spring 1978): 86–104.

Nicolson, Harold George, Sir. *The Development of English Biography.* London: Hogarth, 1928; New York: Harcourt, Brace, 1928.

Noland, Richard. "Psychohistory, Theory and Practice," *Massachusetts Review,* 18 (Summer 1977): 295–322.

Novarr, David. *The Lines of Life: Theories of Biography, 1880–1970.* West Lafayette, Ind.: Purdue University Press, 1986.

Oates, Stephen B., ed. *Biography as High Adventure: Life-Writers Speak on Their Art.* Amherst: University of Massachusetts Press, 1986.

Pachter, Marc, ed. *Telling Lives, The Biographer's Art.* Washington, D.C.: New Republic Books, 1979.

Pascal, Roy. *Design and Truth in Autobiography.* Cambridge, Mass.: Harvard University Press, 1960.

Passler, David L. *Time, Form, and Style in Boswell's Life of Johnson.* New Haven: Yale University Press, 1971.

Pearson, Hesketh. *Ventilations: Being Biographical Asides.* Philadelphia & London: Lippincott, 1930.

Plagens, Peter. "Biography," *Art in America,* 68 (October 1980): 13–15.

Powers, Lyall H., ed. *Leon Edel and Literary Art.* Ann Arbor, Mich.: UMI Research Press, 1987.

Quilligan, Maureen. "Rewriting History: The Difference of Feminist Biography," *Yale Review,* 77 (Winter 1988): 259–286.

Reed, Joseph W., Jr. *English Biography in the Early Nineteenth Century, 1801–1838.* New Haven: Yale University Press, 1966.

Reid, B. L. *Necessary Lives: Biographical Reflections.* Columbia: University of Missouri Press, 1990.

Rose, Phyllis. *Writing of Women: Essays in a Renaissance.* Middletown, Conn.: Wesleyan University Press, 1985.

Runyan, William McKinley. *Life Histories and Psychobiography: Explorations in Theory and Method.* New York: Oxford University Press, 1982.

Said, Edward W. *Beginnings: Intention and Method.* New York: Basic Books, 1975.

Schaber, Ina. "Fictional Biography, Factual Biography and Their Contaminations," *Biography,* 5 (Winter 1982): 1–16.

Scholes, Robert E. *Structuralism in Literature: An Introduction.* New Haven: Yale University Press, 1974.

Shelston, Alan. *Biography.* London: Methuen, 1977.

Siebenschuh, William R. *Fictional Techniques and Factual Works.* Athens: University of Georgia Press, 1983.

Smith, Barbara Herrnstein. *On the Margins of Discourses: The Relation of Literature to Language*. Chicago: University of Chicago Press, 1978.

Sontag, Susan. "On Style," *Partisan Review,* 32 (Fall 1965): 543–560.

Spence, Donald Pond. *Narrative Truth and Historical Truth: Meaning and Interpretation in Psychoanalysis*. New York: Norton, 1982.

Stauffer, Donald A. *The Art of Biography in Eighteenth-Century England*. Princeton: Princeton University Press, 1941; London: H. Milford, Oxford University Press, 1941.

Stauffer. *English Biography before 1700*. Cambridge, Mass.: Harvard University Press, 1930.

Thayer, William Roscoe. *The Art of Biography*. New York: Scribners, 1920.

Vance, John A., ed. *Boswell's Life of Johnson: New Questions, New Answers*. Athens: University of Georgia Press, 1985.

Veninga, James F., ed. *The Biographer's Gift: Life Histories and Humanism*. College Station: Published for the Texas Committee for the Humanities by Texas A&M University Press, 1983.

Vernoff, Edward, and Rima Shore. *The International Dictionary of 20th Century Biography*. London: Sidgwick & Jackson, 1987; New York: New American Library, 1987.

Weintraub, Stanley, ed. *Biography and Truth*. Indianapolis: Bobbs-Merrill, 1967.

Wendorf, Richard. *The Elements of Life: Biography and Portrait-Painting in Stuart and Georgian England*. Oxford: Clarendon Press, 1990; New York: Oxford University Press, 1990.

Wheeler, David, ed. *Domestick Privacies: Samuel Johnson and the Art of Biography*. Lexington: University Press of Kentucky, 1987.

Whittemore, Reed. *Pure Lives: The Early Biographers*. Baltimore: Johns Hopkins University Press, 1988.

Whittemore. *Whole Lives: Shapers of Modern Biography*. Baltimore: Johns Hopkins University Press, 1989.

Winslow, Donald J. *Life-Writing: A Glossary of Terms in Biography, Autobiography, and Related Forms*. Honolulu: Published for the Biographical Research Center by the University of Hawaii Press, 1980.

Woolf, Virginia. *Collected Essays*. London: Hogarth, 1967; New York: Harcourt, Brace & World, 1967.

Contributors

Ayse Agis ....*Yale University*
Sondra Miley Cooney ....*Kent State University*
Ian Duncan ....*Yale University*
Ann W. Engar...*University of Utah*
John J. Fenstermaker..*Florida State University*
Steve Ferebee...*North Carolina Wesleyan College*
Richard Greene....................................*Memorial University of Newfoundland*
David Hopkinson ....*Elstead, Surrey, England*
Paul R. Johnson ....*Conception Seminary College*
Alun R. Jones ....*University of Wales*
John L. Kijinski...*Idaho State University*
Elise F. Knapp ....*Western Connecticut State University*
Phillip Mallett..*University of St. Andrews*
Elizabeth McCrank ....*Boston University*
Brian McCrea...*University of Florida*
Natalie J. McKnight ....*Boston University*
Barbara Mitchell...*University of Leeds*
Dennis Paoli ....*Hunter College of the City University of New York*
Glyn Pursglove ....*University College of Swansea*
John Henry Raleigh ....*University of California, Berkeley*
Meredith B. Raymond............................*University of Massachusetts – Amherst*
Fiona Robertson ....*University of Durham*
Pat Rogers..*University of South Florida*
Gert Ronberg ....*University of Aberdeen*
W. A. Sessions ....*Georgia State University*
Fiona Stafford...*Somerville College, Oxford*
Hugh Wilson ....*Texas Tech University*

Cumulative Index

Dictionary of Literary Biography, Volumes 1-144
Dictionary of Literary Biography Yearbook, 1980-1993
Dictionary of Literary Biography Documentary Series, Volumes 1-11

Cumulative Index

DLB before number: *Dictionary of Literary Biography,* Volumes 1-144
Y before number: *Dictionary of Literary Biography Yearbook,* 1980-1993
DS before number: *Dictionary of Literary Biography Documentary Series,* Volumes 1-11

M

Q

R

W

ISBN 0-8103-5558-2

Documentary Series

Yearbooks